Underdevelopment and
Economic Nationalism
in Southeast Asia

Underdevelopment and Economic Nationalism in Southeast Asia

FRANK H. GOLAY

RALPH ANSPACH

M. RUTH PFANNER

ELIEZER B. AYAL

Cornell University Press

ITHACA AND LONDON

First published 1969

PREPARED UNDER THE AUSPICES
OF THE SOUTHEAST ASIA PROGRAM
CORNELL UNIVERSITY

Standard Book Number: 8014-0493-2

Library of Congress Catalog Card Number: 69–18210

PRINTED IN THE UNITED STATES OF AMERICA
BY VAIL-BALLOU PRESS, INC.

THIS VOLUME IS DEDICATED TO

Itshak Zvi Hershler-Ayal
David E. Pfanner
Ruth Mary Rogin Anspach
Clara Wood Golay

FOREWORD

The impact of economic nationalism on economic policy and development in postwar Southeast Asia is the subject of this study. Economic nationalism, in the context of underdevelopment in countries recently freed of colonial rule, is dominated by the drive to increase the share of nationals in the ownership and control of productive assets outside subsistence agriculture and by the desire to increase their share of material rewards and prestige from economic activities.

Development under colonialism proved to be economically dualistic and racially pluralistic. Relatively modern, commerce-oriented, large-scale enterprises developed alongside traditional, technologically backward, subsistence-oriented smallholders agriculture. Not only were these two sectors poorly articulated, but the ownership of modern assets tended to be vested in Asian and Western aliens. Business acumen and a willingness to "plow back" earnings were handsomely rewarded by the liberal economic system imposed on Southeast Asia by the colonial powers. Such qualities were slow to appear in the tradition-ridden host societies, however, and Southeast Asians tended to remain on the sidelines as colonial development took shape.

In the postcolonial era, Southeast Asians have displayed uniform determination to match their hard-won political independence with meaningful economic sovereignty. They envisage their nationalist revolutions as incomplete until they have transformed the colonial economies they inherited into national economies owned and controlled by members of the national society. On the other hand, economists have tended to approach the challenge of economic development as if that goal, as conventionally defined in terms of economic expansion, enjoyed an overriding priority.

The possibilities of conflict are obvious. Economic development is concerned with the size of the "pie" without regard to its racial dimensions; economic nationalism is concerned with the racial and ethnic distribution of the "pie" rather than its size. For societies seeking to escape pluralism, extreme racial specialization, and underdevelopment, these goals are alternatives rather than joint products. The priority assigned to economic development as such tends to be subordinated to that of economic nationalism.

The competition between these two goals admittedly is seen more clearly in the short run and hopefully will prove illusory over the longer haul as members of the national society develop values, attitudes, and skills appropriate to effective participation in national economic development. Admitting this possibility, however, only reinforces the need for the outside world to adapt its participation in the modernization of the underdeveloped world to the demands of economic nationalism if the hoped-for benefits of economic and social development are to materialize more promptly.

The authors seek to communicate awareness of the priority given economic nationalism to economists who have accepted major responsibility for assessing and prescribing development policy. At present economists readily admit the existence of economic nationalism but casually exclude it from development models as having little consequence. Such insensitivity to this major determinant of economic policy is an important explanation of the meager results of our efforts in Southeast Asia and, therefore, it lies behind the creeping malaise that erodes the will of Southeast Asians and their outside collaborators to persevere in joint efforts.

We emphasize also that our study is not a comprehensive survey of economic nationalism in Southeast Asia. We are concerned only peripherally with the efforts of Southeast Asian societies to control economic relations with the outside world and with the array of policies installed in each country to mobilize national capabilities for social and economic development.

It is not our objective to produce policy prescriptions. Obviously, economic nationalism can be resisted, and there are strong moral arguments as well as economic ones for doing so. We emphasize, however, that such a stance precludes effective participation until Southeast Asian nationalists have completed their revolutions by transforming the colonial economies they inherited. Outside efforts can be adapted to the requirements imposed by nationalism with minimum compromise of the goal of economic development, and we believe this approach offers the best chance for effective participation.

Economic nationalism is a fact of life which, if ignored, will upset the most careful economic calculations. It is not an attractive phenomenon, and our intention is not to gloss over the basic inhumanity it propagates. The conditions that have molded it in Southeast Asia are a legacy of colonial rule, and the societies that exercised imperial power have a responsibility to understand it rather than merely deplore it. Only if economic nationalism is understood can the outside world adapt to this complex force and, in the process, hope to mitigate its discriminatory encroachment on human liberty. The authors are motivated to contribute to such understanding. The choice of the subject of this study reflects no single value judgment; it mirrors the belief that economic nationalism probably has been the most important determinant of economic policy in postwar Southeast Asia and will almost certainly remain a prominent influence in the foreseeable future.

The collaboration that produced this study arose from a shared awareness of the significance of economic nationalism which was impressed upon the authors during extended periods of research and residence in Southeast Asia. Over the decade before 1962, when this study was begun, the authors spent a total of eight years in Southeast Asia. Five of the country studies were the direct result of field research; two—South Vietnam and Cambodia—were produced from library reference materials.

Frank Golay is responsible for the studies of the Philippines and Malaya and for the shorter essays on South Vietnam and Cambodia. Ralph Anspach produced the study of Indonesia, Ruth Pfanner that on Burma, and Eliezer Ayal the Thailand study. The introductory and concluding sections were drafted in two conferences held at Cornell University, one in the spring of 1964 and a second in the following year, and through a laborious process of circulating successive drafts for criticism and refinement. Although this process was inefficient, it has resulted in statements all of the authors support.

We acknowledge our substantial debts: to the Cornell Southeast Asia Program for liberal financial support; to many friends in Southeast Asia—civil servants, scholars, librarians, legislators, and others— who gave generously of time and energy; to colleagues who patiently and insightfully subjected our ideas to scrutiny; to wives, husbands, and children who endured the inefficiencies of our collaboration.

Finally, we take this opportunity to state that the views expressed herein are those shared by the authors and do not necessarily reflect those of the United Nations, the employer of Ruth Pfanner.

F. H. G.
R. A.
M. R. P.
E. B. A.

October 1968

CONTENTS

TABLES

The Philippines

Indonesia

Burma

Thailand

Malaya

*Underdevelopment and
Economic Nationalism
in Southeast Asia*

1

ECONOMIC NATIONALISM IN SOUTHEAST ASIA

Economic nationalism is an elusive, emotion-laden concept meaning many things to many people. Although the basic elements of a thoroughgoing policy structure of economic nationalism emerged in the mercantilist system of the seventeenth and eighteenth centuries, the use of the term is of recent origin. References to economic nationalism appeared first in the years following World War I when the international economy was subjected to stresses arising out of the economic and political dislocation inherited from the War.[1] Governments seeking to escape from the external constraints on their freedom to make decisions sought to insulate their economies from external forces in order to exercise greater autonomy in stimulating internal economic expansion. By the mid-1930s, the term had come into widespread use to describe the power-oriented systems of fascist Italy and Nazi Germany.[2] Use of the term has continued to the present, though its interpretation has shifted markedly.

Although economic nationalism lacks precise definition, it is possible to identify common and related elements in its various uses over time and thereby establish a minimum content for the concept. First, there is uniform agreement that economic nationalism refers to a system of national policies; that the relevant social unit is the nation-state or-

[1] Economic nationalism is not a topic discussed, as such, in the *Encyclopedia of the Social Sciences* or in any of the standard encyclopedias including *Encyclopedia Britannica*.

[2] See G. G. Hodgson, *Economic Nationalism* (New York: H. W. Wilson Co., 1933). The earliest use of the term "economic nationalism" reported in this survey was in a reference published in 1927.

ganized to pursue the national interest as identified through the political process.

At this level, one is tempted to define economic nationalism as a system of policies and institutions created to promote national economic development and, by so doing, to ensure that progress toward goals of material welfare, power, and sovereignty takes place. Such a definition is unexceptional and deceptively plausible but is of little value because, to their advocates, all policies are national policies guided by a defensible concept of the collective interest. Controversy can arise, therefore, only in challenging particular policies on the ground that they confuse the real with an illusory national interest. Clearly a government can adopt a policy, or combination of policies, of protectionism, insulation, autarky, international co-operation, and free trade, any or all justified by a defensible image of the national interest.

A second element common to all concepts of economic nationalism and its antecedents back to the mercantile system is the central role assigned to regulation and control of economic relations between a country and the outside world. Such regulation is never an end in itself but is a means to the national interest, however defined. The mercantile system in its crudest form was power-oriented and tended to identify the national interest in terms of a strategic reserve of "treasure." Such a system was organized to produce a surplus in exports of goods and services which would add to the nation's stock of precious metals.[3]

With the erosion of the intellectual underpinnings of mercantilism by the persuasive ideas of economic liberalism and free trade, systems of policies involving regulation of external economic relations were placed on the defensive and remained so throughout much of the nineteenth century. Economic thought and policy controversy remained focused on commercial policy, however, and two powerful ideas with direct roots in mercantilism competed with considerable success with economic liberalism for influence upon economic policy. One was the system of economic protectionism for economic development *cum* industrialization which was formulated consistently by Alexander Hamilton (1791) and elaborated more fully by Friedrich List (1841). Advocates of this system postulated divergence between the interna-

---

[3] The theory of mercantilism became increasingly complex and sophisticated as colonialism was integrated into the system. The basic power orientation remained intact, however, as productive capacity and economic self-sufficiency were increasingly recognized as critical dimensions of national power.

tional interest furthered by multilateral specialization and the national interest, which required that protection be used to guide national economic development. Although subject to continuous controversy and under heavy attack by economists generally, protectionism as a system strongly influenced policy and development in the United States, France, Germany, and Russia.

A related intellectual development with roots in the mercantilist emphasis on precious metals as a war chest was the controversy over a system of insulation and autarky to promote national power which initially was synthesized by the German philosopher Fichte (1800). In an important sense, the sporadic development of this type of system focused on power and ultimately diverted to aggression, culminated in the fascist regimes of Italy and Germany. The system of commercial, monetary, and exchange control policies developed by Nazi Germany to support rearmament and aggression prompted the revival of controversy over economic nationalism in the 1930s, which gave the concept its essentially pejorative connotation.

The period following World War II has seen subtle but important accretions to the concept of economic nationalism. Although it has retained its previous emphasis upon control of external economic relations and economic independence, the concept has been broadened to connote the planned integration of diverse policies to pursue social goals. This change is related, first of all, to the widespread concern for underdevelopment and the problem of initiating and maintaining accelerated modernization in the less developed world. The challenge to mobilize national resources for this task has been discussed in terms of planning, and the state, often by default, has been assigned formidable economic responsibilities. Modernization requires the transformation of the existing underdeveloped society and economy, usually associated with colonialism, and there is widespread recognition that policies of "colonial *laissez faire*" offer little assurance of accelerated economic growth or industrialization.

A similar emphasis emerged in the industrialized world in the years immediately following World War II. This was a period of bilateralism, and stringent controls over external economic relations were in widespread use to manage the disequilibria inherited from the war. At the same time, it was a period of planning for economic rehabilitation and expansion which formed a continuum with the earlier planning of economic mobilization to support the war effort. The emphasis on planning was reinforced by the postwar resurgence of socialism with its priority on welfare and its image of capitalist instability. Under the circumstances, prevailing concepts of the role of the state in organizing productive resources and in managing economic change underwent rapid evolution.

Economic nationalism today connotes insulation usually for planned economic development and is applied not only to the control of external economic relations, but also to the mobilization of internal resources. In the industrial West, such a system is used to maintain progress toward goals of material welfare and social integration. In the Soviet bloc, a system of policies similar in concept but more authoritarian in execution promotes expansion of the industrial base and enhanced security. In the underdeveloped world, insulation and control are sought to promote economic modernization. Not surprisingly, industrialization occupies a central position in the aspirations and plans of less-developed societies, and universal concern for independence and sovereignty enhances the priority of industries believed to be strategic. In the earliest stages of development such a role is attributed to a steel industry; later the priority may shift to more complex metalworking industries or even to an atomic energy industry. Economic nationalism in the context of underdevelopment very frequently manifests a preference for directly productive public enterprise. In some instances this results from socialist ideology; in others, from insistence upon control believed necessary to planning; and with at least equal frequency, it is a pragmatic response to the inadequacy of private initiative and managerial skills.

The current concept of economic nationalism described above is illustrated by reference to the writings of two economists who have concerned themselves with this phenomenon: Gunnar Myrdal and Michael Heilperin. Although they represent ideologically divergent positions, it is clear that their concepts of economic nationalism are similar. For Heilperin, economic nationalism is an unmitigated evil associated with growing collectivism and the baneful influence of Keynes which is leading the world to irrationally sacrifice the bounties of economic liberalism.[4] The essential element in his concept is "isolation," or at least "insulation," since he defines economic nationalism as

[4] For an exposition of Heilperin's position as well as a concise history of the concept of economic nationalism, see Michael A. Heilperin, *Studies in Economic Nationalism* (Geneva, Switzerland: Librairie E. Droz, 1960).

"the desire to plan the economic life of the country as independently as possible of the condition of the world economy." [5] Autarky is the result of economic nationalism, not for its own sake, but because autarky offers escape from the "disturbing effects" of international economic interdependence.

For Myrdal, on the other hand, a system of economic nationalism is necessary to insulate economies not only from uncertainties, but from "cumulative causal relationships" inherent in specialization and trade in a world of economic inequality and which are insurmountable obstacles to "national integration." Myrdal's national integration is a vague concept, central to which are the egalitarian implications of the modern welfare state which he believes must be achieved if the national society is to be stable internally and peaceful internationally. In other words, all countries—rich and poor—must pass through a period of economic nationalism, insulation, and internal mobilization to achieve national integration. Only societies that are internally integrated and egalitarian can be integrated into "an international economy"—just, stable, peaceful, and blessed with high and expanding levels of welfare for all.[6]

More recently, the concept of economic nationalism has been perceptively refocused in a series of contributions by scholars motivated to understand Canadian economic nationalism and to generalize from that phenomenon.[7] These contributions sharpen the concept by explicitly recognizing the priority of nationals over non-nationals in the distribution of income and in the ownership and control of wealth as a goal of economic nationalism, and second, the symbolic role of these manifestations of economic nationalism as collective or public capital goods. Such public capital goods are "consumed" (enjoyed) by in-

---

[5] *Ibid.*, p. 20.

[6] For a brief exposition of Myrdal's position, see Gunnar Myrdal, *Economic Nationalism and Internationalism* (Melbourne: Australian Institute of International Affairs, 1957). See also his *Economic Theory and Underdeveloped Regions* (London: Gerald Duckworth and Co., 1957) and *An International Economy* (New York: Harper and Bros., 1956).

[7] Harry G. Johnson, *The Canadian Quandary* (Toronto: McGraw-Hill, 1963), pp. 11–21, and "Nationalism in Canadian Economic Policy," *Lloyds Bank Review* (64), October 1964, pp. 25–35; Albert Breton, "The Economics of Nationalism," *Journal of Political Economy* (72), August 1964, pp. 376–386. Professor Johnson's study of economic nationalism was extended to the less-developed world in "A Theoretical Model of Economic Nationalism in New and Developing States," *Political Science Quarterly* (80), June 1965, pp. 169–185.

dividuals or groups other than direct beneficiaries as psychic income without reducing the "consumption" (enjoyment) of them by other individuals or groups.[8]

Because these contributions are strongly colored by the Canadian experience, they emphasize the relationship of economic nationalism to income distribution both as between nationals and non-nationals and among nationals. The new dimension of economic nationalism is defined narrowly in terms of the reservation of employment to nationals, and analysis is focused on the effects on income distribution of policies designed to encourage greater entrepreneurial participation by nationals. Insofar as economic nationalism is related to underdevelopment, the new dimension emphasizes intervention by the state in economic processes, and public ownership of enterprises to provide "employment for the educated directly in the central control system . . . and to give the government social control over the allocation of jobs to nationals."[9]

This brief survey of the history of the concept of economic nationalism serves to bring out the elements to be found in any system that today would be labeled economic nationalism. First, and in the historical tradition, there is the regulation and control of economic relations between a country and the rest of the world to enhance sovereignty by insulating the economy from foreign influences. Second, there is the extension of regulation and control to internal economic processes in order to mobilize national capabilities for increased welfare and/or power through economic development. Finally, such a system is concerned with the share of members of the national society in the ownership, management and control of productive assets, and their share in the allocation of prestigeful and materially rewarding economic functions.

The elevation of the latter dimension to a position co-ordinate with the traditional elements in a system of economic nationalism does no more than recognize the emergence in recent years of nation-states in which the national economy and the national society, in substantive aspects, are not coterminous with and adequately specified by the national boundaries. Such a state of affairs prevails in much of the underdeveloped world where economic nationalism has been strongly

---

[8] Breton, *op. cit.*, p. 377.

[9] Johnson, "A Theoretical Model of Economic Nationalism in New and Developing States," p. 183.

colored by the struggle for independence and by the nature of colonial economic development.

Central to nationalism in the context of underdevelopment and unstable political institutions is the goal of national integration with major dimensions of political, economic, social, religious, and cultural unity. Inherent in nationalism as a movement is a "society" made up of members sharing basic ingredients of nationality which is striving for homogeneity, separateness, and distinctiveness—a society inclusive of those possessing the requisite qualifications and exclusive of those who fail to present the necessary credentials.

The proper credentials for membership in the national society cannot be defined for all societies and for all time. There obviously will be a core of people possessing minimum common ethnic and cultural qualifications. Such credentials, however, are neither necessary nor sufficient to ensure membership in the national society. Membership is ultimately conferred by recognition on the part of those elements of the society that have monopolized political power. Such recognition, providing access by outsiders to membership in the national society, represents a pragmatic response to the racial and ethnic pluralism inherited from colonialism, wars, migration, and commercialism. It is a means through which the ethnically and racially diffuse societies of Southeast Asia move toward meaningful nationality.[10]

This line of analysis leads to a dimension of economic nationalism that emphasizes, not the nation state defined by physical boundaries but the national society with its emphasis on membership, which may or may not be conferred upon particular groups within the resident population. This dimension of economic nationalism is reflected in the use of the powers and institutions of the state to transfer the sources of

[10] The significance of recognition is illustrated by diverse societies strongly driven by nationalism. For example, following the nationalist revolution in Egypt in the 1950s, those Egyptians of the economic aristocracy who failed to support the revolution found that they were denied recognition and their access to resources, markets, and political participation was restricted. A similar fate befell the Chinese comprador and commercial classes following the Communist takeover in 1949. The "sins" of such elements may be expiated by expropriation of their wealth, which will serve to erase their distinctiveness in the homogeneous national society, and full recognition may be accorded to the next generation. In Southeast Asia an analogous situation arises in Malaya where Chinese and Indian citizens are not "recognized" as entitled to all of the economic rights of Malay citizens. The authors are indebted to Professor Kimon Valaskakis for this important insight.

wealth and income, and control over the national economy, to the members of the politically dominant national society. It is the thesis of this study that economic nationalism in the context of underdevelopment tends to be dominated by this goal.

The problem of integration of the nation-state, the national economy, and the national society is one of bringing them into congruence. Absolute congruence, of course, is unattainable and integration must be relative. Examination of economic policies in Southeast Asia produces convincing evidence that acceptable congruence is a *sine qua non* of nationhood, and economic nationalism is dominated by the immediate goal of making the colonial economy over into a national economy. In other words, an early and necessary stage in national economic development is completed only when the share of members of the national society in ownership and control of productive assets (outside subsistence agriculture) and their share of prestigeful and materially rewarding economic functions are sufficiently large that concern to increase them further no longer commands a dominant priority.

This drive behind economic nationalism is a quality universal in man and will be latent or prominent in diverse environments. Our study reflects the conviction that economic nationalism in Southeast Asia lends itself to comparative study because the drive to transform the diverse economies of the area has been molded by a shared heritage of colonialism, racial pluralism, and twentieth-century contrasts in development and underdevelopment. Needless to say, this dimension of economic nationalism exists today and has existed in the past in states that have not undergone colonial rule.[11] Similarly, racial pluralism is neither a necessary nor a sufficient condition for economic nationalism to become prominent.[12] The necessary condition for the system of economic nationalism which is the subject of this study is recognition by members of the politically dominant national society— or at least by the elites wielding political power—of the lack of some critical minimum level of congruence between the nation-state, the economy, and the national society.

---

[11] Thailand is a state that avoided colonial subjection and has displayed many manifestations of economic nationalism common to other countries of the area.

[12] That underdevelopment is not a necessary condition is attested by Canadian economic nationalism which became virulent in the postwar period as American investment and, therefore, control over economic decisions increased in prominence.

We shall use the term "indigenism" to describe the structure of policies and institutions created to transform the racial dimensions of the colonial-type economies inherited by Southeast Asian societies.[13] In the various studies that make up this volume we will refer to this type of system in particular countries as Filipinism, Burmanism, Thaiism, and so forth.[14]

Indigenism does not substitute for more conventional dimensions of economic nationalism, but normally will be found in combination with protection for industrialization, insulation to facilitate control of economic processes and internal mobilization, and other aspects of policy motivated by considerations of national sovereignty, to form a comprehensive policy system of economic nationalism. The significance of indigenism arises in its dominant priority as a social goal when a disproportionate share of the productive assets and prestigeful and materially rewarding economic functions are preempted by aliens. Under such circumstances, and particularly where they are compounded by underdevelopment and political nationalism nurtured under colonialism, economic policy becomes intelligible in terms of the goal of indigenism rather than goals of economic growth and welfare.[15]

[13] The word we have adopted, "indigenism," has the merit of descriptive preciseness and promises to serve our goal of communicating awareness of an important feature of underdevelopment in Southeast Asia.

[14] "Indigenism" will also be used to refer to the *process* by which control over wealth and sources of income is transferred to members of the national society. Moreover, as the end result of this process, indigenism is a *social goal* of high priority. Depending upon the context in which it is used, "indigenism" will be used to refer to the *system* of economic nationalism, to the *process,* and to the *social goal.* The reader will be aware that "indigenization" (a term first used in Ralph Anspach's doctoral dissertation) would be grammatically preferable in the latter two uses. We have used indigenism, however, because it is more pronounceable.

[15] Examination of the literature dealing with economic nationalism indicates that scholars considered indigenism—if it occurred to them at all—as a peripheral aspect of nationalism. An exception was the economist T. E. Gregory who provided an insightful analysis of indigenism in the early 1930s when developments in Germany and Eastern Europe focused attention on this phenomenon. Gregory, seeking to understand economic nationalism, said: "I will make clear what I mean by taking a fairly normal case. What is the position of Poland? As a result of the Great War you have a previously submerged nationality now in a position to impose its political will upon formerly dominant political bodies, Germans and White Russians. A policy of economic nationalism appears to be almost self-evident because if you ruin the Russians in those portions of Russia absorbed into Poland, and if you ruin the Germans at Upper Silesia you deprive yourself of very dangerous political enemies. Economic nationalism is, therefore, part of the policy of

Indigenism is a prominent feature of the social environment in Southeast Asia, and it serves to distinguish the systems of economic nationalism found in that part of the world from the traditional neomercantilist system described by Myrdal and Heilperin. In the Philippines and Thailand, indigenism has evolved by accretion—pragmatically and erratically—and is implemented in an enterprise type of economic system. In others, such as Burma and Indonesia, it tends to reflect a fuzzy ideological commitment to socialism. Whether pragmatic or ideological, it is a major determinant of economic policies. As such, it can be and frequently is, but need not be, an obstacle to long-run economic growth. Effective participation in organizing accelerated economic development requires that economists understand this phenomenon and appreciate its priority in less developed societies only recently removed from colonial status.

Economists have displayed little interest in indigenism partly because, with few exceptions, they project themselves imperfectly from the confines of Western tradition and experience. The ethnocentricity of economists is reflected in the implicit assumption that diverse social goals can be subsumed under the objective of economic growth, which is almost universally defined as "increasing per capita real income." Implied in such a definition is faith in income in the social accounting sense as the appropriate measure of social progress, that income is homogeneous and impersonal and, therefore, selection among alternative policies and activities can and should reflect "rational" economic considerations.

Western faith in income as the appropriate criterion for economic policies in the context of underdevelopment reflects the dominance of rationalism in Western outlook. More specifically, it can be traced to three related factors. First, in developed economies the gap between aspirations and accumulated resources—capital, knowledge, and human capacities—available to satisfy aspirations is small relative to past progress and is in dynamic equilibrium. Economic growth proceeds in Western societies at rates that keep the gap between aspirations and resources from widening. Under such circumstances the demand for

---

racial ascendancy, because if you increase the economic power of your own people and weaken that of alien elements, you are strengthening the political power of those people in the state whose ascendancy you desire on grounds which have nothing whatever to do with economic conditions" ("Economic Nationalism in the Modern World," *International Affairs* [10], May 1931, pp. 291–292).

particular goals will be moderated, and material progress can substitute for a wide range of social objectives. Social scientists and politicians alike recognize the capacity of material progress to submerge social tensions and conflicts.

Second, Western economies are characterized by institutional arrangements evolved over long periods of sovereignty which provide more or less automatic fulfillment of minimum social goals. Such institutions include progressive taxation, government promoted and subsidized research, comprehensive social insurance, and systems of transfer payments which ensure appropriate development of human and material resources. These institutions function in ways that make us confident that the fruits of material progress will be widely distributed, that the nature of specialization will contribute to industrialization and sovereignty, that the benefits of growth will accrue to our nationals, and that our communal demand for expanding social services will be satisfied.

Finally, expanding welfare can be taken for granted where viable political parties must recognize the responsibility of government to intervene in the economy to maintain high levels of employment. In a society characterized by high per capita incomes and savings, the pursuit of high levels of employment ensures economic growth because achievement of employment goals depends upon government investment and upon monetary and tax policies that create strong incentives to private investment.

The conditions that permit industrial societies to equate economic growth with social progress are not duplicated in substantive aspects in the countries of Southeast Asia. There the goal of economic growth competes with other social goals to a degree not comparable with that found in wealthy industrialized societies. In particular, the goals of economic nationalism cannot be subsumed under increasing per capita real income and, therefore, they generate priorities independent of, and frequently in substantial conflict with, the priority assigned to material expansion.

To the extent that they acknowledge any development under colonialism, Southeast Asians are convinced that such development was not in the interests of the legatee national states in their part of the world. They believe that the nature of their economic development and specialization can either be attributed to the exploitative nature of colonialism or is due to their late entry into the mainstream of material progress. They are quite aware of the long history of actions by policy makers to control the direction of national specialization in developed countries—actions frequently taken over the protestations of economists concerned with short-run relationships between specialization, foreign trade, and real income.

Colonial economies tended to develop a dualistic character in which relatively modern and foreign trade-oriented, commercial, industrial, financial, mining, and plantation enterprises existed in enclaves surrounded by the traditional, technologically backward, subsistence-oriented, agricultural sector. These sectors were not only economically isolated one from the other, but the ownership of assets in the modern sector tended to be vested in aliens, including the economically rational Chinese, Indian, and Arab minorities as well as the dominant Westerners. This state of affairs resulted primarily from superior business acumen and the willingness of members of alien minority groups to save and invest productively. The process was enhanced by the favorable returns to capital in an environment in which that factor was combined with accessible natural resources and abundant and cheap labor, both native and immigrant. Capitalistic behavior was liberally rewarded by the *laissez-faire* economic organization exported to Asia by the West. The relative absence of any background of experiences that might have prepared Southeast Asians to engage in capitalistic activities, however, precluded the extensive appearance of indigenous entrepreneurship.

The determination of Southeast Asians to convert their colonial-type economies to national economies represents to them an essential and presently missing stage in the consummation of their nationalist movements whether revolutionary or evolutionary. This fact of the economic environment is readily acknowledged by the outside observer but in our preoccupation with economic growth, tends to be forgotten or dismissed as of little importance.

The indigenism that is the subject of this study is an integral element in the comprehensive policy systems of economic nationalism found in Southeast Asia. Each of the studies is concerned with understanding the spectrum of policies and activities motivated to reduce the importance, prominence, and functional specialization of alien participation in the national economy. The determination to indigenize is as central to nationalism—particularly the nationalism of societies only recently removed from colonialism—as is the goal of political autonomy, because it is an indivisible ingredient of independence and sovereignty. In Southeast Asia the ramifications of nationalism, economic as well as political, can be understood only in terms of colonialism and colonial development.[16]

To understand the central process of colonial economic development, one can benefit by returning to the controversy over economic imperialism which was intense around the turn of the century. This literature includes the perceptive protests of the economic heretic Hobson as well as the Marxist and neo-Marxist contributions of Lenin, Hilferding, Luxemburg, and others.[17] The leitmotif of this controversy was the role of capital in imperialism, and embedded in the polemics are insights into the process of colonial capital formation which help us to understand the virulence of economic nationalism today.

The forty years prior to 1914 represented a period of massive outflow of foreign investment from Western Europe to the less-developed world. The bulk of this investment moved to the so-called "areas of recent settlement"—North America, Australia, New Zealand, South Africa, and Russia—rather than to the countries that today are underdeveloped. However, a substantial amount of capital moved to the tropical colonies and to Latin America—the present underdeveloped world—and was a major ingredient in such economic development as took place. At the same time that this movement of capital was taking place, Europe's merchandise trade was basically balanced. The trade returns show, moreover, that the colonial world experienced substantial export surpluses in commodity trade at the time they were receiving substantial injections of foreign investment from the developed world. This characteristic export surplus was the so-called "colonial drain."

[16] The failure of economists to appreciate the importance of indigenism as a motivation of policy in underdeveloped countries is explained, in part, by the voluminous and relatively sterile controversy over the sharing of the gains from trade between primary products and manufactures and between underdeveloped and developed economies. In their attempts to explain the erratic and limited achievements of colonial economic development, and incidentally, to "explain" the determination of newly sovereign ex-colonial societies to transform their economies, economists have emphasized the alleged deterioration of the terms of trade of underdeveloped countries. The case against colonial-type specialization erected on such grounds is ethnically and racially neutral and provides no understanding of an economic nationalism that insists that membership in the national society be required for access to resource and product markets.

[17] Consistently obtuse were the contributions of economists who concerned themselves with the "economic cost" of colonies in expenditures required of the government of the colonial power.

Originally associated with the extraction of export produce through such institutions as monopoly companies and indirect rule, this pattern of trade continued following the relative liberalization of colonial policy in the twentieth century.

The theory of capital transfers tells us that foreign investment is transferred through a surplus of exports of goods and services on the part of the investing country and a corresponding import surplus in the capital receiving country. How could the colonial world be receiving foreign capital at the same time that it was experiencing a "colonial drain"? The answer is a simple one. The services of capital, shipping, insurance, of the colonial bureaucracy, and so forth, provided by the developed world were sufficiently in surplus that net earnings from exports of such services could pay for the persistent import surplus of commodities received by the developed world in trade with the colonies and still have earnings left over to account for the accumulation of foreign capital which was "transferred" to the colonies.

In other words, foreign investors in the aggregate were entitled to a flow of income from the services of capital which they had accumulated in the colonies. Foreign investors collectively chose to consume a part of the investment income to which they were entitled, and such consumption is measured by the import surplus of goods and services (net of investment income) enjoyed by the developed world in trade with the less developed colonies. The remaining part of their investment income, the investors in the aggregate chose to "plow back" into the colonies. Behaving as capitalists, they added to the capital equipment— mines, plantations, transportation facilities, commercial enterprises—in the colonies and at the same time enlarged the share of the total income of the economy accruing to foreigners.[18]

The roles of capital and the capitalist outlined above, are central to economic development in which production is organized on the basis of individualism. In the absence of participation by Southeast Asians as capitalists and entrepreneurs, however, ownership of the assets in the "modern" sectors of the colonial economies ended up in the hands of foreigners. Southeast Asians were confronted by the anomalous situation in which the modern enterprises in their part of the world

---

[18] This assumes, of course, that the rate of capital accumulation by foreigners exceeded the rate at which the indigenous elements of the population saved and invested. This state of affairs was supported by the favorable returns to capital where it was combined with abundant labor and natural resources.

came into existence and grew to impressive size as the result of the mobilization of local labor and natural resources through the critical participation of alien entrepreneurs and their capital, the latter consisting largely of earnings plowed back into enterprises. Southeast Asians, possessing neither capital goods nor entrepreneurial experience, did not immediately comprehend the nature of capitalist development. In time, however, their awe at the capacity of their colonial rulers to organize resources and create large-scale modern enterprises was replaced by acute awareness that their labor and local natural resources made an essential contribution to this process.

In a number of prominent instances, political power was abused by aliens to obtain natural-resource concessions and to divert public revenues to social investment that lowered costs to Western and other alien enterprises. Such cases should be acknowledged and deplored, but they should not be allowed to obscure the essential nature of the process of colonial development. "Exploitation" was probably no more characteristic of such development than it was of early capitalist development in the West with its well documented abuses of political power and the privileges of wealth. The inequities that resulted were inherent in the institution of private property and the differential rewards reflecting property ownership and the proportions in which productive factors were combined.[19]

In the process of colonial economic development the interstices between the large Western enterprises organized to produce raw materials for industrial markets were filled by smaller enterprises associated with commerce, foreign and domestic, wholesale and retail. Western enterprise tended to dominate in foreign commerce, but Western businessmen could not be recruited in sufficient numbers to provide the smaller scale retail and wholesale trading functions. Best equipped

---

[19] The application to the colonies of the classical economic prescription discriminated against Southeast Asians who were unprepared by any background of experience to participate in the market other than as sellers of their labor, either directly as unskilled workers or indirectly as peasant smallholders. At still another level, the *laissez-faire* prescription discriminated against the colonies as latecomers and ensured that they would remain specialized as producers of primary products for export to industrial markets. The process of specialization and exchange does not reduce initial differences in human capacities or available resources but instead tends to accentuate and perpetuate them. The pejorative connotation of "colonial *laissez faire*" also reflects the double standard frequently found in the application of the policy prescriptions of economic liberalism to the colony as compared to their observance in the metropolis.

to fill this vacuum were the economically rational members of alien minority groups: Chinese, Indians, and immigrants from the Middle East. The enterprises of these aliens flourished because of the industriousness of the proprietors and because, as "capitalists," they were motivated not to consume, but to plow back their earnings.

The objective circumstances of colonial development in Southeast Asia provide the basic explanation of alien domination of the prestigeful and materially rewarding economic roles. Of even greater importance, however, in understanding the virulence of economic nationalism in that part of the world, is the image held by Southeast Asians of their colonial experience and the consequences for their economic, political, and social development which they attribute to the policies and practices central to that image.

Colonial policies and practices, as they were adapted to societies with diverse cultural heritages and to economies with great variety in resource endowments, were distinguished by heterogeneity rather than uniformity. Major differences resulted from diverse ideological influences at work in the colonizing powers, the timing and motivation of imperialism, the adaptation of such institutions as direct and indirect rule, changes in transport and other technologies, the available markets, and so forth. Because of this diversity, generalizations about colonial policy and practice should be treated with caution.

Contrasting sharply with the diversity in colonial policies and practices is the uniformity of the images held by Southeast Asians of their colonial experiences. Nationalism is seen as a movement to liberate the national society from the constraints—at best, incidental to misguided policies; at worst, reflecting the deliberate exploitation inevitable in the colonial relationship—which prevented the fulfillment of individual and collective capacities for economic and political development. The racial correlation of economic roles and inequalities is believed to have resulted from policies and practices that blocked access by members of the indigenous society to jobs, markets, and resources.

The nationalist image of colonial economic development includes a stereotyped immigration policy imposed by the colonial power and reflecting the needs of Western enterprise. Such a policy permitted, and in many cases subsidized and recruited, the immigration of Asian aliens who subsequently specialized in commerce and credit—with the discriminatory encouragement of the colonial administrators—

thereby establishing a formidable barrier to the economic mobility of members of the indigenous society.

Equally uniform, is the image of the neglect and perversion of education under colonial rule. The "plural" colonial economy as Furnivall described it was characterized by "disorganization" and the absence of effective social demand for educational and other social services.[20] Such services, in excess of minimum and inadequate levels, became the responsibility of each of the racial communities, and facilities and services available to the indigenous population were maintained at woefully inadequate levels. Moreover, such universal education as was provided was focused upon preparation for clerical positions in the bureaucracy and hence was unsuited to the full development of the capabilities of Southeast Asians.

Similarly, colonial policy and practice is believed to have prevented indigenous participation in commerce and export specialization based upon absolute advantage and exploitation of the patrimony of natural resources. The fact of alien domination of this sector was convincing evidence for Southeast Asians that, at worst, discriminatory obstacles to their participation existed, or at best, that the colonial administrators had failed to provide training, capital resources, and avenues of mobility which would permit balanced racial participation.

Still another facet of the image concerns colonial commercial policy which denied protection to the colonies and therefore is believed to have prevented industrial development. Exchange reserve currencies in which the supply of money and credit were tied inflexibly to the balance of payments subjected the colonial economies to the extreme instability attributed to world trade in primary products. In the eyes of Southeast Asian nationalists, the most charitable explanation of such policies lies in their consistency with *laissez faire,* while more common is the belief that they were an aspect of colonial exploitation which

---

[20] J. S. Furnivall, *Netherlands India* (Cambridge: Cambridge University Press, 1939), pp. 446–469. Furnivall sought to understand the consequences of applying the *laissez-faire* prescription in the Southeast Asian environment dominated numerically by tradition-bound, indigenous populations. He analyzed powerfully the consequences of colonial economic policy and development in terms of "disorganization" and "pluralism" and pointed out the consequences for the militancy of Southeast Asian nationalism. In later writings, he pushed his insight unnecessarily hard and labeled the consequences of colonial *laissez faire* "disintegration," but this should not be allowed to obscure the fundamental value of his contribution.

prevented Southeast Asia from entering into the mainstream of industrial progress.

The validity of the nationalist image of colonial policies and development is not the concern of this study.[21] The existence of such an image and its nature are "facts" as real as the fact that successful nationalist movements fell heir to alienized and relatively underdeveloped economies. The belief that colonial policies maintained overpowering obstacles to the economic and social mobility of members of numerically dominant indigenous populations was a powerful idea behind the nationalist movements that brought an end to colonialism in Southeast Asia. With the achievement of independence, the nationalist elites were challenged to indigenize their economies as well as to initiate economic development, as it became clear that removal of colonial rule was not a sufficient condition to ensure progress toward these goals. Our study is concerned with the persistence, initiative, and ingenuity evident in the response to the challenge to indigenize.

The colonial experience tended to discredit capitalism; political elites, and populations generally, have been receptive to the establishment of government corporations and nationalization of existing enterprises. The willingness to resort to public enterprise has been reinforced, in some cases, by the strength of socialist ideology and in all of Southeast Asia by the weakness of indigenous entrepreneurship. Throughout Southeast Asia the newly sovereign states sought to expand the economic functions of the public sector to include commercial, industrial, mining, and plantation enterprises. Expansion of the sector of bureaucratic enterprises obviously helps to satisfy the deep-seated urge to transfer important economic activities from alien to indigenous control.

More important to indigenism has been the widespread use of public

---

[21] This is a statement of fact and not a value judgment. The nationalist image of colonialism has produced both human progress and inhumanity. Nationalism has been a powerful liberating force for some societies, and it has consigned others to privation, inequality, and arbitrary authority. Webster defines patriotism as "devotion to the welfare of one's country," but someone else observed that it "is the last refuge of scoundrels." The validity of the nationalist image is a question of fact, but after a century of analysis and controversy, there is no consensus in the developed world on the facts, or even among the populations of the ex-colonial powers. This is not to suggest, of course, that the consensus in the ex-colonial, underdeveloped world which is described above establishes any objective facts. Thinking man must be concerned with ex-colonial nationalism in order to deplore its excesses and applaud its accomplishments. This concern, the authors share, but the purpose at hand is more modest; it is to describe and understand economic nationalism in Southeast Asia.

policies and institutions to redress handicaps that have limited participation by Southeast Asians in business activities. In a number of cases, government monopolization of foreign exchange has been developed into a powerful weapon for increasing the share of nationals in commerce and manufacturing. As is well known, restriction of imports is followed by increases in the domestic prices of such imports, and indigenous importers and industrialists, allocated foreign exchange at the official rate, are granted a windfall which helps to ensure their competitive survival. Equally important has been government monopolization of the power to create and distribute credit as managed currency systems have replaced the exchange reserve currency systems which were associated with colonial status. Establishment of central banks has been followed by the proliferation of government-controlled specialized credit institutions which often serve to reserve credit resources to nationals. Commercial and exchange control policies have also been used to indigenize the production and marketing of exports. In a number of cases, government monopolies established to implement exchange controls and to produce government revenues have nationalized export functions. Moreover, inflation and currency over-valuation, which have been widespread in Southeast Asia, have adversely affected export production and trade, traditional strongholds of foreign investment.

Finally, Southeast Asians have not hesitated to use the police power of the state to indigenize. Laws and administrative procedures denying aliens the right to engage in specific economic activities or to practice professions are to be found in every Southeast Asian country. Strict immigration and naturalization policies have minimized alien access to resources and markets. Sporadic but extensive expropriation of alien assets has also occurred. Expropriation has ranged from overt nationalization with and without compensation to gradual indigenism through discriminatory taxation.

There follows below a series of country studies of indigenism in the Philippines, Indonesia, Burma, Thailand, and Malaya, together with shorter essays which tentatively survey this phenomenon in South Vietnam and Cambodia. Each study includes a brief survey of the cultural, historical, political, and economic factors that have shaped indigenism, followed by examination of the structure of policies and institutions through which this goal is pursued. In a concluding chapter, we seek to distill from our efforts those generalizations, qualified as necessary, in which we are confident.

2

THE PHILIPPINES*

The Environment of Policy

Current efforts on the part of the Philippine society to ensure that
material progress is Filipino as well as Philippine, have roots reaching
far back in colonial rule. Repressive measures and violence directed at
the Chinese, particularly in Manila, occurred sporadically throughout
the Spanish era.[1] While the sources of Spanish and Filipino animosity
are complex, dependence upon and inability to compete with Chinese
commercial enterprises undoubtedly contributed to this reaction. More
recently, the upsurge of nationalism and revolutionary activity in the
closing decade of the 19th century was sustained in considerable part
by Filipino resentment over the land holdings of the Spanish-staffed
missionary orders.[2]

* The field research behind this study of indigenism in the Philippines was
made possible by generous fellowships received from the John Simon Guggenheim
Foundation, the Social Science Research Council, and the Cornell Southeast Asia
Program. The author is indebted to his collaborators for perceptive criticism and
advice, for their patience and unruffled dispositions, and for their faith in our
enterprise—F. H. G.
[1] As early as 1586 Governor Vera and other prominent Spaniards in Manila
petitioned the Council of the Indies to forbid the Chinese from remaining in
Manila to retail their goods since this business should be in the hands of the
Spaniards. In 1722 an official in the colony reported to the king that "The Sangleys
(Chinese) have gained control of all the commerce in provisions and other supplies
and of the mechanical trades" (William L. Schurz, *The Manila Galleon* [New
York: E. P. Dutton and Co., Everyman Edition, 1959], p. 96).
[2] By the end of the Spanish period, the missionary orders owned about 165,000
hectares of agricultural land or some 6 per cent of the total area in private ownership. Missionary land holdings were concentrated in the irrigated and relatively
fertile areas in central Luzon. In the five Tagalog provinces adjacent to Manila

During the American period, an early issue between the Colonial administrators and Filipino nationalists was that of public land and natural resource policy. The Americans sought to promote economic development through liberal land and other natural resource concessions to all comers. Filipino leaders insisted on a policy of strictly limiting the extent of land and natural resource concessions and confining the benefits to Filipinos and United States nationals. This issue served to mobilize Filipino opinion and to vitalize the nationalist movement in the early years of the American rule.[3] More important, the Filipino position prevailed and gave economic development in the colony a direction and character that molded Philippine nationalism.[4]

During the American period until the establishment of the Philippine Commonwealth in 1935, indigenism remained a subdued and gradualist movement subordinated to the achievement of independence. Recognition that aggressive nationalism might serve to delay independence was brought home to Filipinos by controversy over the so-called "bookkeeping laws" and the public stalls ordinances which were ultimately declared unconstitutional by the United States Supreme Court. The former acts provided that all accounts must be kept in a language familiar to Filipinos, and the latter that space in the public markets could be leased only by Filipinos and United States nationals.[5] The opposition of Chinese in the Philippines as well as official resistance by the Chinese Government had important repercussions in the islands and abroad. The controversy, moreover, was seized upon by the American

---

such holdings accounted for 48 per cent of the agricultural land. See Cesar A. Majul, *The Political and Constitutional Ideas of the Philippine Revolution* (Quezon City: University of the Philippines Press, 1957), pp. 123–136.

[3] For an account of Philippine public land policy, see Alice M. McDairmid, "Agricultural Public Lands Policy in the Philippines during the American Period," *Philippine Law Journal* (28), December 1953, pp. 851–888.

[4] It is true, of course, that evasion of limitations on land alienation has been prominent. The essence of the policy was maintained, however, and it exercised important influence on Philippine economic development. Cf., Frank H. Golay, "The Nature of Philippine Economic Nationalism," *Asia Papers* (1), Spring 1964, pp. 17–19.

[5] The United States Supreme Court in Yu Cong Eng *vs.* Trinidad, 271, U.S. 500 (1926) ruled that "the intent of a statute is the law," and that the intent of the Bookkeeping Act of 1921 was to force the Chinese from the retail trade business and not to ensure the full collection of taxes. In declaring the act unconstitutional, the Court, in effect, held that protection is to be extended not only to citizens but to everyone within its jurisdiction including aliens.

opponents of independence as an argument for prolonging the period of preparation for self-government.[6]

Once independence was scheduled and the commonwealth government began to take form in the Constitutional Convention of 1935, the suppressed goals of indigenism emerged. Policies and institutions for achieving these goals developed erratically however, over the next quarter century. In spite of the "trial and error" nature of this process, the last decade and a half has seen rapid Filipinization in an environment of economic growth and reliance upon individualism and private enterprise.

Although the Philippine society, as other national societies in Southeast Asia, assigns dominant priority to achievement of an acceptable congruence between the nation-state, the national society, and the economy, the process by which progress toward this goal has been achieved in the Philippines is unique in the area. In each of the countries, the system of indigenism initially reflected determination to create an indigenous bourgeoisie class—entrepreneurs, managers, and professionals—and powerful rewards were established for individualistic behavior by members of the national society. The results of such efforts to encourage individualism, however, have been uneven and generally disappointing. In Burma, Indonesia, and Cambodia, frustration with the meager accomplishments of this policy led to its abandonment for one of indigenism through nationalization of alien enterprises and denial to aliens of access to activities they formerly dominated. In Thailand and South Vietnam, attempts to create an indigenous middle class were compromised by the priority assigned to assimilation of the Chinese, and only minor inroads have been made on the racial patterns of ownership and functional specialization. In Malaya, policies of indigenism have merely "scratched the surface" of the problem of introducing Malays into commerce, finance, and industry.

Filipino nationalists also visualized indigenism as resulting from a combination of large-scale public enterprise and expanded private Filipino participation. Directly productive bureaucratic enterprise was tested thoroughly, was found wanting, and has been abandoned. On the other hand, the Filipino entrepreneurial response, vigorous compared

---

[6] Cf., Katherine Mayo, *The Isles of Fear* (New York: Harcourt Brace and Company, 1925), and Nicholas Roosevelt, *The Philippines, a Treasure and a Problem* (New York: J. H. Sears and Co., 1926).

to that found in any other Malayo-Polynesian society, has sustained rapid postwar Filipinization and modest economic development.

Philippine indigenism is a complex and distinctive phenomenon understandable in terms of features of the social environment that give form and substance to the movement. A major parameter is the relative size of the alien population which, for the Philippine society, has maintained a meaningful choice between a minority policy of repression and isolation and one of accommodation and assimilation. Still another major influence is the character of the nationalist movement which, in important aspects, is unique in Southeast Asia. The economic conservatism of the land-based cacique oligarchy which captured the leadership of the independence movement established a rigid commitment to an individualistic economic system and ensured that efforts to create an indigenous middle class would persevere. Third, the postindependence economic growth facilitated indigenism because it is easier to increase the Filipino share of a growing pie. Moreover, economic expansion moderated the priorities assigned to other goals that might have competed successfully with the priority assigned Filipinism. Finally, it is necessary to understand the accelerated transition of the Filipino as "economic man"—his changing attitudes and values, his self-image and his world-image, and the evolving pattern of his responses to the opportunities in the system of indigenism. The peculiarly Filipino adaptation of the enterprise economy produced national economic development only because a significant number of Filipinos modified entrenched patterns of thought and behavior as they assimilated to entrepreneurial roles.

The Philippine society throughout its history has absorbed infusions of foreign blood—most prominently, Chinese and Spanish—through a process of assimilation in which the racial elements absorbed slowly lost their distinctiveness. This process is going on today and the non-Malay members of the society make up a complex continuum including, at one extreme, alien elements that identify with the culture from which they emigrated and, at the other, elements which are "more Filipino than the Filipinos." Although administrative discretion in the system of indigenism has given rise to distinctions in the treatment of ethnic Filipinos, native-born citizens of alien descent, and naturalized citizens, these distinctions have remained relatively minor. The pressures of indigenism impinge on the aliens—five-sixths of whom are

Chinese nationals—whose participation in the economy is conspicuous to Filipinos.

The first census under the American regime in 1903 tabulated 56,412 residents born outside the Philippines, including 41,035 born in China.[7] The ratio of foreign-born to total population was 0.81 per cent with the China-born accounting for 0.59 per cent. The most recent census in 1960 recorded a total population of 27,087,685, including 219,686 aliens of whom 181,626 were Chinese citizens. The ratio of aliens to total population was 0.81 per cent and that for Chinese citizens was 0.67 per cent. For the intervening censuses of 1918, 1939, and 1948, these ratios depart slightly from the remarkable correspondence found in the above comparison, but the maximum proportions of aliens and of Chinese nationals recorded in the census of 1939 were only 1.04 per cent and 0.73 per cent respectively.

The proportion of aliens in the population is unlikely to increase because it is Philippine policy to minimize immigration for purposes of permanent residence. For the eight years through 1961, such immigrants averaged only 393 annually. There is every reason to believe that this negligible rate of immigration will be maintained in the future.

The stability of the proportion of aliens in the population in this century conceals substantial shifts in the sex and nationality composition of the alien minorities. For example, in 1903 only 517 Chinese women were resident as compared to 40,518 men. This imbalance was steadily reduced, however, until in 1960 Chinese women were outnumbered by men 103,569 to 78,057. The most significant change in the nationality composition of the alien population occurred at the end of World War II when the Japanese, who numbered 29,057 in 1939, were repatriated.

Census aggregates also conceal the fact that historically and today the alien minorities, both Western and Asian, are concentrated in urban centers. The census of 1960 reported one-half of the alien Chinese resident in Manila and surrounding Rizal Province, and another quarter were in provincial cities and larger towns. Similarly, such aggregates conceal the extreme functional specialization which has sustained the intensity of economic nationalism.

[7] For various estimates and censuses of the Chinese minority, see Victor Purcell, *The Chinese in Southeast Asia* (London: Oxford University Press, 1951), pp. 569–581.

The small ratio of aliens to the total population contributes to the distinctiveness of Philippine indigenism by freeing that society to pursue goals of Filipinism with minimum concern for maintaining avenues of assimilation. The Chinese remain involuntary and patient victims because they have no place to go. As for the Western elements, they display little willingness to assimilate on any significant scale and their departure for home would be welcome to Filipino nationalists.

Philippine nationalism emerged in and was nurtured by the alternation of liberalism and conservatism in nineteenth-century colonial policy which corresponded—with some lag—with the domestic political cycle in Spain. The collapse of the Spanish colonial empire in the Americas during the nineteenth century, moreover, served to communicate to Filipino elites awareness of the possibility of autonomy and ultimate independence.

The origins of the nationalist movement can be traced to two proximate sources. One branch developed as an intellectual movement among Filipino students seeking professional training which flourished in the comparatively liberal environment in Spain in the last two decades of the nineteenth century. Members of this group, in most instances mestizos with infusions of Chinese and Spanish blood and with origins in the cacique class, were strongly influenced by the masonic-liberal ideas they found in Spain and were increasingly estranged from clerical-class loyalties. Filipino nationalists of the "Propaganda Movement" led by José Rizal were evolutionary in philosophy and visualized social progress in terms of reform and minimum self-government. Another branch of the nationalist movement had rural roots in the long history of dissidence and violence associated with the semi-feudal organization of agriculture and urban roots in the insecure proletariat in Manila which was the "window" opening toward new ideas and institutions. This movement, initially led by Andres Bonifacio, was revolutionary in outlook and demanded independence.

Although the revolution of 1896 was precipitated by the Katipunan, the underground revolutionary political club led by Bonifacio, the two branches of the nationalist movement merged in their common opposition to Spain. In the confusion and fluidity surrounding military reverses and internal jockeying for power, the leadership of the nationalist movement passed to Emilio Aguinaldo whose strength was based in the ethnic loyalties of the Tagalogs and in his own competence as a military leader. In the leadership vacuum that persisted following the execution of Rizal and the military reverses of Bonifacio and subsequently of Aguinaldo, the leadership of the nationalist movement shifted increasingly to members of the cacique class. The economically conservative, land-based aristocracy steadily tightened its hold on the nationalist movement in the early years of American rule, and it is this factor, more than any other, which has given Philippine nationalism a Latin quality distinctive in Southeast Asia.

The second major influence was American colonial policy, which subverted the nationalist movement with self-government and paternalism. Extensive liberty to engage in political activity was granted to Filipinos in 1902, and the Jones Act of 1916 established substantial Filipino autonomy in internal affairs. Rapid Filipinization of executive departments was initiated in 1913, and by 1920 the nationalists (Nacionalista Party), for most practical purposes, had achieved internal self-government. Colonial policy gave the nationalists broad scope to develop their movement through self-government which contributed to its nonradical, centripetal nature.

Philippine nationalism has also been molded by the depth of Filipino identification with the West, which resulted in dominant patterns of emulation in social behavior and a willingness to adapt Western economic and political institutions to the Philippine environment. The depth of such identification was made possible by the early conversion of the Filipinos to Catholicism which weakened their ties to a Malay heritage. Such identification with the West is also explained by the public school system installed by and initially staffed with Americans. The public school system was not so much an instrument for conventional education—the use of English as the language of instruction precluded this—as it was a means of communicating to the grass roots of society the possibility of social change. The public school system was instrumental in intensifying the Western identification of Filipinos who had been by-passed by the Spanish cultural impact.

Philippine nationalism is also distinguished by the requirements of sovereignty acceptable to that society. Once independence was assured, external security became the dominant concern of the political leadership, and during the Commonwealth period there was considerable discussion of this problem in terms of Philippine "neutralization" guaranteed by major interested powers. In the immediate postwar period, the problem was approached in terms of the collective security afforded by the United Nations as augmented by regional security arrangements, and the Philippines displayed—and still displays—considerable initiative in trying to promote regional collaboration. The sharp rebuff they received in the abortive Baguio Conference of 1950 called following the collapse of Nationalist China, however, prompted a major reexamination of the problem of external security.

The Philippines astutely used leverage arising out of American desire for a Japanese peace treaty to obtain a firm commitment from the United States to defend the islands. This commitment was established in the Mutual Security Treaty signed in Washington, August 27, 1951 and was subsequently reinforced by the pact creating the Southeast Asia Treaty Organization. Philippine foreign policy has differed from that of the United States in significant aspects, but such differences have tended to be submerged in the shared strategic interest. Although there has been vigorous controversy between the two countries over issues of sovereignty and jurisdiction arising in the existence of United States military bases in the islands, the Philippines, up to the present, has shown no sustained inclination to change existing security arrangements. Paradoxically, the "compromise" of political nationalism to establish an acceptable external security encouraged the upsurge in Filipinism in recent years as it freed Philippine policy makers from constraints that otherwise would arise in the international position of their country.

Philippine nationalism has also been given a distinctive flavor by the role of the Catholic church and its missionary orders. For a number of reasons, the Church has been unable to recruit adequate numbers of Filipinos for the clergy. As a result, the Philippines has remained a missionary territory, and a major part of the dominant Catholic population continues to be served by non-Filipino priests. In addition, the Church as a universal, cosmopolitan institution is, in important respects, antithetical to nationalism.

Finally, Philippine nationalism has been subverted by economic concessions and benefits flowing from the "special relationship" with the United States. During the decade and a half following World War II, the Phillippines benefited from an import surplus of approximately $3 billion, made possible by equivalent United States government disbursements. Presently, the United States is subsidizing the Philippines with economic aid, a military assistance program, substantial Veterans Administration payments, plus the sugar quota which enables the Philippines to market approximately one million tons of sugar in the United States at prices substantially above world market prices. It has been traditional Philippine policy to retain and if possible to expand the preferences in the United States market.[8] The valuable economic concessions established by the United States in favor of the Philippines have produced a streak of objective "rationality" in Philippine nationalism, and their existence goes far in explaining the skepticism with which this phenomenon is viewed elsewhere in Asia.

Reinforcing this rationality is the "grass roots" reservoir of good will toward the United States, reflected in widespread Filipino confidence in United States actions and policies. The explanation of this confidence is complex, but its existence is undeniable. Anti-Americanism has not been, up to the present time, a profitable issue in Philippine politics. This is not to say that frictions do not characterize mutual relations or that anti-Americanism will not become resurgent at any time. The Philippine society, however, has not responded widely to anti-American slogans, in part, because of the prolonged period of relations based on good faith and mutual understanding.

Also significant in shaping indigenism has been post-independence Philippine economic development. Colonial development and specialization following the middle of the nineteenth century, reflected the amalgam of economic liberalism and exclusiveness that characterized colonialism. Export expansion based on absolute advantage led to increasing specialization in production of tropical agricultural crops and minerals until, by the late 1930s, over three-quarters of export earnings were provided by sugar, abaca, coconuts, and gold. Similarly, the colonial policy of mutual free trade resulted in increasing concentration of Philippine trade with the United States until, for the same period, over three-fourths of exports and seven-tenths of imports were traded with the metropolitan country. Not only was Philippine trade concentrated, but mutual free trade precluded development of manufacturing in the Philippines.

Colonial economic development was not impressive. Sufficient progress was maintained to more than keep abreast of population growth, but it did not provide Filipinos generally with an advanced level of living. Agricultural resources engaged in export production were owned for the most part by Filipinos, and food crop production for the internal

[8] See Frank H. Golay, *The Revised United States-Philippine Trade Agreement of 1955*, Cornell Southeast Asia Program Data Paper No. 23 (Ithaca, New York, November 1956).

market was exclusively in Filipino hands. Alien minorities were functionally specialized and economically and politically powerful. Western interests—American, British, Spanish, Danish, and Swiss—were active in exporting, importing, and wholesaling, and they provided important entrepreneurial and capital resources in the development of mining and forest resources and in the processing of agricultural crops for export. Asian minorities, mainly the Chinese, were important in the assembly of agricultural and forestry products both to supply the domestic market and for export. They dominated internal trade, particularly retailing, and participated extensively in importing and wholesaling. The extent of foreign ownership and participation in non-agricultural enterprises at the end of colonial rule is summarized in Table 1.

Manufacturing was concentrated in the processing of export commodities, and ownership was dispersed among the various ethnic groups, including Filipinos. Under the exchange reserve currency system, commercial banking was dominated by foreign branch banks which made funds available for commerce and little else. Monetary and credit institutions to mobilize and divert financial resources to production for the domestic market were undeveloped with the important exception of the government-owned Philippine National Bank which provided limited banking services outside Manila.

Government was minimum colonial-type government, smug in its "efficiency," reflecting inadequate levels of social investment and services, and relying heavily on excise-type taxes. Political decision making was shared by the leaders of the Nacionalista Party, dominated by landowners who maintained voting discipline among peasants in local areas, and the colonial administrators lead by the Governor-General. The latter, ten thousand miles from the United States, led a cheek-by-jowl existence with American businessmen seeking profits from the Philippine economy. Under the circumstances, the conservative bias in political decisions and economic policies was not surprising.

The pressures sustained by the Philippine nationalist movement culminated in the passage by the United States Congress of the Philippines Independence (Tydings-McDuffie) Act of March 24, 1934. Independence was scheduled to follow a transition period of ten years during which the islands would be governed as an autonomous Commonwealth. The economic preferences which had served to bind the Philippine economy tightly to the United States were scheduled to be

(millions of pesos)

Type of enterprise	Total	Filipino	American	Chinese	Japanese	Spanish	British Commonwealth
Logging	4.4	3.0	.3	.2	.8	—	—
Sawmills	26.8	9.6	12.2	.2	1.8	.3	2.4
Fisheries	46.1	43.7	—	.1	.4	—	—
Gold mines	188.2	91.9	68.5	3.3	.3	6.1	11.4
Iron mines	4.4	.6	3.5	—	—	.1	.1
Chromite mines	3.6	2.7	.4	—	—	—	—
Manganese mines	2.1	1.3	.5	.1	.2	—	—
Copper mines	2.4	.8	1.0	—	—	—	.6
Electric utilities	56.3	14.7[a]	41.2	.1	—	—	—
Manufacturing[b]	356.4[c]	197.3	66.5	26.4	4.7	49.2	4.0
Commerce[b]	587.6[d]	203.6	121.0	149.5	23.0	15.3	35.2
Total	1,278.3	569.2	315.1	179.9	31.2	71.0	53.7

31

Abbreviations used in tables:

n.a. = not available

n.r. = not reported

— = negligible

Source: R.P., Bureau of Census and Statistics, *Census of the Philippines: 1939*, Vol. IV, Reports for Economic Census (Washington, D.C., 1943). Rows do not add to totals because of omission of minor interests from tabulation.

[a] Including assets owned by government agencies.

[b] R.P., Bureau of Census and Statistics, *Statistical Abstracts of the Philippines* (Manila, July 1950). Summaries of the 1939 economic census.

[c] Major components included food products, which accounted for 237.2 (including, *inter alia*, coconut oil, 22.3, desiccated coconut, 4.6, sugar centrals, 170.3, and rice and corn mills, 28.3); textiles and manufactures of textiles, 19.1 (including embroidery products, 5.9 and tailors and dressmakers, 7.3); and miscellaneous manufacturers, 92.8 (including beverages, 13.2, cigars and cigarettes, 14.9, cordage and twine, 5.0, printing and publishing, 9.6, and footwear, 5.5).

[d] Major components included retail trading which accounted for 425.3, wholesale trading, 36.8, combined retail and wholesale trade, 28.2, and importing and exporting, 91.7.

dismantled over the period of the Commonwealth. Filipinos would thus be given a breathing spell in which to adjust their economy to the loss of these concessions.

In the years immediately following establishment of the Common-wealth in 1935 and prior to the Japanese invasion at the end of 1941, the Philippine government experimented persistently with bureaucratic entrepreneurship and the public corporation as the instruments with which they hoped to industrialize the economy and transfer control to Filipinos. The accomplishments of the Commonwealth period, how-ever, produced little basic change in the colonial-type economy that the Filipinos had inherited.

Following World War II, which had thoroughly shaken up custo-mary patterns of behavior, shifted populations, and destroyed much of the capital equipment, a period of rehabilitation and reconstruction with liberal United States participation resulted in the restoration of the prewar economy and structure of policy. Such a restoration of the prewar *status quo* proved to be a stop-gap, however, as processes of far-reaching social, political, and economic change had been initiated.

Rapid economic expansion was maintained throughout the postwar period. Within the three years following 1945, the economy, which had suffered destruction, damage, and dislocation, was rehabilitated and prewar levels of output restored.[9] In the next eight years, through 1956, real output increased by two-thirds, and in the nine years following 1956 real output is estimated to have increased further by one-half.[10] Over this period of seventeen years, population is estimated to have increased from 19.1 million to 32.3 million, a rate of increase somewhat less than half the rate of increase in real output.

The expansion in output was widely distributed with the largest absolute increase in income taking place in the agricultural, forestry, and fisheries sector where income (at current prices) increased from ₱ (pesos) 2.3 billion in 1949 to ₱5.8 billion in 1965, or by 152 per cent. The real output of agricultural, forestry, and fisheries products over the

[9] Cf., Marvin Goodstein, *The Pace and Pattern of Philippine Economic Growth: 1938, 1948, and 1956*, Cornell Southeast Asia Program Data Paper No. 48 (Ithaca, New York, July 1962), p. 6.

[10] See the successive April-June issues beginning with 1956 of the *Statistical Reporter*, quarterly journal of the National Economic Council, in which the Philippine social accounts are published. Gross national product at constant (1955) prices is estimated to have increased from ₱9,132 million in 1956 to ₱13,670 million in 1965. Combining the Goodstein and the official series results in the estimate that gross real output increased following 1948 through 1965 by 150 per cent.

sixteen years through 1965 is estimated to have increased by 131 per cent.[11]

Following the establishment of high levels of protection by import and exchange controls at the end of 1949, income generated by manufacturing expanded rapidly. In the sixteen years through 1965, income originating in manufacturing increased from ₱440 million to ₱3,072 million or from 8 per cent to 18 per cent of national income. The real increase in manufacturing output, however, was more modest as protection raised prices of manufactures produced in the Philippines or imported. The official index of the physical volume of manufacturing production increased over this period by 326 per cent.[12]

Another feature of postwar economic growth gratifying to nationalist ambitions has been the decline in the relative importance of exports and in the political power of exporting interests. In contrast to rapid growth elsewhere in the economy, exports handicapped by overvaluation of the peso slowly expanded during the postwar period through 1961. The influence of exporting interests, which traditionally had dominated economic policy making, declined as competing interest groups benefited from policies of Filipinism and acquired political power. Foreign capital and entrepreneurship which had played a central role in development of the export sector under the powerful incentives of colonial "mutual free trade" were steadily replaced by Filipino resources as virulent nationalism reinforced the incentive to disinvest in continued peso overvaluation.

By early 1962 when exchange and import controls were abandoned and the peso effectively devalued to approximately half of the previous rate, substantial Filipinization of the export sector had taken place. Devaluation of the peso stimulated sharp expansion in the value of exports from an average of $530 million annually during 1960–1961 to an average of $769 million in 1963–1965, a change that promises the Philippine economy an escape from the foreign exchange constraint which had become a formidable obstacle to continued economic expansion and industrialization. The strong incentives to expand exports established by the peso devaluation have not aroused Filipino apprehensions as they would have if the colonial pattern of alien dominance of the export sector existed today.

The economic growth sustained by the postwar Philippine economy

[11] Central Bank of the Philippines, *Statistical Bulletin* (17), December 1965, p. 247.
[12] *Ibid.*

could not help but satisfy nationalist longings. Visual evidence of industrialization was widespread. Experience in successfully managing their economy contributed to the self-confidence of Filipino policy makers. Moreover, dependence upon the export economy for welfare was rapidly reduced, and the establishment of commercial policy autonomy by exchange and import controls was followed by geographic diversification of Philippine trade, thus reducing traditional dependence upon the United States market. Such progress toward a more genuine independence reinforced the self-confidence which, after 1949, Filipinos derived from the reduction of the Huk insurrection and the evident improvement in the functioning of the political processes and institutions. These mutually reinforcing changes contributed to the environment of social stability and material expansion in which Filipinization was rapid.

It was relatively easy to increase the Filipino share of a growing "pie" by taking policy actions to ensure that new activities, new investments, and new production would be Filipino. The strong incentives to Filipino initiative and enterprise "worked" because the relative attractiveness of remaining a rural or urban landlord eroded in an atmosphere of economic expansion. Equally important, the adjustments forced upon the displaced alien businessmen by Filipinism were eased. The opportunities in manufacturing were not closed to aliens, and the appearance of Filipinos with commercial and entrepreneurial experiences stimulated joint enterprises to produce for the protected internal market.

The experiences of Filipinos with self-government and management of their economy since World War II have confirmed them in their decision to rely on an enterprise-type economy with liberal rewards for entrepreneurial initiative. This is not to say that it is a competitive economy—which it is not—but rather to emphasize the role of entrepreneurial initiative in organizing resources. The profit motive is the goad, but competition is not the regulator. Instead, the state by dispensing the various items of largess inherent in its powers to tax and to spend—and not to tax—to create money and credit, and to intervene in market processes, regulates private economic activity. Such a system reflects, in large part, the quality of Philippine politics and the persistent incompetence displayed by bureaucratic managers and entrepreneurs. Philippine experiments with public enterprise over the two decades following 1935 established a strong case for reliance on private initiative and enterprise.

Discretionary intervention by the state in the economy—exchange and import controls, price controls, creation of institutions to distribute credit, as well as constant experimentation with all kinds of government enterprises—has established a system which, in important respects is the antithesis of *laissez faire*. The pervasive intervention by the government is characterized by minimum concern for competition and efficiency. The system is in the *laissez-faire* tradition, however, insofar as the expectations of the businessmen are treated with tenderness.

The Philippine economic system is capitalist in that there is a conjunction of strong forces tending to concentrate income in the form of profits. So long as the peso remained grossly overvalued, the foreign exchange windfall was allocated as "profit" from commercial and industrial activity. The fiscal system is extremely dependent upon excise-type taxes which impinge directly on consumption rather than profits. Moreover, it is government policy to grant exemption from all internal revenue taxes to so-called "new and necessary industries." High levels of protection established by new tariffs, as well as tight controls on imports, also help to insure the profitability of entrepreneurial activity. Rapid urbanization tends to maintain a disciplined, competitive industrial labor force and limits the capacity of labor to bargain for higher wages and thereby encroach on profits. Credit is easy, profit prospects overpowering, and indigenism ensures that Filipinos are favored in the allocation of the valuable privileges. Under the circumstances, the emergence of Filipino entrepreneurship is not surprising.

Agricultural expansion more rapid than population growth has been sustained as rural Filipinos, restless and mobile as the result of the dislocation of war and the population pressure in high tenancy areas, have settled the frontier and brought idle land in previously settled areas under cultivation. The expansion in agricultural output has contributed immeasurably to social stability by ensuring that the material progress of the postwar period was shared widely in increased consumption. The rapid growth in output, moreover, has been sufficient to turn the internal terms of trade against the agricultural sector and has made possible the remarkable stability that characterized the composite indexes of Philippine prices through the 1950s. Agricultural expansion also enhanced the profitability of entrepreneurial activity to the extent that agricultural imports are a cost of production and insofar as improved consumption contributes to the productivity and passivity of the urban labor force. The decline in the internal terms of trade for agricultural output, combined with the increasing willingness of the government to intervene to redress the traditional imbalance in land-lord-tenant relations, has encouraged healthy competition among the traditional political elites. Subordination of the interests of the agricul-tural producers in favor of the emerging Filipino commercial and in-dustrial interests is an important aspect of the structure of incentives which recruits scions of the *rentier* class to commerce and manufac-turing.[13]

The fiscal performance of the government remains circumscribed by two basic considerations. First, the Philippines has a long tradition of economically conservative, minimum colonial government and the postcolonial government, identified with an evolutionary nationalist movement dominated by the cacique oligarchy, continues the basic features of colonial fiscal policy. The second consideration is the con-straint upon revenues inherent in the structure of the economy and the level of development. Where government revenues represent a sub-stantial share of aggregate output, this situation tends to result from the socialization of the means of production or, in enterprise economies, is attributable to the enlarged role of the corporation, as industrializa-tion proceeds and tax withholding is developed to generate revenues.[14] Limited economic development presently precludes a major fiscal role for these two institutions in the Philippines.

Conservative fiscal policy combined with rapid expansion in output to ensure relative stability of prices throughout the 1950s. At the same time, conditions were favorable for rapid growth in money and credit which was shared between the government and business. In contrast to the situation in many underdeveloped countries, the expansion of credit to the private sector in the sixteen years through 1965, amount-ing to ₱3,952 million, was virtually double that diverted to the govern-ment sector. This increase in domestic credits was absorbed by the growing economy with minimum inflation, thereby facilitating modest expansion in government functions and services and at the same time providing ready command over resources to the emerging Filipino en-trepreneurs.

[13] For an informative study of entrepreneurial recruitment in the Philippines, see John J. Carroll, S.J., *The Filipino Manufacturing Entrepreneur, Agent and Product of Change* (Ithaca: Cornell University Press, 1965).

[14] Strong external demand conditions in conjunction with inelastic supply con-ditions for smallholders output have permitted a limited number of less developed countries to obtain large amounts of revenues for limited periods of time from taxation of export commodities.

Credit and savings resources are distributed by an expanding structure of functionally specialized capital market institutions. Commercial banking, in which participation of branches of foreign banks was prominent during the colonial period, by the end of 1966 included 41 banks of which 37 were Filipino-owned and these banks operated 447 branches and agencies scattered over the country. There were 7 savings banks operating 29 offices, 338 rural banks, a postal-savings banking system with 1,423 offices, the government-owned investment bank—the Development Bank of the Philippines—with 36 branches, 25 private development banks, and 4 development corporations engaged in investment banking. As of the end of 1960, there were 7 building and loan associations, 83 pawnshops, as well as a flourishing system of 136 private insurance companies, and a government-capitalized Agricultural Credit and Cooperative Financing Administration with 524 local co-operatives. A Government Service Insurance System, the retirement system for civil servants, and a rapidly growing contributory social security system play increasingly important roles in the mobilization of savings.[15] The rapid growth in this system of institutions contributes to Filipinism by channeling credit to nationals who respond to the entrepreneurial incentives.

Finally, Philippine economic nationalism has been shaped by the postwar acceleration of change in the Filipino—the transformation of the human environment. Students of the Philippines are in agreement that the society is embarked upon a transition in which patterns of social, political, and economic behavior are undergoing rapid change. The expanding goals of Filipinsm are one aspect of this process of change and at the same time advances toward these goals propagate further change.

As elsewhere in Southeast Asia, the traditional and basic social organization is familial. The building blocks of Philippine society are the elementary family and the bilateral extended family which embraces all relatives of the father and mother. The intense family loyalties of Filipinos have resulted in minimum identification of individual welfare with activities of a group larger than the family. Security and status are attributable to family membership and basic loyalties are to the family. Universal recognition of the loyalties and responsibilities of family membership has handicapped the development of co-operative business

[15] For information on the rapid proliferation of credit and capital market institutions, consult the *Annual Reports* of the Central Bank of the Philippines.

organizations, expansion of governmental activities, and the establishment of functional efficiency as a criterion in economic decision making.

Although identification with and loyalty to the family are basic characteristics of Filipino behavior, this pattern has eroded in recent years. Far-reaching changes were an inevitable result of World War II. Activities necessary to survival as the economy collapsed under pressure of allied blockade and bombing contributed to the deterioration of values and standards which reinforced the stability of the traditional society. Large numbers of Filipinos forced underground into the guerrilla forces devoted themselves to subversion of the existing political order, including that of the constituted Filipino authorities. Commitment to individual and group violence contributed to new patterns of behavior and thought that resisted confinement in the stylized, formal relationships of the prewar society.

The war created an environment favorable to the emergence of individualism. Access to new and varied experiences—military command, administrative and organizational responsibilities, and others— generated Filipino aspirations as well as capabilities. As the economy ground to a halt under the impact of the submarine blockade and bombing, problems of survival forced Filipinos to become more mobile and this change persisted in postwar urbanization and land settlement. Similarly, the constraints and opportunities of the Japanese occupation forced Filipinos into new patterns of improvisation and innovation which deeply influenced the self-image of the Filipino. The war also contributed directly to reduction of alien participation in the economy: the Japanese were repatriated and pressures were maintained on Western nationals who had been interned to accept repatriation. The war also weakened colonial relationships and influences that otherwise would have persisted to resist Filipino freedom to develop and adapt their political and economic systems.

The economic system in which indigenism has flourished is peculiarly Filipino in that it is essentially a continuum of the familiar political system. Philippine political activity is organized on the basis of the bilateral extended family and regional and ethnic loyalties. Abstract ideas play a minor role in Philippine politics, party loyalties are weak, and power tends to reside in unstable coalitions of local leaders. As a result, political activity tends to be concerned with the creation of personal relations of obligation and reciprocity, the endless

seeking of influence and security through patronage and the maintenance of power through relationships of personal fealty. Such a system, inherently unstable, places a premium on behind-the-scenes
manipulation and intervention and maintains a willingness on the part
of the society to tolerate unusual levels of executive discretion.

The system of overpowering entrepreneurial incentives rewarded
political activity as much as it did economic initiative. The Filipino
seeking to become an entrepreneur found himself engaged in familiar
political manipulation—to obtain foreign exchange allocations, to obtain credit, to seek items of reparations equipment, to obtain protection
against imports, and so forth. Initially, he was half businessman and
half politician, and in the latter activity he could bring to bear his long
experience and skills. Such an adaption of the enterprise economy made
the transition from traditional patterns of economic behavior—and
from political behavior—to entrepreneurship much less abrupt.

Filipino educational values have encouraged new patterns of economic behavior. The public school system traditionally has served as
an instrument for introducing new ideas raising aspirational levels
and offering new symbols of prestige, and in the process served to
erode the foundations of traditional authority and value patterns.
Despite progressive Filipinization of the teaching staff, the system
retained its American orientation in curricula, philosophical attitudes,
and many aspects of content.

Filipinos look upon education as an end in itself, as a symbol carrying prestige and status, as much as it is viewed as an avenue to economic well-being and security. The strong drives to obtain an education and to provide an education for one's offspring have been reflected
in the proliferation of institutions of higher education and enrollments.
For the most part, these institutions have not been distinguished by
their quality but they have provided a socially and economically useful
education. Prolonged schooling, frequently capped by a period of study
abroad, has created a generation of Filipinos receptive to Western-
oriented patterns of individualistic behavior.

Such developments have contributed to a significant behavior pattern—a pattern of Filipino willingness to emulate things American.
Such a generalization, of course, has more validity for the urban, fluid
Philippines than it does for the traditional, peasant-dominated agricultural sector, but the visitor to the Philippines is struck by the extent of
such emulation. The educational system, political institutions, and the

economic system are, in important respects, in the American pattern. The press, service clubs, labor unions, "society," and the like, are modeled upon the same institutions in the United States. The pattern of emulation also carries over into values associated with individualism. The folk hero in the Philippines today is the businessman. He receives universal approbation and approval. He is asked to pontificate on social issues. His departures by airline and by steamship are elaborately chronicled in the press. When he opens a new plant or office building the occasion will be graced, in all likelihood, by the participation of the President and by a cardinal of the Church. The prestige accruing to those who achieve business success is a strong stimulus to such activity. When studying the Philippines, one is struck by the one-way flow of talent out of the universities and professions into business pursuits—a flow that has proved debilitating to Philippine scholarship.

Students of the Philippines have frequently commented on the stability of the Philippine population, both social and geographic. Today the opposite is true; the population is restless. Urbanization is proceeding with major impact on values and patterns of behavior. Social, economic, and political relationships become impersonal in an urban environment as the individual is forced into a far wider range of human relationships and new attitudes are generated by diverse experiences involving functional and transient relationships. Similarly, migration to the frontier of land settlement is proceeding with consequent weakening of kin-oriented social relationships, traditional attitudes, and behavior patterns.

Major consequences flow from the acceleration of population growth in an environment of economic change. The capacity of the extended family with its patriarchal trusteeship of family wealth held in agricultural and urban real estate to maintain the social and economic position traditionally enjoyed by individual family members is doomed to frustration as the family grows. The younger, well-educated family members tend to become restless in the face of foregone economic opportunities and in the face of well-publicized achievements of individualistic contemporaries. The impact of bilateral and equal inheritance in an environment of rapid population growth has resulted in heavy strain on the cohesion of the extended family. Filipino entrepreneurship, in large part recruited from the cacique class, has been pulled into new activities by powerful incentives and at the same time pushed by the relative decline in the capacity of the extended family to ensure the material well-being and social prestige of its members.

Other factors have hastened the changes in the Filipino which make him more responsive to economic incentives and opportunities. The proliferation of communications media has tended to erode the monopoly of political and economic leadership of the *rentier* class. Literacy has expanded at a respectable rate until in 1960 somewhat more than three-fifths of the population was functionally literate. English has been accepted, at least for the time being, as the *lingua franca* of the economy, and this has contributed to the receptivity of Filipinos to ideas and patterns of behavior that reinforce individualism. The range of publications is wide and circulation figures are impressive. The country is blanketed with radio stations, and the transistor radio today occupies the position on the horizon of material aspirations of the average Filipino that the Parker Pen occupied fifteen years ago.

Although the processes of social change which have begun to remold the human environment have accelerated, the consequences should not be exaggerated. The impact, as of the present, remains marginal. It is concentrated in the urban centers, particularly Manila, and has radiated outward from the cities and larger provincial towns. The impact has been widespread in the provinces surrounding Manila and is evident in the barrios of these provinces. In the remote provinces of Luzon and in much of the rest of the country, the changes described herein have been slow and halting. What is important in understanding economic development *cum* Filipinization, however, is the fact that these changes have generated a flow of Filipinos willing to engage in entrepreneurial activities and possessing diverse skills—managerial, professional, and craft—in quantities adequate to sustain the economic development of the postwar period.

Filipinos have been energetic in seeking import licenses and foreign exchange allocations, perhaps initially as "dummies" for aliens but increasingly in order to perform entrepreneurial functions. Similarly, Filipinos have sought credit, reparations equipment, tax exemption, and the like to become manufacturing entrepreneurs. Some Filipinos have used political skills to obtain various kinds of natural resource concessions and have developed them into viable enterprises. Other Filipinos of less fortunate economic status, moreover, have made sacrifices to acquire educational qualifications of diverse kinds; they have migrated to the cities and have assimilated to the disciplined industrial work force which has materialized in advance of the job opportunities in manufacturing and commerce.

The economic system on which the Philippine society has chosen to rely is nothing more than a reflection of a component part of the human environment: the urban, transitional Filipinos. The marginal changes described herein have been sufficiently rapid to make the system work. It is not a particularly attractive system—wealth and income tend to be concentrated in profits and *rentier* income, the former inflated by a regressive fiscal system and rapid urbanization. The bulk of Filipinos, as in the colonial era, remain passive bystanders as the organization of economic resources based upon individualism proceeds. There is, however, a significant and growing group of Filipinos who are making the transition from traditional, stylized schemes of thought and behavior and in the process have sustained the indigenism which is the concern of this study.

The Nature of Philippine Indigenism

CONSTITUTIONAL CONVENTION

Enactment by the United States Congress of the Philippines Independence (Tydings-McDuffie) Act,[16] was followed by an upsurge of indigenism, and in the Constitutional Convention convened on July 30, 1934 the objectives of Filipinization became clearly delineated.

The principle of public enterprise was accepted without controversy and the Constitution (Art. XII) provides that "The State may, in the interest of national welfare and defense, establish and operate industries and means of transportation and communication, and, upon payment of just compensation, transfer to public ownership utilities and other private enterprises to be operated by the Government."

Although controversy arose in the Convention over provisions for citizenship, it quickly became evident that the delegates would reject, on economic grounds, the principle of *jus solis*, which had prevailed during the American colonial period. A spokesman for this change, Miguel Cuaderno argued: [17]

---

[16] Public Law (P.L.) No. 127, 73rd Congress, 2nd Session.

[17] Cuaderno, a career civil servant, was appointed Secretary of Finance by President Roxas and subsequently was named governor of the Central Bank when it was established at the end of 1948. As governor of the Central Bank, Cuaderno exercised greater influence over postwar economic policy than did any other person, and he played a major role in the rapid Filipinization of the economy.

I am against the precept (*jus solis*), Mr. President, for economic reasons. The very preamble of our constitution says that we are to maintain and conserve the national patrimony. A child without a drop of Filipino blood could . . . select Filipino citizenship perhaps for economic reasons, perhaps, Mr. President, in order that he could take advantage of the limitations contained in this draft for the acquisition and enjoyment of our natural resources. Who knows that, behind the idea of adopting local citizenship, he is not mentally reserving the citizenship of his blood, the citizenship of his parents.[18]

The Convention accepted, without recorded opposition, the principle of *jus sanguinis* as the basis for citizenship.

Filipinization of natural resources generated a sympathetic response exemplified by the contention of a delegate that, "with the complete nationalization of our lands and our natural resources it is to be understood that our God-given birthright should be one hundred per cent in Filipino hands . . . otherwise, our independence will be just a mockery, for what kind of independence are we going to have if a part of our country is not in our hands but in those of foreigners." [19]

Debate tended to moderate the more xenophobic proposals for natural-resources policy, but the basic nationality requirement was retained. The Constitution as finally approved provides (Art. XIII) that "all . . . natural resources of the Philippines belong to the State, and their disposition, exploitation, development, or utilization shall be limited to citizens of the Philippines, or to corporations or associations at least sixty per centum of the capital of which is owned by such citizens."

Filipinization of the retail trade, long dominated by the Chinese, received strong support. The Committee on Commerce recommended that "five years after the inauguration of the Commonwealth, only citizens of the Philippine Islands and of the United States, and firms, partnerships or corporations . . . at least seventy-five per centum owned by said citizens, may engage in the retail business." [20]

In the draft Constitution, however, this article was not included and extensive debate produced a compromise draft article, stating that "the National Assembly may by law prescribe that only citizens of the

[18] Jose M. Aruego, *The Framing of the Philippine Constitution,* Vol. I (Manila: University Publishing Co., 1936), pp. 211–212. Aruego, lawyer and educator, was a delegate to the Constitutional Convention.
[19] Speech of delegate Enrique J. C. Montilla, Negros Occidental. Reported in Aruego, *ibid.,* Vol. II, p. 592.
[20] *Ibid.,* p. 658.

Philippine Islands and/or the United States and firms, partnerships, or corporations . . . at least 75 percent owned, and controlled by said citizens may engage in the retail business." [21]

Subsequent debate was tense and a vote was delayed in order to hold a caucus of Nacionalista Party delegates. The caucus, counseled by Senate President Quezon, the dominant leader of the independence movement, agreed not to press for an article Filipinizing retail trade and settled for a convention resolution stating "that it is the sense of the Convention that the public interest requires the nationalization of retail trade." [22]

The report of the Committee on Commerce proposed still another draft article providing that "only citizens of the Philippine Islands and of the United States, and firms . . . at least seventy-five per centum owned by said citizens, may engage in the business of warehousing, milling, selling or in any way dealing in rice, corn and other cereals of food value produced in the Philippines." [23] This recommendation, however, was not included in the draft Constitution, as the issue was dropped once the article providing for Filipinization of retail trade was abandoned.

A number of proposals to nationalize public utilities were introduced, and the Convention readily approved an article limiting the operation of public utilities to Filipinos and firms at least 60 per cent Filipino-owned.[24]

Proposals to Filipinize employment were also popular. The report of the Committee on Labor and Social Welfare included a draft article authorizing the State "by means of laws based on the principles of social justice, to regulate the nationalization of labor." The draft Constitution did not include this article but in subsequent debate three alternative amendments calling for Filipinization of employment were presented, and it became evident that a majority of the delegates were determined

[21] *Ibid.*, p. 662. It was contended that such an amendment was necessary to give the National Assembly power to nationalize retail trade in view of the fact that the Constitution guaranteed equal protection of the laws to every person.

[22] *Ibid.*, p. 663. The Constitutional Convention subsequently rejected the proposed amendment and approved the caucus resolution.

[23] *Ibid.*, p. 665–666. The report of the Committee on Commerce concluded: "This situation (alien monopolization) has given rise in the past to serious troubles. It is very harmful to our economic self-sufficiency and may cause grave social disorders. The evil is so deeply rooted in our soil and is of such harmful consequences that it is imperative that the same be corrected."

[24] *Ibid.*, p. 669.

to include such an article. At this point, Quezon intervened again, and advised the delegates to reject such an article as it would invite the antagonism of those countries (China and Japan) whose nationals in the Philippines would be affected. The well-disciplined Nacionalista Party delegates fell into line.[25]

While the Convention witnessed frequent outbursts of sentiment for indigenism, the Constitution, as approved, was only moderately nationalistic. To a considerable degree, this reflected external influences. It had to be approved by the President of the United States, and the important economic interests that had been built up during the colonial period could bring heavy pressure to bear on his decision. Equally significant was the awareness, shared by the delegates, of the necessity to "get along" with China and Japan if Philippine sovereignty was to become a reality.[26]

The nationalist aspirations of the Filipino people were clearly defined in the process of drafting the Constitution. The State was given wide economic powers, including the right to demand compulsory civil service of citizens and the right to participate in all kinds of economic activity through public enterprises. Similarly, the Constitutional Convention reflected the determination to Filipinize major economic activities.

Although the Constitution received overwhelming approval from the Philippine society when submitted to vote, the provisions reserving the exploitation of natural resources and the operation of public utilities to Filipinos were later breached in favor of Americans and their enterprises by the so-called "parity amendment" adopted in 1946. Immediately after World War II with Philippine independence scheduled to materialize on July 4, 1946, the United States Congress hastily drafted two laws of major importance to the Philippines. One law, the Philippine Trade Act of 1946, stipulated terms to be included in a trade agreement to be negotiated between the two countries.[27] Among other provisions, the trade agreement required the Philippines to extend national treatment for Americans and their enterprises in the exploitation of Philippine natural resources and the operation of public utilities. The second law, the Philippine Rehabilitation Act of 1946, provided

[25] *Ibid.*, pp. 654–655.
[26] Cf., J. Ralston Hayden, *The Philippines: A Study in National Development* (New York: Macmillan Co., 1955), p. 41.
[27] P.L. 371, 79th Congress, 2nd Session.

for war-damage payments totaling $620 million.[28] The law authorized the payment of war-damage claims in excess of five hundred dollars, however, only after the Philippines ratified the proposed trade agreement. After prolonged and divisive controversy, the Philippine society resentfully accepted the humiliating "parity" requirement of the Trade Act by amending their constitution.

CITIZENSHIP, NATURALIZATION, AND IMMIGRATION

It will be recalled that the Constitutional Convention rejected *jus solis,* place of birth, and adopted *jus sanguinis,* descent of blood, as the basis of nationality. Under the Constitution (Art. IV), citizenship is conferred on those whose fathers are citizens of the Philippines, and those whose mothers are citizens and who, upon reaching the age of majority, elect Philippine citizenship.

Insofar as the principle of *jus solis* had prevailed during the American regime, all persons born in the Philippines during that period were entitled to citizenship.[29] The change to the principle of *jus sanguinis* was quickly made retroactive, however, by a succession of court decisions which culminated in the Tan Chong decision that an individual born in the Philippines prior to ratification of the Constitution was not a citizen. In reaching this position, the Court, after discussing the issues at length, admitted that the doctrine of *jus solis* had been recognized in many Philippine decisions. The Court concluded, however, that this principle had not been applicable to the Philippines because of restrictions on Philippine citizenship found in the Philippine Act of 1902 and therefore had not, in fact, been the law during the American period.[30]

---

[28] P.L. 370, 79th Congress, 2nd Session. For more extensive treatment of the economic aspects of the transfer of power, see Frank H. Golay, *The Philippines: Public Policy and National Economic Development* (Ithaca: Cornell University Press, 1961), pp. 60–67.

[29] Roa *vs.* Collector of Customs, 23 Phil. 315. See also United States *vs.* Ang, 36 Phil. 1958 and Haw *vs.* Collector of Customs, 59 Phil. 612. The United States Congress in the Philippine Act of 1902 (P.L. 235, 57th Congress, 1st Session) decreed "that all inhabitants of the Philippine Islands . . . who were Spanish subjects on April 11, 1899 (date of the ratification of the Treaty of Paris ending the Spanish-American War) . . . and their children born subsequently . . . shall be held to be citizens of the Philippine Islands." For a concise survey of the evolution of legal aspects of Philippine nationality, see Cornelius J. Peck, "Nationalistic Influences on the Philippine Law of Ctizenship," *The American Journal of Comparative Law* (14), Summer 1965, pp. 459–478.

[30] In 1939, the Supreme Court in Paz Chua *vs.* Secretary of Labor, 68 Phil. 649, bluntly stated that the mere fact of birth in the Philippines prior to ratifica-

An aspect of citizenship and nationality that has concerned Philippine courts and legislators has been the right of a child of a Filipina mother to "elect" citizenship as provided in the Constitution. Early in the Commonwealth, legislation was enacted which provides that a Filipina loses her citizenship, "if, by vesture of the law in force in her husband's country, she acquires his nationality." [31] It was subsequently established that the children of such a Filipina have no right to elect Philippine citizenship.[32]

Philippine naturalization requirements are not unduly harsh,[33] but as implemented by court decisions, naturalization policy is distinguished by a vigilant concern to prevent any abuse of acquired citizenship. The philosophy has been expressed time and again in court decisions that the naturalization laws are to be strictly observed and that the rights and privileges of citizenship acquired by naturalization are not inalienable, but must be continuously merited by behavior expected of loyal and patriotic Filipinos.

That naturalization confers something less than full citizenship is also evident in the steady increase in the number of legislative proposals and laws and administrative measures designed to limit economic benefits and privileges to "native born" Filipinos. For example, House Bill No. 2053, which would have limited the benefits of the Philippine Flag Law to "natural born" citizens was passed by Congress in 1949, but was vetoed by President Quirino.[34] Beginning in 1957, the Monetary

---

tion of the Constitution was not sufficient to confer citizenship. One year later the Court reversed itself in Ramon Torres *vs.* Tan Chim, 69 Phil. 518. In 1947, the Court settled the question in Tan Chong *vs.* Secretary of Labor, 79 Phil. 249. For a brief survey of the Court's reasoning, see Peck, *ibid.*, p. 469. Although the Court wavered slightly in 1952 in Talaroc *vs.* Uy, 92 Phil. 52, the principle was reaffirmed in 1957 in Teo Lam *vs.* Republic, 54 Official Gazette 1364.

[31] Commonwealth Act (C.A.) No. 63 of Oct. 21, 1936. In view of the Chinese principle of dual nationality, the obvious goal of this law was to prevent the children of Chinese married to Filipinas from acquiring citizenship by birth.

[32] Secretary of Justice, *Opinions*, No. 14, Series of 1938; No. 83, Series of 1939; No. 201, Series of 1947. The Filipina also loses her citizenship if the relationship is a common law marriage. More recently, the Supreme Court moved to tighten citizenship policy by decreeing that an alien woman marrying a Filipino becomes a citizen only by naturalization. This decision, which upset long standing practice, deprived thousands of women of citizenship which they must reestablish by naturalization. See *Manila Times*, January 31, 1967, p. 1.

[33] See C.A. No. 473 of June 17, 1939 as amended by Republic Act. (R.A.) No. 530 of June 16, 1950.

[34] *American Chamber of Commerce Journal* (25), July 1949, p. 287.

Board of the Central Bank used its power to license banks to require that the ownership of banks established thereafter be limited to natural-born citizens.[35] Pressure for such a qualification resulted in the enactment and subsequent approval by President Garcia in 1959 of Republic Act No. 2261, which provided that the lucrative privilege to barter specified exports outside the system of exchange control "shall be granted only to natural born citizens of the Philippines." [36]

In recent years, Congress has moved to prescribe cancellation of naturalization as a penalty for violation of the provisions of economic laws. Such a provision first appeared in the Anti-Dummy Law (C.A. No. 473 of June 17, 1939) and more recently in the barter export law of 1959 described above, and the Price Control Act (R.A. No. 2610 of July 16, 1959).

In spite of the strictness of existing policy, efforts on the part of Congress to further restrict naturalization have persisted. During the First Congress (1946–1949), three bills were introduced that would have sharply reduced the number of aliens who might qualify for naturalization. In the Second Congress (1950–1953), such bills numbered seven, in the Third Congress, eleven, and in the first two years of the Fourth Congress, fourteen such bills were offered.

This concern on the part of Filipino nationalists has arisen because naturalization proceedings are a function of the Courts of First Instance, the lower courts in the Philippine judicial system. Petitions are made to the Court and after approval are filed with the Department of Justice for the executory period of one year during which they may be challenged. It is widely believed that the present decentralized system —in the American tradition—is abused, and there is considerable discussion of the need to centralize the naturalization process in the Department of Justice.[37] Under the present procedure, the understaffed Department of Justice can intervene only in a minimum number of naturalization cases.

In view of the persistent concern of legislators over alleged abuses of the naturalization system, what, in fact, has occurred under this

[35] See below, section on banking and credit.

[36] Precedents for distinguishing between native-born and naturalized citizens existed in the Public Land Law (C.A. 141 of November 7, 1941, Sec. 44) and the law creating the Anti-Dummy Board (R.A. 1130 of June 16, 1954).

[37] It is rumored that naturalization cases are a lucrative source of illicit payments which augment the meager pay of provincial fiscals (prosecuting attorneys), police officials, and judges.

policy? First, there has been steady increase in the number of naturalization petitions. During the first three full years of independence, 1946–1948, such petitions averaged 159 annually, whereas, in the three years ending with 1959, the average number of petitions was 905. The rate at which petitions have been granted has also increased but somewhat more slowly, reflecting the period required for their processing. During the postwar period to the end of 1949, petitions granted by Courts of First Instance numbered 189 annually, whereas, in the three years ending with 1959, petitions granted averaged 587 annually. During the postwar period to the end of 1959, there were 6,336 naturalization petitions. As of mid-1960, some 4,003 of these petitions had received final approval, 929 had been withdrawn, dismissed, or rejected, and the remainder presumably were still pending.[38]

A Department of Justice survey of postwar naturalization cases covering the period to the end of 1959, indicated that Chinese applicants, numbering 6,306, accounted for 93.7 per cent of petitions filed, with petitioners of Spanish nationality and stateless persons accounting for 1.7 per cent and 1.4 per cent respectively.[39] The ratio of successful Chinese petitions to total petitions filed by this nationality group was 53 per cent as compared to 57 per cent for all other petitioners. The ratio of Chinese petitions denied to total Chinese petitions acted upon (total Chinese petitions less those pending at the end of 1959) was 19.3 per cent as compared to 30.4 per cent for all other petitioners.

Although the rate at which petitions for naturalization are submitted has increased, there is no evidence that the courts have taken

[38] The statistics presented here were compiled by the author from the records of the Naturalization Section of the Department of Justice. The condition of the available records left much to be desired and officials admitted that the records were subject to errors arising out of the failure of officials of provincial courts to report the outcome of naturalization cases to the Department. While the statistics presented here are subject to errors of various kinds, they are probably accurate to within 5 per cent. They are confirmed in essential respects by the Census of 1960 which tabulated 26,867,999 citizens of whom 1,282 acquired citizenship by marriage, 1,649 through election by virtue of being born to a Filipina citizen, 3,500 by naturalization, and 4,900 by operation of law, i.e., through the principle of *jus sanguinis*. Native-born citizens accounted for 99.96 per cent of Philippine citizens tabulated in 1960. See R.P., Bureau of Census and Statistics, *Census of the Philippines, 1960*, Vol. II, Summary Report, Table 23.

[39] R.P., Department of Justice, *Naturalization Cases from April, 1945 to December 1959* (typescript, undated). Over this period, naturalization cases numbered 6,728. As of the end of 1959, petitions approved totaled 3,593, with 904 denied, and 2,231 pending.

longer to process petitions or that petitions of Chinese are treated less favorably.[40] On the other hand, during the first decade and a half of Philippine independence, the number of Chinese naturalized amounted to about 2 per cent of the alien Chinese population. In other words, the Chinese in their reluctance to assimilate to the Philippine society and the Filipinos determined to maintain obstacles to such assimilation have combined to produce a rate of legal assimilation that is only a minor fraction of the natural increase in the resident alien Chinese population.

Immigration for permanent residence is regulated by national quotas originally set at five hundred immigrants annually but subsequently reduced to fifty.[41] Once policies were established covering immigration and alien registration and surveillance, Congress thereafter intervened only to increase the various fees imposed on aliens. The original law established an annual head tax of ₱16 on immigrants which, together with various fees "for services" rendered to immigrants totaled some ₱60 annually. By 1960 the Immigration Act as amended provided for various fees to which immigrants were subject and which could result in a total cost to the immigrant of ₱540 annually.

Grounds for deportation are harsh and have increasingly included grounds related to economic activity. Deportation was provided in the Immigration Act of 1940 for conventional grounds such as conviction of crimes involving moral turpitude, an alien who becomes a public charge, belief in the overthrow of the government by force, and so forth. In 1950, Congress amended the Immigration Act to provide for deportation for conviction, among other things, "of profiteering, hoarding, or black marketing . . . , or any offense relating to the acquisition of Philippine citizenship."

In recent years economic legislation has tended to include automatic deportation for alien violators. This type of provision originated with the Import Control Law of 1950 (R.A. No. 426 of May 19, 1950) which

[40] This probably would be interpreted by many Filipino nationalists as confirming their suspicions that naturalization is abused as a result of the corruptibility of provincial officials.

[41] The Immigration Act of 1940, C.A. No. 613 of May 26, 1940 as amended by R.A. No. 503 of June 12, 1950. Over the four years following 1961, the number of aliens registered with the Bureau of Immigration declined from 152,738 to 141,586. This decrease was accounted for by the decrease in the number of alien Chinese from 137,519 to 125,468 (R.P. Bureau of Census and Statistics, *Journal of Philippine Statistics* [18], April-June 1967, p. 5).

provides, "that in the case of aliens, the penalty (for violation of the act) shall consist of payment of fine and immediate deportation . . ." [42] Still another variation on this theme occurred in Republic Act No. 1093 of June 15, 1954, which provides that "any alien who shall knowingly and fraudulently evade the payment of any internal revenue tax . . . shall be liable to deportation." Even more harsh is the Retail Trade Nationalization Law (R.A. No. 1180 of June 19, 1954) which provides for automatic deportation after payment of "a fine of not less than ₱3000 . . . and imprisonment of not less than three years." [43]

The existence of such provisions reflects a broad grant of executive and judicial authority typical of the Philippine political process, but there is little evidence that these harsh provisions are strictly enforced. For example, one observer reported that in the case of two hundred Chinese convicted of violating price control laws and against whom charges were filed with the Deportation Board, none were actually deported.[44]

NATURAL RESOURCES AND PUBLIC UTILITIES

Basic policy governing access to natural resources and the right to operate public utilities was established in the Constitutional Convention which limited these activities to Filipinos and enterprises at least 60 per cent owned by Filipinos. The various laws governing access to specific natural resources and the operation of specific utilities have repeated the nationality requirement of the Constitution (Art. XIII) and in some cases have extended it substantially.

Although the nationality requirement of the Constitution was specifically limited to "agricultural lands," Congress, in the Public Land Act of 1936, extended the requirement by interpreting "agricultural

[42] For similar provisions, see Price Control Act, R.A. No. 509 of June 13, 1950, Sec. 12; Import Control Act, R.A. No. 650 of June 15, 1951, Sec. 18; Price Control Act, R.A. No. 729 of June 18, 1952, Sec. 12; and Price Control Act, R.A. No. 1168 of June 18, 1954, Sec. 9.

[43] For similar provisions, see Margin Fee Act, R.A. 2609 of July 16, 1959, Sec. 8; Price Control Act, R.A. 2610 of July 16, 1959, Sec. 9; and Coffee Import Control Act, R.A. 2712 of June 18, 1960, Sec. 2.

[44] A. V. H. Hartendorp, *History of Industry and Trade of the Philippines* (Manila: American Chamber of Commerce of the Philippines, Inc., 1958), pp. 655–656. The author concluded: "In general, however, it appears that the courts considered the penalties provided for in the law too extreme and humanely refrained from imposing them."

land" to include residential, commercial, and industrial lots both rural and urban.[45] Subsequently, the Secretary of Justice in 1941 issued the opinion that "agricultural land" as specified in the Constitution did not apply to the transfer of title to land held privately for use as a residential lot. This interpretation proved short-lived, however, as in 1947 the Supreme Court in the Krivenko decision decided that "agricultural land" included urban residential, commercial and industrial lots.[46] The Krivenko doctrine was later breached in substantive aspects when the Supreme Court ruled that privately owned land could be leased without nationality restrictions on the lessor for as long as ninety-nine years as allowed by the Civil Code.[47] A decade later, in September 1967, the Court reversed itself and ruled that aliens may not circumvent by lease the "intent of the Constitution" to reserve access to land to Filipinos.[48]

During the American period, title to mineral lands was initiated by discovery of minerals therein, and the right to such land could be maintained indefinitely subject to the annual performance of a specified amount of development work. The Constitution reverts to the regalian doctrine vesting ownership of mineral resources in the state. The granting of mining concessions is governed by the Mining Act of 1936 which established stringent conditions for access to mineral resources.[49] As of the present time, virtually all mining enterprises of any size are working claims established prior to inauguration of the Commonwealth. The titles to such lands which were established during the American period have not been modified by legislation or court decisions.

Access to timber concessions on public lands is governed by provisions of the Revised Administrative Code, which provides for leases

[45] C.A. No. 141 of November 7, 1936, Secs. 58, 59, 60. See also Secs. 12, 22, 23, 33, 44, 47, 48, 61, 118, 122, 123, 124 and 132.

[46] Krivenko vs. Register of Deeds of Manila, 79 Phil. 461. Subsequent decisions affirming the doctrine of the Krivenko decision include Pindangan Agricultural Co. vs. Schenkel, 83 Phil. 529; Rellosa vs. Gaw Chee Hun, 93 Phil. 827; and Register of Deeds of Rizal vs. Ung Sui Temple, Official Gazette (51), June 1955, p. 2866.

[47] Smith, Bell and Co., Ltd. vs. Register of Deeds of Davao, G.R. L-7084, 1957. For the Civil Code provision, see R.A. No. 386 of June 18, 1949, Sec. 1643.

[48] Philippine Association, *Weekly Economic Review*, September 15, 1967, p. 93.

[49] C.A. No. 137 of November 7, 1936. This law (Sec. 74) substitutes 25-year government leases for the outright patents that had been issued during the American colonial period.

"not exceeding twenty-five years" in duration to "any Filipino citizen or association of persons . . . authorized by the Constitution to acquire lands of the public domain." [50]

Exploitation of Philippine fisheries resources is governed by the Fisheries Act of 1932 as amended. The nationality provision of the Constitution is repeated with a slight modification raising the required ownership by Filipinos in licensed fishing enterprises to 61 per cent.[51]

Since the drafting of the Constitution as modified by the "parity" amendment, the various laws enacted to regulate access to public utility franchises have steadily extended the principle that such activities are to be reserved to Filipinos and their enterprises.[52] For example, air transportation franchises "except as otherwise provided in the Constitution . . . shall be issued only to citizens of the Philippines." [53] Similarly, the privilege of operating in Philippine interisland shipping is limited to vessels owned by citizens of the Philippines or by enterprises at least 75 per cent owned by citizens.[54]

The determination of the Philippine society to reserve the exploitation of natural resources to nationals has remained unambiguous since the early controversy with the American colonial administrators over public land policy. Similarly, Filipinos have moved firmly to reserve the right to operate public utilities to nationals. Although the parity amendment established national treatment for Americans and their enterprises in these activities, virulent economic nationalism has dampened American initiative and investment.[55] The administrative discretion inherent in these policies has been used to obstruct and delay non-Filipinos and to favor and expedite the interests of Filipinos.

[50] Act No. 2711 of March 10, 1917, as revised by R.A. No. 121 of June 14, 1947, Sec. 1838. The wording of the section refers to Art. XIII of the Constitution as modified by the "parity" amendment of 1946 establishing national treatment for United States citizens and their enterprises in access to Philippine natural resources and public utility franchises.

[51] This ratio of required participation by Filipinos (or United States nationals) first appeared in Act No. 3674 of June 30, 1930 which provided for access to timber concessions.

[52] C.A. No. 146 of November 7, 1936, Sec. 14 specifies the various economic activities to be included in the term "public utility."

[53] R.A. No. 776 of June 20, 1952, Sec. 12.

[54] Act No. 2711 of March 10, 1917, Sec. 1112. For a firm to qualify under the law, the president and managing director must be citizens. The law further provides that only one deck and one engineering officer may not be citizens and that all other crew members must be citizens.

[55] See below, section on foreign investment policy.

ROLE OF GOVERNMENT ENTERPRISE

Beginning with the establishment of substantive self-government by the Jones Act of 1916,[56] Filipino nationalists persisted in efforts to industrialize and Filipinize through public enterprise. Prior to 1916, the Philippine government was involved with *ad hoc* arrangements to provide financial aid to the Manila Railroad Company. This process culminated in the acquisition of the railroad in 1916 and its operation since that time as a government corporation. The Manila Hotel, which was opened in 1912, ran into financial difficulties and was taken over by the Manila Railroad Company in 1923. Meanwhile, in 1919 the National Development Company (NDC) was organized as a semi-public holding company to acquire and operate agricultural estates as well as to establish manufacturing enterprises. The initial flurry of development by government enterprise terminated in the early 1920s, however, as the shift to Republican Party government in the United States in 1921 produced a sharp change in the complexion of the colonial administration. Reassertion of greater executive authority by the American Governor-General was followed by an abrupt halt in the formation of government enterprises.

The policy of government participation in directly productive activity, which received strong support in the Constitutional Convention, was revived by the Commonwealth Government in the mid-1930s. The National Development Company was converted into a government-owned corporation in 1936 and received large capital appropriations. The NDC subsequently established the National Rice and Corn Corporation (1936), the National Food Products Corporation (1937), the People's Homesite Corporation (1938), the National Footwear Corporation (1940), and purchased the Insular Sugar Refining Corporation (1938). The National Power Corporation was established as a separate corporation in 1936 and subsequently initiated hydroelectric surveys and a modest construction program.

The National Abaca and Other Fibers Corporation (1936) and the National Tobacco Corporation (1940) were formed to engage in diverse operations, including limited procurement and marketing activities with overtones of Filipinism. Similarly, the National Trading Corporation and the National Cooperative Administration were organized in 1940 and assigned various functions including participation in wholesale and retail trade long dominated by aliens.

[56] P.L. No. 240, 64th Congress, 2nd Session.

These ambitious plans for development and Filipinism through government enterprise were interrupted by World War II, however, before the policy was adequately tested. Following the war, the government, stimulated by the opportunity in promised industrial reparations from Japan as well as large amounts of industrial materials declared surplus by the United States armed forces, quickly revived the policy. The NDC created a sawmill project (1946), a pulp and paper mill (1948), a nail factory (1948), the National Shipyards and Graving Dock (1949), and the National Shipyards and Steel Corporation (1950); the Philippine Sugar Institute (1951) was established to take over the assets of the Insular Sugar Refining Corporation. In addition, the government through the NDC provided minority but substantial equity capital in the De La Rama Steamship Company, which operated three ocean-going freighters owned by the government; Celulosa de Filipinos, Cia. a small mill manufacturing paper from sugar cane fibers; and the Philippine Electrical Manufacturing Company, producing incandescent bulbs and fluorescent tubes.

The National Power Corporation flourished during the postwar period experiencing sound management and adequate financing. In addition to limited development of hydroelectric sites and transmission facilities, the NPC also built and operated a fertilizer plant and a small electric-arc steel plant in northern Mindanao using power from the Maria Cristina hydroelectric site.

A number of other corporations were created to provide social overhead services, including the National Airports Corporation (1938), Philippine Air Lines (1946),[57] and the National Waterworks and Sewerage Authority (1955). The Manila Gas Corporation, a private firm which had suffered heavy war damage, was acquired by the NDC in 1951 and was subsequently rehabilitated.[58]

[57] Philippine Air Lines was founded in 1941 as a private enterprise. The Government through the NDC acquired majority control in 1950.

[58] The government also resumed the policy of establishing public corporations with diverse marketing and Filipinization functions. These included the Philippine Relief and Rehabilitation Administration (1945), subsequently reorganized as the Philippine Relief and Trade Rehabilitation Administration (1947), subsequently replaced by the Price Stabilization Corporation (1950), subsequently dissolved and superseded by the National Marketing Corporation (1955), as well as the National Cooperative and Small Business Corporation (1947), the Rice and Corn Production Administration (1950), and the Philippine Tobacco Administration (1954). For details of the reincarnations, permutations, and combinations involved in the extensive history of government enterprises, see A. V. H. Hartendorp, *op. cit.*, pp. 49–63.

Analysis of the role of the public corporation in Philippine economic nationalism must distinguish between the directly productive manufacturing enterprises and public enterprises providing essential services of a public utility nature. Social services—power, transportation, water supply, and the like—are essential to economic expansion, and provision of such services by public corporations is common practice and only incidentally gratifies longings for indigenism. On the other hand, the greater part of over-the-road and interisland transportation, as well as local power services are provided by private Filipino enterprises.

The efficiency with which social overhead services have been organized by government enterprise has varied widely. The National Power Corporation, and the major public financial institutions command confidence. On the other hand, the Agricultural Credit and Cooperative Financing Administration, the National Waterworks and Sewerage Authority, the Manila Gas Corporation, the Manila Railroad Company, the various corporations engaged in agricultural and commercial activities have had spotty records, and in many cases their operations have been characterized by persistent inefficiency and faulty judgment, if not worse.

Attempts on the part of the government to directly participate in manufacturing are more direct manifestations of indigenism. Such enterprises do not represent an inescapable public responsibility so much as a choice among alternative means of ensuring national economic development. Filipino faith in bureaucratic manufacturing enterprises was clearly delineated in the Constitutional Convention, and the two decades following 1935 witnessed extensive testing of this policy.

By the early 1950s the national government was operating railroads, hotels, electric power, gas and water works, as well as directly producing coal, cement, steel, pulp and paper, textiles and yarns, operating a shipyard for both repairs and construction, and engineering shops. In addition, the government had majority equity interests in firms manufacturing incandescent bulbs and fluorescent tubes, and pulp and paper, a "national" domestic and international airline, and a "national ocean-going" steamship line. Finally, the government through a government-owned holding company was, or had been, engaged in production of nails, marble, lumber, footwear, sugar, textiles and yarns, food preserving and packaging, and warehousing. While the extensive list of manufacturing activities on the part of the government indicates persistent faith in the capacity of the government to participate directly in industrialization, the disappointing results produced a radical change in this policy beginning in 1954.

It will be recalled that the principal issue in Magsaysay's successful presidential campaign in 1953 was corruption and inefficiency in government, including nepotism, mismanagement, and corruption in the operation of government enterprises. Following his inauguration in January 1954, the government initiated action to sell or lease to private management those manufacturing plants and other enterprises of the government in which private enterprise was interested and to liquidate public enterprises with a wide variety of price support, marketing, and land colonization functions.

On January 15, 1954 the Office of Economic Coordination in a candid self-appraisal concluded: "The high incidence of political considerations and the 'padrino' system in the appointment, promotion and tenure of office of officials and employes . . . is the root cause of abuses and heavy losses and waste of public funds and property and contributes to the loss of people's faith in government corporations." [59] The report went on to admit:

Some projects and activities of government corporations involving the expenditures of huge sums of largely borrowed funds have fallen far short of their goals and failed to meet time schedules, resulting thereby in waste and misuse of public funds and properties. These projects and activities lack thorough planning and programming, competent management, direction and supervision, and are hampered by complicated administrative procedures and poor personnel selection and administration.

With respect to the National Development Company, the government holding company for manufacturing enterprises, the Report concludes: "The Company is saddled with considerable investments which do not even earn enough profits to cover administration expenses. The financial structure of the NDC is in extremely precarious situation. NDC is hardened with large overhead and inefficient management." [60]

---

[59] The government corporations under direction of the Office of Economic Coordination, all of the directly productive public enterprises, included the Cebu Portland Cement Company, National Shipyards and Steel Corporation, the National Power Corporation with its subsidiaries, the Maria Cristina Fertilizer plant and steel mill, and the National Development Company with its various manufacturing subsidiaries.

[60] R.P., Office of Economic Coordination, *Report on Government Corporations in the OEC Group* (Manila, January 15, 1954), pp. 3–4.

Curtailment in the manufacturing activities of the government began early in the postwar period. In 1949 the National Footwear Corporation was abolished. The nail plant of the NDC was sold to the Marcelo Steel Corporation which was formed to purchase and operate the plant; the lumber mill of the NDC was transferred to the Bureau of Prisons. The National Food Products Corporation, a subsidiary of the NDC, was abolished in 1950 and the remaining assets were sold to the Rose Packing Corporation. In 1953 the Manila Hotel Company, heretofore operated by the Manila Railroad Company, was leased to a private operator. In 1957, the Cebu Portland Cement Company (CEPOC) sold its Bacnotan plant to a private firm organized to acquire and operate the plant. In August 1957, the Celulosa de Filipinos, Cia. redeemed its preferred stock, owned by the NDC, and a month later the CEPOC sold its small paper and bag plant, which had been inactive since 1954, to a private paper firm. Another of CEPOC's minor activities, a marble quarry and mill, was sold to the newly-formed Romblon Marble Corporation in 1958. Finally, in mid-1960, the sale of the remaining Naga plant of the Cebu Portland Cement Company to a private firm was announced and the sale of the Maria Cristina fertilizer plant of the National Power Corporation to the Marcelo Rubber and Tire Corporation had been approved by the cabinet. These transfers, together with those manufacturing enterprises that have disappeared after a process of asset consumption, resulted in the virtual liquidation of the extensive system of government-owned manufacturing enterprises built up following 1935.[61]

For more than two decades following establishment of the Commonwealth, the Philippine society displayed persistent faith in bureaucratic entrepreneurship. The accomplishments of such public manufacturing corporations were sufficiently disappointing, however, that this policy was abandoned and government enterprise, at present is

[61] The lapse of time will undoubtedly color the role of directly productive public enterprise in Philippine economic growth, and economists so inclined will attribute a dominant role to this policy. The available evidence strongly suggests that the manufacturing enterprises of the government were, with minor exceptions, inept and inefficient. To place the role of such enterprises in perspective, it should be pointed out that the net worth of the National Development Company, the holding company for government manufacturing enterprises, was less than 5 per cent of the value of fixed assets of all large (more than twenty employees) manufacturing establishments in 1956.

virtually limited to public utilities and functionally specialized financial and credit institutions.[62] Current policy also reflects the vigor of postwar Filipino private entrepreneurship.

COMMERCE: IMPORT TRADE

An early goal of Filipinism was the import trade which in the Philippines, as in Southeast Asia generally, was dominated by foreign firms. During 1948 and 1949, for example, imports by Filipinos and their firms accounted for only 23 per cent of total imports. Filipinization of the import trade was relatively easy as currency overvaluation and exchange and import controls could be used to transfer this activity to Filipinos and ensure the viability of their enterprises.

During the period of relief and rehabilitation, 1945–1948, when shipping and imports were in short supply, Filipinization was the responsibility of the government-owned National Trading Corporation, the Filippine Relief and Rehabilitation Administration (PRRA), and its successor, Philippine Relief and Trade Rehabilitation Administration (PRATRA), which imported directly and allocated imports to Filipino firms. As shipping and trade returned to more normal conditions, the windfall in importing evaporated, many Filipino enterprises succumbed to competitive pressures, and the ethnic pattern of prewar import trade reappeared.

The unprecedented postwar import surplus, stimulated by changes in Filipino consumption patterns and peso overvaluation, ultimately had to be halted as foreign exchange reserves drained away. To restore a tolerable equilibrium in external payments, the Philippines at the end of 1949 resorted to exchange and import controls which were applied with increasing stringency. Restriction of import quantities resulted in increases in their peso prices, and those traders allocated exchange for imports received a windfall equivalent to the difference between the peso cost of imports and their peso selling prices.

The possibility of using import and exchange controls to Filipinize

[62] The government currently has plans for a substantial "integrated steel industry" with participation, if possible, by private enterprise and management but with majority ownership by the government. The National Shipyard and Steel Corporation has been retained to serve as the nucleus for the planned integrated steel industry. The Philippine society's insistence upon a domestic steel industry is an understandable manifestation of nationalism but is only remotely related to considerations of efficiency.

import trade was recognized by the first exchange control order which provided that 20 per cent of imports would be allocated to "new importers." [63] Although it contained no nationality provision, the effect of the order was to modify the historical distribution of imports among established and largely alien firms. Within three months a second regulation was issued stipulating that "not more than twenty per cent of the quota fixed for each article shall be set aside, to be allocated exclusively to Filipino importers who had no importation during the base period." [64]

With the authorization for import controls scheduled to expire at the end of 1949, Congress moved to renew the authority and to schedule further Filipinization. The resulting legislation (Republic Act No. 426 of May 22, 1950) provided:

The [Import Control] Board shall reserve thirty per centum of the total import quota for any article, goods or commodities for the fiscal year 1950–51, forty per centum for the fiscal year 1951–52, and fifty per centum for the fiscal year 1952–53 in favor of *bona fide* new importers. . . . To qualify as a new importer, one must be a Filipino citizen or a juridical entity at least sixty per centum . . . owned by Filipino citizens.

Legislative promotion of Filipinization remained in abeyance during the remainder of the Quirino administration although a comprehensive import control law covering fiscal years 1952 and 1953 was enacted in the Congressional session of 1951.

With the expiration of the legislative authorization for import controls, Congress, which had passed to Nacionalista control and which was feuding with President Quirino, allowed the controls to lapse. The Central Bank under blanket authority to manage the international reserve stepped in, however, to take over exchange licensing.[65] Regulations were issued which provided that foreign exchange allocated to an "old importer," defined as one who was in business when controls were initiated, should not exceed 40 per cent of the value of imports by

[63] Executive Order No. 193 of December 28, 1948. The law authorizing the President to impose import controls, R.A. No. 330 of July 15, 1948, contained no nationality provisions.

[64] Executive Order No. 209 of March 20, 1949.

[65] The Central Bank Act, R.A. No. 265 of June 15, 1948, provides (Sec. 2) that the Central Bank is responsible for the maintenance of the par value of the peso. It was under this authority that the Central Bank took over administration of exchange and import controls.

the importer in 1950.[66] Inasmuch as 1950 was the year in which import controls were applied most intensively, the regulation, if enforced, would have limited imports by "old importers" to about one-quarter of their shipments in 1948 and 1949.[67]

Although Filipinism was proceeding rapidly, Congress persisted in efforts to hasten this process. In 1954, five bills (H1369, H2252, H2253, H2289 and H2454) were introduced which, among other things, would have accelerated Filipinization of the import trade. The year 1956 saw seven bills (S408, S451, H4614, H4750, H5210, H5538 and H5775) proposing changes in this direction. Two of the bills (H4750 and S408) provided that 75 per cent of foreign exchange allocations would be reserved for Filipino importers.[68] In debate over the proposed legislation, the percentage reserved for Filipino (and United States) importers was increased from 75 to 90 per cent after a Central Bank official pointed out that allocations to Filipinos and Americans and Philippine government entities already exceeded 75 per cent of the available foreign exchange.[69]

Although none of these legislative proposals to accelerate Filipinism received approval, the administrative discretion inherent in exchange and import controls was used to rapidly shift importing to Filipinos at the expense of other participants, particularly the Chinese. For details of this process, see Table 2.

Nationalist pressures increased in intensity in the year and a half following the presidential election of 1957 in which Carlos P. Garcia, a long-time Nacionalista Party leader who had succeeded to the presidency on the death of Magsaysay, was returned to office. The Central Bank, struggling to contain pressures on the balance of payments, tightened exchange controls. Because of the substantial commitments of foreign exchange to firms designated "new and necessary industries," cuts in foreign exchange quotas tended to fall most heavily on imports of consumer goods for sale. Also at this time the various interest groups

[66] Central Bank *Circular* No. 44 of June 12, 1953. Subsequently, Central Bank *Regulation* No. 10 of July 1, 1954, defined "new importers" as Philippine or United States citizens or enterprises at least 60 per cent owned by such citizens.

[67] The index of the volume of imports declined in 1950 to 58 per cent of the 1949 level.

[68] Inasmuch as the Revised Philippine-United States Trade Agreement of 1955 provides (Art. VII) for reciprocal nondiscrimination by each country in the treatment of citizens of the other country and their enterprises, the proposed legislation would have to include American enterprises as co-beneficiaries.

[69] *American Chamber of Commerce Journal* (32), May 1956, p. 203.

Table 2. Imports by nationality of trader (in million pesos; per cent of total imports)

Year	Total value of imports	Filipino nationals and enterprises[a]	Percentage of total	U.S. nationals and enterprises	Percentage of total	Chinese nationals and enterprises	Percentage of total	Other nationals and enterprises	Percentage of total
1948	1136	260	23	319	28	438	39	119	10
1951	959	354	37	275	30	257	27	73	6
1954	903	380	42	233	26	216	24	74	8
1957	1243	669	54	300	24	175	14	99	8
1960	1285	775	60	316	25	90	7	104	8
1963	2487	1608	64	520	21	122	5	237	10
1965	3237	2261	70	709	22	119	3.6	148	4.6

Source: R.P., Bureau of Census and Statistics, *Foreign Trade Statistics of the Philippines*, annual numbers as indicated. The dramatic increase in the peso value of imports between 1960 and 1963 includes the devaluation of the peso from the official rate of 2 pesos per dollar to 3.90 pesos per dollar.

[a] Includes imports by government and government entities.

created by the policies of Filipinism began to coalesce into a politically-oriented "Filipino-First Movement," and under the leadership of the Philippine Chamber of Commerce, this movement began to flex its political muscles.

By the beginning of 1959, conditions had developed to the point where final elimination of foreign exchange quotas for alien enterprises, other than those of United States citizens, importing commodities for resale was undertaken. On January 5, the Monetary Board issued "special rules which govern the distribution of allocations among importers . . . in consonance with the Government's 'Filipino First' policy." [70] Exchange allocations to alien importers except United States citizens were to be gradually reduced until, beginning in the fourth quarter of 1959, such allocations were to be eliminated. Later that year, the Monetary Board decreed that only Filipino (and United States citizens) importers and producers would be permitted to import decontrolled items.[71] Inasmuch as this exchange control category of commodities received liberal foreign exchange allocations, the resolution would have sharply reduced the share of the import trade remaining in alien hands.

The final elimination of exchange allocations to "alien importers" failed to materialize as the Monetary Board subsequently reversed itself and decided to maintain the quotas of "alien importers" at the level established for the first quarter of 1959. This decision reflected the strong protests made by alien importers through diplomatic channels and commercial associations. More important in explaining the reversal of the decision, however, was the improvement of the balance of payments resulting from the exchange premium tax imposed in mid-1959.

Filipinization of the import trade has proceeded steadily since the imposition of effective exchange and import controls. Moreover, the statistical evidence of the shifting proportion of "imports by nationality" understates the Filipinization of importing proper as an expanding proportion of foreign exchange has gone to finance raw materials and capital goods imported directly by producer-exporters and producer-manufacturers. From a tactical point of view, the policy has been remarkably successful as final elimination of quotas to alien importers was proposed only ten years after initiation of the policy. Although this end goal was postponed, essentially for economic reasons, Filipinization

[70] Central Bank of the Philippines, *Eleventh Annual Report*, 1959, p. 153.
[71] Monetary Board, *Resolution* of January 23, 1959.

of imports of consumption commodities for resale has continued until this activity is virtually a Filipino monopoly.

COMMERCE: RETAIL TRADE

As elsewhere in Southeast Asia, alien participation in retail trade was a prominent feature of colonial development. Alien firms, mostly Chinese with minor Indian participation, tended to be relatively large and to account for a disproportionate share of the total trade.[72] In the postwar period, two major approaches to Filipinizing retail trade can be identified: direct legislative encroachment on the rights of aliens, and subsidization of Filipino participation in retailing.

In attempting to trace the pattern of Filipinism, one is beset by the succession of proposals to achieve this goal that were introduced in Congress each year, as well as the continuous political controversy over the issue. This pattern emerged during the American period when Filipinism measures were frequently enacted by the legislature with the full knowledge that the Governor-General would not approve them; the aim being to embarrass the American authorities.

There was every likelihood that, with independence, efforts to speed the pace of Filipinization would materialize. Two factors operated to limit such efforts; the new government was preoccupied with the tasks of reconstruction and rehabilitation and, moreover, in the early post-war period, Filipinos participated in importing and retailing to an unprecedented degree. The relative scarcity of goods, the undiscriminating "G.I." customers, and the inability of older firms to re-establish

[72] The Census of 1948 compiled the following information on Philippine retail trade:

National-ity of retailer	No. estab-lishments (000)	Per cent of total	Value of assets (₱000,000)	Per cent of total	Gross sales (₱000,000)	Per cent of total
Filipino	113.6	90	213	67	467	61
Chinese	12.1	10	93	29	295	38
Other	.4	—	11	3	10	1

The Bureau of Census and Statistics reported that in 1951 there were 119,352 retail stores owned by Filipinos, 17,429 by Chinese and 36 by other nationalities. In that year, Filipino-owned stores accounted for 61.1 per cent of total assets of retail stores and 53.1 per cent of gross sales of such stores (reprinted in the *Answer of Solicitor General Ambrosio Padilla to the petition filed with the Supreme Court by Lao H. Ichong* [Manila, 1956]). The Economic Census of 1961 reported 121,860 retailing establishments of which 110,513 were Filipino and 11,044 were Chinese.

distribution and selling organizations ensured the temporary viability of the new firms. With improvement in the shipping situation, disbursement of war damage payments, and the easing of shortages of consumer goods in the United States, the larger and more experienced firms quickly drove the new Filipino firms out of business. One observer has described the plight of the displaced Filipinos in the following terms: "The new movement was but a brief materialization of hopes and dreams which appeared not only to vanish, but which left behind a cloud of frustration and bitterness." [73]

The burst of Filipino commercial activity, however, did not prevent early moves to indigenize the retail trade. Within three months after the transfer of power, two laws were enacted reversing decisions galling to Filipino nationalists which had been imposed by their colonial administrators.[74] The first, Republic Act No. 37 of October 1, 1946, provides that "All citizens of the Philippines shall have preference in the lease of public market stalls." The second, Republic Act No. 48 of October 3, 1946, requires that accounts be kept in a native language or in English or Spanish, and established harsh penalties for failure to do so.

In the first session of the First Congress in 1946, three bills were submitted (H38, H438 and H652) proposing to Filipinize retailing and in the first session of the Second Congress (1950) there were six such bills (H280, H398, H467, H704, H1241, and H2334). Presidents Roxas and Quirino consistently refused their support and none of the measures were approved by Congress. During this period, retail trade nationalization was limited to the promotion of Filipino participation through education and training facilities, encouragement of retail co-operatives, and the funding of special credit institutions, as well as half-hearted attempts to divert to Filipino retailers the windfall arising out of import restriction.

By 1954 conditions had changed sufficiently that legislation to Filipinize retailing was enacted by Congress and approved by the President. The Magsaysay landslide of 1953 placed the Nacionalistas, with a long tradition of nationalist activity, in control of both the Congress and the Executive. Moreover, earlier attempts to offset the competitive handicaps confronting Filipinos had proved ineffective, and the assets of government agencies created for this purpose had been

[73] A. V. H. Hartendorp, *op. cit.*, p. 273.
[74] See above, section on the environment of policy.

dissipated with little lasting benefit. The rapid change in the international situation and the deepening of the United States commitment to defend the Philippines also encouraged greater freedom of action to pursue Filipinism. This development was interpreted by Nacionalista politicians as *carte blanche* to proceed to "wrest" the retail business from alien (Chinese) hands.

In the first session of the Third Congress in 1954 a wide variety of bills to Filipinize the retail trade were introduced, including nine bills (S104, H4, H174, H275, H377, H1247, H1889, H2523, and H2524) which would have Filipinized this activity by legislative fiat. In the closing days of the regular session, President Magsaysay "certified" an administration bill which was described as a compromise measure.[75] Congress promptly enacted the bill into law and, despite strong protests, Magsaysay signed it on June 19, 1954.[76]

The law, which climaxed at least four decades of nationalist agitation, provides that "No person who is not a citizen of the Philippines, and no association, partnership, or corporation the capital of which is not wholly owned by citizens of the Philippines, shall engage directly or indirectly in the retail business." The law allows alien retailers to continue in business for ten years before the law becomes fully executory.

The legal test of the law was completed in May 1957 when the Supreme Court in the Lao H. Ichong case upheld the act with only one out of eleven justices dissenting and with one other justice refusing to participate in the decision.[77] This decision vests the government with

[75] H2523. Presidential certification of a bill as urgent and necessary not only carries Executive approval but is necessary toward the close of a congressional session to by-pass certain normal procedures designed to ensure legislative deliberation.

[76] R.A. No. 1180. In his message to Congress accompanying the signed bill, the President stated: "I have discussed H.R. 2523, which seeks to nationalize retail trade, with experts and political leaders, and have devoted considerable time to evaluating the arguments for and against the measure. I am fully aware that the bill has imperfections, but notwithstanding this, I am constrained, in concurrence in its primordial objectives, to sign this measure. I have taken this action after carefully considering representations from diplomatic sources and alien chambers of commerce for its disapproval, because I firmly believe in the principle that it is for the best interests of our people and posterity. To my mind, there is nothing in this bill that contravenes our fundamental law or our treaty obligations."

[77] Lao H. Ichong *vs.* Jaime Hernandez, Secretary of Finance, and Marcelino Sarmiento, City Treasurer of Manila (G.R. L-7995 of May 31, 1957). The Court said: "We are fully satisfied upon a consideration of all the facts and circumstances that the disputed law is not the product of racial hostility, prejudice or discrimination, but the expression of the legitimate desire or determination, of the

adequate power to "wrest" the retail trade from alien hands. This goal has long been evident, and there can be no question that it represents an objective widely approved by the Philippine society. The sympathies of the outside observer, however, instinctively go out to the Chinese— the underdogs—who are penalized for their thrift and industry.

Shortly after passage of the Retail Trade Nationalization Act, the Secretary of Justice, Pedro Tuason, expressed the opinion that Philippine commitments assumed in the Philippines-United States Trade Agreement of 1946 exempted "American citizens and juridical entities from the provisions of R.A. No. 1180." [78] Subsequently, in 1963 nationalist pressure on American firms was intensified when Secretary of Justice, Juan R. Liwag, in another opinion concluded: "We cannot agree to the contention that . . . it is not necessary for an American corporation to be wholly owned by American citizens in order that its subsidiary in the Philippines could qualify to engage in the retail business here . . . the agreement of non-discrimination [Revised United States-Philippines Trade Agreement of 1955, Art. 7] does not carry a commitment to place United States citizens or enterprises on a better footing than Filipino citizens or enterprises." [79] As the principal American firms engaged in "retailing" in the Philippines are subsidiaries of public corporations whose shares are widely traded, certification of 100 per cent American-Filipino ownership becomes impossible.

Extension of the effect of the retail trade nationalization law to areas of commerce beyond any conventional definition of retail trade resulted

---

people, through their authorized representatives, to free the nation from the economic situation that has unfortunately been saddled upon it rightly or wrongly, to its disadvantage. The law is clearly in the interest of the public, nay of the national security itself, and indisputably falls within the scope of police power, thru [*sic*] which and by which the State insures its existence and security and the supreme welfare of its citizens."

[78] Republic of the Philippines, Department of Justice, *Opinions*, Series of 1954, No. 175. R.A. No. 1180 provides (Sec. 1) that "nothing contained in this Act shall in any way impair or abridge whatever rights may be granted to citizens and juridical entities of the United States of America under the Executive Agreement signed on July 4, 1946."

[79] R.P., Department of Justice, *Opinions*, Series of 1963, No. 71. Legal testing of this issue is still under way. In December 1966, a lower-court decision reaffirmed *Opinion* No. 71 and at the same time specifically denied the petition of an American corporation that United States-owned enterprises are exempt from the 100 per cent ownership provision of the Retail Trade Nationalization law by virtue of the non-discriminatory treatment provisions of the 1946 Trade Agreement and its successor Laurel-Langley Agreement of 1955.

from still another Justice Department opinion [80] which states that "in determining whether a transaction is retail or wholesale, the criterion is the character of the purchaser or the disposition of the goods bought; if the purchaser is the ultimate user or consumer who utilizes the products or goods 'resulting in the diminution of their utilities,' the transfer is a sale at retail." [81] In other words, this interpretation, if enforced, will displace aliens, including most American-owned enterprises, from retail trade as conventionally defined. Moreover, it also will effectively displace aliens from importing and distributing most capital goods and industrial raw materials and confine them to importing for direct use. Direct sales—of a tractor to an agricultural producer, wire rope to a mine, raw cotton to a textile mill, fuel oil to an electrical generating plant or bunker oil to a shipping company—are interpreted as retail trade and can be made legally only by wholly-owned Filipino or American firms.

For two decades following establishment of the Commonwealth, nationalist efforts to Filipinize retailing were diverted by a succession of sporadic and half-hearted attempts to ensure the competitive viability of Filipino retailers by subsidies in various forms. The policy was initiated in 1940 by the National Trading Corporation (NTC) which proposed to function as wholesale supplier of imports to Filipino retailers and in the process, it was alleged, would pass on the "exploitative profits" of alien middlemen who dominated the activity.[82] The NTC resumed operation after the war and during 1945 and 1946, when shipping was tight and relief and rehabilitation supplies were being chan-

---

[80] *Ibid.*, No. 75.

[81] R.A. No. 1180 defines retail trade (Sec. 4) as "any act, occupation, or calling habitually selling direct to the general public, merchandise, commodities, or goods for consumption." Legal testing of the definition of retail trade is still under way and ultimately will be resolved by a decision of the Supreme Court. On December 1, 1966, a lower court reaffirmed *Opinion* No. 75 by defining retail trade as including "not only sales in limited quantities to the general public of consumers goods for personal or household consumption . . . but also sales for industrial or commercial consumption, that is, sales to manufacturing establishments of goods and products for use in the production of other goods." In August 1967 this position was directly contradicted by still another lower-court decision which asserts that the law is applicable "only to owners of small sari-sari stores or establishments engaged in the resale of goods 'for personal or household consumption or utilization'." See *Philippines Free Press*, August 5, 1967, pp. 68–69.

[82] The President of the NTC announced that one of its purposes was to "break the strangle hold of foreign retailers on Philippine trade" (*Manila Daily Bulletin*, October 18, 1940).

neled through the Philippine government, the NTC was able to divert a part of the windfall in importing to Filipino retailers. As conditions returned to normal, the capacity of the NTC and its successors, the Philippine Relief and Trade Administration (PRATRA) and the Price Stabilization Corporation (PRISCO) to subsidize Filipino retailers dwindled away.[83]

With the imposition of exchange and import controls at the end of 1949, conditions analogous to those prevailing immediately after the war were restored and efforts to pass on a part of the windfall in the peso prices of imports to Filipino retailers were resumed. Although laws and administrative orders ostensibly requiring the sharing of the windfall promptly appeared, they were emasculated by loopholes and enforcement was half-hearted. The shared interest of the dispersed and economically weak Filipino retailers could not sustain an organized pressure group with strength to match that of Filipino importing interests concentrated in Manila and dominated by political entrepreneurs recruited from the cacique oligarchy.

The expectations of Filipino retailers during this period were also inflated by the ambitious plans of the Bureau of Commerce and the National Cooperative Administration to organize Filipino retailers into co-operative marketing associations.[84] These plans were never backed by substantial funds, however, and the co-operative movement made a negligible contribution to Filipinization of retailing.

With the passage of the Retail Trade Nationalization Act, Congress moved promptly to appropriate funds to support the creation of a Filipinized retailing system. Republic Act No. 1292 of June 15, 1955 states that "it shall be national policy to encourage Filipino retailers"

[83] The PRATRA, created by Executive Order No. 90 of September 10, 1947, was charged "to find ways and means of encouraging and assisting Filipino retailers and businessmen such as by supplying them with merchantable goods at prices which will enable them to compete successfully." The PRISCO, created by Executive Order No. 350 of October 3, 1950 to succeed the PRATRA, was capitalized with a revolving fund available, among other purposes, to finance imports of commodities and to make loans to Filipino retailers. For legislative "lip service" to this policy, see the import control laws, R.A. No. 509 of June 13, 1950, Secs. 4, 5, and R.A. No. 650 of June 15, 1950, Sec. 13, and the law creating the Filipino Retailers Fund, R.A. No. 1292 of June 15, 1955, Sec. 3.

[84] The Director of the Bureau of Commerce reported that "the idea behind the movement is not to wrest totally the control of trade from the hands of alien traders, but to educate Filipinos in every phase of business in order to enable them to assume control of the domestic trade." See Philippine National Bank, *Business Letter*, March-April 1954.

and creates a "Filipino Retailers Fund" to assist such retailers "in securing liberal credit facilities, extending them technical assistance, teaching them merchandising techniques and skills, and, in general, equipping them with the necessary tools to compete more effectively with aliens in the retail business to the end that Filipino merchants wrest control of this important phase of the national economy from the hands of foreigners."

The Fund, which received an initial appropriation of 20 million pesos was destined to display the characteristics of the other revolving funds created by the government. By 1959 lending by the Retailers Fund had virtually ceased as the resources of the Fund had been converted to illiquid loans. In mid-1959 the government took steps to limit loans to Filipinos who had been in business for at least six months in the hopes that such a policy "would arrest the increasing numbers of retailers delinquent in the payment of their loans." [85]

Creation of the Filipino Retailers Fund was followed two days later by Republic Act No. 1345 which established the National Marketing Corporation (NAMARCO). The law declares (Sec. 1) that it is "the policy of Congress to assist Filipino retailers and businessmen by supplying them with merchantable goods at prices that will enable them to compete successfully . . . In order to do this, it is necessary that a government corporation be created for the purpose of engaging in the activities of procurement, buying and distributing merchantable goods to Filipino retailers." To implement this policy, NAMARCO was capitalized by an initial appropriation of ₱30 million.[86]

In creating the Retailers Fund and the National Marketing Corporation, the Congress recognized that it is not only necessary to eliminate alien retailers, but to actively promote a substitute Filipino trade organization. Past history strongly suggests that Filipinization of the retail trade will be costly to Filipino taxpayers and consumers who can

[85] *Commerce* (56), July 1959, p. 4. See also, *Commerce* (56), September 1959, p. 4.

[86] R.A. No. 1601 of August 14, 1956 amended R.A. No. 1345 to authorize NAMARCO "to establish and operate distribution offices . . . to enter contracts with wholesale business . . . that may be deemed essential for carrying out the purposes of the Corporation authorized in this act: Provided, that the distribution of such [NAMARCO] commodities shall be done through Filipinos only." The NAMARCO experienced the fate of its various predecessors, succumbing to mismanagement and overstaffing. In May 1967, it was announced that the Corporation would suspend operations "because of bankruptcy." See *Manila Times,* May 7, 1967.

expect deterioration in retailing services and higher prices. It seems quite clear, however, that the Philippine society does not question such a price for attainment of a goal that has been evident since early in the Spanish colonial period.[87]

COMMERCE: ASSEMBLY AND MARKETING OF AGRICULTURAL PRODUCTS

Still another goal of Filipinism has been the elimination of alien (Chinese) middlemen from the assembly and marketing of agricultural crops. Initially, this policy concentrated on indigenizing the rice and corn trade, but there is strong evidence that it will be extended to other agricultural products.[88]

Filipinism was initiated by the National Rice and Corn Corporation (NARIC) which was established as a subsidiary of the National Development Company in 1936. The NARIC was reorganized by Republic Act No. 663 of June 16, 1951 for the purpose of "developing and improving the rice and corn industries in all their phases." To carry out these responsibilities, the NARIC was empowered "to buy, sell, import, export, deal in, barter, exchange and handle in every other manner, rice and corn, . . ." NARIC was capitalized by an initial appropriation of 20 million pesos and exempted from various taxes.

Following imposition of import controls NARIC was given a monopoly of rice imports and during the 1950s was occupied with the maintenance of stocks of imported rice in the interests of consumer price

[87] The writer visited the Philippines early in 1965, nine months after the end of the ten-year period of grace extended by the Retail Trade Nationalization Act. At that time, some fifty Filipinos—legislators, civil servants, businessmen, and professionals—were asked their impressions of the extent to which the policy had been enforced. Not one of those questioned was of the opinion that the law was not effectively enforced. When asked about the existence of individuals who were operating retail establishments and who were not ethnic Filipinos, the respondents confidently asserted that such individuals were naturalized Filipinos.

[88] The broad outlines of the role of alien enterprise in the "rice and corn trade" were established by the Economic Census of 1961. The census of manufacturing establishments reported 6,444 rice and corn mills of which 6,180 were Filipino and 260 Chinese. Of the 190 large mills (ten or more employees), 110 were Filipino and 80 Chinese. Gross value added by rice and corn milling totaled ₱45.2 million of which ₱20.3 million was contributed by large mills. The census of retailing and wholesaling establishments reported 358 wholesalers of rice and corn of which 226 were Filipino and the remainder Chinese, and 1,555 retailers of rice and corn of which 1,370 were Filipino and the remainder Chinese (R.P., Bureau of Census and Statistics, *Economic Census of the Phlippines, 1961.*, Vol. VI, Commerce, Table 2).

stabilization.[89] Steady expansion in agricultural production tended to maintain the Philippines on the margin of rice self-sufficiency through the 1950s, and the NARIC engaged in only minor trading in domestic rice.

The NARIC is also assigned responsibility to import and market corn. Here too, improvements in production have maintained marginal self-sufficiency and NARIC trading in corn has been at minimum levels.[90] In recent years, moreover, limited appropriations have tended to restrict the activities of NARIC as its consumer orientation aroused strong opposition from the powerful National Federation of Rice and Corn Producers.[91] As a result, NARIC's role in Filipinizing the domestic cereals trade has been inconsequential.

The first major step taken to create an indigenous marketing structure occurred in 1952 with the creation of the Agricultural Credit and Cooperative Financing Administration (ACCFA).[92] The ACCFA was allocated large budgetary appropriations, Central Bank credit, and American aid, and was assigned responsibility to develop a country-wide system of Farmers Cooperative Marketing Associations (FACOMAS).

The FACOMAS grant loans on either a pledge by the farmer to deliver his next crop or the actual deposit of palay (unhusked rice) as collateral. The producers stand to gain in relatively low interest rates and on improved prices for rice which can be stored and marketed when prices are relatively favorable. The initial working capital was provided by an appropriation of ₱100 million to serve as a revolving fund to be loaned to FACOMAS for further lending to farmer members. Although FACOMAS were initially established among cereals pro-

[89] United Nations, ECAFE, *Food and Agricultural Price Policies in Asia and the Far East* (Bangkok, 1958), pp. 95–96.

[90] *Ibid.*, pp. 96–97.

[91] In the 1957 congressional session the Federation was able to push through R.A. No. 2017 of June 12, which imposes full import duties on NARIC imports of rice and corn. The government initially was able to by-pass this law by importing marginal rice and corn requirements through the National Marketing Corporation which is specifically exempted from payment of import duties. In 1963, the incumbent Macapagal administration, hoping to influence the outcome of the congressional elections, circumvented the intent of Congress by importing large amounts of rice directly by the Philippine Armed Forces. By the time the action was declared illegal by the Supreme Court, the election was over. For details, see Frank H. Golay, "Obstacles to Philippine Economic Planning," *Philippine Economic Journal* (4), Second Semester 1965, p. 306.

[92] R.A. No. 821 of August 14, 1952.

ducers, operations were subsequently extended to tobacco and coconuts. By the end of 1959, FACOMAS numbered 502 with total membership of 289,121 farmers. Loans outstanding amounted to ₱86 million.

While the language of the legislation creating the ACCFA is moderate, the role planned for the Administration was made clear by its General Manager, Osmundo Mondoñedo, who reported to the Cabinet in March 1957:

Alien palay traders have been totally eliminated in Bulacan, and that their participation in the trade in Pampanga and Pangasinan had been reduced to 50 per cent and in Tarlac and Nueva Ecija to 30 per cent, and that with the added funds it was safe to predict that they would soon be ousted from the whole of Central Luzon.[93]

In spite of strong financial support, by the end of 1958 the capital of ACCFA had become tied up in illiquid loans and operating losses, and the loan fund had ceased to "revolve." In March of 1959 the results of a survey of the co-operative organization by an American firm of economic consultants was made public. The survey disclosed extensive mismanagement of both FACOMAS and ACCFA. Of ₱86 million of outstanding ACCFA loans at the end of 1958, two-thirds were delinquent. Loans to individual farmers accounted for only one-third of the delinquency, with the balance representing loans to FACOMAS. Over four-fifths of the FACOMAS were reported as operating at a loss in early 1959.[94]

The failure of the co-operative system to provide a satisfactory substitute for the traditional marketing structure led to renewed efforts in Congress to use the police power of the state to Filipinize this activity. In the 1958 Congressional session, no fewer than twelve bills were introduced to indigenize the rice and corn trade [95] and in 1959 a further eight bills were introduced.[96] Congress adjourned both in 1958 and 1959 without enacting legislation, but in the regular session of 1960 such a law was passed. The bill (H3925) provided that "no person who

[93] *Manila Daily Times*, February 21, 1957.

[94] The report was prepared by Arthur D. Little, Inc. The conclusions of the Little survey were confirmed in December 1959 by the *Report on the Activities of ACCFA* of the Committee on Good Government of the House of Representatives.

[95] S16, S74, H136, H163, H235, H248, H252, H364, H377, H420, H733, and H1900.

[96] S327, S455, H2146, H2168, H2685, H2889, H3135 and H3193.

is not a citizen of the Philippines, or association, partnership or corporation, the capital of which is not wholly owned by citizens of the Philippines shall directly or indirectly engage in the rice and/or corn industry."

The bill also provided that non-Filipino retailers of rice would be allowed to continue in business for six months, "only for the purpose of liquidation," non-Filipino wholesalers for one year, and millers and warehouses two years. To create a substitute Filipino-owned rice and corn industry the bill directed the Development Bank of the Philippines, the Social Security Commission, the Philippine National Bank, and the Government Service Insurance System to contribute ₱50 million each to a revolving loan fund. Half of the funds were to be lent to Filipinos for purpose of "milling, processing, warehousing and marketing." The other half would be available for cultivation and production, including crop loans.

President Garcia chose to veto the bill and, in his message returning the bill to Congress, emphasized the hardships imposed on aliens by the short period permitted them to liquidate their businesses as well as the dangers to the promising and actuarily sound social insurance systems which were directed by Congress to invest in risky assets.[97]

During the special session of Congress in 1960, a modified law restricting the rice and corn trade to citizens of the Philippines or enterprises wholly owned by such citizens was approved.[98] To meet the objections raised in the earlier veto message, the new law stipulates that aliens engaged in the "retail, wholesale, culture, transportation, handling, distribution or acquisition for the purpose of trade of rice and/or corn" will be allowed to continue in business for two years "only for the purpose of liquidation," while those aliens engaged in milling and/or warehousing are allowed three years. The law also directs the Development Bank of the Philippines and the Philippine National Bank each to "set aside an adequate revolving fund for loans of at least fifty million pesos" to be lent to Filipinos for milling, processing, warehousing and marketing facilities as well as for cultivation and production loans. This law also instructs the Central Bank to rediscount such loans "at the lowest possible rate in order to insure the maintenance of financial assistance to the rice and/or corn industry."

[97] The recent difficulties of the ACCFA must have influenced the veto decision.
[98] R.A. No. 3018 of August 2, 1960.

The law went into effect on January 1, 1961 and at the beginning of 1964 this industry was formally Filipinized. The pattern followed that established in indigenizing the retail trade. Initial steps reflected the belief that Filipinization would proceed at a rewarding rate if credit resources were allocated to set Filipinos up in business. Such measures proved ineffective as credit resources allocated to revolving funds became immobilized in illiquid loans, and Filipino enterprises tended to succumb to competition and to mismanagement. Frustrated in efforts to Filipinize these major activities by such measures, Congress resorted to use of the police power of the state to dispossess aliens.

Still another agriculture industry that has been Filipinized in recent years has been the Virginia-type tobacco industry. Although the Philippines has traditionally been an important tobacco producer and exporter, output in the past was concentrated in cigar tobacco. The liberation and early postwar period produced a major shift in Philippine consumption patterns, however, as American cigarettes were freely available, both from military stores and from commercial imports. As the result of postwar changes in smoking habits, the Philippines became a large importer of Virginia-type tobacco, both as manufactured cigarettes and later as a raw material input for the cigarette industry. Cigarette output, protected by import restrictions and differential excise taxes which discriminate against imported cigarettes, expanded rapidly.

Filipinization was initiated by Republic Act No. 698 of May 9, 1952 which scheduled rapid reduction in imports of leaf tobacco. Evolution of tobacco policy was completed in 1954 by the enactment of Republic Act No. 1194 of August 25, which terminated tobacco imports, and directed the ACCFA to purchase "all locally grown and produced Virginia-type leaf tobacco." The Central Bank was instructed to loan the ACCFA the necessary funds. Reservation of the domestic market to Filipino tobacco farmers and Filipinization of marketing activities through a public monopoly was accomplished with relative ease.

As in the case of the rice and corn trade, the termination of the financial activities of ACCFA promised distress for Filipino farmers.[99] Congress responded, however, by quickly passing legislation creating

[99] Both the Arthur D. Little Report and the report by the House Committee on Good Government were critical of the tobacco price-support functions of ACCFA which had resulted in the accumulation of large tobacco stocks.

the Philippine Virginia Tobacco Administration to continue the price support and marketing functions of ACCFA.[100] The law empowers the PVTA "to take over . . . and control, all functions and operations with respect to the processing, warehousing, and trading of Virginia tobacco." The PVTA is given exclusive right to sell locally-produced Virginia tobacco to *"bona fide* tobacco manufacturers and exporters." To finance the PVTA, the Central Bank is directed to "grant the PVTA the necessary loans with which to effect the purchase of all locally grown flue-cured Virginia tobacco." [101]

A repeat performance of Filipinization is promised for coffee by Republic Act No. 2712 of June 18, 1960. This law provides (Sec. 1) that "The importation of coffee beans of the Arabian variety shall be gradually reduced . . . and completely banned beginning with 1964." Coffee plantings have been strongly encouraged in recent years by various activities of the Bureau of Plant Industry, and output has steadily increased. It seems safe to predict that production in excess of domestic requirements will materialize, and the government will resort to price supports and monopolization of marketing functions as occurred in the case of tobacco.

Still another minor agricultural crop that has been Filipinized by a government trading monopoly is ramie.[102] Both ramie fiber and finished textiles can be marketed only through designated government agencies. Imports of textiles of non-Philippine ramie are prohibited, while the ACCFA supports prices to Filipino producers of ramie fiber at artificially high levels.

Recent years have seen persistent moves to Filipinize the assembly and marketing of coconuts by creating an alternative Filipino marketing organization. Initially, the ACCFA sought to extend the system of FACOMAS to the coconut industry but with limited success. To overcome the financial constraints on ACCFA, Congress in Republic Act No. 1369 of June 18, 1955, appropriated ₱30 million for investment in government-owned and operated coconut centrals and loans to Filipinos and corporations "owned by citizens of the Philippines to establish centrals." More recently, Republic Act No. 2282 of June 19, 1959

---

[100] R.A. No. 2265 of June 19, 1959.

[101] The law specifies that no part of such loans shall be used in the purchase of sun-dried (low quality) Virginia leaf tobacco. Such purchases by ACCFA had accumulated as high cost, illiquid inventory since this grade of tobacco is not suitable for cigarettes.

[102] See R.A. No. 1392 of August 23, 1955.

created the Coconut Financing Fund of ₱30 million to be made available over a period of five years to finance coconut co-operatives and production loans to coconut producers. The Act specifies that the "Coconut Financing Fund shall be a revolving fund."

The postwar period has also seen a succession of bills introduced into Congress to Filipinize trade in copra by law. Such bills first appeared in the 1954 session when two bills (S14 and S105) were introduced in the Senate and six bills (H155, H1164, H1769, H1996, H2291, H2518) in the House of Representatives. In the first three years of the Fourth Congress (1958–1960) a further six bills (S45, S499, H3003, H3793, H3825, H3851) were introduced. It seems safe to predict that the pattern followed in Filipinizing retail trade and the rice and corn trade will, in all probability, be repeated in the copra industry as frustration over costly failures to create an alternative Filipino marketing structure encourages more direct action.

Further Filipinization of trade in agricultural products is an obvious goal. The "fields to conquer" are limited, however, because the major targets—coconuts and abaca—are export commodities and commercial policy cannot be used to reserve foreign markets to Filipino producers.[103] In other words, government policies can reserve the internal market to domestic producers, but the dominant export markets for these commodities in all likelihood will remain competitive. Because this is a fact of life, the incentive to Filipinize such industries is relatively weak.

EXPORT PRODUCTION

Colonial development in the Philippines followed the historical pattern of specialization in primary production for export. Table 3 reveals that foreign investment was attracted to the export industries and tended to dominate in the processing of coconut oil, copra meal, desiccated coconut, abaca, and tobacco, the production and processing of pineapples, forestry products, and minerals, and the production of embroideries and cordage.

On the other hand, Filipino nationalists, over the opposition of Amer-

[103] Alien participation in abaca trading has generated relatively little nationalist concern, and legislative proposals to Filipinize this activity have not been prominent. This situation is explained, in part, by the steady postwar decline in the abaca industry in the face of competition from substitutes and severe plant-disease problems.

Table 3. Assets in export industries by citizenship of owner, late 1930s
(in million pesos; various years)

Industry	Total investment[a]	Filipino	American	Spanish	British
Sugar					
Centrals	196.5	93.4	61.2	30.0	n.r.
Land and improvements	362.6	340.9	10.9	7.3	n.r.
Coconuts					
Mills and refineries	23.8	1.8	11.1	1.1	7.0
Land and improvements	418.6	389.3	16.8	8.4	–
Abaca					
Mills and cordage factories	21.6	2.0	7.9	n.r.	2.8
Land and improvements	400.2	352.5	11.0	n.r.	–
Tobacco					
Factories	18.6	.2	n.r.	12.1	n.r.
Land and improvements	42.0	40.8	n.r.	.8	n.r.
Forestry products					
Sawmills and logging equipment	15.2	4.6	6.4	n.r.	.8
Gold mines	188.2	91.8	68.5	6.1	11.4
Other mines	13.0	5.4	5.8	0.1	0.7
Embroideries	15.0	1.0	14.0	–	–
Canned pineapple factories	2.0	–	2.0	–	–
Cordage factories	6.0	2.5	3.2	–	–
Total investment	1,723.3	1,326.2	218.8	65.9	22.7

Source: Philippines Commonwealth, Technical Committee to the President, *American-Philippine Trade Relations.* (Washington, D.C., October 1944), pp. 51, 70, 95, 99, 105, 115, 122, 123, 140 and 149. Also published as appendix to U.S. House of Representatives, Committee on Insular Affairs, *To Provide for Rehabilitation of Philippine Islands,* Hearings on S. 1610, 79th Congress, 1st Session. Japanese investment in abaca lands and improvements totaled 33 million, in abaca mills, 1.5 million, sawmills and logging equipment, 0.6 million and in mines 0.6 million. Chinese investments listed included gold mines, 3.3 million, other mines, 0.1 million, cordage mills, 0.4 million, and forestry products, 1.5 million. A substantial part of the residual of investment in tobacco factories and in the coconut industry undoubtedly was Chinese.

[a] Rows do not add to total investment as residual nationality categories are omitted.

ican colonial administrators, were able to limit drastically the amount of land that could be acquired by individuals and corporations, thereby preventing wholesale development of plantations.[104] At the end of the American period, smallholder production accounted for virtually the entire output of coconuts, and sugar production was concentrated in the output of small to medium-sized Filipino-owned holdings farmed by tenants and hired labor. Production of abaca in Davao Province, accounting for half the total output, was dominated by Japanese capital and entrepreneurship, and a semi-plantation technology prevailed. Elsewhere, abaca was a smallholders crop. In the case of tobacco, there was substantial Spanish investment and a few medium-sized plantations, though the principal part of output came from smallholdings.

Filipinization of export production and trade has proceeded steadily during the postwar period, although this sector has not been the object of special attention or policies. An early step occurred as the result of the defeat of Japan when the United States Enemy Property Custodian transferred some 232,000 hectares of agricultural land to the Philippine government. These lands which had been seized from Japanese operators were concentrated in Davao Province and accounted for approximately one-third of the area planted to abaca in the late interwar period. Republic Act No. 477 of June 9, 1950 provided for subdivision of

---

[104] The Census of 1939 reported the following distribution of agricultural land in farms by nationality of owner:

Nationality	No. of farms	Farm area (000 has.)	Cultivated area (000 has.)
Filipino	1,631,379	6,538.9	3,890.4
Japanese	2,807	44.9	35.7
Chinese	299	22.8	8.7
American	150	22.3	9.6
Spanish	61	59.0	8.6
Other	30	2.0	.9

Filipinos owned 99.7 per cent of all farms, 97.7 per cent of the total farm area, and 98.6 per cent of the cultivated area in farms in 1939. In view of (a) the expansion in farm area and cultivated area following 1939, a process reserved to Filipinos, (b) the repatriation of Japanese residents following World War II, and (c) the steady disinvestment of agricultural holdings by Americans and other aliens, the above ratios are undoubtedly above 99 per cent in all categories as of the mid-1960s. See Commonwealth of the Philippines, Commission of the Census, *Census of the Philippines, 1939*, Vol. II, Population and Agriculture (Manila: Bureau of Printing, 1941), Table 8.

these Japanese lands and their distribution to *"bona fide* occupants" and veterans of World War II. As a result of this transfer, production of abaca was Filipinized and in the process became almost entirely a smallholders crop.

Production of coconuts, with the exception of a few medium-sized plantations associated with processing enterprises, has remained in the hands of Filipino smallholders. Important in the processing of coconut oil into products consumed domestically are the Philippine Manufacturing Company, a wholly-owned subsidiary of Procter and Gamble, and the Philippine Refining Company, a wholly-owned Lever subsidiary. In addition, there are a number of medium-sized firms with Chinese, naturalized Filipino (Chinese), and Filipino participation which process the bulk of coconut oil exports. As coconut meal is the by-product of coconut oil manufacture, these firms also dominate in the production and export of that product. For a survey of information on the nationality of the controlling interest of the major export processing and mining enterprises in 1961 see Table 4.

The remaining coconut export product is desiccated coconut. In the early 1960s, the two largest firms accounting for almost three-fifths of

Table 4. Nationality of controlling interest of selected large enterprises
in nonagricultural export industries, 1961
(number of enterprises)

Type of enterprise	Total	Filipino	American	Chinese	Other
Sugar centrals	25	20	3	–	2
Desiccated coconut mills	6	2	2	–	2
Coconut oil mills	10	7	–	3	–
Logging, including rough cutting of lumber	1,658	1,636	16	–	6
Plywood and veneer mills	21	20	1	–	–
Gold, copper, and chromite mines	20	17	3	–	–
Embroideries	31	23	7	–	1
Pineapple canneries	1	–	1	–	–

Source: R.P., Bureau of Census and Statistics, *Economic Census of the Philippines, 1961,* various volumes. Not all of enterprises tabulated engage in exporting.

exports were Franklin Baker Co. and Peter Paul Philippine Corp., wholly-owned subsidiaries of United States firms.

Filipinization of a sort has occurred by reason of the decline, both absolutely and relatively, in the share of this crop exported as coconut oil and desiccated coconut, which are processed by alien enterprises. Coconut oil exports, which averaged 171,000 metric tons during 1937–1940, averaged only 65,500 metric tons during 1957–1960. Coconut exports in copra equivalent increased from approximately 635,000 metric tons in 1937–1940, with almost half of the crop exported in processed form as coconut oil and desiccated coconut, to 958,000 metric tons in 1957–1960, with approximately four-fifths of exports shipped as copra.[105]

Foreign participation in the sugar industry, the second major export crop, tended to be concentrated in sugar mills (centrals) serving an extensive planting district of small and medium-sized farms of planters.[106] Foreign participation in sugar planting was never extensive and as of 1960, virtually all sugar lands were Filipino-owned. On the other hand, centrifugal sugar manufacturing capacity resulted from foreign initiative, and as recently as 1940 a substantial part of such capacity was alien-owned.

A number of factors, however, have contributed to Filipinization of this industry in the postwar period. To begin with, rehabilitation after the war resulted in transfers of centrals to Filipinos as the Philippine National Bank and the Rehabilitation Finance Corporation liberally allocated credit to Filipinos to rehabilitate their centrals and to buy out foreign interests. More important was the steady process of disinvestment as profit prospects remained bleak under the impact of peso overvaluation and stringent exchange controls. Because of the close regulation of sugar production and exports under the quota in the sheltered United States market, the sugar industry had less capacity to evade exchange controls and thereby improve the effective exchange rate realized from sugar exports. Moreover, the postwar period wit-

[105] Trade statistics were compiled from R.P., Bureau of Census and Statistics, *Foreign Trade and Navigation of the Philippines*. Prewar statistics were compiled from Philippines Commonwealth, Bureau of Customs, *Annual Report of the Collector of Customs*. Exports of coconut oil, stimulated by the devaluation of the peso in 1962, have increased sharply in recent years.

[106] Such centrals maximized their own sugar plantings, but such holdings were limited by law to 1,024 hectares.

nessed intervention by the government to establish a crop distribution between planters and the centrals favorable to the planters. This intervention occurred under the Agricultural Relations Act (R.A. No. 1199 of August 30, 1954) which was designed to establish tenant security in landlord-ridden rice provinces by fixing ratios for dividing crops between landlord and tenant. The sugar planters seized upon the legislation as grounds for litigation which ultimately resulted in a substantial increase in the planters' share of the sugar output from cane delivered to centrals.

In 1951, the small American-owned Hind Sugar Co. passed to Filipino ownership. In mid-1956 the Pampanga Sugar Mills, originally a Spreckels (U.S.) enterprise, became 100 per cent Filipino-owned. More recently, in 1958 the Central Azucarera de Tarlac passed from Spanish management and control to Filipinos. As of mid-1960, the only large sugar centrals with majority foreign ownership were the Hawaiian-Philippine Co. and the Bogo-Medellin Central. These two centrals accounted for less than 8 per cent of estimated average annual production.[107]

The fourth most important export crop in recent years has been canned pineapple. Prior to the mid-1960s, the entire crop was produced on a single (6000 hectares) plantation combined with a cannery in northern Mindanao. The export firm, Philippine Packing Co., is a wholly-owned subsidiary of a United States firm.[108]

The export industry most attractive to foreign investment during the later colonial period was gold mining, which was stimulated by the increase in the price of gold following the devaluation of the dollar in

[107] Majority ownership of the Victorias Milling Co., Inc., one of the largest Philippine centrals in mid-1960, was held by the Ossorio family. The head of the family (recently deceased), of Spanish-Filipino origin, was an American citizen. The majority ownership of the firm was reported as Filipino by reason of the fact that the family shares were registered in the name of a family member who had retained Filipino nationality.

[108] To escape the legal limit (1,024 hectares) on land that can be alienated to a corporation, land for the plantation was obtained on a sublease from the National Development Company. In 1962, Dole (U.S.) interests were able to obtain land for the production of pineapples under a similar arrangement. Use of this type of arrangement for American participation in plantation-type development in the Philippines was abruptly halted in 1964 when Senator Lorenzo Tañada convened a Senate investigation of a proposal of the Program Implementation Agency to lease lands of the Davao Prison Colony to United Fruit Company interests for the production of bananas. President Macapagal, faced by aroused nationalist concern, chose to repudiate the negotiations.

1933. For the four years ending in 1932, production of gold averaged 254,000 ounces annually whereas for the four years ending 1941, production averaged 1,018,000 ounces annually, a four-fold increase.

Philippine gold mining, handicapped by the fixed price of gold and the relative inflation in peso costs and prices, has made only a partial recovery in the postwar period. During the four years ending with 1960, gold production averaged 404,000 ounces annually. The absolute and relative decline in the gold mining industry has resulted in an obvious contribution to Filipinization.

Pressures for Filipinization of mining have been alleviated by a number of factors. Because of the risks of development, capital has traditionally been raised by the public sale of shares. The Manila Stock Exchange was established in 1934, and trading in mining shares, issued in such quantities that their prices range down to fractions of a peso, has dominated exchange activity. Trading in "penny" mining shares is an exciting diversion for Filipinos and has gradually increased their ownership share in this industry though control and management have been Filipinized more slowly. Also important has been the dominant role of American prospector-investors who have been protected under the "parity rights" extended United States interests. American "old timers" often became permanent residents, proved relatively assimilable, and in some cases acquired citizenship. Finally, the risky nature of mining and the privations and hard work involved in exploration and development have not appealed to Filipinos.

While gold mining has remained depressed during the postwar period, production of copper, chromite, iron and other ores and concentrates has expanded rapidly. Through public subscription and trading in shares, Filipino participation has tended to become dominant outside of a limited number of major firms. As of mid-1960, the largest gold producer, Benguet-Consolidated, was over 90 per cent American-owned but other important gold producers had major Filipino ownership. Copper production is dominated by two mines, Atlas-Consolidated in Cebu and Lepanto in Northern Luzon. Majority ownership of the former mine, a Soriano enterprise, is American.[109] The Lepanto mine

[109] The late Andres Soriano, ethnically Spanish, was the most energetic entrepreneur in the postwar expansion of Philippine natural-resource industries. Following World War II, he acquired United States nationality and his activities have become diversified internationally. Soriano interests in the Philippines have enjoyed considerable relief from the pressures of economic nationalism. Because of Soriano's longstanding identification with the Philippine society and culture and

was essentially Filipinized following World War II when 10.7 million shares of stock were turned over to the Philippine government by the United States Enemy Property Custodian. In subsequent stock transactions alien ownership has increased until, as of mid–1960, Lepanto was a widely owned, cosmopolitan corporation with predominant Filipino ownership. Virtually all chromite is produced by a single mine, Consolidated Mines, Inc., in Zambales Province. All officers and directors of this firm are Filipinos and more than three-fifths of the shares were Filipino-owned in mid-1960. In the case of iron ore, Philippine Iron Mines, Inc., is the largest producer. As of the early 1960s Filipino ownership was about three-fifths, American one-fifth, with the remainder of the shares held by Chinese and other interests. Top management is American. The second largest iron producer, The Samar Mining Co., is a Filipino firm controlled and managed by Elizalde interests.

The remaining major export industry is forestry products including logs, timber, and lumber, exports of which averaged 2,138 million board feet annually during 1962–1964 as compared to 84 million board feet in 1937–1940. Currently there are more than two hundred medium-sized and small firms engaged in logging and lumbering for export, with the four largest firms accounting for no more than one-fifth of total exports.[110] Administrative discretion in the allocation of lucrative timber concessions has ensured that the postwar expansion of this industry has been in Filipino hands. The few remaining alien firms are pre-war enterprises and they have declined in relative importance. Pressures to Filipinize further remain strong because of the extensive participation of naturalized Filipinos of Chinese descent and also because of the alleged prevalence of Chinese using Filipino "dummies."

Filipinization of export production and trade has proceeded steadily throughout the postwar period. This change is attributable only in part to clear-cut policies of economic nationalism. The relative decline in the share of export production and trade in aggregate income, and the

---

his association with political leaders, Filipinos tend not to identify Soriano enterprises as alien. Moreover, Soriano enterprises are publicly held corporations, and Filipinos derive satisfaction from the knowledge that they can buy shares in these enterprises whenever they choose to.

[110] Golay, *The Philippines,* p. 46. The 1961 Economic Census tabulated 313 large (ten or more employees) logging establishments of which 306 were Filipino and the remainder American (R.P., Bureau of Census and Statistics, *Economic Census of the Philippines, 1961,* Vol. I, Part A: Forestry and Logging, Table 3, pp. 3–4).

substantial decline in the share of alien enterprise in this sector also resulted from the prolonged period of peso overvaluation and exchange and import controls which adversely affected profitability.

With the minor exception of pineapples and a few medium-sized plantations in other crops, agricultural production for export has been Filipinized. Sugar refining capacity has been substantially transferred to Filipino ownership. On the other hand, the processing of copra and the growing and canning of pineapples have remained strongholds of foreign investment. Although foreign holdings and management remain substantial in mining, the "foreignness" is essentially legal and technical as ownership in mining is largely Filipino or in the hands of residents who identify with the Philippines and arouse little nationalist concern. Production and export of forest products are widely dispersed among medium- and small-sized firms. Steps have been taken to favor nationals in the allocation of concessions and this activity has been substantially Filipinized.

MANUFACTURING

Central to the national economic development to which the Philippine society aspires is industrialization, and major postwar economic policies are intelligible in terms of this objective. Protection established by import controls was developed into a strong and precise instrument for directing resources into manufacturing, and the windfall in exchange allocation was used to assure the profitability of Filipino firms.

Although the Philippine society displayed dogged faith in the capacity of the state to participate in industrialization as capitalist and entrepreneur, the performance of government manufacturing enterprises was so disappointing that this policy was abandoned in the mid-1950s. Subsequently, manufacturing development became increasingly dependent upon a system of strong entrepreneurial incentives including tax remission, high levels of protection from competing imports, and the windfalls and subsidies in allocation of scarce credit and foreign exchange resources, reparations, and imported raw materials. Although industrialization policy up to the present has permitted a substantial role for foreign and resident alien enterprises, Filipino nationalists have moved steadily to reserve the overpowering incentives to nationals. The distribution of the controlling ownership at large (more than ten employees) manufacturing enterprises in 1961 is summarized in Table 5.

A basic component of Philippine industrialization policy has been

Table 5. Nationality of controlling ownership of large manufacturing enterprises, 1961

Category of enterprise	No. of enterprises	Filipino	American	Chinese	Others
Food, beverages, and tobacco products	1,154	604	27	514	9
Textile manufactures	101	84	2	14	1
Wearing apparel and footwear	853	695	19	126	13
Wood products including furniture	547	394	16	134	3
Paper and products, including printed material	324	234	6	80	4
Leather products except footwear	42	27	2	13	0
Rubber products, chemicals, and chemical products	240	163	30	44	3
Products of petroleum and coal	6	3	3	0	0
Non-metallic mineral products	147	119	5	19	4
Basic metal products	53	33	1	19	0
Metal products except machinery and transport equipment	160	102	7	51	0
Machinery except electrical machinery	125	106	5	14	0
Electrical machinery and apparatus	73	55	5	13	0
Transport equipment	136	114	9	12	0
Miscellaneous manufactures	124	109	0	15	0
All industries	4,085	2,842	137	1,068	37

Source: R.P., Bureau of Census and Statistics, *Economic Census of the Philippines, 1961*, Vol. III, *Manufacturing*, Table 25.

the use of tax concessions to subsidize "new and necessary industries" which was inaugurated by Republic Act No. 35 of September 30, 1946. Inasmuch as tax exemption was limited to the first four years of the life of the new firm—a period when volume of business and profits would be relatively low—the strength of the incentive was unimpressive and it exerted little influence on economic development in the early postwar years. The process of rehabilitation was primarily one of restoring prewar productive capacity, and few industries qualified as "new and necessary."

The introduction of exchange and import controls produced conditions that sharply enhanced the economic value of designation as a "new and necessary industry." Protection proved highest for less essential imports and established strong incentives for "industries" that could perform some minor processing of imported "raw materials," the importation of which, in manufactured form, was embargoed or heavily restricted.[111] Given these conditions, applications for designation as a new and necessary industry increased. In 1953, the policy was revised to extend the period of tax concessions. Although nationality was not formally introduced as a qualification for preference in the allocation of tax exemption until 1961,[112] administrative discretion in implementing the policy was used aggressively to Filipinize the growth of the manufacturing sector.

Government promotion and subsidization of functionally specialized credit institutions also facilitated the emergence of Filipino entrepreneurship. Following establishment of the Central Bank in 1948, the commercial banking system was rapidly Filipinized and credit to support manufacturing expanded rapidly. Of total credit granted by commercial banks, savings banks, and rural banks during the seven years through 1964, over four-fifths was granted to Filipino individuals and enterprises, 7 per cent to Americans, and 9 per cent to Chinese. Of total credits extended, 56 per cent went to corporate enterprises and 30 per cent to manufacturing enterprises.[113]

Of growing importance as a source of longer-term industrial finance

[111] Initially there was considerable official Philippine enthusiasm for this type of development and the potentialities of such protection to bring about industrialization were widely discussed. Cf., Miguel Cuaderno, "The Bell Trade Act and the Philippine Economy," *Pacific Affairs* (25), December 1952, pp. 324–325.

[112] See Basic Industries Act, R.A. No. 3127 of June 17, 1961.

[113] Central Bank of the Philippines, *Statistical Bulletin* (17), December 1965, Tables 21, 22, and 23.

are the private development banks, entirely Filipino-owned and dominated by the government-owned Development Bank of the Philippines.
Loans and investments outstanding of development banks, as of the
end of 1964, totaled ₱1,115 million, of which 61 per cent had been
allocated to industrial enterprises. Of total bank credit outstanding,
other than that of the Central Bank, at the end of 1964, over one-third
had been allocated to uses classified as "manufacturing" or "industrial." [114]

Overt economic nationalism in industrialization policy first appeared
in 1957 in the "System of Determining Industrial Priorities" adopted by
the National Economic Council "to govern the extension of credit by
government banking and financing institutions, the grant of foreign
exchange allocation, tax exemption, acquisition and distribution of
reparations materials, application of foreign aid to industrial development, the allocation of scarce materials owned or produced by the
government or government corporations, and other actions involving
other forms of government assistance or protection to industry." [115] The
Industrial Priority Formula provided that "a firm that is financed entirely or mostly by nationals [Filipino citizens] will be given preference.
. . . This is justified by the fact that there is relatively greater stability
in an enterprise that is operated by nationals. Furthermore, the enterprise would provide or expand better opportunities for training Filipinos to acquire management skills and techniques. This is not to
mention the fact that the earnings of nationals are likely to be plowed
back into the national economy—something that cannot be guaranteed
in the case of the profits of foreign investments." [116]

Evidence that nationality was introduced as a criterion in granting
"new and necessary industry" designation is difficult to pin down.

[114] *Ibid.,* Tables 15 and 28. Progressive Filipinization is also indicated by the
fact that, of the paid-in capital of new businesses registered with the Securities
and Exchange Commission over the six years ending with 1965 totaling ₱1,789
million, five-sixths was classified as Filipino. For the six years ending with 1954,
the share of Filipino capital was two-thirds (*ibid.,* Table 58). Over the six years
ending with 1964, the SEC reported that 93 per cent of the paid-in capital of
newly registered corporations was classified as Filipino, whereas for the six years
ending with 1954, the share of Filipino capital was 50 per cent (Central Bank
of the Philippines, *Statistical Bulletin* (16), December 1964, Table 56).

[115] R.P., National Economic Council, *The Five-Year Economic and Social Development Program for FY 1957-1961* (Manila, January 3, 1957), pp. 261–262.

[116] *Ibid.,* p. 259. In the priority system, "investments of aliens shall have priority
over investments by foreigners, but investments by nationals shall have priority
over all." Chinese residing in the Philippines are classified as aliens.

Nevertheless, the expansion in purely Filipino firms and joint ventures with Filipino participation strongly suggests that this was the case.[117] As of mid-1958, slightly more than half of all firms designated "new and necessary" were exclusively Filipino, and these firms accounted for slightly more than half of the approved applications.[118] Firms in which Filipino entrepreneurship was participating, either alone, or jointly with other nationalities, accounted for 78 per cent of the firms designated for which nationality is identified.[119]

Following the election of 1957, the Filipino economic interests benefiting from postwar economic nationalism coalesced into the "Filipino First" movement, and economic nationalism became more vigorous and open. Early in the new Congress in 1958 a bill was introduced (H1308) which provided that the privilege of designation as a "new and necessary industry" be limited to proprietorships and partnerships owned by Filipinos and corporations at least 60 per cent Filipino owned. Although the proposed legislation did not receive Congressional approval, the objective of the bill was strongly supported by actions of the National Economic Council and Central Bank. On August 21, 1958, the National Economic Council issued Resolution No. 204 which stated "it is the policy of the Government to encourage Filipinos to engage in enterprises and industries vital to the economic growth, stability, and security of the country." The National Economic Council also announced that "in instances where Filipino enterprises seek to enter a field now predominantly in the hands of non-Filipinos, such steps shall be taken as will enable Filipino enterprise to participate." It was subsequently reported on September 5 that the National Economic Council had taken steps to set up "absolute production ceilings" for all alien

[117] A Filipino study of joint business ventures concluded: "Approval of a project by the Central Bank and more recently by the National Economic Council has become a prerequisite to any substantial venture in which there is foreign participation; at the same time the Central Bank seems to have made local equity participation in any such project a prerequisite for approval. Under the circumstances, foreign investors have been shifting to the joint venture approach as a means of obtaining government approval" (Columbia University, *Joint International Business Ventures in the Philippines* [Manila, July 1956], p. 147).

[118] American Chamber of Commerce of the Philippines, *New and Necessary Industries Granted Tax Exemption under Republic Acts 35 and 901* (Manila, 1958, mimeographed).

[119] The tendency for Filipinos to associate with Chinese in "new and necessary industries" is a promising development. Firms with joint Filipino-Chinese participation, alone or in conjunction with other nationalities, numbered 128 or 16 per cent of the firms for which nationality is identified.

firms. It was stated that the "proposed restrictions would require such firms to operate under quotas based on current levels of business." [120]

In October 1958 the Monetary Board announced that no new industries would be approved except dollar-producing industries and 100 per cent Filipino-owned and highly essential dollar-saving industries.[121] Eighteen months later, Monetary Board Resolution No. 635 of April 16, 1960 announced that Filipino-owned industrial enterprises engaged in any basic industry (chemicals, iron and steel, agricultural and machine tools, ship building, etc.) would be given top priority in allocations of foreign exchange at the preferential rate of two pesos per dollar.

During the initial phase of postwar industrialization, non-Filipinos shared in the high levels of protection to domestic manufacturing and the indirect subsidies resulting from tax exemption, peso overvaluation, and exchange and import controls. Meanwhile, the Central Bank and the National Economic Council, under the cloak of administrative discretion, moved steadily to reserve the "new and necessary industry" privileges to Filipinos and to reduce alien participation to a minor share.

BANKING AND CREDIT

The priority for Filipinizing money and capital market institutions has been encouraged by widespread belief that the colonial structure of commercial banking discriminated against Filipino enterprises. It was generally accepted that the resources of foreign-owned banks, concentrated in Manila, were allocated for the most part to financing foreign trade in which Filipino participation was minor. The need for wider distribution of banking facilities led to the establishment in 1916 of the government-owned Philippine National Bank. Although the early years of the PNB were plagued by mismanagement and political chicanery, the Bank was instrumental in extending commercial banking services and steadily acquired stature as an efficient enterprise. In the process, it also became the largest commercial bank in the Philippines.

Establishment of independence was followed promptly by passage of banking legislation which reserved the future growth in this activity predominantly to Filipinos. The General Banking Act, Republic Act No. 337 of July 24, 1948, specifies that "at least 60 per cent of the capital stock of any banking institution which may be established after the approval of this Act shall be owned by citizens of the Philip-

---

[120] *American Chamber of Commerce Journal* (34), September 1958, p. 401.
[121] Central Bank of the Philippines, *Press Release*, October 7, 1958.

pines." [122] The rapid Filipinization of the commercial banking system is summarized in Table 6.[123]

Although Congress has not changed the nationality restriction established in the General Banking Act, the Monetary Board on February 19, 1957 established the requirement of 100 per cent Filipino ownership for commercial banks established thereafter. This policy was modified slightly on December 10, 1965 by Central Bank Resolution No. 1573

Table 6. Changes in the commercial banking system, 1951–1966

Measures of change	1951 [a]		1966 [b]	
	Filipino	Foreign	Filipino	Foreign
Number of banks	10	4	37	4
Number of branches and agencies	91	10	430	10
Deposits (per cent of total)	68.3	31.7	90.1	9.9
Assets (per cent of total)	70.5	29.5	92.0	8.0

[a] Central Bank of the Philippines, *Third Annual Report, 1951,* and financial statements of foreign banks.

[b] Sycip, Gorres, Velayo and Co., Research Division, *A Study of the Commercial Banks of the Philippines* (Manila, 1967), and Central Bank of the Philippines, *Eighteenth Annual Report, 1966.*

which requires that 80 per cent of the individually held shares of commercial banks organized after February 19, 1957 must be held by natural-born Filipinos and the remaining 20 per cent may be held by naturalized citizens.[124] Where bank shares are held by corporate entities, the corporation must be 70 per cent owned by natural-born Filipinos. The remaining shares may be held by naturalized citizens and aliens, with the total holdings of the latter limited to 10 per cent. In 1959, the Monetary Board announced that establishment of new branches of existing banks required prior approval of the Board. Recent

[122] Although ample authority to reserve expansion in banking to Filipinos exists in the wording of the General Banking Act, the nationality requirement of this Act is repeated in the Rural Banks Act (R.A. No. 720 of June 6, 1952, Sec. 4), the Development Bank Act (R.A. No. 2081 of June 14, 1958, Sec. 8), and the Investment Company Act (R.A. No. 2629 of June 18, 1960, Sec. 15).

[123] As of the end of 1966, there were 338 rural banks, 25 private development banks, and 7 savings banks, all established following 1948 and therefore subject to the nationality requirement of the General Banking Act.

[124] See Philippine Association, *Weekly Economic Review,* February 11, 1966, p. 4.

proposals by American banks operating in the Philippines to obtain permission to open branches in the burgeoning Makati financial district were not approved.[125]

Efforts to ensure that credit resources are diverted to Filipinos also have been vigorous. Domestic credits outstanding of the Central Bank and commercial banks expanded from ₱808 million at the end of 1949 to ₱7,418 million at the end of 1965, with credit outstanding to the private non-bank sector increasing from ₱568 million to ₱4,732 million.[126] Of the total credits extended by commercial banks, savings banks, and rural banks over the seven years ending with 1964 amounting to ₱32 billion, ₱26 billion or 81 per cent were granted to Filipinos and their firms.[127]

Efforts to ensure Filipinization of capital market institutions have been aggressive and successful. Similar success has attended moves to reserve financial and credit resources to Filipinos. These are aspects of sovereignty that are little questioned in principle and which proved easy to establish.

FOREIGN INVESTMENT POLICY

The impact on the flow of foreign investment of the system of Filipinism is illustrated clearly by the evolving role of American private direct investment in the postindependence Philippines. Over the thirteen years following 1950, the United States Department of Commerce estimates that American direct investment in the Philippines increased from $149 million to $415 million.[128] The fastest growing sector of United States direct investment was manufacturing (including petroleum refining) which increased from $23 million to at least $190 million. Close behind was commerce (including petroleum distribution) where the increase was from $30 million to $150 million. In other words, the growth of

---

[125] Central Bank Circular No. 97 of August 27, 1959. Only two American banks provide commercial banking services in the Philippines. These banks established five banking offices, one of which was closed in April 1968.

[126] Central Bank of the Philippines, *Statistical Bulletin* (17), December 1965, Tables 4 and 14.

[127] *Ibid.*, Table 21.

[128] U.S. Department of Commerce, Office of Business Economics, *U.S. Business Investments in Foreign Countries* (Washington, D.C., 1960) and *Survey of Current Business* (45), September 1965, pp. 24–25. For analysis supporting this survey of American direct investment in the Philippines, see Frank H. Golay, "Economic Collaboration: The Role of American Investment," in Golay (ed.), *The United States and the Philippines* (Englewood Cliffs, N.J.: Prentice-Hall for the American Assembly, 1966), pp. 106–111.

direct investment in these two sectors exceeded the total growth in American direct investment in the Philippines.[129] This pattern directly reflects the system of indigenism which maintained powerful incentives to foreigners to invest in manufacturing for the domestic market and in final processing and distribution facilities in order to get inside the wall of protection that was integral to the system.

Inasmuch as the increase in direct investment in commerce and manufacturing more than accounted for the total increase in United States direct investment, investment in public utilities and natural resource industries declined following 1950. The Department of Commerce reports that investment in public utilities dropped from $47 million in 1950 to $27 million in 1963, or from one-third of total American direct investment to 6 per cent. As is well known, the major American enterprise in this area was the Manila Railroad and Electric Company (Meralco) which supplies electricity to Manila and environs and which was sold to Filipinos at the end of 1961.[130]

Direct investment in the agricultural sector has remained minor despite American efforts to maintain access to agricultural resources. The Department of Commerce estimated that such investment totaled $15 million in 1950. In the ensuing seven years, a period in which American direct investment doubled, such investment in agriculture declined to $14 million. Although estimates of direct investment in Philippine agriculture have not appeared since 1957, isolated reports of transfers of American holdings suggest that investment in this category has not increased.

Although the Department of Commerce has not provided estimates of direct investment in mining and forestry industries, reference to financial statements of the principal firms and information of ownership by nationality indicates that American direct investment in mining was concentrated in four enterprises and was of the order of magnitude of $40 million in 1963. Examination of American participation in the forestry sector indicates that direct investment was between $5 million and $10 million in 1963.

The steady closing of access by foreign investors to Philippine re-

[129] Of the estimated increase in American direct investment of $266 million, the international oil industry accounted for about three-quarters. Direct investment that can be identified in oil refining increased by $80 million and in oil distribution by about $105 million.

[130] Late in 1967, the sale to Filipino interests of American holdings in the Philippine Long Distance Telephone Company was announced. This was the last major American direct investment in a Philippine public utility enterprise.

sources and markets—other than commerce and manufacturing for the internal market—has been attended by controversy and uncertainty which have inhibited the inflow of foreign capital. At the same time, Filipinos generally—elites as well as the "man in the street"—have avowed persistently that foreign capital is necessary if economic development and expansion in employment opportunities are to keep pace with the growth in population. This national concern has been reflected in the succession of legislative proposals—many of them sponsored and supported by the Executive in office at the time—to establish a foreign investment policy that will accommodate the basic nationalist aspirations of the Philippine society and, at the same time, generate an inflow of foreign capital appropriate to Philippine goals of economic development and industrialization.

The long-debated foreign investment policy is defined in conjunction with investment policy generally in the Investment Incentive Act of September 16, 1967.[131] The law leaves intact the basic constitutional constraints on foreign investment in natural resource and public utilities industries, the legislative limits on alien participation in banking and commerce, and the common law and administrative rulings which have curtailed alien access to Philippine resources and markets.

Under the new policy, a Board of Investment is charged with drawing up an annual Investment Priorities Plan of "preferred" and "pioneer" areas of investment. If an undefined but significant gap—called "measured capacity" in the legislation—exists between the present capacity of an industry and the current or likely future demand for the output of that industry, such an industry shall be declared a preferred area of investment. A "preferred" area, or a line of production within a "preferred" area may be declared "pioneer" if it either involves the manufacture, not merely the assembly or packaging of materials that are not currently being produced in the Philippines on a commercial scale, or uses a new "design, formula, scheme, method, process or system" to transform any raw material into another raw material or finished good which is new and untried in the Philippines.

A wide variety of incentives is provided—tax remission, protection from imports, accelerated depreciation, deduction of various categories of costs from tax obligations, loss carry-over for tax purposes, tax credits, and so forth—and the duration of the various incentives is subject to complex provisions in the law. Suffice it to say that the basic

[131] R.A. No. 5186 of September 16, 1967.

incentives should go far toward eliminating all tax obligations over the first ten years of the life of a preferred or pioneer enterprise. The law is also permeated with complex provisions which ensure that Filipinos will be favored in access to the various incentives.

Foreign capital is given permission to engage in "pioneer" areas of manufacturing in which Filipino capital is unwilling to venture because of lack of funds or because of risks or technical complexities. Foreign capital also is permitted a residual role in "preferred" areas of investment following a period of three years during which Filipinos and enterprises at least 60 per cent Filipino-owned are given an absolute priority in registering to fill the "measured capacity" gap in such industries.

The invitation to foreign investors proves less than wholehearted, however, as the foreign firm that qualifies to engage in a "pioneer" or "preferred" activity must begin promptly to transform itself into a Filipino enterprise. A foreign enterprise is obligated to begin selling out to Filipinos not later than the tenth year following "registration" of the enterprise as "pioneer" or "preferred," and the proportion of Filipino ownership must build up to at least 60 per cent within twenty years following registration.

Given the postindependence history of Filipinism, the evident concern to reserve incentives to nationals and the obligation to transform foreign-owned firms to Filipino enterprises should surprise no one. The act makes explicit certain aspects of existing foreign investment policy, and it changes policy only to curtail the access of foreign investors to the manufacturing sector.

The law creates a new institution, the Investment Board, to plan Philippine industrial development. One cannot be sanguine about the effectiveness of the Board in introducing efficiency and rationality in Philippine industrialization. It is strategically placed to maintain discretionary control over the distribution of lucrative windfalls and if postindependence history is a guide to the future, we can expect this authority to be used to promote the interests of a few favored Filipinos rather than the general interest.

Philippine foreign investment policy as confirmed by the Investment Incentives Law can be criticized as inappropriate to Philippine economic growth. Certainly it is inappropriate to a large role for foreign capital and entrepreneurship. On the other hand, it is not inappropriate to the creation of a Filipinized economy. Over the past two decades,

Filipinos have been engaged in refining their foreign investment policy and in doing so, they have made crystal clear the minor role they intend foreign capital to play in the development they seek as a society.

ANTI-DUMMY POLICY

An inevitable problem accompanying Filipinization has been the "dummy;" the national who acts as a "front" for the alien entrepreneur. The anti-dummy law, (C.A. No. 108 of October 30, 1936),[132] provides for severe penalties for Filipino dummies and their alien principals.

The original anti-dummy legislation was directed against Filipinos in Davao Province who, it was widely believed, were co-operating with Japanese farming extensive abaca holdings to circumvent the public land laws.[133] During the first eighteen years under the anti-dummy policy, however, only one case was brought to court.[134] This case involved a violation of the flag law (Commonwealth Act No. 138) in which an alien created a dummy corporation headed by a Filipino to bid on government contracts. The case resulted in conviction and the Supreme Court, in affirming the trial court decision, increased significantly the penalty on the Filipino dummy.

Congress in 1939 broadened the scope of anti-dummy policy by providing that intervention by aliens "in the management, operation, administration or control thereof [of a business requiring specific nationality qualification], whether as an officer, employee or laborer" is prohibited.[135] Following the upsurge in economic nationalism in 1954, the policy was further strengthened by creating an Anti-Dummy Board in the Department of Justice responsible for the enforcement of all laws requiring Philippine citizenship for the exercise or enjoyment of a right franchise or privilege.

[132] As amended by C.A. No. 421 of May 31, 1939 and R.A. No. 134 of June 14, 1947.

[133] In 1936, in a special report to the President of the Philippines, the former chief of the Public Lands Division of the Bureau of Lands estimated that in Davao Province alone, the Japanese had acquired 32,000 hectares of public lands through dummies. The initial anti-dummy law was enacted in that year following the recommendations of a joint legislative executive committee to investigate fraudulent registration of land in Davao Province. See Leon O. Ty, "The Davao Problem Again," *Philippines Free Press* (38), January 18, 1947, pp. 2–3.

[134] People *vs.* Padilla and Von Arend, 71 Phil 261.

[135] C.A. 421, Sec. 1. With enactment of the Retail Trade Nationalization Law it became necessary to issue orders permitting Filipino-owned restaurants to employ Chinese cooks (R.P., Department of Commerce and Industry, *Administrative Order*, November 17, 1959). Similarly, a lower-court decision affirmed the right of a Filipino to employ an alien meatcutter in his retail business.

As of the end of 1959, 1,824 cases alleging dummy activities had been reported to the Board. A majority of the cases arose as the result of unsolicited information from persons in all parts of the Philippines.[136] At that time, 622 of the cases had been investigated, of which 396 had been dismissed by the Board either for lack of merit or jurisdiction. Of the investigated cases, 125 had been recommended for prosecution, and disposition was pending in 101 cases. The remaining 1,202 cases were pending as of the end of 1959. Of the 125 cases recommended for prosecution, 47 had been dismissed or referred to other agencies, 70 were in the courts, 6 had resulted in acquittal, and there had been 2 convictions.[137] As of October 1960, there had been two additional convictions under the Act making four in all.[138] Both the alien principal and the Filipino dummy in all of these cases received stiff prison sentences and fines.[139]

BUREAUCRACY, PROFESSIONS, AND EMPLOYMENT

The first decade and a half of the American colonial period saw the creation of a career service of American colonial administrators. The service was built upon the merit principle and security of tenure until in 1913 there were some 2,600 Americans serving in the Philippine civil service.[140]

The transfer of political power to the Democratic Party with the election of Wilson in 1912 was followed by rapid Filipinization of the colonial civil service. When the new Governor-General, F. B. Harrison,

[136] R.P., Anti-Dummy Board, *General Case Progress Report*, covering the period from October 16, 1954 to December 31, 1959 (Manila, 1960, mimeographed).

[137] Two-fifths of the cases involved alleged violations of land alienation laws, while a further one-third of the cases involved alleged violations of the Retail Trade Nationalization Law (*ibid.*, Table A, p. 23).

[138] People *vs.* Go Seoc Kieng, G.R. No. 16671-R; People *vs.* Pedro Ty Belizar, *et al.*, Criminal Case No. 4108, Court of First Instance, Catbalogan, Samar; People *vs.* Aurora Valeng, *et. al.*, Criminal Case No. Q-2936, Court of First Instance, Rizal; and People *vs.* Saturnino Datoy, *et al.*, Criminal Case No. 4593, Court of First Instance, Negros Occidental.

[139] As of February 1964, the Board had referred 274 cases to provincial and municipal officials for prosecution. The referrals had resulted in ten convictions at that time. See Cornelius J. Peck, "Administrative Law and the Public Law Environment of the Philippines," *Washington Law Review* (40), August 1965, pp. 434–435.

[140] J. Ralston Hayden, *op. cit.*, p. 87. Hayden reports, "This body of officials and employees from the United States . . . were regarded by the responsible authorities as being absolutely essential to both the good government and the political education of the Filipino people."

arrived in the Philippines, "only two positions as high as that of bureau chief or assistant chief were held by Filipinos." [141] When the Republican Party returned to office in 1921, only nine Americans remained as bureau chiefs out of thirty-nine positions of that rank. Moreover, the number of Americans in the service had been reduced from 2,623 or 29 per cent of the total in 1912 to 614 or 4 per cent of the total in 1921.[142] By 1926, Governor-General Leonard Wood could report that "outside of schoolteachers there is only a handful of Americans holding positions in the insular government." [143]

Filipinization has motivated persistent efforts to tighten the nationality requirements for professional practice. In the Commonwealth period and in the first years of the Republic, a policy of reciprocity was followed. The pattern was established in Commonwealth Act No. 294 of June 9, 1938, regulating the profession of mechanical engineering, which provides, that a foreign engineer shall not be permitted to practice "unless the country of which he is a subject or citizen specifically permits Filipino engineers to practice . . . on the same basis as the subjects or citizens of such country." [144] This reciprocity pattern was repeated after World War II for electrical engineering, chemical engineering, veterinary medicine, and dentistry.[145]

Legislative efforts to establish a harder policy became prominent following independence. During the First Congress (1946–1949), twenty bills were introduced to regulate various professions which, almost without exception, would have introduced strict nationality requirements. Two of the bills (H695, 1946 and S129, 1957) were comprehensive bills proposing nationality requirements for all "professions,

[141] Francis B. Harrison, *The Cornerstone of Philippine Independence* (New York: The Century Co., 1922), p. 86.

[142] *Ibid.*

[143] U.S., Governor-General of the Philippine Islands, *Report to the Secretary of the Army for 1926*, p. 26.

[144] Sec. 42. See also the Accountacy Law, Act No. 3105 of March 17, 1923, and the Revised Administrative Code, Act No. 2718 of March 10, 1917, as amended, Chapters 31 and 32 of which regulate the licensing of physicians and dentists respectively.

[145] See R.A. No. 184 of June 21, 1947, R.A. No. 318 of June 19, 1948, R.A. No. 382 of June 18, 1949, and R.A. No. 417 of June 18, 1949. An exception to this policy was the practice of law as the *Rules of the Court of the Philippines* promulgated July 1, 1940 provide (Rule 127) that "every applicant for admission to the practice of law must be a citizen and resident of the Philippines." Presumably, the privilege of practicing law in the Philippines cannot be denied to qualified United States citizens by virtue of Article VII of the Revised United States Philippines Trade Agreement of 1955.

trades and callings." During the Second Congress (1950–1953), twenty-seven bills were introduced including one blanket bill. In the Third Congress (1954–1957), thirty bills were introduced. In the first two years of the Fourth Congress, an additional twenty-seven bills including one comprehensive bill were introduced. In addition to the customary professions, the bills introduced covered such exotic callings as naturopathy, the advertising profession, cosmetology, embalming, midwifery, geodetic engineering, dietetics, psychology, real estate brokers, and travel agencies.

The reciprocity pattern was substantially modified with enactment of the Civil Engineering Act (R.A. No. 544 of June 17, 1950) which provides (Sec. 25) that a foreign engineer cannot qualify to practice "unless he can prove . . . that, by specific provision of law, the country of which he is a citizen . . . either admits citizens of the Philippines to practice the same profession without restriction, or allows them to practice it after an examination on terms of strict and absolute equality . . . including the unconditional recognition of degrees issued by institutions of learning duly recognized for the purpose by the government of the Philippines." It is obvious that if the intent of the law is to Filipinize the practice of civil engineering, the Board of Examiners can make the proof of strict reciprocity an impossible task to the applicant.[146]

The reciprocity provisions of the Civil Engineering Act have been repeated for architecture, sanitary engineering, master plumbing, and optometry.[147] On the other hand, Republic Act No. 954 of June 1952, regulating chemical engineering and chemistry reverted to the more liberal reciprocity pattern established for mechanical engineering, as have the laws regulating nursing, midwifery, and dietetics.[148] Still another strict version of reciprocity was established in the Medical Act of 1959 (R.A. No. 2382 of June 20), which limits the practice of medicine to citizens or to qualified aliens who submit "competent and conclusive documentary evidence" that their country's laws permit Fili-

---

[146] The requirement of "unconditional recognition of degrees" is also a manifestation of Filipinism. As is well known, Philippine institutions for professional training are, with few exceptions, profit-making enterprises with many characteristics of "diploma mills." The low standards of staff training, equipment, and facilities are evident in the very low percentage of passing marks achieved in various professional examinations given periodically in the Philippines.

[147] R.A. No. 545 of June 17, 1950, R.A. No. 1364 of June 18, 1955, R.A. No. 1378 of June 18, 1955, and R.A. No. 1998 of June 22, 1957, respectively

[148] R.A. No. 877 of June 19, 1953, R.A. No. 2644 of June 18, 1960, and R.A. No. 2677 of June 18, 1960, respectively.

pinos to practice under the rules governing citizens. Finally, Republic Act No. 768 of June, 1952 requires Philippine nationality for anyone to be licensed as a dental hygienist and does not provide for reciprocity.

Filipinization has proceeded steadily and alien professionals who were prominent in law, medicine, and engineering before the war have become inconspicuous in the Philippine economy. The growth of Philippine professional schools will sustain the output of laws serving both to define new professions and to establish strict nationality requirements for their practice.

Beginning with the Constitutional Convention, political leaders have been vocal in their support for Filipinization of labor, and diverse legislative proposals to further this goal are frequently tabled. Although a comprehensive statute reserving employment to nationals has not been acted, occasional laws applying to specific industries and activities have been approved, but their enforcement has not been prominent.[149] The reason for this state of affairs lies in the direct conflict of interest between the politically powerful entrepreneurial beneficiaries of Filipinism and the relatively unorganized and poorly led laboring class.

In the Industrial Priorities Formula Filipinization of labor is specifically recognized as a goal. The formula provides: "Other considerations being equal, preference shall be given to an industrial project that will make the most use of domestic labor. . . . Firms that employ more Filipinos per unit of capital invested will be given preference." [150]

The objective of labor nationalization also has been supported by the courts. In an early decision in this area, the Supreme Court, in sustaining a decision of the Court of Industrial Relations, said: ". . . the court [C.I.R.] may specify that a certain proportion of the additional laborers to be employed should be Filipinos." [151] In the same decision, the Supreme Court said, "A majority of the laborers employed should be native [Filipino]." A more recent decision of the Court (Macario King *et al. vs.* Hernaes *et al.*, of March 31, 1962) makes it illegal for any non-American alien to be employed in any capacity in any retail business.

Pressures to Filipinize executive and management positions have

---

[149] See the Petroleum Act of 1949, R.A. No. 387 of June 18, 1949; the Surigao Minerals Reservation Act, R.A. No. 1828 of June 22, 1957; and C.A. No. 421 of May 31, 1939.

[150] R.P., National Economic Council, *The Five Year Economic and Social Development Program for FY, 1957–1961*, pp. 254, 260.

[151] Dee C. Chuan and Sons *vs.* Court of Industrial Relations, 85 Phil. 365.

also been evident. Up to the present, such moves have been moderated as economic expansion and industrialization have provided employment for available Filipino executive and managerial resources. At the same time, Western and other alien firms have adapted to nationalism by increasing management opportunities for Filipinos, and the expansion in joint ventures has maintained avenues for Filipinos to advance to executive roles.[152] A survey of Filipinization of managerial personnel in 61 wholly-owned United States firms at the end of 1958 revealed that for thirty-four such firms established before World War II, the number of Filipino executives had increased from 52 in 1941 to 211 at the end of 1958, while the number of foreign executives had dropped from 201 to 103. For twenty-seven such firms established after World War II, the number of Filipino executives at the end of 1958 totaled 187 as compared to 59 at the establishment of these firms. Over the same period, the number of foreign managerial personnel had declined from 85 to 69.[153]

Filipinization of professional, labor, and managerial positions has persisted as a goal of economic nationalism. In spite of the many harsh legislative proposals in this area, the laws enacted have remained relatively moderate. Progress has been steady, however, as administrative discretion was used to limit professional practice to nationals and postwar economic growth has sustained Filipinization of employment. Alien employers, moreover, have adapted to pressures of nationalism by throwing open all levels and varieties of positions to Filipinos.

Summary

Examination of public policies and the pattern of legislative activity reveals the preoccupation of Filipino political leaders with Filipinism. Progress toward this goal has been rapid and has occurred without overt expropriation of the alien communities which characterized indigenism in Indonesia and Burma. Filipinization has been facilitated by economic expansion as it was essentially a process in which new

[152] See Columbia University, *Joint International Business Ventures in the Philippines* (Manila, July 1956), passim.

[153] See *American Chamber of Commerce Journal* (35), June 1959, p. 227.

opportunities and new enterprises were reserved to Filipinos, and the contraction in the alien role in a number of economic activities has been relative rather than absolute.

The economic system with which the society has sustained modest postwar economic growth and rapid Filipinization is based on individualism. As has been true of enterprise systems historically, the Philippine version of capitalism treats the expectations of individuals who respond to the opportunities presented by the system with tenderness. To generate adequate Filipino entrepreneurship, the system has depended upon powerful incentives in foreign exchange allocation, tax remission, subsidized credit, export drawbacks, Japanese reparations, and the like. Discretionary intervention by the state in economic processes and the police power of the state have also been used to minimize competition from alien enterprises which, prior to 1950, stifled the emergence of Filipino entrepreneurship.

It is true, of course, that many of the policy measures of Filipinism have their counterparts in other countries, including the industrialized, high-income economies of the West. The distinction between economic nationalism in an industrialized country and in the typical developing, ex-colonial country is essentially qualitative and not a difference in kind. The economic progress that takes place in the typical industrial society is capable of dampening the drives of indigenism. On the other hand, colonial economic development in the Philippines created a dualistic economy in which alien control of productive assets and economic activities of the modern sectors was prominent. The nature of international specialization, moreover, ensured that industrialization would bypass the Philippines leaving her strategically and economically vulnerable and, in the eyes of Filipino nationalists, making a mockery of her sovereignty. The social tensions arising in the conjunction of this type of economic development and the achievement of independence were not to be submerged by economic growth within postwar Philippine capabilities. Priority was enhanced, therefore, for policies designed to transform the colonial-type economy into a national economy with little concern for their direct impact on aggregate growth.

Another observer seeking to understand Philippine economic nationalism might very well erect an explanation in terms of the economic interests of the beneficiaries—avarice, if you will—in conjunction with the political power they exercise. This feature of Filipinism is undeniable and is of obvious importance. The personalization of the appeal of confiscation ensures that those favored will be clamorous supporters of a vigilant and aggressive economic nationalism. I choose, however, to identify a more basic initiative in the influence of the nationalist political elites, nurtured in colonialism and the independence movement, and driven to achieve what they consider to be the essential requirements of independence and sovereignty.

Central to the structure of policies with which the economy was rapidly Filipinized following 1949 were exchange and import controls. These controls, combined with peso overvaluation, gave the economic policy makers a powerful, responsive policy instrument for allocating protection and the windfall in importing. They also established strong incentives to dispossess aliens from lucrative activities dependent upon exchange allocation. At the same time, the system contained the seeds of its destruction in the equally strong incentives to evade the controls that existed for exporting interests who were subjected to heavy and discriminatory "taxation" and for those who were denied foreign exchange in the discretionary system of allocation.[154] Over time, the controls were undermined by corruption and evasion—both legal and extralegal—until early in 1962 the peso was effectively devalued and controls were abandoned. Subsequently, the value of the peso was stabilized at approximately half the unrealistic official rate.

Withdrawing the "crutch" of the windfall in foreign exchange allocation and the transition to protection implemented by tariffs was greeted with apprehension by entrepreneurs, economists, and policy makers. The survival of Filipino enterprises, long nurtured by protection and subsidization, was brought into question. The decision to devalue is now far enough behind us to permit convincing evidence to accumulate that the economy weathered the devaluation with a minimum of dislocation. Few Filipino enterprises failed to survive the drastic changes in the policy environment in which they emerged.

The stimulation to exports in the new exchange parity generated rapid expansion in foreign exchange earnings, which promises to ease the task of sustaining further economic growth. That the dislocation of the devaluation has been successfully weathered is indicated by the recovery in aggregate growth rates which had slipped markedly following 1957 as the strains on the control system became severe. Although an occasional article or speech looks back with nostalgia on the period

---

[154] Cf., Golay, *The Philippines*, pp. 140–162.

of controls, there is general relief at the reduction in corruption and political chicanery. A continuing threat to the more rational postdevaluation economy persists, however, in the inflationary expansion in bank credit which was necessary to ease the difficulties confronting hard-pressed manufacturing and commercial entrepreneurs.[155]

These changes have gone far toward elimination of the opportunities for graft on the part of policy administrators and the incentives to avarice on the part of potential Filipino entrepreneurs which obscured the basic nature of Philippine indigenism. Over time, the experiences of Filipino businessmen in surviving the transition to a more rational economy will enhance their security and self-confidence and should accelerate their assimilation to values and behavior patterns more appropriate to their functional role.

A major ingredient of the system of Filipinism surveyed herein was abandoned with devaluation, because it had outlived its objective economic usefulness and because it had declined to minor importance in furthering Filipinization. The remarkable change attributable to the post-1949 Philippine economy was not the modest economic growth and industrialization which was initiated, but the rapid transfer to ethnic Filipinos of ownership and control of the modern sectors of the economy. The extent to which this transfer has been accomplished is surveyed in Table 7.

The economic census taken in 1961 revealed that the controlling ownership of 79.3 per cent of all large non-agricultural establishments and 90.2 per cent of all small establishments was Filipino. Moreover, these proportions, particularly that of small establishments, were scheduled to increase with the full implementation in 1964 of the laws prohibiting alien participation in retail trade and trade in rice and corn. If non-agricultural enterprises with controlling alien ownership engaged in retailing and trade in rice and corn in 1961, and presumably subject to these prohibitions, are removed from Table 7, the proportion of all large enterprises with controlling ownership by Filipinos increases slightly to 80.5 per cent, and for small enterprises, the proportion jumps to 97.2 per cent.

The sectoral concentration of the minor alien participation remaining

---

[155] Credit expansion has also been sustained in recent years by the self-evident "boom" in urban construction, particularly commercial, financial, and industrial building, which shows few signs of easing.

in the Philippine economy emerged clearly in the 1961 economic census. Four out of the eleven sectors, manufacturing, wholesale trade, retail trade, and services, accounted for 96.4 per cent of all large non-agricultural establishments tabulated with alien controlling ownership. The proportion in manufacturing was 30.5 per cent, in wholesale trade 36.0 per cent, retail trade 22.7 per cent, and services 21.7 per cent. For the remaining major industrial sectors, the proportions were less than 5 per cent in the forestry and logging, fishing, utilities, transportation, and communication sectors. For mining and quarrying the share was 10.9 per cent and for construction, 8.4 per cent. In the case of small establishments, the proportion of those with controlling ownership by non-Filipinos was less than 10 per cent in all sectors except wholesale trade and retail trade. Beginning in 1964, alien controlling ownership of small non-agricultural enterprises became negligible outside of the manufacturing, wholesale trade, and services sectors.[156]

Indigenism promises to be muted and down-graded in priority in the future precisely because of the Filipinization of the past decade and a half. This process will be facilitated, moreover, if changes in the "special relationship" with the United States—in "parity," trade concessions, conditions of military bases tenure, and defense commitments—assist Filipinos to establish the credibility of their sovereignty. So long as Filipino political elites remain frustrated by the skepticism with which the outside world views Philippine independence, political nationalism will remain aroused and Filipinism virulent.

It is abundantly clear that indigenism is not merely an anti-Chinese or anti-Asian alien phenomenon. Tactical considerations and expediency provide sufficient explanation of the twists and turns of Filipinism without invalidating the basic unity of indigenism strategy.

Pressures on the legally sheltered American economic presence have increased steadily. Retail trade nationalism initially may have been directed at the Chinese community, but it has become a powerful threat to the activities of large-scale American commercial and manufacturing enterprises. The "parity" amendment served to sustain the fervor of Philippine nationalism rather than to ensure national treatment of American enterprises. The sale to Filipinos of American holdings in public utilities since 1950 has more than offset the growth of American

[156] Data adequate for a suggestive and basically reliable appraisal of the pace of Filipinization since the late 1930s are presented in Tables 1, 3, 4, and 7.

Table 7. Nationality of controlling ownership of nonagricultural enterprises by major industrial sectors, 1961

Sector	Total no. of enterprises	Filipino	American	Chinese [a]	Other
Forestry and logging					
Large	354	344	8	n.r.	2
Small	1,625	1,622	1	n.r.	2
Fishing					
Large	1,314	1,310	1	n.r.	3
Small	15,064	15,026	13	n.r.	25
Mining and quarrying					
Large	101	90	10	n.r.	1
Small	414	414	0	0	0
Manufacturing					
Large	4,085	2,842	137	1,068	38
Small	33,284	30,643	40	2,576	25
Construction					
Large	261	239	13	n.r.	9
Small	387	381	0	n.r.	6
Utilities					
Large	162	161	1	0	0
Small	693	693	0	0	0
Wholesale trade [b]					
Large	1,357	869	71	376	41
Small	4,668	3,229	38	1,358	43
Retail trade [c]					
Large	616	476	13	121	6
Small	121,244	110,037	103	10,923	181
Transportation					
Large	1,094	1,065	24	n.r.	5
Small	16,105	16,034	13	n.r.	58
Communication					
Large	160	153	5	n.r.	2
Small	1,025	1,022	3	0	0

Table 7. (continued)

Sector	Total no. of enterprises	Filipino	American	Chinese [a]	Other
Services (business, personal, and recreational)					
Large	1,556	1,219	37	276	24
Small	21,178	19,525	40	1,589	24
Total					
Large	11,060	8,768	320	1,841	131
Small	215,687	198,626	251	16,446	364

Source: R.P., Bureau of Census and Statistics, *Economic Census of the Philippines, 1961*. Large enterprises employed an average of ten or more persons during 1961.

[a] Number of Chinese firms was listed only for Manufacturing, Wholesale Trade, Retail Trade and Services.

[b] Alien wholesale rice and corn trade establishments other than those wholly owned by Americans became illegal in 1964. Rice and corn trade establishments with controlling ownership by aliens other than Americans in 1961 numbered 26 large and 106 small enterprises.

[c] Alien retail establishments other than those wholly owned by Americans became illegal beginning in 1964.

investment in natural resources.[157] United States direct foreign investment moved into manufacturing and trade and today is heavily concentrated in oil refining and distribution. American investment in manufacturing and commerce proved relatively acceptable to the Philippine society and was attractive to Americans because it helped to ensure access to the highly protected and lucrative internal Philippine market. Such investment accumulated for the most part through a process of

[157] A survey of member firms of the American Chamber of Commerce of the Philippines revealed that 64 reporting firms acquired title to 3,836 hectares of land in the two decades following passage of the "parity amendment." Of the firms polled, 57 reported that they did not own land. The land acquired amounted to one-tenth of one per cent of the increase in land in Philippine farms between the two census years 1939 and 1960. The principal part of the land acquired is being used for commercial and industrial purposes; only four firms reported that land acquired was being used for agricultural purposes. See the Philippine American Chamber of Commerce, Inc., *A Study of the American Business Stake in the Philippines and Article VI of the Laurel-Langley Agreement* (New York, October 5, 1967, mimeographed), pp. 6-7.

"plowing back" earnings from existing investment, frequently earnings blocked under the exchange controls and not eligible for remission to owners abroad.[158]

Beginning in 1957, intensification of balance of payments pressures was followed by imposition of tight restrictions on the remission of earnings from foreign investment. This change, together with the militancy of the "Filipino First" movement, produced a change in the investment climate which initiated steady decline in the inflow of American and other foreign capital. Further contraction followed the devaluation at the beginning of 1962 which virtually cut in half the dollar value of pesos earned. Moreover, uncertainty arising in the scheduled termination of the Laurel-Langley Agreement, as well as litigation arising over the position of American enterprise under the retail trade nationalization policy and the "parity" amendment, offer bleak prospects for improvement in the climate for American investment in the Philippines.[159]

We can expect Filipinism to be relegated to a lower priority but this will take place haltingly and will be obscured by political controversy and the resistance of affected economic interests. It cannot be expected to culminate in conditions where resident aliens and foreign investors receive national treatment in access to Philippine resource and product markets. It is quite certain that the transition will be facilitated by new institutions and the adaptation of old institutions which will open avenues for effective collaboration between Filipino and alien capital and entrepreneurship. Hopefully, the transition will be accompanied by and facilitated by the assimilation of the resident Chinese into the Philippine society.

The clear capability of the Philippine society to assimilate alien minorities is measured by Chinese names of leading nationalist politicians, business leaders, and statesmen such as, Locsin, Lim, Lacson, Puyat, Cuenco, Yulo, Tanco, and Tuason. Encouragement is also to be found in the social acceptance and prestige of entrepreneurial families of Spanish origin, for example, Elizalde, Soriano, Ayala-Zobel, Aboitez, and Ossorio.

Immigration of Chinese has been virtually halted and the past history of the Philippines suggests that absorption of the Chinese into the

[158] Golay, "Economic Collaboration: The Role of American Investment," pp. 109–110.

[159] *Ibid.*, pp. 111–120.

national society will gradually take place. This assessment is supported by the muffling of outbursts against the Chinese and the easing of Filipinism pressures following their formal legal exclusion from retailing and trade in cereals. In part, these changes reflect a peculiarly Filipino obsession with legal form rather than economic substance. In part also, they reflect the diverse spectrum of informal, frequently illegal arrangements sanctioned by the Filipino and Chinese communities representing a pragmatic, and more-or-less humane accommodation acknowledging the existence of the Chinese and their usefulness in the economy. Such accommodation becomes acceptable to Filipinos, generally, as they are reassured by evidence of Chinese willingness to assimilate. It promises to the Chinese an acceptable outlet for their individualism at a tolerable cost, particularly to new generations of Chinese for whom the attractions of the "inner kingdom" become steadily more obscure.

3

INDONESIA*

The Environment of Policy

The vast Indonesian archipelago, stretching from Australia to the Asian mainland, consists of about three thousand islands rich in largely untapped wealth. At the time of independence in 1950, which forms the starting point for this analysis of economic nationalism, her population was estimated to be about 77 million which made her the sixth most populous nation in the world. The 1961 census revealed that population growth in the first ten years of independence accelerated to reach 2.3 per cent per annum in 1961, and today Indonesia's population is well over the 100 million mark—an indication of the growing Malthusian dilemma confronting her policy makers. About three-fifths of her population is concentrated on the island of Java, with Sumatra accounting for another 15 per cent. While 90 percent of the people adhere to Islam, their religion, especially in Java, is strongly diluted by beliefs and customs dating to an earlier Hindu period. The major Indonesian ethnic strain (Malayo-Polynesian) is actually composed of many sub-groups, such as the Javanese and Sundanese of Java, the Atjehnese, Menangkabaus, and Bataks of Sumatra, the Menadonese and Buginese in Celebes, and the Ambonese in the Moluccas.

The country is largely rural, and if one had to choose a commodity to symbolize the economy, it would be rice. Thus, about 55 per cent of the nation's output in 1951 was produced in agriculture, and of this, two-

* The author is indebted to Ruth Pfanner, Eliezer Ayal, and Frank Golay for advice and criticism which helped to refine and improve this study. Donald Pond and Daniel Lev read the manuscript in one of its reincarnations and provided valuable comments. The author is responsible, of course, for the final product—R. A.

thirds was accounted for by peasant food crops. Rice, in turn, made up about half of the peasant food output. Peasant export products, mainly rubber and copra, constituted about 17 per cent and estate crops, largely rubber, tea, tobacco, and palm oil, about 6 per cent of the agricultural output. In the crucial foreign trade sector, however, commodities produced by nonindigenous industry and estate agriculture accounted for nearly 48 per cent of total export proceeds in 1951.[1]

Estimates of per capita incomes in postwar Indonesia vary widely from \$25 to \$91 in terms of American money, but such statistics must be taken with a grain of salt because of the difficulties involved in international price comparisons and in assessing intercultural living standards. Suffice it to say, the Indonesian income level is very low by Western standards but probably does not compare unfavorably with levels prevailing elsewhere in Southeast Asia.

It is the distorted ethnic composition of economic functions, however, which is the concern of this study. This feature of the Dutch East Indies was first emphasized by Furnivall when he coined the term "plural economy" to describe an economic structure "in which distinct social orders live side by side, but separately within the same political unit." [2] His definition may be sharpened by specifying that these social orders are ethnically distinct and constitute horizontal strata in an economic hierarchy of which the indigenous people form the base.

The social orders engaging our attention are the indigenous population (ethnic Indonesians), the Chinese, and the Dutch. The ethnic Indonesians (or *aseli*, which means "root" in the Indonesian language) will be defined as Malayo-Polynesians of the same origins as peoples found in Thailand, Indochina, Malaysia, and the Philippines. These were the people classified as "Inlanders" or "natives" by the Dutch.

The composition of the Dutch group is self-explanatory except that we will include herein the offspring of Dutch-Indonesian intermarriage (Eurasians). This can be justified on the ground that 89 per cent of the total Eurasian population of about 120,000 living in Indonesia in 1952 chose Dutch citizenship because "the great majority of the Eurasians have not been able to bring themselves to accept being merged

---

[1] For export statistics, see *Bank Indonesia Report for the Year 1952–53* (subsequently these annual reports will be cited as *BI Report*), p. 119, and Douglas S. Paauw, *Financing Economic Development* (Glencoe: Free Press, 1960), p. 208.

[2] J. S. Furnivall, *Netherlands India* (Cambridge: Cambridge University Press, 1939), p. xv.

with a people whom they have always considered inferior, and losing their identity as a group which they have long sought to maintain." Furthermore, it was estimated by a government commission that actually 97,000 out of about 100,000 Dutch citizens living in Indonesia in 1952 were Eurasians.[3]

It is the Chinese, about 2,100,000 strong in 1950, who present the greatest classification problem. Because of widespread intermarriage with Indonesians, a definition along racial lines is unsatisfactory. An expert in the field, Skinner, concludes that "a person of Chinese ancestry *is* Chinese when he functions as a member of, and identifies with, Chinese society" and that such self-identification is demonstrated by "the use . . . of a Chinese surname." [4]

Furthermore, the Chinese group is sometimes subdivided into the *peranakans* and the *totoks*. Strictly speaking, the *peranakans* are the Indonesia-born Chinese and the *totoks*, the foreign-born. However, because there was less assimilation by the large number of Chinese immigrating in the self-consciously nationalistic twentieth century, these terms have acquired a slightly different connotation. Skinner, for example, defines *peranakans* as Chinese oriented to the Indonesian culture and *totoks* as Chinese who remain devoted to Chinese custom.[5]

The extent to which the early Indonesian economy conforms to a plural economy model may be gauged by the distribution of economic power which, as a first approximation, may be measured by the ownership of the productive resources. While such estimates are crude and useful only as orders of magnitude, a considerable part of Indonesia's national income in the early 1950s can be assigned ethnic origin. In the following statistics, the national income figures cited will exclude the "Trade, Banking, and Insurance" sector—mainly in foreign hands—because this sector plays a vastly greater role than would be indicated by the fraction of the national product which it generates.

Virtually the entire output of peasant agriculture (including smallholders exports and inland fisheries), which accounted for an estimated three-fifths of such national income, exclusive of income generated by trade, banking, and insurance in 1952, came from indigenous

[3] Virginia Thompson and Richard Adloff, *Minority Problems in Southeast Asia* (Stanford: Stanford University Press, 1955), pp. 141–142.

[4] G. William Skinner, "The Chinese Minority," in Ruth T. McVey (ed.), *Indonesia* (New Haven: Yale University Press, 1963), p. 97.

[5] *Ibid.*, p. 106.

enterprises.[6] Similarly, the output of small-scale enterprises, mainly cottage industries, which accounted for 3 per cent of such income, can be attributed almost entirely to indigenous business.[7] On the other hand, nearly all the value added by modern plantation-type agriculture and by large- and medium-scale industries, comprising some 11 per cent of such income, was contributed by alien enterprises, Chinese and Western. The output of mines, distributed roughly equally between government and alien business, generated a further 2.5 per cent. The contribution of transport and communications accounted for some 3 per cent, about half to be imputed to alien enterprises and the remainder distributed between indigenous enterprises and government. The fragmentary nature of the information does not permit allocation by ethnic origin of the value added by construction, imputed rent, and miscellaneous services, which accounted for another 11 per cent of this income. The remaining 9 per cent was accounted for by government activities.

Using this method, we can attribute, therefore, about 15 per cent of Indonesia's noncommercial and nonconstruction income to enterprises owned by aliens. In other words, the alien population, which represented no more than 3 per cent of the population residing in Indonesia toward the end of the colonial period,[8] owned, or managed for foreign owners, enterprises contributing about one-sixth of income. The share of alien income, moreover, was highly concentrated in the modernized sector. On the other hand, these estimates indicate that the indigenous sector did account for more than three-fourths of the productive resources. If this were the whole story, the ethnic distortion of the economy could not have been as serious as is often claimed. However, the bulk of Indonesian economic power, as expressed in ownership shares, is found in the areas of peasant agriculture and small-scale industry, and it is precisely in these sectors that the omitted and largely alien "Trade, Banking, and Insurance" sector exerted a leverage far beyond that indicated by its weight in the national income. The effect of this leverage was to divorce formal indigenous ownership from significant

[6] For national income estimates, see S. D. Neumark, "The National Income of Indonesia, 1951–52," *Ekonomi dan Keuangan Indonesia* (7), June 1954, pp. 354, 371.

[7] For information on the ethnic composition of industrial output, see J. J. Polak, *The National Income of the Netherlands-Indies in 1921–1939* (New York: Institute of Pacific Relations, 1939), pp. 29–32.

[8] Based on the Census of 1930.

aspects of economic power. As a result, most Indonesian peasants—whose titles to land enjoyed some legal protection from alienation—and tool-owning cottagers were subordinated to the alien merchant who linked them to the market through an intricate credit and distribution system. In other words, if one could construct a continuum of economic power, Indonesian peasants and cottagers would be closer to the factory worker than to the entrepreneur.

The process by which peasants and fishermen were thus alienated from property prerogatives and economic power has been extensively documented.[9] The system was animated by the indebtedness of the peasant to the retailers of consumer goods, usually Chinese. The retailers, in turn, were financed by wholesalers, importers, and exporters, usually Europeans and occasionally Chinese. As collateral, the peasants pledged their crop while it was still unharvested because land was inalienable.[10] The produce subsequently passed up the chain through the intermediate trader to the wholesalers and exporters. In effect, the peasant owned the land but not the usufruct thereof.[11]

The situation was similar in export production by Indonesian smallholders. Thus, Sutter concludes that the output of copra, kapok, sugar, coffee, tea, tobacco, and rubber was effectively controlled by foreigners who assembled these commodities for export.[12]

Analysis of industrial output also substantiates the general picture of the inferior economic position of the Indonesians. Their role in the modern sector was limited almost exclusively to common labor, and the situation in the cottage industry sector was analogous to that prevailing in peasant agriculture. Working capital for cottage industries in the form of raw material was advanced through a putting-out system under which Chinese merchants supplied the goods and sold the prod-

[9] See, for example, J. H. Boeke, *Economics and Economic Policy of Dual Societies* (Haarlem, Netherlands: H. D. Willink & Zoon, 1953), p. 36; Liem Twan Djie, *De Distribueerende Tusschenhandel op Java* (The Hague: Marinus Nijhoff, 1952), *passim*; and Ralph Anspach, "The Problems of a Plural Economy and Its Effects on Indonesia's Economic Structure: A Study in Economic Policy" (Ph.D. dissertation, Department of Economics, University of California, Berkeley, 1963), pp. 17–18.

[10] This was called the "idjon" (green) system because the peasant pledged the crop while it was still green. For a description, see Boeke, *ibid.*, pp. 10–11.

[11] Perhaps this system functioned to articulate the peasant to the market better than any alternative process, though this is debatable. What is certain is that its ethnic configuration was a breeding ground for Indonesian nationalism.

[12] John O. Sutter, *Indonesianisasi*, Cornell Southeast Asia Program Data Paper No. 36 (Ithaca, 1959), pp. 14–15.

uct.[13] Similarly, it is generally agreed that medium-scale industry was largely in the hands of the Chinese, while large-scale industry was in those of the Europeans.[14]

Little deviation from this pattern can be identified in three important industrial branches that deserve special attention: batik cloth, kretek

[13] Sutter, *ibid.*, p. 35. See also, Dexter Wright Draper, "Industrialization in Indonesia" (Master's thesis, Department of Economics, University of California at Berkeley, 1959), p. 16, and P. W. H. Sitzen, *Industrial Development of the Netherlands Indies* (New York: Institute of Pacific Relations, 1943), pp. 15, 75.

[14] Sutter, *ibid.*, pp. 34–57. Tabulation of the information presented in this reference results in the following picture of the ethnic structure of all major industries except kretek cigarettes, textiles, and printing.

Commodity	No. of plants	Ownership
Beer	2	Western
Margarine	2	Western
Oxygen plants	4	Western
Rubber products	1	Western
European shoes	1	Western
Automobile assembly	1	Western
Light bulbs	4	Western
Dry-cell batteries	1	Western
Packaging material	1	Western
Paper	6	2 major plants, Western; ownership of 4 smaller plants not given
Paints	1	Major plant controlling 70% of production, Western; other plants not given
Cigars	3	1 Dutch; 2 Chinese
Glass	5	1 Dutch; 4 "Foreign Asiatics"
Soft drinks	130	Largest producer: British; most of remainder Chinese
Soap	13	Largest producer: Dutch; most of remainder Chinese
Western-type cigarettes	24	Leading producers: 1 Dutch, 1 Belgian; most of remainder Chinese
Stationery supplies	Not known	Leading producer: Dutch, remainder not known
Rice mills	1,137	Nearly all Chinese
Ice manufacturing	204	Leading producer: Dutch; most of remainder Chinese
Dairies	Not known	All Dutch
Engineering workshops	110	Nearly all Dutch
Sawmills, ice cream plants, perfumed cigarettes, modern furniture, repair and workshops		Predominantly Chinese

cigarettes and printing. Indonesians dominated that part of the batik industry located in Solo and Jogjakarta but the rest of batik manufacturing was largely in Chinese and European hands. Such development occurred even though batik cloth and kretek cigarettes (consisting of a mixture of tobacco and crackling cloves wrapped in the outer leaf of an ear of corn) were peculiarly Indonesian products. Indonesians were also able to establish themselves to some extent in the printing industry which, in its Indonesian-language sector, provided indigenous businessmen with obvious advantages.[15]

Thus, the economic power structure of the society inherited from colonialism is represented validly by the following diagram.

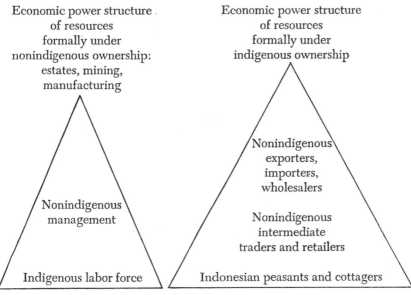

Economic power structure of resources formally under nonindigenous ownership: estates, mining, manufacturing

Nonindigenous management

Indigenous labor force

Economic power structure of resources formally under indigenous ownership

Nonindigenous exporters, importers, wholesalers

Nonindigenous intermediate traders and retailers

Indonesian peasants and cottagers

This economic power structure was faithfully reflected in Polak's estimated income distribution for 1939, according to which per capita income received by the European, Chinese, and Indonesian communities in 1939 was distributed in the ratio 61:18:1.[16]

The coexistence of unassimilated ethnic groups with sharply differentiated economic roles in the same geographic area is fairly common. Generally, it is only in colonies like the Dutch East Indies that one finds extreme economic pluralism where the high ground of the economy is almost exclusively monopolized by numerically small and

[15] Anspach, *op. cit.*, pp. 59–62.
[16] Polak, *op. cit.*, p. 5.

ethnically foreign groups. The reason for this is probably that most ethnic majorities, except those that have lost political power, resort to state power, where such intervention is necessary to block the ascendancy of foreign elements. Furthermore, the emergence of an ethnically plural economy was frequently abetted by policies imposed by the metropolis for the benefit of its own people and to the detriment of the indigenous population. Such measures may even take the form of "colonial *laissez faire*" if the economic power position of the nonindigenous groups is so well entrenched that they can outcompete—or outmonopolize—the indigenous population without government intercession. However, the specific forms of Dutch economic nationalism that contributed to the formation of the Indies plural economy will not be discussed in this chapter.[17] Our concern is with the causal connection between the existence of a plural economy and the development of Indonesian economic nationalism.

In any strongly inequalitarian society that is not socially inert, one may expect to encounter among the dispossed hostility toward the economically powerful. Such feelings are an amalgam of envy and warranted resentment toward institutionalized blocks to upward mobility. In plural economies, these animosities are greatly intensified as exaggerated income distinctions are brought into sharp relief by ethnic or racial differences, and are reinforced by that unpleasant human characteristic, xenophobia. In addition, pressures to redress economic inequalities associated with ethnic differences are intensified with independence as enterprising members of the triumphant indigenous majority see some of their expectations of upward economic mobility disappointed because many of the higher slots in the economy have been preempted by members of minority groups.

In the Indonesian case, generalized nationalistic demands are intertwined with pressures for an economic "new deal" for Indonesians. The first great Indonesian nationalist movement was the *Sarekat Islam* (Union of Islam), founded in 1912, which "burst upon the heretofore tranquil colonial scene with a suddenness and force which quite astonished not only the Dutch but also Indonesians as well."[18] What lay behind the phenomenal growth of this organization to a membership of

---

[17] See Anspach, *op. cit.*, pp. 22–85, for an extended discussion of some of the historical factors behind the impotence of the Indonesian economic sector.

[18] George McT. Kahin, *Nationalism and Revolution in Indonesia* (Ithaca: Cornell University Press, 1952), p. 65.

about two and a half million within eleven years of its foundation? In
the last analysis, an answer must take account of all the negative aspects
of colonialism in general. However, the specific provocation for this
development was related to the plural economy. Kahin writes:

The outstanding immediate cause for the emergence of an Indonesian
political-nationalist leadership resulted from the suddenly increased impinge-
ment of aggressively competitive Chinese entrepreneurs upon the interests of
the vestigial Javanese merchant class that attended the gradual lifting of
travel restrictions on the Chinese in the interior of Java between 1904 and
1911. . . . [The *Sarekat Islam*] was reorganized on a cooperative basis and
geared to launch boycotts against the Chinese in defense of the interests of
the large number of Javanese merchants it had attracted.[19]

The founder of the *Sarekat Islam* was Raden Umar Sayed Tjokroami-
noto. His protégé and son-in-law was the young engineering student,
Sukarno. Due to his ability to symbolize and articulate national aspirations springing from the facts of the plural economy, Sukarno was able
to stamp his personality forcefully upon the Indonesian state.

The gist of Sukarno's ideology is summarized in his 1957 address
entitled "Marhaen and Proletarian," which he considered to be his most
important speech.[20] Although an understanding of this system of
thought is probably fundamental to grasping the pressures under which
Indonesian policy operated, it was not taken too seriously in the West.
What is significant, however, is not the validity of Marhaenism as such,
but the fact that it reflected the self-image and world-image of Indonesia's leadership echelon.

Marhaenism involves a reformulation of one of the principles of the
Marxist theory of historical development in terms of Indonesian conditions.[21] It will be recalled that traditional marxist theory, *inter alia*,
postulated that a capitalist society which has changed from a progressive society to one that protects the moribund class interests of the
capitalists at the expense of economic advance is overthrown by pro-

[19] *Ibid.*, p. 67.
[20] Sukarno, *Marhaen and Proletarian*, Cornell Modern Indonesia Project (Ithaca,
1960), p. III.
[21] Sukarno himself seems to have been most directly influenced by several of
Kautsky's writings, in particular *Sozialismus und Kolonialpolitik* and *Der Weg zur
Macht*. See Roeslan Abdulgani, "Perkambangan Tjita-Tjita Sosialisme di Indonesia," *Mimbar Indonesia*, July 30, 1960, pp. 11–12.

letarian mass action. The proletariat presumably serves this function gladly because, as producers dispossessed from the means of production, it is said to be most directly injured by the decadent capitalist system. Sukarno's reformulation, on the other hand, asserts that the vehicle of change in Indonesia is not merely the proletariat as found in Western countries, because, under the type of colonialism practiced by the Dutch, it was not only the proletarian who was exploited and pauperized. On the contrary, says Sukarno, "almost the whole of the Indonesian people are paupers. . . . They are the poor common people, yes, the poor worker, yes, the poor peasant, yes, the poor fisherman, yes, the poor clerk, yes, the poor stall vendor." [22] Sukarno then traced the relative pauperization of the Indonesians to a colonial system which emphasized export production of primary goods and which hence benefited from low wages and low rents.

In our terms, Marhaenism asserts that the Indonesian economy was handicapped by its plural structure, and economic improvement could be meaningfully implemented only after the overthrow of ethnic pluralism and the establishment of a "national" economy. It also implied a rejection of the conventional Marxist concept of class struggle which distinguishes classes on the basis of property ownership criteria.[23]

The political parties played an important but varied role in the Marhaenistic drive to a national economy which ensued after independence. For this reason, it will be useful to provide a highly capsulized review of the attitudes of the five major political parties toward economic nationalism.[24]

The Masjumi was the major Islamic party drawing support from "social groups with an interest in such governing as would restrain the

[22] Sukarno, *op. cit.*, p. 7. Actually, Marhaen was the common name of a typical West Javanese peasant supposedly accosted by Sukarno—a peasant who owned his land and his tools of production but who was nevertheless pauperized.

[23] A political theorist identified with the Indonesian statist economy that emerged in 1959–1960, Roeslan Abdulgani, interpreted Sukarno's message in the following terms: "In Indonesia, in fact, class warfare happens to have taken the form of strife between the races . . . [and therefore, Sukarno's slogan was not] 'workers of the world, unite' [but] Smiths of Indonesia, unite'." (Roeslan Abdulgani, *op. cit.*, p. 9). This should not leave the impression that Sukarno is a racist. On the contrary, he has been a moderating influence on ethnic conflict because of his stress on nation-state building.

[24] A capsule description cannot do justice to the complex and subtle permutations that characterized Indonesian political strife in this period. For a comprehensive review of Indonesian politics, see Herbert Feith, *The Decline of Constitutional Democracy in Indonesia* (Ithaca: Cornell University Press, 1962).

pace of social change." [25] The Masjumi stood "against any major nationalization moves . . . and advocated . . . that steps should be taken to protect existing foreign enterprises and attract larger amounts of foreign investment." [26] Citing the position of the Masjumi, or its leaders, is convenient for illustrating the conservative viewpoint within the Indonesian political spectrum. This is not to gainsay that some minor parties, or factions within a major party such as the Nahdatul Ulama, stood farther to the right.

Partai Kommunist Indonesia (PKI) was Indonesia's major communist party. It strongly opposed foreign private capital but, for tactical reasons, took a conciliatory position toward "national" capital. In line with Marxist-Leninist principles and also because of its pro-Chinese attitude, it defined as "national" all capital, indigenous or not, which has no need to transfer profits abroad.

Partai Sosialis Indonesia (PSI) was a small elite party led by Western-trained intellectuals. It was social-democratic in the sense that its socialist ideology was tempered by a preference for evolutionary change. It emphasized economic development and planning and opposed "extreme nationalism and anti-foreign feelings." [27] At the same time, the PSI and its leaders would normally be found to the left of the Masjumi.[28] The PSI as an elite party of intellectuals, moreover, was not tied to any economic interest group, and its policies tended to be relatively pragmatic and flexible.

Partai Nasionalis Indonesia (PNI) attracted the largest vote in the only parliamentary election held in the postwar period. It was closest to President Sukarno and espoused the strongly nationalist and anti-colonialist ideology of Marhaenism. At the same time, it was so riven by factionalism that generalizations about its position must be treated cautiously. Its leadership came largely from the vestigial aristocracy that had been utilized by the Dutch in their native civil service and, therefore, it was closely tied to the bureaucracy. Although it also represented groups interested in preserving the *status quo*, the PNI differed from the Masjumi in two important respects. First, while Masjumi support came from the older indigenous capitalist groups, the loyalties

[25] Herbert Feith, *The Wilopo Cabinet, 1952–53*, Cornell Modern Indonesia Project (Ithaca, 1958), p. 41.

[26] *Ibid.*, p. 43.

[27] *Ibid.*, p. 32.

[28] Bruce Glassburner, "Economic Policy-Making in Indonesia," *Economic Development and Cultural Change* (10), January, 1962, pp. 120–121.

of the "small, new bourgeoisie of the larger cities, largely an outcrop of the bureaucracy and developing rapidly as a result of government support" went primarily to the PNI. Second, the PNI leaders lacked empathy with the cause of private enterprise because "virtually none came from a commercial background." [29]

Nahdatul Ulama (NU) was a Java-oriented, Islamic faction which split off from the Masjumi because it felt that its type of Mohammedanism, strongly influenced by Hindu-period animism, was slighted by the dominant Masjumi faction, especially in regard to political patronage.[30] This disaffection of the Nahdatul Ulama tended to weaken those forces opposed to drastic structural and social changes.

The fact that popular support was shared by four of these five parties with the support of no one party approaching a majority ensured the instability of parliamentary government. Seven governments were installed in about as many years following 1949.[31] In the 1955 parliamentary election, the five parties received the following percentages of the total votes: PNI, 22.3, Masjumi, 20.9, Nahdatul Ulama, 18.4, PKI, 16.4, and PSI, 2.0.[32] In spite of this instability, however, there was remarkable continuity in the policies and actions by which the various cabinets pursued the goals of economic nationalism. A major exception was the tenure of Iskaq Tjokrohadisurjo as Minister of Finance in the first Ali Sastromidjojo cabinet when relatively radical steps were taken against the plural economy.

A more detailed analysis of the policies of indigenism would have been simplified had policy actions been logically designed in terms of indigenism. One of the characteristic features of the struggle against the plural economy, however, was that it was largely unplanned and sporadic. Nevertheless, dominant patterns are discernible. The Marhaenistic principle that indigenism should be assigned highest priority

[29] Feith, *The Wilopo Cabinet,* pp. 45, 48.

[30] *Ibid.,* pp. 44–45.

[31] Prime Ministers, their parties, and their terms of office were: Hatta, nonparty, Dec. 20, 1949–Sept. 6, 1950; Natsir, PNI, Sept. 6, 1950–April 27, 1951; Sukiman, Masjumi, April 27, 1951–April 3, 1952; Wilopo, PNI, April 3, 1952–August 1, 1953; Ali Sastromidjojo, PNI, August 1, 1953–August 12, 1955; Burhanuddin Harahap, Masjumi, August 12, 1955–March 20, 1956; Ali Sastromidjojo, PNI-Masjumi Coalition, March 20, 1956–April 9, 1957; and Djuanda, nonparty, April 9, 1957–June 29, 1959 when "guided democracy" was installed.

[32] Herbert Feith, *The Indonesian Elections of 1955,* Cornell Modern Indonesia Project (Ithaca, 1957), p. 58.

became increasingly influential in postindependence Indonesia.[33] At the same time, however, there was also clear evidence of a willingness by some groups to subordinate indigenism to other goals. Conservatives, like Sjafruddin, were quite ready to postpone it for the sake of short-run output increases.[34] Less conservative but still inclining to gradual change were leaders such as Sumitro of the PSI who stressed general developmental objectives like industrialization as the best means of furthering Indonesian interests, or Vice President Hatta (nonparty) who saw the co-operative system as the lever with which to dismantle the plural structure.[35]

This conservative-moderate-extremist division was also reflected in other aspects of indigenism. It becomes apparent when nationalistic measures are differentiated in accordance with the degree of government intervention in the market required for their implementation—a classification that has high explanatory value in the Indonesian case. Thus, conservatives preferred to minimize state interference in the market, which led them to favor subsidization of indigenous business without further restrictions upon existing or even new alien enterprises. This will be called "credit indigenism." From the viewpoint of productivity, such policies have the advantage of compelling indigenous businessmen to be efficient to meet the demands of competition, unless they can count on new loans and subsidies if their enterprises remain continuously unprofitable.

Less moderate are policies that employ the police power of the state to intervene directly in the market for the benefit of indigenous business. These policies will be called "decree indigenism." Most extreme is outright nationalization of foreign enterprise.

Credit indigenism itself may involve different degrees of government interventionism. The more conservative position reflected the belief

[33] Douglas Paauw concludes that by the end of the first decade of free Indonesia's existence, it has become apparent that the highest priority in economic policy had been assigned to "establishing Indonesian control over economic activities carried out by foreigners and minorities" (Douglas S. Paauw, "From Colonial to Guided Economy," in McVey, ed., *Indonesia,* pp. 231–232.

[34] Hans Schmitt, "Some Monetary and Fiscal Consequences of Social Conflict in Indonesia, 1950–58" (Ph.D. dissertation, Department of Economics, University of California at Berkeley, 1959), pp. 110–112.

[35] For Sumitro's viewpoint, see Schmitt, *ibid.,* pp. 112–114, and for Hatta's position, see Mohammed Hatta, *The Cooperative Movement in Indonesia* (Ithaca: Cornell University Press, 1957), pp. 8, 54.

that indigenous enterprises would flourish if only Indonesian business-men were given the same opportunity to raise capital as their Dutch and Chinese colleagues. This implied, first of all, that the big Western banks and the informal Chinese credit system gave preferential treat-ment to their respective compatriots. Moreover, it was believed that credit resources were being channeled to the alien-dominated trade and estate sectors at a time when industry appeared to offer the best op-portunity for nascent indigenous business. Credit indigenism was vis-ualized accordingly as an economically logical offset to the tradition-bound behavior of alien banks.

However, if the true credit worthiness of indigenous entrepreneur-ship was lower than that of the Westerners and the Chinese, this ap-proach would accomplish little indigenization. For this reason, moderate policy makers who were somewhat less conservative saw credit in-digenism as a kind of government scholarship in the school of business experience. Thus, Finance Minister Wibisono admitted in defense of his discriminatory credit policy that if the requirements for credits by national entrepreneurs were to be processed in accordance with "bank-technical consideration," more than 90 per cent of national enterprises would have been disqualified.[36] As a result, institutions like the Jajasan Kredit (Credit Foundation) were established with the express purpose of providing guarantees to enable Indonesians to qualify for bank loans.

Decree indigenism also can assume more or less radical forms. On the one hand are edicts that reserve only entry into a sector to members of the indigenous group. On the other hand are the more extreme measures which exclude all aliens from a sector by licensing arrange-ments.[37]

Actually, both credit and decree indigenism were practiced at the same time under the various governments with the more statist Ali Sastromidjojo cabinet emphasizing decree indigenism more than the others. Furthermore, Indonesian entrepreneurs tried to maximize their access to both types of assistance. The ideal situation, from their point of view, prevailed when state subsidies or credit financed their entry into business and the government subsequently protected them against alien competition. Opposition to such government intervention normally came from indigenous businessmen who had benefited from all the

[36] *Indonesian Observer* (Djakarta, English Language newspaper), February 26, 1957.
[37] For further discussion of these issues, see Anspach, *op. cit.*, pp. 185–207.

credit and decree indigenism they needed and who did not want to share the market with other Indonesians.

What lessons does the Indonesian experience provide for selecting among alternative policies designed to promote a national middle class? Both types of measures engendered corruption and failed in the last analysis to create an indigenous business class strong enough to cope with alien competition. However, it is not surprising that corruption should arise under the circumstances and, in any case, history demonstrates that corruption does not preclude the formation of a middle class—or economic development. Also, it was inevitable that the aided businessmen would be comparatively inefficient and unskilled, for otherwise there would have been no need for indigenism in the first place. The important question is which policies, consistently and persistently applied, would be most effective for promoting a healthy middle class? Unhappily, this question was never adequately tested because of the sporadic and capricious pursuit of diverse and frequently conflicting goals of economic nationalism in this period.

What is surprising about this period is that policies designed to encourage the formation of indigenous private enterprise preoccupied Indonesian policymakers. After all, the socialist rhetoric to which the Indonesian leadership was addicted would have led one to expect a greater reliance upon nationalization. Thus, Glassburner concluded that although the leaders of the 1950–1957 period almost unanimously professed socialist ideals, "no cabinet [of this period] undertook a major program of economic retooling [in the direction of socialism]."[38]

However, in 1957–1958, large chunks of foreign private enterprise (Dutch and Kuomintang Chinese) were suddenly nationalized, and various official Indonesian spokesmen proclaimed that these expropriations bespoke of socialist intentions. Furthermore, many foreign and Indonesian observers predicted confidently that these seizures augured the end of Indonesian private enterprise and yet, taking the independence period as a whole, there has been very little change in the position of Indonesian private business though some other foreign enterprises were temporarily taken over in 1964–65. To what should one ascribe these paradoxes?

[38] Glassburner, *op. cit.*, p. 121. Apart from isolated instances, the only general exception occurred when some public utilities were nationalized. Obviously, public ownership of utilities is quite compatible with a private enterprise orientation.

One explanation is provided by Glassburner who argues that the Indonesian leadership was both socialistic and nationalistic, but that progress toward socialization and indigenization of the economy was doomed to frustration so long as key sectors of the economy belonged to the Dutch. He argues that Indonesian economic policy, feeling itself constrained by lack of expertise and capital, experienced what psychologists might call a "fugue" and that the consequent inaction was bound to persist until the Dutch roadblock was removed.[39]

The present writer, however, leans to the belief that the early avowals of socialism by much of the Indonesian leadership involved lip service rather than deep devotion. For many elite figures, "socialism" expressed but an emotional predilection, a vestigial sentiment from the revolutionary struggle against the capitalistic Dutch. Furthermore, in terms of practical politics, vote appeals couched in the language of socialism found a ready response in a constituency conditioned by the slogans of the revolutionary period. The fact that the 1950–1957 period saw few structural changes toward socialism is therefore explained essentially by the lack of real socialist orientation of the leadership.[40] Furthermore, it will be argued that only the failure to accomplish indigenism via private enterprise solutions led to the large-scale nationalization/socialization of Dutch enterprise in 1958 and other takeovers of foreign enterprises in 1964–1965. Moreover, the differences within the leadership elite over policies of economic nationalism that did emerge in this period are to be related less to a socialist-capitalist conflict than to a conservative-radical split. The split reflected frustration with the speed with which indigenism was being accomplished by the instrument of a national bourgeoise and not rejection of the national bourgeoise as the appropriate instrument.[41]

The drives of economic nationalism are imperative and conversion of the plural to the national economy will, in the absence of progress, reflect feasibility rather than economic and political philosophy. Nationalization in Indonesia by government seizure initially reflected the priority goal of indigenism rather than socialism. Failure to recognize this distinction leads to unreliable predictions regarding the future

[39] *Ibid.*, p. 130. The proposition that the continued Dutch presence paralyzed Indonesian economic policy is also found in the dissertation by Schmitt, *op. cit.*

[40] This statement excludes, of course, the Indonesian communist party which was not in a position to make policy during this period and which was easily crushed in 1966 when it began to pose a threat to existing power groups.

[41] See Anspach, *op. cit.*, pp. 154–157.

course of economic policy in underdeveloped countries. If a country "nationalizes" in order to indigenize, such a country may revert to a dominantly private-enterprise system in the future; whereas nationalization occurring as an outgrowth of socialist convictions must be seen as a stepping-stone in the direction of socialism.

Having discussed the environment of indigenism in Indonesia, there follows a catalogue of the Indonesian experience in the various economic sectors during the 1950–1957 period when policy was mainly oriented toward the promotion of an indigenous capitalist class. The study will then analyze and describe the dramatic events of 1957–1958 when Dutch economic power was suddenly eliminated and when the Indonesian economy was transformed into an *économie dirigée*. The present state of Indonesian indigenism is discussed in the last section.

The Nature of Indonesian Indigenism

IMMIGRATION, NATURALIZATION, AND CONTROL OF ALIENS

The Netherlands East Indies practiced an "open door" immigration policy. Admission into the country was refused only to those with criminal records, potential subversives, and potential wards of the state.[42]

Independent Indonesia, in contrast, admits only those foreigners deemed to be helpful to the Indonesian economy but not competitive with local manpower.[43] This selective system operates through a multitude of regulations so complex that only a trickle of immigrants enter, although up to 8,000, including 4,000 Chinese, are technically admissible each year. For example, before an entry permit is granted, the prospective newcomer must obtain clearance from the ministry having jurisdiction over the candidate's place of future employment, from the Manpower Placement Office, from the local civil service and from the Attorney-General's office. Clandestine immigration, especially of

[42] Netherlands East Indies (NEI), Department of Agriculture, Industry and Commerce, Division of Commerce, *Handbook of the Netherlands East-Indies, 1930* (Batavia, Java: G. Kolff, 1930), pp. 60–61.

[43] Republic of Indonesia (R.I.), Department of Immigration *(Petundjuk Imigrasi), Immigration Guide (Djawatan Imigrasi),* Djakarta, 1960, p. 302.

wealthy Kuomintang refugees, occurred in sizeable numbers, however, in the early 1950s.[44]

Immigration policy was a matter of little consequence compared to the problem of naturalization of the nonindigenous people residing in Indonesia at the time of independence. Here a conflict arose between the urgent need to integrate the fragmented Indonesian society and the desire to deny citizenship to alien residents who were felt to hold disproportionate economic power.

The exclusion of as many nonindigenous residents as possible from citizenship in the new state would have simplified the task of economic nationalism since it is relatively easy to establish citizenship requirements for a gradually expanding circle of economic activities. Examples of such policies can be found in every country, developed or undeveloped, and there is little criticism of policies that favor the citizen over the noncitizen.

Such a policy, however, would have saddled Indonesia with a large disaffected and disruptive minority. In part to avoid this result, formal government policy has consistently been to assimiliate into Indonesian status as many of the nonindigenous, Indonesia-born residents as possible. Thus, in its Political Manifesto of November 1, 1945, the Government of the Republic of Indonesia affirmed: "In our internal policy we intend to implement the sovereignty of our people by putting into effect citizenship regulations which will in the shortest possible time encourage all groups of European and foreign Asian descent to become true Indonesians, that is, Indonesians who love democracy and their native country." [45]

In any case, even had the Indonesian leadership been rigidly xenophobic, the Dutch procured some safeguards for the citizenship status of minorities during the negotiations that set the terms for the transfer of sovereignty. At that time, however, there arose a controversy over procedures for naturalizing resident aliens. The more extreme economic nationalists who wished to circumscribe the bestowal of Indonesian citizenship, preferred the so-called "active system" whereby non-

[44] Thompson and Adloff, *op. cit.*, pp. 49, 122, and Donald W. Willmott, *The Chinese of Semarang: A Changing Minority Community in Indonesia* (Ithaca: Cornell University Press, 1960), p. 70.

[45] Willmott, *ibid.*, p. 77. Willmott cites additional evidence of the pro-assimilationist attitude of Indonesian leaders, including Sukarno, Hatta, Sjafruddin, and Sjahrir even during the independence struggle (1946–1950) when many Chinese were siding with the Dutch.

indigenous but Indonesia-born persons could acquire citizenship only by formal abjuration of other nationality. More moderate was the alternative "passive system" under which Indonesia-born aliens and those naturalized under the Dutch regime would accede to Indonesian citizenship automatically unless they took the trouble of renouncing it.

The Roundtable Conference Agreement that emerged favored the assimilationist position. All *peranakans,* who made up about 70 per cent of the country's Chinese population, and foreign-born, naturalized Chinese were given two years to opt formally for Chinese citizenship. Failure to do so was to be tantamount to naturalization. For those of Dutch origin, including Eurasians who would have opted mainly against Indonesian citizenship under any procedure, an "active" system was imposed.[46]

What was the response of Indonesia's nonindigenous population to this option? The best estimate is that about 90 per cent of those of Dutch origin rejected Indonesian citizenship, thereby simplifying the indigenization of activities of this group. Furthermore, 20 to 30 per cent of the *peranakans* reported to the Chinese embassy to assert their allegiance to China. This choice of Chinese nationality by nearly 300,000 Indonesia-born Chinese is generally ascribed to resurgent Chinese nationalism, as well as to some rather justified suspicions that naturalized Chinese would be at the mercy of a hostile government. Nevertheless, approximately 1,200,000 *peranakans* technically became Indonesians with full citizenship rights guaranteed by the law of the land.[47] The Constitution (Art. XXV) declares that "the authorities shall not attach any advantages or disadvantages to the fact citizens belong to a particular group of the population" and, in addition (Art. VII), specifies that "all are entitled to equal protection against any discrimination and against the incitement to such discrimination." Similarly, the human rights provisions of the Roundtable Conference Agreement in effect prohibited discrimination between citizens. Furthermore, the leaders of the revolutionary nationalist movement, Sukarno and Hatta, have stood formally against ethnic discrimination and "even when anti-Chinese feelings were running high, they publicly opposed any measure against 'non-indigenous' citizens."[48]

[46] *Ibid.,* pp. 2, 25–29; Thompson and Adloff, *op. cit.,* p. 51.
[47] For the above statistics, see Willmott, *op. cit.,* pp. 68–69, and Thompson and Adloff, *op. cit.,* p. 51.
[48] Willmott, *op. cit.,* pp. 78–79.

This initial commitment to a policy of easy access to citizenship and nondiscrimination among citizens withered, however, as frustration with the speed of indigenism accumulated. Pressures for preferential treatment of ethnic Indonesians as against alien residents and naturalized citizens intensified and increasingly confronted the legal constraints that technically sheltered over half the Chinese population from economic discrimination. Over time, the pent-up pressures forced various modifications in immigration policy, not to mention contradictions and equivocations evident in governmental actions and declarations.

An early step in this process was to make it difficult for citizen *peranakans* to prove their citizenship status and thereby to differentiate themselves from the *peranakans* who had repudiated Indonesian citizenship and the foreign-born *totoks*. Without adequate proof, they often found themselves treated as foreigners particularly in regard to those economic activities reserved to Indonesians. As a result, the Bureau of Minority and Alien Affairs (UPBA) issued a citizenship certificate to those who were qualified and who requested it. Because of inadequate registration of vital statistics, however, many *peranakans* did not possess the birth certificate required to substantiate their Indonesian birth.[49] Furthermore, because many *peranakans* balked at obtaining papers that were not required by indigenous Indonesians, only a limited number of these certificates were requested and issued. Somewhat later, Djakarte agreed to accept as citizens those *peranakans* who produced birth certificates and filed depositions that they had not rejected Indonesian citizenship.

Citizenship certificates continued to be in demand since they enabled the holders to quality for various permits and privileges, such as foreign credit or recognition as "national enterprises." Eventually, in 1957, the UPBA certificate was replaced by an affidavit issued by district courts. At about that time, it was also ruled that affidavits would be required only in cases where government agencies were obligated to distinguish between citizens and foreigners. Nevertheless, confusion persisted over the substantiation of citizenship as many officials continued to give priority to indigenism over the civil rights of naturalized citizens.[50]

The demands of indigenism also induced a range of subterfuges to

[49] Civil registration of the Chinese was introduced in Java only in 1916 and in the Outer Islands only in 1926 (*ibid.*, p. 37).
[50] *Ibid.*, p. 79–84.

deprive nonindigenous Indonesians of their full citizenship rights. Article II of the Roundtable Conference Agreement, which had been inserted at the insistence of Djuanda (afterwards Prime Minister), and which empowered the fledgling state "to make such regulations as are necessary for the protection of national interests or economically weak groups, proved very convenient.[51] The "economically weak group" euphemism saw frequent service in rather ludicrous attempts to reconcile the conflicting goals of nondiscrimination and protection of indigenous interests. Thus, a leading cabinet minister, in rationalizing an indigenization decree, declared:

The requirement . . . is based on the Government's view that although it does not practice racial discrimination, it has full right to make regulations to protect economically weak groups. As is known, indigenous Indonesian nationals as a group are included in the economically weak. Of course, a few indigenous Indonesians are economically strong, but most of them are economically weak. Nationals in this country who are not indigenous Indonesians form the economically strong group. Of course, in that group there are also economically weak persons, but these are only exceptions while most are in an economically strong position.[52]

The citizenship laws were also circumvented by restricting certain economic activities to Indonesian citizens whose parents were born in Indonesia. Economically more significant were the cases in which the civil rights of Indonesians of Chinese descent were abridged by biased exercise of the discretionary lending authority by officers of the various governmental credit agencies. Occasionally, access to financing was so glaringly discriminatory as to evoke unavailing protests in Parliament by Chinese members.[53]
A frequently used tactic employed to square indigenism measures with the legal protections extended to all citizens exploited the fact that overseas Chinese held simultaneously Indonesian and Chinese citizenship.[54] Thus, economic licenses or other privileges were fre-

[51] Sutter, *op. cit.*, p. 1292.
[52] Statement to Parliament by the then Minister of Communications, Djuanda, quoted in *ibid.*, p. 1019.
[53] See for example, N. Amstutz, "The Development of Indigenous Importers in Indonesia, 1950–55" (Ph.D. dissertation, Fletcher School of Law and Diplomacy, Tufts University, 1958), p. 169. See also Sutter, *op. cit.*, pp. 978–979.
[54] This contentious issue can be traced back to 1909 when the Imperial Chinese government decided to base its citizenship law on the principle of *jus sanguinis* whereby Chinese nationality was conferred on every child of a Chinese father or

quently withheld from Indonesian citizens who "held citizenship other than Indonesian citizenship." This subterfuge was rendered inoperative, however, when Indonesia and the People's Republic of China signed the Method of Implementing the Dual Nationality Treaty in 1960. This agreement, which divested the Chinese of the right to be citizens of more than one country, in effect imposed an "active" system of naturalization on Indonesia-born Chinese. *Peranakans* opting for Indonesian citizenship were to present themselves at a local court, provide acceptable proof of Indonesian birth and formally choose Indonesian and reject Chinese nationality.[55] Although the Chinese negotiators advocated more liberal access by Chinese to citizenship, the Indonesians retained the formal rejection of Chinese citizenship as a demonstration of loyalty by the *peranakans* and as a means of restricting citizenship.

Many *peranakans* objected strenuously, though vainly, to the new dual nationality treaty. They were incensed that Indonesian-born Chinese, who had already become citizens through the "passive" system and who had voted in national elections and even had held government positions, were nevertheless still forced to submit to yet another naturalization process.[56] If nothing else, it could not help but make them anxious over the permanence of their citizenship status and rights. On the other hand, Willmott argues that in the long run, the new system will actually redound to the benefit of the *peranakans*:

Native Indonesians will be more satisfied with an active optive system. It will therefore probably improve the attitudes of government officials and the In-

---

mother, no matter where its birthplace. This ruling beclouded the status of the Indies-born Chinese who, according to a 1910 law, had become Dutch "subjects." After some negotiations, the Netherlands and China agreed in 1911 that the expression "citizen" should be interpreted in each case according to the law of the country of domicile—which was a way of shelving a problem without really resolving it. The Republic of China in 1929 strengthened the *jus sanguinis* principle by announcing that a Chinese wishing to become a national of another country could only lose his Chinese citizenship with the permission of the Ministry of the Interior in Peking. See Willmott, *op. cit.*, pp. 14–17.

[55] *Ibid.*, Chapter IV; see also David Mozingo, "The Sino-Indonesian Dual Nationality Treaty," *Asian Survey* (I), December 1961, pp. 25–27.

[56] Technically, *peranakans* who could prove their Indonesian birth were able to pass naturalization procedures either by formally choosing Indonesian nationality or by providing proof that they had previously voted in national elections. In the absence of birth certificates, a document signed by two witnesses attesting to their Indonesian birth was also acceptable. Willmott, *ibid.*, p. 55; Mozingo, *ibid.*, pp. 26–27.

donesian public toward citizen Chinese. The latter, having actively rejected their Chinese citizenship, may actually receive more equalitarian treatment than they would have if they had acquired Indonesian citizenship passively.[57]

Although naturalization procedures are available, aliens now residing in Indonesia—the foreign-born, mainly *totoks,* and the *peranakans* who rejected Indonesian citizenship—now find it very difficult to gain citizenship.[58] This situation raises the question of the civil rights status of the some one and a half million noncitizen Chinese residing in Indonesia at present.

Initially, their position was safeguarded by the 1950 Provisional Constitution which guaranteed equal treatment under the law and equal protection against discrimination to all residents. The first deviation from this principle came in November 1951, when the government ordered all aliens to register, ostensibly to tighten its control over the increasing number of illegal immigrants. Although this registration law was not enforced, in 1954 all foreigners had to register with a newly-formed Alien Control Bureau.[59] A further edict obligated them to report all births, deaths, and other census data to the authorities, undoubtedly to facilitate governmental surveillance. In 1955, a provisional law compelled all aliens to renew their entry permits at specified intervals during a period of fifteen years. At the end of that time, foreigners could apply for a certificate of residence. In 1958, foreigners were prohibited from working without a permit issued by the Ministry of Labor. Later, under the state of war clamped on the country during the 1958 rebellion, places of residence and internal travel of foreigners came under strict supervision of the military. In short, as pressures of economic nationalism have increased, the civil rights and economic opportunities of foreigners living in Indonesia have steadily deteriorated.[60]

INDONESIANISASI—MANAGERIAL INDIGENISM

In the eyes of Indonesians, the almost complete monopolization of managerial and technical positions by aliens under colonialism was a

---

[57] Willmott, *ibid.,* p. 62.

[58] It is estimated that between 65 and 90 per cent of the affected Chinese elected Indonesian citizenship. See Mary F. Somers, *Peranakan Chinese Politics in Indonesia,* Cornell Modern Indonesia Project (Ithaca, 1964), p. 34.

[59] Thompson and Adloff, *op. cit.,* p. 49.

[60] Willmott, *op. cit.,* pp. 70–72; *Petundjuk Imigrasi, op. cit.,* pp. 238–241, 253–255.

glaring affront and an obvious priority target of indigenism.[61] Although the Dutch were beginning to respond to this pressure toward the end of their rule, discussion of what was then called "Indianization," was not matched by substantial recruitment of Indonesians into staff positions in government or private enterprise.[62]

Under colonialism, the bureaucracy, as shown in Table 8, reflected the ethnic pyramid of the plural economy except that the Chinese were somewhat underrepresented.

Table 8. Distribution of government personnel by racial origins, 1938
(in per cent)

Nationals	Lower	Lower middle	Middle and higher middle	Higher
Europeans	.7	35.5	60.1	92.7
Indonesians	99.0	62.1	38.1	7.3
Chinese and other Asiatics	.3	2.4	1.8	—

Source: Netherlands-Indies, Department of Economic Affairs, Central Bureau of Statistics, *Statistical Pocketbook of Indonesia, 1941* (Batavia: G. Kolff and Co., 1941).

With independence, the Indonesian state moved vigorously to place ethnic Indonesians in the higher ranks of the civil service. To facilitate the transition, experienced nonindigenous personnel, usually Chinese, were frequently assigned to work at the side of Indonesians who, therefore, initially filled their managerial posts only formally. This contrivance, however, was self-terminating as Indonesian officials gained experience.

The civil service at all levels was readily indigenized by the virtual elimination of Dutch personnel, mainly Eurasians, of whom there had been approximately 17,000 in 1932.[63] This was done by restricting the civil service to citizens. The Eurasians, for the most part, obligingly refused Indonesian citizenship, and their numbers in the bureaucracy

---

[61] In general, the only Indonesians who managed to rise to semiresponsible positions were the aristocrats through whom the Dutch governed under their system of "indirect rule."

[62] For example, see Boeke, *op. cit.*, pp. 147, 194.

[63] See *Indisch Verslag, 1938* (The Hague: Department of Overseas Territories, 1939), Vol. II, p. 424.

were reduced to 7,000 by 1952. Those remaining were chiefly technicians, and the government announced that it planned to replace all but
2,000 with Indonesians by 1957.[64]

In the case of private enterprise, the new Indonesian state pressed
foreigners to pass on their skills and experience to the indigenous
population, a practice with deep historical roots. For example, while it
is common knowledge that England in its early development phase
encouraged the immigration of skilled foreigners, it is less well known
that aggressive steps were taken to ensure that technical skills were
transferred to Englishmen. Such measures included forbidding immigrant craftsmen from taking alien apprentices, other than their own
children, or from employing more than two alien journeymen, or from
withholding trade secrets from Englishmen.[65]

Thus, Indonesia insisted that the Roundtable Conference Agreement
provide that alien employers should co-operate in

. . . the inclusion within the earliest possible period of eligible Indonesians
into the direction [and management] and staffs of the enterprises, and co-
operate in establishing training courses with the objective that after a
reasonable period, the predominant part of the leading staff personnel of the
enterprises will consist of Indonesian nationals.[66]

The available evidence suggests that modern foreign enterprise
substantially complied with this demand. The Standard-Vacuum Oil
Company (Stanvac) reported that the proportion of Indonesian employees in technical, administrative, and supervisory positions increased
from 27 per cent in the beginning of 1949 to 72 per cent at the end of
1954.[67] The large Anglo-Indonesian Plantation Ltd. reported that,
whereas in 1940 its managerial staff had consisted of 55 Indonesians and
268 foreigners, the ratio had shifted to 225 Indonesians and 16 foreigners by 1960. Goodyear Rubber Co. announced that it had replaced 40
per cent of its foreign technical personnel with Indonesians by 1960.[68]

[64] Thompson and Adloff, *op. cit.,* p. 142.

[65] W. Cunningham, *The Growth of English Industry and Commerce in Modern
Times,* Vol. II (Cambridge, Cambridge University Press, 1923), p. 78.

[66] Secretary-General of the Roundtable Conference, *Roundtable Conference
Results* (The Hague, undated), p. V-2.

[67] John P. Meek, "The Government and Economic Development in Indonesia,
1950–54" (Ph.D. dissertation, Department of Economics, University of Virginia,
1956), p. 145.

[68] *Indonesian Observer* (Djakarta English-language newspaper), April 21, 1960,
May 24, 1960.

The National Carbon Company's Indonesianization program had progressed by that time to the point where only four non-Indonesians remained out of a total of 600 employees.[69]

There was also significant compliance by Western enterprises with the demand for training courses for Indonesians. Thus the Association of Dutch Importers and Exporters organized an Academy of Trade and Commerce with 208 enrollees in 1954; the General Agricultural Syndicate offered a course in plantation agriculture with 130 enrollees in 1954; Royal Dutch Shell set up a training school for oil workers; and Stanvac had an intricate training program including elementary schools for 3,000 employee children, special technical job training for 150 to 200 employees each year, and a series of scholarships to Indonesian technical schools.[70]

While statistics are inadequate to estimate the rate at which managerial positions were indigenized, it seems clear that these examples were not unusual. No doubt, the Indonesian government did much to encourage this process by restricting residence and immigration permits granted to foreign personnel. Foreign companies experienced great difficulties in keeping foreign technicians and bringing in new ones as they were required to prove that trained Indonesians were not available to fill the jobs.

Confidential interviews with foreign management conducted by the writer in 1960 support the view that older firms which had experienced the halcyon days of colonial protection of foreign enterprise were resentful of staffing pressures applied by the government. They complained that such pressures involved unwarranted meddling in managerial prerogatives and resulted in serious lowering of managerial performance. In contrast, foreign managers and entrepreneurs who had become established after independence tended to feel that Indonesian staff personnel were satisfactory and that complying with the Indonesianization requirements was not a major problem. On the other hand, there seemed to be general agreement that if nationalist pressures culminated in the demand that top executive positions be staffed by Indonesians, the companies would seriously consider closing down their operations.

[69] Information obtained in interview, Djakarta, June, 1960.
[70] Meek, *op. cit.*, pp. 139–140.

BANKING AND CREDIT

The degree to which Indonesia's inherited banking and credit system was alien owned and controlled is impossible to establish because, alongside the organized credit system, there subsisted a complex, informal money market of unknown magnitude. Here Indonesian peasants conducted a multitude of credit transactions with the intermediaries who linked them to the modern market. Since these middlemen were predominantly Chinese, this informal money market was largely nonindigenous.

At the same time, the commercial banking system was also dominated by aliens. In addition to the Dutch-owned Java Bank, with major central banking functions, seven commercial banks were licensed to handle foreign exchange, three Dutch, two Chinese, and two British. Indonesian participation extended initially only to a few financial intermediaries that had been owned and operated by the colonial government and to several small private banks.

Capturing control of the money market was an important prerequisite to effective promotion of Indonesian private enterprise in other sectors of the economy. Initial measures of indigenism included nationalization of the bank of issue, establishment of state banks to compete with alien foreign banks, promotion of the growth of national private banks and encouragement of co-operative credit societies to break the Chinese hold over the informal money market.

The abrupt nationalization of the Java Bank was essentially non-controversial since control of money and credit is generally recognized as an essential ingredient of sovereignty. Newly-independent, under-developed countries seeking to modernize and industrialize inevitably turn to their inherent power to create money and credit to mobilize resources for these purposes.

The Dutch worked hard to retain control over the Java Bank with a view to blocking those central banking activities which could conflict with their interests. Credit expansion to finance indigenism posed a direct threat to their economic position and also promised to dilute the real value of remaining Dutch financial claims against the new state.[71] Consequently, the Roundtable Conference Agreement, negotiated at a time when Dutch troops still occupied large parts of the archipelago, stipulated that changes in the Java Bank Law, extension of credits by

[71] For an insightful exposition of these issues, see Schmitt, *op. cit.,* pp. 42–49.

the Java Bank to the Indonesian government, and changes in the personnel of the bank's board of directors would require prior consultation with the Netherlands. The latter condition suggests that the Dutch also hoped to maintain indirect control over the Indonesian monetary system through the personnel of the central bank which were then overwhelmingly Dutch. At the time of independence, the board of directors counted only one Indonesian member; the top executive positions of the bank's main office at Djakarta were nearly all in Dutch hands, all chief agents of branches were Dutch, and with one exception, the boards of directors of the branches were Dutch-controlled.[72] In Indonesian eyes, there was considerable doubt whether these bankers, no matter how competent, would interpret national interests as Indonesians would.

The vehemence of Indonesian nationalism ensured that all these noxious infringements on sovereignty would be repudiated although concern for the lack of Indonesians capable of operating a central bank moderated the speed of this process. Thus the Natsir government argued that nationalization would be an empty gesture unless the bank could be staffed with qualified Indonesians. This viewpoint was also shared by Sjafruddin, the economic expert of the Masjumi, who warned against making nationalization a dogma. There was little patience with this minority viewpoint and even the conservative Masjumi at its Fourth Congress (1949) called for the immediate nationalization of the Java Bank though it supported nationalization in no other case. The proponents of expropriation argued that without nationalization, Indonesianization of the bank's personnel would take excessive time. It was recalled, for example, that civil service "Indianization" had been a much discussed but little implemented objective of the Dutch before independence.[73]

In any case, the Sukiman cabinet, through its Finance Minister Wibisono (Masjumi) announced its intention to seize the Java Bank (henceforth called Bank Indonesia) three days after taking office. The seizure was carried out on December 15, 1951 without the required prior consultation with the Netherlands, and the reluctant Sjafruddin was himself appointed governor of the new central bank.

Nationalization of the central bank not only vested control of monetary and credit policy in the government, but also transferred to the state the important commercial department of the Java Bank. Although

[72] Sutter, *op. cit.*, p. 958.   [73] *Ibid.*, pp. 959–960.

the 1953 law governing the operations of the central bank provided that the Bank Indonesia was to give up its commercial banking business in time, this process was not started until the late 1960s. Because this commercial bank shared the prestige of the central bank, its competitive position vis-à-vis the foreign banks was strong, and its usefulness to the government prolonged its life and ensured its growth.[74]

The Indonesian government also proceeded to construct a powerful system of state banks and other credit institutions. First to be established and very active in credit indigenism was the Bank Negara Indonesia (BNI). The BNI had been the official bank of the national revolutionary government located at Jogjakarta during the independence war against the Dutch (1946–1948). Immediately after the cessation of hostilities in 1949, the BNI found itself demoted when central banking functions were assigned to the Java Bank, but it acquired a new role by switching to credit indigenism on the basis of an original capitalization of Rp. (rupiah) 17.5 million provided by the state. For example, it financed the first indigenous commercial insurance company, the N. V. Maskapai Assuransi "Indonesia," helped establish the first Indonesian motor vehicle assembly plant, and underwrote an Indonesian paint and varnish factory (P. T. Sidi Tando). It also helped finance various manufacturing companies producing consumer goods, as well as dockyards in Sumatra.

As government attention focused on credit indigenism in the import field, the BNI was assigned primary responsibility for the financing of Indonesian importers. In July 1950, an additional Rp. 40 million of capital was appropriated by the government for this purpose, and the following month it began taking over the work of the Algemene Import Organisatie, which up till then had provided credit to Indonesian importers. In September, the BNI became the first indigenous bank allowed to operate in the foreign exchange field. The government capital contribution was increased as needed until in 1955 it totaled Rp. 340 million and outstanding credits had risen to Rp. 660 million.

In this year, a new law, the 1955 Bank Negara Indonesia Emergency Law, stated that the bank's task was "to help promote the property of the people and national economic development in the field of commerce in general and the import and export trade in particular." In

[74] Domestic credits granted by the central bank to the private sector grew from Rp. 47.7 million in 1950 to Rp. 283.5 million in 1957. See *BI Report 1953–54*, p. 158, and *BI Report 1959–60*, p. 240.

pursuit of this objective, the BNI set up a subsidiary, the Central Trading Corporation (CTC), which became the leading national enterprise in international trade.[75]

With the BNI preoccupied with supporting indigenous traders, another major credit institution, the Bank Industri Negara (BIN) was established on April 4, 1951 to provide long-term credit needed for indigenous development of manufacturing, mining, and agricultural industries. By 1957, government capital contributions to the Bank Industri totaled Rp. 453 million with another Rp. 140 million provided by the proceeds of bond sales made almost exclusively to government banking institutions.

The Bank Industri operated both as an industrial development corporation and as a long-term investment bank in providing financial assistance in the form of share capital and long-term loan capital. When the bank financed indigenous entrepreneurs by buying shares in their firms, it frequently became the majority stockholder and provided the management of such companies which therefore remained "private" in name only. The bank also made loans both to the general public and to firms it either owned outright or *de facto.*

Regulations issued by Minister of Finance Sumitro in August 1952 provided that even if loans might be unjustifiable by conventional banking standards, the Minister of Finance could underwrite the risks involved and order the Bank Industri to undertake them. In time, the Bank Industri acquired control of five sugar and three tea estates and of twenty-four other corporations, half of which the bank initiated.[76]

The fourth major institution in the state banking system was the Bank Rakjat Indonesia or BRI (Bank of the Indonesian People). This bank was an offshoot of the Dutch Algemene Volkscredietbank, a public institution which gave small-scale credits to peasants and also aided cottage and handicraft industries and merchants in the countryside. The BRI continued these functions to some extent but, in accordance with government plan, tended to concentrate increasingly upon loans to small, rural Indonesian businessmen and industrialists. By 1957, the

[75] For further information on the BNI, see Sutter, *op. cit.,* pp. 973–983, and Harold K. Charlesworth, *A Banking System in Transition* (Djakarta: New Nusantara Publishing Co., 1959), pp. 92–102.

[76] For further information on the BIN, see Sutter, *ibid.,* pp. 782–786, Charlesworth, *ibid.,* pp. 117–130, and Mohammad Sadli, "Structure and Operative Aspects of Public Enterprises in Indonesia," *Ekonomi dan Keuangan Indonesia* (13), June 1960, p. 233.

Treasury had contributed Rp. 350 million to its capital. According to Charlesworth, 30 per cent of its Rp. 797 million loan portfolio in 1957 represented small credits (below Rp. 1,000 per person) while 50 to 60 per cent represented credits extended to small manufacturing, commercial, and agricultural enterprises.[77]

The achievement of these state banks in substituting for alien banks may be gauged from the fact that by 1955, national banks disbursed 39 per cent of all credits granted by foreign exchange banks as compared with zero per cent in 1950. Moreover, 84 per cent of credits emanating from national foreign exchange banks went to Indonesians.[78] Through the government-owned banks, "the government attempted to launch a massive financial assault upon the position of the vested interests represented broadly by the customers of the seven foreign commercial banks." [79] Nevertheless, in 1955, 72 per cent of the credits disbursed by the seven alien foreign-exchange banks still went to non-Indonesians.[80]

The Indonesian government also created a somewhat bewildering array of functionally specialized credit institutions to serve both the aims of economic development and those of economic nationalism. Such institutions included the Jajasan Kredit (Credit Foundation), the Djawatan Kooperasi (Cooperative Service), the Kredit Industry Ketjil (Small Industry Credit Services), the Jajasan Fonds Keradjinan (Institute for Handicraft Loans), the Kantor Gerakan Tani (Office for the Peasant Movement), the Jajasan Perkebunan Rakjat (Small-holder Estate Service), and Biro Rekonstruksi Nasional (Bureau for National Reconstruction). These operated mainly by providing government guarantees for loans by the banking system to indigenous businessmen who would otherwise not have qualified.[81] The volume of credit guaranteed by these institutions grew rapidly from Rp. 15 million in 1952 to Rp. 400 million in 1956. The total of such credits granted up to the end of 1956 was Rp. 665 million.[82] Government outlays for these credits, plus expenditures in support of the BNI, BIN and the BRI, accounted for roughly about 15 per cent of the total government deficits in this period.

A closer look at the distribution of state-guaranteed credits shows that the first Ali Sastromidjojo cabinet, which was in office throughout

[77] For further information on the BRI, see Charlesworth, *ibid.*, pp. 101–117.
[78] *BI Report 1956–57*, p. 89.　　[79] Schmitt, *op. cit.*, p. 89.
[80] *BI Report 1956–57*, p. 89.　　[81] Meek, *op. cit.*, p. 163.
[82] *Indonesian Observer*, Dec. 20, 1956 and Feb. 26, 1957.

1954, used credit indigenism less than the other cabinets. This fits the previous comments on political preferences between credit and decree indigenism. On the other hand, the pace of state-guaranteed credits reached a crescendo in 1956. When Wibisono, the Masjumi Minister of Finance during much of that year, was attacked in Parliament for his generosity in granting such loans, he replied that he was merely carrying out the second Ali Sastromidjojo government's mandate to protect national enterprise from foreign competition and that it was better to finance private enterprise than to subsidize nationalized business.[83]

The same theme is found in the Masjumi Urgency Program, written by Sjafruddin and adopted in December 1954 by the Masjumi Party Conference when the party was out of power and decree indigenism was being stressed. The program asserted that all aid to weak national enterprise should be given in subsidies, provision of cheap labor, raw materials and tools, and the granting of low-cost credits. Indirect aid such as special licenses or special inducements was deplored.[84]

Indigenous private banking was also fostered by the state. The Bank Indonesia reported eighteen such banks in existence in 1952 although statistics were not published on their lending activities.[85] The governor of the central bank complained in 1952 that too many such banks were capitalized on state handouts rather than on their ability to attract private capital.[86] He was nevertheless obligated by the statute of the newly-nationalized central bank to help "promote . . . the national banking and credit system." [87] On the basis of this policy, implemented through large doses of government financial aid, indigenous private banking experienced some expansion. By December 1956, the Bank Indonesia reported forty-two indigenous national banks that accounted for 11 per cent of domestic credit outstanding.[88]

Subsidization of indigenous national banks enhanced their profitability and led to a certain amount of "wild-cat" banking as unscrupulous operators took advantage of government largess. The government reacted by announcing in 1955 that only banks possessing a minimum paid-up capital of Rp. 2.5 million would be licensed.[89] Furthermore, the state established certain supervisory powers over the national banks

---

[83] *Ibid.*, Feb. 6, 1957.
[84] *Keng Po* (Djakarta, Indonesian-language newspaper), December 28, 1954.
[85] *BI Report 1952–53*, p. 78.   [86] *Ibid.*
[87] *BI Report 1952–53*, p. 221.   [88] *BI Report 1956–57*, p. 94.
[89] *BI Report 1954–55*, p. 71.

which were, however, hard to enforce "through lack of qualified personnel for this control." [90] Nevertheless, three indigenous banks (Bank Dagang Nasional Indonesia, Bank Persatuan Dagang Indonesia, Bank Umum Nasional) acquitted themselves well enough in the banking field to be formally admitted into the select circle of commercial banks empowered to handle foreign-exchange transactions.

Indigenous credit was also aided through promotion of the co-operative sector, which for ideological reasons, has occupied a special position in Indonesia. A prominent leadership echelon headed by Vice-President Hatta argued that Indonesian socialism could be realized only through co-operatives. These were felt to be readily adaptable to traditional social institutions and would be ideal for moderating feared excesses of individualism on the one side and state bureaucracy on the other. One also gets the impression that many Indonesians regarded co-operatives as the best method to give Indonesians the business experience that would enable them to supplant aliens in the economy.

The development of the co-operative sector in the 1950–1957 period, however, failed to live up to these hopes largely because it was obliged to grow organically from the grass-roots level with a minimum of government aid. This put it at a great disadvantage in competition with heavily subsidized private business. However, multi-purpose village co-operatives operating mainly in the credit field did increase their membership from 559,160 in 1951 to 1,624,441 in 1957.[91] Despite this impressive numerical growth, there was general agreement that these indigenous rural credit institutions failed to reduce materially the Chinese hold on village credit.[92]

PUBLIC UTILITIES

Industries providing electricity, water, gas, communications, and transport services, are generally classified as public utilities because of the indispensability of their services to modern life. Such services frequently are provided by nationalized industries, or, where organized by

[90] *BI Report 1955–56*, p. 82.

[91] Included in these figures are desa, lumbung, and credit co-operatives which provided credit both in money and in kind. See Central Bureau of Statistics, *Statistical Pocketbook of Indonesia, 1957* (Djakarta, 1958), p. 194, and *Statistical Pocketbook Indonesia, 1958*, p. 206.

[92] See Mohammad Sadli, "The Public Sector, Private Sector and Economic Growth Experience in Indonesia," *Ekonomi dan Keuangan Indonesia* (15), No. 1/2, 1962, pp. 5–7, 19–21.

private enterprise, standards of service and rates are fixed by the state. Therefore, because there is less resistance to government intervention in public utilities, this sphere was rapidly indigenized.

Many public utilities, characterized by structural monopoly,[93] were nationalized against the opposition of moderate cabinets. These take-overs were foreshadowed by the Roundtable Economic and Financial Agreement (Art. 1) which stated that "The possibility that public utilities, such as privately owned rail- and tramways and powerplants (gas and electricity) will be nationalized by the Republic of the United States of Indonesia which will be carried out by way of expropriation . . . shall have no influence upon the reinstatement of the rightful claimants in the actual exercise of their rights." On the other hand, in cases where the public utility was amenable to competition, indigenism took the form of measures to strengthen the position of indigenous operators within the private enterprise framework.

Structural Monopolies [94]

The ownership pattern of Indonesia's gas and electricity firms was complicated during the political turmoil of World War II and the subsequent civil war, when Dutchmen, Japanese, Indonesians, Englishmen, and then Dutchmen again took turns in governing. Outside of Java and Sumatra, prewar privately-owned companies reverted to private, foreign ownership when peace returned. On Java, there were in 1950, two major firms generating electricity, the state-owned PENUPETEL of West Java and NIWEM of East Java which was 50 per cent in private hands. The largest distributors of electricity (ANIEM and OGEM), which accounted for 70 per cent of Indonesia's electrical power distribution, were owned by Dutch companies with head offices in Holland. In addition, OGEM was also the largest producer and distributor of commercial gas.

The Indonesian state declared in June 1950 that it favored nationalization of both gas and electricity companies but only eventually. On the other hand, the Congress of the Electric and Gas Workers Union in

[93] By "structural monopoly" is meant an industry structure in which free entry and competition among many small firms may result in providing services at higher prices than if the same services had been provided by a single or a few firms. The explanation of structural monopoly is usually found in a relatively large capital outlay compared to annual gross revenues.

[94] Unless otherwise stated, this section will be based on Sutter, *op. cit.*, pp. 867–904, 932–953.

April 1950 had asked for an immediate takeover. The conflict was intensified August 1, 1950, when the state-owned PENUPETEL and NIWEM raised their prices by 64 and 50 per cent respectively. A few days later, rises of 58 and 48 per cent for the Dutch ANIEM and OGEM were approved by the government. The Indonesian public reacted strongly against the Dutch companies, and various political leaders, aside from the economic conservatives, responded to public opinion by proposing that the "offending" companies be nationalized.

The government, in the face of pressure, reaffirmed its intention to postpone nationalization and stated that the country's capital could be used better for development than for compensation of expropriated existing facilities and that Indonesia lacked technicians to run these companies. Committees in opposition to the electricity rate increases sprang up, and ANIEM aggravated matters further by quickly cutting off electricity to those customers who did not pay the new rates. A formal motion, which in its final form asked the government "to carry out the nationalization of all electric and gas companies in Indonesia within as short a time as possible," was submitted to Parliament. After the government reluctantly swung behind this motion, it was approved overwhelmingly by a vote of 120–19.

With political power held by moderates, there was at first only slow implementation of this directive. The Natsir cabinet in power at the time of the resolution fell before it could act. The next cabinet (Sukiman) declared that the needs for construction of new electric power facilities must not be neglected, suggesting that nationalization of established gas and electricity companies had a low priority. Almost a year later, an Electricity and Gas Company Nationalization Commission was set up which then took another year to send its recommendations to the government. The Wilopo cabinet of that time finally decided on December 23, 1952 that all electricity companies throughout Indonesia were to be nationalized. Gas companies were exempted, but this decision was not published.

A new commission was set up, however, to study nationalization terms. This committee resolved to seize first the companies owned 100 per cent by private capital. Finally, on September 2, 1953, the new Ali Sastromidjojo cabinet, always ready to push indigenism, made public the December 1952 decision and proceeded to take over various electric companies.

Nationalization then engulfed nearly all the electric companies on

Java. After the fall of the Minister of Economic Affairs, Iskaq, moderates like Roosseno who were strongly concerned with the budgetary burdens from compensation for seized property took over and no further nationalization of gas and electric companies was undertaken prior to the mass expropriations of 1957–1958.

The reluctance of most Indonesian governments prior to 1957 to submit to radical nationalization pressures also affected air transport. The Round Table Conference Agreement committed Indonesia to honor the 1940 monopoly concession granted the KNILM, a subsidiary of the Dutch airline KLM. Nevertheless, the KLM management was persuaded in 1950 to form a company, called Garuda Indonesian Airways, in equal partnership with the Indonesian government which had inherited the planes owned by the previous government. The Indonesian state was given an option to obtain a majority of the shares after ten years. KLM was granted managerial rights over the new company for a ten-year period but had to agree to train Indonesian personnel to take over the service gradually. Garuda was also given a thirty year concession with monopoly rights over domestic air services.

Still, the more radical economic nationalists pressed relentlessly to nationalize Garuda. The *status quo* was maintained by the Natsir, Sukiman, and Wilopo administrations which argued that nationalization should come only in ten years, after the personnel of the company had been adequately staffed with trained Indonesian personnel. Wilopo, however, did persuade KLM to begin selling its shares to the Indonesian state. On the other hand, KLM resisted demands that it relinquish its managerial rights over Garuda.

The nationalization of the airline was subsequently completed rather abruptly by the first Ali Sastromidjojo cabinet, which, seven days after assuming office, declared that it intended to buy out KLM's shares during 1954 and take over Garuda's management at the same time. This transaction was completed on schedule and KLM's role was reduced to providing technical assistance to Garuda.[95]

At the time of independence, about half of Indonesia's railroad

[95] Garuda since then has had a commendable operating record. All of its pilots, of whom there were 265 by 1967, are Indonesians trained at the Indonesian Aviation Academy. Garuda has had only two major accidents in twelve years of service. This, then, was an act of economic nationalism which was forced through ahead of a cautious time schedule and which did not lead to any noticeable loss of efficiency. See *Far Eastern Economic Review* (40), May 9, 1963, p. 326, and June 8, 1967, p. 562.

mileage was still Dutch-owned but with the exception of two urban railroads in East Sumatra (Batavische Verkeers Mij. and the Deli Spoorweg Mij.), the Dutch-owned railroads were integrated into and managed by the Indonesian state railway system (DKA). This arrangement moderated demands for expropriation because it precluded friction between the Indonesian public and alien owners. Although a government commission studying nationalization problems under the Wilopo government did recommend eventual nationalization of the Dutch-owned railroads of Java, this did not occur until the mass expropriations of Dutch property during the West Irian campaign.[96]

The Djakarta municipal transportation system's fate provided a minor but instructive episode in the nationalization process. After independence, this Dutch-owned and managed transportation service became a direct target of public hostility which took the practical form of widespread refusal to pay fares. As a result, the company in question, (BVM) announced that it was unable to continue service. The Wilopo cabinet then placed the company under state custody.

The first Ali Sastromidjojo Cabinet began to buy up its outstanding shares with a generous payment 60 per cent above the maximum price quoted on the stock market during 1953. Resentment persisted, however, because the company was still operating under Dutch management. Consequently in June 1954, the Ali government nationalized the BVM. Shares of the company were "expropriated" with the same rate of compensation used before, and management was transferred to Indonesians. With unintended humor, the nationalization decree stated that the "legal consciousness" of the public demanded that transportation in Indonesia's capital city be operated by Indonesians.[97]

Public Utilities Amenable to Competition

Bus transportation was one of the rare sectors in which indigenous entrepreneurship had gained a foothold in the colonial period. Exactly

[96] An interesting sidelight was that the Dutch-owned and *operated* East Sumatran railroads not only were permitted to operate until the West Irian action but the communist-dominated railroad unions even opposed their nationalization. It appears that the State Railroad Service provided less favorable labor conditions than the Dutch-run railroads.

[97] The number of free rides was reduced by the nationalized company which soon claimed that it was able to operate at a profit. Whether this is to be ascribed to the public's legal consciousness or the ability of Indonesians to enforce rules more rigorously than their Dutch counterparts is a moot point.

how much is not clear; Dutch figures claim that 45 per cent of all buses were operated under "native" ownership in 1940, but the Indonesian government asserted in 1952 that 90 per cent of all franchised buses had been in alien hands before the Second World War.[98] Be that as it may, a parliamentary investigation team after independence reported that most of the buses were operated by "old timers," i.e., by businessmen who were mainly Chinese. Since this was a nonmonopolistic industry which provided an opportunity for indigenous small business, it became an early target for decree indigenism.

In January 1951, Djuanda, who held the Communications portfolio in three successive cabinets, circulated to all state governors a "guide" for granting bus franchises, which provided that half of the franchises should be given to those Indonesian citizens who had operated such routes successfully before the war and another quarter should be given to Indonesian citizens who might be expected to operate such companies in the public interest; bus companies should be managed by Indonesian citizens; and a company qualified as Indonesian if its presidency, managership, and 75 per cent of its stock are held by citizens. The "guide" also reminded the governors of the regime's obligation to assist and protect those citizens who are "economically weak."

Shortly thereafter on January 16, 1951, the central government obtained from parliament the right to grant bus franchises. The stated reason was to facilitate "the development of a national transportation apparatus formed of transport companies most of which are national." Somewhat later, it was reported officially that half of the bus companies and two-thirds of the buses had come into the hands of "economically weak Indonesian citizens." To further promote indigenism, regulations were issued limiting the number of buses per company to a maximum of twenty, which discriminated against the larger Chinese-owned companies. Finally, in November 1954, it was decreed that all board members of bus companies had to be citizens. This was directed at nonindigenous owners of bus companies who had transferred themselves to the board of directors while nominally staffing the position of manager and president with Indonesian citizens.

These edicts did not eliminate the Chinese completely from the bus transportation field, but they did weigh heavily against them. For example, for the period from November 1952 and December 1953, the

[98] See NEI *Indisch Verslag, 1940, op. cit.,* p. 421, and Sutter, *op. cit.,* p. 918.

government reported that 78 per cent of the franchise applications by indigenous Indonesians were granted but only 24 per cent of those made by Chinese applicants.

After launching decree indigenism in the bus field, Djuanda turned to the trucking industry, another public utility amenable to competitive conditions. On April 22, 1953, ethnic qualifications for trucking franchises were promulgated, which resembled those applied to the bus sector. This new "guide," ominous enough for Indonesian citizens of Chinese descent, was issued during the moderate Wilopo administration which ordinarily eschewed the more radical measures of decree indigenism.[99] Officially, the government rationalized the decree by arguing that it had to reserve licenses to Indonesian citizens since truck transportation was a public utility.

In the case of water transport, the major thrust of decolonization was leveled at the Koninklijke Paketvaart Mij. N. V. (KPM), a world-wide Dutch shipping company. Although the formal monopoly concession granted the KPM by the colonial government had expired in 1945, the company enjoyed virtually a *de facto* monopoly on interisland shipping at the time of Indonesian independence. This was intolerable to an archipelago nation for which interisland shipping is a matter of survival.

At the same time, the festering antagonism of the Indonesian public against their erstwhile colonial rulers was inflamed by conditions in shipping where the public was in continual, direct contact with the Dutch. Because of the postwar shipping shortage, KPM provided only infrequent service to smaller ports, and the company also tended to favor old customers, whereas the new customers were often Indonesians. Finally, because of the war-caused shortages and the chaotic harbor conditions, the KPM ships were frequently behind schedule. Yet, paradoxically, the power of the Indonesian state over the KPM was limited because the company, as a last resort, could always sail its ships out of Indonesian waters. As a result, the process by which interisland shipping was indigenized was distinctive.

At first, Indonesia offered the KPM a contract similar to the one already negotiated with the Dutch airline, which called for an equal partnership between Indonesia and the KPM, with the Indonesian state granted an option to take over the enterprise in ten years. The company, emboldened perhaps by its favorable bargaining position,

[99] See Anspach, *op. cit.*, p. 196.

turned down the offer. During the subsequent hiatus and prior to 1957, the KPM wrote off many of its Indonesian assets and repatriated as much of its invested capital as possible.[100]

Sometime before KPM's recalcitrance became evident, the Indonesian government had established a Central Shipping Authority (PEPUSKA) to promote national private shipping in coastal and ocean transport. PEPUSKA was initially capitalized by an appropriation of Rp. 30 million which was to be used for loans and direct subsidies to private enterprise. Leading Indonesian businessmen and public figures began to show interest in the industry and a private shipping company, INACO, was incorporated.

After KPM's stand was announced, policy toward the shipping industry underwent a radical change. Indonesia declared that while KPM still would be allowed to operate, a state-owned shipping company, Indonesian National Shipping Co. or PELNI, would be set up to compete with KPM in interisland shipping. At the same time, the government de-emphasized its previously outlined effort to promote a national private shipping industry. One of the first victims of the new policy was PEPUSKA which was liquidated in April 1952, a few weeks after the Wilopo administration took office. PEPUSKA's assets were turned over to PELNI.[101]

Why the changed policy? Sutter argues that the establishment of a company to rival KPM presupposed enormous outlays—some estimates ran as high as Rp. 900 million in foreign exchange—which induced the government to cut its financial commitments to aid private industry. However, it also seems reasonable that the government, once launched on an ambitious shipping enterprise of its own, would be less inclined to subsidize potentially competitive private shipping. Whatever the

[100] From 1953 on, the KPM ceased adding new vessels to its Indonesian fleet, though four or five ships were being retired each year. See the statement of the general manager of the KPM to Antara, printed in the *Indonesian Observer*, October 5, 1956.

[101] The Department of Sea Transportation reported the following composition of Indonesian shipping as of January 1, 1957:

Company	No. of ships	Tonnage
KPM	104	207,720
PELNI	55	35,150
Private Enterprise	88	40,928
Chartered	32	53,630

Source: *Pos Indonesia* (Djakarta, Indonesian-language newspaper), March 14, 1960, p. 1.

reason, we have here a case where the resistance of foreign private enterprise to indigenism tipped the balance for socialization and against domestic private enterprise. When the KPM vessels sailed out of Indonesian waters in 1957–1958, state-owned ships served most of the routes KPM had operated. By 1961, the government fleet accounted for 70 per cent of Indonesia's modern vessels.[102]

In addition to interisland transport, pressures developed to indigenize harbor services that were provided largely by alien firms. Minister of Economic Affairs Iskaq settled the matter by decree indigenism with the promulgation on December 15, 1954 of the Regulation Covering the Handling of Ship Cargo. This required all stevedoring, harbor transport, and warehousing to be licensed and that licenses should not be issued in contravention of the development of a "balanced middle-class."

AGRICULTURE

As far as the legal ownership of land resources was concerned, Indonesian nationalists had minimum grounds for complaint. In 1959, about 90 per cent of the arable land was in indigenous hands, a situation that could not have differed much from the preindependence period (see Table 9). This was attributable to long-standing colonial policy which assured that all cultivated land outside certain "self-governing" principalities and sultanates belonged to individual peasants or to the villages, where communal property rights obtained under the customary (adat) law. In addition, the agricultural laws of 1870 and 1875 prohibited further alienation of land from their native owners. However, all unused or "waste" lands were adjudged to be the freely disposable property of the state and were available for lease to foreign estates.[103]

In spite of this favorable ethnic ownership pattern the agricultural sector proved sensitive to the pressures of economic nationalism. This response reflected the role of foreign estate output in the crucial area of export production, the friction between foreign estates and indigenous farmers, and the considerable economic control exerted by foreign middlemen over indigenous peasants.

---

[102] *Statistical Pocketbook of Indonesia, 1962,* p. 175.

[103] Unless otherwise indicated, this section is based on G. C. Allen and Audrey H. Donnithorne, *Western Enterprise in Indonesia and Malaya* (London: Allen and Unwin, 1957), Ch. 3; Karl J. Pelzer, "The Agricultural Foundation," in McVey (ed.), *Indonesia;* and Sutter, *op. cit.,* pp. 26–33, 695–712.

Table 9. Major agricultural landholdings by form of title, 1940 and 1959
(hectares)

Title	1940	1959	Percentage in 1959
Indonesian-owned lands			
Irrigated lands privately owned	n.a.	4,984,000 [a]	23.5
Unirrigated land, compound or mixed garden land, and fresh-water fishponds	n.a.	14,773,000 [a]	69.0
Modernized agriculture on lease			
"Erfpacht" or long-lease tenures	1,015,500 [b]	695,100 [b]	3.0
Agricultural concessions (all in Outer Islands)	936,000 [b]	785,500 [b]	4.0
Short leases from Indonesian private owners	89,700 [b]	59,000 [b]	0.3
Land fully owned by foreign interests			
"Private Lands" or "Free Holds"	351,300 [b]	71,000 [b]	0.3

[a] Karl J. Pelzer, "The Agricultural Foundation," in McVey (ed.), *Indonesia* (New Haven: Yale University Press, 1963), pp. 121–123.
[b] *Statistical Pocketbook of Indonesia 1962,* p. 62. One hectare = 2.47 acres.

Indonesian agriculture is dominated by smallholders food production, which includes staples such as rice, sweet potatoes, and corn, and also export crops. All commodities raised for export enter into the money economy and, moreover, a considerable portion of the output of staples enters the market. The various export crops are grown either in the modern, capital-intensive estate sector or by Indonesian smallholders, in the proportions shown in Table 10.[104] With the exception of the most important crop, rubber, all export commodities experienced serious declines in output between 1938 and 1959. In the case of crops where estate production played an important role, the declines were due both to the increased importance of the less efficient smallholder sector and to the nationalization of foreign estates. In other cases, attempts to

[104] All agricultural crops that played an important role in the export trade of the Netherlands Indies are commonly called export commodities. This classification has been retained even though in some cases, of which sugar is a prominent example, major so-called export commodities are now consumed domestically because of the changed consumption conditions in postindependence Indonesia.

Table 10. Structure of export production [a]

Crops	Percentage of total export earnings [b]		Percentage of crops raised by peasants [c]		Percentage of change in production (or exports) between 1938 and 1959 [d]
	1938	1959	1938	1959	
Raised both by estates and smallholders in 1938					
Rubber	22.6	33.1	48	63[e]	(+127)
Coffee	2.0	2.3	58	80	−32
Raised largely by estates in 1938					
Tea	8.2	3.1	18	35	−46
Sugar	6.5	.9	1	33	−39
Tobacco	5.6	3.7	30	90	(−70)
Palm oil	2.4	3.0	0	0	−39
Raised largely by smallholders in 1938					
Coconut products (largely copra and copra cakes)	5.6	2.3	95	99	−63
Pepper	1.2	.6	99	100	(−46)

[a] The table includes only those export goods that account separately for more than one per cent of total value of agricultural exports in 1938.

[b] *Statistical Pocketbook of Indonesia, 1962,* p. 144.

[c] See Karl J. Pelzer, "The Agricultural Foundation," in McVey (ed.), *Indonesia* (New Haven: Yale University Press, 1963), p. 120.

[d] Based on *BI Report, 1959–60,* pp. 157–158, 162–163, 170, 174–175, 178–179. The year 1959 was chosen for comparison because 1958 was a year of civil war which distorted normal economic performance.

[e] Exports rather than production.

indigenize the collection of exports and the trade sector in general also took their toll in economic efficiency.

Policies of economic nationalism in agricultural export production during the period 1950–1957 included measures that shifted estates from alien to indigenous ownership, those which diverted production from alien estates to indigenous smallholders, as well as actions to strengthen the smallholder's position vis-à-vis the aliens who linked him to the market. Before the nationalization of Dutch estates in 1958, emphasis was placed on the latter two activities.

As a matter of fact, the foreigner's control of estate lands was actually reinforced in this period by the government. This occurred because much estate property had come into the possession of squatters immediately after World War II and during the subsequent independence struggle. The situation confronted Indonesia in 1950 with the hard choice of either regularizing the *de facto* possession by cultivators or of returning the lands to their erstwhile owners, as was provided by the Roundtable Conference Agreement.[105] With the foreign exchange needs of the society establishing a strong incentive, the government chose to resist the demands of economic nationalism. This policy was made more palatable by the formation in March 1950 of an Alien Estate Restoration Commission empowered to compensate evicted Indonesian peasants financially or with other lands. By 1953, 70 per cent of the estates on the islands of Java and Sumatra were back in the possession of their foreign owners.

The course of this restoration, one of the few examples of counter-indigenism, however, was not smooth and squatter problems plagued estate agriculture throughout this period. Conflict was particularly bitter in the Outer Islands where lands were returned to foreign estates even though they had historically been under various types of communal tenure. These disputes carried serious consequences for internal stability and order because they affected the peasant masses in a situation where their immediate interests came into direct conflict with those of their former colonial rulers.

A case in point was the attempt of the Wilopo government to end the peasant occupations of East Sumatran lands leased for a seventy-five-year period to Dutch tobacco companies. The Sumatran peasants resisted eviction strenuously since they had been encouraged to repossess estate lands by the Japanese occupation authorities concerned for increasing food production during 1944 and 1945. This resentment intensified even though the Tobacco Estates Association renounced its claim on about half of the area under contention.[106] With leftwing

---

[105] The Roundtable Conference Agreement pledged Indonesia to recognize "all rights concessions and licenses granted according to law and still in effect at the time of the transfer of sovereignty" and to restore these rights "so far as such has not yet occurred" (Sutter, *op. cit.*, p. 1290).

[106] *Ibid.*, This renunciation followed upon negotiations based on another clause of the Roundtable Conference Agreement which allowed for exceptions to such restorations in cases where the Japanese occupiers had induced the squatting in the first place.

organizations taking the part of rebellious peasants, sporadic violence occurred, including the killing by the police in the district of Tandjung Morawa of one Indonesian and four Chinese farmers.

The Tandjung Morawa incident aroused strong emotional reactions against the use of force to return property to the unpopular "colonial" enterprises. The ruling PNI party withdrew support of its own government's squatter policies, and the Wilopo cabinet resigned. With the temper of the country accordingly revealed, this was the last time that any government attempted to directly resist decolonization pressures in such dramatic circumstances.[107] Furthermore, in spite of subsequent cautious state actions, the squatter problem remained largely unresolved until the 1958 takeover.

Other foreign estates, particularly sugar estates in overcrowded Java, procured their land directly from Indonesian peasants under short-term leases (see Table 9). Following independence, the sugar estates could not, or would not, offer rentals high enough to compensate peasants for foregoing the two rainy season crops and one dry-season crop necessary to harvest a crop of sugar. This was due, to some extent, to the decreased profitability of the Javanese sugar industry which was concentrated in areas particularly unstable in the chaotic revolutionary and post-revolutionary period. In the first two growing seasons after independence, between one-fifth and one-sixth of the cane crop was stolen. The decline in the production of sugar led to government intervention to fix maximum land rentals in an attempt to restore output. This policy, which favored foreign estate owners, also aroused nationalistic resentment but nevertheless received parliamentary approval.[108]

Although the large-scale elimination of foreign estate operations was stemmed in the 1950–1957 period, indigenism did progress somewhat through the growing importance of the smallholders sector. This process was encouraged by liberal financial and technological assistance channeled directly to farmers through newly-established government institu-

[107] For more on the Tandjung Morawa incident, see Anspach, *op. cit.*, pp. 161–166.

[108] The Minister of Agriculture in explaining the policy to Parliament asserted: "For the time being sugar and tobacco estates must still be operated by foreign capital. In view of the fact, the Government does not agree . . . that it is impossible for a "community of interest" to be formed in the estate industry among capital, landowners, and labor . . . there must be cooperation between the groups possessing the three factors of production, free of the question of whether or not the proprietors are alien" (Sutter, *op. cit.*, p. 708).

tions. Particularly important among these were the Smallholders Rubber Institute Service, established in 1953 by the Department of Agriculture, and the Indonesian Small-Holders Institute which specialized in providing credits to peasant farmers.[109]

Indigenism occurred in this way where estates had shared the market with smallholders or where estate production had been clearly dominant (see Table 10). Unfortunately, this often did not reflect improvement in indigenous production but deterioration in estate agriculture. The declines in the estate sector were due to the continuing problem of squatters, to policies favorable to indigenous labor unions which resulted in higher wage costs, and to the persistence of pilferage, especially on tea plantations. Thus, estate production of tobacco fell from about 35,000 net tons in 1938 to about 7,000 in 1956, while smallholder output was largely unchanged. Similarly in coffee production, estate output declined from 45,000 net tons in 1938 to 12,000 tons in 1958, while smallholder production experienced only a minor decline.[110]

There were other cases, however, where smallholders agriculture expanded as the new state dismantled colonial arrangements which had inhibited peasant enterprise. For example, peasant sugar production, which had been effectively banned by the Dutch, leaped from 71 hectares in 1950 to 24,031 hectares in 1955.[111] More significant from the economic viewpoint was the response in smallholders rubber production when colonial policies that favored estate production were abandoned.[112] With the removal of such restrictions, smallholder rubber exports rose from 264,000 tons in 1940 to an average of 458,000 tons during 1950–1957. Estate exports, in the same period, declined from 281,000 to 242,000 tons. These cases demonstrate once again that indigenism is not necessarily accompanied by setbacks in production, although smallholders rubber production has been plagued by chronic problems of inadequate replanting and quality maintenance.

---

[109] See Kenneth D. Thomas, *Smallholders Rubber in Indonesia* (Report by Institute for Economic and Social Research, University of Indonesia, Djakarta School of Economics, undated), pp. 27–43; *BI Reports 1953–54*, p. 125; and *BI Reports 1956–57*, p. 162.

[110] *BI Report 1959–60*, pp. 175, 178.

[111] *BI Report 1959–60*, pp. 175, 178; Sutter, *op. cit.*, p. 705.

[112] Boeke characterized Dutch policy as designed "to protect the far more weighty interests of Western Enterprise" (Boeke, *op. cit.*, p. 214). See also P. T. Bauer, *The Rubber Industry* (Cambridge, Mass.: Harvard University Press, 1948), p. 79.

Indigenism efforts in export agriculture and in food production for the domestic market also tackled the problem of control exercised by alien middlemen. Smallholder production was financed by traders, largely Chinese, who advanced consumer goods against future repayments in the marketable export products, and there was great interest in displacing these middlemen by co-operatives or state marketing agencies.[113]

Such trading organizations were frequently established in the first instance for purposes other than indigenism. For example, the Copra Fund was set up by the Dutch in 1940 to control the quality and pricing of the copra output to keep it competitive with other producing areas. For similar reasons, the Kapokcentrale was founded in 1937. Co-operatives in rubber marketing were organized after independence to raise the proportion of the price received by the smallholder and to help upgrade the quality of his rubber. N. V. Karet, a rubber processing and marketing co-operative in which the state held majority stock ownership, was organized in 1954 to rationalize rubber collection after the government had temporarily prohibited the export of raw rubber in order to stimulate domestic processing.

Over time, these agencies became concerned with encouraging indigenous entrepreneurship in the trade sector. Where this was done by giving inadequately financed indigenous commercial enterprises monopolistic rights, smallholders were frequently worse off after such indigenism measures than when they were still dealing directly with Chinese middlemen. For example, in 1954 when steps were taken by Iskaq to channel copra exports from the Copra Foundation through national exporters, the result was such a deterioration of the smallholders terms of trade that the Copra Foundation came under heavy attack and was liquidated in 1956.[114]

In fact, there is general agreement that the government's attempts to indigenize the marketing structure of smallholders export products was an over-all failure because of inexperience, inefficiency, corruption, and inadequate capital. In the case of rubber and copra, the disorder and confusion that followed these measures contributed to the general discontent in the Outer Islands which eventually led to the 1956–1958 uprisings. Furthermore, these efforts had little effect on the ethnic

---

[113] For marketing of rubber, see Thomas, *op. cit.*, p. 48; for copra, kapok, and coffee, see Sutter, *op. cit.*, pp. 14–16.

[114] *BI Report 1956–57*, p. 145.

composition of marketing activities prior to the drastic changes of 1958–1959.

Finally, land nationalization made a minor contribution to indigenism prior to the wholesale expropriation of Dutch property in 1958. Estates owned by Axis subjects were confiscated by the government in the aftermath of World War II. This virtually doubled the landholdings of the government estate service, State Plantation Center (PPN) but the fraction of the total estate average held by PPN after these expropriations was still only some 2.5 per cent of the land in private estates.[115]

Land nationalization also occurred in the case of the feudalistic "private lands," which had been alienated to private interests by the Dutch colonial administration during financial crises in the nineteenth century (see Table 9). The buyer also acquired administrative rights over the inhabitants including the privilege to levy taxes, to set market prices, and to exact compulsory labor. Although the largest single "private estate" was the British-owned P. and T. Lands on Java, 40 per cent of all such property was held by the Chinese in 1935.

To free tenants from the abuses of absentee landlordism and excessive exactions and also to prevent the sale of some existing large freeholds to non-Dutch nationals, the Netherlands government in 1910 instituted a policy of liquidating these estates by repurchase. By 1940, more than two-thirds of such "private estates" had been repurchased leaving only 351,300 hectares outstanding. The Republic of Indonesia continued this policy and reduced the freehold area to 72,300 hectares by 1957. But even this liquidation pace was considered too slow, and in 1958 all freehold estates were abolished by law. Landlords had to sell their lands at fixed prices either to private persons or to the government. By 1962, this category of landholding had almost disappeared.[116]

MINING

Foreign participation in mining is particularly resented by economic nationalists because it involves the visible extraction and shipment abroad by aliens of a portion of the proven resource patrimony of the country. The heavy capital investment required by mining, however,

[115] Probably the most significant result of this development was that the PPN recruited and trained the Indonesian cadres who in 1958 would assume much of the responsibility for operation of the seized Dutch estates.

[116] Pelzer, *op. cit.*, p. 137.

frequently leads capital-short underdeveloped countries to turn to foreign investment to develop their mineral potential.

In the Indonesian case, these conflicting pressures led initially to a policy of noninterference with existing foreign enterprise, combined with rejection of further concessions to foreign investment.[117] Thus, the Teuku Hasan Motion, approved by the Parliament on August 2, 1951, ordered the government to set up a State Commission on Mining Affairs to draft an Indonesian mining law grounded on the principle of a national economy. The motion also urged the government "to postpone all granting of concessions and exploitation permits or extending expired permits, pending the results of the work of the State Commission on Mining Affairs." [118] Since this Commission failed to draft a law until 1958—possibly an example of judicious procrastination—the mining law of the colonial regime remained in operation "provisionally," but no new concessions were granted to foreigners.

Outside of the North Sumatra oil field, Indonesia implemented an oil policy of accommodation with foreign enterprise. The facilities in North Sumatra belonging to the Dutch-British Batavsche Petroleum Maatschappij (BPM), a subsidiary of Shell Oil, had been almost completely destroyed, first by Dutch scorched-earth tactics during the Japanese invasion, then by Allied bombing, and finally by Indonesian military action during the revolution. With a minimum of fixed plant, they were operated after independence by the Indonesian government at about 2 per cent of their prewar capacity, mainly to satisfy the local demand for oil for cooking and lighting.

An initial government decision to return the wells to the BPM was subsequently reversed on the grounds that the Dutch, by destroying the installations, had also destroyed their investment and their claims to the wells. Consequently, in accordance with the Constitution, "new" mineral exploitation rights were not granted to BPM. The final rejection of the foreign claim occurred when the second Ali Sastromidjojo cabinet formed a government corporation, North Sumatra Petroleum Operations, Inc., to exploit this resource.[119]

These wells represented an insignificant proportion of Indonesia's

[117] Both the 1945 and the 1950 Constitution stated unequivocally that "the land and air and natural riches to be found therein are administered by the state and are used for the greatest welfare of the people."

[118] Sutter, *op. cit.*, pp. 820–821.   [119] *Ibid.*, pp. 831–846.

important oil output, which accounted for 20 to 30 per cent of export earnings. The foreign companies which provided the bulk of this income—Shell Oil, Caltex and Stanvac—experienced more tolerant treatment, in part, because they controlled the distribution facilities through which Indonesia's oil traditionally had been marketed.

The relationship with the big three producers was governed by the so-called "let-alone agreements," which were negotiated by the Netherlands-Indies government in 1948 during the Dutch period. Under these agreements, the oil producers were exempted from Indonesian foreign-exchange controls and, in return, the companies agreed to rehabilitate damaged oil installations without recourse to Indonesia's foreign-exchange funds. The companies further agreed to pay profit taxes in foreign exchange and also to purchase with foreign exchange their rupiah requirements in excess of the rupiah proceeds from sales in the local market.[120]

In the production of tin, which provides about 6 per cent of Indonesia's foreign exchange, economic nationalism involved the issue of managerial control rather than ownership. Indonesian tin was produced in two mines, Bangka, which accounted for three-fifths of production, and Billiton, which accounted for the remainder. At the time of independence, the Billiton mine was operated by the N. V. Gemeenschappelijke Mijnbouwmaatschappij Billiton (GMB) in which five-eighths of the shares were held by the Indonesian state as legal successor to the Netherlands Indies government and three-eighths by a Dutch company, N. V. Billiton Mij. Under a management contract, the Dutch minority stockholder was given complete administrative control over the GMB. At the same time, under a similar management contract, the Bangka mines, owned by the government, were operated by the GMB. Under these arrangements, the private Dutch firm managed Indonesia's production of tin even though it owned only about 15 per cent of the producing companies.

As early as 1950, a Bangka labor leader and PNI member of Parliament complained that Dutch personnel employed at Bangka were being replaced by Dutch employees of the GMB. He asserted that the GMB was trying thereby to make itself indispensable at Bangka in order to

---

[120] The Indonesian government was thereby motivated to keep the prices of locally sold oil products as low as possible, not only as an anti-inflationary measure but also to force the oil companies to turn over more foreign exchange. This led to continuing friction between the producers and the government.

induce the government to renew its management contract when it lapsed in February 1953. Actually, the Teuku Hasan motion approved by Parliament in 1951, was motivated, in part, to prevent such a contract extension. After the PNI party council had resolved that all tin mines should be owned and operated by the government, the Wilopo cabinet decided not to renew the management contract over the Bangka mines. In spite of dire predictions, the Indonesian managers acquitted themselves well in operating the mines in the early years after the takeover.

On the other hand, the Wilopo cabinet did extend the GMB contract to manage the Billiton mines for another five years. However, the first Ali Sastromidjojo cabinet, during its Iskaq period, proceeded to end the government's role as a silent partner by appointing Indonesians to top positions on the board of the GMB and directed that the staff be progressively indigenized.[121]

In March 1958, in the wake of the wholesale expropriation of Dutch enterprises, Billiton passed entirely into Indonesian hands when the government refused to renew the GMB management contract. The enterprise was subsequently operated by the Biro Urusan Perusahaan Tambang Negara, or BUPTAN (State Mining Enterprises Bureau).[122]

The bulk of the coal mines, about 70 per cent, were owned by the Netherlands-Indies government and therefore became indigenous with the transfer of sovereignty. Most other small prewar mining operations failed to resume work because of the unsettled economic conditions and because of nationalist constraints spelled out in the Teuku Hasan motion. In two minor cases, the Indonesian state displaced and operated alien mining properties by routine processes. When the government contract of the nation's only asphalt producer, the N. V. Mijnbouw Mij. Boeton, expired in 1954, its operations were continued by the Ministry of Public Works. Similarly, the government operated a gold mine at Tjikotok, West Java after buying out a private company that had failed to resume operation.[123]

MANUFACTURING

During Indonesia's colonial period, modern manufacturing was largely restricted to the processing of exportable raw materials, and such activities have been considered by Indonesians to be a part of

[121] Sutter, *op. cit.*, pp. 846–850.   [122] *BI Report 1958–59*, p. 211.
[123] Sutter, *op. cit.*, pp. 860–863.

agriculture and mining rather than manufacturing, a practice that is continued herein.[124] A rudimentary consumers goods industry, initiated when import supplies were interrupted during the First World War, collapsed when trade resumed after the war. The shrinkage of foreign markets during the Great Depression, however, led the colonial government once again to undertake serious promotion of industry. While some success attended this belated industrialization policy, by 1952 income generated by manufacturing represented only about 9 per cent and that generated by modernized industry about 6 per cent of national income.[125] Moreover, the factories that had been established as a result of this policy were almost wholly in alien hands.

Indonesians, in common with underdeveloped ex-colonial countries generally, attributed their economic backwardness to the colonial regime's neglect of manufacturing outside the export sector. Hence, attainment of independence signaled an industrialization drive. Because of the paucity of statistical information, the precise dimensions of the accomplishments of this drive cannot be established. Insofar as national income figures are reliable, they indicate that manufacturing output did not change significantly as percentage of Gross Domestic Product from 1951 to 1958.[126] On the other hand, absolute changes in the licensed capacity of those industries subject to government controls indicate encouraging growth.[127]

Because of the priority assigned to industrialization, alien enterprise in this sector enjoyed security from economic nationalism not available to foreigners engaged in other activities. Although Indonesia took steps to reserve the future growth of the manufacturing sector to indigenous enterprise, the existing manufacturing sector was left largely untouched in spite of its alien character.

Important for efforts to promote output of manufactures was the encouragement of the largely indigenous handicraft sector set up through the *induk* (management center) system. This was a revival of a prewar Dutch program of setting up central finishing establishments to provide marketing outlets, credit, and technical aid to village cottage

---

[124] Indonesian statistics of manufacturing, for example, still generally exclude industries processing raw materials for export.

[125] See Anspach, *op. cit.*, pp. 14–15.   [126] Paauw, *op. cit.*, p. 195.

[127] *BI annual reports* from 1952 through 1959. The reader should be cautioned that licensed capacity tells only part of the story, since shortages of raw materials due to foreign-exchange crises often prevented factories from working at capacity during this period.

industry. These efforts were combined with the Loan and Mechanization Program under which credit for mechanization together with technical assistance was made available to eighty-two firms in the handicraft sector. Unfortunately these programs were plagued by inexperience, administrative incompetence, and inadequate planning and, therefore, had only a minimal effect upon the progress of Indonesian industry. An evaluation of the program covering results up to November, 1956 concluded that only six of the eighty-two firms were using the provided machinery to a satisfactory degree.[128]

The most ambitious component of the industrialization drive outlined by the Economic Urgency Plan involved sponsorship of large-scale industrial plants. In 1952–1953 alone, about Rp. 160 million were budgeted for this purpose, compared to an over-all total of Rp. 30 million for the *induk* and Loan and Mechanization programs.[129] Factories, which were to be principally financed by state capital, were eventually to be turned over to private, co-operative, or joint public-private management. In general, however, the government had to assume ownership functions in the absence of private indigenous entrepreneurship. New plants in rubber remilling, printing, cotton spinning, cement, caustic soda, and coconut flour were built under the program.

The implementation of the Economic Urgency Plan in all its phases, however, was spotty and slow. Many new plants often operated with disappointing results and this, together with growing fears of inflationary pressures generated by developmental spending, led to the scrapping of the Plan in 1956 in favor of the First Five Year Plan. The latter not only called for a significant slowing down in scheduled industrialization but also ended financial assistance to private enterprise and concentrated on the development of state enterprises. This reflected a growing disenchantment with the prospects of industrialization and indigenism within the framework of a noncentralized private enterprise economy.[130]

The Economic Urgency Plan, which was based on the Regulation for

[128] Wanda Mulia, "Mechanization of Small-Scale Industry," *Ekonomi dan Keuangan Indonesia* (11), March-April 1958, p. 200; and Sumitro Djojohadikusumo, "The Government's Program on Industries," *Ekonomi dan Keuangan Indonesia* (7), November 1954, *passim*.

[129] Sumitro, *ibid.*, pp. 4–25.

[130] Adamantios Pepelasis, Leon Mears, and Irma Adelman, *Economic Development* (New York: Harper & Brothers, 1961), pp. 441–45; and Paauw, *op. cit.*, pp. 214–220.

Enterprise Ordinance of 1934, set strict limits to the role of nonindigenous industrial capital.[131] In part this was done by reserving to the state a dominant ownership share in new plants built in "essential" industries, including defense, basic chemicals, cement, power, water, and transportation. Participation by aliens in the management of these "key-industries" was severely restricted. Although foreign capital was more acceptable in industries not considered to be essential, even here, Sutter concluded:

Where private Indonesian interests in such factories was in reality or potentially great, a mixed enterprise might be set up so long as Indonesians acquired a majority of the stock . . . and of the seats on the boards of directors, with the Government serving as temporary financier "to bridge any possible gaps." The corporation charter would provide for the gradual transfer of shares from alien stockholders to Indonesians and would require alien members to train an Indonesian staff. Where private Indonesian capital displayed no interest, alien capital could invest within the framework of the general economic plan. Such companies too, however, would have to be willing to accept eventual Indonesian stock participation and staff personnel or to train Indonesians to take over staff functions.[132]

The plan enjoined the authorities to give preferential treatment to "national capital," though this concept was not defined. The Department of Industries, which was concerned with the implementation of the large-scale industry component of the plan, however, interpreted "national" to mean "indigenous."[133]

Actually, the Department of Industries, in all its activities, proved to be a center of determined indigenism and as such was continually under attack from indignant citizens of Chinese descent. For example, in December 1953, *Keng Po,* an influential journal speaking for Chinese-Indonesian interests, complained that although the Ministry of Eco-

[131] This regulation gave the colonial government wide authority to intervene in all branches of industry to control both the development of established firms and the entry of new ones. It was drawn up to prevent "destructive competition" during the depressed Thirties but, ironically enough, the colonial government also used it to eliminate Japanese competition with Dutch or Chinese firms and to "prevent local industries from entirely displacing imports in categories for which quotas had been assigned to the Netherlands" (Jack Shepherd, *Industry in South East Asia* [New York: Institute of Pacific Relations, 1941], p. 63).

[132] Sutter, *op. cit.,* p. 775.

[133] See, for example, the statement of the Governor of the Bank Indonesia, *BI Report 1951–52,* pp. 40–41.

nomics had ended ethnic discrimination, its subordinate Department of Industry had not.[134]

The position of the government was stated most bluntly by the second Ali Sastromidjojo cabinet toward the end of 1956 when it established the following order of priority for the granting of licenses to new enterprises of all types.

1. Enterprises 100 per cent managed and owned by indigenous nationals.

2. Enterprises managed and owned on a 50:50 basis between indigenous and nonindigenous national capital.

3. Enterprises run and owned by 100 per cent nonindigenous nationals.

4. Mixed enterprises of indigenous, nonindigenous nationals, and foreigners.

5. Foreign-owned enterprises.

At the same time, this administration also reassured Parliament that in practice no new licenses had been granted to foreign enterprises since the beginning of 1956, except in a few cases where the foreign companies were obliged to accept indigenous participation.[135]

Beside this major effort to direct new industrial capital into national ownership, there were also a few cases of indigenization of existing factories. A cigar factory (N. V. Negresco) and a plant producing farm implements and other metal wares (N. V. Construktiewinkel) were sold voluntarily to the Special District Government of Jogjakarta in Central Java. In Djakarta, the Carya Shipbuilding Company bought out the Dutch-owned N. V. Scheepwerf Antjol in 1952, and only indigenous citizens and Indonesian organizations were allowed to hold stock in the new firm. In the Outer Islands, there were also a few cases of sales to Indonesians of saw mills, coconut oil mills, and of a ramie fiber plant.[136]

Although it was not the dominant theme of policy, the state occasionally interfered by edict to change the existing ethnic and racial structure of industry. The first cases of such decree indigenism occurred

[134] *Keng Po,* December 7, 1953.

[135] *Times of Indonesia* (Djakarta, English-language newspaper), October 17, 1956. The list is also suggestive of the high degree of refinement to which decree indigenism was carried.

[136] Sutter, *op. cit.,* pp. 801–802.

in the batik and kretek industries. The traditional batik industry of Solo and Jogjakarta was still in Indonesian hands at the time of independence, but the modern batik industry at Pekalongan and the kretek industry had by that time been largely captured by Chinese interests. With independence, the Indonesian stake in these areas, paradoxically enough, was further jeopardized as these industries were plagued by rising world prices and chronic speculation in their two most important raw materials, cloves and cambric cloth. Indonesians, who were mainly the smaller manufacturers with the lowest financial reserves, were being squeezed out by their bigger Chinese competitors. At this point, the Wilopo government stepped in and set up monopoly import organizations in both fields, which were linked up with manufacturers' associations including all producers.[137] These Indonesian-controlled cartels were then given the sole right to import and allocate the raw materials among their membership, which ensured supplies for the smaller producers.[138]

Finally, the promulgation in 1954 of the Paddy-Milling and Rice-Polishing Restriction by the first Ali Sastromidjojo government extended the more radical type of indigenism by fiat to the industrial sector. It was extreme because it sought to shift existing rice mills into indigenous ownership by use of governmental licensing power. Actually, even before this ordinance was enacted, no new licenses for rice mill operations had been issued to aliens. Nevertheless, this regulation included the sweeping provision that no one would be allowed to hold a license for rice milling after a year except Indonesian citizens who were not also citizens of other countries. In practice, however, the ordinance was not implemented because of the lack of indigenous entrepreneurs and the unwillingness of the various governments to jeopardize the critically important rice industry. Instead, temporary one-year licenses were issued to Chinese mill owners, regardless of their citizenship status.[139]

These measures signaled a more radical approach to indigenism in the manufacturing sector which came in response to growing impatience with the accomplishments of the policy of reserving the growth

---

[137] Technically, these manufacturers' associations were co-operatives but, in practice, they were "a cluster of capitalistic enterprises . . . grouped together in a cooperative so as to reap the benefits of a monopoly, state protection and subsidy" (Mohammad Sadli, *op. cit.*, p. 20).

[138] Sutter, *op. cit.*, pp. 1049–1051.

[139] *Indonesian Observer,* July 24, 1956.

sectors of industry to private national capital. It culminated in the nationalization of the bulk of existing industrial capital during and after the West Irian action.

THE IMPORT SECTOR

Indonesian commerce was dominated by two interrelated circuits of commodity movements. The first involved the export of commodities produced in the modern sector of foreign-owned estates and mines. These goods were shipped out either directly by the producers or through large foreign-owned trading companies, including the prominent "Big Five" Dutch concerns (Borsumij, Jacobson van den Berg, George Wehry, Internatio, and Lindeteves) and the British firm, Mac-Laine Watson. These merchant houses also held a dominant position in the general import field. This distribution circuit largely survived the pressures of economic nationalism until the 1958 nationalization of Dutch enterprises.

The other trade circuit linked the small holder to the money market. It encompassed the collection of raw materials from indigenous producers, either for export or for the domestic market, and the counter-flow of finished goods, either imported or locally produced, to Indonesian consumers. Except for some indigenous firms in small-scale domestic industry and a few medium-sized, modern retail stores, Indonesians in this trade circuit were largely restricted to participation in the retailing of consumer goods and the collection of marketable goods from the peasants. The levers of economic control, based on financial strength and business experience, were centralized in the large, alien merchant houses. Indonesia's leadership decided early not to jeopardize her sorely needed foreign-exchange earnings by forced indigenism in the export sector. On the other hand, the so-called "national middle-class" traders, mainly Indonesian owners of Western-style retail or general stores, benefited from a variety of preferential measures, particularly in regard to import licenses. The government also bestowed special privileges on the co-operative movement, organized in part, to provide a substitute indigenous market organization to compete with larger alien financial interests.[140]

However, the major indigenism drive in the area of trade, as else-

[140] See, for example, Wanda Mulia, "The Processes of Changes in the Marketing Structure Since the Implementation of Guided Economy," *Ekonomi dan Keuangan Indonesia* (14), January-February, 1961, pp. 58–70.

where in Southeast Asia, occurred in the import sector. Indigenous merchants could set up business with a minimum of overhead investment, could concentrate on commodities sufficiently standardized to require a minimum of business experience, and could deal in goods that enjoyed a seller's market because of import restrictions. Furthermore, Indonesians had before them the example of the "Big Five" companies which had used the import field as a springboard into plantation agriculture, internal distribution, insurance, and the manufacture of import competing goods.[141] The pattern of the Dutch success story had been imitated by several indigenous import firms such as Dassaad Musim Company, which had diversified into weaving and tea growing; Djohon Djohor, which had moved into rubber planting and brick manufacturing; and Rahman Tamin, active in the textile manufacturing field.

On April 1950, only four months after the formal creation of the Indonesian state, the then Minister of Prosperity, Djuanda, launched the drive to transfer the import trade to Indonesians. It was called *Benteng* which is the Indonesian word for "fortress." The *Benteng* program, which relied on private enterprise rather than efforts to lay the foundation of a socialist state, quickly became the focus of Indonesia's indigenism efforts.

The *Benteng* plan used both credit and decree indigenism as easily saleable consumer goods were reserved to national importers by decree, and various government-owned banks and credit agencies were directed to provide the requisite financing. Between 1950 and 1953, about seven hundred Indonesian firms benefited. Although the *Benteng* program involved only about 10 per cent of total imports through 1951,[142] this was, nevertheless, a substantial achievement, particularly since *Benteng* was intended to be a cautious rather than a radical indigenism program.

Almost immediately, two problems arose that were to bedevil *Benteng* throughout its history. First, plainly discriminatory conditions against nonindigenous citizens were spelled out for entry into the *Benteng* club. Although indigenism is intrinsically discriminatory, many

---

[141] The Dutch, upon their return after World War II, had given further proof of the importance of imports by seeking to restore by decree the Dutch dominance of this activity by the "historical rights" system. This involved reestablishing the prewar Dutch-controlled import structure—with Indonesian newcomers assigned the small percentage of the import share previously held by Japanese or German firms.

[142] Amstutz, *op. cit.*, p. 49; Meek, *op. cit.*, p. 169.

Indonesians were uneasy with the blatant official ethnic bias which conflicted with the ideals of the new state. Thus, protected firms had to be managed by *"bangsa Indonesia aseli"* (indigenous Indonesian nationals) and at least 70 per cent owned by such Indonesians. Such requirements were aimed directly at the Chinese wholesalers who had moved in strength into importing with the departure of some of the less important Dutch firms. Because the *Benteng* program initially covered but a minor part of imports, however, the protests of Indonesian citizens of Chinese descent were restrained.[143]

Second, *Benteng* encountered economic difficulties even in this period when Indonesia was still benefiting from the "Korean Boom" in export prices. The difficulties began with the disappointing rice harvest of 1951 which caused substantial increases in rice prices. As a result, consumers allocated more of their income to rice and less to textiles which were among the most important *Benteng* commodities, and alien middlemen apparently were able to capture most of the increased expenditures on rice. Furthermore, these middlemen apparently did not increase their purchases of textiles out of their increased income sufficiently to maintain demand for textiles at the previous level. The resulting pressure on textile prices was intensified as overextended importers dumped stocks on the market,[144] and many underfinanced *Benteng* importers found themselves in serious financial straits.

The government came to their rescue by postponing loan repayments and by the end of 1951, state credits totaling Rp. 90 million granted to importers were in arrears. More important, with the termination of the export boom, planned budgetary deficits maintained inflationary pressures which restored the profitability of importing *Benteng* commodities. This was the last time Indonesia could plan budget deficits and reflation, however, because of the subsequent dissipation of Indonesia's foreign-exchange reserves, built up under Korean boom conditions. As shown in Graph 1, Indonesia's reserves thereafter consistently stayed at low levels primarily because of unfavorable terms of trade which, through 1958, remained below the 1952 level except for the brief but crucial period between August 1955 and February 1956.[145]

[143] Amstutz, *op. cit.*, p. 47; Sutter, *op. cit.*, p. 1019.
[144] Textile prices dropped as much as 37 per cent during 1951.
[145] Furthermore, the 1952 net barter terms of trade stood far below 1950 and 1951 levels. For extended treatment of the following exposition, see Anspach, *op. cit.*, pp. 207–292.

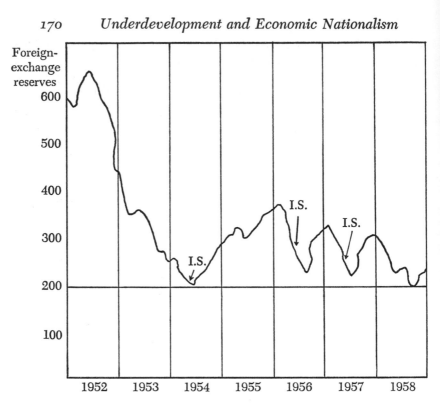

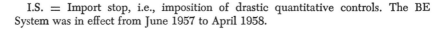

Graph 1. Foreign-exchange reserves, 1952–1958
(millions of U.S. dollars)

I.S. = Import stop, i.e., imposition of drastic quantitative controls. The BE
System was in effect from June 1957 to April 1958.

The Wilopo government eventually faced the necessity of a series of
defensive measures to reduce imports and to control the inflation
which jeopardized foreign-exchange reserves. Unfortunately, neither
the Wilopo nor succeeding cabinets were able to carry out the structural changes in the tax system needed to provide budgetary balance.
Instead, recourse was had to various *ad hoc* measures, and economic instability and vacillation in policies confronted *Benteng* importers with
formidable problems.

A foreign-exchange rationing (*tranche*) system was instituted according to which the government released only a specific amount of foreign
exchange each four-month period. To ration the reduced amount of
foreign exchange and to dampen the chronic inflation, the government,
beginning in August 1952, obligated importers to deposit 40 per cent of

the import value as advance payment on the day the import license was granted. The latter measure imposed hardships on Indonesian new-comers because of their inadequate liquidity and limited access to credit.

Wilopo's Minister of Finance Sumitro, who was responsible for these measures, was severely criticized particularly in view of his admission that he had not given enough aid to Indonesian traders while in an earlier cabinet.[146] This failure, he wrote before taking office in the Wilopo cabinet, had had "unfortunate results on public opinion as if thereby the government had ignored aspirations for an Indonesian economy." [147] Nevertheless, the tightness of the foreign-exchange position forced him to deny additional credits to *Benteng* importers, and the advance payments policy was continued. To placate his critics, he resorted to decree indigenism to moderate the pressure of competition of alien firms and on November 20, 1952 it was announced that 25 per cent of "free" imports were to be reserved for national importers and that the government would channel most of its own imports through them. The effect of this move was to increase the share of these im-porters to 21 per cent of commercial imports plus the enlarged share of government imports diverted to them.

To the extent that indigenous importers lacked capital or access to credit, the new policy provided a powerful incentive for Indonesians who had a quota but not the money to gravitate to alien businessmen who had the money but not the quota. "Briefcase importing" in which foreign businessmen operated behind a facade of indigenous "im-porters"—whose offices were their briefcases—flourished. The govern-ment responded to this development with persistent but ineffective attempts to legislate "briefcase importing" out of existence—a largely futile gesture and the practice remained a festering sore in the body politic.

The government's first anti- "briefcase" move was to set prerequisites for entry into the *Benteng* club, including minimum capitalization of Rp. 100,000, offices big enough to accommodate several employees, and officers who could demonstrate prior business experience. These were

---

[146] Kosasih, Chairman of the Indonesian Importers Association, led the chorus of complaints. Indonesian industrialists, dependent on imported raw materials, were discontent for the same reason. See *Keng Po*, September 1 and 24, 1952.

[147] Sumitro Djojohadikusumo, *Persoalan Ekonomi di Indonesia* (Djakarta: Indira, 1953), p. 127.

followed in May 1953 by regulations raising the necessary capitalization to Rp. 250,000, and requiring that *Benteng* enterprises be 100 per cent owned by nationals and furnished with an "adequate" bank account.

These steps were accompanied by steady expansion in the categories on the *Benteng* list until by August 1953, 40 per cent of all imports were technically in the reserved sector. The Chinese community responded to this situation by protesting strenuously and with some success. In the face of growing demands from such organizations as the Indonesian Chamber of Commerce for further moves against the Chinese, the government reiterated its formal opposition to ethnic discrimination and the qualification for *Benteng* membership was changed from "*bangsa-Indonesia aseli*" to "*bangsa Indonesia*" (Indonesian nationality). Administrative discretion in import licensing, however, ensured that indigenous importers would continue to enjoy favorable treatment.

More significant to the fate of the *Benteng* policy was the economic climate. Continued internal inflation intensified pressure on the available foreign exchange, and the government gradually extended exchange rationing. In January 1953, allocations for "free list" imports were reduced to 50 per cent of allocations for all imports by the Wilopo cabinet and surcharges were further increased. In April 1953, bankers' import credits were frozen at the March 1953 level and importers' prepayments were increased from 40 to 75 per cent. Simultaneously, all quantitative restrictions on imports were temporarily dropped to force goods out of hoards. These measures temporarily stabilized prices of imports through April 1954, but they obviously favored alien importers with adequate financial resources. The resultant indignation went far beyond the immediately affected importers, and the Wilopo cabinet lost a vote of confidence on June 3, 1953. Although the Sumatran squatter issue was the immediate cause, the policies of economic retrenchment which tended to frustrate aspirations for indigenism left the Wilopo government vulnerable.[148]

The successor second Ali Sastromidjojo cabinet promised to work assiduously for the indigenous business class, but did so mainly by "decreeing" greater business participation for indigenous merchants— again without providing the financial wherewithal to make the decree

---

[148] For example, the Masjumi leader, Tjikwan, moved in Parliament that all import surcharge alterations be subjected to legislative approval. All parties, except the Finance Minister Sumitro's PSI, signed the motion which passed by a vote of 97–0.

meaningful. On September 8, 1953, the Central Office of Imports issued a circular that allotted fifteen categories of imports completely to *Benteng* traders and increased the proportion of their imports in total imports by 20 per cent. Protests over certain ethnically discriminatory clauses caused the circular to be withdrawn in spite of the objections of the Indonesian business community, but in practice ethnic discrimination was continued. Still another step in decree indigenism came in November 1953 when each importer was restricted to imports of three of the nine import categories remaining on the free list. This was designed to prevent big, established firms, usually foreign, from preempting all free list goods.

The extent of decree indigenism of import trade was revealed in August 1954, when the Minister of Economic Affairs Iskaq announced that 85 per cent of all import licenses would henceforth be allocated to national importers. The Ali Sastromidjojo government also moved to support *Benteng* importers financially and on October 1, 1953, advance payments for the import of raw materials and capital goods were decreased from 75 to 50 per cent. Otherwise, tight credit policies were continued as the government was unable to eliminate budget deficits which maintained inflationary pressure.

In the spring of 1954, Indonesia's foreign exchange reserves began to approach $200 million (see Graph 1), which covered only about 25 per cent of the total imports of 1953, and the country was confronted by a clamorous balance-of-payments crisis.[149] Quantitative restrictions on imports were tightened in May, 1954, and the foreign-exchange holdings promptly began to recover. The inflation-moderating effects of foreign-exchange depletion were, however, replaced by the inflationary pressures associated with tightened import restrictions as well as modest accumulation of foreign exchange. Moreover, the continued budgetary deficits and decreases in output due to cutbacks in the imports of raw material strengthened inflationary forces. In the face of strong protests by various organizations representing indigenous importers, advance payments on import letters of credit were returned to the previous 75 per cent level.

The measures of the Ali government proved inadequate. Inflation worsened and speculative activities burgeoned. The response of the

[149] Inspection of Graph 1 suggests that Indonesia considered $200 million the minimum ("iron") reserve during this period, although later, in the 1960s, reserves were allowed to dip much lower.

government was to impose price controls on various commodities, including cotton thread, cambrics, cloves, tin plate, newsprint, flour, and automobiles. In the case of textiles, all importers were obligated to sell their goods at fixed prices to a state enterprise, Supply Service for Industrial Raw Materials (JPBP). Furthermore, all textile importers and wholesalers had to report their stocks each month.

This jerry-built structure of policies not only failed to stop price increases, but the indigenous importers, together with the rest of private enterprise, heartily resented government intervention of this magnitude. Also, continued inflation, stringent import controls, and tight credit maintained strong incentives to continue "briefcase" importing. The director of the Central Office of Imports estimated at that time that 90 per cent of the registered national importers were not *bona fide,* and Iskaq himself acknowledged that licenses were marketed at from 200 to 250 per cent of nominal value.[150] Neither the legitimate national importers who failed to get the licenses which actually ended up in foreign hands nor the Indonesian political elites took kindly to these developments. The government reacted to this situation with a futile decree outlawing briefcase importing.

The flourishing corruption now became enmeshed in Indonesia's first general election. The Masjumi, which had the backing of the wealthy, and the PKI, which was alleged to receive funds from communist countries and also from parts of the Chinese community, were able to liberally finance their campaigns. The PNI, which was preeminently the party of the underpaid bureaucracy, did not have comparable access to financial support. Under these circumstances, the PNI Minister of Economic Affairs Iskaq chose to raise campaign funds by demanding "kickbacks" for his party from applicants for import licenses. This led to a major political scandal and the resignation of Iskaq on November 5, 1954.[151]

Following the resignation of Iskaq, the policy of government intervention and control of the import sector was reversed until December 1955, and control through market forces became official policy. Such a change imposed still another radical adaptation on *Benteng* merchants. Roosseno, Iskaq's replacement as Minister of Economic Affairs, eliminated all special licenses in foreign trade and, for all practical purposes, abolished the JPBP. More important, he instituted a foreign-exchange

[150] See Amstutz, *op. cit.,* p. 145; *Keng Po,* October 11, 1954.
[151] Later, in 1960, Iskaq was tried and found guilty of corruption.

auction system in the textile sector. Although *Benteng* was kept alive formally, discrimination on ethnic grounds was banned, and the Chinese were allowed to participate in importation, both directly as *warga negara* importers and indirectly using *warga negara* as dummies.[152] In terms of revenues collected and improvement in the graft-infested, bureaucratic tangle, the changes were considered such a success that a few days before the Ali cabinet was forced to resign on July 24, 1955, Roosseno announced that the textile auction system would be extended to all goods except basic subsistence commodities.[153]

The auction system was a disaster, however, for the indigenous businessman with inadequate access to financial resources. Dassaad, a leading Indonesian entrepreneur, said that such a scheme could work where "national firms have economic power but in Indonesia, foreign traders could use national briefcase importers as fronts to take all the textile import business away from *bona fide* Indonesian importers." The Indonesian Chamber of Commerce (DEIP) formally asked the government to abandon the auction system, and three East Javanese indigenous business organizations (Union of National Importers, Retail Shopowners and Importers of East Java, and Textile Wholesale Association of East Java) demanded that drastic state controls be reimposed on all textile trading.[154]

The Harahap cabinet, which brought back Sumitro as Minister of Finance in August 1955, introduced changes in the format though not the substance of the anti-inflationary policy. These were made possible by a drastic, though short-lived, improvement in Indonesia's balance of payments which permitted liberalization of imports.[155] This in turn made possible the abandonment of the unpopular auction system in favor of increased surcharges on imports and higher advance payments.

---

[152] *Warga negara* is the colloquial phrase for "Indonesian citizen of Chinese descent" or "*Warga negara Indonesia turunan tionghoa.*"

[153] The immediate cause of the resignation involved the cabinet's handling of a case of military insubordination, but contributing to it was the general economic malaise and the consequent frustration of indigenism.

[154] These business organizations declared with unintended irony that even though certain difficulties arose in connection with the JBPB, nevertheless "thanks to the cooperation and understanding existing between national business and state offices, these difficulties were in process of being resolved to the satisfaction of all concerned." For the reaction to the auction system, see Anspach, *op. cit.*, pp. 251–258.

[155] The recovery in Indonesia's balance of payments was due to a steep but temporary improvement in the terms of trade.

In effect, these policies encumbered the import business with a more realistic exchange parity under a system of import surcharges but otherwise freed it from government interference. At the same time, to insure that imports materialized, all national importers, Chinese as well as indigenous, were given free access to foreign exchange. Indonesian businessmen found little improvement in their position, and under the prevailing tight credit conditions many Indonesian traders continued to serve as agents for Chinese businessmen.[156]

This policy was to be quickly reversed, a fate that also befell various other policies during the ensuing two years, as the economy and the course of government policy wavered erratically under the conflicting pressures of indigenism, inflation, foreign-exchange crises, and regional disintegration. A major change occurred on September 30, 1955, seven weeks after the new government took office, when banks were given permission to finance importer's prepayments. A week later, limits on credits to the import sector were cancelled, the Bank Indonesia was directed to provide rediscount facilities to commercial banks, and surcharges on cotton and cotton thread were abolished and imports of these were reserved to Indonesian importers. On November 3, 1955 prepayments on the import of industrial goods were cut in half, and eleven different categories of goods were taken off the permitted import list to protect Indonesian manufacturers of competing goods. On December 1, 1955 all textiles, stationery products, and various categories of drugs and paper were designated *Benteng*.

Simultaneously, the Harahap government was forced to compromise its anti-discriminatory policy, and a decree was issued restricting *Benteng* to citizens whose fathers had been born in Indonesia. The use of the market to eliminate importers who were not *bona fide* was abandoned, and the state moved to screen importers by direct investigation which resulted in discrimination through administrative discretion.[157]

---

[156] A Rp. 5 million tax levied on foreign importers by Sumitro appears to have succeeded in changing the means of trade financing by foreigners rather than in shifting the import sector into national hands in any real sense. For a fuller discussion of this tight money period, see Anspach, *op. cit.*, pp. 251–269.

[157] These changes were due in part to the fact that the parliamentary elections had demonstrated the strength of radical economic nationalism. The parties which were more oriented toward structural changes in the plural economy (PNI, PKI, PSSI, Murba, and Buruh) won 108 seats while the more conservative parties (PSI, Masjumi, Parkindo, Partai Katolik) won 76 seats out of a total of 256. With the NU leaning toward the stronger, nationalist side, this faction had 153 seats. See Herbert Feith, *The Indonesian Elections,* Cornell University, Modern Indonesia Project, Interim Reports Series (Ithaca, 1957), p. 58.

Such actions, however, were insufficient to enable the underfinanced Indonesian businessmen to overcome the challenges posed by the pause in the price inflation of import commodities, high surcharges on imports, and competition from Chinese enterprises which continued to find ways to participate in the import market. This became evident as a radical movement in support of more aggressive measures of indigenism, the Assaat movement, emerged and briefly flourished during this period.[158]

The second, and this time rather conservative, Ali Sastromidjojo (PNI) government, took office with a few gestures in favor of *Benteng* to demonstrate its support for economic nationalism. By this time, however, the reserves were again tumbling toward the $200 million mark, both because of renewed weakness in the terms of trade and because of the heavy imports authorized during the Harahap period (see Graph 1). Consequently, on June 1, 1956, the new Finance Minister Wibisono warned the country of an impending economic emergency, and the government moved to choke off the stream of imports and resorted to various deflationary measures. This led the secretary of the Indonesian Chamber of Commerce to proclaim in turn that national capital also faced a crisis. The Ali government, almost as if by reflex, sought to placate economic nationalism by further decree indigenism. Seventeen consumer goods were added to the *Benteng* list, but the financing problem continued to be assigned low priority and relief for the indigenous business community was limited. The seriousness of the situation was underlined when, at the beginning of July, 1956, Vice-President Hatta met with directors of the three major state banks and Finance Minister Wibisono and demanded that the government subsidize the national banks so that they could come to the aid of embattled "national capital." This was the same Hatta who persistently had supported co-operatives and inveighed against the use of state funds to aid national capitalists. Wibisono granted an aid package of Rp. 75 million—much less than had been requested—and a briefly postponed date for paying surcharges.

In the meantime, interest in indigenism by private enterprise began to wane as the country's attention turned toward the growing regional discontent that threatened to Balkanize the new nation. Smuggling from the export-rich Outer Islands, now in quasi-rebellion, reduced the foreign exchange available to the central government at the

[158] See below, section on the expulsion of the Dutch.

very time it had to step up its military expenditures. Furthermore, foreign-trade policy was used increasingly to reduce frictions between the Outer Islands and Java, and an export certificate system (BE) was installed by the Djuanda cabinet in June 1957. This system, which combined a fluctuating exchange rate with limited rates of export taxation, was designed to protect exporters, often alien enterprises domiciled in the Outer Islands, against the cost squeeze inherent in domestically rising prices and a fixed exchange rate. It also protected the exchange reserves because no more than the approximate amount of foreign exchange generated by exports was made available for foreign payments. Although it was meant to pacify the Outer Islands which generated a disproportionate share of export proceeds, the insurgents disliked the system since they wanted to control foreign exchange for their own purposes rather than have its uses determined by market forces.

The Export Certificates, which were sold in a competitive market, signaled a significant de-emphasis of the *Benteng* program. They eliminated all preferential treatment for the underfinanced Indonesian importers and thereby removed the prop by which many of them had survived.

Benteng, Indonesia's most ambitious and sustained attempt to promote an indigenous capitalist class, had failed to come up to expectations and ultimately was repudiated. Foreign-exchange crises dogged the country throughout the period of experimentation with indigenism through private Indonesian enterprise. In the absence of basic fiscal reform, the various governments resorted intermittently to *ad hoc* measures that impinged heavily on the import sector. Such measures usually took the form of higher taxes on imports which were meant to absorb money from the economy and discourage imports.[159] Often such measures involving advance payments, complete cessation of import licenses, or temporarily establishing free markets in foreign exchange, tended on balance to injure the Indonesian importers. Furthermore, the vary rapidity of the policy changes prevented most indigenous traders from accumulating the capital and experience necessary to become competitive. At the same time, imprudent measures, often not attuned to economic realities, encouraged corruption.

The decline of *Benteng* provided the prelude for harsher moves against alien enterprise. Many Indonesians considered *Benteng* the

---

[159] It is of course typical for less developed countries to concentrate taxes on the foreign-trade base.

touchstone of private-enterprise indigenism, and its failure contributed to a new climate of opinion favorable to direct nationalization of those alien businesses which were thought to block the emergence of Indonesian entrepreneurship.

THE FRUSTRATION OF ECONOMIC NATIONALISM: 1950–1957

The Indonesian community was dissatisfied with the pace of indigenism achieved during the years between 1950 and 1957 even though Dutch economic power was drastically curtailed. The latter change was measured in part by the rapid decline in the Dutch population, which had fallen by about half to 160,000, during World War II and the subsequent revolution. Emigration of the Dutch continued until by 1957 only about 23,000 remained to be expelled after the West Irian action.[160]

Dutch enterprises saw the handwriting on the wall and, like businessmen generally, displayed ingenuity in cutting their losses. Statistics on such transactions are fragmentary, but disinvestment proceeded rapidly as Dutch estates were not maintained by proper replanting [161] and amortization funds were exported by other enterprises to set up branches outside Indonesia.

The full magnitude of the Dutch capital flight became apparent only after the 1957–1958 expropriation of what was left of Dutch property. The American magazine *Business Week* published then the following candid account which had been provided by one of the Big Five trading companies, probably to reassure its stockholders.

Since 1949, Borsumij has gradually transferred a large part of its capital and its operational base to Holland and other countries. Other companies operating in Indonesia have followed this same program of getting out and diversifying. While official figures put Dutch assets in Indonesia at roughly $1.2 billion, their present market value is closer to $200 million . . . since the end of World War II, Borsumij has opened 25 offices outside Indonesia. . . . In 1955, it bought a large interest in Twentsche Oversee Handelmatschappij of Enstrede—a Dutch trading company with 17 offices mostly in East Africa. . . . Borsumij and other Dutch traders are using a variety of techniques to get

[160] W. F. Wertheim, *Indonesian Society in Transition* (The Hague: W. Van Joeve, Ltd., 1959), p. 28; and *Statistical Pocketbook of Indonesia, 1960*, pp. 15–16. During the same 1950-1957 period, there was a net departure of only 36,636 Chinese.

[161] The Indonesians passed a law in 1956 giving the authorities the right to cancel the concession of any plantation not carrying on production in an appropriate manner, precisely to prevent such capital flight.

what they can out of their Indonesian holdings . . . several companies have set up "dummy companies" to get along better with Indonesian laws. They have shipped goods in and out of Sumatra without going through Djakarta formalities . . . and the trading companies have frequently used Chinese and other middlemen to make shipments—and looked the other way.[162]

That this was not an isolated case can be inferred from the share prices of some of the major expropriated Dutch enterprises. Their seizures led to rather heavy declines in share prices in early 1958. By the end of 1958, however, the major estate companies had more than recovered and the Dutch shipping line, KPM and Internatio of the Big Five had done almost as well. Interestingly enough, Borsumij, which, in the above citation, claimed to have been particularly active in capital transfers, actually did less well than some of the other companies.[163]

This is not to say that Dutch economic power had disappeared completely in the period under review. About 50 per cent of all estate acreage remained in Dutch ownership in 1957; and, according to one observer, 60 per cent of Indonesia's foreign trade was still Dutch controlled.[164] Furthermore, a substantial fraction of total bank credits was still accounted for by Dutch banks in 1956.[165] Nevertheless, the transfer of Dutch interests to Indonesians was proceeding rapidly.

[162] *Business Week,* January 11, 1958, pp. 90, 94.

[163] Stock quotations of some major expropriated Dutch companies, from Dutch press reports:

Company	July 1957	Jan. 21, 1958	Dec. 4, 1958
Estates			
H. V. A.	124	80	127
Deli Mij	92	54	131
Senembah	63	39	119
Shipping			
KPM	157	99	133
Trading Co.			
Internatio	91	50	85
Borsumij	72	31	40
Lindeteves	142	72	98
George Wehry	57	30	32

[164] Kenneth D. Thomas, "Indonesia's Approach to Socialism, 1950-60, An Historical Analysis in Political Economy" (M.A. thesis, Department of Economics, University of California, Berkeley, 1962), p. 123.

[165] In 1956, the seven non-Indonesian foreign-exchange banks granted about 50 per cent of all bank loans, and three of these banks were Dutch. See Charlesworth, *op. cit.,* pp. 84–85.

The real frustration of indigenism, therefore, resulted less from Dutch activities, which were declining in relative importance, than from the expanding economic role of the Chinese in post-independence Indonesia. Ascendancy of the Chinese trading class was initiated by features of colonial policy that had the effect of interposing the Chinese between the Dutch rulers and the natives.[166] The Chinese, however, even without the help of the Dutch, had certain advantages in entrepreneurship over the Indonesians.[167] Not only are immigrants in general particularly venturesome and enterprising, but the Chinese immigrants also organized themselves into an informal monopolistic structure, based on dialect groupings, which magnified the advantages arising from their frugality and industry. A student of the prewar Netherlands-Indies wrote:

When considering the economic position of the Chinese population we must always remember this striving for communities of interest, which may be considered as the basis of Chinese business life. This is particularly the case regarding the numerous forms of granting credit, between which the Chinese always clearly discriminate, according to whether or not it is a form conducive to mutual business interests.[168]

Whatever the cause, the economic vacuum created by the withdrawal of Dutch enterprises was filled to a disquieting degree by Chinese rather than indigenous private capital. Most successful appeared to have been the Chinese not born in Indonesia (*totoks*) rather than the more assimilated Indonesian-born Chinese (*peranakans*).[169]

The Chinese expansion can be traced back to the brief Dutch interregnum between Japanese and Indonesian control when the unsettled conditions in the countryside forced many Chinese to move to the

---

[166] Anspach, *op. cit.*, pp. 79–81; Willmott, *op. cit.*, pp. 11–12.

[167] See, for example, Skinner's remarks on the Hokkiens, who formed the dominant group among immigrants until the middle of the nineteenth century (Skinner, *op. cit.*, p. 102).

[168] W. L. Cator, *The Economic Position of the Chinese in the Netherlands Indies* (Chicago: University of Chicago Press, 1936), pp. 59–60. Recent studies of the overseas Chinese have further documented this spirit of mutual aid with its obvious advantages for business competition in a plural society. See, for example, Willmott, *op. cit.*, p. 108; Ju-K'Ang T'ien, *The Chinese of Sarawak*, London School of Economics, Monograph on Social Anthropology, No. 12 (London: Lund Humphreys, 1953), pp. 17, 79–80; and Alice Dewey, *Peasant Marketing in Java* (Glencoe, Ill.: Free Press, 1962), pp. 44–46.

[169] See, for example, Willmott, *op. cit.*, p. 64.

cities for protection. There they established small manufacturing enterprises and, *inter alia,* soon won control over the important weaving industry in West Java. In addition, they frequently bought up shops jettisoned by small Dutch businessmen who decided to leave the country after returning from Japanese internment camps. It was also reported that by 1949 the Chinese had increased significantly their share of public motor transport and that the rubber remilling plants, subsidized by the Indonesian state, tended to end up in Chinese hands.

Comprehensive statistics describing Chinese economic power at the beginning of Indonesian statehood are lacking but the following scattered figures are indicative.[170] In East Java in 1952, 138 out of 154 rice mills belonged to aliens, mainly Chinese. Similarly, in the same area, aliens owned 116 out of 150 printing presses, all of the 24 ice plants, all of the 6 machine-made cigarette factories, and 98 out of 183 weaving mills. In South Sumatra, at the same time, the Chinese owned 635 out of 1,112 "industrial enterprises." In Atjeh, they owned 64 per cent of all such enterprises. Only in Tapanuli, home of the unusual Toba Bataks, were the Chinese kept to a 34 per cent ownership of industry.[171]

In 1951, in the important weaving industry, the Chinese owned about 85 per cent of all mechanical looms. Ninety-five per cent of the bus companies of East Java and East Sumatra were Chinese, and nearly 100 per cent of those of Central Java. At about the same time, 819 of the 1,130 public trucking companies operating in West Java and most of the smaller harbor warehouses were Chinese. Furthermore, the Chinese rather than the Indonesians were buying up the smaller estates thrown on the market by the departing Dutch. Thus, by 1952, 19 per cent of the estates of Java were Chinese-owned whereas in 1929 they owned none. It was also generally understood that Chinese merchants moved in to fill the vacancies left by the departing Dutch in wholesale, import, and export trade.

In addition, there are also strong indications that Chinese enterprise, backed by experience, financial capacity, and associative spirit, proved highly resistant to the pressures of indigenism in the 1950–1957 period. Chinese business tenacity was brought home to this writer in the

[170] See Anspach, *op. cit.,* pp. 302–311, for the sources of the statistics in this and the following paragraph.

[171] Certain Indonesian subgroups, such as the Toba Bataks, the Menangkabaus and the Menadonese, have shown themselves to be particularly adept in business. Different specific conditions appear to have produced this deviant behavior.

course of a 1959 interview of an army major directing a state plant for processing textiles. The plant had originally been built to dye yarns under the government industrialization plan because it was felt that modern dyeing methods would be especially helpful to small Indonesian producers. However, it was discovered that the producers were working under a putting-out system with Chinese businessmen who provided capital in the form of raw material and who preferred to do their own dyeing. As a result, the government plant got little business. With Djakarta complaining about the new enterprise's failure to make profits, the management adopted this putting-out system which seemed to fulfill local needs. The Chinese responded by offering such good terms to producers, that the new plant remained underutilized.[172] The state plant then capitulated and began to process finished textile goods for the Chinese textile merchants. Thus, the government venture motivated largely by the goal of indigenism ended up subcontracting for nonindigenous business.

Other scattered data suggest that this incident was not unique. For example, in the important weaving industry around Bandung, the ethnic distribution of capital in the late 1950's was reported as follows:

Alien enterprises using all alien capital	Rp. 90,000,000
National enterprises using all or part alien capital	26,000,000
National enterprises using capital supplied by Warga Negara	24,000,000
National enterprises using all indigenous capital	5,000,000 [173]

At the National Printers Congress held in 1956, it was disclosed that the Chinese had a 59:41 ownership advantage over indigenous enterprise, in spite of the language advantage enjoyed by Indonesians. Similarly, the well-protected and subsidized West Javanese *aseli* retailers announced in 1955 that indigenous owners of Westernized stores accounted for only 5 to 10 per cent of the business transacted by such stores in West Java.

Sole agencies, formerly monopolized by the Dutch, were taken over

[172] How could the Chinese outlast a modern plant? The major related that the Chinese worked harder, used the free labor provided by large families, and sold at a loss to eliminate the competition.

[173] Pramudja Ananta Toer, *Hoa Kiau Di Indonesia* (Djakarta: Bintang Press, 1960), pp. 185–187.

so extensively by the Chinese that the government acted to reserve them for "national" entrepreneurs.[174] For the same reason, the Minister of Communications ruled that government-subsidized national shipping firms could be sold only with permission of the government. Also typical was the case of the South Sumatra Rubber Corporation set up by the government to buy slab rubber from smallholders in order to process it in Indonesia rather than in Singapore. Within a short time, the government discovered that those shares of the corporation set aside for the private sector had been bought up by Chinese remillers.

The same dismal results accompanied much of the drastic decree indigenism. For example, it will be remembered that it was decreed that all rice mills were to be in Indonesian hands by March 1955. In early 1956, only six medium- to large-scale mills were owned by *aseli* while the other 269 were still in Chinese ownership, and the terminal date for compliance with the decree was postponed to March 1957. Also, all stevedoring, harbor transport, and wharfage enterprises were ordered to be transferred to national ownership by 1956, but this date had to be continuously extended, with the last extension set for June 1959. In another instance, Indonesian retailers complained that a Regulation (No. 61), which barred aliens from erecting warehouses, had only succeeded in replacing Dutch companies by Chinese *warga negara* enterprises. Characteristically, the spokesman complained bitterly that even Indonesian businessmen often preferred the more efficient Chinese storage facilities but concluded nevertheless that "unfair" Chinese competition had led to a deterioration of the position of indigenous enterprises in this sector.[175]

The spreading awareness of this noncompetitiveness of many Indonesians vis-à-vis the Chinese was matched by a sense of futility over the possibility of indigenizing private enterprise within an acceptable time span. It was this frustration of economic nationalism that formed the backdrop behind the dramatic events of 1957–1958 which drastically accelerated the pace of indigenism through massive socialization.

THE EXPULSION OF THE DUTCH

Against the background of frustrated economic nationalism, a sudden nationalization of all Dutch property struck at the roots of Indonesia's plural economy. The seizures came in the wake of the abroga-

---

[174] Sole agencies are trading firms holding exclusive rights for the distribution of specific trade-marked imported goods.

[175] The above section is based largely on Anspach, *op. cit.*, pp. 302–315.

tion of the Roundtable Conference Agreement (RTC) and were triggered by a sequence of unpredictable events associated with the struggle over political control of West Irian.

The RTC, as will be recalled, had sought in various ways to protect alien economic interests in Indonesia. At the same time, the Agreement also reserved to the Indonesian government the right "to make such regulations as are necessary for the protection of national interests or economically weak groups," which, in effect, provided ample legal scope for pursuit of indigenism. The Agreement, nevertheless, remained a restraint upon economic nationalism. It symbolized Indonesia's acquiescence in the basic continuity of the economic power relationships inherited from Dutch times and as such became the target of nationalist agitation. Tedjasukmana, Minister of Labor in the Sukiman, Wilopo, and Harahap cabinets, wrote, for example:

Since the transfer of sovereignty, the activities of the political parties and the trade unions have centered around relations between the Republic and the Netherlands. . . . The Financial and Economic Agreement was nothing more than the continuation of Dutch domination in the economic field which would in effect leave the country's natural resources in the hands of Dutch monopolists and would make impossible the liquidation of the colonial economic system and the development of a national economy . . . [and because of the alleged inflexibility of the Dutch] many trade unionists gradually arrived at the conviction that the only remedy for abuses, was a radical change of the economic structure itself, with, as condition *sine qua non,* the liquidation of the RTC Agreements, because it was these Agreements with the Dutch government, they believed, which formed the basis of the supremacy of Dutch capital in Indonesia.[176]

Indonesian efforts to whittle down the RTC, although resisted by the Dutch, finally culminated in its unilateral abrogation by the Indonesian Government on February 13, 1956. This unexpected denouement came only after the Dutch rejected modifications of the agreement proposed by the Harahap government.[177] Feith depicted the significance of this abrogation in the following terms: "Now for the

[176] Iskandar Tedjasukmana, *The Political Character of the Indonesian Trade Union Movement,* Cornell University, Modern Indonesia Project (Ithaca, 1959), pp. 119–122.

[177] Subsequently, a political comedy ensued as opposition parties balked at letting the Harahap cabinet reap the credit for this anti-Dutch act. Finally, the RTC was abrogated for a second time on April 23, 1956, by the elected parliament during the second Ali Sastromidjojo administration. See Anspach, *op. cit.,* pp. 293–301.

first time since the days of the Revolution, Indonesia had broken through legality to act in defiance of the Dutch . . . Indonesia had stopped playing the game on the Dutch home ground of agreements and formal regulations. It had seized the initiative in a symbolic assertion of national self-reliance." [178]

Pressures for drastic steps against the plural economy multiplied after the abrogation. Some groups attacked Chinese interests and others the Dutch. Indigenous private enterprise, largely represented by small business and hence directly in competition with the Chinese, tended to be particularly hostile to Chinese interests. This animosity was focused in the Assaat movement which emerged about a month after the abrogation in the National Importers Congress (KINSI) held in Surabaya. A resolution presented to the Congress by Assaat declared that the overpowering strength of the Chinese, especially in the trade sector, obstructed Indonesian efforts in all sectors.[179] Therefore, continued adherence to the RTC principle that all citizens must be treated alike under law would prevent amelioration of the conditions of the indigenous elements in the population. Consequently, the resolution demanded firm governmental protection in all areas for indigenous business and declared that the category "national enterprise" should include only firms either wholly owned by indigenous businessmen or owned jointly by *aseli* and *warga negara*—but with power in the hands of the *aseli*.

The motion was passed by the convention, and Assaatism, which was unique in Indonesian history with its explicit demand for ethnic discrimination, was set loose to spread like a brushfire over the country.[180] In June, Kaum Assaat, a political party was founded in Macassar. Its policy was to elect representatives pledged to transfer all enterprises into indigenous hands and among its leadership were found not only businessmen, but also journalists, government servants, and artists. A convention of the National Middle Traders (merchants owning modernized retail stores) unanimously voted support for Assaatism. The National All-Indonesian Economic Conference

[178] Feith, *The Decline of Constitutional Democracy in Indonesia*, p. 456.

[179] Assaat was a prominent politician who had been chairman of the Governing Council of the Revolution (KNIP) and President of Indonesia during the federal period, and who, at that time, was being mentioned as a possible heir to Sukarno.

[180] Feith observes that Assaat had "expressed with shattering directness feelings which many Indonesians had long had, but hesitated to express in public" (*The Decline of Constitutional Democracy in Indonesia*, p. 481).

(KENSI), held in August 1956, demanded that national enterprises be given two years to conform to the Assaat definition of "national." Furthermore, in reaction to the buffeting indigenous business had taken as a result of rapid cabinet changes and the *ad hoc* measures to cope with foreign-exchange crises, KENSI also demanded that indigenism be embodied directly in law. Their seriousness in this matter, was indicated when KENSI members precipitated an ugly confrontation by blocking the participation of the Federation of National Cigarette Factories because some of its members were not Indonesians.

Nevertheless, the meteoric career of Assaatism proved to be short-lived, and news about it disappeared from the press after August 1956. The blatant racial and ethnic intolerance of Assaatism spent itself; Assaat himself repudiated ethnic discrimination—and returned to "weak group" euphemisms.

The recoil from overt ethnic discrimination occurred because Assaatism failed to receive support from any of the three major political parties (Masjumi, PNI, PKI) or from the influential elite party, the PSI. The two parties that should have been particularly well-disposed to Assaatism because of the latter's sympathy for indigenous private enterprise, the Masjumi and the PSI, argued that, apart from all other considerations, indigenous business needed the aid of Chinese capitalists—foreign and national—to develop. The PNI, the most important secular, nationalist party, was even less patient with an ethnic discrimination which, when openly avowed, conflicted with its nationalist ethos. Thus, the PNI party congress, meeting at the height of the Assaatism agitation, declared that indigenous and nonindigenous citizens had the same legal rights and obligations and that therefore aid to "weak groups" could not be rendered on the basis of racial distinctions. Finally, the communist party (PKI) was essentially friendly to the Chinese, in part, because of its affinity for the People's Republic of China but also because it distinguished on principle between acceptable national capitalists, often Chinese, and "imperialist" capitalists, who transferred profits abroad.[181]

Turning to the other component of the plural economy, we find that

[181] See, for example, *Keng Po*, December 3, 1956, April 4 through 20, 1956, May 2, 1956, and November 10, 1957. Hatta took the same position. See *Indonesian Observer*, July 30, 1956. Also, see Willmott, *op. cit.*, pp. 93–94, for indications of the ambivalence of the PSI and Masjumi on this issue.

attacks against the remaining Dutch business concerns also multiplied. The PKI, of course, participated in these sallies, but they also arose in the general hostility against the vestigial interests of the colonial power which had resisted the independence movement with violence. It is important to keep this in mind, for otherwise decolonization may be confused with anticapitalism, *per se*. After the RTC abrogation, however, it must be admitted these two tendencies frequently overlapped and the distinction lost its sharpness.

It was to this deep reservoir of anti-Dutch sentiment that Sukarno appealed when he called for the abrogation of the RTC and criticized the leaders who did not dare to act. It was a similar sensitivity to public opinion that led the otherwise moderate PSI to join the clamor for anti-Dutch actions. For example, in May 1956, one of the leading PSI members of parliament castigated the second Ali government for its timidity in eliminating Dutch influence, and Sumitro accused the Ali government of dismissing the head of the Foreign Exchange Bureau for allegedly withstanding pressures from the Bank Indonesia to facilitate Dutch capital flight via exchange manipulations.[182] This public agitation, however, led to few concrete acts against the Dutch.

Subsequently, at its December 1956 congress, the Masjumi moved hesitantly to support the transfer of certain key sectors to "national" interests, but only over a fifteen-year period and only if the needed technicians and money became available during this time. It also proposed that foreign business be allowed to erect new enterprises even in the field reserved for national enterprise if national capital was not forthcoming. The only exception to this theme was the prophetic recommendation that all small shops be transferred to citizen ownership within a period of two years, which articulated the Masjumi's cautious policy of embarking upon indigenism at the lowest level of trade where experience and monetary requirements were at a minimum. Politically, it implied anti-Chinese action without resorting to outright ethnic discrimination, since Europeans did not own small retail shops.[183]

---

[182] *Indonesian Observer*, April 23, 1957, and *Keng Po*, May 9, 28, 1956.

[183] This policy of restraint, which represented the conservative side of the spectrum, should not be construed as a rejection of economic nationalism. Rather, it represented the Masjumi's belief that any drastic disorganization following the abrogation would only boomerang against indigenous private business interests which would evolve most readily and successfully in a stable business climate and in co-operation with foreign capital.

Although the governments in power following the abrogation of the RTC were not Masjumi, the cautious behavior advocated by the latter was imposed on them by the exigencies of Indonesia's balance of payments. Gold reserves in the summer of 1956 again dropped close to the critical $200 million level. There were also growing indications of deterioration in military discipline as certain army officers participated in smuggling operations from June 1956 on, and as a series of *coup d'état* attempts broke out, starting August 1956.[184] With minimum foreign-exchange reserves and a possible civil war in the offing, the government became understandably reluctant to embark on new adventures.

Djuanda, head of the Planning Bureau in the Ali Cabinet, warned on July 20 that Indonesia must follow up the abrogation prudently because a shortage of foreign exchange would be dangerous at that time. The new chairman of the PNI, now a government party, pointedly assigned the highest priority to economic stability and economic development in his speech to the PNI convention. In October 1956, the Council of Ministers took an even more conservative stand than had the Masjumi when it stated that while the permanent ownership of large estates by foreigners could not be sanctioned in principle, the necessary structural changes could be completed only in thirty years. Finally, the Djuanda cabinet announced on May 18, 1957 that in regard to the abrogation, it would take only those steps which would be of the greatest benefit to the nation and that this left the way open for continued co-operation with the Dutch.[185]

This is not to say that policies of economic nationalism were completely absent. A dramatic step occurred with the unilateral annulment on August 15, 1956, of Indonesia's debt to Holland, though this was probably a measure to conserve foreign exchange more than an attack on the plural economy. The Bank Indonesia branch in Amsterdam was also closed in 1956, but since other Indonesian banks continued to operate there, this was only a symbolic gesture. Furthermore, the Djuanda government in July 1957 imposed an annual head tax on foreigners residing in Indonesia, most of whom were of course Chinese. The government declared that the tax was "to protect Indonesian citizens in their work." Only about 40 per cent of the tax was col-

[184] *Coup d'état* attempts occurred August 13, October 5, the middle of October, and in November 1956. See *Times of Indonesia*, December 14, 1956.

[185] Anspach, *op. cit.*, pp. 327–332.

lected in 1958 because the amount assessed was beyond the means of many lower-income Chinese.

Finally, in September 1957, alien enterprises, operating in industry or trade, were brought under the provisions of the Bedrijfreglementerings Ordinantie, 1934 which, it will be recalled, imposed licensing as a requirement for business operation as well as for the establishment, expansion, removal, and transfer of the assets of business enterprises. The new rules allowed foreign enterprises to continue to operate pending further regulations but denied them permission, in principle, to set up new enterprises, to expand, or to move the site of existing enterprises. The measure did not, in fact, lead to immediate moves against foreign enterprises, but it did give the government adequate legal power to reduce the competitiveness of foreign enterprises and ultimately to close them down.

The Indonesian government acted simultaneously to reassure foreign capital. For one thing, land-hungry peasants had stepped up the occupation of estate lands subsequent to the RTC abrogation. This occurred under the leadership of a Committee to Distribute Concession Lands which argued that the abrogation had removed the legal basis for existing concession rights. The Ali Sastromidjojo government responded by decreeing heavier penalties for new illegal occupations which were endangering badly needed foreign-exchange revenues, and the decree appears to have been quite effective. The government also ordered a Dutch printing press, seized in Macassar in September 1956 by a citizens committee acting as self-appointed executors of the abrogation, returned to its rightful owners. In addition, the Ali cabinet also submitted to parliament a moderate foreign investment bill designed to fill the legal vacuum left by the abrogation and thereby normalize the status of existing foreign capital.

The draft foreign investment bill included surprisingly liberal provisions although full discretionary authority was vested in a Committee of Foreign Investment to determine the length of time an enterprise had to be in operation before it could repatriate capital and the number of aliens who could be employed in each foreign enterprise. Only the following public-utility type industries were closed, in principle, to foreign ownership: railways, telecommunications, shipping, aviation, irrigation, water supply, electric power, arms and ammunitions, and atomic energy.[186]

[186] Benjamin Higgins, *Indonesia's Economic Stabilization and Development* (New York: Institute of Pacific Relations, 1957), p. 105 and Appendix I.

All these moderate Indonesian reactions to the abrogation were suddenly submerged in the final expulsion of the Dutch and the expropriation of their assets. This occurred during the "West Irian Action," a government-sponsored complex of manifestations designed to put pressures on the Dutch and to impress uncommitted United Nations members with the seriousness with which Indonesian society and government viewed its claim to West New Guinea.

The "West Irian Action" was officially launched with mass demonstrations and torchlight parades on Youth Oath Day, October 28, 1957, organized by the BKS-PM, a co-ordinating committee for youth groups and military organizations formed by order of the Army Chief of Staff, Nasution. Aroused public opinion was kept at high pitch by carefully stated official pronouncements and a variety of separate actions during the course of the General Assembly debates on the issue.

On Saturday, November 30, 1957, the Indonesian-supported West Irian resolution failed to get the necessary two-thirds majority in the U.N. General Assembly and that same night, an assassination attempt against Sukarno occurred. This inflamed the atmosphere further and events moved rapidly. On Sunday, the cabinet announced reprisals against the Dutch, including a twenty-four hour strike against all Dutch enterprises, withdrawal of landing permission for Dutch airlines, and prohibition of all Dutch-language publications. On Tuesday, the government prohibited Netherlands nationals from entering Indonesia. On Wednesday, nationalist, non-communist labor unions seized the KPM and one of the largest Dutch merchant houses, Geo. Wehry Co. This set off a wave of labor union seizures of other Dutch businesses. On Thursday, the army terminated the syndicalist phase of the takeovers by taking control of the sequestered firms. Finally, on December 6, the cabinet moved to reassume control and closed all Dutch consulates, expelled all Dutch nationals "whose presence was not essential," stopped all money transfers to Holland, and assumed responsibility over all enterprises confiscated by their workers. On the same day, Chief of Staff Nasution swung the central military authorities behind the economic revolution, by declaring in a nationwide address that recent events meant the end of Dutch colonialism and that Dutch capital would no longer be tolerated in Indonesia. On December 13, Nasution ordered all Dutch property throughout the nation placed under military control.

The Outer Islands followed the central government's lead when military authorities began taking over Dutch property on December 7, the day after the cabinet's decision to legalize the seizures. Only central Sumatra, which was the center of the incipient rebellion, did so with obvious reluctance as it appended to the takeover order the statement that "the action was designed as a preventive measure in the security field to insure the stabilization of daily life . . . in view of the arbitrary action taken in the rest of the country." [187]

Somewhat later, Prime Minister Djuanda on December 30, 1957 claimed that the takeovers, far from being spontaneous, fitted into the government's scheme for the abrogation of the RTC. It was only in the matter of timing, he added, that the state's plans had been by-passed by the unions. Since the government's pre-expropriation actions gave no hints of imminent radical moves, however, it appears likely that the actual takeovers were unplanned. Moreover, they were fortuitous, because had the Dutch given up West New Guinea in 1957 rather than in 1962, or had the United Nations voted to support the Indonesian claim, the path to Indonesian indigenization might have been different. In the long run, reduction of Dutch economic power in Indonesia was inevitable, but there existed alternative paths to this dominant social goal.

This is not a trivial point because of the critical importance of the timing of the expropriations. They occurred prior to the formation of an Indonesian capitalist class sufficiently vigorous and competent to replace Dutch enterprise. At the same time, a return of the enterprises to the Dutch was unthinkable at a time when public opinion was already highly resentful of the slow pace at which indigenism was proceeding. Consequently, the state had to fill the vacuum. Indigenism through nationalization became a necessity and a turn to statism, if not socialism, concluded almost a decade of persistent but indecisive attempts to generate Indonesian private entrepreneurship. The frustration of indigenism associated with these attempts was a necessary but not a sufficient cause of the radical turn of events.

INDIGENISM AFTER THE EXPULSION OF THE DUTCH

The expropriation of Dutch economic power was formalized by an act of parliament unanimously passed on December 4, 1958. Only the conservative Masjumi and the small Catholic Party abstained during this momentous vote.[188] This nationalization represented a massive

---

[187] See Anspach, *op. cit.*, pp. 344–353, for a more detailed description of these events.

[188] Anspach, *op. cit.*, pp. 353–355.

leap forward to a national economy. Indonesians, for example, increased their share of estate ownership to about 90 per cent of total plantation output.[189] The takeover of the Big Five trading houses indigenized an estimated 60 per cent of Indonesia's foreign trade.[190] Indonesian dominance of the modern industrial sector was established by the absorption of 246 Dutch factories and mining enterprises.[191] In modern banking, Indonesian banks increased their portion of bank loans from about 50 to 75 per cent and only four non-Indonesian commercial banks survived.[192] Interisland shipping was completely indigenized though this proved a hollow victory, since the seized Dutch ships had to be returned to their owners because of pressures from an international marine insurance consortium.

Although the goal of indigenism had been brought within sight by this economic revolution, the survival of non-Dutch Western enterprise and, even more important, the survival of Chinese business kept alive a significant degree of pluralism. As a result, during the period of "guided economy" under Sukarno (1958–1965), foreign enterprise continued to be attacked on a wide front.

During this period, objectives of indigenism were furthered by measures that could also be interpreted as being due to the increased statism (socialism à la Indonesia) of that period. Thus, when the state extended its control over the economy by means of various cartel-type arrangements within which the state enterprises expropriated from the Dutch were given the leading roles, it also magnified the power of indigenous decision makers.[193] In the import trade, nine of the most important commodities were reserved for eight state-owned import houses, seven of which had previously been Dutch. With these commodities added to the four goods—cloves, batiks, fertilizers and rice—already under state or Indonesian control, the greater part of importing was indigenized. At the same time, nationalization of this trade deprived private Indonesian importers of access to a lucrative activity.[194]

---

[189] See the statement by Minister of Production Suprajogi, *Indonesian Observer*, September 9, 1960.

[190] Thomas, "Indonesia's Approach to Socialism, 1950–60," p. 123.

[191] *Ibid.*   [192] Charlesworth, *op. cit.*, pp. 84–85.

[193] Anspach, *op. cit.*, pp. 372–374. For a more general discussion of the economic reorganization, see Paauw, "From Colonial to Guided Economy," and Bruce Glassburner and Kenneth D. Thomas, "'The Swing of the Hoe: Retooling Begins in the Indonesian Economy," *Asian Survey* (1), June, 1961, pp. 3–11.

[194] Anspach, *op. cit.*, pp. 353–355.

Early in the Sukarno period, the government also moved against those foreign enterprises belonging to noncitizen Chinese. The first to be affected were the Kuomintang Chinese who had become stateless after they rejected both Indonesian and People's Republic of China citizenship, as Indonesia does not recognize the Republic of China on Formosa. Their position was further compromised by the widespread belief that Nationalist China was aiding the rebels in the Outer Islands. Their organizations were proscribed, and all schools and business enterprises partially or wholly owned by them were closed down or seized.[195]

Next, the government moved against the remaining Chinese aliens with a decree (Government Regulation 10) which summarily terminated the licensing of foreign-owned retail shops operating at the village level. At that time, Chinese enterprises were reported to account for 83,783 out of 86,690 registered foreign retailers.[196] This move can be traced back to the Masjumi Congress of 1956 where Sjafruddin had advocated that all small shops should be in national hands within two years.[197] However, its timing was also significant since it occurred about three weeks after the *Benteng* program had been reduced to impotency by the granting of monopoly privileges over major import commodities to the state import enterprises. It was probably issued, therefore, to offset the resentment felt by the indigenous business class which had suffered another serious setback.

Minister of Distribution Leimena estimated that Government Regulation 10 affected 25,000 shops, which indicates that perhaps another 60,000 alien Chinese retailers were operating outside the village level and hence were exempted from the decree. This confirmed the widely held belief that many of the Chinese shop owners fled the villages for urban centers during and after the revolution. While alien Chinese were permitted to sell their shops to co-operatives formed by citizen Chinese, such transfers were allowed only if no ethnic Indonesians came forward to purchase them. Although the most desirable stores could not be transferred directly to *warga negara*, the restriction did

---

[195] B. H. M. Vlekke, *Indonesia's Struggle 1957–58* (The Hague: Netherlands Institute of International Affairs, 1959), pp. 56–59.

[196] *Spectator* (Djakarta, political magazine), September 15, 1959, p. 18.

[197] At that time, Sjafruddin argued that a healthy national entrepreneurial class could be formed most effectively by inducing Indonesians to enter business at the lowest level where the needed financing and experience was at a minimum— a "natural selection" approach to indigenism. See Anspach, *op. cit.*, p. 375.

result in the emergence of another type of "briefcase" Indonesian who, for a fee, purchased shops for *warga negara*.

Regulation 10 forced tens of thousands of the smallest and poorest Chinese retailers to repatriate with their families to China.[198] However, the policy soon became moribund largely because of Sukarno's tolerance of Chinese interests which supported his policy of national integration and also his developing friendship for Peking. As a result, Regulation 10 did little at that time to advance indigenous economic power.

In contrast, hostility towards non-Dutch Western capital increased during this period until another wave of seizures nationalized those interests almost completely. The initial rules of conduct toward such foreign capital were outlined in the Foreign Investment Law (October 27, 1958) and in the "Political Manifesto" speech of Sukarno (April 17, 1959) which became the credo of Indonesia's guided economy. These rules promised noninterference with the remaining Western capital, preference for foreign loans over direct foreign investment and, in the case of direct investment, preference for joint Indonesian-foreign ventures over purely foreign investment.

The Foreign Investment Law of 1958 was very similar to the draft foreign investment act which had been approved by the Ali Sastromidjojo cabinet in 1956. One major change provided that "mining of vital materials" be added to the other sectors previously banned for foreign investment. This raised the question of the status of the oil companies when their concessions came up for renewal. Furthermore, in contrast to the 1956 draft which provided that land occupation rights for vital industry could be granted in principle for up to thirty years, the 1958 law reduced this period to twenty years. On the other hand, guarantees against expropriation of agricultural enterprises were extended from twenty to thirty years. Finally, the 1958 law added to the earlier draft the clause that "priority shall be given to applications for the joint operations of foreign capital and entrepreneurs, on the one hand, and national capital and entrepreneurs, government as well as private, on the other." [199]

[198] For a lengthy discussion of Regulation 10, see Anspach, *op. cit.*, pp. 374–378.

[199] For the text of the Foreign Investment Act, see Commercial Advisory Foundation in Indonesia, *Circular No. H 269*, June 8, 1960.

Subsequently, Sukarno, in his "Political Manifesto," declared:

Though we take our stand on the principle that for construction and development, we give priority to our own capital, and that, if nevertheless foreign capital is needed, we would prefer credit rather than foreign investment . . . despite this, we are nevertheless tolerant enough of foreign non-Dutch capital which is already here and which possibly will come here.[200]

The preference for loans over private investment became evident as the government sought and acquired substantial credits from foreign governments to help finance projects on the priority listings of the Eight Year Plan to begin January 1, 1961.[201] Some security against potential pressures from any one country was to be obtained by distributing foreign assistance among a large number of countries on both sides of the cold war frontier.[202]

In the case of foreign private investment, a modified production-sharing agreement resolved temporarily the anomalous situation created by the 1958 investment law for the Big Three foreign oil companies. The 1963 contract between the Government of Indonesia and Caltex, Shell, and Stanvac specified that, in principle, oil exploitation was reserved for state enterprises but since such enterprises were not yet capable of fulfilling this function, their work was to be subcontracted to the foreign enterprises for a period of twenty years. The foreign firms, moreover, were given full control over management. Indonesia also obtained formal agreement for a 60–40 profit split which confirmed the *status quo* of the previous two years.[203]

Amicable relations with Dutch capital underwent a minor revival after the settlement of the contentious West Irian issue. Indonesian political elites, now no longer fearful of Dutch economic power, initiated a rapprochement with Dutch business interests. The Netherlands-Indonesian thaw commenced with the reopening of Dutch airline

[200] Republic of Indonesia, Department of Information, *Political Manifesto, Republic of Indonesia of 17th August, 1959*, p. 67.

[201] The Eight Year Plan, a document of 4,657 pages, is more an inventory of development resources and a listing of planned projects than a conventional development plan. For an analysis, see Paauw, "From Colonial to Guided Economy," pp. 222–231.

[202] Indonesia received grants and credits totalling about $850 million from the West and $1,100 million from the Communist Bloc from 1950 up to 1961. These totals were derived from Donald Hindley, "Foreign Aid to Indonesia and Its Political Implications," *Pacific Affairs* (36), Summer 1963, *passim*.

[203] *New York Times*, June 2, 1963.

service with Djakarta, exchange of Chargés d'affaires, and a lifting of a ban on Dutch shipping in Indonesian waters.[204]

But the *de facto* position of foreign private investment in Indonesia eroded steadily in the three years beginning with 1962. The business climate of the statist economy was characterized by overregulation, monetary instability, and economic uncertainty. As a result, very little direct foreign investment came in after passage of the Foreign Investment Law. With little at stake, therefore, Sukarno announced on August 13, 1962 that private foreign investment requiring profit transfers abroad would no longer be welcome. Such investment would be restricted to production-sharing arrangements run by joint Indonesian-foreign ventures with management lodged at all times in the hands of Indonesian nationals. Sukarno rationalized the change in policy as a measure to save foreign exchange. He added, however, that direct foreign investment offended nationalist feelings and merely led to demands for nationalization.[205] Subsequently, Indonesia launched a drive to procure foreign investment in the form of production-sharing joint ventures.

The status of direct foreign investment deteriorated even further when Sukarno's government reacted vehemently to what it considered to be improper Anglo-American political and military intervention in Southeast Asia. The establishment of Malaysia with British assistance, which Indonesia interpreted as an expansion of neocolonialist power in her sphere of influence, led to the takeover of British concerns in 1963–1964. United States support of Malaysia and her military intervention in Vietnam led to similar seizures of American property. Then in 1965, all remaining Western foreign property was nationalized.[206]

In this climate of confrontation with Malaysia and the West, Sukarno's government leaned increasingly on the support of the Communist bloc and China. This shift in the direction of foreign affairs benefited the more radical anticapitalist groups within Indonesia's political spectrum and accelerated the internal drift to the left. In reaction to this, however, serious counterpressures against the left-moving Sukarno regime also began to develop.

[204] *Indonesian Observer*, May 6, 7, and 11, July 5, and November 13, 1963; April 13, 1964.
[205] *The Times* (London), August 14, 1962, p. 12.
[206] Australian National University, Research School of Pacific Studies, *Bulletin of Indonesian Economic Studies*, No. 1, June 1965, p. 22.

Probably most damaging to the "guided economy" was the galloping inflation which pushed the cost of living index to 10,141 in July 1965, compared to a base of 100 in January 1958. This monetary collapse, caused by vast budgetary deficits, was due mainly to bureaucratic mismanagement and the central government's inability to collect taxes rather than to bloated governmental expenditures in real terms or to a failure in production.[207] Regardless of cause, however, the hyperinflation, with its attendant foreign-exchange crises, tended to discredit the Sukarno regime, particularly with the salaried urban elite which was especially vulnerable to monetary instabilities and foreign-trade disturbances.

In addition, internal strains of a more direct nature developed in agriculture where land-reform measures, moderate in any case, were obstructed at the local level by a growing landlord class. In turn, poor peasants, often organized by communist farmer associations, occasionally resorted to force to support their claims. At the same time, tensions rose in the cities as labor and other low-income groups were organized by the PKI to confront a developing alliance between bureaucratic managers of state enterprises and indigenous private entrepreneurs.[208]

Still another factor weakening Sukarno's position was his protective attitude to the Chinese minority. Sporadic anti-Chinese outbreaks during this period made it painfully clear that xenophobic emotions, once aroused, are difficult to control. Extreme anti-Chinese riots erupted in West and Central Java in May 1963, leaving in their wake thousands of smashed shops.[209]

All these forces culminated in the reaction to the attempted palace revolution of October 1965—a coup by a small clique of military officers which, in its first hours, gained at least tacit support from the Communists and Sukarno. In the wake of this bungled coup, the majority elements of the army teamed up with frustrated students, religious forces, and the beleagured indigenous landlords and entrepreneurial groups to settle accounts with Sukarno and his "guided

---

[207] For a review of the economic conditions toward the end of the "guided economy" period, see the *Far Eastern Economic Review*, April 28, 1966, pp. 216–217; July 21, 1966, pp. 107–109; and October 6, 1966, pp. 25–29.

[208] Australian National University, Research School of Pacific Studies, *Bulletin of Indonesian Economic Studies*, No. 1, June 1965, pp. 19–20, 38–39.

[209] *Ibid.*, p. 30.

economy." [210] Sukarno himself was eased out of office by a process that was kept deliberately gradual in order not to stir up his considerable following, especially among the peasant masses. Communists, together with their sympathizers and families, were subjected to an army-led massacre of savage proportions.[211]

The successor regime, called the "New Order" and headed by General Suharto, has executed a drastic right turn in economic policy. With statist and anti-Western policies in bad repute and the far left of Indonesia's political spectrum decimated, indigenous private enterprise is now back in favor and the welcome mat is out once again for Western private foreign capital.[212] Western enterprises seized by Sukarno since 1963 without compensation have been returned to their foreign owners.[213] A new investment law highly favorable to foreign capital was passed in December 1966, followed by the conclusion of an investment guarantee agreement with the United States in June 1967.[214]

This does not mean that the goal of indigenism was abandoned. If anything, it was at first stepped up in another direction. The new nationalistic attack focused on the Chinese community which had adapted to overcome nationalistic barriers to some extent by moving into areas that were being poorly served by the inefficient state trading companies.[215] Symptomatic of the resentment against the resilient Chinese were the demands of the organization representing Indonesian business interests in the Suharto front that all Chinese, regardless of citizenship status, be deprived of trade licenses and expelled from

[210] A perceptive analysis of this coup is found in Daniel S. Lev, "Indonesia 1965: The Year of the Coup," *Asian Survey* (VI), February 1966, pp. 103–111.

[211] This carnage and its aftermath, estimated to have taken up to 500,000 lives, is reliably surveyed in a series of articles by Jean Coutenay in the *Far Eastern Economic Review*, November 23, December 14, 1967, and January 11 and January 25, 1968.

[212] *New York Times*, April 4, 1968. Indigenous private enterprise had at times been well treated even during the last years of the "guided economy," but its position at that time was at best precarious because of the unfavorable political climate.

[213] *Business Week*, December 31, 1966, p. 26.

[214] This action did not affect the status of the former Dutch enterprises seized during the West Irian action (*New York Times*, January 14, 1967; Australian National University, Research School of Pacific Studies, *Bulletin of Indonesian Economic Studies*, No. 1, June 1965, p. 22).

[215] *Bulletin of Indonesian Economic Studies*, ibid., p. 30.

Indonesia.[216] The Suharto regime, closely allied to indigenous private business interests and perhaps anxious to maintain an internal image of vigorous indigenism in face of its rapprochement with foreign Western capital, tended to act less forcefully to restrain xenophobic emotions than had the previous government.[217]

The anti-Chinese drive was punctuated by frequent and violent rioting. The lapsed regulation that banned noncitizen Chinese from trading in rural areas was revived and vigorously enforced. Even in the cities, noncitizen Chinese had to get permission from street organizations before they could open up new businesses. In East Java, all noncitizen Chinese were banned from engaging in wholesale and intermediary trade. As a result of these moves, an estimated 100,000 Chinese have emigrated since the establishment of the Suharto regime.[218]

There is still hope, despite these short-run developments, that Indonesia's Chinese will be able to overcome this setback to their assimilation as one of the many subcultures accepted as an integral element of the Indonesian nation. In the first place, it is generally acknowledged that the *peranakans* have been the most assimilated of all the Southeast Asian Chinese; and with the ending of Chinese immigration, all Chinese in Indonesia will soon be *peranakans*. Furthermore, assimilation of the *peranakans* continues to be official policy and, undoubtedly, is desired by the majority of Indonesians. Regulations are issued forbidding Indonesians of foreign descent from going to foreign schools, exhortations are circulated to encourage *peranakans* to assume Indonesian-sounding names, and even the use of the Chinese language in public has been banned.[219] As one observer concluded recently:

Today one can find genuine cooperation between indigenous Indonesians and Peranakan Chinese in a small number of special-interest associations, business firms, professional offices, churches and even government agencies. An increasing number of WNI (warga negara) Chinese are committed to broadening the scope of inter-ethnic cooperation . . . [and as a result] . . . one may now entertain the possibility that the WNI Chinese will eventually be accepted as true compatriots by their fellow citizens.[220]

In the last analysis, however, the future of the remaining alien ele-

[216] *Far Eastern Economic Review,* June 2, 1966, p. 452.
[217] *Ibid.,* November 9, 1967, p. 286.
[218] *Ibid.,* p. 282, and May 4, 1967, p. 265.
[219] *Ibid.,* November 9, 1967, p. 282.
[220] Skinner, "The Chinese Minority," p. 117.

ments in Indonesia's economy depends on the country's ability to provide a decent living standard for her people. There had been hopes that the successors to Sukarno would set Indonesia's course to recovery and development. Unfortunately, the performance of the increasingly militaristic "New Order" gives scant evidence that it is likely to resolve the fundamental socio-economic problems obstructing growth.

This doleful estimate is not based simply on the fact that Indonesia is having some difficulty getting the massive injections of Western governmental aid and private investment that she had counted on as a reward for her shift toward the West and for her renewed experimentation with a market economy.[221] The major difficulty, rather, is that her new leadership appears to lack the feeling of urgency and the commitment necessary to call forth the drastic austerity measures required to extricate Indonesia from its economic morass.[222] Should the economic situation continue to erode, however, we can expect to see further social upheavals in Indonesia with tragic consequences for the remaining nonindigenous groups and foreign economic interests which can easily be cast into the role of scapegoats.

[221] *New York Times,* April 4, 1968, p. 2.

[222] For a description of the unsatisfactory economic performance of the "New Order," see the *Far Eastern Economic Review,* December 24, 1967, p. 570, and January 14, 1968, p. 92. Perhaps symptomatic of this failure of will is the following statement by one of the chief economic advisors to the present government: "We have to go slowly, develop discipline and educate the people as we go . . . otherwise we will go backward rather than forward in the long run" (*New York Times,* December 2, 1967).

4

BURMA*

The Environment of Policy

Burma gained political independence on January 4, 1948 to become a constitutional republic outside the British Commonwealth. The achievement of independence was the culmination of a process of increasing nationalist pressure which first received articulate expression in the early twentieth century. Since independence, the Burmese Government has consciously and consistently sought to achieve a comparable economic sovereignty.

With a population of about twenty-five million, Burma is relatively rich in agricultural, fishery, timber, mineral, and water resources, which are unlikely to be subject to population pressure for years to come. Most important are the agricultural resources, and the most important single crop is rice, of which Burma was the world's largest exporter until 1964. In 1962–1963 approximately 35 per cent of the gross domestic product was produced in agriculture, fisheries, and forestry, while an estimated 84 per cent of the population lived in rural areas.

Before annexation by the British, Burma was a geographically isolated absolute monarchy. The society was agricultural and essentially

* Research for this study was conducted in the Union of Burma during 1959–1960. The author is indebted to many people in the University of Rangoon, in the Burmese government service, and in business who gave generously of their time and information. The views expressed in this study are solely the responsibility of the author and do not necessarily reflect the opinions of her Burmese friends or informants nor do they necessarily reflect those of the United Nations. Mr. David E. Pfanner read and criticized the manuscript and gave generously of his experience as a student of modern Burma—M. R. F.

feudal, and was unified by the strength of Buddhism and the tremendous influence of the Sangha, the Buddhist monastic order.

British annexation opened Burma to the world, and economic nationalism was profoundly influenced by two consequences of British colonial policy. First, Burma was absorbed into the Indian Empire and, until the dyarchy system of parliamentary government was introduced in 1923, was administered by the Indian Civil Service. It was only natural, therefore, that the administrators of the new colony were recruited from among the British service trained in India who brought with them subordinate Indian civil servants. Burma's earlier isolation further contributed to the influx of Indians into her economy, and her previous self-sufficiency contributed to the economic disadvantage of the Burmese. Burma had never developed ocean-going shipping, nor had the Burmese any experience with foreign trade. Industry and commerce had never been organized on modern lines, and the Burmese knew nothing of machinery or steam power. They were isolated by the barrier of language and knew nothing of Western law or methods of administration. Burma had no supply of cheap and unemployed labor accustomed to working with Europeans. All these deficiencies India could and did supply.

The second important result of British rule was the opening of Burma to the influence of an economic policy of *laissez faire* which was superimposed on the existing tradition-bound, subsistence-oriented, and technologically static rural economy. The most far-reaching result of the application of the liberal prescription of competition and free trade was the colonization of the Irrawaddy delta by the Burmese rice farmers in response to the economic incentives that appeared following the opening of the Suez Canal and the growth of the Indian market. Burmese cultivators, quick to respond to these incentives, migrated from their traditional village communities to an economy based upon credit and market forces. This was the only sphere, however, in which the Burmese rose to take advantage of the opportunities in the new economic organization. Shipping and foreign trade sprang up; forests, mines, and oil fields were developed; modern banking was introduced; but the Burmese had neither the knowledge, opportunity, nor the ability to compete in these activities, and, as a result, colonial Burma took shape under foreign economic as well as political control.

The plural society that developed in Burma was composed of four main groups: Burmese, Europeans, Indians, and Chinese. In 1872 aliens comprised 5.5 per cent of the total population; by 1900 they

Table 11. Racial composition of the population, 1901–1931

Year	Total population (thousands)	Percentage		Percentage of non-Buddhists in	
		Total alien	Indian	Large towns	Other towns
1901	10,491	6.97	5.84	–	–
1911	12,115	8.02	6.15	62.8	22.3
1921	13,212	8.98	6.69	63.5	25.3
1931	14,667	9.74	6.95	62.7	28.1

Source: J. S. Furnivall, *Colonial Policy and Practice* (New York: New York University, 1956), p. 117.

formed 7.0 per cent including 5.8 per cent Indian and by 1931, 9.7 per cent with 7.0 per cent Indian.

Not only was the alien population large, but it was concentrated in the large towns where aliens controlled almost all commercial and industrial undertakings. Although figures for urban population by race are not available until 1931, the ratios of the non-Buddhists in Table 11 may be roughly equated with the urbanized alien community which undoubtedly was somewhat larger, as many Chinese classified themselves as Buddhists. This conclusion is supported by the fact that the ratios of non-Buddhists in 1931 were approximately equal to the ratios of the nonindigenous population in large towns and other towns presented in Table 12.

More important than the actual size of the alien minorities in Burma was their functional specialization and dominance of major economic

Table 12. Racial composition of the urban and rural population, 1931

Race	Racial population		Racial percentage			
	Large towns	Other towns	Large towns	Other towns	All towns	Rural areas
Indigenous	210,796	679,170	36.0	72.7	58.5	93.9
Indian	290,124	173,090	49.6	18.5	30.5	4.2
Chinese	39,262	32,871	6.7	3.5	4.7	0.9
Indo-Burmese	24,497	39,708	4.2	4.2	4.2	0.9
Others	20,555	9,964	3.5	1.1	2.0	–

Source: Furnivall, *op. cit.*, p. 118.

activities. The mining and petroleum extracting firms were European, as were the cement works and general engineering enterprises. The large rice mills and saw mills were European, with medium-sized mills owned by Indians and Chinese. The export trade was in the hands of Europeans, Indians, and Chinese, and Indians handled most importing and the retail distribution of imported goods. The Burmese retained control of the retailing of local products, and, of course, agricultural production.

With the growth of the rice export trade in the last quarter of the nineteenth century, the demand for labor in the new rice mills rose. The colonial administration decided to encourage the immigration of Indian laborers with, initially, a subsidy for their transportation. The subsidy was withdrawn in the 1880s, but recorded arrivals of immigrants continued to increase from 84,000 in 1883–1884 to over 400,000 in 1927. The Indian coolies arrived in time for the harvest, followed by work in the rice mills and then repair work in the fields. Although a large proportion of this labor was seasonal and returned home when work was not available, Indians came to predominate as year round factory workers, mine workers, and coolie labor on the docks. An inquiry into Indian immigration reported that in 1938–1939 Burmese constituted 29.7 per cent of the nonagricultural unskilled labor force and Indians 69.5 per cent. Among skilled workers Burmese numbered 36.7 per cent and Indians 58.4 per cent, and among the industrial labor force, including mining, Burmese accounted for only 30.7 per cent.[1]

The exclusion of the Burmese from modern economic life occurred also in the professions, the members of which, apart from the Westernized community, were largely incorporated in the colonial administration. This situation was exacerbated by the British education policy which provided inadequate opportunities for the Burmese to acquire professional training.[2] In many of the public services there was also a predominance of Indians, especially at the lower levels. Indians understood the administrative system, were used to working with British officers, and had a long start over the Burmese in knowledge and use of the English language.

Apart from a small minority of Burmese who were able, through

---

[1] James Baxter, *Report on Indian Immigration* (Rangoon: Superintendent, Govt. Printing and Stationery, 1941).

[2] J. S. Furnivall, *Colonial Policy and Practice* (New York: New York University Press, 1956), pp. 123–130.

acquiring Western education, to enter the ranks of the civil service, the professions, and modern economic activities, the bulk of the indigenous population remained on the land. It is often argued that in the nineteenth century and up to the 1920s the cultivators participated in the prosperity occasioned by the phenomenal increase in the value of rice exports from K. (kyats) 20.55 million in 1868–1869 to K. 381.71 million in 1926–1927. Furnivall maintains, however, that the increased wealth in the towns did not reflect conditions in the villages in Lower Burma where, after the turn of the century, the "great mass of the people were steadily growing poorer." [3] Rents were continually rising, as was indebtedness, tenancy, and land alienization. Home weaving and other local crafts became unprofitable as cheaper imports became available. Further evidence of growing poverty was the increasing difficulty of collecting the capitation tax and the estimated decline of from 10 to 15 per cent in per capita rice consumption. With the fall in the price of rice during the depression of the 1930s, the cultivator's position deteriorated even further.

The opening of Burma to the free play of economic forces led finally to agrarian distress and the increasing disintegration of Burmese society. The social relationships, based on stability of land tenure and the strength of custom and power of the Sangha, which had existed in Upper Burma before British annexation, never developed in Lower Burma. [4] Two changes combined with the economic to hasten disintegration. The first was the weakening of Buddhist ecclesiastical authority which had previously regulated conduct largely through the monastic schools and monastic courts. The prestige of the Sangha eroded with the decline in the economic value of a monastic education and the increase in opportunities that were opened to those who could obtain education in Western government schools. Secondly, British secular law was introduced and, except for minor disputes and matters of marriage, divorce, and inheritance, it replaced the customary and monastic law with a system that was alien to Burmese society and was not understood by the Burmese.

Out of this situation arose increasing nationalist pressures—political and economic—which culminated in the race riots of the 1930s. The

[3] *Ibid.*, p. 103.
[4] For the development of this thesis, see David E. Pfanner, "Rice and Religion in a Burmese Village" (Ph.D. dissertation, Department of Anthropology, Cornell University, 1962), *passim.*

virulence of economic nationalism in Burma and the grass-roots nature of the movement reflected two peculiar features of the British colonial period in that country. Unlike the situation in a number of colonies where economic development by the metropolitan power took the form of a plantation system, the development and cultivation of rice was undertaken by small-scale Burmese cultivators. The services necessary to bring this product into the world market—credit, transport, and processing—were provided by aliens, but agricultural production remained in indigenous hands. In other words, dualism, as has been described in Indonesia, did not exist in colonial Burma; subsistence farmers did not produce in juxtaposition with capitalist plantations. The Burmese cultivators were brought into close contact with Western economic forces, however, and were subjected to market uncertainty and instability. This had a great deal to do with the equation of capitalism and imperialism by the Burmese and contributed to the ideological bias in Burmese economic nationalism.

Secondly, the Burmese peasant was brought into close contact with the economically successful alien in the person of the Indian (Chettyar) moneylender, who provided agricultural credit in the rice villages. His success contrasted sharply with the declining welfare of the peasant, who, gradually deprived of land, found himself in competition with cheap Indian labor.

It is not necessary here to trace the rise of the nationalist movement from its genesis in the Young Men's Buddhist Association in 1908, through the 1920–1921 University and school strike and the emergence of the *pongyi* (monk) politicians. These events were followed by the period of the ineffective Dyarchy beginning in 1923, the boycott of the Simon Commission in 1929, and the race riots and the Saya San rebellion of the 1930s. Economic distress and racial friction increased throughout this period.[5] In view of this history it is understandable that the Burmese should have been driven to rid their country of aliens in order to benefit from the material progress being extracted from the patrimony of natural resources by their own economic endeavors.

The group that led Burma to final independence in 1948 was the young educated Thakins, led by Aung San.[6] They had come together

[5] John F. Cady, *A History of Modern Burma* (Ithaca: Cornell University Press, 1958).

[6] "Thakin" was the respectful term of address to Europeans in Burma. This revolutionary group gave themselves this name to show they were now the masters. One of the Thakins' slogans was "Thakin-myoe hae Do Bemar," meaning "We Burmese belong to a master or ruling race."

as students at Rangoon University in the 1930s, supported the Japanese as liberators in the early years of the war, and later shifted their support to the British when the Japanese proved the more oppressive rulers. In the first postwar elections of 1947, the Anti-Fascist People's Freedom League (AFPFL), under the leadership of Aung San, was given an overwhelming mandate. After Aung San was assassinated later that year, the leadership fell to U Nu who continued as Prime Minister through the elections of 1951 and 1956 until the assumption of power by the military caretaker government of General Ne Win in the fall of 1958. In early 1960, Ne Win voluntarily relinquished power to a civilian government again headed by U Nu. The second U Nu government proved short-lived, however, as its inadequacies led to a coup by the military, headed by Ne Win, early in 1962 and rule by a Revolutionary Council of officers. After a brief period of vacillation in economic policy during which internal strains were evident in the ruling Council, the government moved abruptly to socialize and Burmanize the economy by nationalization.

The anti-European aspects of the Kuomintang revolution in China encouraged Burmese nationalist sentiment. During the thirties, the Thakins were influenced by the radical left in India, and socialist and Marxist literature was regularly brought into Burma. The Thakins were violently anti-British and revolutionary, and the group contained a strong communist minority which became influential. They were attracted by the "people's front" orientation of European socialist and communist parties, but many of the Thakins were devout Buddhists and were offended by communism's repudiation of religion. The intensity of their nationalist fervor kept the group working together until the eve of independence. With the return of the British, the Burmese wartime resistance movement, the Anti-Fascist Organization (AFO), became the AFPFL, to emphasize that its goal was not merely Japanese defeat but also independence. The Thakins who formed the leadership of the AFPFL ranged in ideology from democratic socialism on the right to Trotskyism on the left. There was no leadership to the right of the moderate socialists. In 1946 the communists split amongst themselves. The Red Flag communists who wanted to conduct armed rebellion against the British went underground and began military action. The White Flag communists, led by Thakin Than Tun, wished to work within and capture the AFPFL. Than Tun made a bid for leadership but failed and then declared a general strike against the AFPFL. The AFPFL leader, Aung San, countered by expelling the communists from the party and from all key positions in trade unions and workers' and peasants' organizations. The AFPFL then became the party of democratic socialists. Immediately following independence the White Flag communists announced a revolutionary program and also went underground in active revolt against the government. The seriousness of the insurrection that engulfed the country for the next four years is well known.

The economic success of the British, Indians, and Chinese in colonial Burma accentuated the economic distress for the Burmese, caught up in the capitalist process. As a result of their experiences, many Burmese made no distinction between "imperialism" and "capitalism." Prime Minister U Nu verbalized the tendency to equate the two concepts when he said, "Burma has been for over a century under Imperialist domination, and Capitalists have during the entire period been regarded as the handmaids [*sic*] of Imperialism. During the entire course of our struggle for freedom therefore Capital and Imperialist domination have been closely associated in the minds of all of us who have taken part in that struggle, and it has been impossible to view the two in isolation." [7]

The draft constitution was drawn up in 1947 and in his speech moving for its adoption, U Nu made it clear that

Burma [would] be a Leftist country. And a Leftist country is one in which the people working together to the best of their power and ability strive to convert the natural resources and produce of the land . . . into consumer commodities to which everybody will be entitled each according to his need . . . there will be no such thing as a handful of people holding the monopoly over the inexhaustible wealth of the land while the poor and the starving grow more and more numerous . . . there will be no distinction between the employer class and the employed class . . . (between) the master-class and the slave-class, the governing-class and the governed-class.[8]

The Constitution does not include any reference to Burma as a socialist state, but it is quite clear that the intention of its framers was to create such a state. Although the right of private property and of private initiative in the economic sphere is guaranteed, this right cannot be used to the detriment of the general welfare. Private monopolis-

---

[7] U Nu, *From Peace to Stability* (Rangoon: Supt., Govt. Printing and Stationery, 1951), p. 75.

[8] U Nu, *Towards Peace and Democracy* (Rangoon: Supt., Govt. Printing and Stationery, 1949), p. 2.

tic organizations and practices are forbidden, and "private property may be limited or expropriated if the public interest so requires" (Sec. 23). "The State is the ultimate owner of all lands" (Sec. 30) and has the right to regulate or abolish land tenures and can resume and redistribute land. "The State shall direct its policy towards giving material assistance to economic organizations not working for private profit" (Sec. 42). All public utility undertakings and the exploitation of all natural resources will be operated by the State, by local bodies, or people's co-operatives (Sec. 44).

Political power, which the Burmese achieved with independence, was applied promptly to reserve positions of economic control to the Burmese. The war had rid the country of almost all the Indian money-lenders and landowners, and left the cultivators in Lower Burma temporarily free of their interest and rent obligations. A large proportion of European capital in mines, shipping, and oil production had been destroyed. The Burmese, moreover, were determined that aliens would not resume their former positions of economic control in the economy. The moment we have the power, U Nu had said, we will put an end to

this unfair, one-sided economic system. The wealth of Burma has been enjoyed firstly by the big British capitalists, next the Indian capitalists, and next the Chinese capitalists. Burmans are at the bottom, in poverty, and have to be content with the left-over and the chewed-over bones and scraps from the table of foreign capitalists.[9]

Burmanism became a key policy of the new republic. It was introduced into all economic sectors of the economy: agriculture, internal and external trade, retailing, industry, banking, and the professions. Burmanism was carried out by nationalization of existing assets, by reserving certain economic functions to Burmese citizens or the State, by direct competition of the State with alien enterprises, by giving economic advantages to Burmese nationals vis-à-vis aliens, and by measures to limit the number of alien residents.

This study is concerned with the process of Burmanization following independence during a period when the Burmese society was committed to two other major goals, the pursuit of which affected the political and economic environment. First, the Burman leadership continuously grappled with the problem of integrating the indigenous non-Burman ethnic groups—mainly the Kachins, Shans, Chins, Karens,

[9] *Ibid.*, p. 3.

and Kayahs—into a national, Burmese, society.[10] Although the indigenous minorities were organized into states in which they controlled education and the preservation of their cultures, integration was encouraged by the spread of the language, religion, customs, and dress of the Burmans.

The principal militant ethnic minority group, the Karen National Defense Organization (KNDO) rebelled against the government along with the communist insurgents during the first decade of independence. Beginning in 1959 segments of the Shans, Kayahs, and Kachins also went underground in their fight for increased political autonomy. The 1962 *coup d'état,* moreover, was in part a response to the growing threat posed by the dissident minorities to the stability and unity of Burma.

The containment of the dissident forces has required a major drain on Burmese resources since independence, and thus far no real unity of the Burmans and the other indigenous groups has been achieved. The desire of the government to promote internal stability and unity, moreover, may have had some retarding effect upon the vigor of its efforts to dispossess and force the migration of certain economically prominent alien minorities.

The priority assigned by the socialist-oriented leadership to nationalization also had an impact upon Burmanism. Many nationalization measures have been undertaken solely for the purpose of transferring ownership from the private to the public sector, and such efforts have impinged upon indigenous and alien enterprise alike. In a number of cases, however, the government has used nationalization measures for the direct purpose of removing aliens from the control of an economic activity. This has occurred where private Burmese enterprise has been unwilling or unable to replace existing aliens or where the government has wished to transfer ownership from aliens directly to the Burmese public sector. In this connection the execution of the Burmanism policy was hampered between 1948 and 1962 by the ambivalence of the Burmese toward socialism and nationalization, which was evident in their persistent and unsuccessful efforts to promote private Burmese enterprise. The frustration generated over time by the failure of such efforts led to the abrupt changes effected by the Revolutionary Council beginning in 1963.

[10] "Burman" is used here as an ethnic term identifying a particular indigenous group; a Burmese is a citizen of Burma.

This survey will treat nationalization measures only insofar as they were clearly motivated by the goal of Burmanization or where their execution contributed significantly to achievement of that goal.

The Nature of Burmese Indigenism

IMMIGRATION, NATURALIZATION, AND
RESTRICTIONS ON FOREIGNERS

The outbreak of war with Japan and the first bombing of Rangoon in December 1941, caused a mass exodus of Indians and Chinese from Burma. At the end of 1943, a census taken by the Government of India of the "Asiatic British subjects" who had entered India since December 8, 1941, revealed that of approximately one million Indians who had been in Burma in 1941, 400,000 had returned to India and many others died on the way.[11]

After the war, Burma had no immigration laws until the passage of the Burma Immigration (Emergency Provisions) Act, No. XXXI of June 14, 1947, and in the meantime, a considerable number of the Indian evacuees had returned. The Act provided that aliens who had evacuated on account of the war might return, provided that, "if Indians, they were armed with Burma Evacuee Identity Certifications and if Chinese, were repatriated under the sponsorship of the International Refugee Organization." Both categories were subject to thorough checking by the Burmese authorities. Re-entry of Indian evacuees was stopped abruptly on December 31, 1950 and of Chinese in 1951 when the International Refugee Organization disbanded.

The Government of the Union of Burma has continually evidenced concern with the fact that Burma forms a "population vacuum between the two large countries with overflowing populations,"[12] and the present immigration policy seeks to minimize immigration in order "to preserve national homogeneity" and "to protect the interests of nationals."[13] U Saw Htin Lin Mya, Deputy Controller of Immigration, said in 1960 that Burma had no quota system, and that virtually no new

[11] Union of Burma (UOB), Director of Information, *Burma, The Tenth Anniversary Yearbook* (Rangoon, 1958), p. 288.
[12] *Ibid.*, p. 290.   [13] *Ibid.*

Table 13. Recorded movement of population
(sea, air, and land)

Year	Arrivals	Departures	Net movement
1949	65,414	118,382	−52,968
1950	72,036	75,574	− 3,538
1951	68,950	65,595	+ 3,355
1952	87,052	82,621	+ 4,431
1953	97,265	94,582	+ 2,683
1954	89,059	94,509	− 5,450
1955	95,906	94,787	+ 1,119
1956	96,232	102,229	− 5,997
1957	94,010	94,055	− 45
1958	92,888	99,507	− 6,619
1959	88,315	103,681	−15,366
1960	89,863	98,240	− 8,377
1961	85,913	92,309	− 6,396
1962	55,023	58,264	− 3,241
1963	34,966	42,398	− 7,432
1964	14,887	103,170	−88,283
1965	13,537	87,624	−74,087

Source: Union of Burma, Central Statistical and Economics Department, *Quarterly Bulletin of Statistics,* 4th Quarter, 1959 (Rangoon: Supt., Govt. Printing and Stationery, 1960), Table 1, p. 1, and *ibid.,* 4th Quarter, 1966 (Rangoon: Supt., Central Press, 1967), p. 1.

immigrants were permitted except for some Chinese refugees from the north.[14] The extent of net emigration in recent years is shown in Table 13.

Entry visas are no longer granted except for employment in one of the government or quasi-government departments. The entrance of seasonal labor has been banned. Before the military takeover in 1962, alien firms remaining in Burma, were entitled to apply for a visa for the temporary residence of an alien to replace an alien employee who was returning home. According to the chairman of the Burma Chamber of Commerce in 1960, it was very difficult to obtain such a visa as the immigration authorities considered managerial skills to be services that

[14] Interview with the author in Rangoon, April 7, 1960. For the Immigration Act as amended and the various decisions of the High Court and Supreme Court of the Union of Burma in relation to the law, see S. L. Verma, *The Law Relating to Foreigners and Citizenship in Burma* (Mandalay: Rishi Raj Verma, 1960).

a Burmese could supply without training and, therefore, it was almost impossible to arrange for the entry of an alien to fill a managerial post.[15]

Dislike of and fear of competition from immigrants persists in Burma. It can be seen in public statements, in the press, and in the public reaction to efforts of the government to prevent illegal immigration.[16] The number of aliens who were subject to surprise checks, or against whom action was taken under the Immigration Act or the Foreigners Registration Act, increased under the military caretaker government in 1959 and 1960, which was interpreted widely as indicating increased effectiveness on the part of the Immigration Department. After the return to civil government in 1960, critical outcries in the press resumed. "The danger of the Burmese race being swamped by foreigners entering the country illegally is so great." No "effective action has been taken by the Government." The "Burmese are gravely menaced by foreign infiltration." [17]

Economic restrictions imposed by the Revolutionary Council following the coup in 1962 have closed many spheres previously favored by enterprising aliens. The import and export trade, retailing, money-lending, and many of the professions are now either nationalized or open only to Burmese citizens. Severe restrictions have been imposed upon the remittance of any earnings to dependents abroad. These changes have virtually eliminated economic incentives to emigrate and have caused a mass exodus of aliens since 1963.

Provisions for Burmese citizenship apply the principle of *jus sanguinis*. Under the Constitution (Sec. 2) a person "both of whose parents belong or belonged to any of the indigenous races of Burma, or . . . who was born in Burma, and at least one of whose grandparents belong or belonged to the indigenous races . . . or both of whose parents are . . . Union citizens, is a natural born citizen of the Union of Burma." [18]

---

[15] Interview with C. A. McDowall, Chairman, Burma Chamber of Commerce, and General Manager of the Bombay Burmah Trading Corp. Ltd., Rangoon, June 24, 1960.

[16] UOB, Director of Information, *Is Trust Vindicated?* (Rangoon, 1960), pp. 86–88.

[17] Editorial, *The Nation* (Rangoon), June 7, 1961, p. 4.

[18] At the time of independence, certain persons resident in Burma were allowed to elect Union citizenship or they could choose to remain British nationals as provided in the arrangements for transferring power in the Burma Independence Act, 1947.

Naturalization is provided by the Union Citizenship Act as amended, No. LXVI of 1948. The applicant must be over the age of eighteen, have resided continuously in the Union for five years previous to the application, be of good character and be able to speak an indigenous language, and intend to reside in the Union.

The problem of dual citizenship, especially involving Communist China, exists for Burma as it does for other countries of Southeast Asia. The Union Citizenship (Amendment) Act of 1954, requires persons with dual citizenship to renounce their foreign nationality to retain their Union citizenship. Although the Constitution of the People's Republic of China contains no provision for renunciation of citizenship, at present Union citizens of Chinese origin have been able to retain their citizenship in Burma.[19]

In the first twelve years of independence, only 21,433 certificates of naturalization were issued, of which three-fifths were issued during the last thirty-two months of the period.[20] Between January 1948 and April 1957, an average of only seventy-seven certificates was issued monthly, and pending cases accumulated especially in the District Courts. The hardship occasioned by the delay in the naturalization process, moreover, has tended to increase since 1962 as economic nationalism has become more radical and xenophobic.

The Burmese constitution makes no distinction between a naturalized and a natural-born citizen, but persistent and increasing pressures have arisen in Burma to deny certain citizenship rights to naturalized persons.

In 1961, U Raschid, the Minister for Industry, cautioned the members of the Rangoon Chamber of Commerce, which is made up of non-Burmese businessmen who have become citizens, that "every utterance and action of a new citizen is suspect in Burma." [21] In the same year, the Immigration Minister proposed that naturalization regulations be tightened by deleting the provision of the Union Citizenship Act, 1948, under which a foreign national can apply for Union citizenship if he and his parents were born in and have continually resided in the Union.[22] Indigenous elements in the business community also have pressed for differential treatment for natural-born and naturalized citizens. For example, an Association to Prevent Economic Domina-

---

[19] Maung Maung, *Burma's Constitution* (The Hague: Martenus Nijhoff, 1959), p. 96.

[20] UOB, *Is Trust Vindicated?*, p. 86.   [21] *The Nation*, July 24, 1961, p. 1.

[22] *Ibid.*, July 10, 1961, p. 1.

tion by Foreigners was set up in Rangoon in 1960 with its stated aim to "wrest control" of Burmese economic life from the hands of aliens and naturalized citizens. The Association criticized the naturalization regulations as too lax.[23]

Such pressures have sustained sporadic tightening of naturalization policy until in 1962 certain economic misdemeanors, if committed by naturalized citizens, became punishable by the loss of citizenship. This was the case, for example, if a naturalized citizen "was found by the Government to be disloyal and faithless to the Union on account of the import policy." [24]

At other times, however, officials have made efforts to counter these pressures. Brigadier Aung Gyi, Head of the Army delegation to the Economic Seminar in September 1959,[25] deplored the tendency to discriminate against Burmese nationals of not "too pure" stock. "The general policy [is] to accord full recognition to all Burmese nationals, regardless of their origins, so long as they become completely Burmese in character." On their part, he said, "these Burmese nationals should assimilate themselves completely into the national culture." [26]

All resident aliens in the Union of Burma must hold a valid Foreigner's Registration Certificate which, beginning in 1956, they were required to renew annually. The fee for the initial certificate, its annual renewal, and for its replacement if lost was set at K. 50 (1K. = U.S. $.21) which for the majority of resident aliens in Burma— poor farmers, laborers, or domestic servants—is a heavy burden. There has been some pressure in the Rangoon press for its reduction.[27] It was reported late in 1960 that there were 201 Pakistanis, 127 Indians, and 66 Chinese who had been in jail for over three years because they were too poor to renew their certificates.[28] Many of them had been born in Burma but had been "unable to get the authorities to pay attention to" their "applications for citizenship," and continued, therefore, to be liable for the annual fee.[29]

[23] *Ibid.*, July 14, 1960, p. 1.

[24] Statement by the Government in Parliament on February 25, 1962 (*Ibid.*, March 1, 1962).

[25] The Economic Seminar, held in Rangoon on September 13 and 14, 1959, was a meeting organized by the Caretaker Government to include government officials and representatives of the mercantile community and the press. The purpose of the meeting was to conduct informal discussions of the government's economic policies and programs.

[26] *The Nation*, September 19, 1959, p. 1.

[27] Editorial, *ibid.*, October 26, 1959, p. 4.   [28] *Ibid.*, August 1, 1960, p. 1.

[29] Editorial, *ibid.*, February 9, 1961, p. 4.

Resident aliens have encountered increasing difficulty in obtaining permission to remit income earned in Burma, though it was announced policy to permit the transfer of one-half of income received to support a wife and children abroad. Such remittances to India declined from K. 25 million in 1949 to K. 3 million in 1960.[30] On June 21, 1961, the government suspended all remittances to India by Indian nationals resident in Burma.[31] After protests by the Indian Ambassador in Rangoon, such remittances were resumed two months later, but subject to tightened restrictions.[32] Remittances to support other dependents were limited to one-fifth of income and permission was subject to the discretion of the exchange control authorities. A high official at the Exchange Control Office reported in 1960 that it was "very difficult" to obtain this permission.[33] By 1963, total net private transfers out of Burma had become negligible.[34]

Prior to 1962, alien residents departing Burma were entitled to remit savings that were in the form of cash or bank deposits subject to proof that such savings were legitimate. Remittance of the proceeds of the sale of immovable property was legally permitted, subject to transfer in installments with the timing at the discretion of Exchange Control. Capital invested in a business could be remitted if the business was wound up, but not if the business was sold, in which case, only dividends from the reinvestment of the capital could be remitted. The same high official mentioned above said that "a great many of these actions [were] at the discretion of Exchange Control, and this way we are able to make it difficult." Subsequently, at a news conference in September 1962, General Ne Win announced that foreigners who had brought no capital into Burma would not be allowed to take out of the country money made while residing there.[35]

Immigration into Burma has virtually ceased, and the economic restrictions confronting resident aliens have caused a growing net emigration in the last few years. Because of the pressures of Burmanism,

[30] *Ibid.*, July 2, 1961, p. 1.   [31] *Ibid.*, July 23, 1961, p. 1.
[32] *Ibid.*, August 19, 1961, p. 1.
[33] Much of the information regarding allowable remittances abroad and the difficulties put in the way of alien residents was obtained during several visits to the Exchange Control Office, the Union Bank, Rangoon during June 1960. Policy statements were confidential but the Exchange Control Manual containing the above regulations was open for inspection by courtesy of U Han Tin, Senior Exchange Control Officer.
[34] International Monetary Fund, *International Financial Statistics* (Washington, D.C.).
[35] *Far Eastern Economic Review,* October 4, 1962.

resident aliens have been forced increasingly into a position of either emigrating or applying for citizenship. The regulations governing naturalization are not restrictive, but the authorities have been very slow in processing naturalization applications, during which time an alien remains liable for a foreigner's registration fee, a heavy burden for many aliens.

AGRICULTURAL LAND

The advent of the steamship, the opening of the Suez Canal, and the growth of the Indian economy, caused an expansion in the external market for Burmese rice. As a result, large areas of virgin land in Lower Burma were brought under cultivation as shown in Table 14, and paddy growing became a commercial venture for export rather than subsistence agriculture.

Table 14. Acreage planted to rice in Lower Burma, 1830–1930

Year	Acres
1830	66,000
1860	1,333,000
1890	4,398,000
1920	8,588,000
1930	9,911,000

Source: J. Russell Andrus, *Burmese Economic Life* (Stanford: Stanford University Press, 1948), p. 43.

Most of this land was brought under cultivation by individual small farmers from Upper Burma who migrated south, became farm laborers for a few years, then took up their own land with whatever savings they had. Most of the land was acquired either by squatting and the subsequent acquisition of legal "landholder's rights," or under the Pattar system in which the government made grants of small areas (10–15 acres) of land. The majority of the cultivators found it necessary to borrow to maintain themselves while preparing the land for cultivation and to buy tools and oxen. The provision of credit by local shopkeepers and Burmese moneylenders, as well as modest programs of government lending, however, proved inadequate.[36]

[36] Chester L. Cooper, "Moneylenders and the Economic Development of Lower Burma—An Exploratory Historical Study of the Role of the Indian Chettyars" (Ph.D. dissertation, Department of Economics, The American University, 1959), p. 26.

Into this situation stepped the Chettyars, a moneylending caste from Madras in South India. As a result of their reputation as moneylenders and their longstanding connections with British banks in India, they were able to borrow funds from the British banks in Rangoon to supplement their own capital. These resources were then lent to Burmese smallholders, a market for credit ignored by the banks which were not interested in small agricultural loans. There were over 1,500 Chettyar firms in Burma in 1930, with an estimated K. 500 million invested in agriculture.[37]

Chettyar agents lived in the villages and made short-term loans for up to three years. Their interest rates were not high compared with those of indigenous moneylenders, and "wherever the Chettyar went, the rates fell." [38] Reports of their rates on land mortgages vary from 15 to 36 per cent (Andrus) to 15 to 25 per cent (Peam),[39] with up to 45 per cent on loans secured on standing crops and movable property. The depression brought down Chettyar lending rates to some extent, and between 1935 and 1942 their rates ranged from 9 to 15 per cent for loans against immovable property, and up to 24 per cent for loans on demand notes.[40]

They were not interested in acquiring land and, as professional moneylenders, they were also not interested in the purpose to which the loans were put. Furnivall maintained that one of the great defects of the Chettyar system was that they actually lent too much to the unsophisticated peasants who were an easy prey to the temptation of easy credit.[41] As a result, at the first reverse, such as a crop failure, illness, or death of his cattle, the cultivator was forced to relinquish his mortgaged land to the moneylender. In the early years the subsequent purchaser was usually another thrifty laborer, but gradually the land was taken up more and more by nonagriculturalists to be let out for rent. Table 15 surveys the steady growth in tenancy. The number

[37] Approximately $105 million at the current exchange rate (J. Russell Andrus, *Burmese Economic Life* [Stanford: Stanford University Press, 1948], p. 75).

[38] G. E. Harvey, *British Rule in Burma, 1824-1942* (London: Faber and Faber, 1946), p. 56.

[39] B. R. Peam, *The Indian in Burma*, Racial Relations Studies in Conflict and Cooperation No. 4 (Leabury, Herefordshire, England: Le Play House Press, 1946), p. 16. Quoted in Chester L. Cooper, *op. cit.*, p. 37.

[40] U Tun Wai, *Burma's Currency and Credit* (Bombay: Orient Longmans Ltd., 1953), p. 52.

[41] J. S. Furnivall, *An Introduction to the Political Economy of Burma* (Rangoon: Peoples' Literature Committee and House, 1957), p. 119.

Table 15. Occupancy of land in Lower Burma, 1925–26 to 1937–38

Fiscal year	Total occupied area in thousand acres	Tenanted area as percentage of total occupied area	Area held by non-agriculturists as per cent of total	Area held by resident non-agriculturists as per cent of total held by non-agriculturists
1925–26	10,340	43	27	25
1928–29	10,654	44	29	25
1931–32	10,734	49	38	21
1934–35	10,926	57	46	18
1937–38	11,300	59	47	18

Source: Based on Knappen, Tippetts, Abbett, and McCarthy, *Economic and Engineering Development of Burma,* Comprehensive Report prepared for the Government of the Union of Burma (Rangoon, August 1953), Table VIII–2, p. 130.

of absentee landlords, for the most part Indians and Chinese, increased and tenancy and rack-renting appeared as the pressure for land increased.[42] The cultivator, now liable for rents of up to 40 per cent of the gross output of his land, was even less able to meet his obligations on his seasonal loans.

The contraction of world markets during the Depression of the 1930s imposed financial stringency on the cultivators in Lower Burma as the wholesale price of paddy after harvest declined in 1934 to roughly a third of its 1929 level.[43] Large-scale default on debts and rents resulted in the alienation of land from tenant to landholder, and small cultivator to mortgagor. The Chettyars were reluctant to acquire land, but as land values fell and the number of buyers declined, they had become by the mid-1930s the holders of 25 per cent of agricultural land in Lower Burma, as Table 16 reveals.

After the onset of the Depression, the Chettyars were loath to lend to any but their own tenants, which forced many cultivators to borrow from local village shopkeepers, mainly Chinese or Indians, at rates that amounted to 250 per cent or more per annum.[44]

As a result of the seriously deteriorating situation in agriculture and

[42] J. S. Furnivall, *Colonial Policy and Practice,* p. 87.
[43] Cooper, *op. cit.,* p. 59.   [44] Andrus, *op. cit.,* p. 80.

Table 16. Classification of occupants of agricultural land in thirteen
principal rice-growing districts of Lower Burma, 1930–1937
(000 acres)

Year	Total occupied area	Area occupied by nonagriculturists		Percentage of area occupied	
		Total nonagri-culturists	Chettyars	Total nonagri-culturists	Chettyars
1930	9,249	2,943	570	32	6
1931	9,305	3,212	806	35	9
1932	9,246	3,770	1,367	41	15
1933	9,266	4,139	1,782	45	19
1934	9,335	4,460	2,100	48	22
1935	9,408	4,687	2,293	50	24
1936	9,499	4,873	2,393	51	25
1937	9,650	4,929	2,446	51	25

Source: Report of the Land and Agriculture Committee, Part II, *Land Alienation* (Rangoon: Supt., Govt. Printing and Stationery Burma, 1949), p. 39. These districts produced 75 per cent of Burma's rice and included the area in which the Chettyars did more than 80 per cent of their business outside Rangoon. The discrepancies in Tables 15 and 16 arise from different definitions of Lower Burma.

the race riots of the 1930s, the government appointed a Land and Agriculture Committee to analyze problems in agriculture and recommend measures for the protection of the cultivator. The Tenancy Act of 1939, based on the Committee's recommendations, was intended to lower rentals and provide more security of tenure, by enabling tenants to bring complaints to government officers who were empowered to fix a "fair rent." The Act proved unworkable in the period prior to the Japanese invasion, however, because of the sheer volume of investigations the officials were called upon to carry out.

A Land Alienation Act was passed in 1941 to forbid the transfer of land from agriculturalists to nonagriculturalists, but it was never put into effect. Similarly, the Land Purchase Act, providing for the purchase of land by the government and its resale to agriculturalists, was passed in 1941 just before the Japanese invasion but was never implemented.

The absentee landlords and moneylenders, particularly the Chettyars, have been accused of using vicious methods to enslave the Burmese peasant. The Burmese despised the Chettyars, in part because of the racial and religious distinctiveness of the latter, and also because they were thrifty. The presence of the Indian landlords and moneylenders was a prominent feature of the rural environment because the Indians were willing to take their business into the countryside, not just into the ports and larger towns. Not surprisingly, the dispossessed cultivators came to identify the Chettyars as the source of all their ills. The anti-foreign slogans of the 1930s were largely directed against the Indian landowner, moneylender, and agricultural laborer, but particularly against the Chettyar. "Alien in appearance and habits, the Chettyar was the butt of the Burmese cartoonist, he was depicted as Public Enemy No. 1, and the violence of the mob was deliberately directed against him." [45] The Chettyar did not come to settle in the country, but came to the village on a limited tour of duty, after which he was moved to another village or the head office in Rangoon. He was never assimilated into the local community, as were many of the Chinese.

The Chettyars in fact, however, were efficient businessmen, "the most moderate of moneylenders, indeed . . . honesty itself." [46] They provided much of the capital needed for the development of Lower Burma. The Chettyars and the Burmese cultivators both became unwilling victims of their own business methods. The Chettyars were willing to lend to the cultivators so long as security was available, for periods that had no necessary relationship to agricultural needs or the crop cycle. The Burmese, on the other hand, borrowed more than was prudent and did not always spend it productively.

The Japanese occupation brought an end to the obligation of the tenants to pay land rents and to repay their debts. Most of the Chettyar landlords fled to India, and the Burmese landlords did not press their claims. When the AFPFL came to power after the war, a number of laws were passed to preserve the security of the cultivator. The Tenancy Standard Rent Act (1947) limited the gross rent for paddy land to twice the land revenue, the tax on such land.[47] The Disposal of Tenancies Act (1948) guaranteed the tenure of a tenant so long as he paid the rent, cultivated the land, and had not defaulted in the repayment of agricultural loans. The Burma Agriculturalists Debt Relief Act (1947), cancelled outright all debts incurred before October 1, 1941 and outstanding on October 1, 1946. Moreover, for debts incurred

[45] Harvey, *op. cit.*, p. 55.   [46] *Ibid.*
[47] Amended in 1954 to limit the maximum rent to the land revenue, approximately K. 3.50 per acre.

between October 1, 1946 and the date of the Act, only the principal need be repaid. These laws gave the tenants security of tenure, nominal rents, and reinstated the titles of many cultivators. Many of the Chettyars who had returned to Burma after the war, chose to return home to India for good at this time.

The war and the immediate postwar measures for the regulation of tenancy and the debt relief of the Burmese cultivators removed most of the aliens from control of agricultural land. Although some remained, Burmanization was completed as a result of two later measures, the nationalization of land and the Land Tenancy (Amendment) Act of 1965.

The Constitution of Burma (Sec. 30) vests the ultimate ownership of all lands in the State. The repossession of land from the Chettyars and Burmese and Chinese moneylenders and absentee landlords, and its distribution to the Burmese peasants was always an aim of the nationalist movement, and the Land Nationalization Act was enacted promptly after independence, on October 11, 1948. The Act provided for the nationalization of all agricultural land and its redistribution to Burmese peasants to a maximum of fifty acres per family. The measure was only applied in one township, however, where it was "an almost total failure" due to the "incompetence and corruption of the politicians and officials." [48]

Insurrection and internal insecurity brought an end to further plans for land redistribution until 1953 when a new Land Nationalization Act was passed. During the five-year period between 1953–1954 and 1957–1958, 3,357,000 acres of land were nationalized, equivalent to 17 per cent of the prewar agricultural acreage in Burma. Implementation of the law was suspended in 1958 by the caretaker government, and little progress was made by the following civil government.

There is no doubt that the primary purpose of land nationalization was its contribution to the socialist program of the government, but its contribution to Burmanism became evident when the Government of India sought to intervene in June 1950 on behalf of the Chettyars who were threatened with expropriation under the Act. The Burmese Government subsequently agreed to draw up a schedule of compensation but refused to meet the compensation rates demanded by India. Prime Minister U Nu asked, "Who is the real owner of the land? Is he the

[48] Hugh Tinker, *The Union of Burma* (London: Oxford University Press, 1957), p. 229.

Chettyar with the bloated abdomen? . . . [No] The ownership of the land is held by the constitutionally elected Government of the people . . . In such a case, it is perfectly legal and morally right to take back our land and there is no obligation at all to pay compensation for the expropriated land." [49]

As of June 30, 1963 it was estimated by the government that agricultural rents were still being paid by tenants to 350,000 landlords, about one-third of whom were aliens.[50] In March 1963, however, the Land Tenancy Act transferred the right to allot tenancies from the landowners to local Land Committees, and the 1965 amendment of the Act abolished the payment of rent by peasants using the land for farming.[51]

NATURAL RESOURCES

Along with the nationalization of land, the Constitution provides that all minerals and natural resources shall be exploited by the Union of Burma. The government may grant (Sec. 219) the right of exploitation to citizens of the Union or associations at least 60 per cent of whose capital is owned by citizens. The Constitution also provides (Sec. 23) that private property may be expropriated if the public interest so requires. Under these two sections of the Constitution the timber, mineral, and oil industries have been reorganized since World War II.

Beginning in the latter part of the nineteenth century, Burma had a strict policy of forest conservation, and timber was extracted from the reserved forests only under license or lease. Considerable long-term capital is required for the extraction, milling, and marketing of teak, the major forestry product, since it takes a teak log an average of four years to reach the mill from the time it has been girdled.[52] The prewar industry, therefore, came to be dominated by five large British concerns and an Indo-Burmese firm of somewhat smaller size.[53] These firms operated under fifteen-year leases on payment of a royalty to the government. In 1924 when forest leases were last renewed, their capital investment was estimated at about K. 100 million (approximately $21

[49] U Nu, "Towards a Welfare State," *Burma Looks Ahead* (Rangoon: Ministry of Information, 1953), p. 113.
[50] *Forward* (3), May 1, 1965, p. 2.
[51] *Far Eastern Economic Review*, May 26, 1966, p. 417.
[52] Andrus, *op. cit.*, p. 105.
[53] The Bombay Burmah Trading Corporation Limited, Steel Brothers Co. Ltd., T. D. Findlay and Sons Co. Ltd., MacGregor and Co. Ltd., Foucar and Co. Ltd., and U Bah Oh and Co.

Table 17. Total timber tonnages handled, 1934–1939
(annual average in per cent)

European leases	78.9
Other leases	2.6
Licensees	11.4
Forest Department	6.6
Other	0.5

Source: U.O.B., Director of Information, *Burma, The Fourth Anniversary Yearbook* (Rangoon: Supt., Govt. Printing and Stationery, 1952), p. 36.

million at the current exchange rate). The extent of foreign control over industry is indicated in Table 17.

During the war organized forestry ceased completely, and a great deal of damage was done by indiscriminate logging of the reserved forests. More disastrous was the dispersal and loss of the prewar elephant force of 6,000-odd on which timber extraction in inaccessible areas depended. Following liberation, the five prewar British firms were unwilling to finance the resumption of operations with their own capital until their long-term lease position had been clarified. They formed themselves into a teak consortium, and a partnership was established with the government, under the management of the Timber Project Board.[54] The government contributed working capital and the profits were divided: 60 per cent to the government and 40 per cent to the consortium.

This arrangement came under constant Burmese criticism as being unfavorable to the Burmese interests.[55] As a consequence, nationalization of the forest industry was one of the first measures of the independent government in 1948. The State Timber Board was established in April with "wide powers to control, extract, mill and market forest produce." [56] It took over the operations of the Timber Project Board and was given control of the exports of all kinds of timber by private firms. The plan was to take over one-third of the Big Five's teak concessions in the first year and the rest subsequently. With the outbreak of the insurrection later in 1948, the teak firms were unable to work their remaining concessions. They therefore surrendered all their

[54] The Timber Project Order, August 15, 1945. See Tinker, *op. cit.*, p. 247.
[55] UOB, *Burma, The Fourth Anniversary Yearbook* (Rangoon: Supt., Govt. Printing and Stationery, 1952), p. 36.
[56] *Ibid.*, p. 37.

forests and assets to the government in exchange for 54,750 tons of teak logs.

The objective of Burmanization was cited by U Nu as the reason for the nationalization of the teak firms. "Our immense forest wealth is of world renown," he said, "but it was only the teakwood which enjoyed the prestige, not the people. The enormous profits of crores and crores [one crore equals ten million] of rupees derived from the teak industry were not received by the [Burmese] people . . . [they] went to the British capitalists. For these reasons, we nationalized the timber industry."[57]

Since 1948 the recovery of teak exports under the State Timber Board has been very slow. In the early years, the continued insecurity undoubtedly was responsible. Walinsky, however, partly blames nationalization for "the lack of imagination and boldness" in implementing the recovery program.[58] By 1960, the production of teak had not returned to its prewar level, whereas the production of nonteak timbers, which had remained the responsibility of the private sector, substantially exceeded the prewar figure.[59] In 1963 the Military Government nationalized the private extraction, milling, sale, or export of all timber and placed the industry under the control of the State Timber Board.

In 1936–1937, 35 per cent of the value of Burma's exports came from the sale of oil-well products (mineral oil, candles, and paraffin wax), most of which were exported to India. This important industry was controlled by British firms; 75 per cent of the production and 85 per cent of the refining being in the hands of the Burmah Oil Company.[60] All the skilled technicians in the industry were European, though efforts were made to train Burmese to become engineers. The unskilled labor in the oil fields was mainly Burmese and in the refineries mainly Indian. Although the Burmah Oil Company was credited with enlightened labor relations, it was a primary target of Burmese nationalists who maintained that it was an outstanding example of "economic imperialism," and the first mass political agitation conducted by the Thakins took place on the oil fields in 1938.[61]

The two other important industrial enterprises in prewar Burma were

[57] U Nu, "Towards a Welfare State," p. 85.

[58] Louis J. Walinsky, *Economic Development of Burma* (New York: Twentieth Century Fund, 1962), p. 322.

[59] UOB, *Economic Survey of the Union of Burma, 1961*, p. 19.

[60] Andrus, *op. cit.*, p. 117.   [61] Tinker, *op. cit.*, p. 283.

the Bawdwin mines, producing lead, copper, and silver, and the Mawchi mine, the greatest tungsten mine in the world at that time. Both were British owned, and the technicians were mainly Europeans. Unlike the oil industry, however, very few of the unskilled workers were Burmese, as the mines were remote and the work hard. The unskilled work force was composed mainly of Gurkhas, Indians, and Chinese.

The scorched-earth policy of both the British and the Japanese during the second World War resulted in the almost complete demolition of Burmese oil facilities. Demolition in the Mawchi and Bawdwin mines was less complete, but the main power plants were destroyed in both areas. After the war, reconstruction had hardly begun before almost all the mining activities were brought to a halt by the insurrection.

It would have been understandable if petroleum and mineral extraction had been among the first targets for Burmanization. The firms were foreign-owned and comprised the main industrial undertakings in the country. The Mawchi and Bawdwin mines employed almost no Burmese, and the Burmah Oil Company had been the object of popular nationalist agitation. Ample nationalization powers existed in the Constitution, and popular opinion appeared to favor their nationalization. Yet these firms were not immediately nationalized.

In 1952, U Nu explained that the Burmese government was unable to provide the necessary equipment or funds needed for the reconstruction of these industries, the technical or organizational skills to maintain them, or the worldwide sales organization. But, concluded U Nu, "as soon as we have rehabilitated these enterprises and acquired all necessary knowledge and ability to manage and operate them, we shall nationalize [them]." [62] As a compromise, the Burmese government and the foreign owners set up joint ventures. This solution promised gradual Burmanization, but without the loss of capital and know-how which would have resulted from complete and immediate nationalization.[63]

Greatest success in the rehabilitation of the mining industries has been in oil. Production has not reached prewar levels but domestic output in 1962–1963 accounted for 90 per cent of gasoline, 89 per cent of kerosene, and 76 per cent of fuel oil needs of the country. In No-

[62] U Nu, "Towards a Welfare State," p. 89.
[63] See below, section on private foreign investment for details of joint ventures in the petroleum and mining industries.

vember 1962, the Revolutionary Council offered to buy out the remaining Burmah Oil Company shares (49 per cent) held by the British and to purchase the fixed assets of the associated marketing firms. The takeover was effected on January 1, 1963 in exchange for payments totaling $13 million to be made over two years. Between 1962 and 1965 the remaining joint ventures in the mining industry were nationalized.

The Burmanism measures used in teak extraction, petroleum, and mining enterprises, which were all under alien control during the colonial period, provide an interesting comparison. The European teak firms returned to Burma after the war, but the Burmese were confident of their ability to operate the industry and nationalized the foreign firms during the first year of independence. The petroleum and minerals industries, on the other hand, though as much under foreign control as the timber industry, were not immediately nationalized. Aware that the Burmese were unable to efficiently operate these enterprises without the assistance of the alien owners, Burmanization was postponed by the government, in spite of popular protests. Joint ventures were set up initially to facilitate the transfer of the necessary technical and managerial "know-how" to Burmese. Such enterprises proved short-lived, as nationalization of these industries was completed by early 1965.

ROLE OF GOVERNMENT ENTERPRISE

In common with many other newly independent countries, Burma has experimented aggressively with the public corporation as a means of achieving goals of industrialization, economic growth, and indigenism. Because the successive governments have been avowedly socialist, it is difficult to make a clear distinction between nationalization measures taken to oust alien enterprises from positions of control in the economy and those motivated purely by socialist ideology. State enterprise also was often justified on the ground that indigenous private enterprise was inadequate.

For various reasons, some valid and some less valid, industrialization is regarded by new and less-developed nations as necessary for, or synonymous with, economic development. Burma was no exception to this, and given her aspirations for Burmanism and socialism, the government readily stepped into the role of industrialist. Recourse to directly productive public enterprise undoubtedly was more vigorous than it would have been in the absence of the drive to Burmanize.

A distinction should be made between directly productive enterprises and the public-utility type of undertaking engaged in supplying transport, communications, and electric power services to the public. Some of these services such as inland water transport, ocean shipping, and electric power were provided in Burma by private organizations before the second World War; others, including railways and postal and telecommunications, were operated under government auspices. In both cases the staffing was largely foreign, with British management and a large proportion of Indians and Anglo-Indians at the middle level. All of these utilities were nationalized after independence and foreign staff was gradually replaced by Burmese. Though the contribution to Burmanism was substantial, the nationalization of these enterprises will not be discussed here since the development of infrastructure is now generally recognized as the province of government in both developed and developing countries.

Industrial development in prewar Burma was concerned almost entirely with the extraction and processing of agricultural commodities and raw materials. The country's integration with India meant that Burma specialized in the production of primary products and obtained manufactured goods from India and Europe. Burmese industry had no tariff protection from Indian goods, and the Burmese who had previously traded in local products often lost their markets to Indians and their cheaper machine-made imports. Most of the industry resulted from the collaboration of British capital and Indian labor. The Burmese owned and operated a number of small establishments, but the larger enterprises were alien owned. These included the large European rice mills at the ports and the oil and mining industries. The British company, Steel Brothers, owned a cotton gin that employed about 2,600, a cotton spinning mill with about 1,300 workers, and a cement factory. The major sugar mill was owned by Indians and employed 800 Indian workers.[64]

The advent of independence found the leaders of the new country determined to pursue a vigorous program of industrialization. The first economic plan, The Two-Year Plan of Economic Development for Burma, published in April 1948 included detailed guidance for the setting up of new industries. A rubber factory, two sugar mills, a steel rerolling mill, sawmill, tile factory, paper and chemicals, and spinning

[64] University of Rangoon, Department of Economics, *The Economic Development of Burma* (Rangoon: University of Rangoon, Department of Economics, Statistics and Commerce, undated), p. 37.

and weaving industries were to be established by the government immediately. Progress was halted, however, by the insurrection, which drove the economy back to the output level of the immediate postwar years. Internal security turned for the better in 1950–1951 and the government was again able to grapple with plans for industrial development. In 1951 a British team of economists spent two months in Burma under United Nations auspices and recommended, among other things, pushing ahead with industrialization. This year also saw the arrival of the American team of economists and engineers (the Knappen Tippetts Abbett Engineering Co., with Pierce Management, Inc. and Robert R. Nathan Associates, Inc.) to produce a comprehensive development program. Their preliminary report, which appeared in 1952, strongly recommended the establishment of an Industrial Development Corporation (IDC) which was subsequently brought into being (Burma Act No. 43, of November 1, 1952) and given control of most of the government's industrial program.

The major enterprises set up under the first flush of enthusiasm for state manufacturing industry included a cotton spinning and weaving mill, a brick and tile factory, jute mill, steel rolling mill, three sugar mills, a brewery, cement and pharmaceutical plants, and enterprises for tea packing and sericulture. Of these, the brewery, the cement factory and one sugar mill were nationalized private foreign concerns.[65] Not until 1959 did the government publish the budgets of its boards and corporations and then only for the single year 1956–1957. Walinsky has published more comprehensive financial data for the government manufacturing enterprises, however, which emphasize the unsatisfactory results obtained under bureaucratic entrepreneurship.[66]

[65] The Burma Cement Co., at Thayetmyo, was a subsidiary of Steel Brothers and Co., and in 1939–1940 provided about nine-tenths of the country's domestic consumption. Its equipment was modern and the annual capacity about 60,000 long tons. The engineers were European and the labor force about half Indian and half Burmese. The factory did not begin operations after the war until 1951, was closed part of 1952 and 1953, and was nationalized on August 1, 1954, the owners receiving K. 3.6 million compensation. The Dyer Meakin Distillery and Brewery at Mandalay was nationalized on October 1, 1954 with compensation of K. 980,000. This was an Indian firm and originally set up to supply beer and spirits to British and Indian troops stationed in Burma. The Indian-owned Zeyawaddy Sugar Factory was also nationalized on November 1, 1954.

[66] Walinsky, *op. cit.*, p. 312. See his chapters 17 and 27 for a discussion of the difficulties encountered by these industries. Financial advances by the government to support the pharmaceutical, jute, cotton, steel, silk, tea, and sugar factories totaled K. 228 million ($48 million) between 1952 and the end of 1961.

The country's foreign exchange and other economic difficulties that developed in 1954 and 1955 put a damper on the expansion of state industrialization, and by 1957 the inefficiency, mismanagement, poor planning and lack of co-ordination in the IDC industries was apparent. Faced with the government's apparent inability to operate these enterprises successfully, U Nu announced in June 1957 an abrupt change in policy. Private entrepreneurs including foreign nationals who had been pushed out of commercial fields were encouraged to enter manufacturing.[67] This encouragement, however, had only a slight effect on the ratio of non-Burmese to Burmese ownership of industry which steadily declined after 1958 (see Table 18).

Table 18. Ownership of industries, 1956–57 to 1961–62
(in per cent)

Year Oct.–Sept.	Owned by		
	Burmese	Non-Burmese	Partly Burmese and partly non-Burmese
1956–57	84.98	7.24	7.78
1957–58	83.61	7.80	8.59
1958–59	86.34	5.04	8.62
1959–60	87.44	4.54	8.02
1960–61	89.70	4.60	5.70
1961–62	90.93	3.53	5.54

Source: The Revolutionary Government of the Union of Burma, Central Statistical and Economics Department, *Statistical Yearbook 1963*, (New Secretariat, Rangoon), Table 79, p. 195.

Initially, the Revolutionary Government continued the policy of encouragement to private capital and individuals in industry, and urged both nationals and aliens excluded from the import trade to turn their capital and skills to manufacturing. In January 1963 government policy was abruptly reversed when it was announced that no new private industry, alien or national, could be established thereafter.

The second major incursion of the state into manufacturing activities in order to displace aliens originated in the military services. The De-

[67] Speech announcing the Four Year Plan on June 8, 1957 (UOB, Director of Information, *Premier U Nu on the Four Year Plan* [Rangoon, 1957]).

fense Services Institute (DSI) was organized in 1951 as a soldiers' nonprofit welfare organization. Initially it operated a department store and a book shop for members of the armed forces. Within a few months after the military caretaker government took office in the fall of 1958, the DSI had expanded into many different fields, including manufacturing, and had become the largest business organization in the country. It was stated that the purpose of this expansion was primarily to contribute to Burmanization by successfully competing with alien firms in cases where private Burmese enterprise had failed; by fostering Burmese enterprise; and by itself entering economic activities in which private Burmese had had no previous experience.[68]

After U Nu's return to office in 1960 many of the DSI establishments were placed under the control of the Burma Economic Development Corporation (BEDC), a new semi-governmental enterprise.[69] The BEDC continued to expand under the Revolutionary Council until January 1963 when the corporation and its forty-two subsidiary companies and the DSI and its five scheduled firms were nationalized and transferred to government departments, boards, and ministries.[70] In 1964 the control of these enterprises was centralized in the New Socialist Economic System Establishment Committee.

In its efforts to establish a modern industrial sector the government vacillated between the use of directly productive government manufacturing enterprises, the encouragement of private Burmese enterprise, and the opening of the industrial sector to aliens. Industrialization through public enterprise was discredited because of the failure of so many of the government's early undertakings, and the vacillation in policy contributed to the ineffectiveness of both Burmese and alien private enterprise. In contrast to priorities evident elsewhere, subordination of the goal of Burmanism to that of economic development occurred in manufacturing. To a considerable degree, this is explained by the absence of a substantial industrial sector in prewar Burma which could have been Burmanized following independence as happened in other sectors. By 1963, however, the political pressures for Burmanism and socialism had accumulated to the point that the manufacturing sector was abruptly closed to new private enterprise.

[68] UOB, *Is Trust Vindicated?*, pp. 225, 227.
[69] See *The Nation*, November 14, 1961, p. 1.
[70] The Enterprises Nationalization Law, October 19, 1963. See UOB, *Economic Survey of Burma, 1964*, p. xi.

PRIVATE FOREIGN INVESTMENT

Before the second World War most of the economic development in Burma had been brought about by foreign capital. Agriculture had been commercialized with the help of Indian moneylenders, rice milling and exporting were largely in the hands of Europeans, and mining and oil extraction had been financed by European firms. All the large factories and most of the small workshops were owned by Indians, Chinese, and Europeans, and much of the social overhead capital had been financed through public debt issues held by foreigners. In 1941, Andrus estimated that private foreign investment in Burma totaled £155 million distributed as shown in Table 19.

Table 19. Private foreign investment, 1941
(£000)

Foreign corporations (mostly British)	£ 47,200
Chinese	2,800
Indian Chettyars	56,000
Government and municipal obligations	45,000
Urban real estate	3,250
Indian industrial establishments not included above	1,000
Total	£ 155,250

Source: James R. Andrus, "Foreign Investment in Burma," *Pacific Affairs* (17), March 1944, pp. 90–93.

Almost all the mining, industrial, and communications facilities were destroyed during the war, but the initial pre-independence government was able to persuade some British firms to return and, with some government aid, to spend considerable sums on rehabilitation. Table 20 presents an estimate of this inflow from 1945 until the time the firms were nationalized after Burmese independence.

In British Burma, most foreign firms held monopolistic positions in their respective spheres, and their returns were high. Most of the companies brought in their own skilled personnel and, on occasion, unskilled staff were also brought in from India. In the struggle for independence, antagonism to private foreign business interests became very bitter, and this bitterness is reflected in sections of the Burmese Constitution and in public speeches of high officials in the early days of the Union.

The Constitution (Secs. 218, 219, and 220) limits the ratio and the duration of foreign capital participation in the operation of public utilities to 40 per cent and to 25 years. The same limits apply to the exploitation and development of natural resources, with the additional proviso that an act of Parliament is necessary to authorize foreign participation. The exploitation, development, or utilization of agricultural land is specifically reserved for citizens.

Table 20. Postwar capital inflow through foreign companies
(£ 000)

Burma Oil Company Ltd. (up to 1948–49)	£ 8,019
Burma corporation (up to 1951)	2,782
Mawchi Mines Ltd. (up to Sept. 1956)	1,065
Anglo Burma Tin Company (up to 1955)	40
Steel Brothers & Co. Ltd. (up to 1957)	2,276
Bombay Burma Trading Corporation Ltd. (up to 1948)	75
Magregar Company	9
Irrawaddy Flotilla Company Ltd.	39
Total	£ 14,305

Source: Columbia University, *Joint International Business Ventures in the Union of Burma,* A Research Project of Columbia University. Country Studies No. 4 (New York, February 1959), p. 19. There is no information available of the extent of the inflow of Indian and Chinese capital into Burma during this period. Since few Chettyars returned to Burma after the war, the inflow from India was probably negligible.

Earlier, the Transfer of Immovable Property (Restriction) Act (1947), provided that immovable property (real estate) could not be acquired by a foreigner or foreign company whether by sale, gift, mortgage, or other means, nor could a foreigner or foreign company lease immovable property for more than one year, though the President of the Union could grant exemptions. This law limited the fields open to foreign investors, created inconveniences where the use of real estate was important to the undertaking, and precluded the use of immovable property as security for loans.

Following independence, the government promptly acknowledged the expectation that private foreign investment would make a valuable contribution to future economic development. In an address before the Burma Chamber of Commerce and Industries on December 10, 1948, Prime Minister U Nu said:

Although we are very keen to transform the Union into a Leftist [*sic*] country, we have a firm conviction that it cannot be done overnight . . . it is the intention of the Union Government to accept whatever cooperation it can get from businessmen both foreign and indigenous . . . the Union Government, while according preferential treatment to the nationals, where qualifications are equal, will not refuse to accept the cooperation of foreigners for the mere fact that they are foreigners.[71]

A resolution adopted by Parliament in September 1949 provided inducements to foreign investment, including protection from competition of imports, a guaranteed period in which the firm would not be nationalized, guarantees of the right to remit dividends and to use a firm's earnings of foreign exchange to import capital equipment. In return, a foreign enterprise would be required to train Burmese nationals in technology and administration, and it could not import unskilled labor into Burma.[72]

In December 1953, the Prime Minister reiterated the government's desire for increased private foreign investment,[73] and the President of the Burmese Trade Union Congress, the largest trade union organization in Burma, repeatedly stressed the need for foreign capital and urged the workers to change their attitudes toward foreign business.[74] In spite of these exhortations, the internal insecurity in the country and the sporadic nationalization of private firms made investment in Burma unattractive during these years, especially in view of the high returns available in more stable countries. The response of private foreign capital to the government's invitations was negligible, and there was a net flow of private capital out of Burma as shown in Table 21.

In a renewed effort to attract foreign capital, the government issued an Investment Policy Statement on June 8, 1955.[75] A number of guarantees and incentives were established, and a set of criteria was laid down for appraising investment proposals. The guarantee against

[71] U Nu, *Towards Peace and Democracy*, p. 166.

[72] Donald Wilhelm, "Development and Administration of Industrial Policy in Independent Burma," *Burma Commerce* (Rangoon), October 23, 1953.

[73] Frank N. Trager, *Building a Welfare State in Burma, 1948–1956* (New York: Institute of Pacific Relations, 1958), p. 91.

[74] Columbia University, *Joint International Business Ventures in the Union of Burma*, Country Studies No. 4 (New York, 1959), p. 46.

[75] For the text of this statement see B. C. A. Cook, *Burma, Economic and Commercial Conditions in Burma*, Overseas Economic Surveys (London: H. M. Stationery Office, 1957), Appendix XVII.

Table 21. Net private foreign investment, 1951–1960

Year or annual average for period	Million kyats
1951–1954 (annual average)	− 14.3
1955–1959 (annual average)	11.3
1960	− 50.0
1961	− 13.0
1962	− 2.0
1963	− 73.0
1964	2.0
1965	−
1966	−
Net total	−136.5

Source: International Monetary Fund, *International Financial Statistics* (Washington, D.C.), various issues.

nationalization was made definite, in most cases, for not less than ten years, but most of the other incentives repeated those made earlier and were vaguely formulated. No clear directives were given to government officials to aid them in appraising investment proposals.[76]

The European business community placed the major blame for the laggard response of foreign investment on the ambiguous administration of the announced policy. "Treatment accorded to most foreign capital has not been in accordance with the declared policy of the Cabinet . . . [the failure to implement the policy at the administrative level] has kept away new foreign capital and acted as a deterrent for the existing firms to make any further investment." [77]

During the first decade of Burma's independence, however, the government was successful in retaining in Burma much of the foreign capital, technology, and personnel that were necessary for the continued operation of the prewar oil and mining undertakings by creating joint

[76] Reinhart Kovary, *Investment Policy and Investment Legislation in Underdeveloped Countries* (Rangoon: Rangoon University Press, 1960), pp. 31–37.

[77] *Burma Commerce,* February 3, 1957, p. 1833. This weekly was published by the Burma Chamber of Commerce, until the late Fifties a European-dominated group.

ventures between the alien interests and the Burmese Government. Six of the most important of these joint ventures were the Burma Oil Co. Ltd., the Burma Corporation Ltd., the Anglo-Burma Tin Co. Ltd., Mawchi Mines Ltd., the Martaban Co. Ltd. and Burma Unilever Ltd. The first four of these oil and mining enterprises, were between the government and companies that had operated in Burma before the war. In all except the Burma Oil Co. Ltd. the government acquired at least a 50 per cent interest, and in most cases the joint venture company accepted the requirement of accelerated Burmanization of staff and established training programs for administrative and technical personnel.

The Martaban Co. Ltd., 1953, was a joint venture between a Japanese fishing firm and a private Burmese company. All the Burmese capital, however, was lent by the government. The initial crews of the fishing vessels were Japanese but efforts were made to train Burmese for these positions. Burma Unilever Ltd. was formed in 1958 with 25 per cent of the shares held by the government and 75 per cent by Unilever Ltd. In this case, however, no formal agreement provided for Burmanization or the right of the government to acquire additional shares in the company.

Between 1958 and 1962, although direct private foreign investment in Burma was negligible, there was considerable expansion in the use of joint ventures as the Defense Services Institute formed a number of them with foreign firms, holding stock and sharing profits equally. The Burma International Inspection Co. was formed as a joint venture with the United States inspection firm of INTECO; the Burma National Housing and Construction Co. Ltd. with the Solel-Boneh Co. of Israel, the Sea Fishery Project, a partnership with the Singapore Fishing Co., and the United Coke and Coal Suppliers and General Trading Co. Ltd., a collaboration between the DSI and the Israeli firm of Peham Israel Coal Co. Ltd. Other joint ventures were set up with Japanese concerns for the manufacture of small electrical products, household appliances, and transistor radios and for the assembly of buses, vans, and trucks.

With the advent of General Ne Win's caretaker government in 1958, security conditions improved, and a fresh attack was made on the problem of attracting direct private foreign investment. The Union of Burma Investment Act (No. XLI of 1959) was passed and came into operation together with the Investment Rules of February 1960. The significant additional incentives guaranteed to foreign investors included exemption from income tax for the first three years of operation of an enterprise, exemption from customs duty on machinery and raw materials for the first three years of commercial production, accelerated depreciation allowances, and permission to remit profits and proceeds from the sale of assets or equity.

The law provided for the transfer of profits and repatriation of capital, but a distinction was made between limited companies and partnerships and sole proprietorships. The latter two, the forms in which most Indian businesses operated, were allowed to remit funds abroad only for family maintenance and in amounts based on individual income. In order to repatriate capital, a company was required to show that the capital had in fact been brought into the country, which was impossible for those firms that had been built up through retained earnings. Moreover, if a successful company was sold, the seller was required to inform the exchange control authorities, as their permission to sell was necessary for the seller to repatriate the proceeds.

The passage of the act made little impact overseas. U Chan Tha, Chairman of the Investment Committee, which had been set up to investigate foreign investment proposals, visited the United States, Canada, and Britain early in 1961. In spite of his endeavors he received no proposals from potential investors.[78]

In 1961 the Ministry of National Planning published the Second Four Year Plan for the Union, 1961–1962 to 1964–1965. The desire for foreign investment was reavowed, the incentives and guarantees repeated, yet the Finance Minister, Thakin Tin, announced in the midst of the intensified campaign to attract foreign investment that because of Burma's need for foreign exchange to implement the Second Four Year Plan, British firms would not be allowed to repatriate funds from the sale of their businesses in Burma.[79]

Immediately following the 1962 military coup, it was announced that the existing Investment Act would be continued in force, and vigorous efforts would be made to invite foreign capital to Burma. A month later, however, the Revolutionary Council announced that "to carry out the socialist plans for Burma, such vital means of production as agriculture and industrial production, distribution, transportation, communications, external trade, etc., will have to be nationalized." [80]

---

[78] *The Nation*, January 17, 1961, p. 1. [79] *Ibid.*, September 8, 1961, p. 1.
[80] UOB, *Policy Declaration, The Burmese Way to Socialism* (Rangoon, April 30, 1962).

The reasons for the small part private foreign investment has played in postwar Burma are obvious. On the one hand, the government continually acknowledged the need for foreign capital and made tentative efforts to encourage it. On the other hand, political necessity and economic uncertainty imposed formidable constraints upon the activities of the government to promote foreign investment.

Fearful of allowing aliens to regain economic control of the Burmese economy, the government half-heartedly encouraged foreign investment. Such efforts were ineffectual because foreign enterprises were threatened at the same time with eventual nationalization, restrictions were maintained on the ownership of immovable property, the repatriation of capital, and remittance of funds abroad, and preferential treatment of indigenous business was continued. In 1963, the government finally abandoned its ambivalent and ineffectual policy of seeking foreign investment, nationalized a number of existing joint ventures, and specifically prohibited all further private foreign investment and aid.

THE EXPORT TRADE

Before the Second World War, rice accounted for nearly half the value of Burma's exports. The other major export items were petroleum, teak timber and minerals. British and European firms, of which the largest was Steel Brothers, handled the bulk of the rice export trade through the port of Rangoon. These firms owned the large rice mills in Rangoon, which were worked in the main by Indian migrant labor, and the firms were often also shipping agents. Indians and Chinese owned a number of medium-sized mills and handled some of the rice exported to India. European, Indian, and Chinese firms in Rangoon were grouped into the Rice Merchants Association and were in a favorable position to influence prices paid to Burmese producers.

After liberation, the British established the Agricultural Projects Board to procure and export rice and other agricultural commodities. In 1946 the Board was succeeded by the State Agricultural Marketing Board (SAMB), an autonomous board under the Ministry of Commerce. Its function was to take over the export of rice and to divert to the government the windfall in the postwar price of rice due to strong external demand conditions. Because there was no takeover of visible assets, no compensation was necessary.

The SAMB gradually extended its grip over the trade. In 1948 the

Board bought 16 per cent of the paddy crop of which about 40 per cent was sold overseas through direct government-to-government deals. In 1950 four-fifths of the exportable surplus was shipped by the SAMB and thereafter, with minor exceptions mentioned below, all exporting was done by the Board.[81]

Not only was the SAMB able to get rid of foreign rice exporters, but by its pricing policy it was able to squeeze the foreign mill owners and middlemen. It did this by setting the prices it paid for milled rice up country and at the ports so that they differed by less than the cost of internal transportation. In this way it was able to discriminate against the port mills which were predominantly foreign-owned.[82]

The attitude of the government was well illustrated by a statement made by U Nu in 1952:

Before the war, although the annual profits from rice trading ran into crores, it was not a difficult undertaking. . . . All the activity related to the rice trade . . . was carried out by Burmese themselves. The British merely poured through account books beneath the ceiling fans in their offices. . . . We longed to substitute the British capitalist monopoly of rice trading with State control and operation.[83]

The SAMB was the largest state organization in Burma. By the late 1950s it controlled both the private and public exports of most agricultural commodities. It issued export licenses to private Burmese citizens for products other than rice, including pulses, potatoes, beans, peas, and so forth. It bought milled rice from millers for export. It accepted paddy from the growers at a set price and released it to the internal market as necessary to stabilize the price of rice within Burma. Following 1951 it made loans to millers for the purchase of paddy, to improve mills, and to build godowns (storage sheds).[84]

Since independence, rice exports have been the main source of foreign exchange for Burma, constituting 75 to 80 per cent of the total earned.[85] One writer has estimated that SAMB net profits have amounted to as much as 8 per cent of gross national product.[86] Recent

[81] Tinker, *op. cit.*, p. 258.
[82] Jonathan V. Levin, *The Export Economies* (Cambridge: Harvard University Press, 1960), p. 224.
[83] U Nu, "Towards a Welfare State," p. 63.
[84] Interview with U Than Maung, Zone Controller, SAMB, April 4, 1960.
[85] Union Bank of Burma, *Bulletin,* various issues.
[86] Levin, *op. cit.*, p. 238.

figures, however, indicate that this percentage declined considerably following 1952–1953.[87] Figures are not available for every year, but the current surplus of the SAMB for the years 1957–1958 and 1958–1959 amounted to 5 per cent and 2 per cent respectively of G.N.P.[88] Part of the SAMB surplus went to the government as a "rehabilitation contribution" for postwar reconstruction, and part of it went as current government receipts in the form of income tax and was not earmarked.

The Burmanization of exports has provided the government with a considerable part of its revenue, but the SAMB profits were not passed on to the Burmese cultivators directly. As of 1960 the procurement price for paddy to the cultivator had been the same for ten years, whereas, during this period, the average annual export price per ton of rice and rice products f.o.b. had fluctuated between K. 446 and K. 838. The SAMB buying price for paddy, as compared with prewar, remained below parity with prices of other goods.[89] There have been frequent criticisms of the government for this pricing policy, but the government has justified its stand by pointing to the indirect benefits to the cultivator of land reform, and in rent, tax, and interest rate reductions.

Since its inception the SAMB was noted for inefficiency and corruption at all levels.[90] Consequently, when the Army took control of the country in 1958, major changes were made in the Board's organization and policy. Most important was the suspension of the Board's monopoly in the export of rice and of other government trading activities in rubber, cotton, and teak. Private exports of rice were encouraged except those traded on a government-to-government basis. Private traders were given first priority in the export business, semi-government organizations such as the joint venture corporations received second priority, and state trade organizations came last. The issuance of export licenses for agricultural commodities other than rice was taken out of the hands of the SAMB.

In order to encourage Burmese participation in private rice exports, certain concessions were made to nationals. Since almost no Burmese existed with the necessary capital and competence to enter this business, a commission was offered to any Burmese national who could sell

[87] Union of Burma, Ministry of National Planning, *The National Income of Burma, 1959* (Rangoon, 1959).

[88] UOB, *Economic Survey of the Union of Burma, 1960*, p. 53; *ibid., 1961*, p. 7.

[89] Trager, *op. cit.*, p. 46.

[90] Tinker, *op. cit.*, p. 269–270; Cady, *op. cit.*, p. 630–631; and Walinsky, *op. cit.*, pp. 424–425, 624.

a minimum quantity of rice annually. As further encouragement, the security deposit required of successful bidders for private rice exports was eliminated.[91] An additional incentive was offered in the form of import licenses to the value of 25 per cent of the value of exports.[92] This was reduced to 10 per cent by the returning civil government[93] and withdrawn completely in February 1963. It appears that most of these incentive import licenses were sold by their recipients to bona fide importers at profits ranging from 120 to 175 per cent.[94]

Prior to 1958 the export of several of Burma's less important agricultural commodities had also been controlled by state monopolies. The Rubber Export Corporation, which bought rubber from estates, was set up in August 1955. The export of cotton was the Wholesale Cooperative Society's monopoly, and teak exports were made exclusively by the State Timber Board. During the 1958–1960 military caretaker regime, these monopolies were abolished and the fields opened to private traders to provide competition for the state organizations.

For a time, the Revolutionary Government continued the policy of encouraging private Burmese enterprise in the export of rice.[95] The policy was changed in February 1963, however, when it was announced that all purchases of paddy and rice exporting would revert to the SAMB, which was renamed the Union of Burma Agricultural Marketing Board. This change was delayed, however, and private domestic trade in rice continued throughout the year; private dealers were paid by the government for finding new markets and arranging contracts with foreign buyers.[96] From the beginning of 1964, the entire export trade was taken over by the government as well as the purchase of paddy and the domestic sale of rice; millers received only a milling charge until the nationalization of the rice mills had been completed.[97]

Since independence, the SAMB has been the principal instrument for transferring control of export trade to Burmese. It replaced the alien exporters and received their income. It lowered the returns to the processors and intermediate traders, many of whom were aliens. It has, therefore, been a successful instrument of Burmanism. Some consider, however, that the price has been high.

[91] UOB, *Is Trust Vindicated?*, pp. 206, 210–211.

[92] *The Nation*, January 14, 1960, p. 4.

[93] *Ibid.*, May 24, 1960, p. 1.   [94] *Ibid.*, July 23, 1961, pp. 1 and 6.

[95] *Ibid.*, March 21, 1962, p. 1.   [96] UOB, *Forward* (1), June 7, 1963, p. 5.

[97] *Far Eastern Economic Review*, March 14, 1963; and UOB, *Economic Survey of Burma, 1964.*

Excessive costs and loss of revenue were due . . . to inefficient procurement, poor milling, extra transport, storage and handling charges, pilferage and poor controls generally. . . . While export rice cost S.A.M.B. £28 or £29 sterling per ton in port cities, it was estimated that private millers, operating far more efficiently, could supply export rice in port cities for about £22 per ton.[98]

This price of indigenous control over the country's largest enterprise has been borne by the Burmese with little protest.

The price of nationalizing the marketing of the output of the country's largest industry became increasingly apparent after 1964. Paddy production declined each year from 8.37 million tons in 1964–1965 to 6.53 million tons in 1966–1967, and rice was rationed in several Burmese towns. Rice exports steadily fell from 1.269 million tons in 1964 to 0.600 million tons in 1967, the lowest in this century. Local observers are certain that the disincentive effects of the government pricing and distribution policies are the cause of these shortfalls. The government has not satisfactorily replaced the middleman for the purchase of paddy, and the farmers are either reducing production or not bringing it forward for sale to the government agencies.

THE IMPORT TRADE

With the opening of Lower Burma to rice cultivation and the subsequent expansion of trade, Burma became a market for imported textiles and other consumption goods, as well as for capital goods used in the extraction and processing of raw materials. In common with exporting, most of the import trade was in the hands of foreigners. The bulk of the consumer goods came from India, although in some cases components were imported from Europe and assembled in India for re-export to Burma.[99] These goods were handled for the most part by Indian firms. British importers handled most of the capital goods that came from the United Kingdom and Europe, and Chinese brought in goods that came from China and from Southeast Asia. The Burmese were almost completely absent from the import field; their commercial enterprises being confined almost entirely to petty trading.

With the return of the British to Burma after the war, an organization was set up to distribute essential import supplies in Rangoon and the rural districts. This was the Civil Supplies Board (CSB) which subsequently served as the organization through which the independent

[98] Walinsky, *op. cit.*, p. 425.   [99] Andrus, *op. cit.*, p. 171.

government moved directly into importing. Many of the Indian importers returned to Burma, and it has been estimated that by 1947, Indian business firms and individuals were handling approximately two-fifths of imports by value.[100]

With independence, the import trade became a major target of indigenization as was true elsewhere in Southeast Asia and for the same reasons. Before the war, aliens had had an almost complete monopoly in this sphere and, therefore, feeling against them ran high. It was expected, moreover, that importing was an activity which the Burmese could take over without undue difficulty. Finally, it was believed that Burmanization could be brought about by import licensing which required only a change in administrative procedure. Burmanization of importing followed a familiar pattern as the government moved to participate directly in the importing of consumer goods and, at the same time, resorted to licensing and regulation of private trade with the object of eliminating alien interests.

Early in 1947, following the recommendation of an enquiry committee looking into losses and waste, the government liquidated the Civil Supplies Board. With the coming of independence in the following year, however, the socialist AFPFL government reactivated the organization and it became a wholesale procurement agency on a national scale. It opened distribution outlets in the districts, and took steps to create a system of consumers co-operatives to replace retailers who were predominantly aliens.

The outbreak of the insurrection and consequent looting, however, forced the abandonment of many of the district offices of the CSB, and subsequently, on October 1, 1951, the Board was reorganized as the Civil Supplies Management Board (CSMB). It became the leading agency for the importation of essential consumer goods and some basic materials required for local industry, and was given a monopoly of the importation of sugar, condensed milk and infant foods, cotton and silk yarns, textiles, cement, asbestos and corrugated steel sheets, and tires and tubes. By 1956–1957, CSMB imports represented nearly one-third of the total imports of the country.[101] In addition to this, the Board

[100] M. Sonayl, "Indian Business in Prewar and Postwar Burma" (M. A. thesis, Department of Economics, Statistics, and Commerce, Rangoon University, 1952).

[101] Maung Maung, "The Role of the Union Government in the Finance of Capital Formation in Burma" (M. A. thesis, Department of Economics, Cornell University, 1960); and UOB, *Burma, The Tenth Anniversary Yearbook*, pp. 239–242.

engaged in the purchase and resale of a number of local products.[102]

The government, however, was apparently not satisfied with the role the CSMB was playing in squeezing foreigners out of the import trade, and in January 1957 five Joint Venture Trading Corporations (JVC) were set up. At the time, it was announced that their "primary objectives were the Burmanization of the import trade and the reduction of the price of consumer goods.[103]

Joint Venture Trading Corporation No. 1 was established to import industrial raw materials. The other four were given a monopoly of import licenses for foodstuffs, textiles, building materials, and general hardware, but were expected to compete with each other in these lines. Each corporation had a nominal capital of K. 5 million, of which 52 per cent was supplied by the government with the remainder to come from Burmese nationals. The following year six more JVCs were set up on the same basis, one of which imported industrial raw materials.

The rapid expansion in the share of the import trade conducted by government trading monopolies was supplemented by policies designed to favor Burmese private traders. In 1947 the Imports Control Act provided for import licensing. Initially, the government decided that 60 per cent of the licenses should be allocated to nationals and only 40 per cent to alien firms and individuals.[104] As a result many Burmese import firms were set up with the purpose of obtaining licenses and reselling them to alien importers. Enterprising Burmese were able to sell their licenses for as much as 50 to 100 per cent of the value covered by the license.[105] U Nu reported in 1952 that "the Government would have liked to grant the entire 100% of the import trade exclusively to national businessmen but . . . nationals are finding it exceedingly difficult to even cope with the . . . allocation of 60%. Ninety eight per cent of the indigenous businessmen," he added, "were dependent . . . upon the big British, Indian and Chinese businessmen." [106]

The economic consultants Knappen Tippetts Abbett Co. confirmed this cautious criticism of import licensing when they reported, "The

---

[102] See below, section on retail trade.

[103] *The Guardian* (Rangoon), June 16, 1960, p. 1.

[104] Tinker, *op. cit.*, p. 259.

[105] UOB, *Report of the Commercial Taxes Advisory Committee, 1951* (Rangoon: Supt., Govt. Printing and Stationery, 1952), p. 4.

[106] U Nu, "Towards a Welfare State," p. 84.

granting of licenses without investigation to wholly unqualified persons provided only that they were Burmese nationals, . . . [resulted in] the open sale of these licenses to foreign trading firms, the accompanying favoritism and sometimes corruption, and the maintenance of exorbitant profit margins on scarce commodities—these things are commonly acknowledged." [107]

With the easing of the economic situation during 1950 and 1951, import licensing was relaxed, and some classes of goods were placed on open general license under which they were imported without nationality restrictions. The policy of allocating 60 per cent of licenses to Burmese was maintained on the goods that remained under license, but in 1953 U Nu admitted that despite this support, little success had been achieved by Burmese traders.[108]

The following year the government took several further measures to stimulate Burmese participation. The Registration (Importers and Exporters) Order (1954) provided that no alien firm could be registered as an importer—which was necessary to apply for a license—unless it had been engaged in foreign trade in Burma before independence and unless it was registered under the Burma Companies Act.[109] The same order required that "at least 50% of [a firm's] staff, whose monthly emolument [was] more than K. 500 and at least 75% of its staff whose monthly emolument [was] less than K. 500" be citizens of the Union.[110]

Following 1951 Burma's trading position deteriorated steadily until in March 1955 she was forced to introduce stringent import rationing and to increase the proportion of imports covered by the licensing system. This gave the government an opportunity to further discourage alien enterprises. The return to licensing automatically gave Burmese firms an increased proportion of the import trade, and the proportion of licenses allocated to them was increased to over 60 per cent for many commodities. Tinker reports that the proportion increased to "from 89% (fountain pens) and 88% (textiles) to a minimum of 65% for

[107] Knappen, Tibbetts, Abbett, and McCarthy, *Economic and Engineering Development of Burma,* Comprehensive Report prepared for the Government of the Union of Burma (Rangoon, August 1953), Vol. 1, p. 73.

[108] Tinker, *op. cit.,* p. 262.

[109] Cook, *Burma, Economic and Social Conditions in Burma,* p. 29. The Burma Companies (Amendment) Act required foreign firms to furnish detailed information about their trading activities and costs and profits at various stages of their transactions. This was not required of national firms.

[110] UOB, The Employment of Citizens of the Union by Importers and Exporters Registration (Importers and Exporters) Order, 1954, Para. 20 (1).

books and periodicals. Altogether Burmese firms received three quarters of the import licenses." [111] Many of these, of course, continued to be sold to alien businessmen. Table 22 indicates the rapid contraction in the share of imports subject to open general license and therefore not subject to nationality restriction.

Table 22. Distribution of government and private imports,
1951–52 through 1958–59
(in per cent)

		Private		
Year	Government imports	Total	Open general license	Licensed
1951–52	17.9	82.1	49.3	32.8
1952–53	21.0	79.0	54.9	24.1
1953–54	18.0	82.0	53.8	28.2
1954–55	24.9	75.1	50.1	25.0
1955–56	44.0	56.0	27.4	28.6
1956–57	43.4	56.6	25.4	31.2
1957–58	48.0	52.0	20.9	31.1
1958–59	51.1	48.9	14.6	34.3

Source: U.O.B., Central Statistical and Economics Department, *Selected Economic Indicators* (Rangoon, February and November 1960), Table 8.

Upon assuming office in 1958, one of the first moves by the caretaker government was to take severe measures to "clean up the mess" in the import sector. A vigorous campaign was started to deregister "bogus" importing firms. Of more than 3,000 registered importing firms, the majority were found to be "fronts" for the alien business interests. They were without capital or business experience in the import trade and were making money by the sale of their licenses. About two-thirds of them, mostly Burmese, were deregistered, mainly on the ground of inadequate finance and trafficking in import licenses.[112]

The caretaker government, however, continued to pursue a strong policy of Burmanism, and the Registration (Importers and Exporters) Order of 1954 was invoked to accelerate the training of Burmese nationals in trade and commerce. In addition, the government reviewed the commodity categories under open general licensing, and most items

[111] Tinker, *op. cit.*, p. 272.   [112] UOB, *Is Trust Vindicated?*, p. 216.

were subsequently brought under license, leaving only a few "non-speculative" items on open general license. Finally, the government ruled that effective from June 1, 1960 all agencies for imported goods must be held by Burmese nationals.[113]

The return of the civil regime headed by U Nu brought attacks on foreign importers with renewed intensity. "In the field of commerce and industry, our principal aim will be to divert control in these fields to the hands of nationals to the maximum possible extent." [114] The battle against the "bogus" importing firms continued, and the Bureau of Special Investigation was asked to move in and conduct inquiries into the resale of import licenses.[115] Early in 1962, however, U Thwin, the Trade Development Minister, admitted that no action had been taken against "bogus" firms. "Eighty five per cent of those receiving import licenses sold them to foreigners," he stated. "It was very difficult, however, to catch them red handed." [116]

Accordingly, two moves were made that year to remove aliens finally from the import trade. It was announced on January 30 that the import trade would be nationalized as of March 1, and no new import licenses would be issued to private importers, either Burmese or alien. Goods under open general license and industrial equipment were excepted for the time being.[117] Five new JVCs, in which Burmese nationals could buy shares, were to be set up to handle the nationalized importing. Trade Development Minister U Thwin said "the scheme had for its motive the supplanting of foreign businesses by indigenous ones." [118]

A furor broke out in the trading district in Rangoon, but the government emphasized that under the existing system the imported goods went into the hands of unregistered foreigners, and continued to press its policy.[119] As a result a three day strike was called for mid-February by nine trade associations in Rangoon. A spokesman for the group declared that if the government wanted to Burmanize it should ask the foreigners to pack up and go home. "But it does not have the courage to do so. So, it beats about the bush and preys upon Burmese

---

[113] *Ibid.,* pp. 214–219; and UOB, *The Nine Months After the Ten Years* (Rangoon, 1959).

[114] U Nu, speech of April 4, 1960. *The Nation,* February 15, 1962, p. 1.

[115] *The Nation,* May 24, 1961, p. 1.   [116] *Ibid.,* February 10, 1962, p. 1.

[117] International Monetary Fund, *International Financial Review,* March 2, 1962, p. 65.

[118] *The Nation,* January 31, 1962, p. 1.   [119] *Ibid.,* February 6, 1962, p. 1.

traders." [120] Over four-fifths of the Rangoon importing firms closed. A day later Rangoon retail traders joined the strike, and it was reported that 95 per cent of retail shops and stores were closed.

In the middle of this upheaval, the Army took control of the country for the second time since independence. With the confidence that had been characteristic of the first military administration, the government considered initially that it could utilize import licensing to indigenize the import trade. Consequently, the nationalization plan was suspended for two years. The proposal to set up five new joint venture trading corporations was dropped, and import licenses were again issued to private firms. The day of the foreign importer was finally over, however, as all licenses were issued to Burmese firms, and from September 30, 1962 all foreign importing firms dealing in goods under open general license were deregistered.[121]

After the resignation of Brigadier Aung Gyi in February 1963, the Revolutionary Council changed its policy from the encouragement of a Burmese private sector to one of complete nationalization, including the import trade. By the end of the year all imports into Burma were being handled by the government.

Beginning with independence, the Burmese government has persisted in efforts to eliminate aliens from the import trade. Until 1963, however, such efforts were frustrated by the inability of the Burmese to successfully operate private importing firms in competition with aliens. The civil government apparently was unwilling to prohibit all foreign participation by decree, yet the Burmese trading sector in Rangoon was powerful enough to prevent the nationalization of importing. Only the military government felt it had the power, first, to prohibit alien activity and, second, to nationalize the trade.

RETAIL TRADE

Since British times, there has been a close connection between the import trade and retailing in Burma. The European, Indian, and Chinese importers retailed their goods largely through firms of their own nationality, as a high proportion of prewar imports into Burma were consumed by aliens or by industries owned by aliens who preferred to deal with their own countrymen. "This was chiefly because

[120] *Ibid.*, February 8, 1962, p. 1.
[121] Commonwealth of Australia, Department of Trade, *Overseas Trading* (14), April 21, 1962, p. 177; *ibid.*, June 15, 1962, p. 273.

most Burmans lived in rather primitive rural surroundings, using very little from the outside world except cloth." [122] Imported consumer goods that found their way to the rural districts were sold mostly by Indian traders. Burmese found in the markets and bazaars engaged in petty trading of local produce or handicrafts.

During the Japanese occupation the role of the large British firms was taken over by Japanese concerns, and Burmese mercantile associations were set up to take over a larger part of the retail trade. Upon their return, the British established the Civil Supplies Board and entrusted it with the distribution of essential supplies. The base was thus laid for the government to increase its activities in the internal trade of the country if it desired to do so.

In the economy inherited by independent Burma, alien firms dominated domestic trade. In 1951 Indian firms outnumbered Burmese at every level (see Table 23). European firms were predominantly large undertakings but after independence were few in number.

Between 1950 and 1958 important political and economic pressure groups in Rangoon repeatedly demanded the direct prohibition of retailing by aliens, but the pressure was resisted by the government. During the 1958–1960 caretaker regime, certain Rangoon business chambers insisted that all but "pure" [123] Burmese stock should be excluded from domestic trade. The military government considered such a plan at that time "as a most economically impractical form of ultra-nationalism." [124] Later in the year, however, U Kyaw Nyein, the ex-deputy Prime Minister, maintained that "Burmanization . . . must embrace every commercial activity including small traders, shopowners and artisans," [125] and the platform of the Stable AFPFL for the 1960 elections stated that only citizens of the Union should be permitted to bid for bazaar licenses.[126]

The Second Four Year Plan of the returning civil government in 1960 stated that "national economic policy cannot succeed if distribution is monopolized by the foreigners." [127] It was planned, therefore, that the channels of distribution would be restricted to private Burmese business and the relevant government agencies; the Civil Supplies Management

[122] Andrus, *op. cit.*, p. 172.
[123] This does not include naturalized citizens or their dependents.
[124] *Burma Weekly Bulletin* (8), September 24, 1959, p. 187.
[125] *The Nation*, October 23, 1959, p. 1.
[126] *Ibid.*, November 23, 1959, p. 1.
[127] UOB, *Second Four Year Plan*, p. 104.

Table 23. Dealers (any seller after the importer) registered by the Commercial Taxes Service, November 1949 through May 1951

| | Business turnover | | | | | | | | | |
| | Up to K. 6,000 | | Between K. 6,000 and K. 12,000 | | Between K. 12,000 and K. 18,000 | | Over K. 18,000 | | Total | |
Community	No.	Per cent	No.	Per cent	No.	Per cent	No.	Per cent	No.	Per cent
Burmese	1,021	35	1,003	38.5	428	39	1,390	37	3,842	37
Indian	1,171	40	1,282	49.0	584	52	1,820	48	4,857	47
Chinese	694	24	304	12.0	95	9	456	12	1,549	15
European [a]	16	1	5	.5	1	–	120	3	142	1
Total	2,902	100	2,594	100.0	1,108	100	3,786	100	10,390	100

Source: U.O.B., *Report of the Commercial Taxes Advisory Committee, 1951* (Rangoon: Supt. Govt. Printing and Stationery, 1952).
[a] Includes seven non-European.

Board and its retail shops; Joint Venture Corporation retail shops; and public co-operatives.

The Burmanization of retail trade has not been the result of direct action on the part of the government but rather the secondary effect of the Burmanization of importing and of the expansion of government agencies into domestic trade. As private importing was transferred to Burmese control, alien retail firms were left with empty shelves. This process was facilitated by the nationalization provision of the Constitution under which bazaars in cities, which were owned by Indians for the most part, were "municipalized," i.e., taken over to be run by the municipal authorities.

The Civil Supplies Management Board and the Joint Venture Trading Corporations were primarily government importing agencies, but each organization distributed goods through its own retail shops and, in the case of the CSMB, such shops sold domestic products as well as imports. Total receipts of the CSMB from sales in 1957–1958 amounted to K. 410 million, representing 12 per cent of estimated private consumption expenditure. Of this, K. 238.4 million came from sales to consumers' co-operatives. Aside from the Defense Services Institute, the CSMB in 1960 was the second largest government-owned enterprise, surpassed only by the State Agricultural Marketing Board.

In addition to the CSMB and the JVCs, the co-operative movement and, after 1958, the Defense Services Institute (DSI, later the BEDC) played major roles in retail trade. The DSI first opened its shops to the public in 1958 and continued to expand during the following two years. The majority of the Burmese business community was fearful of the expansion of the DSI, a giant with which they were unable to compete. The DSI maintained, however, that it fostered Burmese enterprise and that only the "profiteering black marketeers" would suffer; that its expansion into the economy constituted Burmanism because it was a public concern taking over from alien interests.

Government retailing was further expanded under the Revolutionary Council until, with the passage of Law No. 28 on September 24, 1963, the People's Stores Corporation, a centralized government distribution enterprise, was established to take over all existing government importing and distribution agencies and to draw up an over-all scheme for the distribution of foreign and domestic goods throughout the Union.[128]

[128] UOB, *Forward* (2), October 7, 1963.

On March 19, 1964, all remaining wholesale businesses, brokerage houses, department stores, general stores, wholesale co-operatives, and co-operative shops in the Rangoon area were nationalized. In April the nationalization was extended to all of Burma.[129]

Burmanization of retail trade has been completed. The price has been shortages and increased costs to consumers, but in a speech to the Lanzin Party late in 1966 General Ne Win indicated that this was a small price to pay for the elimination of aliens from trade in Burma.[130]

BANKING, CREDIT, AND INSURANCE

In prewar Burma the banking sector was predominantly alien owned and operated. The currency was the Indian rupee and the central banking functions were performed by the Reserve Bank of India. The foreign Western-style banks, concentrated in Rangoon, largely confined their activities to dealing in foreign exchange and financing international trade. On June 30, 1941 there were six banks with head offices in the United Kingdom, six Indian, and six with head offices either in China, the United States, the Netherlands, or Japan.[131] Only one prewar Burmese firm managed to qualify as a scheduled bank. It operated in the Akyab District and not in Rangoon.

There were two major groups in Burma who carried on banking organized on Asian rather than Western lines. The Chettyar firms were, of course, very important in the provision of credit. The other group was the Multanis, who came to Burma around 1900 to take advantage of the high rates the Chettyars were offering to current account depositors. From this they entered the banking business, mainly making advances to merchants in the Burma-India trade. In postwar years, however, no Multani banking firm returned to Burma.[132]

Most of the prewar banks reopened their branches after the war. In 1948 there were seventeen commercial banks in operation, by 1956 the number had increased to twenty-four,[133] and by 1960 to twenty-five.[134]

---

[129] *New York Times*, March 20, 1964; and UOB, *Economic Survey of Burma, 1964*, p. xi. All assets including buildings, warehouses and land of the affected enterprises became government property, but the government was not responsible for the liabilities of the nationalized concerns.

[130] *Far Eastern Economic Review*, December 29, 1966, p. 677.

[131] U Tun Wai, *op. cit.*, p. 26. These banks were scheduled banks, that is, those with a minimum paid-up capital and reserves of Rs. 500,000 and which came under the control of the Reserve Bank of India.

[132] U Tun Wai, *ibid.*, pp. 57–59.

[133] UOB, *Quarterly Bulletin of Statistics*, 4th Quarter, 1957, p. 115.

[134] Union Bank of Burma, *Bulletin*, 2nd Quarter, 1961, p. 22.

The majority of these banks were branches of foreign banks. Only six small banks were owned by Burmese nationals in 1953.[135]

Several important laws set the stage for the displacement of foreign banks by Burmese banks. The Transfer of Immovable Property (Restriction) Act of 1947 and the Amendment Acts of 1949 and 1952 undermined the principal of mortgage equity. Indigenous banking houses were not affected, and, therefore, were favorably placed in comparison with foreign banks. Burmese facilities were limited, however, and as a result, financing available against this type of security remained tight.

The government first moved into the banking field in 1947 when the Union Bank of Burma was established to take over most central banking functions. Currency was issued by the Burma Currency Board until 1952, when this function was also handed over to the Union Bank.[136]

Up until 1963, probably the most significant Burmanism measure affecting the banking system was the establishment of the State Commercial Bank in 1954.[137] It was set up to provide commercial banking facilities for the country as a whole, since private Burmese banks had inadequate resources to do so in the forseeable future, and foreign banks, even if inclined to do so, could not fill this role because they were not permitted to accept immovable property as security. Permission from the Exchange Control was necessary before the State Commercial Bank would lend to a non-national, and this was "very difficult to obtain." [138]

The Bank has been very successful. Since it began operation in August 1954, its declared dividends have risen consistently. By June 30, 1959, it had seventeen branches and four sub-branches operating in the districts, and deposits with the Bank represented 49 per cent of the total deposits of all commercial banks in Burma.[139] In June 1960 its loans and overdrafts represented 36 per cent of the total commercial bank advances.[140] All government and quasi-government business is done through the State Commercial Bank. As the main products of the country were handled by state organizations, and as much of the indus-

---

[135] Knappen, Tibbetts, Abbett, and McCarthy, *op. cit.*, Vol. 1, p. 68.

[136] Act No. IX of 1952.   [137] Act No. XXIV of 1954.

[138] Interview with Daw Yi Yi, Economic Intelligence Officer, State Commercial Bank, Rangoon, July 21, 1960.

[139] UOB, *Is Trust Vindicated?* p. 187; and UOB, *Burma, Eleventh Anniversary Yearbook*, p. 325.

[140] UOB, *Is Trust Vindicated?* pp. 186–187; *The Nation*, December 31, 1961, p. 11.

try and commerce was in state hands, the Bank enjoyed an increasing share of the banking business of the country.

The government, under several schemes, also endeavored to create an alternative credit system to replace the Chettyars and other money-lenders who traditionally provided the credit needs of the Burmese agricultural smallholders. Initially, unsupervised agricultural credit was distributed through agricultural producer co-operatives and government loans direct to cultivators made under the Agricultural Loan Act of 1947, but these efforts were discredited by the nonrepayment of loans.

Subsequently, major emphasis was placed on the State Agricultural Bank, established in 1953 and capitalized by legislative appropriation. In 1961 "village banks" which allocate and supervise the loans of the State Agricultural Bank existed in one-fifth of the 12,000 village tracts in Burma. It was announced in 1961 that the rate of repayment of such loans was approximately 93 per cent.[141]

The government also moved into the field of industrial credit. Under the State Aid to Industries Act of 1939 (No. XXIII, 1939) as amended, cash loans or machinery on a hire-purchase basis were made available to enterprises.[142] Subsequently, one of the functions of the Industrial Development Corporation was to issue loans to private Burmese nationals in order to promote and encourage their industrial enterprises.[143] In September 1955, creation of the Industrial Loan Board of the IDC was announced, to carry out the business of extending industrial loans to private Burmese citizens. In October of that year, the IDC introduced a hire-purchase scheme, under which industrial enterprises could obtain machinery on a hire-purchase basis either from the countries with which barter trade was conducted or from Japan as reparations.

To the end of fiscal year 1957–1958, the Industrial Loan Board had extended a total of K. 5.1 million to 28 industrial concerns, and K. 13.4 million worth of machinery for 136 concerns had arrived under the hire-purchase scheme.[144] When the military caretaker government took

[141] UOB, *Burma, The Fourteenth Anniversary Yearbook*, p. 230.

[142] It was required that not less than half the members of any company receiving aid be citizens of the Union, and that the company give reasonable facilities for the training of citizens of the Union as may be prescribed.

[143] See above, section on role of government enterprise.

[144] UOB, *Burma, Eleventh Anniversary Yearbook*, p. 283; UOB, Ministry of National Planning, National Planning Commission, *Progress Report Analysis, Third Quarter*, 1958–1959, p. 43.

office in November 1958, the IDC was subjected to drastic economy measures and reorganization.[145] The main concern seems to have been the recovery of outstanding loans and the blacklisting of defaulters.

Burmanization of the banking system was completed by the Revolutionary Council by nationalizing all private banks as of February 23, 1963. Fourteen foreign banks were operating in Burma at that time. They were permitted to repatriate only the capital they had originally brought into Burma, plus the value of their fixed assets.[146]

Pawnshops have been and still are an important source of credit in Burma, and nationalization remained a prominent policy objective as pawnshops were operated almost exclusively by Chinese licensees.[147] Under the State Pawnshops Management Board Order (1955), the Board was authorized to take over gradually the private pawnshops as their licenses expired. By 1961 the Board was operating eighty pawnshops, twenty-one of which were in Rangoon and its suburbs. There remained, however, almost four hundred private shops throughout Burma still to be taken over.[148]

The Board employed only Burmese nationals and put its own staff into the shops it acquired. The Board, however, was not able to make a financial success of its operations, and between 1955–1956 and 1959–1960 it borrowed K. 15.5 million from the government to cover its deficits.[149] In June 1961 the Board complained that the Chinese pawnbrokers whom it had displaced were taking out moneylenders licenses, and that the state pawnships were finding it impossible to compete with them. The Board asked the government to increase the minimum amount of a loan that licensed moneylenders could make to K. 1,000, in order to eliminate the competition from the Chinese moneylenders.[150] The government agreed to set a minimum of K. 500, and in an effort to increase efficiency, the Board was taken under the control of the BEDC.[151] Direct prohibition ultimately was necessary to eliminate Chinese competition, however, and in 1962 the Revolutionary Council

---

[145] UOB, *Budget Estimates, 1959–60*, Book III, "Estimates of the State-managed Boards and Corporations" (Rangoon: Supt., Govt. Printing and Stationery, 1959), pp. 18–19.

[146] *The Nation*, February 19 and 24, and April 13, 1963.

[147] Harvey, *op. cit.*, p. 53.

[148] Interview with Mr. I. Pershad, General Manager, State Pawnshops Management Board, Rangoon, July 21, 1960.

[149] UOB, *Economic Survey*, 1955–1961.

[150] *The Nation*, March 6, 1961, p. 1.

[151] *Ibid.*, July 17 and October 3, 1961.

passed a Moneylenders Law providing that moneylenders licenses would be auctioned only to Burmese nationals.

Insurance in preindependence Burma was almost entirely in alien hands. In 1940 there were 110 alien companies transacting insurance business, but by 1957 this number had dwindled to 78.[152] Burmanization of this activity was initiated by setting up the government Union Insurance Board (Act No. XVI of 1950) which was given the monopoly to write all compulsory insurance.

In 1951 the government passed a Nationalization of Insurance Companies Act. The life insurance section of the Burma National Insurance Company, a Burmese enterprise, subsequently was nationalized and became the basis on which the Union Insurance Board built its business. The Board was extended important competitive advantages as all policy monies payable under any insurance to the Union Insurance Board were guaranteed by the government. The Board, moreover, was not liable for income tax or super tax whereas, in 1958, a public company paid an income tax of 32 per cent and a super tax of 18 per cent.[153]

The Life Insurance Prohibition Act of 1959 prohibited the writing of life insurance in Burma except by the Union Insurance Board, and the Compulsory Reinsurance Act, passed on March 8, 1961, made it compulsory for all alien insurance companies in Burma to take out reinsurance policies with the Union Insurance Board. Finally, in 1963, it was announced by the Revolutionary Council that from the following year all types of insurance business would be handled by the Union Insurance Board only.[154]

The Burmanization of banks, pawnshops and moneylenders, and insurance companies has followed a common pattern. A government enterprise was first set up to supplant alien firms by providing indigenous competition. The method was only partly successful as private alien insurance companies and banks continued in business and the Chinese pawnshop owners moved into nonbank moneylending. To remove the alien firms the government ultimately was forced to nationalize the banks and the insurance business, and prohibit the entry of aliens into pawnshop and moneylending activities.

[152] Cook, *op. cit.*, p. 40.

[153] Columbia University, *Joint International Business Ventures in the Union of Burma*, p. 48.

[154] UOB, *Report of the Revolutionary Council to the People on the Budget Estimates of the Revolutionary Government of the Union of Burma for 1963–64* (n.d.), p. 22.

LABOR AND PROFESSIONS

With the growth of Burmese rice exports in the last quarter of the nineteenth century, demand rose for coolie labor, and Indian laborers became dominant in the rice mills, river transportation, on the wharves, in the mines, factories, and as the country's menial sweepers. Agriculture remained the province of the Burmese, but by 1938–1939 Indians constituted seven-tenths of the nonagricultural unskilled labor force in Burma. Only 37 per cent of the skilled workers and 31 per cent of the industrial labor force, including mining, were Burmese.[155]

The decline in agricultural prosperity in 1930 began to force an increasing number of Burmese onto the urban labor market in competition with Indians. As the Depression deepened, competition for employment between the racial groups increased, and violence first erupted in 1930 when Burmese laborers were used as strikebreakers against Indians on the Rangoon wharves. Reports of the number killed range from 100 to 500 with about 1,000 injured, most of whom were Indians. Racial clashes occurred again the following year. The Depression and the racial violence turned the tide of Indian migration, until in 1930 and 1931 departures exceeded arrivals by 30,000 and 57,000 respectively.[156]

In July 1938 violent anti-Indian rioting again broke out and spread from Rangoon to the countryside. The report of the Riot Inquiry Committee set up to inquire into the causes of the riots cited the popular resentment over the competition between Indian and Burmese labor as an important contributing factor.

Except for the return of some of the wartime evacuees, the immigration of Indian labor into Burma since the war has been negligible. The restrictions on immigration, the various regulations governing the employment of aliens, the annual cost of registration required of all aliens, and the increasing difficulties that have been placed in the way of making remittances to India have led to the large-scale postindependence exodus of Indians from Burma and the consequent Burmanization of the labor force.

Although the proportion of Burmese in senior positions in the civil service had risen to 70 per cent by 1940, British officers still dominated at the highest levels, and a large proportion of the teachers in high

[155] Baxter, *op. cit.*   [156] Cady, *op. cit.*, p. 306.

schools and the University, the officers in the Medical Department, and employees in the Post Office were Indians.

Upon gaining independence, Burma dismissed all foreign officials from the civil service, although an opportunity to remain was given to a few Indians and Anglo-Burmans who were willing to take out Burmese citizenship. In some departments these mass dismissals gravely depleted the ranks of the top administrative personnel and caused near chaos in the operation of some services.[157] Since independence, entry into the civil service has been reserved for Burmese citizens.

None of the rules having to do with the qualifications and admission to the practice of law in Burma specifically state that the applicant must be a Burmese national.[158] U.C.C. Khoo, Advocate, Rangoon, and the Chief Justice of Burma, stated in an interview with the writer that an applicant would not be accepted by a High Court or the Bar Council unless he were a Burmese national. Such a decision, however, had not been tested by a foreigner as of April 1960.[159]

A person must be a citizen to be eligible for enrollment on the Register of Accountants. The only exception to this is for persons who were on the Register prior to 1939. In 1960 there remained one foreign registered accountant in Burma and on retirement he would be replaced by a Burmese national. One other foreigner had made application for registration in 1959 and had been refused.

Teachers in state schools in Burma are civil servants and as such must be Burmese nationals. In June 1965 private foreign schools were nationalized, foreign teachers were dismissed, and Burmese became the required medium of instruction. In 1967 the never-dormant, anti-Chinese sentiment of the Burmese erupted when students in the nationalized Chinese schools in Rangoon came to class wearing Maoist arm bands and badges in violation of the prohibition of political activity in the schools. Rioting broke out and Chinese property was damaged or destroyed. Relations with China deteriorated; all Chinese aid projects were frozen or taken over and all Chinese aid technicians left the country. Since the incident, a steady stream of Chinese emigrants have returned to China.

[157] Tinker, *op. cit.*, p. 153.

[158] Cf., The Bar Council Act, India Act No. 38, 1926, as amended by Burma Acts No. 23, 1940; No. 32, 1947; No. 9, 1951. Legal Practitioners Act, India Act No. 18, 1879, as amended by Burma Act No. 27, 1940. See also *Rules and Orders of the High Court of Judicature of Rangoon*, Ch. 1, Advocates.

[159] Interview with U C. C. Khoo, April 4, 1960, Rangoon.

As a result of the Indian evacuation during the war, the number of doctors employed by the government fell from 650 prewar to 400 in 1951. The output of the Medical College of Rangoon University was very small, about twenty or thirty doctors a year, and in 1952 the government recruited three hundred doctors from India and Pakistan on temporary contracts of from three to five years. They were posted to remote areas of the Union where the need was acute, but where Burmese doctors refused to go, and "it was made clear that they [would] be dismissed immediately Burmese nationals [were] available to take their place." [160] These Indian doctors, in fact, were dismissed before the expiration of their contracts. Subsequently, although Burma faced a critical shortage of doctors to man its health services, she remained unwilling to recruit foreigners for these positions.[161]

Until mid-1963 there were no restrictions on resident aliens practicing as private doctors, provided they were qualified, but at the end of June the Revolutionary Council announced that foreign nationals would no longer be permitted to practice medicine in Burma. The rule affected 178 Indians, 1 British, 8 Pakistanis and 5 Chinese. Many of these doctors had received their training in Burma and had practiced there all their lives. The effective date of the new regulation was set only two days after the surprise announcement, but on an appeal by the Indian Embassy, the government granted an extension to the end of the year.

Restrictions against the practice of professions by aliens are widespread. Such restrictions are not abnormal when compared with those existing in many Western countries. They are abnormal when related to the inadequate medical and educational services for which the government is responsible and which cannot be staffed at present by trained Burmese.

Summary

Economic nationalism in Burma has demanded persistent efforts by the state to transfer ownership and control of the economy to the Burmese, and to increase the share of welfare generated that goes to

[160] Tinker, *op. cit.*, p. 215.
[161] UOB, *Burma, Eleventh Anniversary Yearbook*, p. 178.

nationals. The belief is widespread that alien enterprise, because it is alien, is not identified with the national interest and has not in the past, and will not in the future, promote the national interest.

Burmanization has been the major and most consistent economic policy in independent Burma. It has been the avowed goal of all leaders; the process was climaxed in the early 1960s by xenophobic measures of the Revolutionary Council. It has been pursued despite erratic changes in policies of nationalization and industrialization; despite balance of payments difficulties and the recognized need for foreign capital; and at the expense of short-term economic growth and the economic welfare of large sectors of the indigenous population. One knowledgeable observer has said that "of all policies pursued by the Burmese Government, Burmanization was, historically and psychologically, the most deep rooted and most powerfully motivated." [162]

The integration of a plural society into a national society is the concern of political nationalism. The elimination of racial distinctions in economic specialization, whether by assimilation or by the removal of the alien groups that hold economic control, is recognized as necessary for the integration of the plural society inherited from colonialism into the national society. In gaining independence the Burmese assumed political power but predominant economic power remained with the alien minorities which had controlled the colonial economy. Burmanism has been an effort to integrate political and economic control in Burmese hands.

Unlike economic nationalism in the Philippines and Thailand, Burmanism has been ideological and nonpragmatic. Indigenism in Burma arose because of features of colonial development, particularly the juxtaposition within the capitalist system of successful alien entrepreneurs and unsuccessful Burmese peasants. Once indigenism became an accepted ideology, however, it lost its economic roots and was pursued without regard for changing economic and political conditions.

Independent Burma was established as a socialist state, and nationalization has been used to Burmanize many sectors of the economy. Moreover, in the sectors not initially nationalized, government enterprises, rather than private Burmese business, have been more effective in competing with alien enterprise.

The ambivalence that has characterized Burmese nationalization

---

[162] Walinsky, *op. cit.*, p. 493.

policies has reduced the effectiveness of Burmanism. In conjunction with efforts to industrialize, the major nationalization measures were implemented in two periods which were separated by an interval of disillusionment with these policies and, in a number of cases, their relaxation. Immediately upon gaining independence, the export trade, forestry, land, and the major utilities were nationalized. This process was resumed in 1954 with the nationalization of three private industries taken over under the IDC. In the meantime, the government made strenuous efforts to create an indigenous entrepreneurial class which could compete effectively with alien enterprise. Private Burmese firms were given preferential treatment in importing and manufacturing, but the effect of such concessions was undermined as the private beneficiaries were forced to compete with government enterprises.

Given the political commitment of independent Burma to socialism, the government was never really convinced that a Burmese entrepreneurial middle class should or could arise. Attempts were, therefore, made simultaneously to engage in nationalization and to create an entrepreneurial class, but with little success in either direction. By the mid-fifties the government had become disillusioned with the efficacy of socialized industry as the means to economic development and advocated the transfer of some nationalized undertakings to private hands. Rice exporting was even opened to private enterprise by the first Ne Win government, with appropriate preferential treatment for indigenous firms. Burmese private enterprise continued to suffer, however, from the competition of government undertakings and from the continued threat of nationalization. Under these circumstances, private Burmese enterprise made little contribution to Burmanism.

During this period, the government also carried on a half-hearted flirtation with private foreign investment. With the decline in world rice prices in 1953–1954 and the decline in foreign-exchange reserves, some efforts were made to encourage the inflow of private foreign capital, and this invitation remained open until 1963. At the same time, however, no realistic efforts were made to create a suitable climate for such an inflow as the basic commitment to nationalization and Burmanism remained evident.

The failure of the Burmese elites in their efforts to create a private indigenous entrepreneurial class while retaining their commitment to socialism resulted in the gradual accumulation of frustration which was compounded by the obvious capacity of alien enterprises to survive and by the lack of economic development. During the first year in office of the Revolutionary Council government this frustration was contained, but in 1963 it was released by an abrupt and wholesale nationalization which climaxed the heretofore sporadic and hesitant steps toward socialism and Burmanism. An estimated 300,000 aliens fled Burma in the next two years.

Economic growth in Burma during the decade of the fifties was hampered primarily by the insurrection. Output per capita in constant prices and rice exports had not reached their 1938–1939 levels by 1962. Yet, part of the cause of this lag was the removal of foreign factors from the economy, particularly enterprise, technology, and capital, and the maintenance of inadequate incentives to the cultivators as a result of the pricing policy of the state rice marketing monopoly. More recently, between 1961–1962 and 1964–1965 exports of rice fell from 1.8 million long tons to 1.3 million tons. Timber exports declined by 16,000 tons, metals by 5,000 tons, other products by K. 7 million, and crude oil output dropped by 20 million gallons. After 1964 shortages resulted in rice rationing in several major towns and rice exports fell to 600,000 tons in 1967. The economic adjustments of the Revolutionary Council following 1962 were made to rid the economy of aliens and, in Ne Win's own words, "to give back to the Burmese people their national birthright." [163] The short-run cost in foregone output is clear.

The stated aim of the independent government was to increase the welfare of its citizens, yet in two important cases, those of cultivators and consumers, Burmanism measures have led to obvious deterioration in measures of aggregate welfare. There exists a consensus among economists knowledgeable of postwar Burma that rice price policies contributed to a decline in welfare of the cultivators compared with prewar and compared with other sectors of the population. Until the imposition of price controls by the caretaker government, consumers of imported goods paid inflated prices occasioned by the control of a large section of the import trade by quasi-government corporations. The beneficiaries of Burmanism have been the bureaucratic elite, both civil and military, and the cost has been borne by the cultivators, private commercial interests, or consumers in general.

The aim of Burmese indigenism has been the removal of aliens and not their assimilation, especially since the hardening of the exclusive

[163] *Far Eastern Economic Review*, November 10, 1966, p. 289.

policies of the Revolutionary Council. In the short run, the removal of aliens has opened positions of leadership and control to the Burmese, who in many instances, were unable to compete with alien factors of production. In the longer run, it is hoped and expected that the filling of these openings will provide the Burmese with the opportunity to gain the training and experience necessary to pursue economic development effectively.

It could only have been expected that the Burmese, imbued with resentment against aliens that accumulated during the colonial period, would resort to policies to rid their economy of alien economic domination. Independence for the Burmese will be consummated only insofar as economic control is reintegrated with political power. In Burma, as in other countries of Southeast Asia, the pace of economic development has been subordinated to the requirement that the inherited colonial economy be transformed into a national economy.

5

THAILAND*

The Environment of Policy

Each of the countries of Southeast Asia is distinctive in important aspects, but Thailand is unique in that she was never a colony.[1] This historical fact is manifested in distinctive attitudes, social processes and sensitivities. In spite of such differences, Thailand shares common goals with her neighbors, including those of economic nationalism. In her own case, underdevelopment goes far to compensate for the ab-

* The author's debt to the University and especially to the Cornell Southeast Asia Program exceeds that noted in the foreward to this volume. Much of our knowledge of Thailand is due to the pioneering scholarship done under the Program's auspices in that country. Of particular value has been the research of G. William Skinner on the Chinese Community. David A. Wilson and Herbert Phillips read this study at earlier stages and provided helpful suggestions—E. B. A.

[1] For the sake of uniformity throughout this study, "Thailand" is used as the name of the country. This is the present official name. Some references quoted here refer to the country as "Siam" which was its name, especially in foreign languages, for long periods of time. All accessible sources, both in Thai and in English, whether primary or secondary, published or unpublished, were consulted and were supplemented by interviews in Thailand and elsewhere. The footnote references give the English version of a source whenever a reliable English version exists. Unless otherwise specified, all quotations and page references of acts, royal decrees, notifications, and ministerial regulations are from the English version of the Royal Thai Government Gazette as published by International Translations, Bangkok, hereafter referred to as GOT Gazette. In the transcription of Thai names I have conformed to the phonetic system as outlined in the Journal of the Thailand Research Society of March 1941. In some cases, where the spelling of a name is well established through prolonged usage, it is reproduced in that form even when its romanization may differ from the above system. Names and terms that are part of quotations are cited in their original form.

sence of a colonial past, and the process of indigenism displays features similar to those found in other countries in the area. Economic nationalism in Thailand, as elsewhere in Southeast Asia, reflects the presence of a substantial alien minority displaying superior entrepreneurial talents and the adoption by the indigenous elites of Western concepts of nationalism.

There are special difficulties in unearthing Thai policy measures designed to discriminate against resident aliens, especially the Chinese, many of whom are citizens or are long-time residents of the country. Formal policy measures are often deliberately ambiguous, particularly when their legitimacy is doubtful, as in those cases where they discriminate between citizens. Ambiguity also arises in the need to avoid uncomfortable complications, such as might arise with foreign countries. Seldom have the Chinese been explicitly identified in laws directed against them, and occasionally administrative actions have been taken without explicit legal authorization. To understand Thai economic nationalism, we must, therefore, go beyond formal policy pronouncements and beyond the wording of laws, court decisions, and executive regulations. Such documentary evidence has to be supplemented by identification of administrative deviations from the formal aspects of policies, as well as administrative implementation in the absence of law.

Foreign powers stripped Thailand of most of the areas inhabited by non-Thai over which Thailand claimed suzerainty at various periods of her history. As a result, the Thai population is relatively homogeneous and shares essentially the same language and culture. The two major groups that diverge from this uniformity are the unassimilated Chinese and the Malay Muslims of the south. The hill tribes and Vietnamese refugees also diverge from this uniformity but are of minor importance. There is, of course, the separation prominent in developing countries between the rural and urban societies, the latter being represented, by and large, by Bangkok.

There are also differences, minor in terms of cultural diversity, between the four regions. The central region, which is the most densely populated, consists of the wide alluvial plain on both sides of the lower reaches of the Chao Phraya River. The northern region lies around and between the major tributaries of the Chao Phraya. The southern region consists of the mountainous isthmus running from Burma to Malaya.

The fourth region is the dry plateau of the northeast, which is the most economically depressed area of the country.

The way of life in these regions is fairly similar, subject to variations dictated primarily by differences in rainfall and terrain. What is probably more important, however, is that until the last decade or so, with the exception of Bangkok, life for Thai outside the government bureaucracy has not changed substantially for several centuries. During the last hundred years there has been a wide movement of people into the central plain and a great increase in rice production, largely in response to the incentives of expanding foreign markets. Yet the techniques of rice production have been little changed since earliest times. So long as there were empty areas, people moved in, cleared the forests, and established in the new surroundings replicas of the communities from which they came. This continuity in the way of life has contributed to the homogeneity of Thai culture and stability of Thai society.

The Thai value system, as distinct from that of the unassimilated Chinese and the Muslims, is inseparable from Theravada Buddhism. Practically all Thai are Buddhists, and their conception of its teachings is a major factor in their lives. Virtually every village has its Buddhist temple and monks, and the activities of all status groups are directly or indirectly connected with Buddhism. This does not necessarily mean that every action or attitude cloaked in Buddhist terminology necessarily is of pure Buddhist origin.

The Buddhist content of Thai culture emphasizes the primacy of personal values over communal ones. Few commitments or obligations to pursue abstract social goals are expected, and Thai Buddhism does not encourage strong commitment to the sustained hard work required for the establishment and operation of modern commercial and industrial undertakings. The Thai value highly those who are quick to take advantage of opportunities when these present themselves, but it is a rare Thai who actively creates such opportunities or who will cooperate with others in such an endeavour. Accelerated changes in Thai values, especially over the past decade, however, have been accompanied by a growing number of Thais who display economic initiative.

Buddhism has played another important role in connection with the process of modernization in Thailand. Serving as the major integrative force for the Thai culture, it prevented the encroachment of Christianity. Insofar as the adoption of Christianity might have been a major vehicle for Europeanization and modernization, Buddhism served as a barrier to development.[2]

For all practical purposes, the modern history of Thailand begins with King Mongkut (Rama IV)[3] who reigned from 1851 to 1868. More specifically, it starts with the so-called Bowring Treaty of 1855 with Great Britain. As a result of this and subsequent treaties signed with other Western countries, the power of Thailand to levy import duties and inland taxes was severely curtailed, as was her jurisdiction over foreign residents. The major immediate objective of the Western powers in securing these treaties was to minimize the interference with commerce. As for King Mongkut, available evidence suggests that he made these far-reaching concessions by choice more than as a result of British pressure. He realized the implications for Thailand of changes that had occurred in the international power relations and sought to maintain the independence of his country through concessions and gradual Westernization. From that time, Thai national leaders have served as innovators in the gradual modernization of Thailand.

The Bowring Treaty posed a major challenge to the Thai political system. The limitations it placed on access to tax bases imposed far-reaching changes in the methods of financing government and placed constraints on the absolute power of the king. Extraterritoriality for foreigners severely limited Thai legal autonomy and implied a denial of the competence of the Thai authorities and questioned the quality of Thai justice.[4]

Economic changes subsequent to the Bowring Treaty converted the economy of Thailand from a subsistence-dominated and self-sufficient economy into one oriented toward foreign trade with consequent extension of monetization. The major change resulting from the opening up of the country to external trade was the vast increase in rice production and trade. Rice exports increased from a yearly average of approximately 54,000 tons in 1857–1859 to a yearly average of 1,543,000 tons in

[2] This point was made in a slightly different way by Cora DuBois. See her *Social Forces in Southeast Asia* (Cambridge, Mass.: Harvard University Press, 1962), p. 30.

[3] Rama is one of the honorific titles given to the kings of the present dynasty (after the mythical Indian hero by the same name). For convenience, Western-educated King Wachirawut (Rama VI) introduced the method of referring to the kings according to their historical sequence.

[4] See David A. Wilson, *Politics in Thailand* (Ithaca: Cornell University Press, 1962), pp. 4–5.

1930–1934,[5] a total that was not surpassed until 1961. The increase in rice exports was accompanied by related internal changes. As Thai farmers specialized in rice, production of other subsistence-oriented crops such as raw cotton which was processed into cloth by farm families declined. Recent years have witnessed impressive increases in the production of other crops, including maize, kenaf, and tapioca. As in the case of the initial development of rice production, the latter-day changes have resulted mainly from external demand conditions.

All of Thailand's exports have been primary products. The ethnic Thai have concentrated primarily on rice growing and, to a lesser extent, on the new crops. The other major exports—tin, teak, and rubber—have been produced and exported primarily by non-Thai, especially Chinese. Moreover, even the rice trade, as distinguished from rice production, was in Chinese hands. This dominant position of the Chinese in most nonfarm occupations had been both a result and a cause of the failure of entrepreneurship to develop among the Thai.

The Chinese were already prominent in commerce and mining prior to the Bowring Treaty. The new economic opportunities opened in Thailand by the expansion of trade, the continuing political disorder and economic privation in China, and, on occasion, active recruitment by the Thai government which needed labor for various projects, brought in increasing numbers of Chinese immigrants. In a few cases the immigrants took over certain handicrafts formerly in the hands of Thais.[6] In most cases the functions provided by the Chinese had not existed before in Thailand and were a by-product of the expanding

---

[5] Converted from Table III in James C. Ingram, *Economic Change in Thailand Since 1850* (Stanford: Stanford University Press, 1957), p. 38. It should be pointed out, however, that the expansion of rice *production* was much smaller. Also, in the initial period there were other exports that did not experience rapid expansion as did rice and some ceased to be traded.

[6] Although all Thai were subject to *corvée* service up to six months a year, most farmers were rarely called for duty, primarily because of the poor quality of their work. In fact, Chinese laborers were welcomed because they were more dependable as wage laborers. Such labor was needed in the construction of the railways and the dams undertaken by the Thai government toward the end of the nineteenth and the beginning of the twentieth century. The services of Thai craftsmen, on the other hand, were in great demand and consequently they were usually taken for the full term of the *corvée*. This disadvantage was given as the reason for the diminished attractiveness to the Thai of these occupations. The Chinese, on the other hand, were not subject to the *corvée*. See Bruno Lasker, *Human Bondage in Southeast Asia* (Chapel Hill: University of North Carolina Press, 1950), pp. 103 and 284; and Ingram, *op. cit.*, pp. 17–18.

trade. The following quotation, written more than thirty years ago, summarizes the results of this process of development.

> The rice grower has always remained Siamese, and the Chinese have not, as yet, made any attempt to oust him from that basic position. But the rice dealer is Chinese. So are the rice-miller and all his coolies. So is the boat builder, an important handicraft in a country where the rivers and canals form the highroads. So are the pawnbrokers, the tailor, the bootmaker, the dyer of cloth, the furniture maker, the iron-smith, the market gardener, the fish dealer, the old tin can collector and the hawker. One can go on adding to the list, almost ad infinitum, but I have no wish to weary the reader with a recitation of almost every craft known to man. Suffice it to say that, in practically every form of manual labor, the Chinese hold the field, and the Siamese sit by, watching all the requisite services of life being performed by the uniformly impersonal, very vociferous, but intensely industrious celestial.[7]

The Thai government, unlike the individual Thai, was busy introducing changes. King Chulalongkon (Rama V, 1868–1910) sought to accelerate the modernization his father had started. Among other measures, he undertook the building of railways, the reorganization of the government machinery on functional lines, and the adoption of the form, although not entirely the substance, of Western administrative procedure. He introduced postal services, nontemple schooling, all-weather roads, and so forth. His tours, unprecedented for a Thai monarch, of the major centers of European colonization in the Far East, which he made as a boy-king, left a deep impression on him and help to explain many of his actions as a ruler.[8]

One of the most important of his governmental reforms was the introduction of a central government budget in 1892. These budgets, which were audited and published, revealed an unhealthy revenue structure which the Thai government repeatedly cited in later years as an argument for revision of the treaties with the foreign powers.[9] The

[7] Reginald Lemay, *Siamese Tales Old and New* (London: Noel Douglas, 1930), p. 166.

[8] Based on Prince Damrong Rachanuphap, *Khwam songcham* (Bangkok: Klang-witthaya Press, 1951). See Wilson, *op. cit.*, pp. 6–7.

[9] Ingram reports that in the early 1890s, "The two direct taxes, land tax and capitalization tax, accounted for only 8–12 per cent of total revenue. The opium monopoly and gambling farms accounted for about 40 per cent, while commercial services and the royalties on mining and forestry yielded only about 5 per cent of total revenue. The other major sources were excise taxes (15 per cent), inland-transit duties (5 per cent), and customs duties (12–15 per cent). Of the customs revenue, export duties made up about two-thirds, import duties one-third.

latter responded only reluctantly, however, and the revision and ultimately the abolition of the treaties became a dominant Thai foreign policy objective.

In the meantime, the concern of the Thai kings for the maintenance of Thai independence was demonstrated by their extreme reluctance to incur foreign debts or to allow substantial foreign investments. In their determination not to provide foreign powers with pretexts for intervention, the Thai authorities pursued conservative financial policies. For similar reasons, they sought to change the image of Thailand from that of a backward country and exerted efforts to reduce their dependence on such tax bases as the opium regie and gambling.

The succeeding kings, Rama VI and Rama VII, Wachirawut (1910–1925) and Prachathipok (1925–1935), sought to continue the general policies established by Rama IV and V but they were of lesser stature. Changes in goals and policies in the reigns following that of Rama V reflected changes in the nature of the external challenge and also the differences in education and in the personalities of the kings. The only external moves of consequence were the decision of Rama VI to join the Allies in World War I and the revision of the foreign treaties in 1925–1926.

The real challenge to the Thai kings came, however, from internal forces that emerged largely as a result of the modernization of the civilian and military bureaucracies initiated by the monarchs. This was especially true of the reforms in the internal administration and in the educational system, which increased the number of educated Thai recruited from outside the small royal elite. As a result, the conflict between the theory of divine monarchy and the administrative requirements of a Western-type governmental structure became inevitable. Students returning from abroad were particularly prone to note the archaic nature of the absolute monarchy. The growing discontent, primarily among the small but important group of young officials and officers, finally erupted in a *coup d'état* in 1932, which terminated the absolute monarchy in favor of a constitutional regime which relegated the king to the role of constitutional monarch.

The onset of the new regime, however, did not bring about the major social and economic changes sought by some of the coup promoters.

The rates of both export and import duties were fixed by treaty, as were the rates of land tax and inland-transit duties. Furthermore, virtually all *new* taxes were forbidden by the treaties" (Ingram, *op. cit.*, p. 177).

Thus when Nai Pridi Phanomyong (called Pridi) attempted to introduce a development plan involving nationalization of land and capital, it was turned down as "Bolshevist." In fact, the first two post-coup Premiers, Mano (1932–1933) and Phahon (1933–1938), by and large followed policies pursued by the kings before them, although the tempo of change was accelerated. Expansion of the educational system and the introduction of Western administrative paraphernalia continued apace. The major difference was the replacement of the royal princes, who had held the high governmental positions, by new men.

The rise to premiership, in December 1938, of Luang Phibunsongkram (called Phibun) marked the beginning of a strongly nationalistic regime.[10] He was the most durable of the post-revolutionary Premiers and stayed in power from 1938 to 1957, except for a four-year interruption between mid-1944 and April 1948. His main accomplishment during his first premiership was the introduction of extreme nationalism, largely a copy of European and Japanese versions of Fascism. In the years immediately before and during World War II, various measures were taken against aliens, especially the resident Chinese. Yet the Thai version of nationalism, tempered by traditional Thai-Buddhist tolerance, was much less sinister than its prototypes.

The leading intellectual in the coup group was Pridi. After he was cleared of the suspicion of being a communist, he served in ministerial posts under Phahon and Phibun. The policies he pursued in these posts bore little resemblance to his initial and controversial program, and his tenure in office was memorable for the final abolition of all the unequal treaties. Upon the Japanese invasion of Thailand in 1941,[11] he withdrew from the cabinet to become a regent of the boy-king, Ananda-Mahidon, Rama VIII (1935–1946), who succeeded Rama VII following the latter's abdication. While serving as regent, Pridi was active in organizing the anti-Japanese underground. In July 1944, he engineered the overthrow of the Phibun government and installed as Premier another promoter of the 1932 coup, Nai Khuang Aphaiwong. Pridi remained the leading political personality in the new regime which installed a succession of prime ministers. Early in 1946 Nai Khuang, who had been reinstalled as Premier, was removed by Pridi

[10] He had been a leading figure among the young military promoters of the coup of 1932. He achieved national fame in 1933 when he repulsed a royalist counterrevolution and was nominated as the Minister of Defense in the Phahon government.

[11] Phibun would not, or could not, resist the Japanese invasion but joined Japan in declaring war against Britain and the United States.

who assumed the premiership. On June 9, the young king was shot under mysterious circumstances. Pridi was accused of complicity in his death and had to leave office two months later. When his rival, Phibun, who headed the military group, executed a coup on November 8, 1947, Pridi fled the country and has been in exile ever since, the last several years in Communist China.

An abortive navy revolt in 1951, which was suppressed with the help of the army and police, brought into prominence two new figures who played major roles in suppressing the revolt. One was the director-general of the police department, General Phao Sriyanon, and the other was General Sarit Thanarat, the commander of the army units stationed in Bangkok. The competition between these two younger personalities dominated the Thai political scene following 1951 as Phibun was progressively reduced to the role of arbiter between them.

In early 1955, Phibun made a world tour from which he returned with the declared conviction that true "democracy" such as he saw in the United States and Great Britain should be introduced to Thailand. His attempt to do so was not very successful, and there are doubts as to whether it was really sincere.[12] Subsequently, Phao became very active as the organizer of the government party, while Sarit became increasingly cool toward both Phao and Phibun. The latter two were strongly implicated in the elections of 1957, and the suspicion was widespread that their party had rigged the results. Sarit, who had taken no active part in the elections, led the army in a coup on September 16 of that year and Phibun and Phao fled the country. Sarit's deputy, General Thanom Kittikhachon, became the Prime Minister after new elections. His government was short-lived, however, as in October 1958, Sarit returned from medical treatment in the United States and became Premier in what amounted to a benevolent dictatorship. He died in December 1963, and Thanom was returned to the premiership.

The political structure of the Sarit government was not significantly different from other Thai governments after 1932, especially those controlled by the military, which was true of most governments. There was, however, a significant change in policies toward economic development and foreign economic participation. During the Phibun era, the emphasis was on the nationalization and "Thaification" of alien

[12] Cynics allege that Phibun's conversion to democracy was an opportunistic recognition that the introduction of real democracy was the only safeguard that might prevent his being toppled from power by one of his younger rivals through a coup.

enterprises and on direct government participation in industry. Persistent ineptitude and corruption, however, minimized the contribution of the government industries to economic development. Their value was restricted, for the most part, to the recognition they communicated to the Thai that industrial production, commerce, and finance were legitimate occupations to which they could aspire.

Sarit's approach was different. For him and his colleagues economic development took precedence over narrower nationalist objectives, and policies encouraging foreign private investments were implemented from the beginning of the new regime. A National Economic Development Board was established and in 1960, it inaugurated a six-year economic development plan. In May 1963, a new Ministry of National Development was created.

The process of modernization was continuing steadily, however, irrespective of the leader of the government and in spite of the somewhat confusing political situation. The absorption of new ideas was rendered easier for the Thai because, throughout Thailand's modern history, most changes have been initiated, modified, paced, and channeled by their own leaders. Smooth as this process has been, however, Thailand could not escape entirely from stresses produced by the intrusion of alien ideas and institutions. Elements of modern superstructure were grafted on the broad traditional base of Thai society and culture faster than they could be fully absorbed. This is particularly true of the flood of new influences that have become evident since World War II and which tax the capacity of the Thai leadership to maintain earlier patterns of control. The inflow of unintegrated foreign ideas and institutions has contributed elements of psychological conflict and uncertainty. These are probably less intense than in former colonies but are still important.[13]

---

[13] It is my feeling that some scholars attribute an unwarranted adaptability to the Thai personality. For example, Mosel says that the Thai succeed in keeping the conflicts inherent in modernization "at psychological arms-length." His clinical studies of fifteen members of the Thai administration elite "reveal considerable ability in distinguishing between self, and 'modern' roles" (James N. Mosel, "Role and role behavior of Thai Administrators," paper presented at the annual meeting of the Eastern Psychological Association, Philadelphia, March 1964.) Although the writer does not have data with which to refute Mosel's findings, it is not clear, however, how general is the alleged adaptability of the Thai personality and the extent to which it is a characteristic of the increasing number of "nonelite" persons exposed to modern influences. During the few periods when free public expression was permitted, there were clear signs of discontent and confusion of ideas.

This picture of the old interspersed with a spattering of the new, and of uncertainty and plasticity, is reflected in the Thai social structure. In contrast to the popular conception of "traditional societies" as having a feudalistic structure or being composed of castes, the Thai society has few ascribed roles and has been described as a "loosely structured social system." [14] This characteristic of Thai society has been increasingly prominent since the 1932 *coup d'état*, but was substantially true of the society prior to that time.[15] The exceptions were the kings and, to a lesser extent, the hereditary princes (descendents of kings), but even at the level of succession to the throne the rules have not been rigid. Similarly, although prior to 1932 the hereditary princes were likely to secure high posts in government, this was by no means automatic. The special privilege of this group, moreover, was mitigated by the rule that each succeeding generation of princes lost part of its "princehood." The decline culminated with the fifth generation which reverted to the status of commoner. This, and the fact that recent kings have been monogamous, makes the Thai royalty, as a class, an insignificant departure from the generalizations above. At present, being of royal origin carries social prestige but is of little significance in political and economic matters.

While there is no disagreement with the assertion that Thai society is casteless, the question whether it is also classless is controversial.[16] The disagreement arises from the ambiguity of the concept of "class" rather than from divergent images of Thai society. The term "class" has

[14] This phrase originates with J. F. Embree in his article "Thailand, a Loosely Structured Social System," *American Anthropologist* (52), 1950, pp. 181–193.

[15] Besides age, and birth in the case of royalty, one's status has been an achieved status and almost invariably has been synonymous with one's position in the government bureaucracy. Historically, these positions and the equivalent statuses depended on the judgement of the king or his close subordinates. According to this system, called *sakdi-na*, every position was given a numerical value, associated in ancient times with the granting of land by the king, which indicated clearly one's position in the society *at the particular time*. Such positions were not established for life and were not transmitted by inheritance. Although the children of high officials undoubtedly had greater access to prestigeful positions, there were no formal barriers to status mobility. Available evidence indicates that there was considerable mobility both up and down the status ladder.

[16] For recent observations, see Lucien M. Hanks, Jr., "Merit and Power in the Thai Social Order," *American Anthropologist* (64), December 1962, especially p. 1252; Lauriston Sharp *et al.*, *Handbook of Thailand* (New Haven: Human Relations Area Files, 1956), pp. 162–170; and G. William Skinner, *Leadership and Power in the Chinese Community of Thailand* (Ithaca: Cornell University Press, 1958), pp. 18–19.

acquired a connotation of rigid stratification and of clashes of interests. Classes conforming to such an image have never existed in Thailand. Evidence is accumulating, however, that classes in the traditional pattern are coming into existence.

The only concrete organized social groups of significance in the country are the government bureaucracy, the military services, and the rather loosely organized Buddhist "church." The latter, however, has never sought or possessed political or economic power. There have been no other permanent organizations such as political parties, economic interest groupings, and the like, of political significance outside the government bureaucracy.[17] This absence of group structure permeates down as far as the family. In Thai society the extended family does not exist as a corporate kin group, and even the nuclear family is a rather loose affair. Such characteristics help to explain the spatial mobility and land settlement during the century following 1850.

In seeming contradiction of the distinctive individualism of the Thai, one finds that Thai society has a very definite status hierarchy. Thai society, past and present, has been structured on superior-subordinate relationships, fixed in terms of status levels but fluid in terms of the individuals occupying them. This hierarchical structure analogous to military structure, reflects the fact that most nonfarming Thais have been government officials. In such a system, the personal credentials are of little importance as compared to the position one occupies. Prior to 1932, the king, when nominating a person to a position, bestowed upon him not only the title of his rank but also a new name. With the assumption of a new position a person acquired a new personality, as it were, and subsequently behaved accordingly. One's family origin before stepping into a new position is generally regarded as irrelevant.[18] By the same token, the position and status of the individual are not secure and one has to be alert for means to maintain and improve

[17] It is suggested by Wilson that the weak need for affiliation is one of the principal explanations for the indifference to Marxism among the Thai. See David A. Wilson, "Thailand and Marxism," in Frank N. Trager (ed.), *Marxism in Southeast Asia* (Stanford: Stanford University Press, 1959).

[18] A conspicuous exception was Pibun during the last few years of his premiership, when he was repeatedly referred to by the newspaper *Siam Rath* as Nai (Mr.) Plaek, his former, commoner name. Luang Phibun Songkram was his king-given title name. This was done intentionally by the editor, Prince Kukrit Pramot, presumably under the assumption that by reminding the readers of the low origin of the Premier his prestige would be hurt. This was unusual behavior and probably reflected Kukrit's own obsession with his princely origin.

them. The higher one's position, the more largess he requires for distribution to supporters to ensure his tenure in that position.

The kind of insecurities and fluidity discussed above are not shared by the numerically dominant Thai farmers and some other nonelite groups. The farmers are hardly divided into classes, however defined. Some farmers are better off than others, but seldom are the differences great enough to warrant treating them as belonging to distinct social classes.[19] The village headmen are farmers like the rest of the villagers and their position as headman is neither permanent, nor necessarily honored.[20] The way for the farmer to achieve a significant change in his status, therefore, is to leave the village for town, specifically for Bangkok. However, although there are no formal barriers to mobility up the social scale, the farmer's chances for improvement in status are poor because of lack of connections, education, and other relevant experiences. Most of the persons in high places who originated in the villages are those who left at a very young age. The military schools have been an important springboard for such people.

The farmers have little direct political influence and are not represented as such in the National Assembly. This does not necessarily mean that the government is not concerned with their welfare. The important point to emphasize in the present context is that there is no organized group representing the interests of the farmers as a "class" at any level of government. This is significant since the farmers make up the majority of the population,[21] and because almost all of them are ethnic Thai.

The remainder of the rural population comprise craftsmen, store owners (who are often farmers), and middlemen. Most of the latter are Chinese who move between villages and have their permanent abode in the larger centers. Because they are Chinese and because they are not organized into functional interest groups, their overt political

[19] In crowded villages, particularly near Bangkok, class differentiations have begun to appear. Some farmers have acquired more land than they can cultivate without hired help or sharecroppers. Others tend to become landless because of land fragmentation and end up as sharecroppers if they stay in the village.

[20] Michael Moerman's work among the Thai-Lue of North Thailand revealed a low regard among the villagers studied for the position of headman. Although this is not universal, it does emphasize the point that the position of headman does not automatically carry an improvement in status.

[21] According to the 1960 census, 74.6 per cent of the population resided in agricultural households and 81.3 per cent of employed persons aged eleven years and over worked in agriculture.

influence is limited. Nonetheless they occupy a key position in the economy and some of them, especially the rich ones residing in outlying areas, are quite influential. Their importance is evident in their durability in the face of persistent official attempts to displace them.

In the urban areas, the bottom of the social pyramid consists of the unskilled workers, *samlor* (tricycle rickshaw) drivers, house servants, and the like. These Thai have no political articulation although some of them, like the *samlor* drivers, have been used by politicians. Most unskilled workers are migrants, temporary or permanent, from the farms.[22] Employment for wages is a recent phenomenon among the Thai and hired labor is poorly organized and exerts no political influence.[23] Strikes have been limited to disputes over labor conditions, with labor frequently requesting intervention of the government to mediate and arbitrate disputes. Politically insignificant also are the Chinese laborers and the numerous other poor Chinese, many of whom are foreign born, who are primarily engaged in petty trade such as hawking. Many of these Chinese are either members or beneficiaries of Chinese organizations such as benevolent societies organized by dialect groups.[24]

Artisans and shopkeepers are almost exclusively Chinese. It is tempting to classify them as *petits bourgeois* but the validity of such characterization is limited by the fact that they are not considered, nor do they consider themselves as a class. Moreover, most of them are "dynamic" in the sense that they are always alert to exploit opportunities to shift to more profitable functions. The status relevant for them is derived from their position as the head of the family and their role in the Chinese community. The very successful among this group adopt Thai names and seek active involvement in Thai society and public affairs, either directly or through connections with Thai political leaders. Some of them continue to serve concurrently as leaders of the Chinese community.

[22] For an informative study of the *samlor* drivers prior to their eviction from Bangkok, see Robert B. Textor, *From Peasant to Pedicab Driver,* Yale University Southeast Asia Studies, No. 9 (New Haven, 1960).

[23] Labor unions in Thailand were organized by and maintained with the patronage of personalities in high government positions. Unions have been banned since 1958.

[24] These and many other aspects of the Chinese community in Thailand are discussed by G. William Skinner, *Chinese Society in Thailand* (Ithaca: Cornell University Press, 1957); and *Leadership and Power.*

The Thai population does not have a *petit bourgeois* class of any significance. There are Thai petty traders but they are primarily members of farm families, mostly women, who come temporarily to the city to sell their produce. There are also a few independent Thais, mainly in occupations officially barred to aliens and, since World War II, the importance of Thais in such fields as banking and insurance has increased.

Except for these, and the slowly growing class of the professionals, newspapermen, and those connected with large Occidental firms, virtually all other urban Thai are government employees. Their income and status are determined by the rank they hold in the civilian or military bureaucracy or in state-owned enterprises. Many professional people, such as university professors and physicians who, in most other noncommunist countries, would be outside the government, are civil servants in Thailand. The postwar period also has seen the increasing wealth and importance of Bangkok landlords. The influx of foreign businessmen and foreign aid personnel has driven up rents on urban real estate, and since only Thai can own private land, this process has created a small affluent group.

The upper strata of the urban Thai provide the nearest equivalent to political "public opinion" that exists in Thailand. These Thai also serve as the "seed bed" from which the members of the ruling political elite are recruited. As opposed to the old, largely excluded, royal elite, comprised primarily of princes, the new elite, which holds power, is composed of the top military commanders, the highest civilian bureaucrats, and the very wealthy. These subgroups are not mutually exclusive and high office in the army or the police, for example, is often a step toward riches. Wilson subdivides what we called the "new elite" into two tiers. At the top are some ten to fifteen persons

who do or could dominate the ruling class and the country as a whole by manipulating the various political forces. This group includes senior military commanders, a few leaders of great reputation gained in the revolution of 1932 or in the interplay of politics since, and perhaps two or three men around the throne. At any given time there have never been more than six or eight such men in power.

As to the second tier,

It is made up of perhaps 1,000 persons including military officers mostly of general rank, special grade public servants, prominent members of parliament, some princes and some particularly powerful businessmen. While the top group dominates, it is only through their manipulation and control of the second group that they gain, hold and use power.[25]

The old elite, the aristocrats and princes, have exerted little influence as such since the revolution of 1932. However, some of them hold high government positions and/or own substantial property and enjoy the influence derived therefrom.

The Buddhist "priesthood," the Sanggha, while enjoying high prestige, has neither political nor economic power. In Thailand, unlike neighboring Burma and Ceylon, the "hierarchy" of the "church"[26] and its prestige were not challenged by disruptive colonial authorities. Consequently, the monks in Thailand tend to adhere to their strictly religious roles and do not interfere in political affairs. The successive constitutions, moreover, have disenfranchised every "priest, novice, monk or clergy." The "Patriarch" of Thai Buddhism is a functionary of the state, and all church property is held and administered by the government on behalf of the church.[27] Such conditions severely limit the capacity of the "church" to exert independent political and economic power.

Most Occidentals belong economically and socially in the high stratum, but their political importance, if any, is simply a function of the amount of pressure their respective governments can exert. Unlike many Chinese, they cannot properly be considered a part of domestic society.

The 1932 *coup d'état*, although it is called "the revolution," was a mild affair. It was by no means a pervasive social upheaval and its primary achievement was the shift of power from a declining royal elite to a new elite composed primarily of middle-level government and military officials of commoner origin. The new regime was in part a formal confirmation of an already evolving process and at the same time an instrument for further political changes. The fact that the *coup d'état* was bloodless and that its promoters sought to legitimize it

[25] Wilson, *Politics in Thailand,* p. 60. Although minor changes have occurred since Wilson drafted this description, the general picture he presents is still valid. It is too early to judge whether the new constitution scheduled to be adopted in mid-1968 will substantially modify the distribution of political power described above.

[26] I put these terms in quotation marks because their Christian connotation is scarcely appropriate for referring to the loose organization of Thai Buddhism.

[27] A Buddhist priest is not supposed to own any property.

by royal endorsement, after the proper apologies, confirms the narrow base of the change. It is not surprising, therefore, that the constitutional framework was artificial, reflecting concepts of democracy absorbed by the promoters during their studies in the West, rather than any social demand by the Thai society for such a regime.

The first provisional constitution divested the monarchy of its traditional legislative and executive powers. The legislative power was officially vested in the National Assembly, which changed in form and sanction with every new *coup d'état*. The executive became vested in the cabinet or council of ministers. Cabinet members did not have to be members of the National Assembly, though generally they were. The cabinet was nominated formally by the king and was responsible to the Assembly. In practice the ruling group formed the cabinet and the power of the Assembly to control it was very limited. During most of its life, the Assembly was unicameral with half of its members elected and the other half nominated, officially by the king but in fact by the cabinet. For intermittant periods between 1946 and 1952 it was bicameral with a Senate elected by the lower house, or, in the 1949 constitution, appointed by the king. The power granted the cabinet in most of the constitutions to nominate half of the assembly members assured cabinet control over the Assembly.

The "Interim Constitution" promulgated in January 29, 1959, and still in force at the time of writing, established a Constituent Assembly for the purpose of drafting a new constitution. The members were appointed, officially by the king, in fact by the government. Until the drafting of the new constitution is completed, it functions concurrently as the legislative body, substituting for the abolished National Assembly. This has little meaning in practice, as the cabinet is in complete political control of the country.[28]

Since practically all coups have resulted in the abrogation of the existing constitution, whether "temporary" or "permanent," this amounts in practice to the absence of a constitution. Yet it is quite significant that the pretense of having a constitution has been observed. Such behavior reflects a mixture of genuine belief in the importance of having a constitution, together with the need to legitimatize the existing government. With the abolition of the concept of divine kingship in 1932, a substitute mode of sanction had to be created. Therefore, once a coup is successfully executed, it is always meticulously legitimatized through

[28] For a fuller discussion of the constitutions and the functions of the various governmental bodies, see Wilson, *op. cit.*, *passim*.

special acts giving amnesty to those who took part in it—and who violated existing laws by doing so—as well as providing rationalizations for the coup.[29]

The judiciary, though largely independent of the executive, has not proven an effective barrier against changes in the constitutions. Otherwise it provides fairly adequate protection to nationals and their property, especially in cases not involving the government or very high officials. The frequent proclamations of emergency laws prevent similar protection in political cases. These deficiencies notwithstanding, the judiciary is a stabilizing force in an otherwise fluid situation.

Another stable institution is the bureaucracy, which is highly centralized and apolitical, and has transferred loyalty to the successive governments. This has contributed to its stability because new men coming to power have not felt a need to make changes, except for a few positions at the top of the bureaucracy, to ensure their retention of power.

For administrative purposes the country is divided into 71 *changwat* (provinces), which in turn are divided into 411 *ampoe* (districts). The districts are subdivided into *tambon* (communes), each composed of some ten to twenty *muban* (villages). The heads of units below the district are not members of the government bureaucracy, however, but are elected locally. The provincial governors (*khaluang*) and the district officers (*nai ampoe*) by contrast, are professional civil servants of the Ministry of Interior. They are assisted by representatives of various other ministries and departments in handling such matters as education, police, and agriculture.

Following the revolution of 1932, a Civil Service Commission was established and it standardized, largely on British lines, the methods of personnel recruitment, selection, examination, promotion, and grading.[30] In spite of the existence of the Commission, however, promotion is still largely dependent upon one's superiors and their interests. This, coupled with the respect and obedience toward superiors that sub-

---

[29] See, for example, the *Act to Indemnify Promoters of the coup d'état B.E. 2490* of December 23, 1947, *GOT Gazette, 1946–47*, pp. 75–76; and the *Act of Amnesty for those who seized National Government Power on 16th September, B.E. 2500* of September 26, 1957, *GOT Gazette, 1957*, p. 599.

[30] James N. Mosel, "Thai Administrative Behavior," in William J. Siffin (ed.), *Toward the Comparative Study of Public Administration* (Bloomington: Indiana University Press, 1959), p. 319. The first civil service law, however, was enacted in 1928. See Robert L. Pendleton, *Thailand* (New York: Duell, Sloan and Pearce, 1962), p. 26.

ordinates are expected to observe both in the formal structure of bureaucracy and in society in general, curtails initiative among bureaucrats. The nature of the Thai bureaucracy is of special interest because it is involved in more fields than is the case in most other noncommunist countries. For example, the universities, all communication facilities, most hospitals, and various industries are operated by the government, and the officials in most of these institutions are civil servants and are graded accordingly.

With a docile population, rubber-stamp National Assembly, and obedient bureaucracy, the real power rests with the group institutionally represented by the Cabinet. Major shifts in power since the revolution have, almost without exception, resulted from *coups d'état,* and effective challenges to the particular group in power can come, as things stand now, only from another group within this same "new elite." As there are no permanently organized parties that articulate the interests of Thais outside this elite, it is the strength of the various inside groups that determines who will be in control. Since the military maintains the only continuously functioning power-oriented organizations, government has consistently been in the hands of some military group, with the exception of a comparatively short period at the end of World War II.[31]

This picture is complicated by at least two further factors. First, the military itself is not monolithic, and there are interservice rivalries between the army, navy, air force, and the police and even within each of these. Second, is the need recognized by these factions to distribute favors and bribes to secure the votes of members of the National Assembly during periods when the Assembly is permitted to function.

These factors encouraged corruption in high places as the particular group in power had to practice favoritism to secure and maintain the support of enough of the other groups to stay in power. This favoritism often took the form of contracts and monopoly concessions granted without concern for efficiency and experience. Similarly, heads of government departments were permitted to operate economic enterprises without adequate legislative controls and with uniformly poor results. There has been little overt opposition to this state of affairs either from

[31] During the last decade, especially since 1958, the stature of the king has been increasing. This was actively encouraged by Sarit, who was not convinced of the prospects for Western-style democracy in Thailand. One writer goes so far as to question whether any future coup can succeed in the face of opposition by the king. See Donald E. Nuechterlein, "Thailand After Sarit," *Asian Survey* (4), May 1964, p. 848.

within or from outside the bureaucratic elite. This reflects the absence of organized avenues for civilian protest, as well as the longstanding tradition that officials receive tribute for services rendered. This tradition is further strengthened by the Thai Buddhist belief that authority exercised by and the benefits accruing to an individual exercising authority belong to him rightfully by virtue of his deeds in present and past incarnations.[32]

The partial Westernization of "those who count" does not serve as a barrier to corruption and may have aggravated it. The sanctions and restraints of the traditional values have weakened, while the restraining mechanisms operating in the Western social and cultural environment have not yet struck deep roots among the partly Westernized Thai.[33] It thus appears that "favoritism" and "corruption" are inevitable among the culturally transient elements of Thai society, and many of those in control are of this element. These phenomena are not likely to disappear until new social forces and a new system of values compatible with the new circumstances impose appropriate restraints on the behavior of officials.[34]

One symptom of the shallowness of the Westernization of Thailand is the absence of political ideologies. Before the 1932 revolution, political parties with platforms and ideologies were literally unthinkable. At the time of the first *coup d'état*, a pamphlet describing the objectives of the promoters of the coup was distributed. Its contents consisted more of a series of alleged grievances than a coherent platform.[35]

[32] Overt acts morally proscribed by Buddhism might be an exception.

[33] Siffin suggests that the "modernization" and "nationalization" of the Thai bureaucracy proceeded much faster than did changes in the values of the society generally. With the removal of the traditional authority of the king as the head of the bureaucracy, the nonmodernized values of the society reasserted themselves in bureaucratic behaviour and explain the weakness of "nationality" and "productivity" in favor of bureaucratic self-interest. See William J. Siffin, *The Thai Bureaucracy, Institutional Change and Development* (Honolulu: East-West Center Press, 1966), pp. 135–145.

[34] The regime of Marshall Sarit following 1958 saw some reduction in overt cases of corruption. For example, by eliminating the pretense of having to secure the agreement of the National Assembly, the need to bribe the members was eliminated. The basic factors discussed in the text, however, will require a long time to change. The scandal that erupted over Sarit's large estate and the doubtful sources of this wealth dealt a severe blow to efforts of the government to cut down corruption.

[35] A student of Thai political behavior at the time of the 1932 coup insists that the meaning of democracy was by no means clear or interesting to the pro-

Shortly thereafter, Pridi, the political theorist among the civilian promoters of the coup, drew up a comprehensive plan for "national economic policy." It proposed that the government should nationalize all industries and agricultural land, put all citizens, excepting professionals, on its payroll, and thereby provide social security for all. As already explained, the plan was rejected by the more conservative elements, primarily the military men, as *"bolshevist."* Since then no comprehensive ideological platform has even been advanced.

Political parties following the initial coup have been *ad hoc* groupings around prominent personalities. A few groupings, however, have developed the rudiments of political ideology. One such group comprises the scattered admirers of Pridi, primarily disgruntled intellectuals, many of whom used to be his students or friends. It is difficult to determine whether they have a common ideology and what it might be. They can hardly be vocal at this juncture, because association with Pridi, who has been in exile in Communist China, might be dangerous.

Another group is composed of those favoring Nai Khuang Aphaiwong. Although this group is called the Democratic Party, like other Thai "parties" it does not have a permanent party machine nor clear membership. To the extent that it has an ideology, it is liberal in the classical sense of favoring free trade and competition.

A somewhat greater degree of persistence, both organizational and ideological, was displayed during the 1950s by a group of Assembly members elected from the depressed Northeast. Although even this group adjusted pragmatically to current political winds, its members, by and large, have voiced semi-socialistic ideas and have tended toward neutralism in international affairs. Whatever ideology this represents, it is at best half-baked, and so far as nationalism is concerned, they seem to differ from the official position only in greater emphasis on the supposed danger of Western domination.

The only possible exception to the absence of permanent political parties possessing clear-cut political and economic ideology is the Communist Party. It has been underground for so long, however, that it is difficult to assess its numerical strength. The prevailing opinion among Thai officials is that most of its members are Chinese. During

---

moters. He ascribes the failure of the constitutional regime to this lack of ideological commitment or understanding. See Thawatt Mokarapong, "The June Revolution of 1932 in Thailand: a Study in Political Behavior" (Ph.D. thesis, Department of Government, Indiana University, April 1962), pp. 6 and 17.

police raids conducted in 1959 and the following years, however, evidence was uncovered to suggest that Thai are by no means absent from its ranks.[36] At present, the impact of the Communist Party on public opinion and policy is negligible.

The influence of these groupings never amounted to very much. Although Khuang was four times Premier, he never held office for more than a few months at a time and always as a front man for those holding real power behind him. The only functionally relevant "ideology" has been the official one. As ideology it is amorphous and shifting, although a core of Thaification has persisted through the confusing shifts in power. Pridi's blueprint was rejected, but its emphasis on the need to replace the aliens by nationalizing trade and industry has survived, albeit in a milder form.

The origins of economic nationalism as a quasi-ideology can be traced back to the first decade of the present century. The incident that served to focus Thai attention on the dominance of the Chinese over the economy outside of subsistence agriculture was the Chinese general strike and riots of 1910. The immediate cause of the strike was a law imposing taxes on the Chinese, who theretofore were subject to a negligible tax burden. While the change would have imposed the same burden on the Chinese taxpayers as on the Thai, the former chose to use their economic strength to resist the change.

The strike proved to be a grave mistake as it served to open the eyes of the Thai to the complete dominance of the Chinese in trade and manufacture, both of which came to a standstill during the strike. The fears of the Thai ruling elite were aroused by the evidence of Chinese solidarity vis-à-vis the Thai and their ability to mobilize their economic strength on a nationwide scale. A few years later, in 1914, a series of strongly anti-Chinese articles was published. These articles were written by King Wachirawut (Rama VI) under the pen name, "Asavabahn." These articles had few apparent results, however, either at the level of official government policy statements or of concrete action. It was left to the instigators of the 1932 revolution to evolve a nationalist ideology inspired by Western concepts of nationalism and constitutionalism.

[36] According to Coughlin there were actually two communist parties in Thailand, one Chinese and one Thai. See Richard J. Coughlin, *Double Identity, The Chinese in Modern Thailand* (Hong Kong: Hong Kong University Press, 1962), p. 182.

The Nature of Thai Indigenism

MINORITY POLICIES AND ASSIMILATION

Only two minorities, the Chinese and the Malays, are of significance in Thailand, but only the former occupy a leading position in the economy.[37] One cannot discuss Thai nationalism in general, and economic nationalism in particular, without constant reference to the Chinese dominance over key sectors of the Thai economy. Almost every law with economic content in some way, directly or indirectly, affects the Chinese, and most laws directed against aliens have been inspired by fear of the Chinese.

The Chinese are to be found in all cities, market centers, and large as well as many small villages, with the greatest concentrations in the Bangkok area and sections of the South. They have long been an integral part of the Thai scene. In some areas, notably Bangkok and its environs, they comprise one-half of the population, while in the country as a whole, they are estimated to comprise between one-sixth and one-tenth of the total population.[38] Their numbers, combined with their dominance of major economic activities, present a major problem to Thai policy makers.

The problem is further complicated by the vagueness of the definition of a "Chinese" in the Thai context. Here we follow the usual procedure prevalent in Thailand, of considering as Chinese all those who in most social situations will behave as Chinese. Although such a definition may seem vague, it conforms to the consensus shared by both Thai officials and Chinese leaders. The number of Chinese in Thailand

[37] Some writers are inclined to broaden the coverage of the term "minority" to include the Thai-Lao who comprise about one-fourth of the total population. Such a classification is not appropriate for our purposes here. The Thai-Lao are scarcely different from other Thais in their economic behavior, and they have not been the subject of nationalist policies discussed in this study. Instead, the government in recent years has increased activities designed to improve the economic conditions in the Northeast where most of the Thai-Lao live. There are also the Vietnamese refugees and the hill tribes, but these are too small and too scattered to be of interest here.

[38] The estimates vary in different sources because of the absence of firm data. On this see Coughlin, *op. cit.*, p. 5.

who fall within this definition is estimated at present to be about three million. Of these, less than one half-million, having been born outside of Thailand or having registered at birth with a Chinese government agency, are Chinese citizens according to Thai law.[39]

For Thai nationalists, the factor determining the acceptability of a Chinese is not so much his formal Thai citizenship as his exclusive allegiance to Thailand and his assimilation into Thai society and culture. There are hardly any barriers on the Thai side to such assimilation, and throughout Thai history acculturated Chinese were readily accepted as Thai and many prominent Thais today are of Chinese or part Chinese origin. With assimilation, the *raison d'être* of economic nationalism disappears.

The Chinese have been present and active in Thailand for at least five centuries. To encourage their continued stay in Thailand, the kings nominated Chinese to official positions and introduced the most successful among them into the Thai bureaucratic nobility. Following 1850, the services of Chinese were in great demand as the Thai kings initiated modernizing changes, and the Thai showed little inclination to

---

[39] According to the 1960 census, the number of Chinese citizens in Thailand was only 409,508 and, of these, the vast majority were thirty years old and over. Coughlin doubts the census figures and prefers to use the number of Chinese registered as aliens (*ibid.*, p. 207). Unfortunately, the registration figures appear extremely unreliable, as can be seen from the following list, compiled from the Government of Thailand (GOT), *Statistical Year Book, Thailand*, No. 23 (1956–1958) and No. 24 (1963):

	1953	1954	1955	1956	1957
Registered	1,163,838	761,961	761,436	759,430	759,929
Naturalized	108	32	88	119	232

	1958	1959	1960	1961	1962
Registered	358,360	385,175	380,836	383,163	381,603
Naturalized	139	88	95	156	213

It is quite clear that prior to 1958, the number of those registered was far higher than those counted as aliens in the census. (For example, in 1950 the number of registered Chinese aliens was 1,099,084, while the 1947 census reported only 476,582 Chinese aliens. Following 1957 the census figures slightly exceed the number of Chinese registered. Of particular interest are the declines in registration between 1953 and 1954, and again between 1957 and 1958, both irreconcilable with the figures for naturalization or emigration. These changes may reflect increases in alien registration fees in June 1952 and November 1958. Another possible reason was the risk of losing Thai nationality by registry as an alien, as provided in the 1953 Nationality Act. However, this does not explain the decline in registration in 1958. Whatever the reason, it seems clear that the registration figures are not a reliable measure of the number of Chinese aliens in Thailand.

engage in commercial and industrial occupations. It was left to the Chinese to perform practically all functions requiring capital, initiative, and skills, and to provide the manual labor required outside of rice farming.

The Thai government under the absolute kings, in recognition of the contribution of the Chinese to the economy, exempted them from *corvée* services as well as from the capitation tax imposed on Thais. They were subject only to the triennial tax, which was smaller. Moreover, unlike most other aliens, they were allowed to reside in the provinces, thereby distributing their services widely and ensuring that they would become an integral part of the social environment.[40]

The fact that Thailand was an independent country provided the Chinese and other aliens with an incentive for assimilation not present in the surrounding countries. The ruling class was Thai, and upward social mobility was facilitated by Thai identification, whereas in the surrounding colonies power was monopolized by the Occidental rulers and no advantage was to be gained from assimilating to the native society.[41] Chinese assimilation was also encouraged by the low percentage of women among the immigrants during long historical periods which led to intermarriage with Thai women, the near absence of Chinese formal education in Thailand, the mildness of ethnocentric nationalist feelings among both the Thai and the Chinese, and the tolerant nature of Buddhism.[42] These factors have undergone change in the present century, however, and this has contributed to the increasing vacillation in the policies of Thai governments toward Chinese assimilation.

The changes in the Thai position toward the Chinese also have reflected the impact on the Thai elites of more exclusive Western con-

[40] Skinner says that the triennial tax was considered payment for exemption from *corvée* as well as for permission to move freely about the country. (*Chinese Society*, p. 123). A similar, though slightly different view was that the Chinese, unlike the Europeans, were always regarded as owing personal services to the government. Since this service was, in fact, never required of them, they were obliged to pay a special tax in lieu of it (H. G. Quaritch Wales, *Ancient Siamese Government and Administration* [London: Bernard Quaritch Ltd., 1934], p. 68).

[41] I am indebted to G. William Skinner for pointing out this factor to me. This and other factors affecting Chinese assimilation in Thailand are developed in his "Chinese Assimilation and Thai Politics," *The Journal of Asian Studies* (16), February 1957, pp. 237–250.

[42] It should be pointed out that the historical assimilability of the Chinese in Thailand contradicts the stereotype of the "unassimilable Chinese."

cepts of nationalism. At the same time, parallel developments, especially the 1911 revolution of Sun Yat-sen, increased the consciousness of national identity and interests among the Chinese. Other developments also proved divisive. With the increasing number of female immigrants, intermarriage declined, and a formal Chinese school system was established which helped to preserve Chinese culture among the Chinese residing in Thailand. The Thai authorities were faced with a dilemma. The wholesale expulsion of the Chinese was out of the question, yet these developments rendered the alternative and the only apparent solution—the encouragement of their complete assimilation—very difficult indeed. The reaction of the Thai government was to embark upon a many-pronged assimilation policy: curbing Chinese education, limiting Chinese immigration through fees and quotas, and refusing to establish diplomatic relations with the Chinese government.

Beginning in 1919, the Thai government took steps to control all private schools. The number of hours permitted for the teaching of the Chinese language was progressively reduced, and the use of Chinese as a medium of instruction was curbed. At the same time, the number of hours devoted to the Thai language and to the use of Thai as the medium of instruction was increased, and the employment of Thai teachers was required. The Private Schools Act of January 1919 stipulated that the Thai language be taught at least three hours a week and that the teachers pass Thai examinations.[43] The Compulsory Education Act of 1921 signaled more trouble for the Chinese schools, for it required each child to go through four years of regular Thai courses.[44] These acts were not strictly enforced under the absolute monarchy, but enforcement was tightened following the revolution of 1932, especially in 1933–1934. The number of Chinese private schools fell, as a result, from 271 in 1933–1934 to 193 in the following year, and the number of students fell from 5,727 to 4,742.[45] Other restrictive laws followed. In 1935, the Elementary Education Act required, *inter alia*, that instruction in compulsory elementary courses conform to the standard government syllabus and be given entirely in the Thai language. A new Private Schools Act in 1936, as amended in 1937, placed additional restrictions on non-Thai schools. In April 1939, the Education Ministry

[43] Skinner, *Chinese Society*, p. 228.   [44] *Ibid.*

[45] GOT, *Statistical Yearbook of the Kingdom of Siam, B.E. 2476–77* (1933–35), pp. 418 (footnote), 420.

issued new regulations which required that practically all subjects be taught in Thai.

These regulations generated anxiety among the Chinese educators, concerned that their schools would be forced to close down. They predicted the closing of the schools because their continued existence was pointless if they could not teach Chinese language and culture.[46] The expected results of the policies were not slow in appearing, nor were they displeasing to the Thai authorities. Table 24 reveals that the various restrictions and the occasional arbitrary closure of schools by the government on various pretexts, practically eliminated the Chinese school system by World War II.

Table 24. Number of schools classified as "Chinese and other" (not including Occidental and Islamic)

Type	1937–38	1938–39	1939–40	1940	1941	1942	1943	1944
Elementary	197	187	38	6	2	2	2	–
Secondary	20	25	9	2	–	–	–	–
Special	13	6	14	8	1	3	2	2

Source: GOT, Central Statistical Office, *Central Statistical Yearbook of Thailand B.E. 2482 (1939–40) to B.E. 2487 (1944).*

International political developments compelled the Thai government to relax these policies following World War II and the number of Chinese schools shot up to more than four hundred by the end of 1947. The Thai authorities became alarmed and, judging the international situation to have become more favorable, they resumed repressive actions against the Chinese schools. On May 12, 1948 a notification of the Ministry of Education, unusual in that it explicitly referred to the Chinese schools only, restricted the number of such schools in each *changwat*.[47] All Chinese secondary schools were banned. Subsequent restrictions limited the number of hours allowed for the teaching of the Chinese language (five hours per week since 1960), and stiffened the requirements imposed on teachers in Chinese schools.

[46] For the Chinese argument, see *The Bangkok Times Daily Mail,* April 10, 1939.

[47] GOT, *Gazette, 1948–49,* p. 290.

Although the Chinese resented these restrictions, they have come to realize in recent years that Thai instruction is of a great practical value for their children. All dealings with the Thai government as well as all instruction in institutions of higher learning are conducted in Thai. Nonetheless, the study of Chinese is still valued both for reasons of ethnic pride and because of its usefulness in commercial dealings with other overseas Chinese. Such Chinese teaching is done primarily in the evenings and in classes too small to be considered schools under Thai education law.[48]

A parallel development can be traced in immigration policies. Restriction on Chinese immigration was initiated during the absolute monarchy with the Immigration Act of 1927, which provided for the establishment of nationality quotas at the discretion of the Minister of Foreign Affairs. The following year, fees for immigration and residence of aliens were increased, followed by a steeper increase in 1931. These measures produced a decline in immigration, but it was short-lived as the Sino-Japanese war intensified the pressures to emigrate from China. Expanding immigration provoked the passage of the Immigration Act of 1937–1938, which further increased the residence fees (up to 200 baht) and introduced the requirement that an immigrant must show evidence that he would be self-supporting. This act had an immediate impact on immigration which declined drastically, and there was even a rise in emigration. To increase the difficulties of aliens, the Thai government supplemented these laws with a yearly registration imposed in 1939.

After the war, the influx of Chinese into the country soared as the residence fee of 200 baht, the value of which was reduced by inflation, was no longer a deterrent. About 170,000 Chinese immigrants entered

---

[48] In recent years, English has emerged as a serious competitor to Chinese as the language of commerce. As a result, Chinese students enroll in large numbers in missionary schools using English as the language of instruction. The fact that the latter schools enjoy special dispensation from the law requiring all instruction to be conducted in Thai confirms the allegations that the various education laws were directed specifically against the Chinese. This discrimination is against the Chinese language, however, not against schools run by Chinese as such. As long as the Chinese schools conform to the requirements of the Ministry of Education they enjoy government subsidies, as do other private schools. The Thai government encourages private schools because the government school system cannot catch up with the constantly increasing number of children requiring the compulsory education.

the country during the two years 1946 and 1947.[49] This influx alarmed the Thai government and as of May 1, 1947, a new quota system was introduced with the Chinese quota established at 10,000 for the rest of that year and the national quotas for other countries set at 200.[50] The special Chinese quota was abandoned in 1950 by the new Immigration Act which established (Sec. 29) 200 as the upper quota limit from any country, and the residence fee was increased (Sec. 47) to 1,000 baht.[51] The detailed law (67 sections) established elaborate restrictions which effectively stopped all large-scale immigration.

The Thai government, however, has not been entirely consistent in pursuing policies to encourage assimilation, and this ambivalence is particularly evident in naturalization policy. For example, in 1952 the residence requirement for naturalization was doubled to ten years of uninterrupted residence. The same law established knowledge of the Thai language as a requirement.[52] A ministerial regulation issued later that year specified that an ability to read and write Thai, and not merely to speak the language, was required for naturalization. Access to nationality was tightened in 1953 when a new nationality act abolished the provision that anybody born in Thailand automatically acquires Thai citizenship.[53] Moreover, the law specified that an individual qualified for Thai nationality by birth but of an alien father would forfeit Thai nationality if he should take out an identity card under the law governing alien registration.

The most disturbing aspect of the measures taken during 1952–1953 was the discrimination against naturalized citizens, and citizens by birth but of alien ancestry. This discrimination was not confined to the risk of losing citizenship but, in effect, relegated such individuals to second-class citizenship. For example, in order to be a candidate or even eligible to vote, citizens in these categories have had to satisfy special requirements of service, education, and residence. Similarly, they were confronted by difficulties in buying land. During 1952, orders

[49] Skinner, "Chinese Assimilation and Thai Politics," *op. cit.*, p. 246.

[50] Notification of the Ministry of Interior, GOT, *Gazette, 1946–47*, pp. 222–223.

[51] This quota has stayed in force ever since. When in November 1957 the president of the Chinese Chamber of Commerce suggested that the quota be raised to 5,000, his request was rejected by the Minister of the Interior. See *Siam Rath* and *Sathianraphap*, November 4, 1957.

[52] Nationality Act, B.E. 2495 (1952), GOT, *Gazette, 1952*, pp. 47–51.

[53] Nationality Act No. 2, B.E. 2496 (1953), GOT, *Gazette, 1953*, p. 108.

issued by the Ministry of the Interior instructed the *changwat* authorities to take steps to prevent noncitizens from using their naturalized relatives of Thai citizenship as fronts for the illegal purchase of land.[54] In August of that year the *changwat* authorities were ordered to enforce a cabinet decision that only "pure" Thais or ex-servicemen of Thai citizenship should be allowed to lease crown land, and to prevent Thai nationals born of alien fathers and using alien surnames from acquiring rights to land in any form.[55] The discrimination was made explicit in the Military Service Act (No. 6) of January 27, 1953, which excluded "a naturalized Thai subject or person born of an alien father" from those who could be called up for military service.[56]

By mid-1954, the "hard" policy evident in these measures was moderated and new measures aimed at encouraging Chinese assimilation were promulgated. The first step was taken by the Police Department (until then the most actively anti-Chinese department) which established a new Alien Division to "serve aliens by giving them help and advice in their trade and profession," as well as provide them with more security.[57] This was followed by other indications of a major policy shift favoring the relaxation of the anti-Chinese measures. These changes were accelerated after the return of Phibun from his world tour in the middle of 1955, especially throughout 1956, when most of the anti-alien laws were either eased or completely repealed. Both the alien registration fees and the naturalization fees were cut in half in July 1955. The Nationality Act (No. 3) B.E. 2499 (1956) reversed some of the hard measures of the early 1950s. The most significant step in that direction cut the residence requirement in half, to five years.[58] This and other changes encouraging assimilation were accompanied by declarations describing the Chinese as a great asset to Thailand.[59]

---

[54] This issue was raised again as late as November 28, 1960, when the Minister of Interior warned aliens resorting to such practices that they would be severely punished or deported. See *Far Eastern Economic Review*, December 8, 1960, p. 546.

[55] Skinner, *Chinese Society*, p. 374. Coughlin cites cases where only third-generation nonethnic Thais were qualified for land purchase or low-cost housing (Coughlin, *op. cit.*, pp. 140–141).

[56] GOT, *Gazette, 1953*, p. 106.

[57] *The Bangkok Post*, June 11, 1954.

[58] However, the 1960 Nationality Act (No. 4), while easing the requirements for reacquisition of Thai nationality, restored the provision for the loss of Thai nationality by those possessing it by birth but having an alien father.

[59] In reporting on the approval given by the then ruling party to a government draft law designed to ease the naturalization requirements and procedures, *The*

In spite of the shift in policy, beginning in 1955, to one of accommodation and assimilation, misgivings over the economic and organizational strength of the resident Chinese persisted. The strong undercurrent of admiration among them for Red China as the symbol of the rising prestige and power of the Chinese people caused concern to the Thai government, which in turn produced sporadic raids, especially in the early 1950s, on Chinese newspapers, secret societies, and other organizations. This concern has also been manifested in a policy of divide-and-rule capitalizing on internal differences within the Chinese community which has been followed at times.[60] In dealing with the resident Chinese, citizens and noncitizens alike, the Thai authorities prefer to negotiate with local organizations, most notably the Chinese Chamber of Commerce, rather than with the Chinese Embassy.[61] Establishing the chamber as the *de facto* representative of the Chinese community, constitutes, in effect, a recognition of the existence of a separate community demarcated by ethnic rather than nationality criteria. This state of affairs prevails despite the fact that the leaders of the Chinese Chamber of Commerce are Thai citizens and often have Thai names.

The second largest minority in Thailand are the Muslims. The census of 1947 gave their numbers as 670,000 and that of 1960 tabulated 1,025,600, which was 3.9 per cent of the total population. Since the great majority of them live in the four southern provinces and maintain their separate religious and linguistic identity, they present a potentially dangerous challenge to Thai sovereignty over these areas. Those residing in these provinces are actually Malays who were politically but not socially or culturally separated from their kinsmen by the

---

Bangkok Post explained that "the bill is to facilitate assimilation of aliens so that they may contribute toward progress of the Thai nation." One indication of appreciation for such contributions was the authorization given the Minister of the Interior to "grant Thai nationality to aliens who have done deeds beneficial to the Thai nation, irrespective of whether they fulfill requirements of residence period and language" (*The Bangkok Post*, December 26, 1956).

[60] Since 1950 such differences have centered primarily around the competing claims to allegiance advanced by the two antagonistic Chinese regimes.

[61] Fearing the threat of interference in her minority policies, Thailand consistently avoided establishing diplomatic relations with China. It was only after World War II that such relations were established under pressure from the United States. After the Communst takeover in China, Thailand chose to continue recognizing Nationalist China for "ideological" considerations and also because the latter was obviously the weaker of the two Chinas.

expansion of the Thai state to the South. Their way of life is indistinguishable from that of the Malays across the border: they are small-scale farmers, fishermen, and modest rubber growers.

As in the case of the Chinese minority, Thai policy toward the Thai-Malays has vacillated. Mild attempts to assimilate them have failed, and the attempts to strengthen central government control over their areas caused only resentment. Thai-Malay grievances gained new significance after World War II, when a strong drive for national self-assertion manifested itself among the Malay Muslims in Indonesia and Malaya. Thai fear of an irredentist movement led at first to intransigence toward Thai-Malay demands that would tend to perpetuate the separate Thai-Malay identity. The frictions that arose culminated in riots and bloody clashes between the Thai-Malays and the police. This was followed by some Thai concessions, but tension has continued.[62]

The agitation concerning the position of the Thai Muslims has continued up to the present and has appeared in the news from time to time. For example, in the summer of 1957, the Muslims in the South demanded that the Ministry of Interior establish in the southern provinces a university for Thai Muslims, transfer Thai Muslim government officials to the four southern provinces, reserve ten openings in the police academy for Thai Muslim students each year, and hold separate contests for posts in government for Thai Muslims, because they would not be able to win in the general competition.[63] Complaints of alleged discrimination against the Muslim religion by the government have been heard from time to time, especially before elections when various parties have tried to win the Muslim vote.

There are also small communities of Muslims in other parts of the country, mostly in the central plain. Many of these are descendants of Malay prisoners of war. They are hardly distinguishable from other Thai and seem to be well integrated into Thai society. They are called "Thai Islam," as distinguished from the term "Thai Malay," often used in reference to those Muslims residing in the four southern provinces. Neither group has demonstrated economic prowess and, as far as can be ascertained, policies designed to restrict their economic activities have never existed.

[62] At the end of 1951, for example, a Thai Muslim leader, Haji Surong, who was rumored to be in favor of the secession of the four provinces, disappeared. Informants in Bangkok maintain that he was killed by agents of the Thai government. *The Bangkok Tribune* of January 11, 1958 reported the prevailing opinion that he had been thrown into the sea behind Noo Island.

[63] *Chao Thai* (and various other newspapers), July 31, 1957.

The importance of the other minority groups in Thailand, including various non-Thai tribal groups and the hill tribes, in terms of numbers, distinct culture, and economic significance is minor. The explicit policy of the government toward them is one of assimilation. The more Thaified these people become, the more their economic activities resemble those of the Thai. The process is not always easy, since the economy of some hill tribes has been based on slash and burn agriculture and on opium rather than on settled rice cultivation. Recent reports indicate that pressures to assimilate are resented and have caused some tribes to support Communist terrorists. Other reports indicate that insurgency activities of Vietnamese refugees is increasing. Efforts by the Thai government to return refugees to Vietnam have not been successful.

GOVERNMENT PARTICIPATION IN PRODUCTION

Economic nationalism, the nearest equivalent to an ideology to be embraced by the Thai elites following the 1932 coup, was connected in their minds with the nationalization of alien enterprises. There was little in Thai tradition that would oppose nationalization of existing enterprises or the creation and operation of new enterprises by the government. Although the complete nationalization advocated in Pridi's program of 1933 came into disrepute, the theme of Thaification continued.

This was enunciated with great clarity in the official policy statement of the Phibun regime which came to power at the end of 1938. In a radio speech a month after the new government came to power, Pridi, the Finance Minister, declared that a primary goal of the government was the entry of ethnic Thai into the profit-producing activities of the country.[64] Shortly thereafter, in another radio speech the Minister of Economic Affairs, Phra Boriphan Yuthakit, openly accused the Chinese exporters of degrading the quality of rice for export and deplored the dominance of the Chinese in the rice trade. He announced that the government intended to take over all activities connected with production and marketing of rice. He concluded by asserting:

I have been asked what kind of trade this is—is it free trade? socialist? or communist? or what? My answer is that it is Thai-ist. This is a word that you will not find in any dictionary, but its meaning is obvious. It is a system to

[64] *Prajamitra,* February 17, 1939. For an English summary of the speech see Kenneth Landon, *The Chinese in Thailand* (New York: Oxford University Press, 1941), pp. 173–174.

help the Thai. It is not intended to destroy the alien traders, but to create Thai traders. Naturally, there may be some loss to aliens. Our purpose is not destructive and negative but positive. We are going to help the farmers, and to create a Thai business community.[65]

The degree of intensity of Thaification has waxed or waned with changes in government and in Thailand's international relations, but the goal has remained intact, though on occasion, it has been obscured by official and semi-official declarations of good will toward all. The laws passed and the administrative actions taken leave little doubt that Thaification has remained an important policy objective.

The precursor to nationalization policies was the Business Registration Act of November 1936, which provided for the collection of information about the various enterprises in the country, including the race and nationality of the owners.[66] It was after the treaty barriers were completely removed in 1937,[67] and particularly after Phibun became Premier, however, that explicitly nationalistic legislation was introduced. Nationalization was initiated in 1938 by the formation of the government-controlled Thai Rice Company which was formed through the purchase of ten Chinese rice mills.[68] It was expected at the time that this company would progressively take over all Chinese mills, but this objective is virtually as far from realization today as it was when the company started operations.[69]

The immediate targets for nationalization following the coup were the Western-owned oil companies, internal shipping companies, and the British-American Tobacco Company. The most complicated confrontation involved the oil companies with their world-wide connections.

[65] *Prajamitra*, March 9, 1939. Quoted in Landon, *ibid.*, p. 174.

[66] See below section on trade and finance.

[67] Pridi was largely responsible for negotiating the treaty revisions during 1935 and 1936.

[68] The reader will become aware of the rather loose use of the terms "semi-governmental," "government-controlled," etc. This arises from the fact that in Thailand very rarely is the amount of responsibility of the government, as opposed to that of individual cabinet members, clearly defined. As for the Thai Rice Company, mentioned in the text, 51 per cent of its shares were held by the government and the rest by rice co-operatives.

[69] Ironically enough, no Thai with sufficient experience to manage the company could be found, and a Chinese who had sold his three mills to the company became the manager, having been granted speedy naturalization (Skinner, *Chinese Society*, p. 411, note 2). He was still the manager when the author visited Thailand in 1963.

The Liquid Fuel Act of April 1939 established rigorous government controls over the importation of oil and provided for a government distribution agency that would share the market with the two existing companies, Royal Dutch Shell and Standard-Vacuum. In addition, the government agency was to provide all of the liquid fuel needs of the government, while controlling the distribution and prices of the foreign companies. The companies objected to these provisions and terminated their activities in Thailand by the end of July, thus leaving the government agency in complete control.[70]

After the war some of the provisions of the Liquid Fuel Act were repealed, and in 1946 an agreement was negotiated with the interested international oil companies providing for the division of the Thai market among the companies and the withdrawal of the government from this activity.[71] The government refused to renew this agreement when it expired in 1956, and subsequently the Oil Fuel Organization (OFO) in the Ministry of Defense began to operate filling stations and moved in on the markets shared by the Western companies. The OFO was able to compete successfully because as a government enterprise it did not have to pay local taxes. At the time of writing, the government is still active in the oil market and appears determined to expand its participation.

Although no significant oil deposits have been found in Thailand, the government has persisted in its efforts to bring into being a Thai oil refining industry.[72] The problem for Thai policy makers has been to reconcile the need to have experienced oil companies construct and operate the refineries with the objective of Thaification. In the prolonged negotiations conducted with various oil companies over a number of years, the Thai government sought immediate or eventual Thai ownership of the facilities, as well as Thaification of staff at all levels.

---

[70] Lack of experience and the shortage of tankers and of oil supplies, once World War II came to Southeast Asia, contributed to the spotty performance of this monopoly.

[71] The market was shared in the following proportions: Stanvac (Standard Vacuum Oil Company) had the largest share, 48–49 per cent of the market; Shell about 45–46 per cent; and Caltex, a latecomer, about 5 per cent.

[72] The only area in Thailand where oil deposits have been found is near Fang in the *Changwat* of Chiengmai in northern Thailand. These deposits are, however, of low quality and, according to the World Bank mission are "associated with much water" (International Bank for Reconstruction and Development [IBRD], *A Public Development Program for Thailand* [Baltimore: The Johns Hopkins Press, 1959], p. 109).

Although these negotiations failed, an alternative solution was found when five local businessmen incorporated a company, the Thai Oil Refinery Company (TORC), which was granted the authority to construct the refinery and operate it for ten years, after which time it will be handed over to the government.[73] The TORC contracted with foreign companies to construct the refinery, to supply crude oil, to distribute the refined products, and to provide technical assistance in the refining process. Thai nationals have been trained outside the country, and some of them are already working both in the refinery and in the new Thai Petroleum Transport Company which operates coastal tankers. It is still too early to assess the efficiency of the enterprise, as the refinery began operations early in 1965. In one respect, however, it has already been a success in that it established a precedent in which an important industry materialized with provision for automatic Thaification.[74]

The second major target of Thaification policies before World War II was the alien shipping companies operating in Thai waters. The Thai Vessels Act which, like the Fuel Act, was passed in April 1939, provided that all vessels above a minimum size operating in Thai territorial waters had to be owned by Thais or by corporations 70 per cent of whose shares were held by Thai nationals. In addition, the crews had to be 75 per cent Thai. Following enactment of the legislation, two foreign-owned ship companies were liquidated and the British-owned Siam Steam Packet Company, which had held a virtual monopoly over national shipping, was sold to the government.[75] This act, together with an earlier one restricting fishing in Thai territorial waters to nationals, practically eliminated foreign-owned ships from Thai waters, except for ships carrying imports and exports. Not satisfied with Thaification of coastal shipping, the Thai leaders moved to participate in international shipping. This objective was openly admitted by Phibun in May 1940, when he announced that the government would acquire a controlling interest in companies operating ships between Thailand and nearby ports, and that it would develop an ocean-going merchant fleet.[76] To implement this policy, the Thai Maritime Navigation Com-

---

[73] The entrepreneur, managing director, and major stockholder of TORC is a Chinese who came to Thailand barely twenty years ago.

[74] In spite of this success, the Ministry of Defense pressed on with its plans for its own refinery, probably for military reasons.

[75] See Virginia Thompson, *Thailand—The New Siam* (New York: Macmillan Company, 1941), p. XX.

[76] Landon, *op. cit.*, p. 235.

pany was created in 1941 and promptly bought five ocean-going ships.[77]

Related moves, partly motivated by considerations other than economic nationalism, contributed to further Thaification of activities related to shipping and fishing.[78] The dredging of the bar at the mouth of the Chao Phraya River and the completion of the government wharfs at Klong Toei (Bangkok) were followed by a regulation requiring all ocean-going ships to berth alongside these wharfs.[79] Dredging the bar permitted the lightering service which was controlled by Chinese to be dispensed with. With the completion of the government wharfs in 1950, nationalization of shipping and harbor services was virtually achieved.[80]

The other major industry to be nationalized was tobacco and cigarette manufacturing. On March 22, 1939, a Tobacco Act was passed establishing government control over the growth, importation, manufacture, and distribution of tobacco and tobacco products.[81] The major company, the British-American Tobacco Company, had been successful in encouraging Virginia tobacco production by maintaining experiment stations, building curing sheds, supplying farmers with seeds and expert advice, and developing marketing facilities throughout the country. The Thai government complimented the company for its enterprise by nationalizing it in September 1941.[82] Smaller companies, unable to survive under the new restrictions, also sold out to the government company which has maintained a monopoly on tobacco products since that time.[83]

Following World War II, anti-alien laws in general, and measures nationalizing foreign enterprises in particular, were moderated con-

[77] The operation of this company was not a conspicuous success. By mid-1959 it was operating three ships, employing a hundred workers, and was 30 million baht in debt. In October of that year its management was transferred from the Ministry of Economic Affairs to the Ministry of Communications. The excuse given for not liquidating the company at that time was that "Thailand needed a state-owned shipping line because there is no control over international shipping rates" (*Bangkok World*, October 15, 1959).

[78] Thaification of the fishing trade is discussed below in the section on professions and labor.

[79] GOT, *Gazette, 1950*, pp. 438–439.

[80] In the early 1960s about 95 per cent of all imports and 70 per cent of all exports were handled through the Port of Bangkok.

[81] GOT, Ministry of Finance, *Report of the Financial Adviser, 1940*, p. 26.

[82] The owners received 5.5 million baht. See Ingram, *op. cit.*, p. 137.

[83] Aliens for whom no qualified Thai replacements could be found were retained by the nationalized company.

siderably. For one thing, there were few substantial foreign holdings left in Thailand. The Thai government, moreover, was cognizant of Thailand's sensitive position as a former collaborator with Japan, and the administrative capacities of the Thai government were occupied in meeting the obligations imposed by the victorious Allies. The most important obligation, the compulsory delivery of large quantities of rice to the Combined Food Board (succeeded in 1947 by the International Emergency Food Council), provided the Thai government with an excuse to establish a "monopoly" over the export of rice. Although the compulsory rice deliveries were subsequently reduced and then terminated after 1948, the rice export monopoly was continued to the end of 1955.[84]

Following World War II, the emphasis on Thaification through government enterprise shifted from nationalization of existing enterprises to direct creation of manufacturing establishments. The choice of plants to be erected demonstrated no "rational" program of priorities, however, and pragmatic considerations determined the succession of enterprises established.[85]

During the war, the curtailment of outside supplies stimulated attempts to organize the manufacture of import substitutes, but with few permanent results. Government participation in industry after the war, especially after Phibun's return to power in 1948, also was concentrated in import-replacing industries. The viability of such import-replacing industries was enhanced by high levels of protection and by regulations requiring government departments to buy their products.

---

[84] This monopoly involved government control and "profit" sharing rather than actual nationalization since the exporters, mostly alien, continued to operate as agents of the government. For details see Eliezer B. Ayal, "The Impact of Export Taxes on the Domestic Economy of Underdeveloped Countries," *Journal of Development Studies* (1) July 1965, especially pp. 334–335.

[85] The following remarks of the World Bank Mission support this assessment. "A basic weakness in the government's development effort in the past has been a lack of guiding objectives, not only for the effort as a whole but even in individual sectors of the economy. Investments have been authorized without first trying to find out if they would serve urgent needs, if they would be as productive as other alternatives, or if the particular forms of investment chosen were the best means of attaining their objectives. Consequently, public development effort has been unbalanced, uncoordinated and excessively diffused" (IBRD, *op. cit.*, p. 11). I am in general agreement with this assessment of the IBRD report, although it suffers, as does the rest of the report, from failure to recognize economic nationalism as the basic *raison d'être* for many government actions and policies.

Although government enterprises had existed for a number of years, it was only in 1953 that legislation authorizing such enterprises was enacted. The Government Organizations Incorporation Act B.E. 2496 (1953) empowered the government, whenever it deemed such action proper, to "incorporate any organization for the purpose of public interest, economic purpose, or in connection with the cost of living or public service, with capital drawn from the state budget." [86] By that time, the Ministry of Industry, which administered most government industries, operated twenty-four factories, fourteen distilleries, six sugar refineries, a weaving mill, a tannery and two paper mills.[87] This ministry was by no means the only government agency engaged in manufacturing, as other ministries, most notably the Ministry of Defence, and the individual armed services, had established enterprises. Some of these, particularly those sponsored by the branches of the armed forces, tended to compete with each other as well as with private producers.

Government enterprises continued to proliferate and as of 1958, the government, in addition to operating or being directly involved in all public utilities including a large part of public transportation, controlled about sixty manufacturing establishments, fifteen of which were distilleries.[88] These included monopolies over tobacco, potable and industrial spirits, and playing cards; dominant participation in timber, sugar, pepper, gunny-bags, and minerals other than tin; large interests in cement, glass, pharmaceuticals, batteries, tin, tanneries, and textiles. The government also operated small plants producing such products as shoe polish, alum, rubber footwear, metal cabinets, paper clips, ceramics, and so on. About forty government firms were big enough to employ more than fifty workers each.[89]

Although accounts of these enterprises are either unavailable or badly kept, it is common knowledge that, with the probable exception of the tobacco monopoly, none of them could survive competitively. In its highly restrained language, the World Bank mission concluded:

[86] GOT, *Gazette, 1953*, p. 150.

[87] GOT, Central Statistical Office, *Statistical Year Book 1953*, pp. 388–391.

[88] Some reports put the number of government ventures at the time at 130. As noted earlier (note #68), definitions vary as to what constitutes a government enterprise. Also, the larger estimate includes enterprises providing services, including financial institutions.

[89] IBRD, *op. cit.*, pp. 90–91. The picture is substantially unchanged at the time of writing.

"In the industrial field it is noted that the record of government industrial ventures, including nominally private ventures sponsored by the government, has been for the most part poor. Further government ventures into industrial operation are considered inadvisable." [90]

The Thai government has not been unaware that the performance of these enterprises was unsatisfactory or that they have required continual subsidies and other types of aid. However, in the words of Phibun, the role of government in business was transient, "a step toward bringing control of Thailand's commerce from foreign into Thai hands." He asserted that since "foreigners, mainly Chinese, are keeping a tight hold on the business of the country," Thai private businessmen cannot take over speedily. It is, therefore, the purpose of the government "to show the way." [91]

Governmental or semigovernmental enterprises also provided a source of income to men in power and their supporters. The World Bank mission, after a thorough examination of the governmental enterprises concluded:

The enterprises were too often initiated by persons with political influence, who had no special knowledge of the industry or particular concern about ultimate success. Consequently there was little control over expenditures during the course of construction. . . . Because of their political origin, the projects were not properly studied at the beginning. . . . Both assets and liabilities are swollen by loans to and borrowing from other government agencies—a pernicious system which not only makes the balance sheets unintelligible but is obviously open to abuse. . . . The evidence of poor management is to be seen . . . in procurement and marketing methods . . . in idle labor, poor maintenance, inefficient use of plant, and bad housekeeping . . . all establishments [in Thailand] tend to employ more workers than do their Western equivalents. But the disproportion is even greater in the government plants. Political reasons are said to be responsible.[92]

In 1965, a study of the state-owned enterprises conducted under the sponsorship of the USAID mission in Bangkok confirmed the World Bank assessment of the defects of these ventures. The enterprises of

[90] IBRD, *ibid.,* p. 20.

[91] *Bangkok Post,* February 26, 1953. Similar statements were made on numerous occasions by high government officials, but their frequency has diminished markedly in recent years.

[92] IBRD, *op. cit.,* pp. 93–94. These shortcomings are presumably being corrected because of the increasing insistence of the central government on the accountability of their enterprises.

commercial nature—the ones of interest for us here—came in for special criticism on the grounds of their inefficiency and the threat they pose to potential investors. A large part of the report is concerned with identifying those enterprises which should be transferred to the private sector and recommends procedures for making such transfers.[93]

The situation was not much different in the nominally private industries connected in one way or another with the government. The classic example of such a company was the National Economic Development Corporation Ltd. (NEDCOL). This corporation was organized by a number of prominent people, most of whom were already connected with another semiofficial body, the War Veterans Organization.[94] The NEDCOL was founded in 1954 with great expectations and substantial government support and was proclaimed as the first major attempt to develop Thai private industry. The ECAFE Economic Survey of 1956 referred to the establishment of NEDCOL as an important step toward "the participation of private enterprise (with government support) [*sic*] in economic development." [95]

Established with an authorized capital of fifty million baht, only three million baht was actually paid by the private shareholders. Most of the financing was done through loans, especially foreign loans, guaranteed by the government. Foreign loans included ten million dollars from the Bank of America and about twenty-two million dollars medium-term credits from machinery suppliers in Europe.

Part of the proceeds of such borrowing was used to acquire an old debt-ridden jute factory from the North East Jute Mills Company. In spite of purchases of new machines and equipment, this venture failed mainly because of inexperienced management. Somewhat better results were achieved in the case of a large modern sugar mill bought from the Thai Sugar Organization which, under NEDCOL management, made a small profit before debt service.[96] NEDCOL also initiated expansion of a gunny-bag factory and built a second sugar mill and a small marble factory.[97] By the end of 1957, when the first loan repayment was due, it became clear that NEDCOL was bankrupt in spite of

[93] George L. Artamonoff, *State Owned Enterprises of Thailand* (Bangkok: AID, United States Operations Mission, November 1965), *passim*.

[94] See below, section on professions and labor, and section on trade and finance.

[95] United Nations, Economic Commission for Asia and the Far East (ECAFE), *Economic Survey of Asia and the Far East, 1956*, p. 166.

[96] IBRD, *op. cit.*, p. 92.

[97] The latter was subsequently separated from the corporation.

the support it had received from the government in loan guarantees, assured markets, high administered prices, relief from custom tariffs on imported equipment, and the like.

Since NEDCOL was the most ambitious enterprise attempted by the Thais, its failure caused great disappointment. This failure brought into sharp relief the role of prominent people who had used their influence to divert public funds for their own benefit under the guise of promoting Thai industries. According to press reports, the investigation initiated by the government that came to power in the September 17, 1957 coup revealed that less than half of the credit received by NEDCOL was actually invested in plant and equipment; the rest "disappeared." [98] To quote the new Minister of Economic Affairs: "The men who started NEDCOL were interested in exploiting government resources, not the resources of Thailand." [99]

The failure of NEDCOL and of government industries generally, combined with the persistent criticism by visiting missions and experts, have produced a change in the policy of Thaification and industrialization through bureaucratic and semibureaucratic enterprise. There is now an increased emphasis on development as such, with greater reliance on private initiative and somewhat reduced concern that such initiative be provided by ethnic Thai. This change does not mean, however, that apprehensions over the activities of the Chinese have disappeared.

The new approach is manifested in government offers to sell or lease its enterprises to private businessmen. The Minister of Industry, Nai Boon Charoenchai, stated on September 21, 1959 that "the government should only establish and run industries which cannot be handled by private firms." [100] The big government Mekong distillery was transferred on that date to private management on a rental basis, and the government was also reportedly trying to sell a brewery, the machines for which had already been procured by a quasi-government company.[101] Statements confirming the new policy were frequent thereafter. The latest official assurance is contained in the draft of the second development plan: "The Government will not establish new state

[98] For details of this episode, see *Thai Raiwan*, October 12, 1957; *Siam Rath*, October 20, 1957; *Daily Mail*, November 29, 1957; *La Démocrate*, December 1, 1957.

[99] Quoted in *Fortune*, April, 1958.

[100] *Bangkok World*, September 22, 1959.   [101] *Ibid.*

enterprises, except those which will be of unquestionable benefit to the public and will not conflict with the policy of promoting private enterprise." [102] Similar policies will apply to the expansion of state enterprises which "will not be undertaken unless they are economically feasible and will not compete with nor be detrimental to private enterprise." [103]

As for NEDCOL, the government took over and tried to salvage the potentially profitable activities under new management.[104] In order to underline the new approach—preference for private enterprise with a genuine welcome for alien participation—the new management planned to sell a large public equity issue and invited tenders without regard to nationality.[105] Shortly thereafter, the Minister of Industry stated that the government stood ready to sell the sugar factory at Cholbury to a private company if a buyer could be found.[106] The response to these offers was not encouraging.

The government also renewed its efforts to help Thai private enterprise, primarily by providing medium- and long-term credit. This was not a new policy but one that had been dormant during the period of aggressive experimentation with government enterprises. For example, as early as 1934 the government provided substantial financial support to the privately owned Boon Rawd Brewery Company. Similar help was provided to a ginning and weaving factory, the Siam Paper Company Limited, and other firms.[107]

The commercial banks in Thailand, as in underdeveloped countries generally, traditionally concentrated on short-term loans to traders, especially in foreign trade. They shied away from the uncertainties and long waiting periods involved in industrial credit. A government-owned industrial bank, which was established in 1952 to fill this gap, was unsuccessful, primarily because of political interference. Consequently, a

---

[102] GOT, the National Economic Development Board, *The National Economic Development Plan, 1967–1971*, preliminary edition (February 1967), pp. 111–112.

[103] *Ibid.*

[104] According to *Siam Nikorn* and *Phim Thai* of August 5, 1959, the Minister of Industries said that at the time the government acquired "free of charge" 444,152 shares of the total 500,000.

[105] See *Siam Rath* and *Bangkok World*, June 26, 1959; and *Siam Nikorn* and *Chao Thai*, June 27, 1959.

[106] *Bangkok World*, September 26, 1959.

[107] Great Britain, Department of Overseas Trade, *Economic Conditions in Siam, 1937*, p. 20.

Table 25. Distribution of ownership of the Industrial Finance Corporation as of mid-1964

Ownership	No. of shareholders	No. of shares	Percentage of total
Thai			
Banks—Agricultural Bank	1	4,277	14.09
Banks—others	15	6,093	20.31
Insurance companies	20	1,300	4.33
Private corporations	2	110	.37
Private individuals	20	1,885	6.28
Total Thai shareholders	58	13,615	45.38
International Finance Corp.	1	4,000	13.33
Foreign			
Banks with branches in Thailand	10	7,431	24.77
Banks—other	4	4,400	14.67
Private corporations	3	554	1.84
Total foreign shareholders	17	12,385	41.29
Total shareholders	76	30,000	100.00

Source: Industrial Finance Corporation of Thailand, *IFCT-Resume,* September 30, 1964, p. 3.

new approach was adopted in 1959 when a substitute and largely privately-owned development finance corporation was set up with strong backing from the World Bank—which had proposed the enterprise—the Thai government, and the USAID mission. The Industrial Finance Corporation of Thailand (IFCT) was able in November 1959 to market its first share issue of 6.1 million baht of its authorized share capital of 20 million baht. By 1964 the IFCT had expanded to the point that 30 million baht of authorized share capital of 100 million baht had been issued.[108] Very promising have been the high proportions of private Thai and nongovernmental participation in the IFCT as shown in Table 25.[109]

A new share issue was undertaken in 1967 through circulars sent to

[108] For more details see Chamlong Tohtong, "Practice and Problems of the Industrial Finance Corporation of Thailand" (Bangkok, January 1964, mimeographed).

[109] "Thai" here is defined by nationality. Most Thai banks are Chinese by the ethnic definition.

existing subscribers inviting them to subscribe to the additional shares. Of the 20,000 shares offered, foreigners bought 10,510 shares or 52.55 per cent, the Thais bought 4,574 shares or 22.87 per cent, with 4,916 shares remaining. Since this changed the ratio of shareholders in favor of the foreigners, it was decided (September 15, 1967) to sell almost all the remaining shares to Thais.[110]

After a slow start, the IFCT is presently making a useful contribution to the development of domestic private industry, albeit on a limited scale. It not only grants loans but also assists in the complex steps involved in the establishment of enterprises. There have been a substantial number of loan applications rejected on grounds of nonexistent or unsound projects, unreliable accounts, unsatisfactory financial situation, and the like. The IFCT has been accused of excess caution and, therefore, of limited usefulness.[111] Without entering this controversy, there is little doubt that an institution such as the IFCT is badly needed as financing is generally acknowledged to be a major obstacle on the path of development of domestic private enterprise in Thailand.[112]

Should the official attitude favoring private enterprise prove enduring, the share of private enterprise vis-à-vis government enterprise will rise.[113] Such a development could have a number of repercussions including the reduction of the relative economic power of the government, a change in the relative power of departments presently involved in economic activities, and perhaps the creation of a viable Thai middle class with distinct interests. Ultimately, an important effect of such development would be to moderate Thai fears of the economic power of aliens.

[110] The relative reluctance of the Thai appears to be due to rumors of the alleged unmarketability of IFCT shares.

[111] The World Bank mission, which initially proposed the founding of IFCT, favored caution until the latter gains experience and reputation (IBRD, *op. cit.*, pp. 103–104).

[112] For an account of the difficulties, financial and otherwise, of a Thai businessman, see Prachan Guna-Kasem, "Some Problems of a Local Entrepreneur," *Bangkok Bank Monthly Review*, December 1963, pp. 205–209. Incidentally, Mr. Guna-Kasem was one of those who failed to get an IFCT loan.

[113] Doubts are raised from time to time. One example was the unconfirmed report that the resignation in early 1964 of Tawee Bunyaket from the chairmanship of the Investment Board was caused by a reversal of government policy. The immediate point at issue was the government's refusal to allow duty-free import of pulp by a new paper mill. It was rumored that the refusal was based on fear that the new mill would compete with the existing government-operated mill. See *Far Eastern Economic Review*, March 12, 1964, p. 581.

PROFESSIONS AND LABOR

Few Thais are to be found in economic activities and occupations outside of agriculture and government service. Under the *corvée* system, which was abolished during the second half of the nineteenth century, artisans were forced to serve for longer periods than rice farmers, a practice that discouraged artisanship among the Thai. Over time, the Chinese monopolized almost all artisanship and other non-agricultural occupations, including hired labor. Inside the Chinese community, occupations tended to be distributed along lines of geographical origin and dialect groups. Chinese social organizations also developed on these lines with a few exceptions, such as the Chinese Chamber of Commerce and the Overseas Labor Union, which crossed dialect lines.[114]

When a genuine labor union was eventually organized in Thailand following World War II, it was open to both Thai and Chinese but the membership was almost exclusively Chinese, reflecting their predominance in the labor market. With the Thai leadership preoccupied with economic nationalism, it is not surprising that the government showed little interest in improving labor conditions, which would only benefit the Chinese. The suspicion with which the Thai authorities regarded any nongovernmental organization and the dominant role of Chinese labor were reflected in the absence of policies encouraging effective unionization. Instead, the Thai authorities sought ways to replace the Chinese with Thais.[115]

In the years following the coup of 1932, opportunities to Thaify labor were provided by strikes organized originally to ameliorate grievances of Chinese laborers. The first major opportunity was the big rice-mill strike of 1934, which involved Chinese both as mill owners and work-

[114] The latter organization, founded in 1909, was not a real labor union but rather a political arm of the Kuomintang and never amounted to much in membership or general impact.

[115] A typical pronouncement was Phibun's New Years broadcast speech in 1939 in which he said "aliens obtaining shelter in any civilized country whatsoever, . . . should engage in a few forms of livelihood only and not all of them, thus depriving the people in the land of such livelihood in an unjust manner. . . . If we should allow aliens to undertake all kinds of work, then it will not be long before the people in the land die." He also urged parents and guardians of Thai children to instill in them interest in "commerce, industry and agriculture" rather than in government service. See *The Bangkok Times Weekly Mail*, April 10, 1939.

ers. As the strike continued, the workers turned to the government for support but the result was not what the Chinese workers had expected. The government let the strike drag on and made little effort to prevent violence which exacerbated feelings on both sides. The government not only did nothing for the strikers, but when the strike was finally broken, seven of the organizers were deported to China.[116] Moreover, the government, ostensibly in response to a petition from the few Thai workers in the striking mills, used the opportunity to enact a law requiring rice mills to employ a minimum of 50 per cent Thai workers.[117]

A second major strike of both Thai and Chinese workers on the government railroads, declared at roughly the same time, ended in a similar fashion. The major outcome was not a significant change in the working conditions demanded by the strikers, but the gradual easing out of Chinese workers and their replacement by Thais. At the present, only Thai nationals are employed by the railway authority.

Thaification measures also took the form of restricting certain occupations to Thai nationals and the application of pressures to force aliens out of certain fields of economic endeavor. Although various laws were enacted to further this objective, often the authorities preferred the less conspicuous use of administrative directives and regulations. One observer commented:

Often anti-Chinese practices are carried out as the personal policy of an official in the administration of his department, presumably with the tacit approval, if not encouragement, of the government. Thus, Chinese are no longer chosen as retail agents of tobacco, wine, sugar or canned goods produced by government factories. Butchers' permits are not being issued to Chinese. The Ministry of the Interior has forbidden alien vendors of drinks or foodstuffs to sell or bring their goods into Ministry offices, and has instructed municipalities throughout the country not to permit aliens to monopolize stalls in food markets.[118]

The first law explicitly restricting an occupation to Thais was the 1939 amendment to the Vehicles Act which confined taxi driving to Thai nationals.[119] In June 1942, a royal decree was issued listing twenty-

[116] Skinner, *Chinese Society*, p. 219.   [117] Thompson, *op. cit.*, p. 115.

[118] Richard J. Coughlin, "The Status of the Chinese Minority in Thailand," *Pacific Affairs* (25), December 1952, p. 381.

[119] GOT, *Gazette*, April 10, 1939, quoted in Landon, *op. cit.*, pp. 230–231.

seven restricted occupations. These ranged from the practice of law, through hairdressing, to the manufacture of Buddha images and included, among others, the manufacture of bricks, firewood, charcoal, women's hats and dresses, and traditional Thai handicrafts such as lacquer and niello ware, and umbrellas. Aliens were allowed periods ranging from three months to one year to change over to other occupations.

Only two years later, in November 1944, the number of restricted occupations was reduced to four.[120] This was probably one of the measures produced to appease the Allies, particularly Nationalist China, when the defeat of Japan had begun to appear inevitable. A few years later the Thai government felt sufficiently secure to reinstate a number of occupational restrictions on aliens and in February 1949, a royal decree was published raising the number of restricted occupations to ten. These prohibited occupations, virtually all from the original list of 1942, included the manufacture of Buddha images, niello and lacquer work, driving public motor vehicles (buses), and tricycles and motor-tricycles for hire, rice farming, salt farming, haircutting, and Siamese type-setting.[121]

Taxi driving was reintroduced into the list along with six other occupations in August 1951, and in September 1952, a royal decree added three more restricted occupations: hair setting, hairdressing and dressmaking. The last royal decree restricting occupations added, as of January 1, 1961, sericulture, the making of silk products, and the weaving of silk fabric.[122] The choice of restricted occupations reflected the ease with which they were expected to be mastered by Thais as well as concern over the "alien" appearance of Thai cities.[123]

One of the most important occupations denied the Chinese was fishing. The Vessels Act of March 1939 forbade the operation of non-Thai vessels in the territorial waters of Thailand if they were mechanically propelled or if they were of six gross tons and upwards. This was

---

[120] Skinner, *Chinese Society*, p. 278.

[121] See GOT, *Gazette, 1948–1949*, pp. 662–663.

[122] GOT, *Gazette*, Dec. 31, 1960, mentioned in the Bank of Thailand *Monthly Report*, Feb. 1961, p. 11.

[123] Agriculture was always considered to be safely in Thai hands and did not attract the attention of policy makers concerned with economic nationalism. A change seems to have occurred lately, as it was reported that in its meeting on February 23, 1965, the cabinet "considered problems regarding the preservation of agricultural pursuits for Thai nationals" (*The Standard* [Bangkok], February 27, 1965).

followed in August of that year by the Act Concerning Fishing Rights in Thai Territorial Waters, which forbade alien participation in fishing.[124] The few remaining activities connected with the fishing industry, especially the wholesaling and retailing of fish, were closed to aliens in the early fifties. The Business of Fish Wharf Registration Act of January 1953, specifically authorized tight government control of the industry, and thereafter, government officials, as authorized by the new law, refused to renew licenses of aliens.

Less success was achieved through the Act for the Slaughter of Animals for Food, of March 1939, which provided for government control and licensing of slaughtering. Various municipalities, the army, and other Thai institutions, such as the War Veterans Organization, entered the business, and the latter for a time was granted the monopoly over pork distribution.[125] In spite of such monopolies and the difficulties they confronted in obtaining licenses, the Chinese remained prominent in this field.

The Chinese were forced out of other occupations through laws abolishing certain concessions. One such law was the Bird's Nest Concession Act of January 1939 under which the concession was discontinued and the government moved to monopolize the activity. This was a clearly anti-Chinese act, since the production of edible birds' nests had been in Chinese hands for centuries, and the consumers were exclusively Chinese.

Another thinly-veiled anti-Chinese measure was the Salt Act of March 1939, which provided that all salt had to be sold to the government. It was announced that the law was enacted "to encourage more scientific methods of salt production, to protect producer's prices, to control distribution, and encourage exportation of salt." [126] The Chinese were dominant in salt farming and distribution, and the law implied that they could not be expected to achieve the specified goals. Since the act became effective only eight days after it was passed in a secret session of the Assembly, and since the government could not provide adequate facilities on such short notice, waste and confusion resulted.

---

[124] The debate in the Assembly made it clear that fishing by aliens was not to be allowed, regardless of the method of fishing used. See *Thai Nikorn* and other dailies of August 14, 1939.

[125] For more details on the activities of this organization, see the section on trade and finance below, and that on government participation in production above.

[126] GOT, *Report of the Financial Adviser, 1939–1940*, p. 26.

After describing the piling up of salt exposed to the weather because of the inadequacy of government storage facilities, Landon wrote:

It seemed as though most of the salt farmers were deliberately forced into bankruptcy: and they were all Chinese. The cruelty of the whole process could not be glossed over, as far as the people were concerned, by the monotonous repetition of government officials that "Thailand is not anti-anything." The salt merchants, like the food hawkers, learned by bitter experience, that the government was "anti-them." [127]

Currently, the Thai Salt Company is operated by the Ministry of National Development.

Other occupational restrictions established by the Thai leadership were less dramatic in impact because they were not as comprehensive, were not publicized so widely, and did not involve direct replacement of the displaced Chinese by the government. But Thailand, especially Bangkok, is rife with rumors of impending restrictions. Such rumors are published in the local newspapers and, though not always reliable, they create an air of uncertainty which is fortified by the occasional restrictions that do materialize.[128] This practice has diminished since 1960.

As for the Thaification of hired labor, it has been promoted by measures requiring that a minimum percentage of Thais be employed in individual establishments. Although no blanket requirements were enacted before World War II, particular industries were covered by such laws as the Vessels Act of 1939. In addition, government contracts for industrial projects specified that no more than 25 per cent of the workers on the projects could be alien.[129] Similar provisions were included in scattered government regulations, but the available evidence suggests that these were not fully implemented because of the shortage of qualified Thai replacements.

The first so-called Vocational and Professional Assistance Act was promulgated in 1942. It empowered the government to establish a minimum percentage of Thai employees to be required in specified industries and plants. This act was subsequently replaced by the Vocational Assistance to Thais Act of February 1956.[130] In the main, the new

[127] Landon, *op. cit.*, p. 227.

[128] For samples of such rumors see Skinner, *Chinese Society*, p. 373, and Coughlin, *Double Identity*, p. 133.

[129] See Landon, *op. cit.*, pp. 242, 255.

[130] On two abortive legislative attempts in the intervening period, see Coughlin, *Double Identity*, p. 134.

act provided that any owner of a business employing more than ten employees should have no fewer Thai employees than would be required by the royal decrees that were to be issued. However, with few exceptions, the law limits the percentage of Thais to be required by such decrees to 50 per cent. Since then the government has on occasion designated industries to be subject to the act.[131]

With the initiation in 1958 of the drive to attract foreign investments, concern was expressed for the likelihood that prospective investors would be discouraged by the policy of requiring employment of Thai labor. In this connection, the newspaper *Chao Thai*, on July 9, 1959, commented that the policy of requiring some foreign investors to employ 50, and sometimes even 75 per cent Thai employees, would be frustrated unless the training of Thai technicians was speeded up. Premier Sarit made it clear, however, that the government intended to maintain control over those occupations open to aliens.[132] At the time of writing, the Thai government still insists on the employment of Thai nationals in increasing percentages but shows a high degree of flexibility. Most Occidental firms abide by this policy willingly and, in turn, their requests for permission to bring in required specialists beyond the immigration quota usually receive favorable treatment.

These measures to Thaify labor are reinforced by restrictions on the immigration of Chinese. An expanded, albeit inadequate, training program for Thais, combined with immigration curbs has caused a rise in the absolute number and the relative share of Thais in various occupations. Since many of the Thais who replaced the Chinese were ex-farmers, mostly from depressed areas in the Northeast, such replacements were concentrated in low-skilled occupations.

Although these developments are widely recognized as having occurred, data to substantiate them are fragmentary. Postwar Thai statistics do not provide information as to the ethnic composition of the labor force in the various industries. Skinner has made estimates, how-

---

[131] Enforcement is in the hands of the Labor Division in the Department of Public Welfare which also considers new categories where the provisions should apply. There were nine such categories in 1961 (GOT, Labor Division, *Labor Services in Thailand, 1961*, p. 6).

[132] In a cabinet meeting in July 1959, he said that he instructed the Interior Ministry to consider a law designed to control aliens' occupations (*Siam Rath*, July 21, 1959). This refers to all occupations, not only those restricted to Thai nationals. The aim was to maintain surveillance of aliens by requiring them to obtain permission to enter any occupation.

ever, of the relative shares of Chinese and Thai in the production of the four major commercial products of the country. According to these estimates, Chinese labor is not important at all in the actual production of paddy and also of timber logs. Not so in the production of raw rubber where the Chinese have a slight majority, nor in tin ore where they have an "easy majority." The Chinese share is greater in the processing stage in all these industries. They supply almost half of the labor force in rice milling, about half in sawmilling, and well over half in rubber processing.[133] Scattered information on other individual areas and industries confirm the trend toward Thaification, although the predominance of the Chinese in the industrial labor force continues. A recent estimate concluded that they still comprise 60 to 70 per cent of the industrial labor force, and their percentage of skilled labor is even higher.[134]

Direct governmental intervention has maintained a slow process of change in the ethnic composition of employment in Thailand. The success of Thaification policies has been limited, particularly attempts to reserve activities requiring special skills to Thais.[135] Other, less direct government measures such as immigration restrictions and vocational training have contributed toward increased Thai participation in economic activities other than rice farming. Greater progress depends upon the appearance of Thais willing and able to acquire the skills needed to replace the Chinese.

TRADE AND FINANCE

At the time of the 1932 revolution practically all trade, both internal and external, was dominated by aliens.[136] The same was true of finance as, outside of indigenous moneylending, financial institutions existed to

[133] Skinner, Chinese Society, pp. 351–353.

[134] United States Department of Labor, Bureau of Labor Statistics Report No. 267, Labor Law and Practice in Thailand, March 1964, p. 36.

[135] An anecdote involving the barbers in Bangkok illustrates how far Thaification still has to go in spite of occupational restrictions on aliens. Being an occupation long reserved for the Thais, municipal officials were disturbed by reports that many barbers could not speak Thai with a proper accent. The ensuing controversy over the remedies, if any, that might be taken exposed the subtle difficulties encountered in the pursuit of Thaification. See Siam Rath Weekly, January 13, 1963.

[136] In terms of numbers involved, the only exception of significance has been the direct peddling of Thai farm produce in the towns by the girls of the farm families.

service commerce. Such circumstances in other Southeast Asian countries have produced vigorous indigenism and a similar response might have been predicted for Thailand. Since foreign trade is the easiest sector of the economy for the government to control, one would expect it to be a primary target for indigenism. Little was done, however, to Thaify these sectors and the limited efforts met with only partial success. In view of the experience in other countries, the negligible use of exchange and trade controls to transfer these functions to Thai enterprises is particularly interesting.

Various factors contributed to this distinctive experience, not all of them clear. Obviously, experience, connections, and access to credit, all work in favor of already established traders. Less tangible, but not less important, is the culture block that inhibits entrepreneurship. The government can provide financing and even help in establishing adequate commercial connections, but it is not clear how Thai attitudes toward participation in trade can be changed. Because of the reluctance of the Thai to become commercial enterpreneurs, Thaification measures tended to lean on governmental and semigovernmental trading corporations. On the village level, desultory attempts were made to replace the Chinese middlemen and traders with credit and marketing cooperatives.

Progress proved more difficult than Thai policy makers had expected. It also became painfully obvious that curtailing Chinese commercial activities prior to the establishment of adequate alternatives would only dislocate the economy. That these facts of life were only slowly communicated to Thai nationalists was evident in the persistent pronouncements and policies reflecting the belief that Thaification could be achieved merely by restricting the activities of alien businessmen. Such policies led the financial adviser to issue the following warning:

Signs have not been wanting in the Press and in conversations with leading Siamese of a desire to accelerate the displacement of the foreign middleman by the introduction of restrictive measures on his activities in the country. . . . I would like to warn all those, who see in such action a quick road to salvation, that the adoption of such measures will only postpone and in no way hasten the attainment of the objects for which we are all working. At the present moment, the foreign tradesman and shopkeeper is just as integral a part of the national economic structure as the first floor walls are of a tall building: you cannot knock those first floor walls out without bringing the whole house down and, until you have prepared the struts and props to take their place and can safely insert them, things must be left as they are.[137]

Only cautious preliminary steps toward the Thaification of domestic commerce were taken prior to Phibun's rise to the premiership in 1938. An initial step was the Business Registration Act of November 1936. The purpose of this act was to collect information on the business establishments in the country, and commercial representatives were sent by the government to the provinces to collect the relevant information on virtually all nonfarm enterprises. The information demanded of enterprises included the race and nationality of the owners. Indigenism also appeared unambiguously in a minor law requiring businesses to be identified with a sign in Thai, or at least to have a Thai transliteration of any foreign language sign. This apparently was designed to facilitate identification of enterprises as well as to make Thailand look more Thai.

Two additional measures were taken in 1939 to facilitate government control over business establishments. In May, new regulations were issued providing for greater discretionary power in granting and abolishing trademarks.[138] The Accounts Act of November 6, 1939 required all establishments above a minimum size to provide the government with five types of accounts.[139]

Direct measures to interfere with Chinese traders were also undertaken. The first such move, which occurred at the end of 1938, took the form of instructions from the Ministry of Education to ministry officials and to school principals to forbid Chinese food hawkers to sell on and around school grounds. This step was copied by other ministries and affected thousands of Chinese in a trade that had been theirs for generations. A drive to publicize Thai cooking and to encourage Thais to enter the vending business accompanied this measure.

In order to encroach upon the Chinese dominance of wholesale and retail trade, the government established the Government Purchasing Bureau, but the impact of this Bureau prior to World War II was negligible. Within a few years of the war's end, however, the Bureau,

[137] GOT, *Report of the Financial Adviser for the Year 1938–39*, pp. 41–42.

[138] For details, see *Prajamitra*, May 16, 1939.

[139] Articles explaining how to prepare the accounts were published throughout January 1940 in newspapers, especially the *Siam Nikon*. A concise summary appeared in *Prajamitra* of May 1, 1940. For some details, see Landon, *op. cit.*, pp. 218–219. The law came into force on April 1, 1940.

together with the semigovernmental War Veterans Organization, began to exert a significant impact on the economic life of the country.

Reactivation of the Bureau in 1948 was connected with the government's promise to lower the cost of living.[140] For this purpose the Bureau was granted permission to import certain goods at the official rate of exchange. This established a strong advantage for the Bureau, as other importers had to acquire their foreign exchange at the market rate, which was much higher. In addition, the Bureau had a guaranteed market as more and more government departments began to make their purchases through it. It also expanded into the retail trade by opening department stores and other retail outlets, and in the 1950s it expanded its operations to exporting.

The Bureau co-operated in many of these activities with the semi-official War Veterans Organization, a society of demobilized servicemen which acquired strength and importance under the leadership of members of the power elite, notably Field Marshal Phin, one of the original promoters of the coup of 1932. This organization performed contract services for the government, sometimes forming individual corporations to provide particular services. At first it dealt in the sale of soft drinks and controlled products, such as cigarettes. It later expanded to take over certain state services such as stevedoring at government harbor installations and ferry services.[141] It obtained a monopoly over all slaughtering in Bangkok and the dining car concession on the railways, and somewhat later received the railway freight concession, giving it the power to decide priorities in the use of cars on the not yet fully rehabilitated railways. This placed the organization in a strategic position to "squeeze" merchants who wanted priorities for their shipments.

The Chinese businessmen sought increased security by entering into partnership with the Veterans Organization in particular and with influential Thais in general. For example, the Northeast Rice Millers Association, whose members were Chinese millers, entered into partnership with the Thahan Samakkhi, a corporation of the Veterans Organization. In the process, the "squeeze" was regularized "and allocated among the millers." [142] When the Veterans Organization obtained control over the freight cars, these millers had a clear advantage over their

---

[140] See U.S. Department of Commerce, International Reference Service, *Economic Review of Siam*, 1948 (6), July 1949, p. 1.

[141] *Ibid.*   [142] Skinner, *Chinese Society*, p. 347.

competitors. Many of the millers in other areas of the country also organized along similar lines. The Thahan Samakkhi, for its part, extended its activities into the lucrative rice trade, and the Chinese millers, who had become shareholders, had to sell half their output to the corporation.

Beginning in 1954, such connections between Chinese merchants and powerful Thais took the form of so-called syndicates, which were jointly financed and included politically influential Thais as directors. The chairman of the board of the syndicate formed by millers in the North, for example, was General, later Marshall and Premier, Sarit Thanarat. These syndicates were not restricted to the rice business but became widespread. The first syndicate to be formed was the so-called Thai Financial Syndicate, which was followed by the Gold Syndicate, the Pork Syndicate and the Remittance Syndicate. These nominally Thai syndicates excited the imagination of the Thai governing elite, and there were plans to expand the system to other economic fields such as foreign trade, tin, rubber, and so forth. Few of the planned syndicates materialized, however.[143]

Chinese businessmen continued to seek security by entering into such arrangements even after Thaification policies were moderated. As recently as 1959, twelve Chinese transport companies formed a syndicate and invited a police general and six police colonels to join their board of directors. In 1960, the Chinese manager of the Chinese owned Thai Development Bank invited a Thai general to become the chairman of the board.[144]

Although the syndicates were rationalized as a method for taking over activities dominated by the Chinese, in fact they were enterprises in which members of the ruling clique pooled their economic interests with Chinese.[145] Insofar as Thaification is concerned, the syndicates, by demonstrating that prominent Thais found it respectable to engage in business, may have had a positive psychological impact on Thai attitudes toward commerce. Otherwise, they served primarily to enrich a few already powerful Thai individuals, largely at the expense of other Thais. It is doubtful, moreover, whether even these few Thais acquired

[143] *Bangkok Post*, November 9, 1953.

[144] D. Insor, *Thailand, a Political, Social, and Economic Analysis* (London: George Allen and Unwin Ltd., 1963), p. 140.

[145] For more details on the syndicates and the personalities involved, see Skinner, *Chinese Society*, pp. 358–361.

useful business experience, since actual business operations continued to be conducted by the Chinese partners.

In the meantime, the Veterans Organization and the Purchasing Bureau came under severe criticism for their failure to lower prices as had been promised in exchange for the preferential treatment they received from the government. In reply to vehement criticism, both from within and outside the Assembly, officials of these organizations claimed they were forced to charge higher prices because they would not stoop to the practices and "vices" of the Chinese merchants. Such arguments, however, would not stand close examination.[146]

The objectives of Thaification and reduction in the cost of living were ignored, for the most part, because they came in conflict with the narrow interests of men in power. They used these organizations to increase their own wealth and to buy political support by distributing jobs, concessions, and other favors. Trade concessions were sometimes granted to various organizations, such as the Thai Labor Union and the Veterans Organization, which were only remotely related to trade. Since the interests of the men in power were involved, those receiving concessions could survive strong criticism voiced by people out of power.[147] The reshuffling of the men in power after the ouster of Phibun in 1957 led to a change in the fortunes of the trading monopolies. The Government Purchasing Bureau, for example, was dissolved by the cabinet in January 1960, since "it had outlived its usefulness." [148]

Some Thaification of the internal trade also occurred as the fortuitous consequence of policies with other objectives. For example, the government "monopoly" over rice exports was accompanied by increased participation of Thais in the rice trade. By stabilizing the internal price of

[146] A United Nations body ascribes the reasons to "high administrative costs and lax enforcement of governmental regulations fixing prices" (UN, ECAFE, *Economic Survey, 1951*, p. 292).

[147] "Only when a major scandal threatens, as in the case of the recent sugar shortages and soaring pork prices, for which those agencies were held responsible, has the government relaxed or partially removed a monopoly assigned to them" (Virginia Thompson and Richard Adloff, "The State's Role in Thai Economy," *Far Eastern Survey* [21], July 30, 1952).

[148] *Bangkok World*, January 18, 1960. The paper also related that after the Bureau's dissolution its assets would go to the Department of Interior Commerce and its business would be transferred to government departments that possessed sufficient background to take over. The monopoly on paper imports, which had provided 80 per cent of the Bureau's annual income, would be taken over by the Government Lottery Bureau.

rice, the monopoly diminished the risks involved, thereby making it easier for inexperienced Thais to enter this field of business.[149] Participation in commerce was also encouraged through the formation of Thai trade associations. The Bangkok Chamber of Commerce, the membership of which was restricted to Thai citizens, was formed in 1934. Most of the members, however, have been Thai nationals of Chinese extraction.[150] Nonetheless, the Chamber has played a role in making business activity more acceptable to Thais. Measures to promote trade organizations among Thais were renewed after the war, and in March 1953 a Food Trade Promotion Committee was set up with the Minister for Economic Affairs as its head. An announced aim of this committee was "the formation of trade associations by Thai which will take over from alien-controlled bodies." [151]

The limited concern of Thai nationalists to transfer importing and exporting to ethnic Thai contrasts sharply with the experiences found elsewhere in Southeast Asia. Traditionally, foreign trade in Thailand was a royal monopoly, and trading was done directly with foreign traders who found favor with the king. Thais were not encouraged to engage in trade, as they would compete with the throne which had to dispose of the products received as taxes in kind. This monopoly was voluntarily relinquished by King Rama IV (Mongkut) in the Bowring Treaty which allowed British traders to deal directly with individual Thais. While retaining the right to restrict the export of rice, salt, and fish, the Thai King agreed to specified low import and export duties on almost all traded goods.[152] Similar treaties were signed with other foreign powers and for all practical purposes, foreign trade was left to non-Thai traders. Even after the revision of the treaties in 1925 and 1926, the government confined its activities in the foreign trade field to the imposition of custom duties.

As we have seen, the government "monopoly" over rice exports after World War II did not eliminate the alien traders but rather used them as agents. At the same time, the monopoly and the subsequent export taxes and "premiums" did cut into the profits of these traders. With very few exceptions, however, there is little evidence of a serious effort

[149] Although the reduced risk was the immediate reason for this response, the changing Thai attitude toward engaging in trade was also important.

[150] Skinner, *Chinese Society*, p. 221.   [151] *Bangkok Post*, March 17, 1953.

[152] For the Bowring Treaty, the negotiations leading up to it, and other observations see Sir John Bowring, *The Kingdom and People of Siam* (London, 1857), Vol. II.

to Thaify foreign trade. The major exceptions are the government-to-government agreements signed with countries such as Indonesia which insisted on such agreements, but the Thai government relies on the services of private traders to fill the contracts.

Since export and import licenses have been required during most of the post-World War II period, it is surprising that the Thai government failed to use licensing to divert these activities to the Thais. It is true that some officials used their discretionary control over licensing to extract some benefits for themselves, but this cannot be regarded as Thaification. During the period of rice export monopoly, moreover, the government allowed private exporters to export on their own, outside the monopoly, to take advantage of the free market prices when they were higher than the prices specified in government-to-government contracts. This was particularly true in 1951, during the Korean boom, when a lively market for export permits developed.[153] There were rumors that this trading in permits developed because the government allocated permits to "dummy" Thai companies who then sold them to alien exporters. These rumors, however, have not been documented.

Commercial banking in Thailand, especially prior to World War II, was in the English tradition and managed by foreigners who were neither familiar with nor interested in rural conditions.[154] Practically all financial institutions in Thailand were oriented toward external transactions; the commercial banks were preoccupied with providing short-term credit to finance foreign trade, and the Chinese remittance houses were concerned with transactions abroad. In spite of this foreign orientation of the financial sector, little was done by the Thai authorities to modify it before World War II. The one exception was the Bank of Asia, which was established in 1939 in part to provide training ground for young Thais.[155]

With the Japanese occupation, however, the foreign banks, except for the single Japanese one, were confiscated, and their operations suspended. The existing banks of Thai registry, as well as five new ones, filled the gap created by the closure of the foreign banks. Isolated by the war, and utilizing the trained personnel released by the closing of

---

[153] Ingram, *op. cit.*, p. 91.

[154] Of the twelve banks operating in Thailand before World War II, seven were foreign, and the five registered in Thailand were established primarily with domestic Chinese capital and managed largely by non-Thais.

[155] See Paul Sithi-Amnuei, *Finance and Banking in Thailand* (Bangkok: Thai Watana Panich, 1964), p. 45.

the alien banks, the Thai banks reached a level of maturity that enabled them to survive after the war.

Following the war, the foreign banks renewed operations, and five new banks of foreign registry were opened between 1947 and 1952. There is little evidence of official discrimination against these banks. It is significant that, in spite of the termination of the wartime protection, five new banks of Thai registry were also opened during the same period. Moreover, whereas before the war there were few bank branches outside the Bangkok area, the postwar period witnessed a proliferation of branches into most provinces.

In the early 1950s the Thai government, influenced by the warnings of the financial adviser,[156] decided to dampen the postwar expansion in the number of banks. Although the adviser was primarily concerned over the local banks which, unlike the foreign banks, often had flimsy financial foundations, the Thai authorities established a limit on all banks. The number of banks of foreign registry was limited to one for each foreign country, whereas the founding of new Thai banks was curtailed through stricter financial and legal requirements imposed by the Bank of Thailand. Branch offices in the provinces, however, continued to proliferate, and almost all such branches were opened by banks of Thai registry. At present foreign banks are not allowed to open branches in the provinces. On the other hand, the rule that each country can have only one bank in Thailand was slightly relaxed. At present there are in Thailand two banks incorporated in Japan and two incorporated in the United States.[157]

Thaification of insurance followed the pattern of commercial banking, alebit more slowly, as foreign insurance companies were closed during the war and Thai companies expanded. There were, however, fewer experienced Thai personnel and a smaller volume of business as compared to commercial banking. After the war, a substantial expansion in insurance business and in the number of Thai companies has taken place, but branch offices of big foreign firms are still conducting extensive operations.

In the field of agricultural credit, Thaification efforts have been concentrated in the promotion of credit co-operatives to ease the debt

[156] GOT, Ministry of Finance, *Report of the Financial Adviser for the Years 1941–1950*, p. 63.

[157] See Alek A. Rozental, *Commercial Banking in Thailand*, National Planning Association, Center for Development Planning (February 1967, mimeographed).

burden of the farmers by reducing their dependence on the middle-men, most of whom were Chinese. The co-operative movement, founded by the government without significant grass-roots initiative, has continued to require government management and subsidization, and has had only limited impact.[158]

The premises basic to government promotion of credit co-operatives, that the Chinese middlemen have been the primary source of loans, or that they charge the highest interest, is not supported by available data. Relatives and neighbors appear to have been the ones most fre-quently approached by the borrowers. Available surveys indicate that the highest interest rates were charged by landlords and not the Chinese crop buyers (see Table 26). Moreover, the professional money-lenders, who charge high interest, are not primarily Chinese.[159] The credit co-operatives have failed to bring about a general lowering of interest rates in agriculture or to significantly Thaify farm credit. Similarly, marketing co-operatives remain small in number and in impact. There also are so-called co-operative shops—wholesale and retail stores in the cities. Although these have not had an observable impact on internal trade, the government encourages their prolifera-tion.[160]

Indigenism has been surprisingly moderate in commerce especially in foreign trade. Such moderation does not mean that Thaification of commercial activities has been rejected as a policy goal so much as it does the difficulties confronting Thais in their efforts to acquire com-mercial expertise. Most commerce is conducted through the family businesses of the Chinese and such enterprises rarely employ outsiders. The intricacies of credit and commercial connections, therefore, remain a mystery to the Thais. The importance of such "apprenticeship" is

---

[158] In the beginning of the 1960s about 200,000 farmers were connected with co-operatives, out of about 3,500,000 agricultural households. Table 26 shows that the relative importance of the co-operatives as a source of credit has declined in recent years.

[159] That the picture was not much different in the 1930s can be seen from the following quotation: "If the farmer is of good reputation, he is allowed to borrow from the Chinese at interest rates well below the legal limit and, even in a number of cases when it was very evident that the farmer was not a man of good reputation, the interest rates were still below the legal limit. The Siamese farmer, and especially his wife, is much more given to money-lending with the hope of high profits than is the Chinese." James M. Andrews, *Siam, Second Rural Eco-nomic Survey, 1934–1935* (Bangkok: Bangkok Times Press, 1935), p. 332.

[160] *Standard* (Bangkok), January 13, 1965.

Table 26. Farm credit by type of lender, average size of loan, and interest charged, 1953 and 1962–1963

	1953			1962–1963		
Type of lender	Number of loans (per cent)[a]	Average size of loan (baht)	Interest charged (per cent per annum)	Number of loans (per cent)	Average size of loan (baht)	Interest charged (per cent per annum)
Institutional						
Credit co-operatives	13.99	1,505	8.54	7.5	1,949	9.6
Other government	0.19	514	0.00	0.4	2,126	9.6
Commercial banks	0.0	0	n.a.	0.0	0	n.a.
Commercial						
Landlords	1.98	904	44.70	2.1	3,531	42.0
Crop buyers	3.19	2,720	25.64	8.6	1,921	34.8
Village store	11.53	1,231	28.24	16.5	782	42.0
Moneylenders	12.52	2,145	30.90	5.4	3,425	39.6
Other	1.15	1,448	17.91	3.9	1,328	30.0
Relatives [b]	55.43	1,092	18.29	39.9	2,124	21.6
Neighbors	—	n.a.	n.a.	15.7	2,123	31.2

Sources: Data for 1953 were processed from Table 47 in GOT, Ministry of Agriculture, *Thailand Economic Farm Survey*, 1953. Data for 1962-63 were taken from Tables 1, 2, and 4 in Pantum Thisyamondol, Virach Aromdee, and Millard Long, *Agricultural Credit in Thailand* (Bangkok: Kasaetsart University, 1965)

[a] Of the farmers surveyed, 31.3 per cent had obtained loans.

[b] This category may have included neighbors in the earlier survey.

emphasized by the relative success achieved in Thaifying banking and insurance where wartime isolation exposed ethnic Thais to experiences that have contributed to their postwar competitiveness in these fields.[161]

FOREIGN INVESTMENT

Foreign private investments in Thailand were never substantial and were further diminished by the nationalization measures of the late 1930s and early 1940s. Early postwar attempts to assess the aggregate amount of existing foreign investments were deficient because of lack of data and the uncertainty as to what constituted a "foreign" firm.[162] Subject to these limitations, the available estimates attributed 70 per cent of foreign capital invested in firms with capital of over a million baht in 1949 to Chinese enterprises. The British were a poor second, with an estimated 4 per cent, followed by Indian, Swedish, American, and Iranian capital. Since most of the foreign firms with capital less than a million baht were Chinese, the Chinese share of total foreign capital was even greater than the estimated 70 per cent. As for the fields of investment, the same estimates indicated that about 60 per cent of the value of foreign investment in 1949 was in trading firms, 25 per cent in primary production, and about 15 per cent in manufacturing.[163]

A later survey of the foreign investments in Thailand, using different classifications, was conducted by the Bank of Thailand at the end of 1954. According to this survey, total foreign investment at the time was equivalent to forty million dollars. The survey showed that 95 per cent of this was "direct" investment in branch offices or subsidiaries of foreign firms. This distribution was, roughly, 69 per cent in wholesale trade, 23 per cent in mining enterprises, 4 per cent in chemicals, and 4 per cent in other enterprises.[164] These estimates confirm that the major

---

[161] It should be pointed out, however, that most banks of Thai registry are still owned and run by Chinese. Nonetheless, the number of ethnic Thai in most positions has increased substantially.

[162] In the study referred to, investments made by branches of firms incorporated abroad were not included in such estimates. On the other hand, firms registered in Thailand in which foreigners held more than 50 per cent of the capital were considered foreign. See Suparb Yossundara, *A Preliminary Survey on Foreign Investments in Thailand*, prepared for the International Monetary Fund, December 15, 1951 (mimeographed).

[163] *Ibid, passim.*

[164] See Amos Yoder, "Patterns of Foreign Investment in Thailand," *Far Eastern Survey* (26), November 1957, p. 174.

part of the investment was in trade where there is rapid turnover. The National Economic Development Board conducted still another survey of foreign investment in 1964, but the results were not released because of their doubtful reliability.

Data on the share in total investment by the Chinese of Thai nationality are, of course, fragmentary and of doubtful reliability in view of the imprecise definition of such Chinese. However, since this is one of the most sensitive areas of economic nationalism in Thailand, a rough estimate of their share in the four major commercial products is attempted here.[165] There has been practically no Chinese capital or entrepreneurship in paddy production, some in the production of timber logs, and an important but minority role in tin extraction with the rest Australian and European. Among primary products, only in rubber has Chinese capital played a major role although it also appears to be prominent in new export crops such as corn. The share of Chinese capital and entrepreneurship is much greater in the processing stages of primary products and plays the major role, in descending order of relative importance, in rice milling, sawmilling, and rubber processing. Chinese participation is, of course, largest in the marketing stage. They predominate in the domestic distribution of rice and timber and play a major role in the export of all four major products.

During the 1960s there has been a substantial increase in investment in manufacturing and assembling industries with large foreign participation. The details are discussed below. Here we would like to mention that about two-thirds of the registered capital in the new investments was recorded as coming from Thai citizens. There are no data indicating the part that came from persons who are ethnic Chinese by the definition adopted here. Nonetheless, the fact that they predominate in the Thai business community would suggest that they had put up a major part of the new capital.

The generally *laissez-faire* attitude of the absolute monarchy toward foreign investments began to change after the 1932 coup. This change was dramatized by the Pridi plan, which allowed little scope for foreign investment.[166] The substitute program of the Ministry of Economic Affairs, however, adopted a different attitude, declaring that

any persons desiring to set up an industry will be assisted as follows: (1) An adequate protection in respect to patents, trademarks, designs, samples,

[165] Based primarily on estimates in Skinner, *Chinese Society*, pp. 351–353.
[166] See above, section on the environment of policy.

models, copyrights, and similar matters. (2) Any industry which the government desires to create, but which is too big an undertaking for private persons, shall be started by the government in the form of a public corporation, having private individuals as shareholders and conducted semi-officially.[167]

If the first provision was considered a lure to foreign investors, such a view proved naive since, in many lines of manufacture, such protection is not important in a country like Thailand. Foreign investment in Thailand was inhibited by more basic factors such as lack of cheap electric power, limited markets, shortage of trained personnel, difficulties in securing matching local capital, and the like. Government practice, as opposed to occasional declarations by high government officials, continued to intimidate foreign investors. This was particularly evident after the rise of Phibun to power in December 1938. But even the governments headed by Phibun promised national treatment to foreign investors, except in certain specified industries including the owning and operation of commercial vessels, the distillation of alcohol, the manufacture of tobacco, opium and playing cards, the generation of electricity, and the operation of trams.[168] In a number of unspecified businesses and industries, however, the government reserved the right to participate as partner or shareholder. Moreover, land ownership by aliens continued to be restricted except when modified by a treaty between Thailand and the investor's government.[169]

The promise of national treatment in sectors other than those specifically reserved was not very convincing to the foreign investors, particularly as occasional consultations between ministries to discuss the desirability of nationalizing specific industries received wide publicity. It was believed that news of such consultations was planted to test the public reaction. One such trial balloon was a so-called five-year plan for transferring alien rubber holdings to Thais. It was announced that the Ministry of Foreign Affairs had been instructed in September 1951 to analyze the "plan" for possible violation of existing treaties.[170] Similar "plans" have been given publicity on various occasions since then.

[167] *Daily Mail*, September 20, 1933.

[168] Wolfram mining was added to the list in August 1951, when the private concessions were discontinued by the Thai government and were taken over by the Mines Department.

[169] For fuller information see UN, ECAFE, *Foreign Investment Laws and Regulations of the Countries of Asia and the Far East* (Bangkok, January 1961).

[170] See the various Bangkok dailies of that month.

A major change in Thai attitude toward foreign investments was supposed to have occurred in the second half of 1954, when an investment guarantee treaty was negotiated with the USAID mission. This agreement guaranteed American investors against losses caused by expropriation or inconvertability of profits and capital.[171] In October of the same year, the Industrial Promotion Act was passed by the Assembly.[172] This act, which purported to be a milestone in Thai foreign investment policy, was commonly referred to, in private, by both Thai and non-Thai as the "act for the discouragement of investments." The act, most of which concerned the administrative procedures through which an investment proposal is screened, did not foster any discernible increase in foreign investments. A special commission, half of whose members were ministers, was created to pass judgement on industrial priorities. The commission also was assigned responsibility to recommend the type of incentives to be extended to each specific industry. Such incentives included exemptions from taxes and duties, permission to remit profits, and so forth.

The ineffectiveness of the act came as no surprise. The World Bank mission assessed it as "confused in its wording, difficult to administer, and gives the impression that applicants will be penalized rather than helped. . . There is excessive delay in dealing with applications, and the results—as might be expected—are negligible." [173] At the time the IBRD report was written (1958), some ninety-three applications had been submitted, but "no action of practical significance has resulted." [174]

The effectiveness of the Industrial Promotion Act was further reduced by the persistent practice by executive branches of the Thai government of building plants in competition with successful private enterprises. This was particularly true of the Ministry of Defence and its departments. For example, American businessmen complained that the military has shown a "discouraging propensity to move in on the

[171] In 1957 it was amended to permit coverage for damage to physical assets caused by war. See United States Department of Commerce, World Trade Information Service, *Summary of Investment Factors in Thailand*, Part 1, No. 59–69 (Washington, D.C., August 1959).

[172] GOT, *Gazette, 1954*, pp. 312–315.

[173] IBRD, *op. cit.*, p. 98. The World Bank mission proceeded to draft a new act, proposing changes that would, the mission hoped, increase foreign investments.

[174] *Ibid.*

private sector of the economy. Thus when an Australian company began to make money in a glass factory, the Navy set up its own competing plant." [175] Even the Thai Cement Company did not escape this kind of competition in spite of the large Thai share in its ownership. The government built a competing cement factory and, as a result, total capacity exceeded local demand. It was not the fear of the efficiency of government enterprises that disturbed the foreign businessmen but the special privileges usually granted to these enterprises. Moreover, because of the limited Thai market, an additional government plant might invalidate the market calculations on which the initial private investment was based.

From the time of the promulgation of the 1954 Industrial Promotion Act until 1958 only two foreign enterprises of significant size actually started operations in Thailand. One of these was a tapioca company, subsidiary of the International Basic Economy (Rockefeller) Corporation and associated with the Bombay Burmah Trading Corporation, a British firm. This company was the first and only company in Thailand to receive a guarantee under the investment guarantee agreement with the United States.[176] The second foreign investment was a reconstituted-milk plant, one of a series erected by Foremost Dairies in Far Eastern countries, and combined American and Thai capital. The investors naturally believed that the Act was really designed to encourage investment and therefore proceeded to apply for a duty rebate on the import of machinery and raw materials to which they were entitled under the Act. Years later, at the end of 1959, the matter was still "under consideration." [177]

The coming to power of Sarit in 1958 marked a significant change in foreign investment policies. In Announcement No. 33 of the Revolutionary Party, made public on December 5, 1958, two months after their assumption of power, Sarit and his colleagues declared that the promotion of economic development, especially through industrialization, was their major goal. The new government issued regulations encouraging private investment, both indigenous and foreign, and moved to amend the Industrial Promotion Act.[178]

[175] *Fortune,* April 1958.
[176] See UN, ECAFE, *Economic Survey, 1956,* p. 166.
[177] Information was obtained from officials of the U.S. Department of Commerce.
[178] See Announcement No. 33, GOT, *Gazette, 1958,* p. 731.

The Revolutionary Party further promised that all enterprises, whatever their form of organization or nationality, should enjoy similar rights. A commission was created to screen and authorize investments. Once a person or enterprise was approved by the commission it was guaranteed that "the state will set up no new factory in competition," and that "the state will not transfer any private industrial enterprise to the state." [179] Incentives extended included exemption from tariff duties on imports of machinery, accessories, and equipment not produced in Thailand; exemption from internal revenue taxes for two to five years; permission to repatriate capital in foreign currency; and authorization to bring in skilled workers and industrial experts outside of the immigration quotas.

In special cases the commission could supplement the above benefits with further privileges, including exemption from or reduction of import duties on raw materials; exemption from or reduction of export duties; and protection by prohibition of competing imports, or imposition of protective duties on such imports, or direct prohibition of the establishment of competing enterprises. On January 12, 1959, Announcement No. 47 was issued stating that permission to own land would be granted to approved industrial undertakings. It was also announced that all concessions and privileges would apply retroactively.

To implement the new policy, a Board of Investments was appointed on April 28, 1959. The members were representatives of ministries and government agencies under the chairmanship of Nai Thawee Boonyaket, a Thai official with long experience in offices concerned with economic affairs.[180]

Toward the end of 1960 a new Promotion of Industrial Investment Act, B.E. 2503, was promulgated. The main purpose was to consolidate in one single act the various laws and regulations concerned with the promotion and control of industrial investment. It also expanded the coverage to include "cultivation, animal raising, fishery, transportation,

---

[179] *Ibid.*

[180] The high hopes from the new policy were evident at the opening meeting of the Board when Sarit said: "We have been dreaming for a long time that Thailand will turn from an agricultural country into an agricultural and industrial one, that our country can be self-supporting and free from privation and that the people will be provided with housing and have large incomes." Whether this will come about, he said, "depends upon the actions of this Board" (*Samseri,* May 20, 1959). The fact that all the provisions were intended for local, as well as foreign, capital was sometimes lost sight of. See *Kiattisak* of June 30, 1959.

and tourist promotion" [181] and appended a complete list of the types of enterprises eligible for promotion.

Not satisfied with the pace of new investments, the Thai authorities issued yet another investment act, with even more generous provisions, in February 1962. The new features in the Promotion of Industrial Investment Act, B.E. 2505, included provisions for expediting promotional assistance. Tax concessions were made more generous, some tax grace periods were prolonged, and regulations governing the remission abroad of loan repayments and interest were liberalized. [182]

That the new policy has impressed potential investors, is evident in the increasing number of applications for approval of new foreign investments. The accomplishments under the new policy during the first eight years are summarized in Table 27.

It should be borne in mind that the table includes only those industrial enterprises that applied for and received privileges under the new investment laws. A greater number applied for the privileges and a greater number still, mostly small enterprises, did not apply at all. Also, not all approvals actually resulted in investments. Out of about 470 firms granted promotion certificates, only about 300 were in production by the beginning of 1968. [183] Although this discrepancy reflects in part changes in the plans of investors, it is mostly due to the time lag necessary for construction. [184] Classification of the applicants by nationality indicates that a large number are Thai citizens and that more than half of the registered capital of the approved applying companies was Thai. Yet, such figures are misleading because many of the relevant Thai citizens are Chinese by the definition adopted here and, moreover, the registered capital is often but a small part of the actual capital involved. A much larger part of the investment is provided by nonequity capital which in practically all large establishments is supplied by foreign companies and subject to conditions that provide the lender with virtual control over the operations of the recipient

[181] GOT, *Gazette*, Vol. 77, reproduced in Bank of Thailand *Monthly Report*, January 1961, p. 23.

[182] GOT, *Gazette*, Vol. 79, as paraphrased in Bank of Thailand, *Monthly Report*, February 1962, p. 13.

[183] Figures taken from a speech delivered on May 7, 1968 by H. E. Pote Sarasin, Minister of National Development, at the Thailand seminar of the American Management Association in New York.

[184] The enterprises cover a wide range of products and processes. The relatively large ones include assembly plants for automobiles, trucks and tractors, tires, and so forth. At the other end of the spectrum, approved enterprises include those engaging in the drying of corn, production of buttons, and the like.

Table 27. Approved investment promotion applications, April 1959–December 1966
(number, million baht)

Items	1959	1960	1961	1962	1963	1964	1965	1966	Total
					(number)				
Applications approved by the Board of Investment	54	48	66	65	82	69	67	90	541
Applicant corporations or limited partnerships signing contracts and receiving promotion certificates	23	40	34	42	61	58	50	40	348
Classified by ownership									
Thai-owned enterprises	9	18	21	14	20	17	23	17	139
Foreign-owned enterprises	2	2	1	2	5	2	0	4	18
Joint venture enterprises	12	20	12	26	36	39	27	19	191
Classified by stage of operation in Thailand									
Enterprises initiating operations	16	25	23	27	45	39	42	35	252
Enterprises proposing expansion in operations	7	15	11	15	16	19	8	5	96
Capital data:					(million baht)				
Total registered capital in application	212	427	206	368	522	432	219	538	2,924
Thai capital	139	354	166	248	327	240	138	338	1,949
Foreign capital	74	73	40	120	194	192	81	201	974
Total capitalization in Thailand	420	857	1,020	1,105	1,582	1,685	567	1,860	9,097
Machinery costs	270	465	550	591	941	901	304	1,120	5,142
Employment data:					(number)				
Expected increase in employment	4,237	12,407	3,926	5,400	9,908	9,539	6,246	5,308	56,971

Source: GOT, Board of Investment, December 1967. Figures supersede earlier and, in some cases, contradictory official data. The amounts refer to the total value of all applications approved by the Board and are not restricted to applicants granted promotion certificates and who have signed contracts with the government. It appears to be the practice where existing companies make applications in connection with proposals to expand existing facilities, to show their total registered capital and not merely the capital required for expansion.

companies. In terms of nationality, the Japanese have been the largest foreign investors, with Nationalist Chinese and Americans second and third. Most American capital is in joint ventures with Thai capital.

It is significant that there has been no evidence of discrimination against the non-Thai in the implementation of the investment laws. In fact, it sometimes appeared as if the new laws were biased in favor of the foreign investors.

There were occasional relapses, however. A case in point is the new section introduced into the revised Revenue Code at the end of 1959, requiring payment of a 15 per cent tax on profits remitted abroad. The section's wording is vague and has given rise to different interpretations. Foreign investors and representatives of their governments have tended to interpret it as a form of double taxation and as portending the restriction of remittances. Thai government officials, however, insisted that such an interpretation is unwarranted and have refused to eliminate the section or to change it.[185]

Such relapses notwithstanding, Thailand's interest in foreign investments, especially American investments, is greater than ever. Besides the obvious economic considerations, there is now also the consideration of long-term national security to bear in mind. A substantial American economic stake in Thailand would, presumably, provide her with an added incentive to come to the protection of Thailand in time of danger. Whatever the precise motivations, Thailand's efforts to attract American investors are unmistakable.

Summary

Although never a colony, Thailand had to face the problem common to former colonies in Southeast Asia, of economic domination by aliens over important segments of her economy. Concern for this situation

---

[185] The various and sometimes contradictory explanations given by various high officials did not remove the uncertainty. For those of the Minister of Finance and the Governor of the Bank of Thailand, see *Bangkok World*, February 9, 1960. For another and more soothing explanation by a high official of the Ministry of Finance, see *Bangkok World*, February 14, 1960. Some of the apprehensions of American investors were removed by the Thailand-United States tax treaty signed March 1, 1965.

dates back to the first decade of this century, but it was only after the 1932 coup that concrete measures for Thaification were introduced. The members of the groups that achieved power through this revolution were imbued with Western ideas of exclusive nationalism and were therefore more sensitive to the presence and activities of unassimilated aliens in their country. This leadership group embarked upon Thaification policies following the revolution, giving Thailand a head start on neighboring states which had to await postwar independence.

The Thai experience points to the near universality and appeal that economic nationalism has for underdeveloped countries. Although never a colony, and a society the members of which are, by and large, self-assured and tolerant, Thailand has displayed a persistant, if erratic, determination to indigenize. This is all the more significant since the Thai show little inclination to strong commitments and tend to be pragmatic and practical.

The Thai found, however, that there are no shortcuts enabling them to Thaify key sectors of the economy. Restrictions on the economic activities of aliens did not automatically produce Thaification. Only in such occupations as taxi driving, which require a relatively short period of training, did Thais take over completely. In commerce and manufacturing activities, in addition to required skills, experience, and connections, a set of values commensurate with such activities was essential for success. The Thai, in common with most other people in underdeveloped countries, are in the process of slowly acquiring such a system of values. The expanding role of Thais in banking, in some of the professions, and in a few other fields attests to the progress toward modernization that has been achieved.

Government policies of economic nationalism have contributed to this progress, but much of it appears to have been the result of a long process of change stimulated by increasing exposure to outside influences. Moreover, the Thai rank and file have not shared the intense concern over alien economic control demonstrated by members of the ruling elite. It is significant in this connection, that no serious attempt has been made to organize a boycott of alien enterprises by the general Thai public, as has been done by some government offices. Such attempts in all likelihood would have been defeated by apathy and indifference.

A somewhat less obvious lesson to be extracted from the Thai experience has been the demonstrated basic correlation between premature indigenism and corruption. The failure to achieve substantial Thaification can be accounted for, in part, by the lack of perseverence and integrity among nationalist policy makers. This was particularly true when opportunities for personal gains were present, and implementation proved difficult. We have seen that most officials on the policy making level belong to the transient element of Thai society, the members of which have unconsciously parted with a number of traditional restraining values without having developed substitutes more compatible with the new social and economic realities. It proved difficult for them to resist the temptations that modernization and their positions of control created. Often unenforceable policies of indigenism remained on the books to be used by such officials to harass alien businessmen for personal gain, while invoking the "national interest."

We have seen that in order to secure some degree of protection, the alien businessmen sought ways to bribe such officials. The form of this activity varied according to the concrete circumstances. One of the more common techniques was to collaborate with high Thai officials. Alien enterprises were "Thaified" through the nomination of prominent Thai personalities to directorships or through entering into some form of partnership with Thai organizations.

Having thus become accustomed to "easy money," it is not surprising that these politically powerful Thais expected to achieve easy success when they launched their own enterprises. Such an attitude was conducive to failure, the most prominent example of which was the bankruptcy of NEDCOL. The damage done by this failure exceeded the immediate losses involved, since it was widely interpreted as demonstrating the futility of attempts to establish genuinely Thai enterprises. Another technique for industrialization and Thaification that received thorough testing was government participation in commercial activities. The experience of Thailand, however, scarcely demonstrates the efficacy of this method. Corruption and inefficiency were not less evident in governmental establishments than in the government-supported enterprises in the private sector. This Thai experience has been paralleled in a number of other underdeveloped countries in Southeast Asia.

Another lesson to be learned from the longer Thai experience with economic nationalism is the tendency for nationalistic fervor to decline with the passage of time. The successive failures proved a sobering lesson to the Thai, and the governments of Sarit and Thanom have

shown clear willingness to moderate the policies of economic nationalism, especially those directed against non-Chinese. Priority is given to
the economic development of the country, and Thaification policies in
conflict with this goal have suffered loss of priority. The new approach
is especially evident in the positive encouragement now conferred upon
foreign investors. There has also been some moderation of measures
directed against the Chinese, although to a large extent this may reflect
confidence, engendered by postwar economic growth, that the functional specialization of this minority is declining in importance. Such
confidence is also encouraged by the effectiveness of controls over
immigration and Chinese education which, together with appropriate
naturalization laws, will facilitate the assimilation of the resident
Chinese.

If these expectations materialize, the dichotomy that sometimes
exists between the national interests and the narrower interests of the
ethnic Thai vis-à-vis the resident Chinese will become less sharp.
Instead of constraining this most economically active element of the
population, the Chinese will be absorbed into the national society.
This appears to be the most desirable solution, and only time will tell
to what extent it will materialize. Whether economic nationalism in
other societies will follow the same pattern is a matter of conjecture.

6

MALAYA*

The Environment of Policy

The decision to include analysis of Malayan rather than Malaysian indigenism is supported by various considerations.[1] Because Malaysia is young and unstable and its leaders preoccupied with threats to the viability of their new country, an attempt to identify the nature of Malaysian economic nationalism would be premature. The external challenges of Konfrontasi, the withdrawal of the British military presence, and the "spinning off" of Singapore have reinforced the realities of spatially isolated territories, economic diversity, and racial and ethnic animosities to moderate the priority of indigenism. At a more mundane level, analysis of indigenism in Malaysia must confront the paucity of statistical information, not to mention the nagging question of the relevance of aggregates including such diverse economies and societies.

Although study of Malaysian economic nationalism would be premature at this time, indigenism as it has evolved in the Federation of Malaya provides insight into the path this phenomenon is likely to follow in Malaysia—should she prove viable. The initiative and political expertise of Malayan political elites, reinforced by the economic strength of Malaya and the dominance of Malayans in the total population, will maintain strong Malayan influence over the new state. Malaya

* The field research behind this study of Malayan indigenism was supported by generous fellowships from the John Simon Guggenheim Foundation, the Social Science Research Council, and the Cornell Southeast Asia Program—F. H. G.

[1] Malaya will be used to refer to the territory of the Federation of Malaya which in the state of Malaysia is called West Malaysia.

can be expected to maintain autonomy zealously over domestic policies affecting economic change and social integration within her territories and to use the political process to extend such policies to the larger federation.

An attempt to fit Malaya into our comparative study must confront the fact that Malayan indigenism is at once more subtle and more complex than that found elsewhere in Southeast Asia. The dominant influence upon indigenism is the racial balance and the resulting strength of communal identification by the racial elements within the society. The census of 1957 revealed that the Malays (including a substantial number of Indonesian immigrants), who accounted for 49.8 per cent of the population, were a minority in their homeland. The Chinese, of whom a large majority are locally-born "Straits Chinese," accounted for 37.2 per cent, Indians, including Pakistanis, for 11.3 per cent, with others, including the economically important Western elements, comprising 1.8 per cent.

Prior to World War II, Malaya's population was demographically unstable and influenced by heavy immigration as well as natural increase. In the postwar period, net immigration has ceased to be a significant factor and demographic characteristics in the future will reflect the rates of natural increase of the various communal groups. The census of 1921 revealed that only 21 per cent of the Chinese and 12 per cent of the Indians in the states that became Malaya were born in the area of Malaya or in Singapore. In the 1957 census, these ratios were 76 per cent and 65 per cent respectively, and of persons aged 15 years and under, 98.6 per cent of the Chinese and 96.6 per cent of the Indians were born locally. Also contributing to the growing demographic stability of the non-Malay population has been the increase in the proportion of females. Whereas the 1921 census tabulated 371 Chinese and 424 Indian females per 1000 males in each group, in the 1957 census the numbers had increased to 926 for the Chinese community and 746 for the Indian.

The racial composition of the population creates a massive problem of integration if Malayan—and Malaysian—nationality is to acquire significance appropriate to the social stability of the national society. The present situation is one of uneasy equilibrium in which the political dominance of the Malay community is offset by the economic dominance of the rational and energetic Chinese population. The Malay image of integration attaches primary importance to effective economic equality among the Malays and Chinese. To achieve this, the Malays expect to use their monopoly of political power to promote the modernization and material progress of the Malay population.

The political realities of the communal society and mutual recognition by the racial communities of the ultimate goal of a viable Malayan (Malaysian) state have imparted a distinctive character to the policies and institutions of indigenism as compared to other countries in the area. Political leaders of each of the communities have displayed persistent willingness to try to understand and accommodate the apprehensions of the other communities. The Malay community, relatively secure in its domination of political power, accepts an essentially *laissez-faire* economic organization which provides the Chinese with adequate scope for functional specialization and material progress. The Chinese community, relatively secure in its economic superiority, acquiesces in the use of the powers and revenues of the state to promote the economic modernization of the rural Malay society and remains patient in the face of discriminatory educational, language, and religious policies, which contribute to Malay security.

Malayan economic nationalism is presently the nationalism of the Malay community, which is predominantly agricultural and rural. Of the economically active Malay population in 1957 of 1,025,000, 74 per cent were engaged in agriculture, forestry, and fishing. Of those engaged in primary production, half were rice farmers. Four-fifths of the total Malay population of 3,125,474 in 1957 were living in villages and settlements of under 1,000 population. In 1957 almost half of this population (46.2 per cent) lived in the northern and eastern states of Kedah, Perlis, Pahang, Kelantan, and Trengganu, and comprised three-quarters (76.5 per cent) of the population of these five states. In the south and western states of Selangor, Perak, Penang, Negri Sembilan, Malacca, and Johore, the Malay population was a minority element of the total population (38.4 per cent) and in no state did they comprise a majority.

While the Malay population is essentially rural and self-sufficient, the traditional kampongs (villages) are under pressure from outside influences. The processes of modernization, stimulated by the introduction of cash crops and resulting penetration of the market economy, have been under way for some time. The Malay population, as village populations elsewhere in Southeast Asia, is restless and the younger Malays are being drawn to the cities, estates, and mines. Access to agricultural land has increasingly been reserved to the Malays, but rapid population growth, land fragmentation, debt, tenancy, and poverty, have contributed to the spatial mobility of members of this community.

Governmental efforts to modernize the Malay community are concentrated presently in blanketing the countryside with agricultural extension, education, and public health services. At the same time a disproportionate share of public investment is allocated to feeder roads and other communications facilities, land settlement, and rural water supply, and electrification works.[2] Also contributing to change within the Malay society is the recruitment of Malays for higher education, the bureaucracy, the army, and for training in the various schemes and institutes developed by the government to provide them with economic skills.

While transitional elements are prominent in rural Malaya, Islam remains a bulwark of conservatism, and traditionalism in most aspects of behavior remains strong. The isolation of the unfederated states during the colonial period maintained the traditional role and influence of the Malay aristocracy with its close identification with Islam and the conservative teachers of the faith. The strength of this influence is evident today in the Pan Malaysian Islamic Party (PMIP), an economically conservative, racially intolerant, religion-based party which represents a major challenge to the relatively progressive United Malay National Organization (UMNO) leadership. The strength of the PMIP is concentrated in the backward east coast states of Kelantan and Trengganu. In the west coast states, on the other hand, economic development has combined with racial balance to weaken the influence of Islam and to relegate the Malay aristocracy to a limited constitutional role.

Malay indigenism, to a considerable extent, is a religious phenomenon. Islam is an exclusive religion, central to which are revealed truths and the faith of believers as chosen of God. Islam is a relatively intolerant religion with features that contribute to the resistance of its adherents to processes of assimilation, adaptation, and compromise. For example, Malay marriages with nonbelievers are rare and are almost always accompanied by formal conversion of the marriage

[2] For an informative survey of the massive governmental effort to uplift the rural Malay society, see Gayl D. Ness, *Bureaucracy and Rural Development in Malaysia* (Berkeley: University of California Press, 1967), pp. 50–122.

partner. Similarly, dietary rules contribute to racial segregation at the village level. More significant is the role of Islam in the external political identification of the Malay with the broader Islamic world, which represents a symbol to which the conservative and devout attach value. The Sharia, the canonical law of Islam, is described by Raymond Firth as "a unifying force, extra-village and extra-national in character, linking even the most remote mountain farmer spiritually and emotionally with the farmer and townsman of the other Muslim communities in Southeast Asia and far beyond." [3]

In the present context, pan-Islam carries the threat that it may be distorted into a pan-Malaysian (pan-Indonesian) phenomenon. This contributes to the insecurity of the progressive Malay leadership and enhances the need for this leadership to seek constantly to promote the welfare of Malays vis-à-vis other racial communities. Such efforts are concentrated in areas symbolically important to the tradition-bound Malays: the aristocracy, agriculture, education, and religion. The sensitivity of the political elites to the demands of Malay nationalism, moreover, is enhanced by their kin ties with the aristocracy. The sultanates, strongly, but not uniformly, influenced by premodern feudal relationships, are the bridge between the rural peasant society and the Malay political leaders. Malays recognize the role of their sultan as the protector of the Islamic establishment, and the Malay society coalesces around the imams (religious ritual officials in the mosques) and through the kadi (the local Moslem functionaries). Reinforcing the cohesiveness and exclusiveness of the Malay community are such features of Islam as dietary laws and the prohibition of riba, which is identified with interest taking. Although such constraints have eroded for urbanized Malays, they remain strong in rural areas.

The basic factor determining the nature of Malay indigenism, however, is the economic insecurity of the Malays within their own country. Colonial economic development, with its reliance on the forms of indirect rule through the sultanates, isolated the Malay society from the processes of economic change. Malays did not provide the labor necessary to colonial development but instead whole Chinese and Indian populations were recruited for that purpose. Many of these alien Asians, for reasons that have not been adequately studied and satisfactorily explained, displayed remarkable capacity to participate

[3] Raymond Firth, "The Peasantry in Southeast Asia," *International Affairs* (26), October 1950, p. 511.

as entrepreneurs in the capitalistic development that was taking place. The Malay community, however, remained relatively isolated and shielded by British policy and administration. As a result, Malays failed to participate widely in transitional processes, and the community remained essentially rural and self-sufficient.

The exceptions to this generalization are the Malay bureaucratic and political elites who became superbly equipped to participate in the political process. The prolonged period of tutelage under colonial administrators which culminated in the challenging collaboration between the British and the Malays in confronting the "Emergency"—the postwar communist-led insurrection—gave the latter skills, experiences, and self-confidence. The British recognized an obligation to transfer dominant political power to them, and unambiguous constitutional arrangements were made to do so.

Insofar as the Malay political elites are concerned, integration of the racial elements into a viable Malayan society will depend upon accelerated modernization of the Malay community to equip its members to hold their own economically. From their viewpoint, an acceptable solution to this problem would result if the relative economic position of the other racial elements could be held at present levels and Malay economic participation promoted until the gap is closed. Such a solution obviously is unrealistic, and the resulting compromise is essentially a continuation of the colonial-type economy in which wide scope is maintained for private enterprise in the commercial, financial, and industrial sectors at the same time that a disproportionate share of the economic resources of the state are used to raise the rural Malay society to a level that promises a socially stable sharing-out of material progress.

Because the Malay community feels economically insecure, its leaders recognize an interest in maintaining a large Western stake in the economy. This is manifested in the strict impartiality observed in policies affecting foreign investment vis-à-vis investment by nationals. By maintaining the British presence in mines and plantations and in the network of large trading and financial enterprises, the Malay community preserves a feature of their economy that they associate with their political dominance. Inasmuch as the Malays are precluded by their economic backwardness from substituting for existing alien entrepreneurial and managerial resources and capital, policies of indigenism would benefit primarily citizens of Chinese and Indian descent. The absence of pressures on alien enterprise, therefore, is a manifestation of Malayism, rather than a denial of Malayan indigenism. Faced by communal realities, the Malays have not been primarily concerned with containing the economic activities of the Chinese and Indians. With the exception of the smallholders agricultural sector, non-Malay Asians —citizens and aliens alike—encounter only minor discriminatory limits on their access to resources and markets.

Malayan economic nationalism is little affected by Chinese influence. Victor Purcell commented that the Chinese in Malaya are "more ethnographically exact than in any other country of Southeast Asia because since large-scale immigration from China began over half a century ago there has not been miscegenation of any importance. Before that it was comparatively small."[4] This suggests that the Chinese community is integrated and cohesive, whereas, in fact, these characteristics are not prominent. The Chinese in Malaya are fragmented into dialect groups which are geographically concentrated. For example, the Hokkiens are more of an urban people, while the Hakkas form a predominantly rural community associated with mining areas. Together with the Tiechiu and Cantonese Chinese, these ethnic groups account for six-sevenths of the Chinese population. While the various dialect communities are scattered over the country, each tends to predominate in some particular areas to the near exclusion of others.[5]

Insofar as the Chinese are organized politically, they tend to follow dialect community leaders and display a weak tendency to coalesce behind the conservative, national leadership of the Malayan Chinese Association (MCA), that co-operates with the Malay political elites. In part this reflects the traditional political apathy of the overseas Chinese and in part the fact that Chinese political leadership is narrowly based in middle-class urban elements. The leftist-oriented leadership was discredited by the Emergency and where not forced underground, jailed, or deported, has been intimidated by close control and surveillance.

The political passivity of the Chinese in the face of Malay nationalism and their acceptance of second-class citizenship is a prominent feature of the political environment. This is partly explained by Chinese

[4] Victor Purcell, *The Chinese in Southeast Asia* (London: Oxford University Press, 1951), pp. 2–3.

[5] Norton Ginsberg and Chester F. Roberts, Jr., *Malaya* (Seattle: University of Washington Press, 1958), pp. 136–137.

submissiveness to control arising in authoritarian and bureaucratic Chinese traditions which, in Malaya, were reinforced by the British practice of governing the Chinese as an alien group. Under this policy, the Chinese were given little opportunity to participate in formal aspects of government. This passivity reflects also the weakening of ties to the "Inner Kingdom" as the population has become demographically settled and dominated numerically by the "straits-born."

The Chinese in Malaya have found security, which substitutes for formal political power, in their social organization. Cohesion derives from religious concepts, familialism, and such institutions as clan and dialect associations, guilds, and secret societies. These features of social organization provide the basis for small centers of Chinese culture which are poorly articulated with similar centers for other clan and dialect groups. Finally, the Chinese community is diverted from politics by the ample scope for the pursuit of material gain. The Chinese are self-confident not only in the superiority of their culture, but also in their capacity to participate in the individualistic economy. The Chinese are not interested in eliminating competition but in maintaining open access to factor and product markets.

The Indian community is associated with plantation agriculture, almost exclusively as estate workers, and in urban mercantile services and the lower civil service. In 1957, almost three-fifths of the economically active Indian population was engaged in production of rubber and other plantation crops with an additional one-fifth engaged in commerce and government service.[6] There is a pronounced ethnic division within the Indian community with the rural population heavily South Indian (Tamil-speaking) while the urban population of shopkeepers and minor civil servants tends to include a substantial proportion of Punjabis and Sikhs from the north of India. Indian immigration is primarily a twentieth-century phenomenon and as recently as 1947, half of the Indians in Malaya were born elsewhere. In the aggregate, the Indian population is ethnically homogeneous with nine-tenths of the population of South Indian origin and at least four-fifths Tamil-speaking.[7]

---

[6] For an excellent analysis of the most recent census of 1957, see Ronald Ma and You Poh-Seng, "The Economic Characteristics of the Population of the Federation of Malaya, 1957," *The Malayan Economic Review* (5), October 1960, pp. 27–31. Of the economically active Indians engaged in agriculture, less than 2 per cent were tabulated as "self-employed" or "unpaid family workers."

[7] Ginsberg and Roberts, *op. cit.*, p. 319.

The political voice of the Indian population, for a number of reasons, is presently a weak one. Indians comprise a small proportion of the total population, and the ratio of Indians with Malayan nationality is lower than for the Chinese community. The estate workers, who comprise two-thirds of the Indian population, came to Malaya under a closely regulated system of immigration under which a standard wage was established, hospital and maternity benefits were assured, and with the estates required to provide facilities for the compulsory education of Indian children. On the estates the Indians live under conditions controlled and regulated by the Federation Government in co-operation with the Government of India. Primitive educational facilities and the prevalence of illiteracy limit the number of Indians on estates who might acquire and exercise the right of suffrage. The political passivity of the Indian population is also reinforced by the caste origins of the Indian immigrants, more than one-third of whom are of lower caste.

On the other hand, the Indians, with little access to alternative organizations to represent their interests, have proved relatively susceptible to unionization and have acquired experiences in the labor movement that have tended to increase their political participation. The Malayan Indian Congress (MIC), which was formed shortly after the war and which has pursued Indian interests by co-operating with the United Malay National Organization and the Malayan Chinese Association, in the Alliance Party, competes with the labor-oriented Socialist Party as the political voice of the Indian community. The MIC, which draws strength from the powerful Indian commercial elements, is urban-oriented and conservative in outlook.

From many perspectives, the Malayan economy represents the archstereotype of colonial development, with extremes in racial and functional pluralism and specialization in plantation and mining production for export to industrial markets, superimposed on an isolated, tradition-bound, subsistence economy. Occupying the larger number of people is "the modified subsistence economy of rice and squatter mixed farms, situated mainly in the North and East, and along the jungle fringes; an economy of static techniques, poverty, chronic debt subsisting at levels not much above the appalling poverty of most of Asia." [8] Dominating this sector is the production of rice which in 1957

[8] T. H. Silcock, *The Economy of Malaya* (Singapore: Donald Moore, 1957), p. 1.

employed 380,000 Malays and only 16,000 Chinese and Indians. Other activities, including truck farming and fishing, employed an additional 79,000 Malays, 91,000 Chinese, and 4,000 Indians.[9]

Concentrated in the west coast states, is an entirely different agricultural economy producing rubber, coconuts, palm kernels, pineapples, and other crops for external markets. This sector, in which output is divided roughly between smallholders and plantations, provided employment in 1957 for 300,000 Malays, 209,000 Chinese, and 170,000 Indians, with the ratio of smallholders much higher for the Malay community than the others.[10]

The remaining part of primary production is accounted for by mining and logging and lumbering. Tin is the major mineral product and currently provides one-fifth of Malaya's export earnings, with iron ore second in importance. Minerals production is dominated by large-scale dredging operations in tin and open cast mining of iron ore, with a substantial part of tin production contributed by small-scale Chinese-operated gravel mines. In 1957, there were 10,000 Malays engaged in the mining sector, 40,000 Chinese, and 8,000 Indians. The racial distribution of the Malayan population among major activities and industrial sectors is summarized in Tables 28 and 29.

The organization of the foreign trade of Malaya, historically and today, is based upon absolute advantage arising in the climate, soil, and mineral resources. The rubber industry in recent years has contributed about 25 per cent of the gross domestic product with other export industries—tin, iron ore, palm oil, timber, pineapples, and so forth—contributing a further 16 per cent. The value of Malaya's exports on a per capita basis in 1964 equal to U.S. $119, was five times that of the Philippines, the country in Southeast Asia with the second highest value.

Because of Malay's extreme reliance upon primary product specialization, manufacturing has received little development. During the three years 1962–1964, value added by manufacturing contributed 9 per cent of national income with one-third of this accounted for by primary processing activities such as rubber remilling, latex processing, coconut oil milling, rice milling, and saw milling. A further one-third was contributed by "large" industries producing biscuits, soft drinks, tobacco products, furniture, structural clay products, book printing and bind-

---

[9] See Ma and You, *op. cit.*, pp. 10–45.   [10] *Ibid.*, pp. 27 and 38.

Table 28. Economically active population in each industries sector
by industry and major ethnic group
(in per cent)

Sector	Malays	Chinese	Indians
Primary			
Number employed	*759,631*	*350,377*	*181,323*
Agriculture, forestry, hunting and fishing	60.5	28.8	2.4
Agriculture products requiring substantial processing	38.1	59.7	93.8
Mining and quarrying	1.3	11.4	3.7
Secondary			
Number employed	*48,433*	*130,116*	*22,398*
Manufacturing	54.9	75.0	45.1
Building and construction	45.1	25.0	54.9
Tertiary			
Number employed	*190,366*	*269,157*	*101,100*
Commerce	16.8	47.2	32.4
Transport, storage, and communications	14.1	10.8	15.9
Electricity, gas, and water	2.0	1.1	4.1
Community and government services	57.3	15.2	26.9
Personal and other services	9.8	25.7	20.6

Source: Ronald Ma and You Poh-Seng, "The Economic Characteristics of the Population of the Federation of Malaya, 1957," *The Malayan Economic Review* (5), October 1960, pp. 27, 29, and 31.

ing, foundry and general machine repair, and motor vehicle repair, each of which employed over 1,000 workers. The remaining industries are small in scale and their products diverse.[11] Employment in manufacturing is dominated by Chinese who numbered 98,000 in 1957, with Malays and Indians numbering 27,000 and 10,000 respectively.

As might be expected, commerce is dominated by the Chinese community. In 1957, 35 per cent of the economically active Chinese were engaged in commerce and these numbered 168,000, with Malays numbering 32,000, almost exclusively in retail trade, and Indians 33,000. Public employment including police and armed services, public utilities, and the civil service engaged 113,000 Malays in 1957, as compared

[11] Federation of Malaya (F. of M.), *Official Yearbook, 1961* (Kuala Lumpur: The Government Printer, 1962), p. 485.

Table 29. Distribution of economically active population in 1957
by industries sector and ethnic group
(in per cent)

Ethnic group	Distribution of major industrial sectors by ethnic group			
	Total	Primary	Secondary	Tertiary
Malaysians	48.6	58.8	24.1	34.0
Chinese	36.5	27.1	64.8	48.0
Indians	14.8	14.0	11.1	18.0
Total	100.0	100.0	100.0	100.0
	Distribution of ethnic groups by major industrial sector			
Malaysians	100.0	76.1	4.8	19.1
Chinese	100.0	46.7	17.4	35.9
Indians	100.0	59.5	7.3	33.2
Total	100.0	62.9	9.8	27.3

Source: Ma and You, *op. cit.*, p. 25. Malaysians include Malay immigrants from Indonesia as well as indigenous Malays.

to 44,000 Chinese and 31,000 Indians. Provision of other services, including transport and communications and personal services, provided employment for 46,000 Malays, 98,000 Chinese and 37,000 Indians.

Reliance upon international specialization and trade in primary products is interpreted widely as a source of weakness in an underdeveloped country hoping to accelerate economic growth. There can be little question that Malaya's chief wealth in its plantations and mines is vulnerable wealth, sensitive to volatile demand conditions reflecting instability in industrial markets and threatened by radical advances in synthetic rubber technology. On the other hand, Malaya's specialization has been a source of enormous, if transient, strength in the postindependence period.

Strong external demand conditions and favorable terms of trade have sustained a large and persistent export surplus which has enabled Malaya to freely import requirements of foodstuffs and other consumption goods, as well as the capital requirements for rehabilitation and growth. Among the countries of Southeast Asia, Malaya is unique in that it has never been forced to resort to effective import and exchange controls, and such controls as have been maintained have been for purposes of surveillance. Elsewhere in Southeast Asia, the incentives and opportunities arising in currency overvaluation and balance of payment disequilibrium have been a major factor in explaining the intensification of indigenism.

The strength of Malaya's export industries in the postwar period has moderated economic nationalism as reliance upon external markets restrained policies that might jeopardize Malayan access to such markets. Similarly, policy makers were not free to impose high levels of protection in the pursuit of self-sufficiency without considering the consequences for the competitiveness of the export sector. The buoyant foreign exchange position, moreover, facilitated large-scale repatriation of foreign capital in the postwar period. In the process a substantial transfer of ownership of plantations, mines, and commercial enterprises to Malayan ownership occurred.

Malaya's international trade and specialization have also been a source of fiscal strength as foreign exchange transactions are a productive, easily administered tax base. During recent years, the ratio of Federal Government revenues to national income has been higher for Malaya than for any other country of Southeast Asia, averaging 23.6 per cent over the three-year period 1963–1965. The contribution of export and import duties to Federal Government tax revenues averaged 55 per cent annually over this period, with export duties contributing 19 of the percentage points. A number of countries of Southeast Asia have been able to tax export production at high rates for short periods through currency overvaluation and exchange controls, and through government trading monopolies and dual pricing schemes. Such taxation, however, has been accompanied by disinvestment in the export sector and laggard expansion in export production and trade. Malaya is unique in that she has been able to rely heavily on export taxation since 1950, a period in which rubber output has expanded steadily, the rubber sector has been substantially replanted in high-yielding rubber, and in which expansion of land allocated to the production of rubber and tin has been strictly limited by government policy.

The importance of Malaya's foreign trade as a tax base, moreover, is not measured fully by import and export duties, as the principal part of company income taxes and personal income taxes are paid on earnings generated in this sector. During recent years, from two-thirds to three-quarters of income tax revenue has been obtained from taxes on company income and two-thirds of such revenue has been generated by plantation agriculture and tin mining.

Still another major factor exerting a moderating impact on indigenism is the strong residual colonial influence upon policy. The political elites have been educated in the British tradition and the higher civil service has been nurtured in co-operation with British administrators. Colonial *laissez faire* has been continued with little change, and there are presently few indications that the government plans to resort to directly productive government enterprise on any significant scale or engage in wholesale regulation of credit allocated to the private sector.

Government is a parliamentary system with wide discretionary authority vested in the executive and legislative discipline maintained by racial cohesiveness as well as the specter of parliamentary defeat. The impression that strikes the observer in Malaya of great governmental power bordering on authoritarianism, is, in large part, a heritage of the Emergency, the communist-led insurrection that was only slowly and with great difficulty brought under control during the decade of the 1950s. The experiences of the Emergency served to discredit socialism because of the left-wing Chinese leadership of the rebellion. More recently, Malay militancy has been reinforced by concern for the threat of instability in Singapore originating with the political Left among the Chinese population. Because of these factors, the Malays gravitate toward collaboration with the British rather than to coalesce with the Chinese in opposition to the colonial power.

The character of the politically dominant Alliance Party coalition also contributes to the strong residue of colonial influence. The United Malay National Organization (UMNO) serves to mobilize Malay political power behind the progressive, British-educated bureaucratic elites who seek to modernize the Malay society and integrate the racially divided population into a viable national society. They can be labeled progressive only in comparison with the alternative, tradition- and religion-bound rural Malay leadership. The UMNO leaders are the designated heirs of the colonial rulers and are closely allied with the Malay aristocracy, and this is a sufficient explanation of their economic conservatism. The Malayan Chinese Association is dominated by urban, middle-class, entrepreneurial elements with deep roots in Malaya. Its economic orientation is toward *laissez faire,* and it rejects communism and the revolutionary doctrines of Mainland China. This element of the population prospered under colonial rule and benefited from close collaboration with large British firms as middlemen, and it therefore has little incentive to change the existing economic organization. The leadership of the remaining component in the coalition, the Malayan

Indian Congress, has origins similar to those of the MCA leadership and, likewise, a stake in the economic *status quo*.

Finally, continuity in colonial economic policy is explained by the rapid economic growth and expansion sustained since the early 1950s. In contrast to the interwar period, when instability in foreign markets and low prices for primary products led to intervention by the government in the economic organization, the past decade and a half of material progress and relative stability has contained social tensions and developed confidence in the economic system and the policy decisions of the political leadership.

The Nature of Malayan Indigenism

CITIZENSHIP, NATURALIZATION, AND IMMIGRATION

Malayan citizenship is acquired in three ways: by birth, by registration, or by naturalization. Citizenship by birth, which is referred to in the Constitution as "by operation of law," is automatically conferred on every child born in the Federation on or after Merdeka (Independence) Day, August 31, 1957.[12] For persons born in the Federation before the establishment of independence, citizenship was conferred on all British subjects and upon all subjects of a ruler of a Malay state. Persons born in Penang and Malacca, which were crown colonies prior to formation of the Federation, were British subjects and hence, automatically became citizens. Persons who had acquired state citizenship, whether by birth or naturalization also became citizens as they were subjects of a ruler of a Malay State.

A person with a substantial family connection within the country may obtain citizenship by registration if he or she is of good character[13] and falls into one of four specified categories: an alien woman

---

[12] A child born outside the Federation of a Malayan father is also a Malayan citizen but falls into one of two groups. If the father was a citizen by registration or naturalization, the status of the child must be confirmed by registration at a Malayan consulate within one month of birth.

[13] A person is presumed to be of good character if he has not, at any time within the three years preceding his application for registration, been convicted in any country of a capital offense or sentenced to more than a year's imprisonment on a criminal charge.

who legally marries a citizen; a minor "ordinarily resident" in the Federation whose father is a citizen; persons over eighteen years born in and resident in the Federation on Independence Day and for five out of the preceding seven years and with an adequate command of Malay; and persons over eighteen years not born in the Federation but resident there on Independence Day and for eight out of the preceding ten years and with an adequate command of Malay.

An alien who has no family connection within the Federation may become a citizen only by naturalization. The Constitution provides (Art. 19) that the Federal Government may grant a certificate of naturalization if satisfied (a) that the applicant has resided in the Federation during the twelve years preceding the date of the application for periods amounting in the aggregate to not less than ten years; (b) that the applicant intends to reside permanently in the Federation; (c) that he is of good character; and (d) that he has an adequate knowledge of the Malay language.[14]

The citizenship provisions of the Constitution are complex but liberal by Southeast Asian standards. Basically, the law provides for application of *jus solis* beginning with the establishment of independence. On the other hand, the constitutional provision limiting citizenship at the formation of the new state to British subjects and subjects of a ruler of a Malay state was designed to ensure the political dominance of the Malay community for the following four or five decades. All Malays born in the area incorporated in Malaya met this requirement whereas only about half of the Chinese and Indian populations did so. Prior to formation of the Federation of Malaya in 1948, alien residents in the Malay states had little incentive to establish status as a subject of a Malay ruler, and legal and administrative obstacles had to be overcome to do so. The political imbalance established by discriminatory access to citizenship at the formation of Malaya will be gradually redressed, however, as the present population is replaced by new generations.

The economic effects of the limitations on the access of alien communities to citizenship should not be exaggerated. Malayan nationality is not a requirement for access to markets and economic activities to any major degree. Moreover, acquisition of citizenship by Chinese and Indians has been extensive. On June 30, 1953 it was estimated that of the population in the Federation of Malaya of 5.7 million, 4.1 million were citizens of whom 2.7 million or two-thirds were Malays (see

---

[14] Special consideration is given (Art. 20) to aliens who served in the armed forces of the Federation.

Table 30). An estimated 54 per cent of the Chinese residents were citizens with a further 21 per cent eligible for citizenship by registration. One-third of the Indian residents were estimated to be citizens with a further one-quarter eligible for registration.

Table 30. Citizenship statistics as of June 30, 1953

Nationality	Population	Presently citizens	Eligible by birth for registration as citizens	Residents born outside Federation and eligible only for naturalization
Malaysians [a]	2,803,000	2,727,000	–	81,000
Chinese	2,153,000	1,157,000	443,000	566,000
Indians	666,000	222,000	168,000	243,000
Other	84,000	33,000	36,000	21,000
Total	5,706,000	4,139,000	647,000	911,000

Source: F. of M., *Annual Report, 1953* (Kuala Lumpur: The Government Printer, 1958), pp. 5, 16, and 17.
[a] Indigenous Malays plus immigrant Malays.

Between January 1, 1954 and Merdeka Day a further 283,157 certificates of citizenship were issued: 188,092 to Chinese, 65,342 to Indians, 24,048 to Malays (Indonesion immigrants), and 5,675 to persons of other ethnic origin.[15] In the three months following establishment of independence, acquisition of citizenship by registration continued at a rapid pace, particularly under the Constitutional provision (Art. 170) which provided that "any person . . . qualified [on August 31, 1957] to make application to the registration authority within the period of one year beginning with that day, could be registered as a citizen." During the last quarter of 1957, a further 135,702 certificates of citizenship were issued, 117,361 to Chinese, 10,467 to Indians, 6,413 to Malays, and 1,461 to persons of other ethnic origins.[16]

By the end of 1957, some two-thirds of the Malayan population of Chinese origin had acquired citizenship. For those of Indian origin, the ratio was somewhat less than 50 per cent. Although statistics on those acquiring Malayan citizenship by registration and by naturalization following 1957 have not been made available, it seems clear that at least two-thirds of the non-Malay population as of August 31, 1957

[15] Tabulated from F. of M., *Annual Reports, 1953, 1954, 1955, 1956,* and *1957.*
[16] F. of M., *Annual Report, 1957.*

either possessed citizenship upon establishment of independence or subsequently acquired such citizenship.

Immigration into Malaya has been strictly controlled since enactment of the Immigration Ordinance of 1952 (No. 68 of 1952) which was devised to restrict immigration of Indians and Chinese to those with family connections in the Federation. In the first five years under the law, immigrants numbered 73,040 including 63,053 family members of citizens and residents of the Federation. During this period immigrants coming for prearranged employment, and those coming to pursue an "economic interest" in the Federation totaled 1,560.[17] The remaining immigrants were those persons "entitled to enter of own right," i.e., those immigrants acceptable to the immigration authorities.

Central to Malayan immigration policy are severe restrictions on travel by residents to Mainland China and, beginning in 1951, permission for residents in the 16–30 age group to travel to China was virtually cut off. The effect of this policy was to prevent the education (indoctrination) of young Chinese and also to reduce the number of immigrant wives of resident Chinese, a large proportion of whom returned to China to marry. Chinese who left the country without a re-entry permit were denied permission to return. Application of this policy to residents of Indian origin was not possible under the immigration law because of the status of such residents as Commonwealth citizens.

Parliament in 1959 enacted a new Immigration Ordinance (No. 12 of 1959) which made major changes in policy and enlarged the discretionary authority of immigration officials. The list of "prohibited classes" of persons is unusually exhaustive and includes the blanket provision: "any person who, in consequence of information received from any source deemed by the Minister to be reliable . . . is deemed by the Minister to be an undesirable immigrant." Moreover, "The Minister may . . . where he deems it expedient to do so in the interests of public security or by reason of any economic, industrial, social, educational, or other condition in Malaya . . . prohibit the entry or re-entry into the Federation of any person."

Control of immigration was made the responsibility of the Minister of External Affairs. New regulations covering immigration provided that the issue of re-entry permits is subject to discretionary control by the Minister and not mandatory, and raised the minimum monthly

[17] Tabulated from F. of M., *Annual Reports, 1953, 1954, 1955, 1956,* and *1957.*

income for entry for prearranged employment to M$1200 as compared to the previous minimum of M$500.

Immigration of Asian aliens into Malaya since 1952 has been limited essentially to immediate family members of citizens and residents. Details of immigration policy have not been publicized in recent years and statistics on immigration have become fragmentary. Entry to engage in entrepreneurial activity and for purposes of prearranged employment is permitted, although the latter is subject to a salary constraint obviously designed to exclude potential Asian immigrants. The power to restrict immigration is discretionary and absolute and is tightly held by Malay ministers.

THE SPECIAL MALAY POSITION

In view of the basic economic insecurity and backwardness of the Malay community and, concurrently, the political dominance of that community, it is not surprising to find laws and regulations defining a "special Malay position" in the economy. Such laws and regulations are not directed against non-Malayans, but favor Malays and discriminate against non-Malays, whether citizens or not. It will be recalled that indigenism for our purposes is defined, not in terms of nationality, but in terms of membership in the national society as recognized by those elements in the society which have monopolized political power.[18] In establishing legal preferences for Malays, the elites of this community have used their dominant political power to define the national society by recognition. They obviously do not consider the national society to be defined by the national economy, the nation-state, or in this case, by those holding Malayan nationality. The structure of policies which establishes the "special Malay position" is a basic manifestation of indigenism such as is found generally in Southeast Asia. These policies impinge upon the Chinese and Indians, whether citizens or not, rather than upon Western aliens who are little interested in the various concessions and economic activities reserved to Malays.

Although, in general, the Constitution reflects the principle of equality under the law, the "special position of the Malays" is also recognized. The responsibility of the executive for this policy has roots in the indirect rule of the British period. It stems directly from powers given by the Malay sultans to the British Residents who increasingly exercised executive authority in the unfederated Malay States. The

[18] See Chapter 1, especially note 10.

Malay rulers stood then, and stand today, in a special position vis-à-vis their Malay subjects as compared to their relationship to others. Sanction for constitutional recognition of the "special position" also stems from recognition of Islam as the religion and Malay as the national language of the Federation.[19]

Executive responsibility for the "special position" was explicitly recognized in the Federation of Malaya Agreement of 1948,[20] which provided (Art. 19) that the High Commissioner shall be responsible for the "safeguarding of the special position of the Malays and of the legitimate interests of other communities." The Constitution extends this principle by providing (Art. 153) that the Yang di-Pertuan Agong shall "safeguard the special position of the Malays and to ensure the reservation for Malays of such proportion as he may deem reasonable of positions in the public service and of scholarships, exhibitions and other similar educational or training privileges . . . and, . . . of [business] permits and licenses."[21]

Among the reserved concessions and privileges, the most important is the right to establish Malay reservations. Beginning in 1913, the

[19] Arts. 3, 12. One scholar of Islam has commented that "the question of political power and social organization so central to Islam, has in the past always been considered in yes-or-no terms . . . close to the heart of Islam has been the conviction that its purpose includes the structuring of a social community, the organization of the Muslim group into a closed body obedient to the law" (Wilfred C. Smith, *Islam in Modern History* [New York: New American Library, Mentor Edition, 1954], pp. 227–228).

[20] The initial postwar political reorganization of present-day Malaya took the form of the Malayan Union inaugurated on April 1, 1946. The Union abrogated the treaties between Great Britain and the Malay sultans and welded the Malayan states into a union in which the Malays had no special privileges and which recognized the equality of all races before the law. The British government forced the Union on the sultans, threatening to depose any who would not co-operate. The Malay community coalesced in a nationalist movement in opposition to the Union and, less than two years later, it was replaced by the Federation of Malaya Agreement. See T. H. Silcock and Ungku A. Aziz, "*Nationalism in Malaya*" in William L. Holland (ed.), *Asian Nationalism and the West* (New York: MacMillan Company, 1953), pp. 298–331.

[21] The Yang di-Pertuan Agong, "Supreme Head of the Federation," is elected for a five-year term by the heads of states comprising the Federation. The Constitution further provides (Art. 153) that an individual cannot be deprived of a right, privilege, permit, or license presently held, and that renewal of a permit or license cannot be withheld if such renewal "might reasonably be expected in the ordinary course of events." Similarly, Article 153 specifically enjoins Parliament from restricting business or trade solely for the purpose of reserving such business or trade to Malays in the future.

various states enacted legislation setting aside large areas in which land alienation is limited to Malays.[22] This process continued until, at Merdeka, about one-fourth of the area of Malaya was so reserved.[23]

The Constitution specifies (Art. 89) that any land in a state which was in a Malay Reservation on Merdeka Day shall continue in that status. After independence, uncultivated or undeveloped land in any state can be declared a Malay Reservation only if an equal area of land similar to that reserved is made available for general alienation. Moreover, further additions to land declared as Malay Reservation cannot be made if the total area of such land exceeds the total area of land in the state available for general alienation.

A second element in the "special position" is the preferential access of Malays to the Malayan Civil Service and to the various functional branches of the bureaucracy: the medical service, police, educational service, public works service, and so forth. Under indirect rule, access to the higher levels of the colonial civil service was monopolized by the British and Malays, particularly those with aristocratic connections. At the end of 1952, however, the High Commissioner, Sir Gerald Templer, announced that in the future, non-Malay federal citizens would be admitted to the Malayan Civil Service in the ratio of one to every four Malays appointed.[24]

Somewhat later, a Constitutional Commission was appointed which met during 1956 and 1957 to prepare a draft Constitution. The Commission concluded that it would be necessary to continue the preferences for Malays but that they should not be expanded and, moreover, should be reduced and ultimately cease; the draft constitution (Arts. 82 and 157) reflected this position.[25] The Constitution subsequently

[22] See "An enactment to amend and consolidate the law relating to malay reservations and to provide for securing to malays their interests in land," *The Laws of the Federated Malay States* (Revised Edition), Vol. III (Kuala Lumpur: Government Printing Department, 1935), pp. 2172–2178.

[23] International Bank for Reconstruction and Development, *The Economic Development of Malaya* (Baltimore: Johns Hopkins Press, 1955), Map 7, facing p. 312.

[24] Lennox A. Mills, *Malaya: A Political and Economic Appraisal* (Minneapolis: University of Minnesota Press, 1958), pp. 83–84. In the functional branches of the bureaucracy, it was policy following 1952 to permit not more than one-quarter of new entrants to be non-Malays.

[25] The Constitutional Commission reported: "Our terms of reference require that provision should be made in the Constitution for the 'safeguarding' of the special position of the Malays and the legitimate interests of other communities. In addition, we are asked to provide for a common nationality for the whole of

adopted does not provide for reconsideration, and ultimate termination, of the "Special Position." There is said to exist, however, an undertaking given by the UMNO leaders to their Chinese and Indian collaborators in the Alliance Party to reconsider this question fifteen years after Merdeka.

Preferential access to bureaucratic positions by Malays is resented by other citizens, particularly in view of the ratios that have been maintained. Such a policy will have adverse consequences for the quality of the bureaucracy as better qualified candidates are rejected for reasons of ethnic origin and standards of entrance are lowered to introduce Malays before the policy is reconsidered.[26]

Akin to the preference enjoyed by Malays in bureaucratic appointments is the existence of the Royal Malay Regiment which is limited to Malays.[27] There are, in addition, a multi-racial Federation Reconnaissance Corps and various supporting units. The significance of the preponderance of Malays in the armed forces in the context of communalism is obvious.

MALAY PARTICIPATION IN BUSINESS

In view of the priority assigned to the economic modernization of the Malay community, persistent efforts have been maintained by the government, with the acquiesence of all racial elements in the society, to increase Malay participation in business.

The constitutional authority to reserve to Malays a reasonable portion of business permits and licenses has been used to a limited extent, most prominently in licensing taxis and road transport. In a speech to the Federal Legislative Council on December 13, 1958, the Minister of

---

the Federation and to insure that the Constitution shall guarantee a democratic form of government. We found it difficult, therefore, to reconcile the terms of reference if the protection of the special position of the Malays signified the granting of special privileges, permanently, to one community only and not to the others" (F. of M., *Report of the Federation of Malaya Constitutional Commission, 1956–1957* [Kuala Lumpur: The Government Printer, 1957], p. 71).

[26] For a concise survey of the impact of the bureaucratic transition following independence on the communal composition of the bureaucracy, see Robert O. Tilman, *Bureaucratic Transition in Malaya* (Durham, N.C.: Duke University Press, 1964), pp. 68–76. Tilman's survey indicates that although Malays monopolized appointments in the First Division level of a general administrative nature, the other communities more than maintained the prescribed ratio in First Division appointments requiring technical and professional training.

[27] F. of M., *Official Yearbook, 1961*, p. 335 reports that the Royal Malay Regiment "forms the great bulk of the fighting forces."

Transport reported: "The Government will continue to give the closest attention to increasing the quantum of Malay participation in the road transport industry." He further asserted that the aim of the government was to "render the proportion of Malay taxi proprietors in each State equivalent to the Malay proportion of the population of that State." [28]

Late in 1966, the Minister of Transport reported to Parliament that the latter goal had been substantially accomplished.[29] Progress toward similar goals in trucking and bus transport has been steady, but as of the mid-1960s, Malay participation remained a minor proportion of the total. At the end of 1957, Malay enterprises controlled 66 out of 1,718 trucks operated by Class A common carrier companies.[30] By the end of 1963 Malay enterprises owned 284 trucks.[31] In November 1966 the Minister of Transport reported that Malay capital in bus transport had increased from M$1.7 million at the end of 1958 to M$7.3 million in late 1966 and comprised slightly more than one-fifth of total investment in this industry.[32]

Malay participation in government contracting has also been encouraged by special preferences. This policy was recommended by a Royal Commission created in mid-1960 "to enquire into the government tender system." [33] When the Commission finally reported in May 1964, it recommended that "the aim of the Government should be to allocate by administrative action not less than 25 per cent of all classes of Government contracts to Malay contractors." [34]

Still another area in which actions have been taken to increase Malay participation has been the development of mineral resources of

[28] The Minister reported that in the Federation as a whole, taxi permits numbered 3,614 of which 1,538 were owned by Malays.

[29] *Straits Budget,* November 30, 1966. Licenses to operate taxis issued to Malays and their enterprises numbered 2,270.

[30] F. of M., *Legislative Council Debates,* Second Legislative Council, 3rd Session, September 1957–October 1958, pp. 4330–4331.

[31] *Straits Budget,* January 15, 1964.

[32] *Ibid.,* November 30, 1966. See also *ibid.,* June 23, 1965.

[33] *Malay Mail,* October 18, 1960. The announcement of the formation of the Commission concluded that "the Commission's most delicate task is to decide on the claim of the Malay Chamber of Commerce that all contracts under $M50,000 should be allocated to Malays. In public, the Chamber have not been able (*sic*) to show that there is capacity available to carry out this work without in fact subcontracting to the present small contractors with the inevitable and distasteful implications that follow." The government considered the appearance of Malay "dummies" inevitable and distasteful.

[34] F. of M., *Report of a Commission to Enquire into the Government Tender System,* CMD 6/64 of 5 May 1964, p. 20.

Malay reservations with government participation and subsidy. This policy was initiated by the recommendation of the National Land Council in 1958 that the government should prospect for tin deposits in Malay reservations and "then select areas for which applications for leases by Malay individuals, companies and cooperative societies will be encouraged." [35] Introduction of Malays into mining has proceeded slowly under the policy. As of mid-1965, the Department of Mines and Geological Survey reported that a total of 73,000 acres of Malay reservations had been prospected of which 12,900 acres had been proved to contain minerals of "good economic value." The report concluded, however, that "only a very small acreage is being worked at present by a Malay company." [36]

The government has also used its administrative powers to encourage Malay participation in the timber and lumber industry. As of the end of 1964, it was reported that timber industry licenses and permits issued to Malays numbered 428 as compared to 802 to non-Malays, and the total area covered by licenses and permits to Malays was 497,000 acres as compared to 861,000 acres to non-Malays.[37] The report goes on to say, however:

looking at these figures, Malay participation in the timber industry appears to be satisfactory; but in practice the position leaves much to be desired as most of these licenses have been subleased to non-Malays who are very active in this business . . . it has been the policy of State governments to encourage Malays to participate in the timber industry . . . but in reality their participation exists only in name.[38]

[35] F. of M., *Land Use: Mining: Mining in Malay Reservations and Malay Participation in the Mining Industry*, National Land Council Paper No. 10, 1958.

[36] Konggeres Ekonomi Bumiputra, *Kertas² Kerja* (Kuala Lumpur: Government Press, 1965), "Mining Land Within Malay Reservations," Working Paper No. 7C/1/65, p. 124. The working paper provides the following summary of Malay participation in mining.

Total acreage in mining leases in States of Malaya	515,085 acres
Acreage held by Malays	9,234
Acreage held jointly by Malays and non-Malays	1,324
Acreage held by non-Malays	504,526
Acreage of leases actually worked by Malays	less than 1,000
Acreage worked by Malays alone and jointly with non-Malays	1,401

[37] Konggeres Ekonomi Bumiputra, *op. cit.*, "Lands," Working Paper No. 7b/1/65, p. 119.

[38] *Ibid.*, p. 120. The survey reports (p. 121) that in mid-1965, there were 44 Malay sawmills and 410 classified as non-Malay. Not only do Malay sawmills represent a small fraction of the total number, but "the Malay set-up is mostly in the form of partnerships with non-Malays in which the latter take a more active part in the business management."

Still another minor phase of the effort to encourage their participation in business is the reservation of industrial sites for Malays. In reporting on the Petaling Jaya industrial site as of mid-1960, the Development Officer reported "that 10 acres of new industrial land . . . had been earmarked for Malay industry. This land had been an offer to Malays for the past four months; in this time there had not been a single application." [39]

At the core of the government's efforts to provide support for Malay participation in modern economic activities have been the credit, training, advisory, and construction activities of the Rural and Industrial Development Authority (RIDA). Established in 1950 to develop the rural areas, RIDA was converted into a public corporation in 1954 and given enlarged responsibilities and funds. RIDA provided medium- and long-term credit for a variety of small private enterprises and housing projects organized, with few exceptions, by Malays. [40] It provided certain economic services and operated enterprises, e.g., a boat-building yard, rubber factory, tractor pool. The RIDA also made grants for the construction or improvement of small community utility plants, minor roads, health centers, and schools. In co-operation with government departments, RIDA provided training courses in various trades, commercial subjects, home economics for women, boat building and carpentry, weaving, and mechanical cultivation. [41]

The RIDA was financed by a modest capital fund and by small annual appropriations. During the nine years, 1950–1958, loans by RIDA totaled M$12.6 million disbursed over 3,238 loans to finance enterprises in commerce, industry, agriculture, animal husbandry, fisheries, and transport. Malay co-operatives, assisted by loans, included, among others, 246 rice mills, 18 in rubber processing, 5 in lumber mill-

[39] *Malay Mail,* July 19, 1960.

[40] Although Malay officials have repeatedly stressed that RIDA is for the rural people and not for Malays only, a survey of lending operations in 1963 revealed that over 95 per cent of loans (by value) had gone to Malays (Ness, *op. cit.,* p. 193).

[41] The Minister of Commerce and Industry reported in mid-1958 that during the three-year period to December 31, 1957, 2,789 persons, all Malays, had received training in five training institutions maintained by RIDA (*Legislative Council Debates,* Second Legislative Council, 3rd Session, September 1957–October 1958, p. 4685). During the same session of the Legislative Council, the Minister of Commerce and Industry also reported that the Ministry has issued rice trade and import licenses to suitable Malay applicants, sponsored applications from Malays for permits and licenses in transport, mining, forestry, and government contract works, and assisted Malays who wished to become agents and distributors for commercial firms (*ibid.,* p. 3389).

ing, 90 retail stores, 5 transport and taxi societies, and 60 fishing credit and marketing societies.[42]

The accomplishments of RIDA were modest in terms of enterprises initiated, credit granted, and repayment experience. The capital fund, which was to serve as a revolving credit fund, tended to become immobilized in illiquid loans while administrative costs and expenditures on nonrevenue producing "physical amenities" constructed in rural areas mounted until they accounted for a substantial portion of the annual appropriation.[43] In 1958 the Minister of Finance reported to Parliament: "Experience has shown that in a substantial number of cases in which loans have been granted, the desired results have not been achieved, due not to any inherent flaw in the enterprise but to lack of energy, experience, acumen and steady application on the part of the borrower." [44]

Increasing Malay participation in the economy through government subsidized training and credit, and the award of licenses and concessions has been a persistent policy. At the same time, accomplishments have been modest and the viability of Malay enterprises precarious. In 1959 a government committee headed by Dato Ahmad Perang, former chairman of RIDA, was appointed to survey the Malay economy. The committee reported in February 1960 that of 89,000 businesses registered in the Federation by the end of 1957, only 8,000 were Malay, that Malay capital invested amounted to only M$4.5 million out of total capital invested in registered companies of M$400 million. Moreover, out of 33,000 income taxpayers in 1958, only 3,000 were Malays and

[42] As of March 31, 1965, RIDA reported loans to 1,780 Malay businesses totaling M$6.2 million of which half had gone to Malays engaged in operating taxis. As of that date, 326 of the businesses had paid off their loans, 88 had failed, 21 had negotiated a settlement of their loan obligations, and loans to 1,332 were outstanding (Konggeres Ekonomi Bumiputra, *op. cit.*, "Capital," Working Paper No. 1/1/65, p. 82).

[43] For the decade 1951 through 1960, expenditures of RIDA totaled M$55.3 million of which 27.6 per cent was expended on administration, 24.0 per cent on nonrevenue "physical amenities" constructed in rural areas, 26.3 per cent on loans to Malays and their organizations for revenue-producing projects, and 17.6 per cent for revenue-producing projects directly managed by RIDA. See Ness, *op. cit.*, p. 140. For a candid appraisal of the early accomplishments of RIDA, see F. of M., *Report on the Rural and Industrial Development Authority, 1950–1955*, prepared by D. E. M. Fiennes and dated June 20, 1956 (Kuala Lumpur; Government Press, 1957).

[44] *Legislative Council Debates*, Second Legislative Council, 3rd Session, September 1957–October 1958, p. 3389.

they paid 4 per cent of all personal income taxes and, the report concluded, "Most of the Malay taxpayers were government officials." [45] The committee commented that Malays prefer to invest in real estate and are reluctant to take part in commerce and industry. A number of reasons for the backwardness of Malays in business were advanced, including the general absence of Malay support of Malay business, the fact that wholesalers are all Chinese, the strong competition, especially from the Chinese, and the lack of capital available to Malays.

Malay frustration over the meager accomplishments of the various policies for increasing Malay participation in business steadily accumulated until in the spring of 1965 the government announced plans for an indigenous congress "to ascertain the views of Malays and native organizations on how they could have a larger share of the economic and commercial life of the country." [46] The resulting Economic Congress of Indigenous Peoples (Konggeres Ekonomi Bumiputra) was held in June 1965 and produced sixty-nine recommendations, five of which the government agreed to implement promptly.[47]

In the fall of 1965, RIDA was reorganized as Majlis Amanah Ra'ayat (MARA) or Council of Trust for Indigenous People. In addition to providing MARA with additional funds to carry on the training, credit, and advisory functions of its predecessor, it was authorized to create and operate directly productive manufacturing, extractive, and service industries to be subsequently transferred to Malays once they were operating efficiently.[48]

Subsequently, in late 1965 Parliament passed legislation creating the Federal Agricultural Marketing Authority (FAMA) to create a new, indigenous marketing system for agricultural produce. Initially concentrating its efforts in rice marketing, the FAMA built and operated

[45] *Malay Mail*, February 3, 1960.   [46] *Straits Budget*, March 17, 1965.

[47] Bank Negara Malaysia, *Annual Report and Statement of Accounts, 1965*, p. 19.

[48] The first annual report of MARA in mid-1966 reported plans to engage in lumbering, textile weaving, manufacture of pulp and paper, and a leather tannery. See *Straits Budget*, July 6, 1966. Earlier in 1964, a government-owned pineapple cannery to provide an outlet for pineapples grown on smallholdings was opened. At the time, it was announced that "it is the Government's intention when the cannery is a going concern, to sell out to a cooperative of smallholders." See *ibid.*, April 1, 1964. Deputy Prime Minister, Abdul Razak announced in January 1967 that MARA-operated bus routes were serving one-quarter of the rural population. He also stated that MARA bus lines would be sold to Malay companies once they were operating efficiently. See *ibid.*, January 4, 1967.

mills and warehouses and provided credit to Malay rice marketing co-operatives. Finally, in 1967, FAMA was given monopoly authority to buy and sell unmilled rice.[49] Shortly thereafter, FAMA moved to use this new authority to implement marketing schemes in four major rice-producing states: Selangor, Kedah, Perak, and Perlis. The schemes were designed to transfer milling and marketing functions to Malay co-operatives and Malay-owned mills and to raise the price of rice to growers who were almost exclusively Malays.[50]

A third recommendation of the Congress was implemented in February 1966 when the government-owned commercial bank, Bank Bumiputra Malaysia Ltd. opened for business with authorized capital of M$20 million of which M$5 million was subscribed by the government. It was announced the capital participation would be restricted to the central and state governments, public authorities, and Malays and their organizations, and that the shares held by government would be sold eventually to Malays and their organizations.[51] It was also announced that Bank Bumiputra would accept land in Malay reservations as security for loans.[52]

The government also undertook to carry out two further recommendations of the Congress: (a) to enact legislation to establish a national land rehabilitation and consolidation authority to prevent further fragmentation of farms and to rehabilitate and consolidate uneconomic agricultural holdings, and (b) to bring into existence a public corporation to develop forestry and mineral resources under the aegis of

[49] See *Government Gazette Notification* of August 4, 1967 which provides that unmilled rice can only be purchased by FAMA or licensed agents of the Authority. FAMA earlier had moved to create a Padi and Rice Purchasing Board to function as the sole legal buyer of unmilled rice from the farmer and sole legal seller of unmilled rice to mills in order to maintain a support price for rice favorable to the growers. See *Straits Times*, April 8, 1967.

[50] In late 1967 the FAMA moved to implement rice marketing schemes covering all of Selangor, Kedah, Kelantan, and Perak. It was also announced that by the end of 1967 the Authority had completed investigations into the problems of marketing fish, pepper, coffee, and coconuts and that "appropriate marketing schemes for these have been formulated." See Bank Negara Malaysia, *Annual Report and Statement of Accounts, 1967*, p. 59.

[51] Bank Negara Malaysia, *Annual Report and Statement of Accounts, 1965*, p. 19.

[52] By law, such land cannot be sold or mortgaged to non-Malays. and existing commercial banks that could not establish title to such land refused to make loans on such security.

MARA.[53] As of the end of 1967, these two institutions were still in the planning stage.

The institutions created as a result of the recommendations of the Konggeres Ekonomic Bumiputra, as well as those yet to materialize, together with the policy changes evident in the functions and activities of these institutions represent major changes in the policy structure of Malay indigenism. The obvious conclusion is that such institutions and policies materialize well in advance of Malay capabilities. There is no dearth of assistance available to the Malay who seeks to engage in business activity and who promises to bring more to the enterprise than his Malayness. At the same time, the political leadership has maintained surprisingly high economic standards in defining access to the various incentives reserved to Malays. This policy serves to reassure the non-Malay communities and sustains their willingness to persevere in the basic developmental strategy of Malay uplift.

NATURAL RESOURCE POLICY

Title to the land resources of Malaya resides in the hereditary rulers of the various states. During the colonial period large amounts of land were alienated upon application by smallholder cultivators and by individuals and enterprises seeking land for plantation development. As of the mid-1950s most alienated land, both urban and rural, was held in perpetuity subject to payment of a fixed annual rent and, in the case of agricultural land, to certain expressed or implied cultivation conditions. In recent years, policy with respect to land alienation has gradually changed, and today virtually all land is being alienated on leasehold basis usually for periods ranging from sixty to ninety-nine years.[54]

Administration of land is recognized in the Constitution as a responsibility of state governments, subject to supervision by the National Land Council which is responsible for formulation of national policy. Malay indigenism appears in the wide discretionary authority exercised by the state governments in the disposal of land. In contrast to most public services in the Federation, the processing of land applications is notoriously inefficient, and obtaining title to land, even in straight-

[53] Bank Negara Malaysia, *Annual Report and Statement of Accounts, 1965*, p. 19.

[54] IBRD, *op. cit.*, p. 223.

forward cases, may take many months and sometimes years to accomplish.[55] As of the end of 1958, applications for land awaiting decision in the Federation totaled 116,000, with 37,000 titles awaiting registration, and 50,000 registered titles awaiting issue. This situation little affects the Malay smallholder who is squatting on and cultivating the land for which he has applied. It is, however, a formidable obstacle for non-Malays who hope to acquire sufficient land for plantation enterprises, and who are frequently dependent in the early stages of development upon credit secured by the land being brought under cultivation.

Discrimination in access to land resources may be found in a number of aspects of the administration and settlement of public lands. At the core of the land colonization effort is the Federal Land Development Authority (FLDA) which clears, or contracts the clearing of large areas of land, plants annual crops, primarily rubber and oil palm, and then turns the land over to settler families in small holdings and provides subsistence allowances for the settlers until their farms are self-sustaining. As of January 1963, Malays comprised 90 per cent of the settlers in FLDA schemes, Chinese 8 per cent, and Indians the remainder.[56] In the 1957 census, Malays comprised 70 per cent of the rural population.

Malayism also arises in the definition of a smallholder as "a citizen of the Federation who owns . . . holdings not exceeding five acres." Since a considerable part of the legislation in recent years to promote agricultural development has applied specifically to smallholders, the effect of both the nationality requirement and the acreage limitation is to exclude a substantial proportion of Chinese and Indian residents.[57] Also reflecting Malayism is the Group Settlement Areas program of government financed land settlement projects. The Land (Group Settlement Areas) Act specifies that no person, other than a citizen, shall be eligible to occupy a rural holding so long as such holding continues to be state land. This provision, together with the exercise of discretionary authority by state officials issuing leaseholds, results in the exclusion of

[55] F. of M., *Report of the Land Administration Commission* (Kuala Lumpur: Government Press, 1958), pp. 22–29.

[56] Ness, *op. cit.*, p. 185.

[57] For example, the various schemes for replanting smallholders' rubber plantings are heavily subsidized by the government. See Legal Notice No. 9 of 31 Dec. 1957, Command Papers No. 3 of 1958, and Legal Notice No. 421 of 30 December 1959.

a substantial portion of the population from the benefits of this important rural development program.[58]

Among the various states, land alienation laws have provided increasingly for nationality restrictions on ownership of land. In Kelantan, only state citizens are entitled to state (leasehold) land, both rural and urban, and applications from Federal citizens must be approved by the Rulers in Council. In 1960, the Selangor government decided that state lands, including urban lots, may be alienated only to Federal citizens. The new law, however, did not apply to industrial sites and mining land.[59]

Malay indigenism also appears in the terms under which land is alienated to various categories of applicants. For example, during the Emergency, substantial numbers of Chinese who had fled the cities into the countryside to escape the harshness of the Japanese occupation were reconcentrated in settlements or "new villages." When leaseholds were eventually offered to resettled persons—citizens and non-citizens—the terms were considerably less favorable than those customarily offered. In Johore, for example, such leases were limited to twenty-one years. In Kedah, where title to most agricultural land is generally granted in perpetuity and shop lots are leased for between sixty and ninety-nine years, resettled persons were offered thirty-year leases for all classes of land. Moreover, the leases provided for annual rents five times the usual maximum. Similarly, leases offered by the Selangor state government were shorter in duration and at higher rentals.[60] In some states, the full rate of rental is applied to holdings of more than ten acres and is reduced for smaller holdings. In Malay Reservations rents are usually reduced by 50 per cent.[61]

Plantation interests in Malaya have continually protested the difficulty of obtaining new land for agricultural purposes.[62] There is little evidence, however, that this reflects indigenism so much as it represents

[58] The law, No. 13 of 1960, provides that "the Ruler in Council may direct that the whole or any part of a group settlement area shall be cleared at the public expense."

[59] *Straits Times*, October 6, 1960. See also editorial "Policy for Land" in this issue.

[60] IBRD, *op. cit.*, p. 233.

[61] F. of M., *Report of the Land Administration Commission*, p. 24.

[62] For example, see the speech of H. I. Thornton-Jones, President of the Federated Malay States Chamber of Commerce, at the 38th Annual Meeting of the Chamber (*Straits Times*, May 7, 1960).

enlightened land policy.[63] Central to postwar Malayan economic policy has been the effort to replant rubber with high-yielding varieties. To accelerate this process, substantial subsidies derived from taxation of rubber have been paid to smallholders and plantation owners to replace existing rubber plantings. During the 1950s when rubber prices were favorable, an obvious incentive existed to maintain production from existing plantings. It was government policy, however, not to make new land available, but to insist on replanting of low-yielding stands.

Malay indigenism also appears to be a relatively minor factor in the management of other natural resources. Forestry resources, with a few minor exceptions, are state owned and fall into two categories: state land forests and forest reserves. State land forests are destined for eventual lumbering prior to the conversion of the land to agriculture and other uses and are worked under annual license. Forest reserves, which include between one-fifth and one-quarter of the land area, are managed as an annual crop, and access to the reserves for lumbering takes the form of an annual permit or long-term agreement. A number of programs, primarily those of the RIDA and its successor MARA, exist to encourage and subsidize Malay participation in this industry. Frustration with the results of such efforts is reflected in the existing government commitment to establish a public corporation to exploit the timber and mineral resources of Malaya, presumably in the interest of the Malay population.[64]

Fisheries policy is similar to that for forestry resources. State laws providing for licensing of fishing gear and boats and enforcement is in the hands of the Fisheries Department of the Federal Ministry of Agriculture. A number of government programs exist to promote Malay participation in the fishing industry and RIDA and MARA have made strong efforts to promote the growth of co-operatives among Malay fishermen and to modernize their equipment and technology.

Ownership of all minerals is vested in the state governments which issue permits to prospect and mining leases. Such leases are issued for a maximum of twenty-one years, subject to renewal. Mining output is

[63] Minister of Commerce and Industry, Lim Swee Aun reported in Parliament that at the end of 1964, of 2,103 rubber estates in Malaya, 1,651 comprising 767,000 acres were owned by "Asian companies" and 452 including 1,126,000 acres were owned by "European companies." See *Straits Budget*, June 22, 1966.

[64] See above, section on Malay participation in business.

dominated by tin, and Malayan production accounts for 30 per cent of world output. Iron ore output, in recent years averaging about one-quarter the value of tin production, is concentrated in two large deposits on the east coast. Bauxite production has expanded in recent years but exports amounted to only 2 per cent of the value of tin exports in 1960.

As of the end of 1964, only 110 out of 1,103 tin mines were operated by European tin mining companies, but they accounted for about 52 per cent of output, with the remaining output accounted for by small-scale gravel-pump mines, almost exclusively Chinese.[65] Government policy of restricting access to new land for tin mining reflects diverse factors. Malaysia is a leading participant in the International Tin Agreement which seeks to maintain stable and high prices for tin by marketing quotas. Under the agreement, increases in tin production in excess of Malaysia's quota would be stockpiled, essentially at the expense of the Federal Government budget. Prejudice against tin mining reflecting both rational and irrational factors is widespread, particularly among Malays. Tin mining disfigures the landscape and it is widely believed to be responsible for the silting of rivers. Moreover, state governments participate to a very minor degree in the heavy taxation of the tin industry and therefore are little inclined to lease new land for tin mining. Also of importance is the fact that tin production in the past has been maintained from existing leases by changes in dredging technology and improved recovery processes which have made the reworking of tin lands profitable.

Malayan indigenism is not a prominent feature of natural resource policy. Natural resources are managed prudently and there is little evidence that access to resources for commercial production involves discrimination between Malayans and aliens.[66] On the other hand, Malay nationalism is prominent in the administration and settlement of public lands by smallholders.

[65] Reported to Parliament by the Minister of Commerce and Industry on June 15, 1966. See *Straits Budget,* June 22, 1966. The account went on to say that "even though tin mining companies were registered as being held by European mining concerns, in some cases as much as 80 per cent of the shares were held by Malaysians [Malayans]."

[66] In 1962, the National Land Council decreed that Japanese and other foreign firms are not to hold more than one-third of the share capital in any iron ore mining company in Malaya (National Land Council, *Foreign Participation in the Iron Ore Mining Industry,* Paper No. 16 of 1962).

MANUFACTURING AND PUBLIC UTILITIES

Malaya is distinctive in Southeast Asia for the role assigned to the state in organizing production. The Malayan government operates a wide range of conventional public utilities but prior to 1965 scrupulously avoided engaging in directly productive manufacturing activities or the operation of marketing monopolies.[67] The government is deeply involved in programs of economic development, but such efforts are concentrated in social overhead investment and in programs to improve welfare and initiate social change in rural Malaya. Insofar as manufacturing, commerce, mining, and plantation agriculture are concerned, the role of government has been to establish well-defined channels, widely accessible to individuals and enterprises, to resource and product markets. Discretionary intervention in economic processes, usually associated in Southeast Asia with graft and corruption, is minimized and bureaucratic morale and discipline have been maintained at high levels.

Malayan public utility services are efficient and provide coverage of the economy not to be found elsewhere in Southeast Asia. Railways are wholly owned by the state and when converted to a per capita basis, mileage of track and freight carried far exceed those found elsewhere in the area. Air service is provided by a mixed company with minority equity participation by the government. All road transport, both passenger and goods, with the exception of the urban transit system in Penang, is operated privately.[68]

Electricity distribution is a central government responsibility, and the principal part of the supply is generated by government plants. Planned expansion of government generating capacity, moreover, will rapidly reduce the relative importance of private generating facilities. Water supply is the direct responsibility of the public works depart-

[67] Recommendations of the Konggeres Ekonomi Bumiputra initiated a substantive change in this traditional policy, and directly productive public enterprises, in existence or planned, will engage in natural resource exploitation and processing and marketing of agricultural products, and in an expanding range of conventional manufacturing activities. These changes reflect the high priority assigned to the economic uplift of the rural Malays and their assimilation to functional roles outside subsistence agriculture. See above, section on Malay participation in business.

[68] In mid-1967, the government announced plans to form a Malaysian national shipping line using ocean-going ships provided as reparations from Japan. See *Straits Budget*, May 31, 1967; *Straits Times*, May 27 and June 6, 1967.

ments of the various state governments. Pure water supplies are provided for the bulk of the Malayan population in urban centers and larger rural settlements.

The postindependence pattern of Malayan industrial development was accurately predicted by the IBRD mission despatched to Malaya in 1955 to make recommendations for the economic development of that country. The Mission concluded that "Malaya's industrial development in the future, as in the past, seems likely to follow the pattern of individually small advances over a wide range of industries catering chiefly to the domestic and nearby markets." [69] The Mission further concluded that "the primary responsibility for progress in the improvement of industrial organization and standards is, of course, that of private enterprise. In the Malayan economy, with its long history of individual initiative in commerce and industry, there is no question of government itself embarking on direct operation of manufacturing industries." [70] The Mission proposed that the government should seek to promote industrialization by providing adequate basic services and by creating a "favorable climate" for the development of individual enterprise.

In elaborating their recommendations with respect to industrialization, the Mission repeatedly emphasized that protection should be limited to industries that initially would be virtually competitive with the outside world and where full competitiveness could be attained within a reasonable time.[71] The Report concluded that "foreign investment remains of major importance to the Malayan economy; as does local reinvestment of earnings from this source. It is most important to maintain an investment climate which will induce foreign capital to remain in Malaya and to reinvest its earnings there and which will attract new foreign investments." [72]

Following the visit of the IBRD mission, the Federation Government in May 1956 created an Industrial Development Working Party of high level civil servants to prepare detailed recommendations for industrialization policy. The recommendations of the working party, which followed closely those of the IBRD mission, included establishment of an Industrial Development Finance Company Ltd., to perform investment banking functions, a Tariff Advisory Committee to consider proposals for protection of new industries, and proposed "pioneer in-

[69] IBRD., *op. cit.*, p. 121.   [70] *Ibid.*, p. 122.
[71] *Ibid.*, p. 124.   [72] *Ibid.*, p. 315.

dustry" legislation providing for tax holidays as an inducement to manufacturing investment.[73] In the spring of 1957, the government threshed out an Interim Statement of Industrial Development Policy which conformed closely to the recommendations of the IBRD mission and the working party.[74]

Central to current industrialization policy is the Pioneer Industries (Relief from Income Tax) Ordinance,[75] which provides for tax holidays of from two to five years for companies that have been granted "pioneer" status by the Minister of Commerce and Industry. The law provides (Sec. 3) that pioneer status may be granted any industry that "is not being carried on in the Federation . . . and it is expedient and in the public interest to encourage the development of the industry." The law also provides (Sec. 3) that the ministerial order establishing pioneer status "may contain such conditions and restrictions as the Minister [Commerce and Industry] may think fit to impose."

Accomplishments under the pioneer industries policy have been substantial. As of the end of 1967, 129 enterprises had been granted pioneer status. Total capital investment of these companies was M$407 million of which 57 per cent was foreign. It was estimated that the value of net output of pioneer companies in 1966 was M$198 million and that employment totaled 14,800 persons.[76]

Examination of the list of industries actually in production and products designated pioneer indicates the importance of light manufactures for the local market. Of 122 industries actually in pioneer status at the end of 1966, 19 were producing foods and beverages and 41 miscellaneous manufactures including textiles and clothing and furniture. Chemicals and petroleum products including plastics and rubber manufactures were produced by 34 enterprises, and 28 were

[73] F. of M., *Report of the Industrial Development Working Party,* Council Paper No. 8 of 1957. The opening paragraph of the Report cited the Election Manifesto of the Alliance Party which proposed to assist the economic development of the country, *inter alia,* by encouraging investment of local capital; attracting overseas capital; amending the income tax law with a view of encouraging the development of new industries; facilitating the development of industrial sites for new industries; providing efficient and reliable transport by road, rail, and air; and giving full employment to labor, including training facilities.

[74] F. of M., *Council Paper No. 30* of May 7, 1957.

[75] F. of M., *Act of Parliament No. 31* of August 28, 1958.

[76] Bank Negara Malaysia, *Annual Report and Statement of Accounts, 1967,* pp. 20–21.

engaged in metal fabrication and engineering goods.[77] Pioneer industries were engaged in cement, rubber tire, fertilizer, plywood, and paper manufacture as well as petroleum refining and aluminum rolling.

Such distinctions as exist between the treatment of foreign investment and Malayan-owned enterprises are surprisingly mild. For example, in the parliamentary debates over the pioneer industries policy, the Minister of Finance asserted "the provisions of the Bill apply equally to local and foreign capital. There is absolutely no differentiation whatsoever between them." He went on to say that with the passage of the bill, Malayans would "be entitled to claim that our investment climate is at least as favourable as can be found in any other underdeveloped country." [78]

A single controversy involving economic nationalism in the pioneer industry policy occurred in 1960 and concerned the designation of a pioneer industry to manufacture rubber tires and tubes. There was an initial flurry of news stories reporting that a proposed Malayan Tyre Corporation, to be organized by local Chinese Malayans, would form a joint venture with a United States firm, Dayton Rubber International Corporation, to manufacture tires and tubes in the Federation. In parliamentary debate on December 2, 1959, an opposition spokesman asserted that "according to reports in the various vernacular papers in the past few months it was stated that a leading tyre (*sic*) factory in this country was not given an opportunity to carry out their trade under pioneer status." The Minister of Finance replied that no application for pioneer status had been rejected because none has been received. Subsequently, a leading British rubber manufacturing firm, Dunlop,

[77] *Ibid.*

[78] F. of M., *Legislative Council Debates*, Second Legislative Council, 3rd Session, pp. 4949 and 4954. In the same speech (p. 4945) the Minister of Finance pledged: "All other factors being equal, I am prepared to give preference to a pioneer factory which is financed wholly by local capital. Next in order of preference will be a factory which is financed by local and foreign capital in partnership." See also F. of M., *Federal Government Press Statement* of October 5, 1960, reproducing the speech of the Minister of Finance, Tan Siew Sin, at the International Bank for Reconstruction and Development, Washington, D.C., October 5, 1960. Only in the case of Japanese foreign investment is there evidence that foreign participation is limited to a minority interest. See *Straits Times*, November 19, 1959 and March 16, 1960 for details of specific joint enterprises with Japanese interests in tuna fishing and structural products of asbestos. The existence of restrictions on Japanese participation was also confirmed in conversations with Ministry of Commerce officials in the spring of 1961.

applied for and received pioneer status to manufacture tires and tubes. There is no evidence that the proposed joint venture involving Malayan Chinese and the United States firm was more than a "fishing expedition."

Two other incidents have occurred which suggest a tenuous relationship to economic nationalism. The Minister of Commerce and Industry reported to Parliament in 1959 that the majority of the firms granted pioneer status were joint enterprises. He further stated that "in cases where pioneer certificates have been issued to overseas firms, provision has been made for local investors to obtain an interest in these companies." [79] On still another occasion, the Minister, in describing policy governing the distribution of employment between Malayans and foreigners in "pioneer" firms, stated, "Conditions are further imposed to ensure that training programs are instituted to enable the Malayans to take over from foreign experts within a reasonable period of time." [80]

Also at the core of industrialization policy is the allocation of protection. The import tariff of the Federation is essentially a revenue tariff with duties on tobacco products, textiles, sugar, alcoholic beverages and spirits, and petroleum products, accounting for more than three-quarters of revenues from tariff duties. The remaining duties are imposed over a wide range of commodities with receipts from no one commodity accounting for as much as one per cent of tariff revenues. Tariff revenues in turn accounted for 36 per cent of the total tax revenues of the central government during 1963–1965. For a number of commodities, the tariff is definitely protective, and the manufacture of a number of products has materialized in response to protection.

Petitions for tariff concessions are considered by the Tariff Advisory Committee (TAC), a nonstatutory body made up of manufacturers, businessmen, accountants, economists, and others. The TAC investigates petitions and makes recommendations to the Minister of Commerce and Industry, who subsequently makes recommendations to the Minister of Finance, who approves or rejects petitions. As of the end of 1960, tariff concessions with respect to eighteen commodities had been approved by the government.

Malayan industrialization policy is moderate in goals and methods. Considerations of market efficiency are given high priority. Public entrepreneurship has been assigned no direct role in industrial develop-

[79] F. of M., *Parliamentary Debates*, Vol. I, No. 9, Column 824.
[80] *Ibid.*, Vol. II, No. 6, Column 685.

ment. Private initiative is encouraged by moderate incentives in the form of tax relief and protection, and is supported by efficient public services, subsidized industrial sites, and liberal support to education and vocational training. Procedures for access to tax and tariff concessions are well defined and incorporate objective economic criteria. There is no evidence that nationality is a major criterion, and up to the present time concessions have been moderate both in rate and duration.

COMMERCE—FOREIGN AND DOMESTIC

In contrast with less-developed countries generally, Malaya has been in the fortunate position of having a steady export surplus and large and stable foreign-exchange reserves. Although receipts from exports increased slowly following 1959 and small current account deficits have been experienced, Malaysia's net official foreign assets totaled almost U.S. $800 million in the close of 1966. On a per capita basis such assets at the end of 1966 amounted to more than U.S. $80, which was substantially above the comparable figure for the United States.

Effective exchange and import controls have not been necessary, and external and internal prices of most commodities imported into Malaya have diverged by amounts explained by transport and other competitive costs and the low levels of revenue duties. Under such circumstances, there has been little opportunity to Malayanize import trade by reserving foreign exchange to nationals, which has been a prominent feature of economic nationalism in a number of other countries of the area. Virtually all commodities are imported on open general license subject to surveillance by the commercial banks, and there is no evidence that nationality is a significant requirement for foreign-exchange allocation. Such a qualification would favor the Chinese and Indian merchants and strict nondiscrimination, therefore, is a mild manifestation of Malay nationalism.[81]

There is no evidence of Malayan nationalism in export trade policy. Such trade is in the hands of private traders with extensive participation by Western and Chinese firms. Malayan nationality has not been a prominent criterion for access to land and other resources employed in export production although, as mentioned earlier, an exception to this

[81] Taxation of imports falls heavily on commodities widely consumed in the urban society and thereby contributes to redistribution of income favorable to the rural Malay society.

generalization arises in the present policy of preserving the remaining patrimony of natural resources for future development, presumably with extensive Malay participation.

In the area of domestic commerce, Malay nationalism is evident in the efforts to introduce Malays into commercial activities. In the rural areas, production and marketing co-operatives have been promoted by the government. Greatest success has been achieved by rice milling societies which benefit from the government price support program for domestic rice. To implement price supports, rice traders proposing to import rice at the lower external price are given import licenses only after they have purchased rice from domestic rice milling co-operatives or from government stocks. During 1960, to obtain permission to import two tons of rice, it was necessary to have purchased one ton of domestically produced rice.[82] Smallholders' rubber co-operatives have also enjoyed modest success in operating processing as well as marketing facilities. Similar modest success has been achieved by other types of Malay marketing co-operatives.

In the area of retail trade, intensive effort has been made to encourage retail co-operatives among Malays. In general, they have been plagued by inefficiency, excessive administrative costs, and indulgent sales on credit to members, all of which have contributed to a persistent pattern of insolvency.[83] To support the co-operative effort, considerable importance has been placed on the training of officials and employees, and the Cooperative College of Malaya was opened in 1956. The training of Malays in elements of commerce and bookkeeping necessary to

[82] *Legislative Council Debates,* Second Legislative Council, 3rd Session, Sept. 1957–Oct. 1958, p. 3390. The Minister of Commerce and Industry reported that "The Ministry of Commerce and Industry has issued to suitable Malay applicants, rice trade and import licenses." Elsewhere (p. 4686), the Minister reported: "We have also issued to suitable Malay applicants import licenses and rice trading licenses and have assisted in every possible way Malays who are desirous of taking up general trading and import and export licenses. For example, during the period 1 June 1957 to 31 March 1958, out of a total of 416 rice licenses issued, 160 or 40 per cent of the total were issued to Malays."

[83] F. of M., *Annual Report, 1955,* p. 427. As of the end of 1966, rural thrift and credit co-operatives in Malaya numbered 1,639 with 60,700 members. In mid-July, 1967, the Minister of Agriculture and Cooperatives, Haji Ghazali bin Haji Tawi acknowledged the generally unsatisfactory condition of rural co-operative societies which he attributed to "lack of supervision and security in extending credit and limited membership which prevented them from engaging full-time staff." He reported that at the end of 1965, rural co-operatives had M$7.1 million of loans in arrears to the central co-operative bank. See *Straits Budget,* July 26, 1967.

operate co-operatives is also provided by the Dewan Latehan Training Institute operated by MARA.

BANKING, CREDIT, AND FINANCE

Conventional and moderate indigenism is evident in a number of moves by the Federation Government to establish control over the supply and distribution of credit. As was true of Southeast Asia generally, the colonial monetary system was an exchange reserve system in which the money supply was directly related to the foreign-exchange assets which were held by the Board of Commissioners of Currency, Malaya, and British Borneo.

The IBRD mission in 1954 recommended the establishment of a central bank and replacement of the exchange reserve system by a managed currency system. Establishment of the Bank Negara Tanah Melayu followed passage of the Central Bank of Malaya Ordinance (October 23, 1958) and in 1960 the exchange reserve system was modified to provide that the assets of the Board of Commissioners of Currency should include the "locally-issued securities of any of the participating governments." [84]

Central banking legislation provides for such conventional instruments of control over banking and credit as liquidity requirements including maintenance of statutory reserves with the central bank. In addition, the bank is empowered to establish a "local assets" ratio under which commercial banks may be required to hold a prescribed ratio of their deposit liabilities in approved assets within the Federation.

Expansion and Malayanization of commercial banking in the Federation has proceeded steadily. At the end of 1958, there were four local banks operating six offices and sixteen other banks operating 75 offices. As of the end of 1967, there were sixteen local banks operating 163 offices, five banks incorporated in Singapore operating 56 offices, and sixteen banks incorporated in other countries. [85]

To perform industrial banking functions, the government provided the initiative in forming the Malayan Industrial Finance Limited. [86]

---

[84] Following the formation of Malaysia, the central bank was reorganized as Bank Negara Malaysia.

[85] Bank Negara Malaysia, *Annual Report and Statement of Accounts, 1967*, pp. 44, 47, and 49. Banks incorporated in Malaysia accounted for 33 per cent of deposits and 32 per cent of loans and advances outstanding at the end of 1967.

[86] This was a major recommendation of the Industrial Development Working Party. See above section on manufacturing and public utilities.

Capital contributions totaling M$15 million were made by the Federation Government (M$2.5 million), commercial banks (M$5 million), the Colonial Development Corporation (M$2.5 million), Malayan and British insurance companies (M$2.5 million), with the remainder (M$2.5 million) coming from various sources including public subscription. There is no evidence to date of overt indigenism in access to the resources and services of this institution.

Foreign firms operating in Malaya encounter a mild discrimination in credit policy in that they are not permitted to borrow locally for capital expenditures. This requirement, however, is not so much a manifestation of indigenism as it is a measure to ensure that foreign investment does, in fact, result in an initial inflow of foreign exchange to pay for the capital assets created or purchased. This restriction, moreover, is limited to capital expenditures and does not apply to working capital which may be borrowed locally.[87]

To increase Malay participation in the ownership of large-scale industrial enterprises, the government sponsored the formation of a Malay-owned and operated investment company Sharikat Permodalan Kebangsaan (National Investment Company) Ltd, which was incorporated in 1961.[88] The share capital of the corporation, reserved to Malays, is used to purchase shares in public corporate issues, and the government subsequently took steps to reserve a portion of all new share issues sold in Malaya to the corporation.[89] Over the six years

[87] See F. of M., *Federal Government Press Statement,* "Local borrowing by foreign-owned companies," December 28, 1959. See also *Federal Government Press Statement* of October 5, 1960 reproducing the speech of the Minister of Finance, Tan Siew Sin, at the meeting of the Board of Governors of the International Bank for Reconstruction and Development, Washington, D.C., October 5, 1960.

[88] The symbolic importance of Malay participation in the ownership of large-scale industrial, commercial, financial, and extractive enterprises permeated the Konggeres Ekonomi Bumiputra. The Congress took the position that "we should judge the success or failure of the policy of increasing participation in industry by Bumiputra [indigenous people] on the question of ownership of companies. If Bumiputra do not own their companies or do not share in the ownership of Malaysian companies, then this policy is a failure" (Konggeres Ekonomi Bumiputra, *op. cit.,* Working Paper No. 6/1/65, "Participation in Industry by Bumiputra," p. 105).

[89] In early 1965, the Minister of Commerce and Industry reported to Parliament that his Ministry attached as a condition for issuing a pioneer industry certificate "that at least 10 per cent of the share capital . . . be reserved for Malays." See *Straits Budget,* January 6, 1965.

ending with 1967, the corporation was allocated M$8.1 million of shares of equities. At the end of 1966, the Corporation held M$4.6 million and had disposed of M$3.5 million of the issues to *bona fide* Malay purchasers.[90]

In August 1962, the Malayan Muslim Pilgrims Savings Corporation was formed under government sponsorship to provide savings facilities for Malays intending to make the pilgrimage to Mecca. It was reported that, as Islamic principle forbids the acceptance of a predetermined rate of return on investments, the outlets for the savings assembled by the Corporation would comprise equities, real estate, and other long-term assets.[91] As of the end of 1967, savings deposited with the Corporation totaled M$5.7 million and well over half of investments were in shares of Malayan companies.[92]

In the case of insurance, Malayan nationalism has been mild, and only in 1963 did the Federation Government write a comprehensive insurance statute. This law provides, among other things, that all insurance companies, both life and general insurance, shall maintain a proportion of their assets in local investments. Beginning in 1963, Malayan assets of insurance companies must be not less than 25 per cent of liabilities in Malaya. This ratio is to increase 10 percentage points per year until in 1966, and thereafter, the required ratio will remain at 55 per cent.

[90] Bank Negara Malaysia, *Annual Report and Statement of Accounts, 1967,* p. 56. Over the five years ending with 1966, the successive annual reports of the Bank Negara Malaysia reported thirty-four public issues which raised M$173 million. Only one issue was unsuccessful, and the reports in most years described the issues as "heavily oversubscribed." Because of the buoyancy of the Malayan capital market, shares tend to sell at a substantial premium after issue. This factor together with the reservation of shares to the National Investment Company ensures the profitability of the latter. The premium to be realized from the rise in share prices after issue creates another problem. In April 1966, Deputy Prime Minister Abdul Razak announced that MARA would buy the unsubscribed shares allocated to Malays in stock issues of Malayan corporations in an effort to put an end to what he referred to as "Ali Baba" deals in which a Malay "Ali" uses the Chinese "Baba's" funds to buy shares allocated to Malays. MARA would later sell the shares to *bona fide* Malay purchasers who intended to participate in the enterprise. See *Straits Budget,* May 4, 1966. In 1967 the MARA Unit Trusts Ltd. was incorporated with initial working capital of M$2 million to buy equity shares allocated to Malays.

[91] Central Bank of Malaya, *Annual Report,* 1962, p. 41.

[92] Bank Negara Malaysia, *Annual Report and Statement of Accounts, 1967,* p. 49.

BUREAUCRACY, PROFESSIONS, AND LABOR

Malayanization of the bureaucracy proceeded rapidly following transfer of political power in 1957. An initial Malayanization Committee proposed in 1954 that replacement of non-Malayan civil service and administrative service officers should take place through normal attrition.[93] As independence approached, however, it became clear that provision would have to be made to prematurely retire and pension non-Malayans, and accelerated but controlled Malayanization was scheduled in three phases to be completed by 1965.[94] Apprehensions concerning deterioration in the efficiency and morale of the bureaucracy in the transitional period proved largely unwarranted and Malayanization was completed, except for a small minority of higher level posts, within four and a half years of independence.

In the case of the professions, overt economic nationalism has been a mild phenomenon. The right to practice most professions is established by licensing (registration) and in the case of physicians, dentists, and pharmacists, registration is automatic for individuals holding a degree from Singapore University, or a degree recognized by the licensing body of the United Kingdom.[95] For individuals with training in institutions not automatically recognized, individual application must be made to the registering body established by the Federation government which is given discretionary authority to recognize degrees from other institutions.

In the case of lawyers, only British subjects may qualify for admission to the bar.[96] Architects registered in the United Kingdom and architects registered in the Federation at the time of enactment of the registration ordinance are automatically qualified for registration.[97] In addition,

[93] F. of M., *Report of the Committee on the Malayanization of the Government Service* (Kuala Lumpur: Government Press, 1954), p. 6.

[94] F. of M., *Report of the Committee on the Malayanization of the Public Service* (Kuala Lumpur: Government Press, 1956). For details of the process of Malayanization, see Tilman, *op. cit.*, pp. 63–76.

[95] Any professional proposing to practice in Malay must, of course, obtain the appropriate immigration permit. Late in 1966 it was announced that visas were no longer being issued to foreign doctors who proposed to practice in Malaya (*Straits Budget,* November 2, 1966).

[96] F. of M., Advocates and Solicitors Ordinance No. 4 of 1947, February 14, 1947.

[97] F. of M., The Architects Ordinance, No. 48 of 1951, October 18, 1951.

others may qualify for registration by examination for which no nationality qualification is specified. Teachers are also registered with general qualifications similar to those of other professions. In addition, the Registrar may, with the concurrence of the Minister of Education, refuse to register a teacher who is not a citizen of the Federation.[98]

Prior to 1965, the right of foreigners to work and practice professions in Malay was not legally restricted. Moreover, no specific trade or profession is reserved to Malayan citizens. On the other hand, entry of foreigners for long-term residence to work in Malaya was subject to strict control through immigration regulations. These include a minimum wage or salary requirement that servies as a supplementary barrier to Asian aliens, as well as the requirement that an employer seeking to bring in an alien to fill a position may be required to show that no trained Malayans are qualified to fill the position.[99] The latter requirement could be and was used to Malayanize positions requiring technical, professional, and managerial skills.[100]

A major drive to extend Malayanization of technical, professional, and executive positions in the private sector was initiated in 1965 when the government created a standing committee of cabinet-level officers on Malaysianization of Commerce and Industry, chaired by the Deputy Prime Minister, Tun Abdul Razak.[101] The report of the standing committee issued in June 1966 proposed that all firms be required to submit plans for the gradual replacement of all technical, professional, and managerial personnel by Malaysians by 1980 and to draft schemes for training Malaysians to take over such posts.[102] In the meantime, a standing committee chaired by the Minister of Commerce and Industry was

[98] F. of M., Registration of Teachers Ordinance, No. 3 of 1957, April 14, 1957.

[99] U.S. Department of Commerce, Bureau of Foreign Commerce, *Establishing a Business in the Federation of Malaya*, World Trade Information Service Report No. 60-36, Part 1, August 1960.

[100] In July 1964, the Minister of Home Affairs reported to Parliament that between January 1, 1959 and May 31, 1964, foreigners permitted entry to work in plantation industries numbered 191; for commercial firms, 150, in mining and engineering, 501, accountants, 95, doctors, 11, and lawyers, 3. See *Legislative Council Debates*, First Session, 2nd Parliament of Malaysia, Vol. 1, No. 5, 6 July 1964.

[101] See *Straits Budget*, December 8, 1965 for report of speech in Parliament by Minister of Home Affairs, Dato Ismail bin Abdul Rahman on December 2, announcing the formation of the standing committee.

[102] On June 21, the Minister of Home Affairs, Dato Ismail presented the recommendations of the standing committee to parliament (*ibid.*, June 29, 1966).

established to examine all applications for entry into Malaysia on employment passes.[103] The Chairman subsequently reported to Parliament that "the Government had taken active steps to ensure that Malaysianization would proceed according to plan."

In May 1967 the Minister of Home Affairs reported that about two-thirds "of all executive posts in the private sector will be Malaysianized by 1970." He also stated that except for a few key appointments, all executive posts in nonprofessional and nontechnical firms will be Malaysianized by 1975 and that this goal will be achieved in professional and technical firms by 1980.[104]

Malayanization of labor in the private sector up to the present has not been a central concern of the political leadership. Malay indigenism has been evident, however, in the labor clauses requiring the hiring of and training of Malays which are included in agreements establishing mining and forestry concessions and granting pioneer industry status. Such agreements customarily require that a substantial proportion of the labor force be Malays, as well as the requirement that Malayans—not specifically Malays—be trained to replace foreign employees within a reasonable time.[105]

Summary

Indigenism in Malaya is a subtle phenomenon which "fits" into our comparative study when visualized as Malayism rather than Malayanism. Predominant political power was transferred from the British

[103] See *ibid.*, May 25, 1966 for an account of the speech in Parliament by Minister of Commerce and Industry, Lim Swee Aun reporting on the work of the committee. In February 1967, the Minister of Home Affairs announced that legislation to require work permits of all noncitizens would be tabled. This step suggests that Malaysianization of positions presently held by alien (Chinese and Indian) residents will be an early target. See *ibid.*, March 1, 1967.

[104] *Ibid.*, June 7, 1967.

[105] The Minister of Commerce and Industry reported to Parliament on January 1, 1965 that the requirement that 30 per cent of total employment be reserved for Malays was a condition attached to issuance of a pioneer industry certificate. See *ibid.*, January 6, 1965. See also *Malay Mail*, February 28, 1960; *Legislative Council Debates*, Second Legislative Council, 3rd Session, September 1957–October 1958, p. 4685.

colonial rulers to the Malays. For reasons associated with the exclusiveness of Islam and their insecurity in an environment of dominant Chinese economic power, the Malays have withheld full recognition of the Chinese and Indians—citizens as well as noncitizens—as members of the national society. This denial of recognition takes a number of forms, not the least of which, is a refusal to make economically significant distinctions between the treatment of Malayan and Western and Asian alien enterprises in the plantation, industrial, financial, and commercial sectors. The prevailing nondiscrimination is not a denial of Malayan economic nationalism so much as it is an assertion of Malayism. The Malay stake in the Western (British) economic presence is obvious. Equally obvious is the fact that conventional measures of indigenism would benefit the Chinese and Indian minorities, with little impact on the Malay community.

Malay indigenism is restrained by the political reality of communal balance. This is presently manifested in the widespread recognition by the political leaders of the various communities that the viability of Malaya as a political entity depends upon the evolution of meaningful Malayan nationality. Currently, these leaders recognize that this will be a prolonged and two-fold process. The imbalance in political power is scheduled to be redressed over time by the application of the principal of *jus solis* in determining citizenship. At the same time, the economically more advanced communities acquiesce in vigorous and discriminatory use of the powers of the state to uplift economically the backward Malay population. Such efforts, if successful, will initiate a process of modernization of the Malay community which promises to reduce the abrasive distinctions in the present division of economic functions and rates of material progress.

Visitors to Malaya in the mid-1960s invariably are impressed by the quality of the bureaucracy and by the efficiency and dependability of public services. The comments of informed observers frequently reflect the conviction that a dollar paid in taxes, or for public services, results in a dollar of services rendered. In contrast to Southeast Asia generally, the morale of the bureaucracy is high, salaries are liberal, their real value stable, and corruption is minimal.[106] The high quality of the

---

[106] Concern for deterioration in the efficiency and incorruptibility of the civil service has been frequently expressed since independence. Apprehension is aroused for the impact upon the civil service of rapid Malayanization combined with maintenance of the restrictive ratios that limit non-Malay staff.

Malayan bureaucracy is explained by the strength of the British civil service tradition and the prolonged and challenging period of the Emergency in which the bureaucratic establishment was forged into a flexible, self-confident instrument. It also reflects the favorable economic conditions prevailing since independence and the buoyant enterprise economy in which the absence of government intervention in economic processes and the strong foreign-exchange position have minimized the opportunities for and the incentives to corruption. Not only is there a proven bureaucracy capable of efficiently executing large-scale undertakings, but, at the same time, the resources available to the government, sustained by the strong external demand, are relatively greater than elsewhere in Southeast Asia.

During the period of the First Five-Year Development Plan (1956–1961), public development expenditure totaled M$1,150 million, or some 12 per cent of gross national product.[107] The Second Five-Year Development Plan, moreover, virtually doubled the planned level of public development expenditure to M$2,150 million.[108] It was anticipated that the level of such expenditure in the Second Plan would maintain gross public investment at approximately 10 per cent of gross national product.[109] In the First Malaysia Plan covering the five years 1966–1970, public development expenditures totaling M$4,550 million are planned, of which M$3,714 million is to be spent in Malaya.[110]

During 1963–1965, current expenditures of the government of Malaysia on social and economic services—medical and health, social welfare, education, public works, and communications—totaled M$1,307 million or 37 per cent of total current expenditures. Over this period, public investment expenditures totaled M$1,827 million, of which almost half was allocated in the Second Five-Year Plan to agricultural development,

[107] F. of M., *Official Yearbook, 1961*, p. 329.

[108] Actual expenditures under the Plan totaled M$2,650 million thus exceeding the target by nearly 25 per cent (Bank Negara Malaysia, *Annual Report and Statement of Accounts, 1965*, p. 14).

[109] During the three fiscal years 1958–1960, investment expenditures of the Federation government averaged M$262 million which was 24 per cent of total expenditures and 5.4 per cent of national income. For the three fiscal years 1963–1965, investment expenditures of the Government of Malaysia averaged M$609 million which was 34 per cent of total expenditures and 10.3 per cent of national income of Malaya (not including Sabah and Sarawak). See United Nations, ECAFE, *Economic Survey of Asia and the Far East, 1962* and *1966*.

[110] Bank Negara Malaysia, *Annual Report and Statement of Accounts, 1965*, p. 15.

education, health, and housing. When the volume of current expenditures on social services and investment in agricultural and human development are combined, the magnitude of the effort to uplift the rural Malay society comes into focus.[111] It is clear that the Malay political elites are in a strategic position to utilize annually at least one-eighth of the total output of goods and services produced by the Malaysian economy to initiate and sustain the modernization of the rural Malay economy. The magnitude of this effort is unprecedented among the less developed countries of Southeast Asia and perhaps in the world.

Malayan government expenditures have been little affected by inflation and are undertaken by a self-confident, efficient bureaucracy. Tax revenues are highly dependent upon taxation of foreign trade, both imports and exports, and upon direct taxation of personal and corporate incomes.[112] The massive redistribution of income from the non-Malay modern economy to the rural economy is the core of Malay indigenism. It represents a plausible assessment of the resource requirements of the task of preparing the Malay society for integration with the other communities into a viable national society. From the point of view of the Chinese and Indians, it is the present cost of the promise of a politically egalitarian national society. For Western enterprise, it is the price that must be paid for continued, relatively nondiscriminatory access to profitable resources and markets.

[111] During 1963–1965, aggregate expenditures of the Government of Malaysia averaged M$1,778 million annually. This was equivalent to somewhat more than one-quarter of estimated gross national product of Malaya (West Malaysia) over this period. Developmental investment plus current expenditures on social and economic services averaged 59 per cent of aggregate expenditures of the Government of Malaysia over this period.

[112] During 1963–1965, revenues from taxes on imports, exports, and incomes averaged M$384 million, M$207 million and M$289 million respectively. Such revenues accounted for more than four-fifths of total tax revenues of the Government of Malaysia (United Nations, ECAFE, *Economic Survey of Asia and the Far East, 1966*).

7

SOUTH VIETNAM

❧❧❧❧❧❧❧❧❧❧❧❧❧❧❧❧❧❧❧❧❧❧❧❧❧❧❧❧❧

The Environment of Policy

To round out our comparative study of economic nationalism in Southeast Asia, we must turn to the successor states of the French colonies in the Indochinese peninsula, the Vietnams, Cambodia, and Laos. The period of independence—more or less precarious from state to state—has provided time for the emergence of policies and institutions that permit tentative assessment of indigenism. Our survey, in fact, is limited to South Vietnam and Cambodia. In the case of North Vietnam, governed by a communist regime which is ideologically committed and self-confident with military success, indigenism has been the incidental result of socialist nationalization. The economically prominent French left North Vietnam following the collapse of colonial rule, while nine-tenths of the Chinese residents chose to evacuate to South Vietnam in the mass exodus of refugees in 1954 and 1955.[1] Laos has been excluded from our survey because economic and political modernization have not proceeded to the point where nationalism in its economic manifestations is relevant. Moreover, insecurity and disorder seriously compromise the *de facto* independence of Laos, a condition we specify as necessary for the emergence of indigenism.

The cultural impact of the successive periods of Chinese invasion, rule, and domination is evident in the Confucian tradition which gives the Vietnamese society a moral unity and defined pattern of authority and preserves a distinctive cultural identity in relation to its powerful neighbor to the north. With minor exceptions, the ancestors of the

[1] United States Department of the Army, *Area Handbook for Vietnam* (Washington: Government Printing Office, 1964), p. 59.

Vietnamese were ruled as a province of China during the period from 111 B.C. to 938 A.D. Subsequently, until the advent of the French in the latter part of the nineteenth century, the Vietnamese enjoyed more or less effective self-rule in the face of Chinese power by combining military vigor and preparedness with judicious acknowledgment of tributary status.

Although French contacts with the Vietnamese, initially of a missionary nature, began in the sixteenth century, it was not until the latter half of the nineteenth century that the French undertook the conquest of Indochina. Within ten years of the capture of Touraine (Da Nang) by a French naval squadron in 1858, the whole of present-day South Vietnam and Cambodia had come under French dominance, although in Annam, the central Vietnamese provinces, the Emperor and his officials were left with nominal autonomy. Siam, which in successful competition with Annam dominated Cambodia, was forced to recognize a French protectorate over the Cambodian kingdom in return for two of its provinces. Subsequently, an expeditionary force brought Tonkin in the north under French control, and the signing of protectorate treaties over Tonkin in 1883 and Annam in the following year formally ended the vestiges of Vietnamese independence. The Laotian kingdom, another Siamese protectorate, was annexed by France ten years later. These regions were subsequently organized into French Indochina, a federation under a French Governor-General.

By 1900 the basic governmental structure of French Indochina was completed. Cochin China and Tonkin were ruled directly as colonies. In the protectorate of Annam, where the Emperor was still nominally in power, French rule was somewhat less direct and administration of the kingdoms of Cambodia and Laos followed in this pattern. The economic opportunities in Tonkin and Cochin China, the former relatively well endowed with resources and with a vigorous, economically responsive population, and the latter rich in unoccupied and fertile alluvial land, preoccupied the French. As a result, the social fabric of Annam, Cambodia, and Laos was less disrupted than in the colonies ruled directly.

French colonial policy is usually discussed in terms of two theories of colonization, "assimilation" and "association." Until well after the turn of the century, the formal aspects of colonial policy were shaped by the former concept calling for the absorption of the colony into a culturally homogeneous empire until every part of the colony's life became French.[2] Over time and in the face of social, political, and economic realities, however, the concept of assimilation was moderated to that of association in which France and Indochina were linked in a special relationship of an exclusive nature but accommodating distinctive cultures.

Like the Chinese society, from which it absorbed major values and institutions, the Vietnamese society was strongly resistant to change and innovation. Assimilation, therefore, required a drastic attack on the whole social fabric. Native law was handled roughly and in Cochin China both the French civil and criminal codes were placed in force. In Tonkin and the kingdoms, the native codes were altered to provide a legal frame for the French social and economic systems, with little regard for the consequences. The ancestor cult of the Vietnamese was under pressure from French missionaries, and native converts were favored in bureaucratic appointments, which strengthened the influence of the missionary orders. By World War II, approximately one-tenth of the Vietnamese were Christians who comprised a cohesive, politically vocal minority.

The spread of the French language was regarded as central to assimilation since "it was believed that the mere knowledge of French would bring an insatiable thirst for French ideas and manufactures." [3] Comparable importance was attached to French education, and initially the French even paid the Vietnamese elites to send their children to the French School in Saigon.[4] As might be expected, for the Vietnamese a French education gradually assumed the role previously filled by traditional Chinese classical education.[5]

In the economic sphere, assimilation meant the restructuring of the economy on the basis of French policies and institutions and oriented

[2] Stephen H. Roberts, *History of French Colonial Policy* (London: Frank Cass, 1929), pp. 27–28; Thomas E. Ennis, *French Policy and Developments in Indochina* (Chicago: University of Chicago Press, 1936), pp. 95–110; and Virginia Thompson, *French Indo-China* (New York: Macmillan Co., 1942), pp. 399–401.

[3] Thompson, *ibid.*, p. 399.

[4] J. S. Furnivall, *Educational Progress in Southeast Asia* (New York: Institute of Pacific Relations, Inquiry Series, 1943), p. 39.

[5] Until the French conquest, Chinese was the language of administration and scholarship in Annam and Tonkin. When the triennial bureaucratic examinations were held in 1903, ten thousand persons sat for them. By 1913, the number of candidates had declined to 1,330. The last mandarinate examinations were held in Tonkin in 1915 and in Annam in 1918 (United States Department of the Army, *Area Handbook for Vietnam*, pp. 68, 74, and 114).

toward the mother country. In the Vietnamese kingdom all land belonged, in theory at least, to the Emperor, who parceled out large holdings to his supporters and favorites to be held during the lifetime of
the grantee, after which the title reverted to the ruler. Extensive communal lands administered by local oligarchies of village elders made a
major contribution to peasant welfare.[6] Under the French, all lands
became alienable including the communal lands. The French distributed tracts of land, at first gratis and later for nominal fees, to the
French *colons*. In Cochin China vast new areas were opened to rice
cultivation by programs of public works: roads, canals, and port works.
Large landholdings, including extensive French ownership, worked by
tenant farmers became the pattern.[7] Mining concessions and land
alienated for rubber plantations and other commercial crops proved
less disruptive of the indigenous society, as they were generally in upland regions populated by tribal groups practicing shifting cultivation.

Insofar as Western enterprise was concerned, the French maintained
Indochina as a preserve for Frenchmen and French capital. Subsidies,
bounties, public contracts, a currency linked to the franc, and restrictive
legislation combined to inhibit foreign capital and entrepreneurship.
Only French citizens, subjects, or "protégés" could obtain land concessions, while further legislation required that half of the "managing
body" and one-third of the capital of mining ventures be French.[8] By
the end of the interwar period it was estimated that foreign investment
other than French and that of the resident Chinese amounted to less
than 3 per cent of foreign investment.[9] In 1938, fifteen large French
companies handled nearly all of Indochina's foreign trade.[10]

Very promptly the colonies were declared legally assimilated, which
meant that the French tariff structure was extended to enclose the
colony while mutual trade was free. Specialization of Indochina as an
agricultural hinterland of the French Empire proceeded apace until
for the three years 1935–1937 exports of rice, rubber, and corn accounted for three-quarters of the value of Indochina's exports. At the

[6] Joseph Buttinger, *The Smaller Dragon* (New York: Praeger Publishing Co.,
1958), pp. 146–148, 159–160. See also Le Thanh Khoi, *Le Viet Nam, histoire et
civilization* (Paris: Editions de Minuit, 1955), p. 66.

[7] Of the "European-owned" plantations in 1931, two-thirds were rice plantations and most of these were in Cochin China (Charles Robequain, *The Economic
Development of French Indo-China* [New York: Oxford University Press, 1944],
p. 194).

[8] Helmut G. Callis, *Foreign Capital in Southeast Asia* (New York: Institute of
Pacific Relations, International Research Series, 1942), p. 84.

[9] *Ibid.*, p. 82.   [10] Robequain, *op. cit.*, p. 129.

same time Indochina's trade became highly concentrated with France until during the three years 1936–1938 the metropolis absorbed 55 per cent of Indochina's exports and provided almost 60 per cent of imports. As was true of the other colonies of Southeast Asia, Indochina's trade resulted in a persistent export surplus which for the same three years averaged more than three-fifths of expenditures on imports.[11]

The Chinese were firmly embedded in the economy of Indochina at the time of the French conquest, and although the French made sporadic efforts to bar further immigration, they found that they needed the Chinese. As a result, the Chinese "were rather grudgingly tolerated," and their immigration was strictly controlled and "conducted on a prearranged system for filling up vacancies in the groups of Chinese." [12] The Chinese, excluded from direct participation in the development of Indochina's natural resources, gravitated to commerce, particularly retail trade, the assembly of the rice surplus for export, and rice milling. In the absence of more formal credit institutions, the Chinese merchants provided the working capital necessary for the rapid development of the rice economy of Cochin China and "from the great rice merchants in Cholon, a cascade of credit, all in the hands of Chinese middlemen, extended down to the buyer-retailers at the village level and through them to every peasant rice grower." [13]

Formal relations of the Chinese minority with the host colony were regulated by a succession of treaties negotiated between France and China.[14] Under the French, the Chinese were permitted to retain Chinese citizenship and to appeal to China for protection. For internal

[11] Because the French sought sanction for their colonial policy in the concepts of assimilation and association, it has become a commonplace to distinguish between the exclusiveness of French policy as compared to that of the other colonial powers in Southeast Asia. Although the semantic differences are undeniable, the consequences of colonial policy for economic structure, functional specialization along racial and ethnic lines, concentration on primary production for export, and the persistence of an export surplus, were not materially different in Indochina as compared to the Philippines. The Dutch and British tolerated a greater dispersion of the trade of their colonies to third countries than did the French, but the other consequences of colonial policy in Indochina conformed to the pattern experienced in Burma, the Netherlands Indies, and Malaya.

[12] Victor Purcell, *The Chinese in Southeast Asia* (London: Oxford University Press, 1951), pp. 229–232, 299.

[13] *Ibid.*, pp. 239–240. See also Paul Bernard, *Nouveaux Aspects du problème économique indochinois* (Paris: Fernand Sorlot, 1937), pp. 26–30; and Thompson, *op. cit.*, pp. 165–172.

[14] For details, see Bernard B. Fall, "Viet-Nam's Chinese Problems," *Far Eastern Survey* (27), May 1958, p. 67.

administration they were organized on the basis of dialect and area of origin into a system of autonomous "congregations" (*bang*). The heads of the *bang* were held responsible by the French administration for compliance by *bang* members with the laws of the colony.[15] The successive treaties provided ample scope within which Chinese individualism flourished, and by the end of the interwar period the interstices between the large-scale manufacturing, plantation, commercial, and financial enterprises of the French were filled by the smaller enterprises of the Chinese.[16] At the same time, the French policy of treating the Chinese as a community outside the Vietnamese society enhanced the distinctiveness of this minority and sustained latent Vietnamese hostility.

The Chinese community in Indochina was altered drastically in the decade following the Japanese invasion of China in 1937. Disorder and privation in China led to the influx of an estimated 400,000 Chinese, and by 1960 the number of ethnic Chinese in South Vietnam was estimated to be about one million of whom an estimated 600,000 had been born in the areas of North and South Vietnam.[17]

The French policy of mutual free trade between Indochina and France precluded substantial industrialization as protection was denied to potentially viable industries in the colony. France administered Indochina as a free trade area, and internal specialization reflecting the availability of energetic and disciplined labor, as well as coal and other natural resources, resulted in the concentration in Tonkin of the limited industrial development that took place. Medium-sized coal, cement, and textile industries grew up in the north, as well as smaller industries producing paper and glass. Industrial development in the south was dominated by the government-administered fiscal monopolies in matches, alcohol, and tobacco, together with Chinese-owned rice mills of Cholon and a single medium-sized sugar refinery. The output of handicraft manufactures was substantial and almost exclusively in the hands of Vietnamese. Small machinery-equipped enter-

[15] In the postwar Sino-French treaty of February 25, 1946, Nationalist China exploited a strong bargaining position to extract for the Chinese in Indochina virtually all the economic rights accorded French nationals (Fall, *ibid.*, p. 66).

[16] See Tsung To Way, "A Survey of Chinese Occupations," in Richard W. Lindholm (ed.), *Viet-Nam, the First Five Years* (Lansing: Michigan State University Press, 1959), pp. 118–125.

[17] U.S. Department of the Army, *Area Handbook for Vietnam*, p. 59; and Fall, *op. cit.*, p. 67. It was estimated that 50,000 Chinese remained in North Vietnam following the mass exodus of refugees in 1954 and 1955.

prises existed in diverse lines of production and belonged to the French and Chinese. Rail transportation was government-operated and received limited development. Trucking and bus services were extensive and largely in the hands of the Chinese, as were the river and coastal shipping services. Electric power in the south was provided by medium-sized, privately owned utilities which were almost exclusively French.

Monetary policy was in the colonial pattern with the currency linked directly with the French franc, and the supply of money and credit fluctuated directly with the balance of payments which was strongly influenced by volatile world prices of rice and rubber. The currency was issued by the Bank of Indochina, owned by French private interests. Commercial banking services, provided for the most part by French and Chinese banks, were limited to the urban centers and credit resources were reserved for loans to large landowners producing export crops and for the working capital requirements of commerce, particularly foreign trade. Those Vietnamese who required capital, other than the large landowners assimilated to the French interests, were forced to deal with local moneylenders, mainly Chinese retailers and the more prosperous Vietnamese farmers.

Colonial economic development proceeded at rates gratifying to the French administrators and to the large-scale French and Vietnamese agricultural proprietors, but not at rates that afforded rapid modernization of the economy or high levels of material welfare for the Vietnamese generally. Land colonization in Cochin China, stimulated by public drainage works and transportation facilities, as well as liberal grants of land, expanded steadily. By the end of the 1930s, approximately 2.8 million hectares of present-day South Vietnam were under cultivation, with irrigated rice occupying four-fifths of this area. The ratio of the value of rice exports to total Indochinese exports reached a peak in 1918 when rice accounted for three-quarters of export proceeds. From that time until the onset of the Depression of the 1930s, the share of rice in the total value of exports remained consistently above two-thirds. Although the Vietnamese receiving large land grants were the principal beneficiaries of the development of Cochin China, French proprietors also participated extensively.[18] At the time of the postwar

---

[18] In planning for the land reform in the mid-1950s, it was revealed that of landholdings in excess of 100 hectares, 2,033 were in the hands of Vietnamese landlords and 430 were owned by French citizens and companies (U.S. Department of the Army, *Area Handbook for Vietnam*, p. 75).

land reform in which all French-owned rice lands and Vietnamese hold-ings in excess of one hundred hectares were subject to redistribution, it was reported that one million hectares were subject to transfer. Of this area, 260,000 hectares or approximately one-ninth of all land planted to wet rice in South Vietnam was French-owned.[19]

Large landholdings organized into family-sized plots of two to five hectares and worked by tenants dominated the rice economy. About 2.5 per cent of landowners held roughly half of the cultivated land in Cochin China, and four-fifths of the land planted to irrigated rice was cultivated by peasants owning no land.[20] Under the French, there were few regulations governing leases, rents, or loans, and tenants enjoyed little security. Rentals were high and usurious rates prevailed for the limited supply of credit available to tenant cultivators.

Less extensive but of major importance were the rubber plantations developed in sparsely populated upland areas of Cochin China and Annam. By the end of the French colonial period, approximately 100,000 hectares were planted to rubber, which had supplanted rice as the most valuable Vietnamese export. Another 20,000 hectares, largely in plantations, were planted to coffee, tea, and sugar. The Vietnamese showed little interest in these crops and most of the output came from French plantations. The four largest French-owned plantations ac-counted for about three-quarters of the rubber produced following 1954 and smallholders production accounted for only 12 per cent.[21]

Vietnamese indigenism has also been strongly influenced by the instability, uncertainty, and disorder that attended the struggle to bring a viable state into existence. When the Geneva Agreement of 1954 terminated the fighting, observers conceded South Vietnam little chance of survival. The authority of the government beyond the en-virons of Saigon was untested and uncertain. The police were con-trolled by organized gangsters who ran lucrative vice rackets, while much of the countryside was in the hands of well-armed, politico-religious sects. More ominous was the subversive potential of the political and military cadres left behind by the Viet Minh forces. Such factors justified the general expectation that South Vietnam would succumb to pressures supported by the Communist North.

[19] *Ibid.*, p. 359.   [20] *Ibid.*, p. 356.
[21] David H. McCall, *Effects of Independence on the Economy of Vietnam* (Ph.D. dissertation, Harvard University, Department of Political Economy, 1961), p. 291.

The economic prospects were equally bleak. Prolonged warfare had disrupted many lines of production, and inflation was rampant. The population was exhausted and resentful after a long and unpopular war. The French military which had propped the postwar economy by heavy expenditures for local goods and services was scheduled for rapid withdrawal. Less dramatic but substantial was the erosion in the French economic presence as Frenchmen sought to salvage and repatriate what could be saved from their investments. The partition carried major economic consequences as internal specialization, in which rice from the south was exchanged for coal, cement, and other manufactures produced in the north, had enhanced the vulnerability of both Vietnams to the abrupt amputation. Finally, the Geneva Agreement provided that for ten months following August 1954, people could move freely within and between the two areas. This freedom resulted in the migration of almost a million refugees from north to south, and their relief and resettlement promised to overwhelm the administrative and economic capabilities of the new South Vietnam government.

The government, however, demonstrated surprising capacity to meet and surmount the succession of difficult challenges. With liberal financial assistance from the United States and the participation of international refugee welfare organizations, the refugees were transported and housed and major resettlement projects were initiated. Solid victories were scored over the politico-religious sects in the summer of 1955, and control of the police in Saigon-Cholon was wrested from gangster elements. Finally, the date for the plebescite specified in the Geneva Agreement came and went without a challenge from Communist North Vietnam and the government of South Vietnam proceeded to reorganize and revitalize the army. In October 1955 a plebiscite was held, followed by proclamation of the Republic and by parliamentary elections in March 1956. Although the viability of the new state was not assured by these steps, they did usher in a period of eight years of formal independence and relative stability within which major policy objectives, including those of indigenism, became distinct.

Vietnamese indigenism was restrained, however, by the precarious existence the new state continued to lead. As the challenge from the Viet Cong persisted and intensified, the administrative capabilities of the state declined and were increasingly occupied with the problems of survival. Of comparable importance were the constraints imposed by American participation with military and economic aid which was

necessary to ensure the existence of the new state. To maintain monetary and budgetary stability in the face of formidable military requirements, the United States engaged in a massive commercial import
program to absorb the piaster outlays necessary to maintain Vietnam's
outsize military establishment.[22] The role of the United States tended
to confine Vietnamese indigenism as American advice and influence
reflected the priority of the military effort and of economic rehabilitation and stability rather than a radical restructuring of the economy.
Similarly, United States aid policy was characterized by unimaginative
and rigid advocacy of private enterprise, including a major role for
private foreign investment.

Finally, assessment of Vietnamese indigenism must take into consideration the values and goals of President Ngo Dinh Diem who
dominated the first nine years of South Vietnam's existence. Diem's
arrogant self-confidence and increasing isolation from detached and
reliable political advice contributed substantially to his ultimate down-
fall. In the meantime, the government of Vietnam remained authoritarian and personal, stamped with Diem's image of the world and his
vision of the nature of the economic organization best suited to realize
the aspirations he held for the Vietnamese.

Descended from an Annamese family long associated with the
mandarinate bureaucracy, Diem rose early to a high position with the
court at Hue but resigned while still in his early thirties in protest over
continued French domination. Thereafter, although his services were
sought by both factions, he refused to participate in the colonial government or in the nationalist movement over which Ho Chi Minh was
gradually asserting control. When in 1954 the French and the puppet
Emperor Bao Dai again turned to him, he agreed to head the government of what was to become South Vietnam on condition of a grant of
full power from Bao Dai and of complete independence from the
French.

From the beginning Diem ruled as an autocrat and would tolerate

[22] The economics of this aid program, of course, can be analyzed from several
points of view. The elements of the aid process were obscured by a "veil" of
budgetary expenditures to acquire local goods and services, including the pay of
the armed forces, which were offset by budgetary "receipts" of counterpart
piasters generated by sales of commercial imports. Behind this veil of monetary
exchanges was the barter of aid imports comprising a wide variety of consumer
goods for Vietnamese goods and services necessary to achieve military and economic objectives.

no effective political opposition. Although Diem always insisted that his authoritarian measures were temporary and were dictated by the desperate circumstances confronting his regime, there is little evidence that he understood or sympathized with meaningful democracy. In any case, the government and the structure of economic goals and policies were indelibly stamped with Diem's economic philosophy.

As a mandarin, Diem was steeped in the Sinicized tradition of rule by an intellectual elite for the good of the society as a whole. Diem took for granted his role as the enlightened and benevolent leader protecting and guiding his people. He expounded this concept in Confucian terms: "The elder brother of the family shall never rest as long as his younger brothers are in need. That is why, night and day, I am looking for better means to carry out economic progress for the benefit of the people." [23]

Diem also found sanction for his regime and for the structure of economic policy he imposed on Vietnam in the philosophy of "personalism" which he espoused as an all-embracing ideological alternative suitable for the Vietnamese society.[24] Personalism purports to find a middle ground between the "evil consequences" of capitalist individualism and Marxist collectivism and, according to Diem, provides reliable guidance for Vietnam's advance toward stability, democracy, and industrial development. Although Diem was unambiguous in identifying communism as the greater danger, he maintained a basic skepticism toward Western individualism and capitalist institutions.

Insofar as indigenism is concerned, Diem's personalism contained a strong bias toward direct government participation in industry and the maintenance of administrative restraints on the activities of businessmen which otherwise would be socially harmful. Such economic implications of personalism were also in harmony with the mandarinate hierarchy of human activities in which commerce and entrepreneurial activity outside agriculture were accorded low status. In contrast to indigenism in its initial phases elsewhere in Southeast Asia, little concern can be identified for promoting the emergence of an indigenous bourgeoisie in Vietnam.

[23] *Times of Vietnam*, September 8, 1956, p. 2. Reinforcing this Confucian sanction was the authoritarianism of French colonial rule.

[24] Vietnamese personalism was derived from a philosophical movement identified with Catholic intellectual circles in France in the 1930s. Jacques Maritain and Emmanuel Mounier, among other writers, contributed to the philosophical rationalization of the movement.

Last, but by no means least, Diem was a fervent nationalist.[25] He was single-minded in his determination to protect the independence and autonomy of the new state as American policy makers discovered to their discomfort. He recognized that economic independence was an essential component of sovereignty, and he was articulate in his insistence on the need to oppose foreign economic influence in government and in private business.

The Nature of Vietnamese Indigenism

POLICIES TOWARD THE FRENCH

In the initial years of independence, the pressures of indigenism on the French community were heavy. The French had bitterly opposed the nationalist movement and had been ejected from political power only after a brutal war. Not surprisingly, they reaped a harvest of mistrust that initially sustained Vietnamese determination to match the decline in French power with contraction in the French economic presence. This process was accelerated by the response of French enterprise to the military debacle and prospects of a rapid takeover by the Viet Minh.

Major French lumbering firms sold out, or attempted to do so, as they were squeezed between rising fees and taxes and difficulties in arranging for concessions. The major French-owned street transportation company in Saigon sold out to the government in 1956 for ₱ (piasters) 5 million after asking ₱100 million the year before. In the meantime, however, the government presented the company with a ₱20 million bill for overdue taxes, traffic fines, and for the refund of excessive fares. The French electric utility company serving Saigon proposed various schemes to sell out as it was squeezed between rising costs and persistent refusal of the government to approve rate increases. Finding a buyer was only the initial problem facing the French investor who hoped to repatriate his salvageable assets, as capital exports required government approval and this was granted on a case-by-case basis after prolonged negotiation.[26]

[25] This is not equivalent to suggesting that he seriously competed with Ho Chi Minh for identification as the symbolic leader of Vietnamese nationalism.

[26] For an account of the pressures on French enterprises in this period, see McCall, *op. cit.,* pp. 294–298.

The major French rice plantations in Cochin China were transferred to Vietnamese ownership in the land reform promulgated in 1956.[27] In contrast, the large French plantations in the upland areas were not disturbed. Rubber had increased in importance until in 1957 it accounted for two-thirds of the value of Vietnamese exports. Surveillance and regulation of this trade was a relatively simple matter, and the importance of the foreign exchange to the new government afforded the French owners a security from indigenism that their compatriots engaged in rice production did not enjoy.[28]

Pressures on the French economic presence began to moderate promptly in the new regime. Although the tenacity with which the French had sought to rehabilitate their power after World War II created deep-seated Vietnamese skepticism of their intentions, Vietnamese fears subsided as the French made it clear that they intended to accept a relationship with the former colony that carried no threat to the hard-won independence of the latter.[29] Subsequently, the strength of the long acculturation of the Vietnamese elites to things French was asserted, and French influence revived, albeit, much diminished and discreet as compared to the colonial period. A French cultural mission became active and French businessmen, reassured by the stability of the new regime, began to accommodate their activities to the constraints imposed by Vietnamese nationalism. The Vietnamese were not only reassured by such behavior, but expanding American activities and influence established a positive incentive to maintain a French presence to offset that of the United States which threatened to submerge Vietnamese autonomy.

The pressures of indigenism on French interests were heavy and

[27] In September 1958 an agreement was signed with the French government which provided that 1.5 billion francs of "economic aid" would be available to compensate French owners for land redistributed to Vietnamese cultivators in the land reform.

[28] One observer reports that the Diem regime made a "brief and unsuccessful effort to eliminate French investment and technical skills in rubber production." By 1959 the government was encouraging expansion of plantation output of rubber by subsidized credit. See M. N. Trued, "South Viet-Nam's Industrial Development Center," *Pacific Affairs* (33), September 1960, p. 252, note 5.

[29] Immediately after the Geneva Conference, French support of Diem was lukewarm at best, and there is evidence that the French continued to intrigue with the politico-religious sects that were challenging the new government. The success of Diem in asserting control outran French policy, however, and the French shifted to a policy of disengagement which carried conviction. See William Henderson, "South Viet Nam Finds Itself," *Foreign Affairs* (35), January 1957, pp. 289–290.

were accompanied by steady contraction in the size of the French minority. By the end of 1956, the number of French nationals in South Vietnam was estimated at 20,000 of whom only one-third were estimated to be Occidentals.[30] The improvement in the situation of the French in the south following 1956 did not halt the exodus, and in mid-1962 it was estimated that the French numbered about 10,000 of whom most were of Vietnamese or part-Vietnamese ancestry.[31]

POLICIES TOWARD THE CHINESE

Policies toward the Chinese during the Diem regime were only partly motivated to redress the economic power or functional specialization of this minority. They were at least equally explained by the desire to initiate and sustain a process that would integrate the Chinese into the host society. There are a number of factors that help to explain such a policy structure.[32] In the first place, the cultural heritage of the Vietnamese elites encouraged optimism in assessing the prospects of assimilating the Chinese minority to a society already heavily Sinicized. Moreover, Vietnamese elites were culturally inhibited from performing entrepreneurial functions, and influential economic pressure groups seeking to transfer Chinese economic activities to the Vietnamese did not exist. Still another factor may have arisen in the Vietnamese image of the French experience in which the Chinese community was accorded special treatment and considerable autonomy. The lesson of centuries of Chinese pressure, as well as the ability of the Chinese to extract concessions from the French, were not lost on the new government which was challenged to survive in a hostile world. Policy toward the Chinese minority also reflected concern for the Chinese doctrine of dual nationality and the need to naturalize a substantial minority which might invite an intervention the new state could not hope to resist.

In the mass migration from north to south following the Geneva Agreement, several hundred thousand Chinese were evacuated, and South Vietnam ended up with a Chinese minority numbering close to a million. The drive to integrate this minority began with Ordinance No. 48 promulgated on August 21, 1956, which granted Vietnamese

[30] Henderson, *ibid.*, p. 290.

[31] U.S. Department of the Army, *Area Handbook for Vietnam*, p. 62.

[32] The similarity of policies toward the Chinese in Thailand and in Vietnam is striking.

citizenship automatically to all Chinese born in Vietnam. A few days earlier, the government had ordered a census of all Chinese born abroad. Subsequently on September 6, 1956, Decree No. 53 was issued which barred aliens from the following trades or activities: fishmonger or butcher, retailer of products in common use, dealing in coal or firewood, dealing in petroleum products, dealing in secondhand goods, dealing in textiles and silks if handling less than ten thousand meters annually, dealing in scrap metals, trading in cereals, transporter of persons and merchandise by "surface vehicle" or boat, rice milling and processing, and serving as commission agent.[33]

Chinese engaged in the first seven activities were given six months to liquidate their businesses, while those in the remaining categories were given an additional half year. Since many Chinese had Vietnamese wives, the possibility of formally transferring ownership of their businesses to their wives moderated the consequences of the policy though the Chinese were understandably disturbed by the two decrees. Their unrest was intensified when shortly thereafter the police confiscated the alien identification cards of Chinese born in Vietnam and prepared new cards for them as Vietnamese citizens. Although May 9, 1957 was the deadline set for the newly designated citizens to pick up their identification cards, less than 4,000, out of an estimated 600,000, did so by that date.[34]

Chinese resistance to the compulsory naturalization continued, and the Nationalist Chinese government attempted to intervene to ensure that Chinese born in Vietnam were given the freedom to opt for Chinese nationality. The Vietnamese refused to negotiate, however, and insisted that the affair was an internal matter. Confronted by this deadlock, Chinese born in Vietnam legally could accept Vietnamese citizenship or seek repatriation to Taiwan. The latter alternative was subsequently terminated when the Vietnamese government decreed

[33] An earlier decree of the French administration, dated August 31, 1933 and which had not been rescinded, barred all foreigners except French nationals from the following occupations: customs agent, shipping consignee or maritime agent, detective and private police agent, immigration and emigration agent, proprietor of an employment agency, hotel and barkeeper, dealer in arms and ammunition, manufacturer of or dealer in radio sets or their components, and printer. Extensive participation of the Chinese in a number of these occupations suggests that the decree had not been vigorously enforced. Cf., U.S. Department of Commerce, *Establishing a Business in Viet-Nam,* World Trade Information Service Report No. 58-65, Part 1 (Washington, August 1958), pp. 3–4.

[34] For details, see Fall, *op. cit.,* p. 67.

that if either parent was Vietnamese the option of repatriation would not be permitted. Although the controversy was prolonged throughout most of 1957, the number of Chinese eligible for Vietnamese citizenship who chose evacuation to Taiwan was small, and the Chinese slowly complied with the registration regulations.[35]

Pressures on the Chinese were maintained and even intensified. In late 1956, the Department of National Economy decreed that all business accounts be kept in Vietnamese or French and that Chinese names must be transcribed to Vietnamese.[36] The government also tightened controls over Chinese education, and three days before schools were to begin in the fall of 1956, the Minister of Education asked the directors of thirteen Chinese schools not to open until the schools had Vietnamese directors and could teach the regular Vietnamese curriculum. He ordered that Chinese be taught as a foreign language, along with French, English, and Cambodian. The schools were unable to comply with the new requirements and failed to open as scheduled.[37]

By 1960, the Chinese minority had adapted formally to the assimilation policies of the government, and those without Vietnamese nationality had declined to a small minority of the ethnic Chinese. The official estimates of July 1960 distributed the total population of 14,081,000 into Vietnamese, including those of mixed Chinese and Vietnamese ancestry, 13,135,000; highland tribal groups, 665,000; Cambodians and Laotians, 182,000; Europeans, mostly French nationals, 14,000; Chinese, 15,000; and others, including Americans, 70,000.[38] It appears that by 1960 all but a small element of the Chinese minority had established valid claims to Vietnamese nationality and those who could not were probably not seriously affected. For example, the Director of the United States Aid Mission, while testifying before the Senate Foreign Relations Committee in 1958, reported that an enterprise was considered to comply with the nationality provision

[35] *Ibid.,* p. 68.

[36] *Times of Vietnam,* October 6, 1956, p. 11; and *May Jih Luan Zan* (Cholon), November 24, 1956. Cited in McCall, *op. cit.,* p. 271.

[37] *Times of Vietnam,* October 6, 1956, p. 5.

[38] U.S. Department of Commerce, *Basic Data on the Economy of Viet-Nam,* Overseas Business Report No. 63-5 (Washington, March 1963), p. 2. Vietnamese of Chinese ancestry were estimated to number 546,000. There is a substantial and unresolved conflict between the official estimates for 1960 reported in this reference and the estimate of the number of Chinese born outside the Vietnams which is reported on p. 396.

of Decree No. 53 if 51 per cent of the enterprise was Vietnamese owned. He reported that Chinese could comply by registering the minimum ownership required in the name of a Vietnamese wife or of a child born in Vietnam.[39]

LAND AND NATURAL RESOURCES

The transfer of agricultural land to Vietnamese ownership was substantially completed by the redistribution under the Land Reform Ordinance of October 1956. All French-owned land suitable for wet-rice cultivation totaling more than 260,000 hectares was subject to redistribution. The French plantation holdings of rubber and coffee in the highlands were undisturbed; such lands totaled only about 75,000 hectares in 1956.[40]

Vietnam's mineral resources policy, unchanged from the colonial regime, nominally permits concessions to individuals regardless of nationality. In the case of corporations, however, only those companies incorporated in Vietnam, France, or the French Union, of which three-fourths of the directors and administrators are French or Vietnamese nationals may engage in mining. Mining policy has been economically insignificant, however, as little development of mineral resources has occurred.

Forestry resources are worked on the basis of concessions awarded by the national government. Exploitation has been laggard, however, because of insecurity prevailing in the upland forest areas and also because of the absence of a clear-cut forestry policy.[41] Manufacture of lumber and lumber products is an area of manufacturing in which the intention of the government to participate is unambiguous, and this probably explains the absence of concern for conditions favorable to private development.

Current Vietnamese law calls for close surveillance of transactions in real property and transfers of enterprises to foreigners. Under Presidential Decree No. 26 of April 20, 1956 transfers to foreigners, by gift or sale, of real estate; industrial, handicraft, commercial, or agricul-

---

[39] United States Senate, Committee on Foreign Relations, *Mutual Security Act of 1958* (Washington: Government Printing Office, 1958), p. 350.

[40] The maximum area under cultivation in postwar South Vietnam was approximately 2.8 million hectares.

[41] U.S. Department of Commerce, *Basic Data on the Economy of Viet-Nam*, World Trade Information Service Report No. 59-52, Part 1 (Washington, 1959), p. 6.

tural enterprises; or concessions on public lands must have the prior authorization of the President. In addition, any rental or lease for longer than ten years of property in the above categories must be authorized by the President. Similarly, transactions calling for the transfer out of Vietnam of equipment from industrial, handicraft, or agricultural enterprise must have the prior approval of the President.[42]

INDUSTRIALIZATION AND GOVERNMENT ENTERPRISE

As elsewhere in Southeast Asia, colonial development included little manufacturing and what existed, for the most part, was controlled by French and Chinese. At the end of 1957 it was estimated that there were two thousand "industrial establishments," exclusive of small rice mills and cottage industries, employing an estimated sixty thousand persons. Such industries were heavily concentrated in the Saigon-Cholon area and in the manufacture of consumer goods for domestic consumption. The sector included small factories producing cotton cloth from imported yarn, small foundries and machine shops, match factories, cigarette factories, printing and publishing plants, small mills processing sugar cane, leather tanneries, enterprises producing clothing and footwear, ceramics, lumber, industrial gases, and food-processing industries.[43]

The industrialization policy of the Diem regime was distinguished by vascillation and uncertainty which inhibited substantial development. A Presidential Declaration ostensibly assigning major responsibility to private capital and initiative, both resident and foreign, was issued on March 5, 1957. The Declaration stated that to govern economic development "within the framework of the (Economic) Plan, the state will advise, harmonize and assist free enterprise" and that "participation in the development of the country both by external and internal capital is solicited." The Declaration added, "the State may reserve to itself a participation not less than 51 per cent in enterprises vital to its economy and security." The state also reserved the right to require private Vietnamese participation as a condition for permission to establish a new enterprise. To encourage industrial investment, the Declaration tabulated an extensive list of specific investment incentives

[42] U.S. Department of Commerce, *Establishing a Business in Viet-Nam*, p. 4. It was reported in Saigon in late 1960 that the required approval was very difficult to obtain.

[43] U.S. Department of Commerce, *Basic Data on the Economy of Viet-Nam*, World Trade Information Service Report No. 59–52, Part 1, p. 6.

including guaranty against nationalization without compensation, exemptions from taxes, customs duties and operating fees and royalties, export subsidies, permission to remit profits, to repatriate capital, and so forth.[44]

The definition of "vital" industries proved to be sufficiently flexible that by early 1963 the government had acquired major ownership of a small paper mill processing imported pulp, owned jointly with an American firm;[45] a government-owned cotton spinning mill accounting for one-fourth of the country's spinning capacity;[46] two sugar refineries, both government-owned, capable of meeting about half of domestic requirements; and a government-owned plywood and wood panel plant began operations in mid-1962. In mid-1961, work was begun on cement manufacturing facilities with major government ownership.[47] Finally, the government held major ownership of a mineral water company, a chemical products company, the airline Air Vietnam, and the television network Televietnam.[48]

At the same time that government participation in directly productive enterprises was expanding, a number of plants without government ownership began operations or were under construction. These included a number of foreign-owned firms as well as joint ventures with private Vietnamese participation.[49] A tire factory owned by French interests was under construction in early 1963. A joint French-Vietnamese glass factory with sufficient capacity to supply the glass container requirements of the country went into operation in late 1960.

[44] Subsequently, on September 11, 1957 the Director General of the (Economic) Plan issued a "Note on the Application of the Presidential Declaration of March 5, 1957, Relative to New Investments" specifying in detail the categories of investment funds and the various tax and customs concessions to be extended new investments. The Note also included an appended list of priority industries. See: U.S. Department of Commerce, *Establishing a Business in Viet-Nam*, pp. 2–4.

[45] One of two such mills, the other being in a joint Vietnamese-Italian private enterprise.

[46] Another spinning mill was owned jointly by private Vietnamese and American interests, and a third was Vietnamese owned. Weaving capacity was entirely Vietnamese owned.

[47] For details, see U.S. Department of Commerce, *Basic Data on the Economy of Viet-Nam*, Overseas Business Report No. 63-5, pp. 8–9.

[48] Lloyd D. Musolf, "Public Enterprise in South Vietnam," *Asian Survey* (3), August 1963, p. 365.

[49] "Vietnamese" is not to be equated to ethnic Vietnamese because of the wholesale naturalization of the Chinese. Such participation, almost certainly, was largely confined to ethnic Chinese.

The establishment of three reconstituted condensed milk plants designed to satisfy three-quarters of domestic requirements and with substantial American equity participation was approved in 1961. In April 1962 the government signed a contract with a consortium of Western oil companies providing for construction of a $16 million refinery which, it was announced, would be the largest privately-owned enterprise in the country.[50]

In spite of the need for industrial development, which the Diem government readily acknowledged, unambiguous rules under which industries could be established never materialized. Permission to establish an enterprise had to be obtained through time-consuming negotiations with government agencies that were delegated little authority and, therefore, were not in a position to facilitate the founding of new enterprises. Permission was not forthcoming until specific conditions covering such matters as equity requirements, lines of production, profit remission, capital repatriation, and so forth, were reached through negotiation. As a result, industrialization proceeded slowly and participation by non-nationals carried no major threat to Vietnamese indigenism.

The pace of industrialization also reflected the requirements of the war economy and the tensions arising out of United States participation in the efforts to bring into being a viable South Vietnam. The import program to finance the military effort flooded the country with imports, which precluded effective protection of domestic manufactures. Necessity concentrated the import program in those consumer goods for which a well-defined internal market existed and which, in a number of cases, were suitable for manufacture in Vietnam. To overcome the loss of autonomy over protection to new industries, the Presidential Declaration of March 5, 1957 promised exemption from customs duties for imported equipment and imports of components for assembly in Vietnam. On other occasions, officials implied that the government would look with favor on requests for tariff protection, and on several occasions import controls were used to prohibit the import of articles in competition with local manufactures.[51]

Vietnam's industrialization efforts also came into conflict with United States aid-supported efforts to promote private entrepreneurial develop-

[50] U.S. Department of Commerce, *Basic Data on the Economy of Viet-Nam*, Overseas Business Report No. 63-5, p. 9.

[51] U.S. Department of Commerce, *Establishing a Business in Viet-Nam*, p. 6.

ment. The Diem government overlapped much of the Eisenhower administration when it was United States policy to vigorously espouse private enterprise, both indigenous and foreign. Initially, Diem made half-hearted efforts to adapt to the pattern of industrialization and foreign investment policy advocated by American advisers. The Presidential Declaration on Industrial Policy of 1957 was made with strong American encouragement in the hopes that it would be followed by a substantial inflow of private foreign investment, as well as a burst of initiative on the part of the Vietnamese and resident Chinese.[52]

To encourage private enterprise, the Industrial Development Center (IDC) was established early in 1958 to perform investment banking functions and to provide consulting services.[53] The IDC was authorized to make contributions or loans in cash or material, to guarantee or endorse industrial loans, to participate in enterprises and buy shares, and to create new industries with or without private capital. Although the Vietnamese officials envisaged the IDC as a holding company with major investments in government-owned industries, the agreement negotiated with the USAID mission, which had encouraged the formation of IDC by promising major financial support, established narrow limits to the use of aid funds.[54] Under the bilateral agreement, IDC loan assistance was limited to private industrial ventures and, on a case-by-case basis, to mixed companies. The Americans conceived of IDC primarily as a catalyst for private initiative, especially for small and medium-sized industries.

The conflict inherent in the two images of the IDC was not long in coming, and relations between the American aid officials and their counterparts in the government deteriorated. The conflict also tended

[52] American leverage was applied without success to get the Diem regime to enact a foreign investment law. In early 1958 the Adviser to the President of Viet-Nam on Investment Problems revealed the mandarinate bias when he reported to the influential pressure group, American Friends of Viet-Nam, that "a general law concerning investments would risk being incomplete if it were too summary, and seeming too rigid if it were sufficiently detailed. Moreover, it is advisable to allow new investments the maximum degree of flexibility. . . . Interested businessmen and investors should establish direct contact with the Vietnamese authorities . . . in order to obtain the privileges to which they are entitled." See *ibid.*, p. 2.

[53] Presidential Decree No. 478-KT of November 16, 1957.

[54] M. N. Trued, *op. cit.*, p. 254. The bulk of the initial resources available to the IDC consisted of capital grants from the USAID mission of $6 million and ₱100 million.

to harden the government's attitude toward private initiative, particularly foreign investment, and the discretionary bureaucratic controls over new enterprises intensified rather than moderated.[55] The official point of view in the Presidential Declaration on Investment of March 1957, hesitant as it was, was gradually replaced by the conviction that acceptable private initiative was inadequate in supply, and this reinforced the philosophical bias of the Diem regime toward bureaucratic entrepreneurship and government ownership.[56]

During the remaining years of the Diem regime, industrialization policy was increasingly concerned with public corporations and joint ventures with government participation. The challenge to assert Vietnam's sovereignty in the face of American leverage reinforced the conspiratorial determination to specify closely the conditions under which private enterprise would gain access to economic opportunities. The fact that private enterprise would not be ethnically Vietnamese, whereas bureaucratic enterprise was, made such policies palatable to the Vietnamese generally.

COMMERCE—FOREIGN AND DOMESTIC

The challenge to indigenize foreign trade never preoccupied the Diem government. Comprehensive exchange and import controls were implemented throughout the postwar period, and there are no reasons for doubting the repeated avowals of public officials that Vietnamese importers would be favored in the allocation of exchange and import licenses.[57] On the other hand, the capacity to transfer the import trade

[55] *Ibid.*, p. 259.

[56] Bernard Fall reports that the deterioration in the collaboration between the USAID mission and the Vietnamese officials proceeded to the point that an article describing in favorable terms the socialist industrialization of North Vietnam with Soviet bloc aid was "widely distributed by the Southern authorities as an example of the aid program they desire the United States to implement in their country" (Fall, "South Viet-Nam's Internal Problems," *Pacific Affairs* [31], September 1958, p. 253, note 35).

[57] U.S. Department of Commerce, *Economic Developments in Viet-Nam, 1956,* World Trade Information Service Report No. 57-29, Part 1 (Washington, March 1957), pp. 3–4. This reference reports that "licensing delays were coupled with the fragmentation of approved license allocations . . . to assist new Viet-Namese importers brought the average value of approved licenses down to about $3,500." In 1961, it was reported that nationality had "some influence in the licensing decision" U.S. Department of Commerce, *Licensing and Exchange Control: Viet-Nam,* World Trade Information Service Report No. 61-69, Part 2 (Washington, September 1961), p. 3.

to Vietnamese participants proved to be quite limited as the country was flooded with imports. Under such circumstances, the basic problem was not one of allocating scarce supplies of foreign exchange but that of developing and maintaining a marketing system that would distribute the imports necessary to "mop up" the piasters disbursed in military outlays. Otherwise, the military outlays would generate inflation and add to social instability. Under such circumstances there was little possibility of sheltering inexperienced Vietnamese importers from competition by discretionary controls as was done in the Philippines, Indonesia, and Burma where foreign exchange tended to be chronically in short supply.

In spite of the realities of the situation, the government initially sought to use import and exchange controls to increase the participation of Vietnamese.[58] By 1956, however, delays in licensing coupled with the fragmentation of license allocations to assist new Vietnamese importers prompted widespread criticism that the management of controls was hampering the military effort. It was also alleged that the favored Vietnamese were not importing but were selling their licenses to alien importers. The government subsequently moved to eliminate fraudulent and uneconomic importers by issuing new regulations which limited the number of categories of goods a firm might import and, moreover, required such firms to make substantial piaster deposits for each import category.[59] Subsequent regulations tightened the qualifications for importing until by 1961 an importer was required to possess a legitimate place of business, to furnish proof of access to adequate warehousing facilities, and to have engaged in importing on a substantial level during the twenty-seven months following September 1957. At the

[58] If strictly interpreted, Decree No. 53 of September 6, 1956 would have limited a major part of the import and export trade to Vietnamese nationals. Subsequently, however, the Department of National Economy announced that the decree was not applicable to foreigners engaged in foreign trade. The interpretation is contained in the Department's circular, "A propos de l'application de l'ordonnance No. 53 du 9 Juin 1956, Sur les professions dont l'exercise est onterdit aux étrangers, aux collectivités et sociétés étrangères" of October, 1956.

[59] Between December 1954 and the middle of 1956, the number of importers rose from fewer than one hundred to about twenty thousand. Beginning in June 1956, the number of licensed importers declined rapidly as the result of government screening measures until in October of that year only fourteen hundred remained in business. See *Far Eastern Economic Review* (24), April 3, 1958, p. 428. See also U.S. Department of Commerce, *Economic Development in Viet-Nam*, pp. 3–4.

end of 1961, when it was announced that no further increase in the number of registered importers would be allowed, there were 777 registered importers, 584 of whom were Vietnamese nationals.[60]

In the area of domestic trade, as in foreign trade, there is little evidence that the substitution of ethnic Vietnamese for the dominant Chinese was a major concern of the Diem government. Decree No. 53, if it had been enforced, would have eliminated the Chinese from domestic trade. The significance of this decree arises in its juxtaposition with the regulation imposing Vietnamese citizenship on all Chinese born in Vietnam. The organization of internal trade was little disturbed by Decree No. 53.

BANKING AND CREDIT

Although Vietnamese nationalism appeared in a number of conventional manifestations in banking and credit policy, changes in the structure of financial institutions have been limited. As elsewhere in Southeast Asia, the achievement of independence was followed promptly by establishment of a managed currency system. The government-owned National Bank of Viet-Nam commenced operations in January 1955 with the full panoply of central bank powers and functions.[61]

At the time of independence, eleven commercial banks, eight of which were branches of foreign banks were operating in South Vietnam. These banks were concentrated in Saigon-Cholon, and they engaged mainly in transactions in support of foreign trade. Early in 1964, there were thirteen commercial banks, ten of which were branches of foreign banks, operating thirty-one offices, of which twenty-five were in the Saigon-Cholon area.

To offset the expanded role of foreign banks in commercial banking, steps were taken to create new government-owned capital market institutions to support industrialization efforts. The National Investment Fund capitalized by piaster appropriation was established in 1955 to provide loans to businesses and to become the owner or joint-owner of businesses assisted by loan funds. The government also created and

[60] U.S. Department of Commerce, *Licensing and Exchange Control: Viet-Nam,* p. 50.

[61] A minor move in the area of banking policy clearly motivated by indigenism occurred in 1955 when the government abolished all private pawnshops, almost exclusively in non-Vietnamese hands, and replaced them with a system of government-owned pawnshops.

capitalized the Credit Commercial as a commercial bank to assist Vietnamese businessmen.[62]

The creation of the Credit Commercial and the National Investment Fund proved premature and they quickly subsided into ineffectiveness. The investment banking approach was revived in 1957, however, with the creation of the Industrial Development Center. The IDC quickly became relatively immobilized in the continuing controversy between the Diem regime and American officials over the roles of private and public enterprise in industrialization policy and like its predecessors, it lapsed into ineffectiveness. Finally, in November 1961, the Government created the Société Financière Pour le Développement Industriel au Vietnam (SOFIDIV) to take over the assets and investment banking functions of the IDC, while the latter continued to provide consulting and technical assistance services to new enterprises. Half of the initial capital of SOFIDIV of ₱400 million was subscribed by ten local commercial banks and the remainder was contributed by the USAID mission.

Co-ordinate with the efforts to create investment banking institutions under Vietnamese control and empowered to promote indigenous participation in industry, the Diem regime also took steps to create agricultural credit institutions to substitute for the moneylending of Chinese merchants and Vietnamese landowners. In April 1957 the National Agricultural Credit Office, capitalized by government appropriation and United States aid, was established to take over the assets and lending operations previously performed by various departments of the government.

Intensive efforts also were made in conjunction with the postwar refugee resettlement and land reform programs to expand the co-operative movement, particularly rice co-operatives. In 1959 the Commissariat for Cooperation and Agricultural Credit was created by presidential decree to provide general direction and technical assistance to credit and marketing co-operatives. Growth of the co-operative move-

[62] At the time of the establishment of the National Investment Fund, Diem asserted that his government would "insist on the extremely important role of Vietnamese industrialists and businessmen" who, because of the colonial past, had only filled "secondary roles, those of intermediaries giving useful services to foreign businessmen." Diem went on to ascribe the deficiencies of Vietnamese entrepreneurship to "the absence of a logical industrial and commercial organization as well as the lack of direction on the part of public authorities." Republic of Vietnam, *Major Policy Speeches of President Ngo Dinh Diem* (Saigon: Presidency Press Office, 1956), p. 14.

ment was slow, however, and in mid-1960 there were reported to be only 266 co-operatives with a total membership of only 97,000.[63] Farmers' Associations (Hiep Hoi Nong Dan) were also authorized by presidential decree in 1958 and were, in part, designed to supplement the co-operative organization.

Summary

A survey of the announced policies and economic activities of the Diem regime results in a mixed bag of evidence with which to erect a model of Vietnamese indigenism that conforms to the pattern we have identified elsewhere in Southeast Asia.

There can be no question of the determination of Diem and his associates to sustain the independence and sovereignty of the new state. Their determination to dismantle the French economic and military presences to the point where they comprised no significant threat to Vietnam's independence was unmistakable. Similarly, South Vietnam's sovereignty was aggressively asserted in the difficult aid relationship with the United States on which the viability of the new state was dependent.[64] The South Vietnamese leaders, self-confident in the tradition of the mandarinate and embittered and skeptical of Western intentions, were alert to resist real and imagined encroachment on South Vietnamese autonomy by their aid counterparts.

Then there is the dramatic juxtaposition in less than three weeks in the fall of 1956 of Ordinance No. 48 granting Vietnamese citizenship automatically and without option to Chinese born in Vietnam, and Decree No. 53 which barred foreign nationals from major areas of retailing, rice trade and milling, and highway and boat transportation. The resolution with which the government withstood the attempts of the local Chinese to resist their forced naturalization, confirms the essential purpose of these measures. The Vietnamese were not primarily motivated to exclude the Chinese from their traditional economic func-

---

[63] U.S. Department of the Army, *Area Handbook for Vietnam,* p. 369.

[64] The frustration of American aid administrators is confirmed by the spate of writings they produced in their efforts to understand their experiences and to distill relevant policy implications from them.

tions and to reserve such functions to ethnic Vietnamese. Instead, the government sought to eliminate formally a substantial minority with Chinese nationality which might at some time in the future serve as the pretext for Chinese intervention in Vietnamese affairs.

Vietnamese indigenism was manifested in a few unambiguous policies. First, was the elimination of the substantial French landholdings in the Mekong delta. The French rice lands in their entirety were redistributed to Vietnamese cultivators, which eliminated the major foreign holdings of natural resources. Second, the new government displayed persistent faith in directly productive public and joint public-private enterprises and relied on a proliferation of bureaucratic procedures and regulations to maintain tight control over private activity, particularly in manufacturing. Although this policy was distinctive for its lack of concern for the emergence of an indigenous bourgeoisie which was found elsewhere in Southeast Asia, such an attitude on the part of the Vietnamese leadership was logical.

The United States aid program of commercial imports to generate local currency proceeds to meet military outlays established three major constraints upon Vietnamese indigenism. First, the magnitude of the program and the requirement that imports be saleable precluded the use of protection to encourage industrial development. Second, these same factors made it imperative that the commercial talents of the Chinese and of foreign firms be used. Finally, to maintain the incentive to import and consume, it was appropriate that the piaster be overvalued and this inhibited the recovery and expansion of export production, traditionally concentrated in rice output which, following 1956, was exclusively in Vietnamese hands.

The regime of Ngo Dinh Diem experienced a brief and disturbed existence of some nine years. It was confronted by steady erosion in its control over the economy following 1958 as Viet Cong pressures increased. As a result, the capabilities of the regime were increasingly applied to problems of survival in the face of dissension within and subversion from without. Under the circumstances, the relevance of searching in the Vietnamese experience for evidence of indigenism in the pattern of that found elsewhere in Southeast Asia is questionable. There are good and sufficient reasons why Vietnamese indigenism was restrained during this period, and our survey of the Diem period neither strongly supports the generalizations of our study nor, on the other hand, does it contradict them. A more auspicious start for the new state characterized by greater *de facto* independence, including greater freedom to choose among alternative economic policies, might have resulted in a structure of actions and policies that would confirm strongly our image of indigenism—or it might not have done so.

8

CAMBODIA

The Environment of Policy

Cambodia is all that remains of the once powerful Khmer Empire. At the beginning of the ninth century, the Khmers under the vigorous leadership of Jayavarman II threw off Javanese suzerainty, and in the rich alluvial plain of Siem Reap, the fertility of which was annually renewed by the flooding of the shallow Tonle Sap basin by the Mekong, the Angkor civilization developed. The impressive monuments that remain today—the hydraulic works as well as the temples—attest to the administrative capacity of the bureaucracy, the economic base of Khmer power, and the cohesiveness of religious fervor. The culture was molded by strong Indian influences. The cult of ruler worship (Devaraja) was dominant and persists today in the mixture of awe and affection with which the Khmers regard their royalty. The stability, order, and executive confidence evident in postindependence Cambodia is, in large measure, attributable to this cultural legacy.

The Khmer Empire, at its height at the close of the twelfth century, extended over much of present-day Thailand, Viet Nam, and Laos. It experienced a rapid decline, culminating in the sack of Angkor by the Thais in 1369. During the succeeding four centuries, Cambodia was beset by dynastic rivalries and expansionist pressure from Siam and Annam, and a precarious autonomy was maintained by rendering vassalage to both states and accepting the loss of Khmer territory along the northern and eastern frontiers.

The appearance of French power in the Indochinese peninsula occurred when Cambodia was seeking to rehabilitate Khmer autonomy after a decade of Annamese colonial rule terminated, not by Khmer efforts, but by a devastating war fought over Cambodian territory between Annam and Siam. Following the assertion of French authority over Annam and Cochin China, the French in 1863 offered protectorate status to Cambodia's ruler King Norodom in return for an array of traditional concessions demanded by European imperialism. These included access by the French to land and natural resources, freedom from tariffs for French commerce, and legal extraterritoriality. King Norodom, insecure in the face of revolutionary activity by dynastic rivals that promised to serve as the pretext for Thai military intervention, accepted the French offer. In 1867, France completed arrangements for the protectorate by persuading Siam to renounce its suzerainty over Cambodia in return for the northwestern Cambodian provinces of Battambang and Siem Reap.[1]

In 1884, King Norodom refused to participate with Cochin China and Annam in a French-sponsored customs union and was forced by the French to sign a convention that converted Cambodia to a *de facto* colony. The French continued and supported the monarchy because of its obvious usefulness in preserving stability and order, and indirect rule was observed in principle. The Cambodian administration, in fact, was highly centralized; power was vested in French Residents with Cambodians limited to minor roles. To fill the secondary administrative posts, the French tended to use Hanoi- and Saigon-trained Vietnamese who were more adaptable by reason of their assimilation to the mandarinate tradition and, in many cases, by their conversion to Catholicism. Not surprisingly, this policy offended Khmer sensibilities and ensured that Khmer nationalism would develop independent of that of the Vietnamese.

The significance of the monarchy as the symbol of Khmer nationalism emerged late in World War II when the Japanese occupied Cambodia, took over the colonial administration, and induced King Norodom Sihanouk, grandson of the earlier Norodom, to declare Cambodia's independence. The French administrators returned late in 1945, but the protectorate was not re-established. The French, confronted by the awakened political consciousness of the Cambodian royalty and bureau-

---

[1] The two provinces were recovered by the French in conventions signed in 1902, 1904, and 1907, after Siamese violation of treaties enabled France to reopen the territorial issue. Battambang and Siem Reap were again annexed by Siam with Japanese approval in 1941, but were returned to Cambodia by the victorious allied powers in 1946.

cratic elites, proposed a period of dyarchy leading to eventual independence, and in January 1946 a *modus vivendi* was signed by which Cambodia became an "autonomous state within the French Union." Although France continued to rule Cambodia more or less as it had before the war, Cambodians were allowed greater responsibility for local administrative matters and, in the process, acquired a taste and a capability for self-rule which stimulated efforts to extract concessions from the French.

During the period of tutelage Sihanouk shrewdly capitalized on the strength of the Khmer tradition of ruler worship to capture the leadership of the Cambodian nationalist movement in competition with revolutionary elements. The latter included dissidents who coalesced under the Khmer Issarak label, as well as Viet Minh elements in the substantial Vietnamese minority, who had an obvious claim as "liberators" of Indochina. Sihanouk patiently asserted his leadership, a uniquely personal process in which political institutions and royal prestige were exploited to wield the Khmers into a unified political instrument, the Democratic Party, led and dominated by Sihanouk.

This process of mobilizing and unifying Khmer nationalism culminated in 1953 in what has become known in Cambodia as the "Crusade for Independence." In January of that year Sihanouk went to Paris to convince the French that independence was imperative if nonrevolutionary Khmer nationalism was to prevail in the face of Viet Minh claims that only they were fighting for national independence. Sihanouk's plea was snubbed by the French, and he returned to Cambodia via a "grand tour" in which he publicized French intransigence in newspaper interviews in various countries. Arriving in Cambodia in June 1953, he reported the failure of his mission to his people and then dramatically exiled himself in Thailand, vowing not to return until Cambodia was free. The French responded by offering "to complete the sovereignty and independence" of Cambodia through further negotiations but in reply, Sihanouk demanded immediate independence. The French yielded with some reluctance and with the turnover of military control, Sihanouk returned in triumph.

There remained, however, the problem of the Viet Minh who had "invaded" the northeastern province of Stung Teng in April-May 1954 in anticipation of the looming negotiations that would end the fighting in Indochina. The Cambodian representatives at the Geneva Conference, benefiting from the widespread longing for a settlement that would bring peace to Indochina, stubbornly and successfully held out for a settlement guaranteed by the Soviet Union and China which would ensure Cambodia's independence in foreign affairs and, equally important, would ensure the evacuation of the Viet Minh. Since Geneva, Sihanouk has provided strong, flamboyant, and unquestioned leadership, and the economic system and development process, as well as economic nationalism, display his strong personal stamp.

Cambodian indigenism, as elsewhere in Southeast Asia, has been strongly conditioned by colonial development. Although land resources in Cambodia, as in Cochin China, were plentiful and suitable for rice cultivation, development followed a different pattern. French penetration occurred via the Annamese coast, and the French were diverted by the opportunities in the fertile delta of the Mekong. As a result, Cambodia remained a backwater of little interest to French capital and enterprise, and of political interest primarily as a buffer between Indochina and the strong British sphere of influence to the west. Some 85 per cent of the permanently cultivated land was planted to rice, and production was organized in small, family-sized, subsistence units with relatively little landlordism and tenancy. Although subsistence production was dominant, the absence of population pressure made it possible for the smallholders to produce rice in excess of family needs and as a result, this crop developed as the major export with shipments in the late 1930s averaging 200,000 metric tons per year.

Other crops grown by the Cambodian peasants included corn, which was exported in substantial amounts and almost exclusively to France, and sugar produced from the sugar palm, which was both consumed domestically and exported to Vietnam as sugar and alcohol. Tobacco, kapok, oil seeds (soy beans, peanuts, sesame, castor beans), and livestock were also produced in quantity and entered the export list.

Plantation production was limited in area but played a disproportionate role in foreign trade. The most important plantation crop was rubber, which occupied some 3 per cent of the cultivated area. Four-fifths of rubber production came from thirteen large plantations, most of them French-owned. The principal French plantation produced about half of Cambodia's total production. Over 90 per cent of the area planted to rubber was in Kompong Cham province and represented an extension of the rubber area in South Vietnam. The only other significant plantation crop was pepper, which had been developed by Chinese enterprise and capital. Pepper exports, produced on plantations occupying only about one per cent of the area planted to rubber, earned substantial amounts of foreign exchange.

In addition to being rice farmers, the Cambodian peasants are also animal husbandmen and fishermen. Oxen, water buffalo, pigs, and fowl are produced for family consumption, for the internal market, and for export to Vietnam. Fishing grounds include the Gulf of Siam, the rivers, and the Tonle Sap. The annual fish catch before the war averaged 200,000 to 300,000 tons, and substantial exports of dried fish went to Vietnam.

Large-scale industry was virtually nonexistent. Manufacturing was confined, for the most part, to processing of agricultural output in rubber plants, rice mills, tanneries, distilleries, and oil mills. Other plants produced palm sugar, soy sauce, fish products, syrup, and charcoal. In addition, a number of factories produced consumer items including aluminum utensils, cigarettes, matches, clothing, ice, soft drinks, soap, and so forth. Handicraft industries, traditionally family enterprises, produced pottery, silk and cotton cloth, cordage, leather, wood products, lacquerware, forged metal ware, copper articles, and jewelry.

At the end of the colonial period, the currency system was an exchange reserve system subordinated to the financial requirements of the French military effort. The banking system included eight commercial banks: three French, two British, one Chinese, and two Cambodian banks. Banking offices were confined to Phnom Penh with the exception of two branch offices. Money lenders, Cambodian, Chinese, and Indian, supplied the short-term needs of the peasant smallholders. Because land could not be alienated by foreclosure on loans, security for loans was confined to crops in process and interest charges were usurious. In an important sense, the economic consequences of the relationship of the Cambodian peasant to the moneylender, compounded as it was by borrowing to celebrate the events of the life cycle, was not far removed from the condition of the landless tenant in Cochin China.

Cambodia was economically integrated with the outside world as a hinterland of Cochin China and as a participant in the mutual free trade area of the French Union. Particularly galling to the Cambodians was the necessity to channel exports through Saigon because ocean-going vessels were unable to navigate the Mekong to Phnom Penh and port facilities were undeveloped on the Cambodian coast bordering the Gulf of Siam. The assembly and shipment of peasant produce for export was in the hands of a few well-established firms both French and Chinese, and these same firms tended to control shipping services. As elsewhere in Southeast Asia, the Chinese dominated internal trade both as wholesalers and retailers, particularly in the provincial towns and villages.

Economic pluralism was muted by the relative lack of economic development that would accentuate the distinctiveness of the various alien communities. The Chinese were scattered throughout the country and were functionally specialized in trade. On the other hand, the Chinese community had been relatively stable in modern times, and intermarriage had contributed to assimilation. The Chinese, moreover, had traditionally been useful to and sponsored by the monarchy which moderated the onus that might otherwise arise out of their economic prominence.[2] On the other hand, the perennial indebtedness of the peasant to the rice mill owners, storekeepers, and other moneylenders had the opposite effect. The Vietnamese, totaling about 5 per cent of the population, comprised a second significant ethnic minority. In the economy, they specialized as merchants and artisans, a few were rice farmers, and they made up the larger part of the plantation labor force. They maintained themselves as a community apart from the Cambodians and were spatially concentrated in the Southeast and in Phnom Penh. Because of the long history of enmity between the two peoples, Cambodian animosity toward the Vietnamese minority is prominent. Currently, the distinction between Cambodian attitudes toward the Chinese and the Vietnamese minorities is accentuated by Cambodia's foreign relations.

Cambodia is dominated by one city, Phnom Penh, and by one industry, the government, and modernization is the concern of a small elite comprising the royalty plus the Western-educated professional elements who monopolize the bureaucracy. Social and political stability is dependent upon the existence of avenues by which the elites can gratify personal aspirations, and the government presently provides such an outlet. This has given Cambodian indigenism a strong bias toward public enterprise and bureaucratic intervention in the economy. These tendencies have been reinforced by the leftward trend of Cambodian foreign policy and the expanding influence of Soviet bloc technical assistance and economic aid.

[2] Roger M. Smith, "Cambodia" in George McT. Kahin (ed.), *Governments and Politics of Southeast Asia*, 2nd ed. (Ithaca: Cornell University Press, 1964), p. 635.

A second major influence on indigenism derives from the personality and political role of Sihanouk and his aspirations for the Khmers. Capitalizing upon the traditional position of the monarchy and his own personal achievement of independence, Sihanouk dominates the political process. Initial postindependence policies of Cambodia, as elsewhere in Southeast Asia, were characterized by experimentation and vascillation. Over time, however, there has emerged a clear-cut pattern of indigenism which is reflected in Sihanouk's charge to his all-embracing political party, the Sangkum Reastr Niyum (People's Socialist Community), successor to the earlier Democratic Party, to establish a "true socialist and egalitarian democracy."

The Nature of Cambodian Indigenism

LAND AND NATURAL RESOURCES

Cambodia's colonial economic development did not result in large-scale alien ownership of land. The French were diverted by the opportunities in Cochin China, and the Chinese were legally excluded from land ownership by French policy. Plantation development was limited to rubber and, to a minor extent, to pepper. Rubber plantations were developed with French capital and a Vietnamese labor force, both obvious targets for indigenism measures. Except for a small-scale program to encourage Cambodian smallholders, however, the rubber sector has not been under pressure, and the acreage in plantation rubber has increased substantially since the early 1950s. Alien-owned plantations have been sheltered from nationalist pressures because of their contribution to foreign-exchange earnings and because they are spatially isolated. In 1964 the government, to encourage private investment in rubber plantations, guaranteed not to nationalize the rubber industry.[3]

Shortly after gaining independence, legislation was enacted that prohibits aliens from acquiring title to real estate, urban or rural, constructed or nonconstructed. The law provides, moreover, that aliens who previously had acquired title to real property can transfer such property only to Cambodians, and such transactions are subject to

[3] U.S. Department of Commerce, *Basic Data on the Economy of Cambodia*, Overseas Business Report No. 65-19 (Washington, March 1965), p. 5.

government regulation and approval with the government reserving pre-emption rights in such transfers.[4]

Virtually no mining development occurred during the colonial period, and no economically significant deposits have been proved since then. In 1956 legislation was enacted providing for resumption by the state of the ownership of all mineral resources "not currently exploited." [5]

Fishing is an important source of subsistence output, and commercial fishing for local markets is extensive both in inland waters and the Gulf of Siam. The majority of commercial fishermen are Cambodians and Vietnamese, but the industry is controlled by the Chinese who lease internal fishing grounds from the government and staff the marketing organization. Chinese control also results from the dependence of the fishermen upon credit to acquire boats and gear. The French created a fresh water fishing co-operative to provide an alternative credit and marketing system, but the attempt succumbed to Chinese competition and was abandoned at the end of 1955. Information is not available to suggest that the structure of the fishing industry has changed markedly since independence.

Although Cambodian forest resources are extensive, they experienced little development during the colonial period. Currently, about half of the country is forested and virtually all forest land is owned by the government. About half of the forest lands are reserved for commercial exploitation under concessions granted by the government. Exports of timber products are minor, and the internal market is served by the sawmills of Chinese and Cambodian concessionaires.

PUBLIC UTILITIES

The process by which public utilities were indigenized was one of bringing services into being, rather than nationalizing existing enterprises. The exception to this generalization was the former French-owned electricity and water concession in Phnom Penh, Compagnie des Eaux et d'Electricité, which in the mid-1950s produced seven-eighths of the electricity marketed in the country. This utility was

[4] *Foreign Commerce Weekly*, August 5, 1957. See also, Marvel Clairon, *Droit Civil Khmer* (Phnom Penh, 1961), p. 26. Cambodians are defined as "personnes physiques ou morales de nationalité Cambodgienne."

[5] David J. Steinberg (ed.), *Cambodia, Its People, Its Culture, Its Society,* Human Relations Area Files, Subcontractors Monograph HRAF-21, Chicago-14 (New Haven, 1955), p. 218.

acquired by the government and private Cambodian interests by purchase in 1958.[6]

Inland highway transport is largely in the hands of Chinese trucking and bus companies, and no systematic attempt has been made to shift this activity to Cambodians. Similarly, inland water transport is a major means of communication and is largely in the hands of the Chinese.[7]

Indigenism in the area of public utilities is evident in the development of port facilities for ocean-going shipping to escape dependence upon Saigon for such facilities. Initially, considerable effort was made to dredge the Mekong and construct port works at Phnom Penh. More important has been the construction of a deep-water port on the Gulf of Siam and of a highway linking this port with Phnom Penh.[8] In 1962 the Cambodian government announced that a joint Cambodian-Chinese shipping company had been formed to provide ocean-going shipping services for Cambodian trade.[9]

COMMERCE

Indigenism pressures on Cambodian import trade have followed a pattern to be identified elsewhere in Southeast Asia: initial and disappointing efforts to create an indigenous private entrepreneurial class, followed by nationalization of importing activities by means of government trading monopolies.

Before independence, Cambodian import trade was in the hands of large French and Chinese firms, most of them with head offices in Saigon. Following 1954, the government encouraged Cambodians to enter the import trade by liberalizing the requirements for business and exchange licensing. As a result, over 750 importing firms were operating by the end of 1956.[10] This rapid growth was attended by flagrant corruption, bribery of bureaucrats, and the connivance of Cambodian

[6] *Foreign Commerce Weekly*, March 16, 1959.

[7] Smith, *op. cit.*, p. 635.

[8] The port, Sihanoukville, was constructed by French economic aid and the highway by American aid. The port, designed to handle 200,000 tons of cargo annually, was opened in 1960. In 1962 cargo totaling 370,000 tons was handled and further expansion to 1.4 million tons in 1970 is predicted. U.S. Department of Commerce, *Basic Data on the Economy of Cambodia*, p. 7.

[9] *International Commerce*, February 12, 1962.

[10] One source reports that the number of registered importers increased from fifty in December 1954 to seven hundred in August 1956 (*Far Eastern Economic Review*, April 3, 1958, p. 431).

"dummies," and was subject to such severe criticism that the government in power at the beginning of 1957 announced plans to cut back the number of importing firms to one or two hundred. By late March, the number of licensed import firms had been cut in half when the government fell, in part, because of the new policy. The successor government chose to resume the earlier policy, and by the end of 1957 there were 1200 firms receiving import licenses.[11]

Subsequently, the successive governments moved to minimize the anomalies in the import trade by stricter supervision of business and exchange licensing, and in 1961 the number of authorized commercial import firms had declined to 265.[12] To qualify as an importer, a Cambodian national was required to post a substantial bond for each category of goods he sought to import from a list of fourteen such categories. The bond required of an alien importer was twice that required of a Cambodian firm. All importers were required to have an established place of business and an operating license subject to annual renewal. It was the policy of the exchange control authority, the Commission de Répartition de Devises (CRD), to allocate not less than $5000 of foreign exchange to each importer applying to import a category of goods under the quarterly import plan.[13] Furthermore, to qualify for exchange allocation, an importer must have resided in Cambodia for three years, and 55 per cent of his employees were required to be Cambodian.[14]

Another early aspect of import policy was the creation of the Foreign Purchasing Bureau to acquire directly the import requirements of the administration. Experiences acquired in operating the Bureau and in administering exchange and foreign trade licensing helped to prepare

[11] U.S. Department of Commerce, *Basic Data on the Economy of Cambodia,* World Trade Information Service Report No. 58-4, Part 1 (Washington, January 1958), p. 13.

[12] U.S. Department of Commerce, *Basic Data on the Economy of Cambodia,* World Trade Information Service Report No. 61-65, Part 1 (Washington, September 1961), p. 15.

[13] U.S. Department of Commerce, *Licensing and Exchange Controls: Cambodia,* World Trade Information Service Report No. 61-53, Part 2 (Washington, August 1961), pp. 3–5.

[14] *Board of Trade Journal* (172), February 23, 1957, p. 431. Earlier regulations that came into effect on July 1, 1956 limited each importer to trading in three out of eighteen "classes" of goods. The regulations also specified that "no importer may trade through an importer of another nationality" (*Ibid.* [171], September 15, 1956, p. 616).

the way for the ultimate nationalization of foreign trade. Similarly, in February 1957, the Royal Office of Cooperation was authorized to import directly and market imported goods. For this purpose, the ROC was allocated substantial amounts of United States aid as well as foreign-exchange earnings.[15]

The transfer of importing to Cambodians sharply accelerated on March 1, 1964 when the state trading monopoly, Société Nationale d'Exportation et d'Importation (SONEXIM) was created.[16] Under the new policy, SONEXIM is responsible for all importing in conformity with an annual national import plan drawn up by the Ministry of Economy. Government agencies, private agricultural and industrial enterprises, and merchants must submit their requests for imports to SONEXIM which imports the commodities for the account of the importer. In addition, SONEXIM imports for its own account such essential goods as cement, jute bags, and condensed milk which have an assured market.

In the case of export trade, initial indigenism efforts were concentrated on diverting the export trade from traditional channels through Saigon. Immediately after independence, Cambodia moved to ban exports of commodities to Vietnam that subsequently were re-exported, for example, pepper, kapok, rubber, and oil seeds. Not surprisingly, Vietnam retaliated by banning imports of Cambodian livestock and later extended the ban to include dried fish and other fisheries products for internal consumption.[17]

As in the case of import trade, formation of SONEXIM which was charged with carrying out all export activities under the control of the Ministry of Commerce, formally indigenized the export trade. In most cases, exports are assembled for shipment and sales are arranged by

[15] U.S. Department of Commerce, *Basic Data on the Economy of Cambodia*, World Trade Information Service Report No. 58-4, Part 1, p. 13.

[16] At the time of the creation of SONEXIM it was announced that the purpose of the move "is to give Cambodian nationals a greater role in the country's trading activities" (U.S. Department of Commerce, *Foreign Trade Regulations of Cambodia*, Overseas Business Report No. 65-2 [Washington, January 1965], p. 1). It was also announced that foreign firms could appoint agents in Cambodia only with SONEXIM's approval. The announcement went on to say "ordinarily such approval is given only to persons or firms which have previously handled the particular type of commodity. However, other reputable Cambodians or firms can be approved as agents" (*ibid.*, p. 6).

[17] U.S. Department of Commerce, *Basic Data on the Economy of Cambodia*, World Trade Information Service Report No. 58-4, Part 1, p. 10.

private firms and then approved by SONEXIM. In other cases, primarily government-to-government rice sales, SONEXIM procures the domestic product and exports directly. SONEXIM guarantees payment to producers and may also grant export subsidies under certain circumstances.[18]

Cambodia's domestic trade has been indigenized slowly and haltingly since the establishment of independence. Following a pattern discernible elsewhere in Southeast Asia, the government early announced the creation of a substitute co-operative system to replace the alien-dominated market structure. The Royal Office of Cooperation was created in 1956 to promote the development of credit, production, and retail co-operatives among the rural population. Subsequently, the State Enterprise Office was created within the Royal Office of Cooperation to import directly for distribution through the co-operative system which had opened retail co-operatives in many provinces.[19]

In April 1957 legislation was enacted that prohibited the participation of aliens in eighteen professions and occupations, including those making up a substantial part of retail trade. The list included a number of occupations dominated by the Chinese, including those of rice merchant, shipping agent, freight forwarder, jeweler, printer, and so forth.[20] The dislocation promised by this policy prompted widespread protest and in September a decree was issued which modified the prohibition by permitting the employment of aliens to a maximum of 30 per cent in any enterprise, including those in the eighteen categories subject to the earlier prohibition.[21]

More recently, in November 1964, the government moved to take over domestic trade by creating a joint state-private corporation, the

---

[18] One report on Cambodia made in late 1964 concluded, "what remains is for the government to take over the purchase of rice from the peasants (it already handles purchases of cotton for example) and it is moving towards this by extending the coverage of state organized cooperatives" (*The Economist* [London] (212), September 9, 1964, p. 1013. Within the year, there was formed in the Battambang area a joint state-private enterprise, the Société Khmer de Ramassage des Produits (SORAPA) to purchase and mill rice for export. At the time of SORAPA's formation, an announcement was made that it planned to "extend its operations to the entire country." See U.S. Department of Commerce, *Basic Data on the Cambodian Economy*, Overseas Business Report No. 65–19, p. 6.

[19] *Far Eastern Economic Review*, June 1963, pp. 549–550.

[20] Clairon, *op. cit.*, p. 26.

[21] *Foreign Commerce Weekly*, January 27, 1958. See also the issue of September 30, 1957.

Société Nationale de Distribution de Produits Importes (SONAPRIM), to wholesale and retail imported products and to stabilize prices.[22] At the same time, it was announced that some seventy firms had been authorized to act as wholesalers for SONEXIM, the government foreign trade monopoly. The authorized wholesalers were to be formed into professional associations or syndicates according to the products handled, which were classified into ten broad categories. It was reported that the members of each syndicate would share equally the foreign exchange available for an import category. The syndicates are also required to establish "model" retail stores where official retail prices are maintained, in order that consumers can compare them with the prices charged by other retail outlets.[23]

INDUSTRIALIZATION POLICY

As elsewhere in Southeast Asia, persistent efforts have been made to promote manufacturing with Cambodian participation. Initially, emphasis was placed on foreign investment and Cambodia promptly enacted a series of foreign investment laws.[24] Foreign investment proposals require prior authorization by the Minister of Finance, who, together with the Minister of National Economy is responsible for assessing the usefulness of proposed new enterprises. They require some, though not specified, Cambodian capital participation and also the employment, training, and upgrading of Cambodian personnel. Legislation also specifies that foreign investment can be made only in foreign currencies. Just and equitable compensation is assured, as well as the possibility of a ten- to thirty-year guarantee against nationalization, national tax treatment for foreign investment, and possible exemption, in whole or in part, from taxes on reinvested profits and on imported capital equipment and raw materials.

Primarily permissive, in that it allows wide discretionary powers to

[22] Consumer price controls have been maintained without interruption since independence. As might be expected, such controls in the absence of effective rationing, were unenforceable. In 1958 it was reported that the government "had established a corps of economic police in order to obtain compliance with the controls" (U.S. Department of Commerce, *Basic Data on the Economy of Cambodia*, World Trade Information Service Report No. 58-4, Part 1, p. 13).

[23] U.S. Department of Commerce, *Foreign Trade Regulations of Cambodia*, p. 5.

[24] Kingdom of Cambodia, Law 102-NS of May 31, 1956 and Law 221-NS of September 13, 1957. See also Law on Foreign Capital Invested in Cambodia Prior to May 31, 1956, Law 220-NS of September 13, 1957.

its administrators, the policy has resulted in a negligible inflow of private foreign investment, exclusive of reinvested earnings. In the five years following 1959 such inflow amounted to approximately US$2 million of which more than half was French capital invested in rubber plantations.[25]

Frustrated by the limited accomplishments under the foreign investment policy, the government soon shifted to a policy of direct government participation. Such participation took the form of joint enterprises financed by state funds in combination with private capital, both Cambodian and foreign, and public enterprises created by economic aid, primarily from Soviet bloc countries.

The Mixed Companies Act of 1959 authorized the government to participate in existing or new industries "deemed to be of special importance to the economy of the kingdom." The government's share of "mixed" enterprises may range from 20 to 80 per cent of the capital of such companies; in actual practice the government's share has ranged between 20 and 40 per cent. Late in 1962 a brewery, capitalized at $2.9 million with 20 per cent ownership by the government, 40 per cent French capital, and 40 per cent private Cambodian capital, was in an advanced state of preparation, as were the Cambodian Phosphate Fertilizer Company, 20 per cent government-owned, with the remainder in the hands of private Cambodian interests; the Cambodian Fishing and Canning Company, with 40 per cent government ownership and the remainder divided between private Cambodian and foreign capital; and the Cambodian Lumber Company, with 40 per cent government ownership.[26] Three additional "mixed companies" were announced in 1962: a petroleum refinery, the foreign-exchange costs of which were to be provided by a French oil company; a brewery with extensive French participation; and a jute mill with local private capital.[27]

Subsequently, industrialization policy was given a new direction as the government moved to take over existing industries. During 1963 alcohol manufacture and trade was nationalized when the government

[25] U.S. Department of Commerce, *Basic Data on the Economy of Cambodia,* Overseas Business Report No. 65-19, p. 8.

[26] For details of accomplishments under this policy, see *Foreign Commerce Weekly,* August 27, 1962 and February 12, 1962.

[27] U.S. Department of Commerce, *Basic Data on the Cambodian Economy,* Overseas Business Report No. 65-19, p. 10.

acquired the French-owned distilling company, Société Khmere des Distilleries. This enterprise became the core of a new state monopoly company, the Société d'Etat des Distilleries with minor private equity ownership.[28] Similarly, in December 1964 the pharmaceutical manufacturing industry was nationalized by the government, together with all retail trade in pharmaceutical products.[29] It was also reported that the government had acquired substantial ownership shares in an ice making and bottling plant, an industrial gas factory, and two cigarette factories.[30]

To guide industrial development, the government has designated areas in which further investment would not be approved because local production is considered adequate. Early in 1965 the list of manufactures in which further investment is prohibited included rice alcohol, matches, nails, sterilized cotton and gauze, carbonated beverages, dry cells, pharmaceutical products, jute bags, rubber sandals, soap, fish nets, galvanized iron sheets, and bicycle tires and tubes.[31] The list, not surprisingly, is dominated by the products of government concerns, both state enterprises and mixed companies.

The remaining element of industrialization policy which has grown steadily in importance is the succession of state-owned enterprises created by foreign aid. By mid-1961 three state industries had been built with Communist bloc aid; a plywood factory with an annual capacity of 3,600 cubic meters per year, a paper mill with an annual capacity of 5,000 metric tons of paper products, and a spinning and textile mill with an annual capacity of 1500 tons of yarn and five million meters of cloth. In addition, a state-owned cement plant of 50,000 tons annual capacity was under construction. Furthermore, negotiations were underway for additional plants and, at one time or another, publicity has been given to plans for a state-owned steel mill to be built with Chinese assistance; a palm oil sugar refinery, a tire

---

[28] *Foreign Commerce Weekly,* January 27, 1964.

[29] U.S. Department of Commerce, *Basic Data on the Cambodian Economy,* Overseas Business Report No. 65-19, p. 6. The pharmaceutical industry came into existence only in 1957 following government approval of a firm authorized to manufacture as well as import pharmaceuticals. See *Foreign Commerce Weekly,* August 5, 1957.

[30] U.S. Department of Commerce, *Basic Data on the Cambodian Economy,* World Trade Information Service Report No. 61-65, Part 1, p. 14.

[31] *Ibid.,* p. 8.

factory and a small tractor assembly plant to be built with Czecho-slovak aid; as well as a textile mill, steel rolling mill, and paper mill to be built with East German assistance.[32]

BANKING AND INSURANCE

With the establishment of independence, Cambodia moved promptly to withdraw from the monetary arrangements and customs union that linked the French colonies of the Indochinese peninsula. On January 3, 1955 the National Bank of Cambodia was established to take over management of the currency which heretofore had been the responsibility of the French-managed Institute of Issue. A new national currency, the riel, was issued to replace the piaster, the currency issued by the Institute of Issue. To manage the foreign-exchange reserves, the National Exchange office was created.

Commercial banks numbered eight in 1954, of which two were Cambodian banks. Banking offices were concentrated in Phnom Penh and the system concentrated in financing trade, particularly foreign trade.[33] In the initial years of independence, banking policy was concerned primarily with the creation of new credit and capital market institutions. The Caisse Nationale d'Equipement (CNE), a semiautonomous, government-owned investment bank, was established in 1956 to finance government development projects and it received substantial budgetary allotments for this purpose. Later, the capitalization was increased by United States aid funds and the CNE established a Small Industry Loan Fund to provide medium- and long-term loans to small private borrowers in agriculture and industry.[34]

A second credit institution created after independence was the Royal Office of Cooperatives (OROC) established in 1956 to take over the functions of the state-operated provincial loan agencies. The latter had been established to provide an alternative to the moneylenders who supplied the credit needs of smallholders, fishermen, and artisans at high rates. The OROC, an autonomous agency of the government, extends agricultural credit at subsidized interest rates to small farmers by providing funds to village co-operatives which relend to members.

[32] *Ibid.*, pp. 5–6.

[33] In late 1961 there were still eight commercial banks of which three were Cambodian.

[34] U.S. Department of Commerce, *Basic Data on the Economy of Cambodia,* Overseas Business Report No. 65-19, p. 8.

The banking system was abruptly transformed by nationalization on July 1, 1964 when the National Bank of Cambodia took over all commercial banking activities. Shortly thereafter, the Cambodian Bank of Commerce was established to maintain control over the activities of the government foreign trade monopoly SONEXIM and to implement the foreign-exchange plan drawn up by the National Exchange Office.

A similar pattern of nationalization has occurred with respect to insurance. Initially, the government was content to extend its regulation of insurance.[35] On June 19, 1957 a decree was issued requiring reserve deposits of all insurers. Such deposits were based on the volume of business, and the deposits required of foreign insurance companies were twice those for Cambodian insurers.[36] At this time, foreign insurers were informed that the government did not intend to nationalize insurance. In June 1960, however, legislation established the Mixed Economy Insurance Company. All foreign insurance companies were given the options of confining their activities to reinsurance, of joining the mixed company, or of winding up their business by July.[37]

CITIZENSHIP AND EMPLOYMENT

Cambodia, in contrast to both Thailand and South Vietnam, has made no significant effort to ease the access of aliens to naturalization and thereby facilitate assimilation. Requirements for naturalization are moderately strict and ample discretionary authority exists to permit wide latitude in policy.[38] On the other hand, there is little evidence that members of the two economically significant minorities recognize strong incentives to seek formal assimilation to a host culture they consider inferior to their own.[39]

Basic policy with respect to reservation of employment to Cambodians was embodied in the decree of April 1957 prohibiting the participation of aliens in eighteen occupations and the subsequent decree

[35] Legislation enacted in June 1955 and February 1956 established the policy of government supervision and regulation. See U.S. Department of Commerce, *Basic Data on the Economy of Cambodia,* World Trade Information Service Report No. 58-64, p. 7.

[36] *Ibid.,* p. 8.

[37] *Far Eastern Economic Review,* June 16, 1960, p. 1252 and *ibid.* January-March 1961, p. 420.

[38] Among other requirements, the applicant must be of good moral character, must be fluent in Cambodian and have a knowledge of Cambodian customs and traditions, and must have been a resident for five years. See Clairon, *op. cit.,* p. 32.

[39] Smith, *op. cit.,* pp. 635–637.

of September of that year limiting to 30 per cent the ratio of aliens that may be employed in any enterprise.[40]

Finally, a number of miscellaneous manifestations of economic nationalism restrict access of aliens to Cambodian markets and resources in various ways. For example, a postindependence decree regulating commerce denies to any foreign firm the right to use a Cambodian name or title.[41] Still another, conventional, example is the requirement that all businesses must keep accounts in Cambodian.[42] Also illustrative of economic nationalism is the regulation excluding all foreign nationals from official positions in labor unions.[43]

Summary

Cambodian indigenism has displayed a number of characteristics common to this phenomenon elsewhere in Southeast Asia. Here again we find the initial attempts to create an indigenous entrepreneurial class by using exchange and import controls to subsidize new firms in importing and domestic commerce. Similarly, there was the initial emphasis on the co-operative movement to replace the ubiquitous Chinese merchant and moneylender, and the sporadic and cautious attempts to industrialize through the collaboration of foreign investment with domestic capital and indigenous resources, attempts so hedged by nationalistic constraints that little industrialization of a private nature resulted.

The basic shift to a policy of nationalization resulted from a number of influences. Frustration over the disappointing accomplishments of industrialization policy and the corruption and prevalence of "dum-

[40] The initial foreign investment law of May 1956 requires that at least 50 per cent of the staff of approved enterprises be Cambodians (*Far Eastern Economic Review*, April 3, 1958, p. 431).

[41] Steinberg (ed.), *op. cit.*, p. 218. Enforcement of such a rule communicates awareness of the economic role of aliens, as well as the existence of alternative Cambodian shops and enterprises.

[42] *Ibid.*, p. 187.

[43] *Ibid.*, p. 182. Inasmuch as the wage labor force outside of the bureacracy is predominantly Chinese and Vietnamese, such a regulation is also motivated to try to prevent the development of labor unions as centers of dissension and potential subversion.

mies" attending attempts to create an indigenous bourgeois were significant. Similarly, the influence of foreign events and the slow erosion of neutralism in favor of the communist position enhanced the economic and political influence of Soviet bloc economic aid. Probably more important than anything else was the concentration of Communist bloc aid in manufacturing enterprises transferred on a government-to-government basis, which were particularly welcome because they assuaged the longings of the Cambodian elites for such symbols of industrialism.

More significant, however, is the fact that the Cambodian society is economically polarized into the bureaucratic elite, including the royalty, and the relatively inert peasantry. The pressures for "étatism" are generated primarily by the need to expand constantly the activities of the public sector to absorb the restless and potentially subversive educated elites and at the same time to support the conservative, but prestigeful royalty. The requirements of national unity and stability are a sufficient explanation of the postindependence expansion of bureaucratic enterprise.

The accomplishments of Sihanouk are impressive. The assertion of Cambodian sovereignty in a hostile, potentially explosive political environment commands wide respect. Responsible monetary and fiscal management contributed to economic and political stability. Diverse sources of economic aid have been exploited to produce a veneer of industrial development which is satisfying to the society both because it is evidence of modernization and because it is controlled by Cambodians.[44] The course of policy benefited from the absence of population pressure and the existence of unoccupied land resources which reinforced the stability of the politically passive, numerically dominant peasantry. Finally, it would be a mistake to discount the importance of the Geneva settlement achieved by the Cambodians, which sharply curtailed the threat of subversion by revolutionary elements left behind by the Viet Minh.

[44] This is not to say that the industrial enterprises are efficient in any competitive sense. In mid-1961 it was reported that both the plywood factory and the textile factory built with Chinese economic aid were "losing money." See *The Economist* (200), July 29 ,1961, p 445.

9

THE SUMMING UP

Central to nationalism as ideology is acceptance of the nation as the focus of human loyalties and aspirations. As such, the nation-state is organized both to respond to the social consensus and to mold that consensus with social inventions—ideas, slogans, policies, institutions, and the like—which produce orderly, institutionalized change in the national interest. The indigenism that has appeared in Southeast Asia has resulted, for the most part, from the direct and discriminatory intervention of governments in economic processes. It is unnecessary to review here the intellectual developments of the past half century which have transformed the conception of the role of the state in organizing economic progress. Needless to say, acceptance by governments of an enlarged responsibility to intervene in the economic organization is not confined to underdeveloped countries.

It is obvious that indigenism is always a political as well as an economic phenomenon, and that it is an aspect of the extension of political nationalism—the extension of the nationalist revolution—to the organization of the economy. The drive to indigenize, however, is not necessarily the consequence of a successful nationalist movement. That this is so is demonstrated by the histories of the so-called areas of recent settlement—North America, Australia, New Zealand, and Latin America—where indigenism was not prominent.

The explanation of this contrasting state of affairs is straightforward. So far as the indigenous populations—the Indians of the Americas, the aborigines of Australia, the Maori of New Zealand—were concerned, the economies were alienized. The missing factor, however, was an indigenous nationalist movement and the achievement of political power by the host population. The carriers of the nationalist tradition, Spanish mestizos in Latin America and Anglo-Saxon immigrants elsewhere, were aliens and hence had a higher level of tolerance of functional specialization by other immigrants who followed. With the submergence of the host population—originally sparse and subsequently decimated by the onslaught of rapacious immigrants—in a society numerically and politically dominated by immigrants, the possibility of the appearance of indigenism as we identify it in Southeast Asia temporarily disappeared. In other words, essential to the appearance of indigenism in Southeast Asia (and in Africa, Southeastern Europe, and the Middle East) is the political ascendancy of the numerically dominant population with a strong traditional identification with the patrimony of natural resources.[1]

This is not, of course, the whole story. The emergence in the nineteenth century of nation-states in the "areas of recent settlement" occurred in an intellectual environment of self-confident economic liberalism and Anglo-Saxon homogeneity which contributed to the mildness of indigenism. On the other hand, states in Southeast Asia have emerged after prolonged exposure to exclusive colonialism and in an environment of intellectual and ideological controversy which has eroded faith in the institutions and policy prescriptions of the earlier period. Equally important, nationalism emerged in the areas of recent settlement in an environment of resource abundance relative to population which facilitated rapid economic growth. Immigrants from Western Europe had been conditioned by the ferment of the Industrial Revolution, and in the colonial world they were confronted by only minor discontinuities between their previous experiences and patterns of behavior required to participate in nineteenth-century overseas development. Indigenism was moderated in an environment where growth was rapid and the potentialities for further growth occupied the energies of the society.

In Southeast Asia, nationalist movements must be concerned with

[1] Without exception, the societies of Southeast Asia we classify as indigenous are descended from immigrant populations. Time, isolation, and processes of assimilation erode the identification of members of an immigrant population and their descendants with the "homeland." Obviously, such a population can acquire an identification with the new homeland necessary for its members to become carriers of the nationalist tradition and in this process acquire values and attitudes necessary to the appearance of indigenism. The indigenism that has become prominent in economic nationalism in Canada and Latin America in recent years is essentially the same phenomenon as indigenism in Southeast Asia—and is more or less evident in any national society.

the integration of societies fragmented by geography, religion, and diverse ethnic and racial origins into cohesive, stable national societies. It would appear that indigenism, with its emphasis on exclusiveness, is antithetical to integration or that its contribution, at best, is negative, in the sense that the functionally specialized alien communities are used by nationalist elites as a threat to cement the national society. Nationalists are able to explain away this antithesis between indigenism and integration by appeal to the egalitarian content of nationalism as ideology which carries two implications for the theory of indigenism.[2] First, political elites must provide their followers with avenues of identification with the nation-state. Policies of indigenism, by removing real or imagined obstacles to their material progress, encourage the economically less fortunate members of the national society to aspire to material progress and to associate their welfare as individuals with the new state. Second, the functional specialization of aliens is a denial of equality, and indigenism is necessary if aliens are to qualify for recognition.

In our efforts to understand indigenism in Southeast Asia we have sought to identify and emphasize the comparative aspects of this important motivation of public policy. By emphasizing these aspects, however, we admit to oversimplifying an exceedingly complex social phenomenon which, to another set of observers, may be significant for its uniqueness in each country. Other scholars may be motivated to examine indigenism in Southeast Asia in wider global or historical contexts and develop analogies with the treatment of minorities in other cultures and types of economies and at earlier periods.[3]

[2] Nationalist movements, pragmatic and eclectic, obviously are not bound by this normative aspect of nationalism as ideology. Articulation of concern for greater economic equality frequently represents lip service rather than evidence of serious commitment.

[3] An obvious opportunity for scholarship lies in the parallels between the pressures on the Jewish populations of Eastern and Southeastern Europe and those on the alien mercantile communities in the underdeveloped world. We choose to study indigenism in Southeast Asia, however, at a level of disaggregation for which there are good and sufficient reasons for not trying to force the patterns of indigenism into the European mold. The contrasts in racialism as an environmental factor, qualitative differences between West-European colonialism and the contiguous imperialisms of Germany, Austria, Hungary, Russia, and Turkey in Eastern and Southeastern Europe, and the sharp distinction in the role of religious persecution in the treatment of minorities in the respective areas are obvious reasons.

The remainder of this concluding chapter consists of those generalizations, qualified as necessary, which we have distilled from our study and which we feel are relevant for understanding indigenism and its significance. Although we are confident that the indigenism we identify is fundamentally the same in each of the countries, attempts to generalize about an area so diverse as Southeast Asia must be hedged with qualifications. Admittedly, for each of our generalizations, exceptions or partial exceptions may be found, or a significant reservation may be necessary. The summary is concerned with three general areas of inquiry: major comparative aspects of indigenism in Southeast Asia, the relationship of indigenism to economic growth and development, and lessons for the future.

Major Comparative Aspects of Indigenism in Southeast Asia

THE POLITICAL CONSENSUS

The political consensus behind each of the policy systems of indigenism found in Southeast Asia is to be understood in terms of the common pattern of motivations that mobilize the various elements in the national society to support the goal of indigenism.[4]

The critically important group comprises the inner-driven ideological nationalists, the innovators who use their political power to erect the policy structure. Members of this elite, confident that they understand and articulate the social will, behave predictably in their efforts to lead the society in achieving an acceptable congruity between the nation, the society, and the economy. They are not basically motivated, at least initially, by prospects of personal gain and they are not seeking political power for other ends. They are unambiguous in their determination to transform the colonial-type economy precisely because they see their national revolution as incomplete until this is done.

A second basic element explaining the consensus is the straightfor-

---

[4] For a preliminary analysis of the elements of a model of this political consensus, see Harry G. Johnson, "A Theoretical Model of Economic Nationalism in New and Developing States," *Political Science Quarterly* (80), June 1965, pp. 171–178.

ward materialistic motivation of the political behavior of the beneficiaries of indigenism policies. The relationship between the distribution of income and wealth and indigenism belongs in any model of economic nationalism, and with the lapse of time, class interests will become increasingly causal. The tenure in office and the political autonomy of the nationalist political elites depends in part on the success with which they satisfy the preferences of influential elements in the national society for various types and quantities of governmental action. Over time, those economic elites who stand to gain from their capacity to respond to the opportunities arising in a system of indigenism are welded into interrelated interest groups. Such groups coalesce to support the initiative of the ideological nationalists in maintaining and extending the system. Only to a very limited extent does this interest group function in Southeast Asia through representative institutions and processes. Even in the Philippines, a flamboyant democracy, the avenues of influence tend to be extralegal, cultural, and traditional.[5]

To explain the support of the system of indigenism by the population generally, a powerful concept is that of ownership and control of productive assets outside subsistence agriculture and the preemption of prestigeful and rewarding employment by members of the national society, as communal consumption capital. Such capital—tangible assets or intangible human capabilities—yields income to the direct beneficiaries as owners, managers, and employees and, moreover, by symbolizing achievement of the goals of indigenism, it also yields utility to members of the national society generally as psychic income without reducing the "consumption" of it by other individuals or groups.[6]

Investment in such capital is made in a number of ways. Straightforward is the use of fiscal and monetary powers to establish new public enterprises or to acquire existing enterprises owned by nonnationals. Less direct is the use of the power to create money, or credit, which is used to divert command over resources to nationals who create new enterprises or acquire existing enterprises owned by non-

---

[5] See John J. Carroll, S.J., *The Filipino Manufacturing Entrepreneur: Agent and Product of Change* (Ithaca: Cornell University Press, 1965), pp. 179–207.

[6] Credit for first applying the concept of public capital goods to analysis of economic nationalism goes to Albert Breton in his "Economics of Nationalism," *Journal of Political Economy* (72), August 1964, pp. 376–379.

444 *Underdevelopment and Economic Nationalism*

nationals. The saving necessary to such capital formation is in part forced on the society generally by the diversion of resources to such uses. More subtle is the use of the public power not to tax in such forms as tax remission, windfalls in foreign-exchange allocation, protection, and so forth, to vest nationals with command over resources which enables them to take over enterprises and activities previously in the hands of aliens. The saving necessary to the formation of such communal consumption capital, at least in part, will be forced on the society in higher prices of commodities and services and deterioration in their quality. To the extent that confiscation occurs, the necessary saving will be imposed on the dispossessed aliens. Only a short step remains to argue that the use of the police power of the state to dispossess aliens and replace them with nationals results in the formation of communal consumption capital out of savings forced on the society in the same forms.

The concept of the "taste for nationalism" has also been proposed to explain the broad base of the consensus supporting indigenism. As a result of the "taste for nationalism" members of the national society choose to sacrifice material gain, i.e., per capita real income, in exchange for the psychic gain "derived from avoiding contact with the group discriminated against." [7]

The authors find the concept of the "taste for nationalism" of dubious value in explaining indigenism in Southeast Asia. A clearly analogous phenomenon appears in Malay behavior in Malaya and, somewhat more muted, in Indonesia. The Malay "taste for nationalism," however, is basically an Islamic heritage and clearly it does not apply at present to Malay behavior toward the British and other Western elements. More directly relevant, perhaps, is Burmese behavior toward the Indian minority, particularly that of the urbanized Burmese who competed directly with the Indians for menial employment. In the Philippines, the results of surveys by sociologists concerned with the prestige hierarchy of social relationships cast doubt on the existence of any wide-

---

[7] See Johnson, *ibid.*, p. 172. Johnson acknowledges the analogy between his concept and that of the "taste for discrimination" advanced by Gary S. Becker in his study of discrimination against negroes in the United States (*The Economics of Discrimination* [Chicago: University of Chicago Press, 1957]). In integrating the "taste for discrimination" into his model (pp. 176–177) Johnson transforms the concept into a straightforward preference for nationals over aliens in prestigeful economic functions on the part of members of the national society.

spread desire to ostracize either the Chinese or Western elements against whom the pressures of indigenism are heavy.[8]

In Buddhist Southeast Asia, both historically and today, a willingness ranging to anxiousness to assimilate the Chinese is evident, which is difficult to reconcile with the concept of psychic gain "derived from avoiding contact with the group discriminated against." So far as Westerners are concerned, outside of Burma in recent years it would be far-fetched to equate nationalist pressures to widespread desire to avoid contact with them.

Finally, it should be emphasized that a model of indigenism in Southeast Asia does not have to be seriously concerned with explaining the behavior of the major population element, the tradition-bound, politically isolated, village population. In varying degrees, this element of the population is politically voiceless and stable to the point of apathy. In the absence of leadership from the outside, the relations of the rank and file of peasants in most of Southeast Asia with the Chinese would remain placid while their economic and social contacts with Western economic elements would be fragmentary and involve little more than curiosity. Peasants respond to nationalist slogans and can be mobilized to support charismatic leaders who successfully appropriate the symbols of nationalism. Such support is undiscriminating, however, and is attributable to charisma rather than commitment to nationalism. Because this is the case, an explanation of peasant behavior independent of an explanation of the behavior of the nationalist elites is unnecessary.

ANTI-ASIAN ALIEN OR ANTIALIEN?

Heretofore, students of Southeast Asia have been concerned with indigenism as an aspect of the study of the Chinese and other Asian minorities in the area. This approach has led to a narrow interpretation of indigenism as essentially an anti-Chinese or anti-Asian phenomenon

[8] For an introduction to this extensive literature, see George H. Weightman, "A Study of Prejudice in a Personalistic Society: An Analysis of an Attitude Survey of College Students—University of the Philippines," *Asian Studies* (2), No. 1, 1964, pp. 87–101; Joel V. Berreman, "Philippine Attitudes Toward Racial and National Minorities," *Research Studies of the State College of Washington* (25), June 1957, pp. 186–194; and Chester L. Hunt *et al.*, *Sociology in the Philippine Setting*, rev. ed. (Quezon City: Phoenix Publishing House, 1963), pp. 123–145.

and to neglect of its broader significance. Admittedly, treatment of alien enterprise within a country is not uniform and in all countries of the area there are formal and/or practical distinctions in the treatment of Asian alien and Western enterprises. It is not surprising that such distinctions have been interpreted to bolster a narrow interpretation of indigenism. We feel, however, that variations in the pressures on the different alien communities in Southeast Asia are differences of degree and, for the most part, reflect considerations of strategy and timing.

Such distinctions arise out of diverse factors. To begin with, the prominence of Western enterprise declined rapidly following 1940, as warfare and political and economic instability were accompanied by disinvestment and transfers of ownership to nationals. Westerners in the tropics, for the most part, have not been colonists but relatively mobile, transient residents, and many responded to the demise of colonialism by repatriating what they could of their investment. In Burma and Indonesia this process has been accelerated by vigorous anti-Western policies. In the Philippines, Malaya, and Thailand the anti-Western pressures have been sporadic and more subtle. In all of Southeast Asia, the prominence of Western enterprise has declined which is, of course, an immediate goal of indigenism.

Another source of the narrow (anti-Chinese) version of economic nationalism arises in the fact that indigenism has been paced by the evolving capacities of members of the national society to perform economic functions heretofore dominated by aliens. It is for this reason that some labor services and commerce, in which Asian alien participation has been conspicuous, have been early targets.

Where government entrepreneurship is not an alternative, requirements of scale can be a formidable obstacle to indigenism in many fields. The emotional impact of relatively large Western enterprises, the prestige attached to working for such enterprises, and the discontinuities between the economic horizons of potential indigenous entrepreneurs and the scale of existing Western enterprises have given security, probably transient, to such enterprises in the Philippines and Malaya. To the extent that Western enterprise has specialized in primary production for export, moreover, such production tends to be geographically dispersed and intrudes less upon the consciousness of the urbanized, politically active, and economically responsive members of the national society.

In Indonesia pressures on Western enterprise have been maintained in excess of those maintained against the firms of Asian aliens. In Burma, indigenism has been carried to the point where remnants of Western enterprise have disappeared, and Asian alien enterprise is threatened with extinction. Occupying an intermediate position is the Philippines where the case is confused by the special position established for American enterprise as a *quid pro quo* for various economic concessions and the American commitment to defend the Philippines. In practice, measures of Filipinism have maintained disproportionate pressure on Chinese enterprises as the economic functions performed by the Chinese—retail trade, import trade, rice and corn trade, and so forth—came within the capabilities of emerging Filipino entrepreneurs. In Thailand and Malaya, a clear distinction prevails in indigenism pressures on Chinese and Western enterprise. The relatively favorable treatment of the latter is explained, in part, by current arrangements providing these societies with acceptable assurance of external security and which involve collaboration with and dependence upon Western allies. For Cambodia and Vietnam, the evidence does not indicate that distinctions in the treatment of Asian alien and Western enterprise have been significant.

ELITE OR GRASS ROOTS?

Observers of Southeast Asia are frequently inclined to dismiss indigenism as an elite phenomenon originating with and promoted by politicians seeking power for other ends and by members of a narrow indigenous entrepreneurial element who are motivated by avarice to expropriate alien wealth. Southeast Asians, on the other hand, tend to rationalize indigenism as a broadly based "grass roots" movement emerging in response to the collective will.[9] We believe that, with the partial exceptions of Burma and Indonesia, indigenism has not originated in the "grass roots" but has been an elite phenomenon.[10]

[9] For example, see Remigio E. Agpalo, *The Political Process and the Nationalization of the Retail Trade in the Philippines* (Diliman, Philippines: University of the Philippines Press, 1962), pp. 65–88.

[10] In some countries, indigenism has been dominated by the economic philosophy and notions of a leader of the nationalist movement. Certainly this was true of South Vietnam where Diem's rejection of socialism, which was matched by his skepticism of capitalism, gave Vietnam's system a flavor of its own. Ne Win and his close associates have imparted a distinctive blend of socialism, nationalism, and xenophobia to indigenism in Burma. On the other hand, there are other dominant nationalist leaders—Sukarno seems to be a case in point—who have played minor roles in erecting the system of indigenism.

Exception must be made in the case of Burma where indigenism directed against the Indian minority has a unique grass-roots character. This is explained by the direct confrontation between Burmese and Indians in the process of bringing the Irrawaddy delta under cultivation which was exacerbated by the depression of the 1930s and the wholesale expropriation of the Burmese cultivators. Complicating the Burmese situation was the fact that Burma was administered as a province of India; Indians staffed the civil service positions and in this capacity were conspicuous to the Burmese. Finally, the Indians, in contrast with the Chinese, are racially more distinct and therefore more evident to the rank-and-file Burmese.

Exception must also be made for Indonesia in those cases where the development of Western enterprise adversely affected peasant welfare. For example, in Java peasants were compelled to lease land for sugar estates for rents they considered too low; in Sumatra communal village lands were leased to estates over peasant opposition; and in general, where estate and smallholder rubber production were in juxtaposition, the rural Indonesians became aware that colonial policies favored estate production.

STEREOTYPES

Although indigenism is not essentially a grass-roots phenomenon, it is rationalized in each society by shared stereotypes of alien economic behavior and of aliens as individuals.[11] In each of the countries, the dimensions of the economic role of aliens are generally exaggerated,[12] the personal qualities attributed to aliens—Asian and Western—tend to fall into a common pattern, and the slogans associated with indigenism are those encountered throughout the area.

Economic activities of aliens receive a criminal identification. Fires in an urban environment are always attributed to arson by Chinese (or Indian) shopkeepers. Smugglers are invariably aliens, and this opinion persists in the face of contradictory evidence. Aliens are the violators of

[11] In Chapter 1 we described, without assessing their validity, those features attributed by Southeast Asians to colonial policy and practice that they believe contributed to alienized economies, pluralism, and underdevelopment. Here we describe the stereotype images of alien behavior without assessing their validity. To establish their truth would be exceedingly difficult and at the same time irrelevant. The stereotype images reflect rationalization and belief, and regardless of their basis, they influence indigenism.

[12] For analysis of the Filipino image of the role of one minority, see Michael O. McPhelin, "The Chinese Question," *Philippine Studies* (9), April 1961, pp. 333–338.

price controls, of exchange and import controls, and they evade taxes by keeping two or more sets of books. At another level, it is alleged that their economic activities are actually or potentially subversive. It is necessary to "wrest" control from aliens because they have a "strangle hold" on the economy. They possess monopoly control which enables them to "hoard" and "profiteer." The remittances of aliens are a drain upon the productive capacity of a country and block development. Aliens are the corruptors of naive indigenous civil servants. Western businessmen seek to associate with political leaders in order to corrupt them. In Burma, many aspects of alien activity are labeled "economic insurgency."

Chinese are characterized as "shrewd," "stingy," and "grasping." In one context they are described as "self-effacing," "evasive," and "unreliable." In another they are resented for being "noisy" and are considered to be self-seeking because they use oversized shop signs and billboards. If menials, aliens are labeled "dirty," "obsequious," and "slovenly" in personal hygiene. They are inevitably characterized as immoral and irreligious. Western aliens are described as materialistic, arrogant, and of "loose morals." It is alleged that alien economic communities are cohesive and organized for the mutual support of members while turning a solid front in opposition to indigenous business interests and to the state. It is believed that members of such communities are aided by access to mutual credit resources and discriminatory pricing is used to favor compatriots.

Southeast Asians complain that the Chinese are efficient, frugal, industrious, willing to go to the most remote place to make a living, and to work long hours. They are usually characterized as sober, reliable, and invariably as industrious rather than relaxed. In Southeast Asia, however, these characteristics have acquired a pejorative connotation. They are qualities not possessed by nationals and hence are unpatriotic, if not subversive. It is asserted that "free-fight" competition enables the aliens to acquire monopoly control over the economy because they possess non-national qualities. Once such control is established it will tend to be subversive because aliens are precluded by their "alienness" from recognizing the national interest.

PRAGMATISM AND INDIGENISM

In trying to sort out the essential qualities of indigenism, the pragmatic aspects of this phenomenon are continually encountered. Having been assigned formidable economic and social responsibilities, new governments resort to fiscal innovations and direct controls to acquire command over resources. Not infrequently, the value of such institutions to the pursuit of indigenism is quickly recognized. For example, in the early postwar period, a number of countries experimented with trading monopolies to divert to the state the windfall arising out of strong external demand for rice and industrial raw materials. These trading monopolies were readily accepted and have proved long-lived, in part, because they indigenized a substantial part of the export trade.

Similarly, all of the countries, on occasion, have used import and exchange controls over foreign-exchange transactions and, with the exception of Malaya and Thailand, the administrative discretion inherent in such controls has been used with varying success to transfer the import trade to nationals. In some cases, indigenous entrepreneurship emerged in response to strong incentives; in others, the import trade was transferred to indigenous control through government trading monopolies. The postwar period also has seen the installation of managed currency systems in each of the countries, and establishment of control over credit has been followed by the creation of specialized, and indigenous, institutions to distribute this important resource. Not surprisingly, nationality invariably was introduced as a qualification for credit allocation.

THE ENTREPRENEURIAL RESPONSE

In Southeast Asia, transfers of power (including the 1932 revolution in Thailand) were followed by the creation of constitutional governments. That this should be so reflects not only the strength of the Western heritage, but also the unwavering faith of nationalists in the unity of purpose and in the capabilities of the national society for progress. The good life would materialize with escape from the colonial yoke which had confined and suppressed the chosen society.

Analogous to this was the uniform postindependence response in efforts to create a viable indigenous bourgeoisie to take over the economic functions dominated by aliens. In Indonesia, Burma, Cambodia, the Philippines, and to a lesser extent in Thailand, South Vietnam, and Malaya, policies and institutions were devised to promote the emergence of an indigenous entrepreneurial class. It is an article of faith to nationalists that the process by which productive assets and the managerial and entrepreneurial functions were alienized resulted from discrimination and exploitation inherent in colonialism. To believe otherwise, that alien domination reflected the operation of impersonal market processes, was an unthinkable denial of the messianic future. Indigenism would automatically follow the release of the capacities of members of the national society previously suppressed by colonialism. This process might be telescoped by subsidized credit, allocation of scarce foreign exchange, protection, tax concessions, and the like. Similarly, it was appropriate to restrict the activities of aliens to speed the flow of indigenous entrepreneurship. But, to believe that the flow so stimulated would not be self-sustaining was a denial of nationalism. For the most part, however, the gap between traditional economic activities and required entrepreneurial behavior has been so great that relatively few Southeast Asians have been able to bridge it.

As indigenism has proceeded, the managers and entrepreneurs have been recruited from diverse sources, including, among others, the bureaucracy, the military, political elites—including elements serving as indirect rulers under the colonial power—traditional economic elites, and skilled craftsmen. The only generalizations we are inclined to make are, admittedly, of limited significance. When the path to indigenism is that of socialism and the public corporation, recruitment takes place in the bureaucracy including the army. To the extent that it results from private enterprise, recruitment is concentrated in traditional political and economic elites.

While the bureaucracy, including the military, has proved to be a major source of supply of indigenous entrepreneurship, only in the case of Burma, and perhaps Indonesia, has bureaucratic entrepreneurship become dominant. The formidable administrative responsibilities of governments have moderated the pressures for public enterprises by providing alternative employment for scarce bureaucratic resources. The bureaucracy, by providing an outlet for talented and educated members of the indigenous society, has also served to retard the appearance of pressure groups with a stake in indigenism by private enterprise.

The capacity to respond to the concessions and incentives demanded by indigenism is reinforced when initial entrepreneurial activity represents a continuum from traditional political and economic activity. This is illustrated in the Philippines where entrepreneurs have been recruited from the politically dominant cacique class and where their success as entrepreneurs is highly dependent upon their skill in combining political acumen with entrepreneurial initiative. Their viability as businessmen frequently was more dependent upon their capacity to manipulate political factors influencing the distribution of credit and foreign-exchange resources, than upon their skills as managers and entrepreneurs.

In Indonesia, entrepreneurs were recruited from diverse sources. Political elites responding to incentives and opportunities, together with recruits from elements of the Javanese and Balinese aristocracies, provided much of the early entrepreneurship.[13] Following the extensive expropriations of 1958, the military stepped in to provide a substantial share of management functions. The Indonesian Army includes political activists strongly sympathetic to the goals of indigenism who have been active in preventing apolitical career officers from frustrating politically motivated indigenism. The revolutionary army recognizes a stake in change rather than in the *status quo* and has provided much of the initiative and managerial talent required to nationalize economic activities.

In Thailand, entrepreneurship has been recruited from among the Chinese and their descendants. During the Pibun regime, the politically dominant Thai military elites used their political power to take over existing enterprises and establish others. Many nationalized industries, however, retained Chinese and other aliens in managerial positions. In other cases, Chinese enterprises, to avoid nationalist pressures, have introduced politically powerful Thais on their boards of directors, but the Chinese continue to provide most entrepreneurial and managerial functions.

Burma furnishes an interesting case because the autonomous commercial and industrial experiences of the army served as a training ground for the military cadres who acquired sufficient confidence to precipitate the final transition to full nationalization. The initial Ne Win government was not motivated strongly by indigenism, but it was forced by necessity to create and operate diverse enterprises thereby acquiring further experience and confidence.

DETERMINANTS OF THE PRIORITY OF INDIGENISM

It is self-evident, that, to the extent that a nationalist movement matured in repression and violence, it will be revolutionary and

---

[13] An entrepreneurial spirit, probably related to special colonial circumstances, has been strong among such ethnic groups as the Toba Batak and Minangkabau.

xenophobic.[14] Moreover, where such movements were militant and unified by the opposition of the colonial power, indigenism has been applied strongly against Western enterprise. On the other hand, there are situations, for example, in the Philippines and Malaya, where the nationalist movement matured in autonomy, political tutelage, and collaboration between ruler and ruled. In these countries indigenism is distinctive, at least initially, for moderation toward Western enterprise. Thailand, not having been subject to foreign rule, followed an erratic course. The strongest measures against Western enterprise were taken in the late 1930s when the regime was controlled by military men influenced by fascism, especially its Japanese variety. Policies of indigenism, which remained prominent during the postwar Pibun regime through 1957, were dampened markedly by the Sarit and Thanom governments.

Indigenism is also influenced by the extent to which the ideology of nationalism is socialist. Independence movements in Southeast Asia, to a substantial degree, were recruited from elements uncommitted by ownership of property or job security. Furthermore, because socialism is identified with social and economic reform in the industrial West, it appeals to nationalist elements whether evolutionary or revolutionary. This appeal is reinforced, moreover, by the Western socialist tradition of opposition to colonialism.

The clearest case of indigenism associated with an ideological commitment to socialism is Burma, where both the civilian and military regimes moved to nationalize alien enterprises, Asian and Western. Socialism was of some significance in Indonesia, but more important in explaining pressures on Western enterprise was the Dutch resistance to the nationalist movement. The ideology of Indonesian nationalism is compatible with the creation of a capitalist class of Indonesians, and many policies are intelligible in terms of their contribution to the emergence of Indonesian entrepreneurship. The self-image of the Indonesian society views all Indonesians as proletarian and exploited whether they be peasants or wealthy businessmen.

In the case of Thailand, Pridi advocated a fuzzy socialist blueprint after the 1932 revolution, but his plan was rejected by the revolutionary

---

[14] In the previous draft of this study completed in mid-1967, this generalization was footnoted with the comment: "Kenya comes to mind as a possible exception." The indigenism that subsequently erupted in that country reinforces the validity of our conclusion.

government and was not revived during his tenure as Prime Minister. Such indigenism as took place in postwar Thailand was opportunistic rather than socialistic. In the Philippines, no ideological basis can be identified with the pressures on alien enterprise. Directly productive public enterprises, which were thoroughly tested and found wanting, were motivated by the goal of industrialization based on the domestic market. In recent years, the structure of government enterprises has been rapidly dismantled, and it is clear that the Philippine society is content with capitalist economic development in which the Filipino share of control and ownership is expanding.

Indigenism in Malaya has no socialist content and there are only minor pressures on Western enterprise. The Emergency, a struggle against forces identified as socialist, reinforced the bias of the politically dominant Malays aganist collectivism. The Chinese economic elites who share in political power as junior partners, moreover, have a strong stake in an enterprise-type of economy.

What will be the impact of economic growth and development on indigenism? In the short run, indigenism will in all likelihood be intensified by economic development, the essence of which is change in human behavior. To the extent that such change is accelerated, it will generate an expanding flow of entrepreneurship—private and bureaucratic—and simultaneously will create a politically powerful pressure group motivated to maintain and expand indigenism. Over the longer haul, the drive to indigenize will be moderated by economic growth insofar as growth is accompanied by increased indigenous ownership and management.

What will be the impact of economic stagnation on indigenism? The answer is similar to that produced by the inverse question posed immediately above. In the short run, the priority for indigenism will be intensified because progress toward this goal can substitute for the lack of economic development. This capability of indigenism must decline over time and in the absence of economic development, however, because new activities to indigenize will become scarce. More important, this capability will wither because it is not possible to "turn back the clock" permanently to a condition of socially stable economic stagnation in a world where nationalist movements have revolted against backwardness and dependency status.

The historical tradition of the society can also exert a strong influence upon indigenism. This is illustrated by the isolation and ethno-centrism of the Burmese society in the past which is repeated in the current phase of withdrawal and turning inward which in turn has closed the Burmese society and economy to outside influences in recent years. Less distinct but similar influences are at work in Vietnam with a long history of insecurity in the face of Chinese pressure, and in Cambodia, traditionally subject to pressure from the Vietnamese to the east and the Thais to the west.

The virulence of indigenism also reflects frustration arising from the gap between the promises and accomplishments of successful na-tionalist movements. Escape from colonialism promised the "good life," but the means to achieve social and economic progress continue to elude some societies. Failure to achieve the economic promises of na-tionalism has stimulated recourse to the police power of the state to substitute nationals for aliens in economic activities, to expropriate alien-owned enterprises, and in extreme cases to eliminate alien com-petition by deportation. Insecure political leaders and parties have not been averse to using the emotional appeal of indigenism as an issue to divert attention from the gap between their promises and record of accomplishments. Political leaders out of office have been equally quick to use the issue to charge those in power with betrayal of the society by failing to extend the nationalist revolution to the economy.

The intensity of indigenism also has been affected by urbanization and particularly by the "nationalization" of the traditionally cosmo-politan capital cities. The concentration of the powers of political de-cision making and of economic opportunities arising out of commerce, together with the juxtaposition of nationalist political elites and Western and Asian alien economic elites in the urban centers, have tended to exacerbate feelings of economic nationalism. So long as the capital cities were relatively small, cosmopolitan enclaves with stable native populations and a minimum of communication with the hinterlands, the drive to indigenize remained relatively dormant. Population mobility during and after World War II has contributed to greater awareness on the part of the host population of the aliens and their functional specialization.

The Japanese occupation of Southeast Asia contributed to the viru-lence of indigenism in a number of ways. Japanese expropriation of and operation of modern Western enterprises, the harsh anti-Chinese economic measures, and the use of economic controls and public enterprises to mobilize Southeast Asian resources for the Japanese war effort established precedents appropriate to postindependence indigenism.

The principal change in the Japanese period, however, was the enhanced mobility of Southeast Asian populations. The restlessness of insecure populations produced a diversity of experiences which disturbed traditional patterns of behavior and weakened relationships that contributed to economic and social stability. Social mobility, internal migration, and urbanization awakened consciousness of national identification and weakened regional and class differences. Under the Japanese there occurred a proliferation of paramilitary mass organizations which cut across previous hierarchical patterns and gave indigenous elites administrative and organizational experiences that enhanced their self-confidence.

The Japanese recognized the value of increased literacy for the political and economic organization of the occupied countries and took steps to expand systems of secular national education. Southeast Asians were introduced into administrative affairs and, in the process, obtained access to and skills in using facilities for transportation, finance, rationing, and the like. In performing administrative functions under the Japanese, they acquired experience with propaganda techniques and control over communications facilities which were readily transferable to the service of nationalist revolutions.

Equally important, the disruption of production, internal and external commerce, and credit and finance exposed Southeast Asians to new economic experiences. Western enterprises were closed, and the Chinese and other Asian aliens were subject to severe repression. Initially, Japanese appeared to substitute for aliens who were now out of the picture, but as production and trade were disrupted, each society tended to be thrown on its own resources and at the same time to become more resourceful. To some extent this was manifested in a movement back to the countryside to cope with the production of food crops for subsistence. In terms of the previous economic organization in which trade, finance, and many lines of production were monopolized by aliens, the struggle for survival saw extensive national participation in such activities.

The basic restraint upon indigenism, we believe, is the racial and ethnic distribution of the population. There seems to exist for each underdeveloped society some critical minimum size of an alien minority relative to the total population which imposes the choice of assimilation rather than continued repression and expropriation. This principle is demonstrated by Malaya, Thailand, and Vietnam where the relatively large Chinese minorities have imposed constraints on indigenism that promise to maintain avenues to assimilation. In the Philippines, Indonesia, and Burma, on the other hand, the relatively small Chinese and Indian minorities have not provided their members a comparable security. In Burma, repatriation of the remaining members of the once sizeable Indian minority is proceeding rapidly. There are some encouraging signs that a more humane alternative will emerge in the Philippines in which openings to *de facto* assimilation will be maintained.

Our principle has little relevance for assessing the future of Western enterprise because Western businessmen rarely consider immigration and assimilation to underdeveloped tropical societies. The ultimate response of the Western businessman to the pressures of indigenism frequently has been to return home with that portion of his assets he is able to salvage. Obviously, this process can continue until the relative economic importance and numbers of this minority no longer stimulate nationalist efforts to indigenize further.

The economically important Asian minorities, Chinese and Indian, have origins in large states continguous to Southeast Asia that are presently ambitious for influence and power. This suggests that indigenism will be moderated by the proximity of India and China. In Burma, it is clear that the Indian minority derived little security from India. In the Philippines, Indonesia, and Malaysia, there is little evidence that indigenism has been moderated by the realities of Asian politics. In Thailand, South Vietnam, and Cambodia, on the other hand, the proximity of Mainland China has clearly restrained such pressures.

In a number of cases, indigenism is moderated by the strength of residual colonial influence. In the case of the Philippines, postwar collaboration in organizing and financing economic rehabilitation and in meeting the challenge of communist-led (Hukbalahap) insurrection, the persistence of the prewar pattern of trade dependency, together with large-scale economic subventions, have all tended to maintain United States influence. As a result, the Philippines has continued preindependence policies which probably have served to temper indigenism.

A similar pattern has appeared in Malaya where close British-Malay collaboration in reducing the Emergency, in transferring power, and in creating a Malay-dominated political system, ensured that British influence would continue. It must be emphasized that this is not to be compared to the communal balance in the population in explaining the basic quality of Malayan indigenism, but it is of considerable importance in explaining the relative security enjoyed by Western enterprise. Malaysian membership in the British Commonwealth and the assistance of the Commonwealth in meeting the challenge of Konfrontasi also have helped to maintain the existing pattern of policy.

At the other extreme, we find Indonesia where the former colonial rulers reaped a whirlwind of bitterness and violence. The Dutch in the successive "Agreements" in the postwar period tried to ensure some security for their economic holdings. Given the nature of their struggle, the energies of the nationalists were increasingly exerted to get rid of Dutch-imposed limitations on Indonesian autonomy. Residual colonial influence in Indonesia rapidly drained away, and attempts to exert such influence intensified rather than moderated indigenism, although the legal obstacles written into the agreements may have slowed the pace at which assets and activities were transferred to nationals. In Burma, for various reasons, residual colonial influence withered rapidly and apparently has had little influence upon indigenism.

Has religion exercised a moderating influence? Generalizations are not fruitful in this area although particular situations are interesting. In Indonesia, the major religious reform movement and the major Islamic political party were identified with the nascent indigenous business community, the interests of which clashed most directly with Chinese economic interests. On the other hand, Western enterprises, rarely in direct competition with Indonesians, but under pressure from leftist groups, indigenous labor, and bureaucratic elements, may have benefited from the influence on the pace of indigenism of the anti-Marxist content of Islam. Catholicism in the Philippines helped produce an identification with the West which has contributed to attitudes toward capitalism, private property, and so forth, which may have delayed the pace of indigenism. The influence of Buddhism has moderated Thai and Cambodian indigenism, whereas in Burma and Vietnam the sporadic activist political role of the Buddhist priesthood, on balance, probably has had the opposite effect. The impact of religion on indigenism varies from country to country and has not been strong, although religions in Southeast Asia do produce attitudes and values that directly influence the possibility and rate of assimilation.

Finally, indigenism is influenced by the historical role of alien minorities. This is illustrated by Thailand, Vietnam, and Cambodia where the timing and royal sponsorship of early Chinese immigrants gave members of this minority an identification with the indigenous aristocracy and access to functional roles of high status reflected in present-day values and attitudes that contribute to the security of the Chinese. On the other hand, when the timing and sponsorship of Asian alien immigration—the Indians in Burma and the Chinese in Malaya and Sumatra—is associated with Western rule and where such immigrants initially performed coolie labor, the effect has been to intensify indigenism.

The Relationship of Indigenism to Economic Growth and Development

Introduction of indigenism into the static economic model bounded by the usual assumptions of perfect competition, unchanging techniques, and resources fixed in quantity and in qualitative dimensions results in the assessment that indigenism will sacrifice per capita real income. Insofar as indigenous factors are substituted for alien factors, misallocation of resources results and potential output is sacrificed.

Once the static model is abandoned for a more realistic world in which competition is imperfect, resources are accumulating and their qualitative aspects are changing, and technology is being produced, unambiguous conclusions regarding the relationship between indigenism and economic growth are not possible. The reasoning of the static model supports the conclusion that indigenism will sacrifice potential output in the short run. Once the competitive assumptions are abandoned, however, even this conclusion is no longer rigorously true.

With the lapse of time, the relevance of the static model rapidly erodes and there are various economic arguments that support the conclusion that policies of indigenism might increase aggregate income over levels that would result in the absence of such policies. Such arguments turn on the existence of external economies arising in divergences between private and social returns from various kinds of "investment" in indigenism. When external economies are defined rigorously in terms of the competitive assumptions, they are limited to bucolic examples of little practical significance. On the other hand, the reduction of market shortcomings (reflecting limited size, institutional rigidities, and human frailties) and, above all, the diffusion of all kinds of productivity improvements through market linkages in the context of economic expansion and technical change are of obvious importance in explaining economic development in the real world. Indigenism policies may be necessary to ensure the development of potential national capacities which otherwise would not be realized because of divergences between private and social returns to investments in indigenism. Although unambiguous conclusions are not possible, our study of the relationship between indigenism and economic growth supports the assessment that potential growth is sacrificed in the short run and probably potential growth is foregone over the longer haul.

These tentative conclusions must be modified substantially, however, when the measure of economic growth is defined as increasing per capita real income accruing to members of the national society. In the static model, amplified to reflect Southeast Asian conditions, per capita real income accruing to members of the national society will be less than per capita real income because resident aliens own a disproportionate share of modern enterprises and pre-empt more than their share of rewarding employment. In the case of the static model, substitution of members for aliens may sacrifice aggregate income, but there are good reasons for concluding that income accruing to members will increase. This, of course, is the case for confiscation.

Once we move from the static model to a more realistic image of the world where resources are produced and undergo qualitative change and in which technology is changing, no unambiguous conclusions are possible. In the short run, confiscation almost certainly will raise per capita real income received by members over levels that would prevail in the absence of such a policy. However, future income from the expropriated assets may decline, and it is possible that potential income accruing to members may be sacrificed. This could result where asset maintenance, product quality control, and marketing expertise are critical ingredients in the enterprises indigenized.

This brings us to consideration of the relationship between indigenism and economic development, where the latter is not defined mechanistically as economic growth, but as growth attended by qualitative changes in human behavior productive of output. Here again it is important to distinguish between economic development of the resident population and economic development of the national society. The former concept is useful for many purposes, but the latter defines the economic progress sought by the underdeveloped societies of Southeast Asia. As in the previous analysis, conclusions that emphasize the negative relationship between indigenism and economic development of the total population are substantially weaker and may be reversed when applied to the national society.

Economic nationalism has obviously played an important positive role in the economic development of the United States, Japan, the Soviet Union, Great Britain, Germany, France, and all other countries experiencing accelerated growth and development. This positive relationship can be identified for a wide variety of nationalistic policy systems and for diverse paths to economic development. Alternative types of social organization have demonstrated capacity to promote economic modernization. Similarly, accelerated development has been achieved by alternative types of economic organization. At still another level, nationalism and development are associated with diverse combinations and permutations of industrialization, agricultural development, international specialization, and the like.

Although we believe that the positive relationship in the past between nationalism in its economic policy manifestations and development was frequently a causal one, this experience may be irrelevant for assessing the impact of indigenism in underdeveloped, ex-colonial countries. The priority attached to indigenism establishes a distinct quality of economic nationalism, and postwar experience suggests that, up to the present, its correlation with accelerated economic development has been low. On the other hand, there are no convincing grounds for concluding that the correlation would be higher if economic nationalism had followed a more conventional pattern or if some other system of policy had prevailed. It is clear that the relationship has not been uniform. Moreover, the question is not meaningful without a time dimension.

Where indigenism in Southeast Asia has been implemented by public enterprise and bureaucratic entrepreneurship, the consequences for development have been disappointing, with few exceptions. Similarly, many observers deprecate the private entrepreneurial response because it has been nurtured by overpowering incentives, at high cost to the society generally in inefficiency, waste, and inequality.

Admittedly, indigenism is associated with corruption and chicanery as politicians and civil servants, as well as potential entrepreneurs, respond to the opportunities created by the policy system. Moreover, avarice has been a prominent motivation of the numerically small but strident economic interest groups who actively support indigenism policies. However, after proper emphasis is given to the negative aspects of indigenism, we emphasize the frequency with which a negative appraisal of the likely role of economic nationalism in economic development would have proved wrong in the past.

If we assume away fortuitous changes and if adequate supplies of other resources exist, economic growth will be accelerated if human behavior changes in ways productive of goods and services. Such changes, which increase the availability of labor as a resource or increase the yield from a given supply of resources, include innovation, specialization, risk taking, functional and geographic mobility, and similar aspects of entrepreneurship, as well as decisions to save and invest.

Critically important to the relationship between indigenism and economic development will be the qualitative aspects of the response of nationals to the incentives and opportunities created by the policy structure of indigenism. Powerful inducements to entrepreneurial and other innovative behavior can be established readily, but the response and, therefore, the effect on economic development will depend more upon culturally derived attitudes and values appropriate to flexibility and adaptability of the human factor than upon the intensity and permanence of the incentives. Indigenism will contribute positively to accelerated development in Southeast Asia only if the human response to the opportunities created by nationalistic policies is cumulative.

The only generalization we are inclined to make regarding the relationship between indigenism and economic development, however defined, is to assert that neither case has been proved or disproved. Although our assessment begs the question, we are encouraged by those cases—including the Philippines and Thailand in Southeast Asia— where the human response to the incentives established by policy systems of indigenism promises to sustain rewarding economic growth and modernization.[15]

Lessons for the Future

Indigenism is an imperative goal because it represents a testing of sovereignty which nationalists must undertake because they are nationalists. They see their freedom to make policy choices as illusory so long as disproportionate economic power is in alien hands; they see that integration of the plural society into a national society will remain a mockery so long as functional specialization and stratification of wealth along racial lines persists.

Progress toward the national economy will not be smooth. The path followed will bounce from side to side of the basic trend toward an ever-larger indigenous share in the ownership and control of modern assets and activities. Short-run economic crises, longings for such goals as peace, stability, social integration, contests for political power, and so forth, will cause vacillation about the path to the national economy. Indigenism is underway in economies with diverse structures at different stages of development, with populations of varying racial and ethnic composition, and conditioned by diverse colonial experiences. The duration and nature of the transition to a less abrasive pluralism will depend upon many factors including the willingness of aliens to assimilate—to acquiesce in and even to seek the removal of aspects of social and economic distinctiveness—and the willingness of the host society

[15] Professor Johnson qualifies his generally pessimistic assessment of the impact of economic nationalism on economic development by acknowledging that a policy system of economic nationalism "may be . . . the cheapest and most effective way to raise the real income in less developed countries . . . investment in the creation of a middle class, financed by resources extracted from the mass of population by nationalistic policies, may be the essential preliminary to the construction of a viable national state. This problem however, belongs in the spheres of history, sociology, and political science rather than economics" (A Theoretical Model of Economic Nationalism," pp. 184–185). Later Johnson reverses this assessment by concluding that "nationalist motivations inevitably lead to economic policies that inhibit the economic development they aim to stimulate. See his *Economic Policies Toward Less Developed Countries* (New York: Frederick A. Praeger, 1967), p. 67.

to provide avenues, both formal and informal, for their assimilation. Among the latter will be arrangements that afford alien communities relief from the pressures of indigenism and at the same time promise increased economic participation and control by members of the host society.

A promising approach to accommodation includes diverse arrangements for joint participation by aliens and nationals in enterprises. Large-scale Western enterprise has displayed some initiative in exploring this possibility, and there exist in Southeast Asia a few encouraging examples of mixed enterprises in which alien firms collaborate with the host government. Such arrangements have been acceptable to nationalists, particularly where they prescribe a schedule for the transfer of the enterprise to indigenous control. Joint private participation of nationals with aliens is also relatively welcome for the same reasons, although the transfer to indigenous control may not be formally scheduled and may not be intended by the alien participants.

Alien participation in the form of publicly held corporations has been relatively welcome in some countries, in part, because such enterprises promise ultimately to be indigenized. Such corporations whose stocks are actively traded, though controlled by aliens, escape the onus of such identification. For smaller alien enterprises, joint participation will be more direct. This type of solution will be facilitated by the expertise and flexibility of aliens in adapting to nationalist constraints.

There is also a significant opportunity for alien firms to mitigate pressures of economic nationalism by employing, training, and upgrading nationals. Such inverse discrimination can reduce the stigma of "alienness."

A second avenue to accommodation lies in the priority attached to industrialization in national economic development. Alien enterprises manufacturing for the domestic market are relatively acceptable to nationalists and in a number of the countries under study, alien entrepreneurs are moving into manufacturing. In some cases this is primarily a response to the high levels of protection that have persisted in Southeast Asia, but in others it reflects the pressures of indigenism. By contributing to industrialization, which looms so large as a national goal, resident aliens can hasten their identification with the national society.

Finally, the alien entrepreneur can establish some security through extralegal and illegal institutions including corruption. The opportunities inherent in discretionary economic controls and the inadequate pay scales for bureaucrats facilitate a collusive *modus vivendi* at a tolerable cost to the alien businessman.

The period since World War II has witnessed a remarkable burst of activity designed to accelerate economic growth and modernization in the less-developed world. The governments of Southeast Asia have exerted initiative and ingenuity in exploring the potentialities of economic planning, commercial policy, monetary and fiscal policy, nationalization, and so forth. Similarly, governments in the developed world have created new institutions and adapted old institutions in efforts to participate in the processes of growth and development. These efforts, however, have been attended in both Southeast Asia and the West by growing frustration with the effectiveness of outside participation.

The challenge to identify opportunities through which the outside world can participate is a complex and frustrating one. The difficulties confronting attempts to influence events and to shape the processes of modernization in the skeptical, if not hostile, ex-colonial world are clear, particularly when that world is divided and confused and external events threaten its precarious stability and security. The implications for outside participation to be drawn from our study will be self-evident to any sensitive observer of Southeast Asian nationalism.

A major institution through which the West hopes to participate in the economic development is long-term private foreign investment. While such investment includes a number of diverse, specialized forms, the principal part consists of direct investment, which is distinguished by the element of control exercised by the investor over decisions that determine profitability. The ingredient of control, which the investor compromises only with reluctance, comes into obvious conflict with the Southeast Asian requirements of sovereignty.

The conflicting images of private direct investment in developed and less-developed societies emphasize with depressing clarity the difficulties of outside participation. In the Western image, the receiving country benefits from an increment of foreign exchange which the investor brings to acquire an existing enterprise or create a new one. Southeast Asians, on the other hand, confronted by the problem of living with chronic pressure on their scarce foreign-exchange resources, become acutely conscious of foreign enterprises as claimants upon scarce foreign exchange.

The Western image also attributes to private foreign investment an element of risk-bearing that otherwise would not appear in the tradition-bound cultures of Southeast Asia where savings tend to flow into urban and rural estate, jewelry, foreign assets, and commercial enterprises rather than into long-term productive investment. Southeast Asians, on the other hand, believe that in the past the risk-bearing function of foreign capital has been compensated at excessive rates and that exploitation will continue unless entrepreneurial returns are regulated by taxation, minimum wage laws, social security legislation, restrictions on profit remission, and similar measures.

The Western image of private foreign investment also includes an element of "know-how" which accompanies control and which will "rub off" on the nationals of the recipient country who work for foreign firms. Southeast Asians have little faith in the inevitability of such a transfer and therefore resort to restrictions on the use of foreign personnel and prescribe schedules for the training and upgrading of nationals. In licensing foreign investment they frequently insist on initial national participation, expansion of such participation, and ultimate national control.

The semantic gulf between Southeast Asia and the West is equally evident. The West refers to the flow of foreign investment with its connotation of the movement of resources from the capital rich to the capital poor. Southeast Asians, on the other hand, refer to the accumulation of foreign capital which emphasizes the role of foreign entrepreneurship and economic power in organizing indigenous resources. Conflicting images raised by the term "foreign investor" inhibit communication. Implicit in the Western image is the individual innovating with creativity and at personal sacrifice. As an individual, he can carry no threat to the independence or economic aspirations of the host society. Southeast Asians, however, are quite aware that private direct investment today results from the decisions of large, economically powerful, international corporations with goals and methods that can challenge their country's sovereignty.

Nationalists in Southeast Asia regard the terms under which private direct investment should be permitted as a problem in bilateral monopoly in which the terms will depend upon the bargaining skill and relative power of the opposing state and the investing corporation. Such investment tends to be large-scale and to involve complex questions of depreciation, depletion, levels of return, taxation, vertical integration, arbitrary pricing, and so forth, and there usually exists little objective basis for assessing the relative values contributed by the parties to the bargain.

There are few grounds for expecting the climate of private foreign investment to improve rapidly in Southeast Asia. Direct investment and, in particular, investment in manufacturing for protected domestic markets will flow to Southeast Asia in increasing amounts and will contribute to the improved productivity of indigenous resources. Private foreign investment is unlikely to make more than a marginal contribution to economic development, however, until the gap is narrowed between the terms on which such investment is acceptable to Southeast Asian nationalists and those acceptable to the investing corporations.

Large international corporations with diverse interests and capabilities and generating large amounts of internal savings clearly embody the major potential for private participation in Southeast Asian development. Efforts to realize this potential are likely to be more fruitful if imagination, ingenuity, and a willingness to compromise are brought to the task of devising innovations which facilitate the corporate adaptation to the requirements of Southeast Asian nationalism.

The second major institution through which the West seeks to participate in economic development in Southeast Asia is economic aid, including unrequited transfers of commodities, foreign exchange, and technical assistance, public loans, and transfers of surplus agricultural commodities. Nationalism imposes obvious constraints on economic aid, and we do not consider that indigenism imposes significant limitations independent of those attributable to political nationalism.

Except in cases of severe external threat to the recipient country, aid provides the donor country with unimpressive leverage with which to influence major policy decisions of the recipient government directly. Such leverage should not be wasted in supporting measures that clash with goals of indigenism. The potential gains are illusory as nationalists can readily frustrate such efforts. In particular, little gain can be expected from efforts to promote foreign investment laws or reliance on individualism and competitive market forces. Greater reliance on private enterprise can be expected in Southeast Asia as indigenism proceeds and members of the national society respond to economic opportunities and, in the process, demand greater economic freedom. Outsiders, including representatives of powerful governments, have little capacity to hasten this evolution. Similarly, the use of economic aid leverage to promote "social reform" is not promising, as such efforts play into the hands of opponents of reforms who charge that these efforts encroach on the sovereignty of the recipient country.

Examination of Southeast Asian nationalism indicates two basic adaptations in aid which promise to improve its effectiveness. An obvious opportunity exists in the gains to be realized from collaboration by donor and recipient countries in devising new international institutions and techniques for mobilizing and distributing aid resources. Anxieties arising in sensitive nationalism will be moderated by the substitution of multilateral planning and co-operation for bilateral aid relationships. Equally promising is the potential of economic aid in the form of large-scale social overhead investments. Such emphasis recognizes the need for an effective institutional replacement for the portfolio investment in transportation and other social capital which loomed so large in the movement of international capital to the colonial world in the half-century prior to World War I. Aid in this form would arouse minimum nationalist concern and to the extent that such capital symbolized progress to members of the recipient society, the donor country would benefit.

At the end of this prolonged sifting of indigenism in Southeast Asia, we choose to close on a note of moderate optimism. Although indigenism has been attended by inhumanity and arbitrary abuse of authority, and further excesses can be expected, we feel that the present insecurity facing the alien minorities in Southeast Asia will be resolved by assimilation rather than repression and violence. We are encouraged by the historical patterns of assimilation and the signs, admittedly faint in some countries, that openings to ultimate recognition will be maintained and even enlarged. We are firmly convinced that indigenism in Southeast Asia is not a stage in the perversion of nationalism which may culminate in obscene genocide such as was the fate of Jews in some Christian countries.

Southeast Asians can be depended upon to maintain zealously their autonomy over issues involving nationalism. Western governments, however, should be alert to opportunities both to reassure Southeast Asians of the reality of their sovereignty and to encourage them to maintain and enlarge avenues of assimilation for their alien minorities. We are confident that this is the policy of our respective countries and that it will remain so. We acknowledge the incongruity of the prescription implicit in our analysis which is held out to aliens in Southeast

Asia. This recommendation, that they remain patient and flexible under the harsh and discriminatory burdens of indigenism, is not a reflection of our insensitivity, but instead, it reflects our conviction that assimilation is feasible and the cost tolerable.

Nationalists in Southeast Asia are energetic and predictable in their efforts to ensure that economic development is national and not merely geographic. In seeking to enlarge their sovereignty, they are sophisticated and realistic and can be depended upon to take a skeptical view of threats to their independence whether from the capitalist West or the communist East. Because ex-colonial economic nationalism has been imperfectly perceived and inadequately appreciated, much of the potential effectiveness of past efforts on the part of the outside world to participate in economic development in Southeast Asia has been wasted. On the other hand, the gap between resources and aspirations in that part of the world establishes wide limits to the range of activities and projects that promise to contribute to economic development. There is so much to be done that surely the problems of developing institutions and techniques for effective participation that do not clash with the requirements of ex-colonial nationalism are capable of solution if approached with flexibility, initiative, and understanding.

GENERAL INDEX

Administrative discretion, 19
Agpalo, Remigio E., 447n
Alien enterprise, adaptation to indigenism, 464-465
Alien minorities, 457, 468-469
  nationalist stereotypes, 448-449
  see also Arab minorities, Chinese minorities, Indian minorities, and Western minorities
Alien population, critical minimum size, 456-457
Alienization, see Colonial development
Arab minorities, 12
Areas of recent settlement, 13, 439-440
Aristocracy, see Entrepreneurial recruitment
Assimilation, 445, 457, 463, 468-469
Autarky, 3, 5
Authoritarianism, 445

Bilateralism, see International economy
Bourgeoisie, see National bourgeoisie
Breton, Albert, 5n
Buddhism, see Religion
Buddhist Southeast Asia, 445
  see also Burma, Cambodia, and Thailand
Bureaucracy, 17, 451, 452, 454, 461
Bureaucratic elites, see Nationalist elites
Burma, 9, 10, 444-453, 455, 457, 458
  see also index for Burma
Burmanism, see index for Burma

Cambodia, 447, 450, 455, 457, 458, 459
  see also index for Cambodia
Canadian economic nationalism, 5, 6, 8n
Capital accumulation, 12, 13-16, 443-444, 446
Capital cities, nationalization of, 455
Capital movements, theory of, 13-14

Capitalism, 3, 12, 14-16, 18, 454, 458, 467
Carroll, John J., 443n
Catholicism, see Religion
China, see International relations
Chinese enterprise, 12, 16, 447
Chinese minorities, 445-449, 454, 456-459
  stereotypes of, 448-449
Collective capital goods, see Communal consumption capital
Colonial development, 6, 7, 9, 10-18
  alienization, 12, 14-16, 441
  exploitation, 14-17, 450-451
  pluralism, 16-17
  Southeast Asian image of, 16-18
  see also indexes for countries
Colonial drain, 13-14
Colonial laissez faire, 3, 12, 15n, 17
Colonial policy, 13-16
  nationalist image of, 16-18
  see also Colonial development and indexes for countries
Colonialism, 3, 6, 8, 9, 11-16, 441
  see also Colonial development and Mercantilism
Colonies, "cost of," 13n
Communal consumption capital, 5-6
  accumulation of, 443-444
Confiscation, role of, 444, 460
Congruence, concept of, 8, 442
Consensus, see Political consensus
Constitutionalism, 450
Corporate enterprise, adaptation to indigenism, 464, 465, 467
Corruption, 462, 464-465
Credit policy, 450

Diem, Ngo Dinh, 447n
Direct foreign investment, 465-467

INDEX BY COUNTRIES

Burma

Agrarian reform, 222-225
Agricultural credit, 220-221, 256
  see also Chettyars
Agricultural Projects Board, 240
Agriculture, 203, 204, 207, 208, 219-
  220, 243-244
Alien registration, 217
Andrus, J. Russell, 220n
Anti-Fascist Organization, 209
Anti-Fascist People's Freedom League,
  209-210
Aung Gyi, 217, 250
Aung San, 208, 209

Banking system, 220, 254-255
Baxter, James, 206n
Black market, *see* Corruption
Bogus importers, *see* Dummies
British enterprise, 225-228, 230, 231n,
  234, 240, 244, 250-251
Buddhism, 204, 207-209
Burma Currency Board, 255
Burma Economic Development Corporation, 233
Burmanism, 211, 212, 215, 217, 218,
  228-229, 233, 235, 245, 248-249,
  251, 253-254, 258, 262
  see also Nationalism
Burmanization, 211, 212, 231-233, 260-
  262
  civil service, 259-261
  effects on economic development,
    264-265
  import trade, 244-250
  managerial employment, 214, 251
  pawnshops, 257
  retail trade, 251-254
  rice trade, 240-244

see also Burmese enterprise
Burmese enterprise, 212, 231-232, 237-
  238, 242-245, 250, 254, 263-264
  see also Burmanization *and* National
    bourgeoisie
Burmese socialism, *see* Nationalism *and*
  Socialism
Burmese society, 207, 211-212, 215, 216,
  265

Cady, John F., 208n
Capitalism, 208-210, 227
Caretaker government, 209, 215, 224,
  238, 239, 243, 248
Chettyars, 208, 220-225, 234, 254
China-Burma relations, 260
Chinese enterprise, 206, 234, 240, 250
Chinese minority, 223, 260
Chins, *see* Ethnic minorities
Citizenship policy, 215-217
Civil Supplies Board, 244, 245
Civil Supplies Management Board, 245,
  246
Colonial development, 204, 207-208,
  219-221, 225, 227-228, 230, 234,
  240, 250-251, 254
Colonial policy, 204, 207, 230
Communism, 209-210
Constitution, 210-211, 215, 225, 234
Cook, B. C. A., 236n
Cooper, Chester L., 219n
Co-operative movement, 243, 253, 254
Corruption, 242, 247, 249, 253
  see also Dummies
Coup d'état of 1962, 212, 215
  see also Revolutionary Council
Cultivators, *see* Peasantry

Defense Services Institute, 232-233,
  238, 253

Cambodia

Malaya

The Philippines

South Vietnam

Thailand